POSITIVE EXPECTATIONS OF AMERICA'S WORLD ROLE

Historical Cycles of Realistic Idealism

Frank L. Klingberg

University Press of America, Inc.
Lanham • New York • London

Copyright © 1996 by
University Press of America,® Inc.
4720 Boston Way
Lanham, Maryland 20706

3 Henrietta Street
London, WC2E 8LU England

Library of Congress Cataloging-in-Publication Data

Klingberg, Frank L. (Frank LeRoy)
Positive expectations of America's world role : historical cycles of
realistic idealism / Frank L. Klingberg.
p.   cm.
Includes bibliographical references and indexes.
1. United States--Foreign relations.   I. Title.
E183.K64   1996   327.73'009--dc20   95-52809 CIP

ISBN 0-7618-0262-2 (cloth: alk. ppr.)
ISBN 0-7618-0263-0 (pbk: alk. ppr.)

⊖™The paper used in this publication meets the minimum
requirements of American National Standard for information
Sciences—Permanence of Paper for Printed Library Materials,
ANSI Z39.48—1984

To

My Wife, Daughter and Son-in-Law,

Grandchildren, and the Generations

Which They Represent

Contents

Preface

This study has two aims in relation to the whole sweep of American history: (1) to show the strong thread of realistic idealism which has pervaded the development of American foreign policy, especially as presented by America's presidents and (2) to present certain cyclical trends which appear to have guided and limited policy makers and which have helped prepare America for its expanding world role.

American leaders have often expressed a remarkable faith in freedom and in America as an instrument for freedom, along with a faith in Providence at work. The Farewell Address of Washington is read in Congress annually on his birthday. Jefferson's and Lincoln's shrines contain some of their famous words. Wilson's ideas for peace seem singularly appropriate in the 1990s. America has been built in part by the efforts, devotion, and idealism of its leaders. Presidents, in their statements on foreign policy, have relied not only on their own perceptions and principles, but also on their Secretaries of State and other close advisers, the Department of State, Congress, and evidence of public opinion.

The statements of American leaders need to be viewed in the context of events and challenges of the time, and as they were shaped by changing dominant motivations or moods of America, in cyclical fashion. These motivations seem to arise from different aspects of human nature—bringing successive periods of rationalism, realism, and idealism, for example, and thus leading to "thesis, antithesis and synthesis" in development (in Hegel's terms). Or they may come from major alternative international possibilities—such as pressing outward (extroversion) or turning inward (introversion). Each of the approaches is always present to some extent, but one of each type dominates in a specific period. The regularity of the shifts from one dominant mood to another seems to be promoted by the succession of political or social generations, as a new generation senses the apparent abuse or failure of a particular approach long followed. Most impressive throughout is the continuity and strength of American idealism, even though it rises and falls in influence at different times.

Emphasis is placed on the defining years of the independent nation (1776–1824), on Lincoln and Wilson, and, then especially, on the years since World War II which have witnessed such an impressive stand by America and its leaders on the world scene. Many Americans may not be aware of the dedication of the American Presidents to the search for peace and freedom ever since 1966, when the Cold War began to show some signs of moderating. These efforts must have helped pave the way for the end of the Cold War and the breakup of European communism.

America's pervasive idealism can be a special inspiration for leaders today, and indeed for all Americans who are concerned about the future of their country and the world. Whatever of value was built deeply into American history is capable of being recovered and used to strengthen the spirit of the nation. The faith and courage of past generations can help Americans accept the burdens and perceive the opportunities of world leadership today and in the future.

In the 1990s, realism and idealism seem to be converging in America to produce the probability of continued effective and beneficent world leadership. These dominant moods now appear to include extroversion (a *realist* willingness to use direct pressure on other nations to promote democratic ideals) and an *idealist* liberal democratic internationalism (promoting a freer and more prosperous world and seeking international cooperation for a just and durable peace).

The successive chapters of this study will begin with an introduction concerning traditional beliefs of Americans and the historical cycles, and continue with the colonial outlook (1587–1776), the revolutionary period (1776–1824), the consolidation of the American nation (1824–71), America's rise as an industrial world power (1871–1918), the world crisis for freedom (1918/19–66/67), and the search for world peace, justice and freedom since 1966. The conclusion will summarize America's record and speculate on the outlook for America's role in the "new world age."

Acknowledgements

1. To my wife—for proofreading and indexing—and daughter, and to grandson David A. Lyons for his advice on word processing.

2. To those who encouraged me to write a sequel to *Cyclical Trends in American Foreign Policy Moods* (University Press of America, 1983): Professor Charles W. Kegley, Jr., University of South Carolina, and Professor Jack E. Holmes, Hope College.

3. To other colleagues and former students for their stimulation of ideas.

4. To Terry Mathias for final text preparation.

5. To the University Press of America, including James E. Lyons, Michelle R. Harris, and Helen Hudson.

6. To the following for permission to copy quotations:

a. HarperCollins Publishers, Inc., New York, N.Y. *The Public Papers of Woodrow Wilson*, Authorized Edition, 6 vols., Edited by Ray Stannard Baker and William E. Dodd (New York: Harper, 1925, 1926, 1927). Copyright 1925 and 1952, Edith Bolling Wilson; Stuart Gerry Brown, ed. *We Hold These Truths: Documents of American Democracy* (New York: Harper and Brothers, 1941); John F. Kennedy, *The Burden and the Glory: Public Statements and Addresses in 1962 and 1963*. Edited by Allan Nevins (New York: Harper and Row, 1964).

b. Rutgers University Press, New Brunswick, N.J. *The Collected Works of Abraham Lincoln*, 8 vols., Edited by Roy P. Basler. Copyright 1953 by the Abraham Lincoln Association.

CHAPTER I

Introduction:
American Traits, Beliefs and Cycles

A nation is built on its history—its foundations and birth and its experience, constructive and destructive. The fabric of American history contains pervasive threads of idealism, derived from its Judeo-Christian heritage, plus Greek and British developments toward democracy.

Similarly, there are other threads of realism derived from Rome and Europe, recognizing the need of law and police and military force. Throughout are also threads of rationalism, evidenced in an emphasis on education and on a pragmatism based on experience and common sense.

The degree of American emphasis on idealism or realism or rationalism appears to vary from generation to generation in a cyclical fashion. Similarly, there are alternating emphases in America's international approach (between introversion and extroversion) and on political attitudes (between liberalism and conservatism, and between concepts of "liberty" and "union"). These cycles stimulate various phases of development from the core ideas found in America's origin and experience.

Importance of the Origins of a Nation

America is a nation, unlike most others, with its origin documented in considerable detail. Alexis de Tocqueville and many others have stressed the significance of the origins of a nation as a key to its beliefs and the relative permanence of such beliefs as passed on from generation to generation, and given a special revival from time to time. De Tocqueville has a chapter in *Democracy in America* (written in

1837) on "Origins of the Anglo-Americans and its Importance, in Relation to their Future Condition." In studying men, he writes, we begin with the infant:

> The entire man is, so to speak, to be seen in the cradle of the child.
>
> The growth of nations presents something analogous to this; they all bear some marks of their origin; and the circumstances which accompanied their birth and contributed to their rise, affect the whole term of their being. . . .
>
> America is the only country in which it has been possible to study the nature and tranquil growth of society, and where the influence exercised on the future condition of states by their origin is clearly distinguishable.[1]

The Irish-born British statesman of the 18th century, Edmund Burke, saw a state as a divinely ordained instrument, operating through successive generations of men (he was speaking particularly of the British Constitution):

> . . . A nation is not an idea only of local extent, and individual momentary aggregation; but it is an idea of continuity, which extends in time as well as in numbers and in space. And this is a choice not of one day or one set of people, not a tumultuary and giddy choice; it is a deliberate election of the ages and of generations; it is a constitution made by what is ten thousand times better than choice, it is made by the peculiar circumstances, occasions, tempers, dispositions, and moral, civil, and social habitudes of the people, which disclose themselves only in a long space of time.[2]

Vico, in *The New Science* (1725), stressed the relation between the origins and subsequent development of institutions, such as states, as well as the natural development of history:

> The nature of things is nothing but their coming into being . . . at certain times and in certain fashions. Whenever the time and fashion is thus and so, such and not otherwise are the things that come into being.
>
> The inseparable properties of things must be due to the mode or fashion in which they are born. By these properties we may therefore tell that the nature of birth . . . was thus and not otherwise.[3]

Woodrow Wilson stressed the role of history in guiding and inspiring a nation, in the recognition that the history of a nation is all of one piece:

> It has also a function of guidance: to build high places whereon to plant the clear and flaming lights of experience that they may shine alike upon the roads already traveled and upon the paths not yet attempted. The historian is also a sort of prophet. Our memories direct us. They give us knowledge of our character, alike in its strengths and in its weakness; and it is so we get our standards for endeavor—our warnings and our gleams of hope. It is thus we learn what manner of nation we are of, and divine what manner of people we should be.[4]

This conception of history as an unfolding of potentialities in the original "core" of a nation must also plainly include the idea of new combinations and novel applications. The basic elements in the origin of a nation will have the characteristic of permanence, but we should expect them to appear in different practical forms as they unfold and develop in the face of changing conditions and policies. We should expect America's foreign policy as well as its domestic policy to be derived from the basic "core" of the nation. This seems related to President Eisenhower's affirmation in his First Inaugural Address: "Whatever America hopes to bring to pass in the world must first come to pass in the heart of America."

America, in a sense, was born twice: first, in 1607, 1620 and after, as colonies under England; and second, in 1776 and 1789 and after, as an independent constitutional democratic republic. Some might add a third birth: in 1871, 1898, and after, as an industrial world power, prepared to play a special world role in the 20th century.

The special keys to America's international beliefs and motivation appear in the creation of the independent nation: with its Declaration of Independence (1776); the Revolutionary War (1775–83); the doctrine of equal rights for states, small or large, in the Northwest Ordinance (1787) and the Constitution (1787); and the protection of individual rights in the Bill of Rights (1791). Dr. Frank Tannenbaum has pointed out the larger implication of the principle of the "co-ordinate state" in America's foreign policy, interpreting it as the basis for America's belief in the legal equality of nations and the protection of the rights of small nations as well as large.[5]

American Idealism and Realism

America's idealism is derived from the Judeo-Christian and Greco-Roman heritage. It is expressed in the Declaration of Independence: "We hold these truths to be self-evident, that all men are created equal, that they are endowed by their Creator with certain unalienable Rights, that among these are Life, Liberty and the pursuit of Happiness." America's realism is also shown in the Declaration's list of evils in British policy in 1776, and the determination to use force in defense of freedom and justice. Lincoln openly expressed the Christian ideal when the Civil War was nearly over, as he began the last paragraph of his Second Inaugural Address with these words: "With malice toward none, with charity for all, with firmness in the right as God gives us to see the right . . . ."

Reinhold Niebuhr, American theologian, analyzed what may be called Christian or religious realism, somewhat in the spirit of Abraham Lincoln. Recognizing the necessity of defending Western civilization against aggressive force like that of Hitler or Stalin, he also warned of the dangers on the democratic side of excessive pretenses of wisdom, power and virtue, of hatred and vainglory, and of the expected contradictions between human and divine purposes.[6]

The American liberal tends to be an idealist—in promoting peace based on justice and freedom, believing that "right makes might" (a Lincoln phrase), and expecting most people to be "good." The American realist expects the presence of evil, and is prepared to oppose it by force. The religious realist points out also the potential evils in one's own society and nation. American history shows the pervading presence of a realistic idealism—a willingness to use force to defend the ideals of freedom and justice, while regarding peace as the ultimate goal. Both realists and idealists throughout American history have expected the United States to move toward a position of leadership in the world, in support of freedom, justice and peace.

Special Traits and Key Beliefs

Among the important influences on the American people have been: (1) the dominant English influence at its center (with its growing emphasis on freedom and its dynamic expansionism); (2) the strong impact of Protestant Christianity (followed later by Roman Catholic, Jewish, Orthodox Catholic and Muslim influences); (3) the enlarging mixture of nationalities, races and religious groups; (4) the challenge of building a new society on virgin territory; and (5) the rapid growth of the population with a moving frontier (lightly inhabited by native Americans), in a land with temperate climate and rich agricultural and mineral resources to be developed.

The American frontier helped promote the development of basic democratic attitudes, such as respect for the individual instead of a presumed class and a practical spirit of self-reliance. Among other fairly positive traits fostered in part by the frontier were an emphasis upon material blessings; a natural optimism, along with practical inventiveness and extraordinary wastefulness; and generosity, friendliness, hospitality, cooperativeness and voluntary community projects of all sorts.[7]

Let us note in particular some other commonly held views of major American characteristics.

Some American Traits

There is a danger of exaggeration in attributing certain characteristics to Americans. In fact, some would deny that there is any difference among nations, and affirm that the only important differences are among individuals. Yet somehow the whole history of nations seems to support the concept of special contributions and characteristics of major peoples.

André Siegfried, a French observer, has shown what can be done with one word to describe major nationalities. Perhaps Americans can claim some share in all the traits listed, in so far as these nationalities have been incorporated in American society. These are Siegfried's chapter headings in his book *Nations Have Souls*: Latin Realism, French Ingenuity, English Tenacity, German Discipline, Russian Mysticism, and American Dynamism.[8]

Hector St. John Crèvecoeur, a French-born New York farmer writing in 1769 (published in London in 1782), believed that some strange metamorphosis seemed to convert a European immigrant rather quickly into an "American." In his letter entitled "What Is an American?" he stressed the idea of a free self-respecting individual:

> What then is the American, this new man? He is either a European, or the descendant of a European. . . . *He* is an American, who leaving behind him all his ancient prejudices and manners, receives new ones

from the new mode of life he has embraced, the new government he
obeys, and the new rank he holds. . . . Here individuals of all nations
are melted into a new race of men, whose labours and posterity will one
day cause great changes in the world. Americans are the western
pilgrims, who are carrying along with them that great mass of arts,
sciences, vigour, and industry which began long since in the east; they
will finish the great circle. . . . Their labour is founded on the basis of
nature, *self-interest*; can there want a stronger allurement? . . . [9]

Crèvecoeur stressed the individualism and love of prosperity which he
believed, writing before the Revolution, characterized the American
people.

Dynamism

Perhaps the most inclusive term to characterize Americans is that of
Siegfried—dynamism. The word connotes power and achievement—
and the chief evidence of the validity of the term is the amazing record
of American growth and constructive achievement. Three characteristics
seem to constitute the foundation of this American attribute of
dynamism: (1) a system which promotes individual initiative, enterprise
and practical organization; (2) large reservoirs of restless human energy;
and (3) the self-confidence and faith of most Americans in the
possibility of cooperating in completing hard tasks and meeting
emergency demands.

Americans seem to have had an almost mystical confidence in what
America as a whole can do, in the value of efficient organization,
planning and voluntary cooperation. General Dwight Eisenhower once
remarked, when commanding NATO forces, that the so-called
"impossible" only takes longer to accomplish.

Dynamism by itself, however, is only a virtue when worthwhile
goals are sought. American individualism is tempered by a strong desire
for association, a keen sense of human sympathy.

Human Sympathy

Enough of America's dynamism has been devoted to help and
service of all kinds that "human sympathy" may be regarded as a
second major characteristic of Americans. Its basis is probably found in
Judeo-Christian principles. Voluntary cooperative action, helpfulness and

generosity are pioneer traits as much as is individualism. It is probably a key to much of America's desire for international cooperation and peace.

Among other commonly noticed characteristics associated with the idea of "human sympathy" may be mentioned the spirit of fair play and good sportsmanship; an honest, direct and forthright approach in most matters; a natural curiosity about the whole world of people, and a desire to learn more about other nations; helping rebuild enemy nations defeated in war; a desire to perform helpful and compassionate deeds for the unfortunate and especially for children in any land (demonstrated in particular by acts of many American soldiers abroad and by large contributions to those in disaster areas); a pronounced concern for the whole community—local, state or national; and a notable sense of humor, and willingness to laugh at one's own foibles.

Another element to be stressed in America's humanitarianism is her capacity to mobilize her idealism into action—sometimes into great crusades of action, stimulated by deep emotional fervor. This happened in the Civil War and in World War I. Henry Van Dyke pointed to the emotional power in America's motivation:

> In the minor problems we shall make many mistakes. In the great problems, in the pressing emergencies, we rely upon the moral power in reserve. The sober soul of the people is neither frivolous nor fanatical. It is earnest, ethical, desirous of the common good, responsive to moral appeal, capable of self-control, and, in the time of need, strong for self-sacrifice.[10]

On certain occasions, at least, many Americans may live up to such idealized statements. Philip Gibbs, English correspondent, in his generous book entitled *People of Destiny* (1920), reminded Americans of the moral exaltation they could feel, by describing their mood in entering the First World War:

> . . . The United States declared war, gathered its youth into great training camps, and launched into the world struggle with slow but ever-increasing energy which swept the people with a mighty whirlwind of emotion.
>
> The American people as a whole did truly enter the war in the spirit of crusaders. . . . The materialism of which America had been accused, not unjustly, was broken through by a spiritual idealism which touched every class, and Americans did not shrink from sacrifice, but asked for

it as a privilege, and were regretful that as a people they suffered so little in comparison with those who had fought and agonized so long.[11]

In relation to this trait of "human sympathy," it has often been noted that America has had only one "traditional enemy" among the nations throughout its history—and that was England, the "Mother Country" for 150 years before America's independence and America's closest ally and friend in the 20th century.

Professor D. Lincoln Canfield, a student of Hispanic as well as North American cultures, has stressed the significance of centuries of acculturation:

> We speak English, we think in English, we live in an Anglo pattern of collective existence wrought over centuries of "acculturation" of peoples of many origins. There is no choice! The pillars of this pattern, I believe, are outreach (search for truth, inventiveness, compassion for the weak, love of enemies), debate, and fair play. Outreach, debate, fair play![12]

In his book on *East Meets West South of the Border*, Canfield stresses the behavior patterns which are the essence of national character. For example, in the Hispanic countries he sees an attractive personalism combined with a measure of civic irresponsibility and lack of mutual forbearance. He quotes approvingly from Pedro Lain Entralgo (*Spain as a Problem*) on the norms of modern Western life (including the United States): (1) effective sharing of life between those who do not hold the same political and religious views (genuine public freedom and true representative democracy); (2) the establishment of a state concerned with the achievement and regulation of the general welfare, based upon a civic morality, that morality by which a man feels inwardly bound to fulfill his duties as citizen; and (3) a general and healthy regard for secular achievements of the human intelligence, particularly in science and technology. Free institutions, Canfield concludes, presuppose a force of respect and responsibility within the behavior of the community, and can be spread by example.[13]

James Fallows stresses the importance of America's rather wide "sense of trust" and the feeling of some control over an individual's destiny: "When these two conditions are satisfied—when the radius of trust is broad; when people think they can affect their destiny—then ordinary people will behave in a way that makes the society rich,strong, and fair."[14]

Pragmatism

Pragmatism is regarded here as the habit of emphasizing the values of experience and common sense, and of judging the validity of a policy by its results. It is America's particular approach and philosophy which was doubtless strengthened by the experience of a new land and an expanding frontier, first of territory and then of intellect. The frontier brought unexpected problems and challenges which needed to be squarely and immediately faced. The pragmatic approach also notes the unique experience of America in its foreign relations.

Three American philosophers are regarded as the founders of pragmatism as a school of thought and action: Charles Pierce (1839–1914), declaring that the truth of a proposition is dependent upon its consequences; William James (1842–1910), who included all aspects of life in his approach, such as the emotional, non-rational and religious, as well as the analytical; and John Dewey (1859–1952), emphasizing scientific inquiry, based on democratic values.[15]

The American pragmatic approach to life and to foreign policy includes: (1) the application of man's creative intelligence to problem-solving; (2) moderation and flexibility; and (3) the goal of peace, while evaluating the use of force or war by its expected consequences.

Man's creative intelligence was to be applied to problems and challenges, often unexpected, remaining skeptical of strong ideologies like Marxism or fascism. Social experimentation (creativity) and "trial and error" were appropriate responses to problems, as illustrated by President Franklin D. Roosevelt's New Deal policies to meet the Great Depression. A person must take full account of the specific circumstances. Pragmatists were suspicious of determinism, believing instead in the ability of people to make a difference in the results, expected to be beneficent in the long run, if creative intelligence was applied.

The moderate approach would avoid the extremes of revolution or reaction, of utopian idealism and excessive reliance on power (*Realpolitik*). The aim was to improve the human situation, to create better communities (local, national or world), to promote human welfare, to combine the best elements of idealism and realism. Americans tended to be flexible (note, for example, the special flexibility of the U.S. Constitution), showed a willingness to accept the contributions of individualism and collectivism, and developed a variety of religious approaches. There is a willingness to revise policies to achieve better results, or to drop unsuccessful policies, as in the Vietnam War or the intervention in Lebanon (1982–84).

Pragmatists have generally accepted the liberal approach to force and war, aiming at peace as the goal. They would evaluate the use of force or war by their expected consequences, based on past experience. War should be a last resort, and the limits of American power should be recognized.

In general, most Americans have lived by the pragmatic approach, more or less habitually, judging actions and policies largely by their results. The value of freedom, for example, had been demonstrated by history. A pragmatic approach can be applied to other ideals, as shown by Charles W. Kegley, Jr. in his analysis of empirical evidence showing that nations do indeed behave largely in accordance with certain ethical principles, such as the "Golden Rule," the obligation to fulfill commitments, and the control of force in seeking peace. Thus, he believes it is "realistic" to hope for and to expect international cooperation.[16] Similarly, Jack E. Holmes has shown that a major reason for American shifts in policy and mood between introversion and extroversion is a majority judgment that one of these approaches has failed,or is seen as contrary to the nation's best interest.[17] Another pragmatic approach is that of Samuel P. Huntington, who urges Americans to:

> continue to believe in their liberal, democratic, and individualistic ideals and also recognize the extent to which their institutions and behavior fall short of these ideals; . . . [and] attempt to reduce the gap between institutions and ideals by accepting the fact that the imperfection of human nature means the gap can never be eliminated. . . . [18]

There is a note of encouragement for the future in these basic traits of dynamism and human sympathy and pragmatism which have appeared more or less permanently throughout American history. George F. Kennan, former Ambassador to the Soviet Union, once suggested the probable powerful impact on world opinion and actions if America's potential dynamism were to be mobilized with positive enthusiasm toward great human ends:

> In the lives of nations the really worthwhile things cannot and will not

be hidden. . . . No iron curtain could suppress, even in the innermost depths of Siberia, the news that America had shed the shackles of disunity, confusion and doubt, had taken a new lease of hope and determination, and was setting about her tasks with enthusiasm and clarity of purpose.[19]

American Weaknesses

Before closing this section on American traits, some of America's weaker traits should also be mentioned. In fact, each of America's presumed strong traits becomes a vice, if carried to an extreme. Dynamism can be dangerous; individualism can produce anarchy and confusion; restless energy and tension may bring a "nervous breakdown"; excessive confidence may produce "delusions of grandeur" or at least an insufferable "superiority complex"; "human sympathy" may degenerate into inactive, tearful sentimentality, or on the other hand produce so much activity for others that the innate strength of the actor is dissipated; and pragmatism may seem to be devoid of ideals or goals.

An important potential weakness in American character, in terms of helping create a cooperative and peaceful world, probably lies in the common American feeling of *superiority* to others, as distinguished from a healthy feeling of confidence and self-assurance. This has effects in many aspects of life, as it may promote lack of respect for other nations and their citizens; unfairness to and abuse of non-white races; provincialism and isolationism; impatience with others and unwillingness to attempt to understand their point of view; pressure toward conformity with the majority opinion or standards of the moment; a "too confident sense of justice," which "always leads to injustice," in the words of Reinhold Niebuhr;[20] a virtuous "Phariseeism"; and a general lack of healthy humility.

On the other hand, there is some danger that Americans could lose their sense of confidence through feelings of inferiority and a sense of historical decline (a number of scholars have pointed to this apparent decline), thereby reducing the American hope of effective world leadership. Another aspect of the American spirit which frightens some of America's friends is the alleged American proneness to emotional excess: they fear that we will abuse our physical power, that we may provoke an unnecessary war, that our fears are excessive, that we are too impatient with the processes of history, and that we are immature and unwise in the ways of world leadership.

Yet we may conclude that the dynamism of a democratic Great Power, guided by a deep and sincere human sympathy, as well as a prudent concern for consequences (pragmatism), could be a strong foundation for effective world leadership in the decades ahead, especially in the light of America's key beliefs.

Some Key Beliefs

The real "core" of America should be found in her basic ideas or ideals. For such ideas are what individuals live by, and they constitute the source of foreign as well as domestic policy. Such ideas, despite their varying intensity, constitute a major type of continuous pressure on the people, corresponding to the influence of the physical environment. There seems to be a sort of "spiritual momentum," described as follows by Robert E. Fitch, after he has discussed the reciprocal "give and take" between spiritual and material factors:

> But we are also led on to the conclusion that, once a spiritual tradition has had its genesis and has established itself in the mores of a people, then, to some extent, it leads an autonomous existence, developing its own implications without regard to specific material instrumentalities. Spiritual values are as real as economic conditions; and ideals exist as truly in nature as the mechanisms through which they get expression.[21]

Ralph Henry Gabriel, American historian,, identified (1940, 1955) three basic ideas of the "American democratic faith" dominating the "Middle Period" in America's independent history—beginning some fifty years after the Declaration of Independence. These seem to offer the clue to the inner "core" and development of America throughout its whole history.

The first doctrine was that of the *fundamental law*, derived from the Creator:

> The foundation of this democratic faith was a frank supernaturalism derived from Christianity. . . . The basic postulate of the democratic faith affirmed that God, the creator of man, has also created a moral law for his government and has endowed him with a conscience with which to apprehend it. Underneath and supporting human society, as the basic rock supports the hills, is a moral order which is the abiding place of the eternal principles of truth and righteousness. . . .

Here, then, was the mid-nineteenth concept of the fundamental law. It was looked upon as absolute and immutable and as made up of both moral and natural law. Out of it came ultimately the law which governed the lives of man, in particular the famous common law built up by the courts of England and of the American states as decision was piled upon decision.[22]

This was the fundamental law upon which responsible liberty was based. This was the Judeo-Christian foundation of America in the early colonial period (particularly in New England), and its power was to be revived in the mid-nineteenth century and perhaps again during the last half of the twentieth century and the first decades of the twenty-first.[23]

Further support for the power of the "fundamental law" in American culture is given in Conal Furay's analysis of the "grass-roots mind" in America: " . . . is there not a basic human thirst for, and tendency toward, constancy, absolutes, the eternal, these leading to the development of bedrock principles." Indeed, he writes, "it would be most surprising if major changes in public mentality occurred at any thing more rapid than a glacial tempo." Furay contrasts these basic ethical and religious beliefs of the "common man" with the modern intellectual tendencies toward relativism.[24]

The second doctrine of the democratic faith of the Middle Period was that of the *free and responsible individual*:

> The social thinking of the time focussed on the individual as Jefferson had done in the Declaration of Independence. . . . In the United States free individuals were the ultimate governors of the nation. . . . The age of the common man began in the United States in Andrew Jackson's time—nearly a century before its appearance in Europe.
>
> Power, of necessity, implied responsibility; responsibility suggested something above the individual to which all must be responsible. The aphorism, liberty under law, stated in political terms the doctrine of the free individual.[25]

This belief in the "free and responsible individual," protected and guided by a fundamental law (natural, divine and "legal"), was the key to the development and strengthening of American democracy and to building a balanced economic system.

The *mission of America* was the third doctrine. Gabriel quotes Abraham Lincoln's expression of the meaning of the Declaration:

> . . . something in that Declaration giving liberty, not alone to the
> people of this country, but hope for the world for all future time. It was
> that which gave promise that in due time the weights should be lifted
> from the shoulders of all men, that all should have an equal chance
> (spoken in Independence Hall, Philadelphia, February 22, 1861).

Gabriel pointed out that Lincoln "gave classic expression to the doctrine
that it is the mission of America to cherish and to hold steadfast before
the nations the ideal of the free and self-governing individual" and "held
up before the humble democrat . . . a romantic vision in which he could
see his inconspicuous performance of civic duties invested with a world
significance."[26]

So let us adopt these three doctrines as the key ideas in American
history. The first idea, the fundamental law, has moral and religious
foundations, so let us call it the belief in the *moral law*—the law of
divine origin and power undergirding human life and furthering the
goals of justice and compassion. The second idea of the "free and
responsible individual" is so closely associated with cooperative and
united activity, that the two ideas can be combined in the special phrase
developed in American history: *liberty and union*. America's
individualism and nationalism belong together, bolstering each other.
The third idea of "America's mission" relates to America's influence
on the rest of the world, or rather to humanity as a whole—so let it be
called America's *world mission*.

These three ideas are brought together in the revised Pledge of
Allegiance to the flag (the words "under God" were added by a joint
Congressional resolution approved by President Eisenhower on June 14,
1954): "I pledge allegiance to the flag of the United States of America
and to the republic for which it stands, one nation, under God,
indivisible, with liberty and justice for all."

Three Periods in American History

The preparation of America for leadership is highlighted by the
historical succession of the three major American ideas in dominant
influence. The three beliefs were all present in the origins of America
and at all periods since then, but different periods saw a greater
emphasis upon one of them. It is almost immediately evident that the
concept of the "moral law" was dominant in the early part of American
history; that "liberty and union" were the key to the period from the

middle of the 18th century until the Civil War, at least; and that not until the 20th century was America in a position to regard her "world mission" with great seriousness—indeed it could no longer be "escaped." This order of succession is also logical—for individual moral discipline is necessary to guide liberty toward union (and prevent anarchy), and America would be ready for her "world mission" only after she had rather fully developed and applied her own basic principles (justice and liberty). Thus the three periods could well be identified as follows:

(1) 1587–1729: the building of the *moral law* into the foundations of the country—the establishment of a Protestant Christian society, from the Lost Colony of 1587 (as Sir Francis Drake destroyed a Spanish fleet at Cadiz in 1587 and England defeated the Spanish Armada in 1588), through the Puritan theocracy in New England (1620–80), and to the wider recognition of religious toleration and freedom.

(2) 1729–1871: the building and consolidation of an American *union* based on the principle of individual *liberty*—from the rise of secular liberty and thought in the 18th century, through the Revolution and the War of 1812, down to the "trial by fire" in the Civil War (by 1871, the three Civil War constitutional amendments had been ratified and the legal and political union had been re-established).

(3) 1871– : America's *world mission*—the principles and role of America take on world-wide significance, as the nation becomes an industrial world power and a major actor on the world stage, seeking the building of a more democratic world, based on moral principles and the ideal of freedom (for peoples and individuals).

The first period of "modern history" can be dated similarly, from 1445 to 1587, and can be regarded in part as preparatory to the building of a Protestant and English America—through great explorations, the Protestant Reformation, the rise of "Puritanism" in England and Presbyterianism in Scotland, and the growth of British sea power (climaxed by the defeat of the Spanish Armada).

Cycles in American History

The principle of rhythm is perhaps a basic law of progress in human society. Arthur M. Schlesinger thus described (1949) the contribution of the liberal-conservative alternation he had detected in America's domestic affairs.[27] A different rhythm seemed to operate in the international arena.

Introversion-Extroversion

In the foreign policy area, America has demonstrated a rather regular alternation between a dominant mood of introversion (for an average of 21 years) and one of extroversion (for an average of 27 years), ever since 1776 and perhaps earlier.[28] Extroversion is regarded here as a willingness to use direct pressure (economic, diplomatic or military) on other nations, while introversion stresses domestic concerns as well as normal economic, diplomatic and humanitarian relations with other nations. These cycles have occurred in a spiral fashion: each extrovert phase has heightened American involvement abroad, while each introvert phase has been a time of "leveling-off" or of retrenchment on the world scene. The length of the phases seems to be based on the succession of "political generations," as they have reacted against the application or results of the preceding approaches. The extrovert phases may be longer than the introvert because they are more "sensational" in character, and develop a strong consensus under Presidential leadership. When Americans "turn inward," special domestic and ethnic interests tend to take the place of a recognized "national interest." Thus this alternation has helped develop the United States from a rather small area on the Atlantic seaboard into the superpower it has become, maintaining both external and internal strength. Extrovert phases have, to a large extent, stimulated a "realist" approach—using military force or the threat of force, and expanding territory and/or influence in each of the phases.

The United States seems to have grown to its present influential position by the process of "challenge and response" (a major dynamic factor in history according to historian Arnold J. Toynbee). The idea of freedom and democracy, for others as well as for Americans, appears to have been the positive spark. The American idea of freedom has been powerfully challenged at least four times since 1776. Each time the nation has met the challenge with a double response—first trying the introvert method, and then the extrovert. By the end of each introvert-extrovert cycle, the problem has been solved to a large extent, the world position of America has been strengthened, and a new challenge soon begins.

The first great challenge to the American concept of freedom was that of British "tyranny" and European interference. First, the colonies secured their independence and established a constitutional government (introversion, 1776–98); then, still motivated by the goal of true independence, the new nation moved into an extrovert phase to end the threats of France, Britain, Spain, the Holy Alliance and Russia (extroversion, 1798–1824).

After the Monroe Doctrine (1823) helped protect the hemisphere, the challenge of slavery and secession had to be faced (introvert, 1824–44); in the extrovert phase (1844–71), both South and North sought to expand (the South for slave territory, as with Mexico, and the North for free territory), and the Pacific Ocean was reached. The solution came through the Civil War, in which "free labor" and democracy won and national unity was maintained (the 15th Amendment was adopted in 1870).

The third challenge to democracy was created by America's great industrial development (from a previously agricultural nation) following the Civil War, and by the continuing problem of recreating the union of North and South. Domestically, the response came in the development of the West and in the various populist, progressive and liberal movements designed to help the "common man" (introversion, 1871–91). Then, as before, an extrovert phase developed, stimulated in part by the desire for markets and raw materials abroad for the growing industrial machine and by the new glory of naval power. By 1917/18, the challenge had been surmounted as a strong democratic nation was prepared to step out on the world stage.[29]

The next and perhaps greatest challenge to America came when nations and new ideologies (communist and fascist) openly challenged the democratic nations and the democratic faith in Europe and America. After the brief experience in World War I, America tried to meet this challenge of the new world age in the introvert mood (1918–40)—with political isolation and, later, economic nationalism. But the crisis for world democracy in 1940 saw the United States getting ready to stride to the very center of the world stage and to begin to direct many of the scenes. The security of the whole "free world" was becoming America's major concern (1940–67), first against fascist powers and then against the communist states. By 1967, it was quite clear that the democratic powers (the United States, Britain, France, Italy, Germany and Japan) had gained a major advantage over the communist states, especially as the Soviet Union and China had split apart, so to speak.

The fifth cycle for America seems to have begun around 1967 with the hope of trying to build a stable peace for the world in the face of important third world challenges backed, at first, by the Soviet Union. America's first reaction, however, was to revert again to a relatively introvert mood for the next 20 years (1967–87), except for the major commitments to Western Europe and Japan, and to witness an expansion of Soviet power (as in Vietnam, Angola, Ethiopia and Afghanistan). In the latter part of this introvert phase, America (first under President Carter in 1980 and then under President Reagan) began to rebuild its military and political strength, as it had sometimes previously done near the end of the introvert phase. By 1987 the turn toward extroversion was apparent—as the nation intervened in the Persian Gulf (1987–89), in Panama (1989) and in Iraq (1990–91). President Bush saw the Iraqi crisis, which prompted the United Nations Security Council to pass 12 unprecedented resolutions, as the challenge which would help establish a "new world order" as a response—an order of justice and freedom and peace, backed by international force. If the extrovert period follows the past patterns, it would last until around 2014—time enough, it can be hoped, to be successful, at least to a large extent.

The cycles dealt with in this study seem to be particularly prominent in what might be called "social moods"—widespread feelings, attitudes, loyalties and cherished beliefs, with deep emotional attachment. Logical ideas seem to gain much of their significance from the favorable or unfavorable moods with which people confront them.

The intellect seems to be only a partial source for opinions. Karl Jaspers has suggested that:

> everything which the understanding devises, sets as its aims, or introduces as a means . . . is ultimately guided by motives of which the understanding did not think; these motives may be either interests and passions, or the impulses imparted by faith, or ideas.[30]

George Washington stated this point of view in a letter of June 30, 1785: "The truth is, the people must *feel* before they will *see* . . . . " Such moods may operate in what Carl Justav Jung called the "collective unconscious," developed through the special history of a people.

These cycles occur much more regularly than cycles of events, such as wars or economic depressions. They often seem quite pervasive in society, from government leaders to the mass public. Once the public has adopted a new mood, this approach seems to take on a life of its own for a "social generation." On the average, the moods are consistent one way or the other for a long period, averaging out somewhat like seasonal weather changes.

In considering cyclical phases, the dates of major historical events become exceedingly significant. It is clear, for example, that a new phase of American history began in 1776, a date likewise important as the beginning of a revolutionary phase in Western European Civilization (including America). Thus 1776 is used to date the beginning of both the introvert-extrovert cycle and the tripartite cultural-political cycle dealt with below. The dates for major cyclical shifts usually occur in about the middle of a six-to-eight year transition.

These alternating or successive moods do not take nations in a circular pattern, but, rather, they operate in a spiral fashion to lift a people, by degrees, toward more positive goals or results.

A Tripartite Cultural-Political Cycle

Looking at the periods above, with their introvert-extrovert phases, each period not only deals with a different problem, but has a different major motivation or dominant mood; it is also closely related to two of the other periods. Thus, there is a revolutionary period with great political-military struggles, but it is normally preceded by an age of enlightenment or preparation, and followed by the consolidation of the principles being developed in the two preceding stages.[31]

Democratic Nationalism, 1729–1871

The cycle from about 1729 to 1871 seems to have been initiated by the developments in applied science and technology (the "commercial revolution") which stimulated the formation in the West of a new middle class without much political power. During the first period of the cycle (1729–76), called the Enlightenment, the physical and intellectual preparation took place for the modern concept of democracy and national independence—the *thesis* (in Hegel's terminology). There followed a major struggle (1776–1824) between representatives of the new ideas and the "old regime"—the *antithesis*. It was the third period, from about 1824 to 1871, in which came the consolidation or *synthesis* of the democratic nation-state (in the United States, Britain, France, Italy, and to some extent in Germany and Japan) and the establishment of a fairly stable and peaceful international system. Great Britain had emerged as the predominant power on the world scene, through its navy, colonies, productivity, trade and generally democratic ideals. Holding the balance of power, Britain helped keep the peace on a number of occasions. The Great Powers together endeavored to maintain stability through occasional meetings of the Concert of Europe. International law and trade developed steadily, with diplomacy the regular means of promoting peace. A powerful moral-spiritual renewal was also evident in the United States and Western Europe. Only limited wars were fought, largely for national independence (as in the cases of Greece and Belgium) or for national unification (as for Italy, Germany and the United States). Another limited war was fought against Russia by Britain, France, Sardinia and Turkey, presumably to maintain the balance of power (the Crimean War, 1854–56). Following the Battle of Waterloo in 1815, there were no "world wars" until, say, 1914, or 1917 (when the United States entered the Great War).

Each of these three periods appeared to have a dominant motivation or cultural-political mood. The Enlightenment (1729–76), the time of preparation in the cycle, was intellectual and rational in character, with a decline in religious emphasis; its wars were limited, for economic and imperial power. The second period (1776–1824) was one of bitter struggle, perhaps irrational at times, dominated by seekers of political power or of liberty from international oppression, by military power-politics, and by wars fought for almost unlimited purposes, with goals by some of hegemony (the American Revolution and its wars, the French Revolution and its wars, the Napoleonic Wars, and the Latin American revolutions). The third period of synthesis (1824–71) saw the rise again of moral, ethical and spiritual values as the particular means of consolidating the goal of democratic nationalism, along with seeking international peace, with a rising respect for international law and institutional reform to promote justice and the general welfare. The succession of *rationalism* and *realism* appears to lead ultimately to the triumph of relative *idealism*.

This succession of moods seems to arise out of elements of human nature. In terms of Freud, the succession goes from *ego* (rationalism) to *id* (realism, power and irrationalism) to *superego* (idealism). The political scientist Harold Lasswell described (1932) how the indulgence of one of these aspects of the human psyche gave rise to another, in an essay on "The Triple Appeal Principle: a Dynamic Key": "Prolonged ego and super-ego indulgence produces redefinition in directions gratifying to the id; prolonged ego and id indulgence produces redefinition in directions gratifying to the super-ego."[32] This succession also appears logical in terms of certain social processes, such as a new generation's reaction against long periods or extremes of rationalism, realism or idealism.

Power-Politics Periods

This concept of a 142-year cycle (approximately) is strengthened by noting that it is fairly evident throughout modern history, beginning about 1445, and perhaps much earlier also. Particularly significant are the power-politics or realist periods (with world-shaking revolutions and ideological world wars) which appear as great divides of history in these long cycles. The first such period in modern history, 1492–1540, contained the Protestant Revolution or Reformation, three coalition wars led by France against the Charles V, Hapsburg ruler of Austria and Spain; the drive of the Ottoman Empire deep into Europe, up to Vienna; and the discovery of the "New World." The second period, about 1634–82, saw the British Puritan Revolution and Civil War; the part of the devastating Thirty Years War which was climaxed by the victorious entry of France, and the French threat to the European balance of power under Louis XIV; and another invasion by the Ottoman Empire, again advancing to Vienna. The third period (1776–1824) was that of the democratic revolutions and wars. The last period, say from 1917/18 to 1966/67, began in the midst of a great European struggle in which Germany and Britain appeared to be the major antagonists; but after World War II, which crushed Hitler's Germany, two new super-powers, the United States and the Soviet Union, engaged in a struggle of great ideological intensity, on the edge of an atomic abyss.

Liberal Democratic Internationalism (?), 1871–

It is impressive that the 124 years since 1871 have shown a similar pattern to that after 1729, indicating that the cycle may be completed by 2013/14 or so.

In the 19th century, the industrial revolution was creating across Western Europe and the United States a new laboring class which sought economic security and more equality. During the new "enlightenment" from, say, 1871 to 1917, the "common man" was receiving more government welfare aid (liberalism), especially in Western Europe, and the doctrines of socialism and communism were on the rise. Similarly, international cooperation was being demonstrated through various international conferences, climaxed by the Hague Peace Conferences of 1899 (when the Permanent Court of International

Arbitration was established) and 1907. Preparation was thus apparently taking place for a potential "liberal internationalism," even as nationalism grew strong and a major arms race developed among the Great Powers, divided into two opposing alliances. Another theme—Western, Russian and Japanese imperialism—tied the world more closely together politically and economically, with the special result of bringing Africa into the modern world. Wars were fought for limited imperial purposes—as the Boer War, the Spanish-American War, the Russo-Japanese War, the Italian-Libyan War and the Balkan Wars. As in the previous Enlightenment of the 18th century, science and rationalism were gaining ground, while moral-spiritual forces diminished.

The Great War of 1914 began with hopes of limited imperialist goals, but by 1917/18 the struggle for power between the new and old forces had developed a revolutionary character, beginning the second period—that of realist struggle (1917/18–66/67). After Bolshevism gained control in Russia, a fascist mentality was planted in some Italians and Germans. By 1918, the United States had sent two million men to Europe to join the Allies, and the war was carried to the complete surrender of Germany, thereby planting the seeds of German revenge. The League of Nations, the special dream of Woodrow Wilson, was established, but without either the United States or the Soviet Union (the latter did become a member in 1934), The struggle between Germany and her allies against British-French-Soviet-American forces was renewed in 1939 and 1941. The irrationalism of the time reached a climax in the Holocaust, and perhaps in the invention and use of the atomic bomb. With the Axis powers completely crushed, a new competition began almost immediately between the United States and the Soviet Union, now in the nuclear age. To sum up, the period of realistic power politics (1917–67) was characterized by the struggle between the so-called "free world" and the totalitarian fascist and communist powers; secularism and materialism were prominent philosophies.

Yet during this half-century of intense struggle, the foundations of liberal internationalism were vastly strengthened, especially after World War II: the United Nations and its Specialized Agencies, the Marshall Plan, the North Atlantic Treaty Organization (NATO), the European Community (founded on the political reconciliation of France and West Germany), the reconciliation of Japan and the West, the end of most Western colonialism and many other hopeful events.

It is now fairly clear that by 1967 one of the two super-powers was in a stronger position—namely the United States, with its powerful allies of West Germany and the rest of Western Europe, Japan, and several countries in East Asia and Latin America—altogether the forces which represented democratic liberal internationalism. The Soviet Union was sharply weakened in influence by its split with the Peoples Republic of China. South Korea had been successfully defended against the North Korean and Chinese invasions. Most of the nations of Southeast Asia strengthened their economic and political independence after the United States sent its armed forces directly into South Vietnam in 1965. Israel had been established as a new nation in 1948, and successfully defended her position in wars in 1956 and 1967.

Although the liberal democratic nations were predominant by 1967, those nations scarcely recognized what had happened, even though the cold war between the Soviet Union and the West seemed to have moderated and the Peoples Republic of China had turned inward (in the Great Proletarian Cultural Revolution). The leadership for a new liberal world order appeared weak, particularly since the United States had once again entered upon a relatively introvert stage. Nevertheless the internationalist trend was furthered in some respects during the 20 years after 1967, with the United States playing a positive role in a number of instances, such as President Nixon's opening to China in 1972, China's moves toward the West and her full recognition by President Carter in 1979; various signs of détente between the West and the Soviet Union (1970–79, and 1986 and after); President Anwar Sadat's dramatic trip to Israel in 1977, followed by the Camp David Peace Treaty between Israel and Egypt in 1979, with President Carter as mediator; the U.S.-Panama Treaty of 1977, showing Great Power respect for a small nation. Among other signs of idealism in the United States was a spiritual renewal among the evangelical churches and also in the mainline ones; they made special contributions to relief abroad and to the settlement of refugees. Most wars or revolutions between 1967 and 1987 were basically nationalist in character, as in the 19th century idealist period.

It was not until 1987 and 1988 that some remarkable breakthroughs were apparently made toward greater international cooperation and peace, as America's extrovert mood again became prominent. Chief among the changes was the modification of Soviet policy in a peaceful direction under Chairman (later President) Mikhail Gorbachev, leading to a U.S.-Soviet rapprochement—noteworthy was the collapse of

Communist ideology, the removal of the Berlin Wall, the independence of the Eastern European countries and the reunification of the two German states inside NATO. Very helpful also was the renewed positive role played by the United Nations in helping end regional wars and mobilizing economic sanctions and military force against Iraq (1990–91). A number of nations moved toward democracy, as the Philippines, Haiti, South Korea, Poland and other East European countries, and a number of Latin American countries. The United States continued to press for the reduction of trade barriers, and signed a pact with Canada for free trade by the year 2000.

This series of remarkable events since 1987 indicates a new spirit of world internationalism, in terms of justice and peace. The American government has again become deeply involved, and this period of hoped-for consolidation and synthesis can be expected to last for two more decades or more (as 1967–2014).

The four major lessons of history delineated by the American historian Charles A. Beard, in the form of aphorisms, shed light upon the cultural-political cycle as it moves slowly toward its consolidation. One applies to the total cycle: "the mills of God grind slowly, yet they grind exceedingly small." Two relate to the period of struggle and irrationality: "the bee fertilizes the flower which it robs," and "whom the gods would destroy they first make mad." The last suggests the human tendency to return finally to moral values which promote reconciliation: "when it is dark enough you can see the stars."[33] At such a time, peace seems to be "contagious," as more and more people come to believe in its possibility and necessity.

Domestic Political Cycles

Two different but related cycles have occurred between liberalism and conservatism, and between moods emphasizing "liberty" and "union."

Liberalism-Conservatism

This liberal-conservative alternation in domestic affairs, as delineated by Arthur Schlesinger, has a significant impact on foreign policy. He detected a definite alternation in spiral form, with an average mood length of 16.5 years. His liberal periods turned out to be 60 percent extrovert and 40 percent introvert, and his conservative periods were 52 percent extrovert and 48 percent introvert. Thus these domestic cycles seem to be independent of the foreign policy cycles. The 20th century periods which Schlesinger described were 1901–19, liberal; 1919–31, conservative; 1931–47, liberal; and after 1947, conservative until around 1962, with the new liberal period expected to last until around 1978. These predictions appear to have been fulfilled in policies and events.

Arthur M. Schlesinger, Jr., would rather define the alternation in terms of "public purpose" (liberal) and "private interest" (conservative). Then he notes that the leaders of the liberal or conservative periods and values use "foreign policy to project those values abroad. . . . So the conduct of foreign affairs breathes the spirit of the alternation in the domestic cycle, while the intensity in which this spirit is imposed on the world depends on phases in the foreign cycle." For example, he writes, public-purpose periods would tend to "incorporate into foreign policy ideas of democracy, reform, human rights, civil liberties, social change, affirmative government. Such eras display a preference abroad for democratic center-left regimes."[34]

With the expectation that the conservative period which began around 1978 would move toward liberalism in the early 1990s, the spirit of liberal internationalism should be strengthened at that time for 15 or more years.

Liberty-Union

The study of American history further suggests that each introvert and extrovert phase has shown a tendency to be divided, approximately in half, by an emphasis on "liberty" and then on "union." Major internal struggles have been seen in the effort to secure individual, local, group and states' rights (liberty), and, on the other hand, in attempts to establish a more perfect "union" ((greater cooperation and consensus, often accompanied by more centralization).

Such an alternation is particularly apparent during the first introvert phase (1776–98), when the spirit of liberty and states' rights (with resultant disunity) dominated until 1787, when the new Constitution symbolized the rising spirit of union, supported especially by the Federalists. Yet by 1798, the Jeffersonian Republicans were reviving the mood of liberty, and this was in turn replaced by a spirit of "nationalism" around 1811.

More recent phases suggest a similar division, as in the extrovert phase from 1940 to about 1986. A spirit of liberty and considerable disunity was present from 1940 to 1953, especially after World War II ended, while in 1953 President Dwight D. Eisenhower became the symbol of a new "consensus"—with a renewed spirit of union for the majority of Americans in his two terms in office (1953–61). President John F. Kennedy likewise gained much national support for his foreign policy and his "New Frontier" program (1961–63), and paved the way for a significant growth of national power in the areas of human rights and welfare under President Lyndon B. Johnson and his "Great Society."

Not until 1966 was there an important break in the general spirit of union which had prevailed since 1953. Then, rather suddenly, it seemed, President Johnson's prized "consensus" gave indications of being in serious trouble—with mounting criticism over Vietnam, the Great Society program, the rising cost of living and the alleged "credibility gap." The Vietnam War continued to divide the nation under President Richard M. Nixon (1969–74—an armistice was signed in 1973, but Americans were divided over whether aid to South Vietnam should continue). The Watergate scandal further divided the nation until President Nixon resigned in August 1974, to be succeeded by Vice-President Gerald R. Ford.

By the summer of 1976 a mood of considerable unity was being restored, with special impetus from the celebration of America's bicentennial. President Jimmy Carter's election helped give the deep South new sense of being an equal part of the nation, had a reconciling influence on blacks, and brought the growing number of evangelical Christians into the "mainstream," so to speak. Ronald Reagan was elected President by a landslide electoral majority, November 4, 1980 (489 to 49), and his general popularity continued until 1986, when the Iran-Contra scandal weakened his reputation and began a new phase of "liberty."

It remains to be seen whether the thirteen years or so after 1986 continue to be a time of "liberty," to be succeeded by a period of more union and consensus, say from 1999 to 2013/14. A major area of political disunity in the early 1990s seems to be a stronger sense of pluralism, with the division over racial and sexual policies highlighted. Blacks (now often termed African-Americans), Hispanics, Asians and Native Americans (formerly Indians) all seek special recognition. Many colleges have reduced the emphasis on the origin and principles of Western culture out of which the United States developed. Diverse religious groups have their own contributions to make. Here is a challenge to recognize and prize pluralism, while seeking to work toward the goal of a new and stronger union on the basis of mutual respect and common ideals.

In the area of foreign policy, a time of liberty and extroversion could expect a major debate over the desired goals for the United States on the world scene—for example, whether the nation should seek a new order for the whole world, or concentrate on a few special areas abroad of distinct national interest, with special attention also to strengthening domestic areas of weakness.[35]

Conclusion

The application of the best in American traits and traditional beliefs seems to lay the foundations for world leadership in our time: a dynamic practical human sympathy, based on high moral-spiritual principles (including respect, charity, love and compassion); responsible freedom for individuals and nations; and a helpful American role directed toward a stable and just peace.

Mood cycles seem to result from the succession of social and political generations, with each generation emphasizing different aspects of human nature or of a nation's role. The moral emphasis in this age of "consolidation" should stimulate *idealism*, while the extrovert mood promotes *realism*, resulting in what can be called "extrovert internationalism," guided by America's basic pragmatic approach to problem-solving.

The next task for this study is to look at some of the threads of realistic idealism expressed by America's historical leaders on the nation's hoped-for world role. What America expects to do on the world scene is highly dependent upon the nature of America as a nation. As the meaning and purpose of an individual's life is based on past experience and memories, so is the nation's meaning and purpose founded on its record and its historical memories. A second task is to note how America's extrovert phases have involved the United States in ever wider areas on the world scene, when challenges from abroad have produced positive responses.

The particular hope is to find guidance and inspiration from America's past. The current convergence of the nation's cyclical trends of idealism and realism increases the hope that America's "creative intelligence" will be applied constructively to strengthen the people's sense of high purpose, both for domestic and international problems.

The next chapters will present some positive responses of leaders during each of the major periods of American history: Chapter II, America's colonial development (1587–1776); Chapter III, the origins of American foreign policy as an independent democratic republic (1776–1824); Chapter IV, the consolidation of the land, liberty and spirit of the nation (1824–71); Chapter V, America as an industrial world power (1871–1917/18); Chapter VI, the world crisis for freedom in a new revolutionary age (1917/18–66/67); Chapter VII, the current effort to establish a stable and just peace (1966/67–); and Chapter VIII, conclusion, and the outlook for the future.

Notes

1. Alexis de Tocqueveille, *Democracy in America*, 1 vol. (New York: Edward Walker, 1849), 26–27.

2. From "Reform of Representation in the House of Commons" in *The Works of Edmund Burke* (London, 1896), 6:146 ff, quoted in John H. Hallowell, *Main Currents in Modern Political Thought* (New York: Henry Holt, 1950), 190–91.

3. *The New Science of Giambattista Vico* (Ithaca, N.Y.: Cornell University Press, 1948), 58 (paragraphs 147 and 148).

4. Woodrow Wilson, "The Course of American History" from *An Old Master* in *Selected Literary and Political Papers and Addresses of Woodrow Wilson*, 3 vols., (New York: Grosset and Dunlap, 1927), 3:213.

5. Frank Tannenbaum, *The American Tradition in Foreign Policy* (Norman: University of Oklahoma Press, 1951), 55–56.

6. See Reinhold Niebuhr, *The Irony of American History* (New York: Scribners, 1952), 173–74.

7. See Ray Allen Billington, *Westward Expansion: A History of the American Frontier* (New York: Macmillan, 1949), 743–48.

8. André Siegfried, *Nations Have Souls* (New York: Putnam's, 1932).

9. J. Hector St. John Crèvecoeur, *Letters from an American Farmer* (New York, 1904, reprinted from the Original Edition, London, 1782), 49–56.

10. Henry Van Dyke, *The Spirit of America* (New York: Macmillan, 1910), 192.

11. Philip Gibbs, *People of Destiny: Americans as I Saw Them at Home and Abroad* (New York: Harpers, 1920), 111–12.

12. Letter in the *Southern Illinoisan* [Carbondale, Ill.], March 7, 1991, 8.

13. D. Lincoln Canfield, *East Meets West South of the Border* (Carbondale: Southern Illinois University Press, 1968), esp. 33–34, 39.

14. James Fallows, *More Like Us: Making America Great Again* (Boston:

Houghton Mifflin, 1989), 26–27. Fallows stresses "putting America's native strengths and traditional values to work to overcome the Asian challenge" (especially from Japan).

15. This brief discussion of pragmatism is based in large part on the comprehensive study by Cecil V. Crabb. Jr., *American Diplomacy and the Pragmatic Tradition* (Baton Rouge: Louisiana State University Press, 1989).

16. Charles W. Kegley, Jr., "Neo-Idealism: A Practical Matter" (Carnegie Council on Ethics and International Affairs) *Ethics and International Affairs*, 1988, 2:173–98.

17. Jack E. Holmes, *The Mood/Interest Theory of Foreign Policy* (Lexington: University Press of Kentucky, 1985), esp. 54–58.

18. Samuel P. Huntington, *American Politics: The Promise of Disharmony* (Cambridge: The Belknap Press of the Harvard University Press, 1981), 261.

19. George F. Kennan, *American Diplomacy, 1900–1950* (Chicago: University of Chicago Press, 1951), 146.

20. Niebuhr, 138.

21. Robert E. Fitch, *A Certain Blind Man* (New York: Scribners, 1944), 117–18.

22. Ralph Henry Gabriel, *The Course of American Democratic Thought* (New York: Ronald Press, 1940), 14, 16.

23. Among recent indices of the religious beliefs and practices of Americans are the following polls, in percentages: 87 percent believe in God (Gallup, 1990); 74 percent have nade a commitment to Jesus Christ (Gallup, 1990); 92 percent believe religion is important in their daily lives (CBS/NYT, 1990); 63 percent, religion can answer all or most of today's problems (Gallup, 1990); 68 percent are members of a church or synagogue (Gallup, 1989); 74 percent of church members engage in charitable activities (Gallup, 1988); 43 percent attend a religious service more than two or three times a month (NORC, 1990). Such figures have been fairly high for the last 50 years. From *The American Enterprise*, Nov.–Dec. 1990, 96–104. Polls show that American involvement in religion is far higher than in Western Europe, for example.

24. Conal Furay, *The Grass-Roots Mind in America: The American Sense of Absolutes* (New York: New Viewpoints, Franklin Watts, 1977), esp. 136.

25. Gabriel, *The Course of American Democratic Thought*, 2nd ed. (New York: Ronald Press, 1956), 19–20.

26. Ibid., 22, 25.

27. Arthur M. Schlesinger, *Paths to the Present* (New York: Macmillan, 1949), 91–92. See also Arthur M. Schlesinger, Jr., *The Cycles of American History* (Boston: Houghton Mifflin, 1986).

28. This theory was first presented, with statistical evidence, by Frank L. Klingberg, "The Historical Alternation of Moods in American Foreign Policy," *World Politics* 4(2), (January 1952): 239–73.

29. William Allen White, in 1925, identified the first three cycles in

American history as the "Revolutionary Cycle" to 1823, the Anti-Slavery Cycle, and the Populist Cycle up to 1917. He saw the America of 1925 "pipping at the shell of a larger destiny" related to the new world age. The dates he used correspond to the cycles just described. William Allen White, *Some Cycles of Cathay* (Chapel Hill: University of North Carolina Press, 1925), vi, 1–2.

30. Karl Jaspers, *The Origin and Goal of History* (New Haven: Yale University Press, 1953), 222.

31. This cultural-political cycle is treated more fully in Frank L. Klingberg, *Cyclical Trends in American Foreign Policy Moods: The Unfolding of America's World Role* (Lanham, Md.: University Press of America, 1983).

32. Harold D. Lasswell, *The Analysis of Political Behavior* (New York: Oxford University Press, 1949), 180–94; first published in the *American Journal of Sociology*, January 1932.

33. Charles A. Beard gave these to Professor George S. Counts (from Memorandum on "Beard's Laws of History," Southern Illinois University, 1966).

34. Schlesinger, *The Cycles of American History*, 25–29, 43.

35. The debate was clearly joined in articles in the *Atlantic Monthly* for July 1991: Alan Tonelson, "What is the National Interest?" pp. 35-52 (concluding, "after a half-century of internationalist predominance, internationalism would be superseded by a foreign policy for the rest of us"); Joseph F. Nye, Jr., "Why the Gulf War Served the National Interest," pp. 54, 56–64 ("in a world of interdependence Americans cannot afford to define the national interest in domestic or international terms alone"); Christopher Layne, "Why the Gulf War Was Not in the National Interest," pp. 55, 65–81 ("The Gulf Crisis is proof that old ways of thinking die hard").

CHAPTER II

The Colonial Outlook: Providence and the Moral Law (1587–1776)

Although there was a mixture of motives among the early English colonists in America, a special world historical role was envisaged, particularly by the Puritans of Massachusetts: building a new Protestant Christian society which would serve as an example to the world. In the words of John Winthrop on his way to America in 1630: "we must consider that we shall be as a City upon a Hill, the eyes of all people are upon us." They were setting forth on an "errand" for the Lord; Samuel Danforth stressed this in his election sermon of May 11, 1670, entitled "A Brief Recognition of New England's Errand Into the Wilderness." The colonists felt like the ancient Israelites, moving into a "promised land" under the guidance of Providence, having a firm covenant with God to abide by His principles of justice and love.[1] Another goal was the spreading of the Christian faith, particularly among the native Americans (Indians). Thus was a society and government to be built upon the doctrine of the "fundamental law," based on the principles enshrined in the Old and New Testaments of the Bible. The idea of the covenant with God was basically a belief in the special mission or purpose of the people on the world scene. (Relations with native Americans and African-Americans at this time were seemingly regarded as outside the covenant, except for the goal of their Christianization).

The colonial time can be logically divided into two parts, based on the tripartite cultural-political succession: 1587–1729, the establishment of a distinct American society, based on religious principles; and 1729–76, preparation for an independent nation stressing democratic principles. An earlier period, 1445–1587 (the first period in modern European history), may also be noted as vital in the preparation for the building of a Protestant English America—in terms of the explorations of the New World, the Protestant Reformation (including the development of Puritanism in England and Presbyterianism in Scotland), and the rise of British sea power (climaxed by the defeat of the Spanish Armada in 1588).

The time from 1587 to 1729 may be divided into three periods in which the "moral law" was firmly established in the colonies:

(1) 1587–1634 (preparation): an "enlightenment" in England; the idea of permanent English settlements; and the small-scale demonstration of their feasibility in Virginia (1607) and Massachusetts (1620).

(2) 1634–82 (struggle): the rapid growth of the colonies, stimulated by the British Civil War and the international wars; religious persecution in England and the colonies; the Puritan theocracy in New England, with the issue of colonial liberties remaining in doubt.

(3) 1682–1729 (consolidation): as England restored Parliamentary supremacy in the Glorious Revolution (1688–89), the colonies re-established their legislative autonomy and the spirit of religious liberty and toleration developed; a sense of virtual American "nationality" was growing.

The next major period in American history ("liberty and union," 1729–1871) began at the time of the so-called Enlightenment (1729–76). In looking at each of the colonial periods, it is to be noted that each of the three basic ideas of America were developing—namely, the moral law, liberty (the free individual) and union, and America's world mission. But the emphasis before 1729 was clearly placed upon the moral law—the religious foundation of the colonies.

Preparation for English Colonization, 1587–1634

Two events helped inaugurate the probability of English colonization: (1) the "Lost Colony" under Governor John White (here was born Virginia Dare, the first white baby); and (2) the defeat of the Spanish Armada in 1588, thereby establishing English naval supremacy in the North Atlantic.

The creation of *English* colonies meant the transfer of the English language, religion and political institutions to North America. This was the England of Shakespeare (1564–1616) and the King James Version of the Bible (1611). The first permanent colony was at Jamestown, where the ships arrived on May 13, 1607. The motivation was largely commercial, but religious influence was important and Captain John Smith expressed his sense of Providential guidance. In the following year, 1608, the French established a post at Quebec; and in 1609, the Dutch explorer, Henry Hudson, entered the river which bears his name, and the Spanish founded Santa Fe.

New England was to prove to be the seat of the basic conception and power of the "moral law" in America, and the most influential area in the development of the nation. The Pilgrims left Holland in 1620 and sailed from Plymouth, England, for America on September 16, with a sense of Providential guidance. They had a letter from their pastor, John Robinson, who remained behind. This letter, quoted by William Bradford in 1647–48, described the spirit back of the venture:

> . . . so doth the Lord call us in a singular manner upon occasions of such difficulty and danger as lieth upon you, to a both more narrow search and careful reflection of your ways in his sight. . . .
>
> Now next after this heavenly peace with God and our own consciences, we are carefully to provide for peace with all men. . . .
>
> . . . Whereas you are become a body politic, using amongst yourselves civil government, and are not furnished with any person of special eminence above the rest . . . let your wisdom and godliness appear, not only in choosing such persons as to entirely love and well promote the common good, but also in yielding unto them all due honor and obedience in their lawful administration . . .
>
> Fare you well in him in whom you trust, and in whom I rest.[2]

Bradford wrote that the Pilgrims not only yearned for their *own* home free from religious persecution, but possessed "a great hope and inward zeal . . . of laying some good foundation, or at least to make some way thereunto, for the propagating and advancing of the Gospel of the kingdom of Christ in those remote parts of the world. . . ."[3]

After the successful voyage of the Mayflower, the famous *Mayflower Compact* was adopted on November 11, 1620, in part as follows:

> In the name of God, Amen. We . . . having undertaken for the glory of God, and advancement of the Christian faith, and honor of our king and country, a voyage to place the first colony in the Northern part of

Virginia, do by these presents solemnly and mutually in the presence of
God . . . covenant and combine ourselves together into a civil body
politic. . . .[4]

Following increased persecution of the Puritans and the dissolution
of Parliament by Charles I in 1629, a large emigration of Puritans from
England began in 1630, when John Winthrop led nine ships to Boston.
John Eliot, "apostle to the Indians," arrived in 1631, and the renowned
Puritan theologian and preacher, John Cotton, came in 1633. The spirit
of the Puritan settlers in Massachusetts is shown in John Cotton's
sermon, "God's Promise to His Plantation," delivered in Southampton,
England, in 1630 to the large band of emigrants about to embark on the
Arabella under the leadership of John Winthrop. John Cotton applied
the Old Testament promises directly to these pioneers, who, he said,
"plainly see a providence of God leading them from one Country to
another":

> . . . God is said to plant a people more especially, when they
> become *Trees of righteousness*, Is. 61:8. . . .
> Every plantation that he hath not planted shall be plucked up, and
> what he hath planted shall surely be established. . . .[5]

Moses Coit Tyler wrote that the first generation in New England had
"an historical consciousness; a belief . . . in the large human
significance of its great task of founding a new order of things in
America; an assurance that what it was doing the future would desire
to know about. . . ."[6] A certain degree of "liberty" was established in
the colonies during this period. Representative government was
introduced in Virginia in 1619, when delegates from eleven plantations
assembled at James City (ironically, this was the same year when the
first black slaves were imported to Virginia from Africa). After the
promulgation of the written constitution of 1621, supreme power was
vested in the colonial legislature and in the King, as King of Virginia.
But the stern, unyielding tradition of liberty was established in Puritan
Massachusetts, the state in which the Revolution later began. The annual
election of governors and magistrates there by qualified citizens was the
rule, along with the election of church ministers, who were so
influential. Thus, given almost complete freedom from the start, these
colonists soon showed they were prepared to fight if necessary to keep
their "traditional" political liberties.

As throughout American history, the moves outward from England in colonizing America were concentrated particularly in the latter phase of this first period (1587–1634)—that is, there appeared to be a type of "extroversion" after 1607.

Colonial Growth in a Revolutionary Time, 1634–82

As early as 1634, when Charles I was in the midst of ruling England without Parliament, a special commission for the colonies was established, including the Archbishop of Canterbury, with "full power over the American plantations." Governor John Winthrop wrote of the advice given by the ministers meeting in Boston: "they all agreed, that if a general governor were sent, we ought not to accept him, but defend our lawful possessions, if we were able. . . ."[7] England moved to take away the charter of Massachusetts, while the colonists "protracted" and in 1638 refused to surrender the charter, with their agent in London arguing in terms which foreshadowed the Revolution. The colony was saved at this juncture by the increasing domestic troubles of Charles I, but the spirit of liberty had been made plainly manifest. The first printing done in America was "The Oath of a Free-Man" in 1639.

The stern Massachusetts spirit of ordered liberty, in a theocratic spirit, was a vital element in the American tradition, but a more "modern" type of liberty was established during the same period in Connecticut and Rhode Island. The Rev. Thomas Hooker left Massachusetts for Connecticut in 1636, and led the way to the adoption in 1639 of the Fundamental Orders of Connecticut, constituting such a liberal constitution that it lasted into the 19th century. Rhode Island was founded by Roger Williams, who was banished from Massachusetts in 1635 for his espousal of religious and intellectual freedom. He was able to secure a charter in 1644 from the Long Parliament which gave the colony full power to govern itself, in a democratic manner.

In relation to "union" as well as "liberty," New England in particular experimented with inter-colonial cooperation and organization. Although some relations with the native American Indians were friendly, the Pequot War of 1636–37 witnessed combined military action against them. Further threats from the Indians and pressure from the Dutch and French resulted in the establishment of the New England Confederation in 1643, lasting until 1684. Of course, too, all the British colonies were inside the British "union."

As compared to Europe, which was beginning to feel strongly the movements toward secularism and rationalism, the New England colonies stressed Judeo-Christian principles. In this sense, Christianity was having a virtual new birth in America. Furthermore, while Europe was engaged in bitter warfare, both religious and dynastic (for example, the Thirty Years War, 1618–48), the American colonies were in relative peace. When England was ravaged by the great Civil War (1642–46) and ruled by Cromwell (1649–58), the colonial settlements were developing a sturdy sense of self-reliance.

In Europe, this revolutionary age (1634–82) produced great secular thinkers, such as Descartes (1596–1650) in France and Hobbes (1588–1679) in England. The thinkers in America at this time were the influential Christian ministers. M. C. Tyler stressed the intellectuality, earnestness, asceticism and "intolerance" of the "heroic" ministers of New England. They were the natural leaders of society, somewhat comparable to the judges and prophets in the Old Testament.[8] Education, too, was stressed in New England—Harvard was founded in 1636, particularly for the education of ministers.

Developments in the colonies reflected the major events in the English Civil War, the wars of England with Holland and Spain, and the expansion of French colonial strength. Furthermore, the colonists had their own bitter internal struggles and faced the continuing menace of the Indians, particularly in the climactic King Philip's War (1675–76). Events of the time brought continuous challenges to the Christian leaders of New England, as they sought to interpret Providence to the inhabitants and fight off the "Satanic" tendencies of the revolutionary times.

Stern Christian motivation and discipline may well have been vital to the very existence and permanence of these colonies. Belief and trust in a sovereign God led to an interpretation of all life—individual and social—as guided by Providential purposes. Students of the thought and literature of the time testify to this felt presence of God. Stanley Thomas Williams wrote that all the records of the events of the time "reveal a powerful people engaged in a soul-testing enterprise" and that "the severe views of life taught by English Puritanism were intensified by the realities of the frontier," so that "famine, disease, and warfare breathe new life into such worn phrases as 'God's Protecting Providence.' "[9]

All major events seemed, in one way or another, to lead to the ultimate strengthening of the colonies. For example, Archbishop Laud's persecution of the Puritans in the 1630s prompted the "Great Migration" into New England until 1642 (there were around 50,000 English settlers by 1641), while the Civil War and Puritan victory until 1660 gave New England the time to consolidate its position against further effective challenge. Following Cromwell's ascendancy in 1649, Anglicans, in their turn, poured into Virginia until 1660, to lay the basis for the future greatness of that colony in the 18th century. Under the Stuart Restoration, Rhode Island and Connecticut were able to gain liberal charters which were followed, as constitutions, into the 19th century. King Philip's War induced reforms in New England. The deteriorating situation in Virginia was climaxed by Bacon's Rebellion in 1676, and Culpeper's Rebellion covered the years from 1677 to 1680 in North Carolina.

Throughout all these events the leaders of New England held fast to the Christian faith and exhorted the people to obey the strict moral and spiritual code, laying the foundations of the nation on a closely "reasoned" Christian faith. Thomas Hooker and Roger Williams were ahead of their time in perceiving the special spirit of liberty inherent in the "moral law." Hooker's emphasis on the "free consent of the people" was undergirded with a powerful moral discipline which sought God's guidance for the individual.[10]

Roger Williams stressed liberty of conscience and separation of church and state. He expressed his spirit of toleration in 1644 in these terms: "it is the will and command of God, that . . . a permission of the most Paganish, Jewish, Turkish, or Antichrist conscience and worship be granted to all men, in all matters and countries; and they are only to be fought against with that sword which is only, in soul-matters, able to conquer, to wit, the sword of God's Spirit, the word of God."[11] It should be noted too that the Catholic settlement made in Maryland in 1634 had established freedom of religion for all Christians, and the principle of toleration for all those who believed in Jesus Christ was reaffirmed by legislative act in 1649.

As the colonists in Massachusetts faced difficulties and witnessed the rise of "evil" in their midst, the divines pointed out the guidance and mercy of Providence in the past and God's sure judgment on evil ways. In 1662, Michael Wigglesworth (1631–1705) published *The Day of Doom: Or a Poetical Description of the Great and Last Judgment*—a work reported to be more popular throughout New England for a century than any other except the Bible. The call for spiritual renewal became more powerful during the last half of the revolutionary period, while dangers and disasters increased. Calamities piled up on London in the middle 1660s: a great plague took around 75,000 lives in 1665; the Great Fire burned for four days in 1666 to destroy much of the city; and the Dutch fleet threatened the city in 1666 and 1667.

William Stoughton (1636–1701) delivered an "election sermon" in 1668 on "New England's True Interest." In it, he included a sentence which became famous: "God sifted a whole nation that he might send choice grain over into the wilderness."[12] While stressing the advantages and privileges of living in such a "covenant state," Stoughton reminded a "backsliding" people of their sins and of their possibilities. Troubles for Massachusetts were mounting to a rapid climax, as King Philip's War began in 1675 with sudden Indian raids on border settlements, including a terrible massacre near Deerfield; and the colony too endured a plague.

Increase Mather published a powerful "prophetic" tract in 1676, stating his firm conviction that God was using the Indians to chastise them for their evil behavior, which he described in some detail. Comparing the people of New England to the early Israelites under Moses, he called for a "covenant renewal" and other spiritual reforms, including more concern for the conversion of the Indians and more respect for converted Indians. Mather ended his tract concerning the judgment of God on New England with an admonition to all the nations of the world, and prophecies from Scripture that wars shall end after a time of great tribulation.[13] Within the next few years a powerful spiritual renewal appears to take place in the churches of New England. Mather's Second Church in Boston, and other churches, explicitly renewed their covenant with God and with one another.

The expansion of the colonies proceeded quite rapidly during this period, particularly in the latter (extrovert) phase after 1654. Certain early colonial claims included the Pacific Ocean as their western boundary. For example, Connecticut's charter of 1662, obtained from Charles II, granted to the colony lands extending to the Pacific. After 1660, the colonists pushed the frontier rapidly to the west. The second Dutch War gained for England in 1664 the cosmopolitan area of New Amsterdam, laying the foundations for the colonies of New York, New Jersey and Delaware. King Philip's War (1675–76) reduced the danger of Indian attacks.

By the early 1680s, the special violent revolutionary era was apparently coming to an end. The colonies were ready to enter upon a new phase of consolidation and development. The stern Puritan theocracy in Massachusetts was declining in strength, while the spirit of

Christianity was being renewed in the colonies with a more tolerant emphasis.

Consolidation of the "American" System in the Colonies, 1682–1729

During this period, dominated by a softer but perhaps more pervasive religious tone, the colonies began to demonstrate a more typically American character. The stern Puritan discipline had done its work in laying solid foundations—spiritually and politically. The colonies were now dominated by men born in America; for example, the two best known ministers and writers of the time were father and son, both born in America—Increase Mather (1639–1723) and Cotton Mather (1663–1728). The new "synthesis" in America was demonstrated most clearly in the rise of greater religious and nationality toleration, a broader intellectual development, continued Christian growth, the permanent establishment of representative government, and a decisive weakening of France in North America. Each of these points will be briefly summarized.

The establishment of the new colony of Pennsylvania and the "City of Brotherly Love" (Philadelphia) by William Penn in 1682 was a key development for the new America. Penn was a Quaker who believed in freedom of conscience. His colony attracted a large number of different nationality groups, in addition to the English, notably Germans, Scotch-Irish, Swedes, Dutch, Irish and Welsh. Religions were even more numerous: in addition to the Quakers, there were Presbyterians, Anglicans, Catholics, Lutherans, Reformed, Mennonites, Baptist, Dunkards, and the like. Here was the typical American mixture of nationalities and religions, all loyal to the new colony and its principles. The basic motive of Penn was religious. "I came for the Lord's sake," he said in 1682.[14] Similarly, the growing colony of New York became steadily more cosmopolitan, as it had tended to be from the beginning. There were reported to be a dozen nationalities there when the English took over in 1664, and the first Jews had arrived in 1654. The revocation of the Edict of Nantes by Louis XIV in 1685 led to the early arrival of French Huguenots (Calvinists) in New York, Massachusetts and South Carolina. The general tendency of the Anglican church in America was toward religious toleration, and New England was moving in this direction (where Rhode Island and Connecticut had long led the way).

Although the dominant note continued to be religious, with a new emphasis on freedom of conscience and voluntarism, intellectual interests were beginning to grow outside the field of theology. Students of law, medicine and education were beginning to write pamphlets and books. Almanacs became popular. This was the period in England of the great scientist Sir Isaac Newton (1642–1727), whose notable work *Principia Mathematica* was published in 1687; Newton saw no conflict between science and religion, and was deeply religious himself. William and Mary College was founded in Williamsburg, Virginia, in 1693, and Yale at New Haven, Connecticut, in 1701. The first continuous newspaper was started in Boston in 1704.

The Christian churches continued to expand their size and influence, although as the decades moved along the vital spark of conviction appeared to decline. In New England, Increase Mather was President of Harvard from 1685 to 1701. After that, his prestige declined, but he and his son, Cotton Mather, were still exceedingly influential. Increase Mather published at least 92 titles, mostly sermons. Cotton Mather was described by Tyler as "the literary behemoth of New England in our colonial era; the man whose fame as a writer surpasses, in later times and especially in foreign countries, that of any other pre-Revolutionary American, except Jonathan Edwards and Benjamin Franklin."[15] Williams wrote:

> He outlived the peak of the Puritan theocracy, but, with the exception of Jonathan Edwards, was its most marvelous product. In learning and spiritual effort he excelled his forbears, but in him the old rough Puritan vigor was somewhat tamed. His mood is more often that of the mystic. He was intensely active in the community and his published works were famous. . . .
> . . . There burned in Mather a pure and aspiring spirit, evident in his writings on the soul and its relations with God.[16]

Cotton Mather's best-known works were his *Magnalia Christi American* or "The Ecclesiastical History of New England, from its first planting in the year 1620, unto the year of our Lord 1698" (two volumes, 1702); and *Bonifacius* or *Essays to Do Good* (1710). Although the Salem witchcraft episode in 1692 suggested considerable religious fanaticism, yet the ultimate result was to produce a strong reaction toward more religious tolerance.

The famous *New England Primer* was first published in 1679. Its major emphasis on the Bible caused it to be called "The Little Bible of New England"; with its stern lessons, entirely religious and moral, "the Puritan mood is caught with absolute faithfulness."[17] The Quaker Jonathan Dickenson published a famous work in 1699 in Philadelphia, entitled *God's Protecting Providence, Man's Surest Help and Defence.* The Presbyterian Church was solidly established in America during this period, with its congregations organized into districts known as "presbyteries" and these into larger units called "synods." The first presbytery was organized in Philadelphia by Francis McKemie in 1706, and the first synod in 1718. (The Congregational Church had set the pattern for "pure democracy" as in the New England town meeting while the Presbyterian organization helped establish the system of "representative democracy" for a large area.) James Blair arrived in Virginia in 1685, to inaugurate a phase of important growth in the Anglican Church. He founded William and Mary College in 1693, and was its president for 49 years. His series of 117 discourses on *Our Savior's Divine Sermon on the Mount* was first published in 1722; Tyler described this work and its author in these terms:

> The tone of the author's mind is moderate, judicial, charitable, catholic. . . . The drift of his argument is steadily toward practical results. . . . While he insists upon the highest excellence in outward conduct, he shows that all moral significance attaches to the inward state of a mind. . . .
> . . . James Blair may be called the creator of the healthiest and most intensive intellectual influence that was felt in the southern group of colonies before the Revolution.[18]

Thomas Bray (1656–1730) was another noted Anglican clergyman who spent some time in America. He established the Anglican Church in Maryland in 1695, founded the Society for the Promotion of Christian Knowledge in 1698, and helped organize the very important Society for the Propagation of the Gospel in Foreign Parts. Isaac Watts published his famous hymnbooks in 1707 and 1719, including some of the best-known hymns of all time which he himself composed. Finally, there were early signs of the coming "Great Awakening" after 1720.

The major political developments in this time of "synthesis" in colonial development were the establishment of representative government with a deeper spirit of liberty in general, and the strengthening of the military security of the colonies against the French.

Both of these movements were tied in with England's Glorious Revolution in 1689, the bloodless overthrow of James II which brought William of Orange (William III) from Holland to the British throne. This established the supremacy of Parliament and the principle of representative government in Britain. John Locke's writings interpreting the Revolution were later very influential in America: *Letters on Toleration* (1689) and *Two Treatises of Civil Government* (1690).

The revolution in England brought a similar decisive shift in the colonies. England had cancelled the charter of Massachusetts in 1684, and had moved to tighten the imperial control over the vital colony. Increase Mather was finally sent to England to undertake the delicate negotiations involved in obtaining more freedom; after four years, with the aid of the Revolution, he secured a new charter (1691)—one which gave Massachusetts more legislative freedom and appointive power than perhaps any other colony. Representative government was also firmly established in New York (Leisler's Rebellion, 1688–91), Pennsylvania ("Glorious Revolution," 1688–91, and Charter of Liberties, 1701), Virginia, and the Carolinas (which had been established in the 1660s). A quarrel over church government gave rise to two notable books by John Wise (1652–1725). A project was pressed in 1705 to bring the churches under the control of the clergy. It was defeated by ministers like John Wise, who stressed democratic government in both church and state. Wise wrote *The Churches Quarrel Espoused* in 1710, and a systematic study entitled *Vindication of the Government of New England Churches* in 1717. With less Biblical emphasis, he stressed the equality of men, and an "original liberty" stamped upon man's "rational nature" by the Creator.[19] He has been called the first great American democrat.

The revocation of the Edict of Nantes in 1685 not only helped start the ultimate decline of French power, by forcing thousands of skilled Frenchmen into exile, but greatly increased the fear of French power felt by Protestant areas like the American colonies. The key event which promoted a solid coalition against French expansionism was the alliance of England and Holland under the same king in 1689. The War of the League of Augsburg (King William's War, 1689–97) was inconclusive, ending with all conquests restored (the Massachusetts colonists had captured Fort Royal, but their expedition against Quebec had failed).

Louis XIV's plan to "unite" the two powers of France and Spain brought the War of the Spanish Succession (Queen Anne's War, 1702–13), when the American colonists were presumably in an extrovert mood. Jeremiah Dummer, agent of Massachusetts in London from 1719 to 1721, wrote in 1709 of the necessity for a successful expedition into Canada. Showing "how early and passionate among the English colonies in America was the dread of the American power of France," he wrote "that those colonies can never be easy or happy whilst the French are masters of Canada!"[20] An English-colonial expedition conquered Port Royal in 1710, and the Treaty of Utrecht in 1713 gave England Nova Scotia, Newfoundland, and the Hudson Bay territory. The colonists, in a more secure position (strengthened also by an acknowledgement of their sovereignty from the warlike Iroquois Indians), were able to expand into the west, and to consolidate their position for the final struggle, to come later, with the French. Throughout this period the population of the English colonies had been increasing rapidly—from an estimated 200,000 in 1685 to 435,000 in 1715.

By the end of this period of consolidation for the colonies (1682–1729), not only had the goal of creating Protestant Christian societies, with considerable political and religious liberty, been largely achieved, but also the vision of an expanding English empire on the North American continent was clearly envisaged. George Berkeley, Irish philosopher and bishop who spent three years in America (1728–31), was one of the early foreign observers who felt strong confidence in the future development of America. Around 1725 he penned the poem "Verses on the Prospect of Planting Arts and Learning in America" which included the often-quoted phrase "westward the course of empire takes its way." Three of his verses read as follows:

There shall be soon another golden age,
    The rise of empire and of arts,
The good and great inspiring epic rage,
    The wisest heads and noblest hearts.

Not such as Europe breed in her decay;
    Such as she bred when fresh and young,
When heavenly flame did animate her clay,
    But future poets shall be sung.

Westward the course of empire takes its way,
    The first four Acts already past,
A fifth shall close the Drama with the day,
    Time's noblest offspring is the last.[21]

Preparation for American Independence, 1729–76

This was the beginning of a new grand period in American history (1729–1871), in which the spirit of "liberty and union" occupied the center of the stage. The separate colonies (all except Georgia, founded in 1733) had been firmly established by 1729, on a deep moral and spiritual foundation. The next decades were to prepare the intellectual, economic and political groundwork for a new spirit of "liberty" and of "union" and for the ultimate revolutionary break with England. This was the "Age of Enlightenment" in Europe and in the colonies.

Near the beginning of the period, a spiritual revival, known as the "Great Awakening," swept a number of the colonies. Weigle dates this movement—with its emphasis on a more vital, conscious religious experience—from 1720 to 1744.[22] Some others date it from 1734, the year when the strong Calvinist, Jonathan Edwards, delivered his powerful sermon on "Sinners in the Hands of an Angry God." John Wesley had started his Methodist movement in Britain in 1738. At his suggestion, the great preacher, George Whitefield, toured the colonies, 1738–41, with profound effect. Weigle summarized the effects of the movement:

> The Great Awakening, in spite of the excesses which characterized some of the revival meetings, had a profound influence upon contemporary thought, It quickened, as nothing else could have done, New England Puritanism, steadily losing the influence over the people which it had wielded in the seventeenth century. It helped to strengthen in an American-born generation the ideals and moral principles which in 1776 made men willing to pledge to each other "our Lives, our Fortunes, and our sacred Honor" in the great cause of freedom.[23]

After the early 1740s, a strong rational spirit entered theology, but there is much evidence that the clergy remained an extremely influential group in expounding a moral law which undergirded the growing spirit of liberty.

During this period, American intellectual life began to flourish. The acquittal of Peter Zenger in 1735 helped establish the principle of freedom of the press. Newspapers and periodicals abounded. Books and pamphlets on political science, economics, international relations, history and science began to appear. The typical figure of the time was the cosmopolitan Philadelphian Benjamin Franklin, who won a

European as well as an American reputation as a journalist, scientist, independent thinker and statesman. This was the period in which Virginia developed the remarkable group of men who played such a prominent role in helping establish state and national liberty: George Washington, Thomas Jefferson, James Madison, Patrick Henry, Richard Henry Lee, Peyton Randolph, George Mason, George Wyeth and many others.

The special challenges which fostered the American spirit of union as well as liberty came first from the French and Indians, and later from the British. Two wars were fought with the French. The first, the War of the Austrian Succession (King George's War, 1740–48) was inconclusive—conquests were restored, including Nova Scotia's Louisburg, captured by the colonials. As the French moved into the Ohio Valley, another conflict was seen as inevitable. Benjamin Franklin had stressed the importance of gaining control of sufficient territory for the expanding Americans, and he warned the colonies of the danger of the consolidation of French power in the Ohio Valley as well as in Canada. In his "Observations Concerning the Increase of Mankind," he wrote in 1751, after noting that America already had a million inhabitants and was increasing at a faster rate than Britain:

> This million doubling but once in 25 Years, will, in another Century, be more than the People of England, and the greatest Number of *Englishmen* will be on this side the Water. What an Accession of Power to the *British* Empire by Sea as well as Land. What Increase of Trade and Navigation! . . . How important an Affair then to *Britain* is the present Treaty for setting the Bounds between her Colonies and the French, and how careful should she be to secure Room enough, since on the Room depends as much the Increase of her People.[24]

Franklin spearheaded an abortive plan for colonial union in the Albany Congress of 1754, as the final colonial war with France was beginning—the French and Indian War (the Seven Years War in Europe, 1756–63); this was again in the extrovert phase of the period.

Quebec fell to the English in 1759, and Canada surrendered in 1760. Franklin stressed the importance of keeping Canada, in a letter of January 3, 1760, to Lord James:

> No one can more sincerely rejoice than I do, on the reduction of Canada; and this is not merely as I am a colonist, but as I am a Briton.

> I have long been of the opinion, that the *foundations of the future grandeur and stability of the British empire lie in America*; and though, like other foundations, they are low and little seen, they are, nevertheless, broad and strong enough to support the greatest political structure human wisdom ever erected. I am therefore by no means for restoring Canada. It we keep it, all the country from the St. Lawrence to the Mississippi will in another century be filled with British people. . . . If the French remain in Canada they will continually harass our colonies by the Indians, and impede if not prevent their growth; your progress to greatness will at best be slow. . . .[25]

Franklin also published an influential pamphlet in London in 1760, explaining the interest of Great Britain in acquiring Canada. He assured the British there would be no danger to them from the colonies, for there would be fourteen separate governments, and their union would be impossible "without the most grievous tyranny and oppression." Additional territory would naturally mean increased population and power.[26]

George Washington was another who saw the significance of the Western frontier. From his personal experience there during the French and Indian War, he wrote to Lt. Governor Francis Fauquier (December 2, 1758), stressing the necessity of keeping Fort Duquesne (on the site of Pittsburgh), after its capture in November.

> Unless the most effectual measures are taken early in the spring to reinforce the garrison at Fort Duquesne the place will inevitably be lost, and then our frontiers will fall into the same distressed condition that they have been in for some time past. For I can very confidently assert, that we never can secure them properly, if we again lose our footing on the Ohio, as we consequently lose the interest of the Indians. I therefore think, that every necessary preparation should be making, not a moment should be lost in taking the most speedy and efficacious steps in securing the infinite advantages which may be derived from our regaining possession of that important country.[27]

Also during the struggle with France for empire, the almanac for 1758 in Pennsylvania published a notable essay on "America—its Past, Present, and Future State." The essay forecast the great future development of the physical resources of the continent:

> Our numbers will not avail till the colonies are united. . . . If we do

not join heart and hand in the common cause against our exulting foes, but fall to disputing among ourselves, it may really happen as the governor of Pennsylvania told his assembly, "We shall have no privilege to dispute about, nor country to dispute in. . . ."

So arts and sciences will change the face of nature in our tour from hence over the Appalachian Mountains to the Western Ocean. . . . Huge mountains of iron ore are already discovered; and vast stores are reserved for future generations. This metal, more useful than gold and silver, will employ millions of hands. . . .

O ye unborn inhabitants of America! Should this page escape its destined conflagration at year's end, and these alphabetical letters remain legible when your eyes behold the sun after he has reeled the seasons round for two or three centuries more, you will know in Anno Domini, 1758, we dreamed of your times.[28]

By the Treaty of Paris in 1763, all Canada became British, as did the territory west to the Mississippi River. With the defeat of the Indian leader, Pontiac, from 1763 to 1766, the colonial west became relatively secure for settlement, and colonists poured over the mountains into the areas of West Virginia, Tennessee and Kentucky.

With the French threat eliminated, the colonists were in a practical position to resist the English efforts at tightening control and levying taxes without the consent of the colonial legislatures. The Stamp Act Congress of 1765 showed that the colonies were prepared to cooperate in resistance to what was regarded as English tyranny. Events moved to a quick climax, while the colonies grew rapidly in population—from 1,500,000 in 1754 to 2,600,000 in 1774. Massachusetts, the colony in which the "moral law" had been so solidly founded, was the center of the drama—with leading figures such as John Adams, Samuel Adams, John Hancock and James Otis.

Carl Becker has emphasized two main sources of the American drive for independence: (1) the strength of the "natural rights" philosophy in the American colonies and (2) the development, after the defeat of France, of the theory that the British Empire was a voluntary federation of practically independent states.[29] The natural rights theory has been stressed by John Locke at the time of the Glorious Revolution (1688–89), and developed by the French philosophers, Montesquieu (*The Spirit of Laws*, 1748) and Rousseau (*The Social Contract*, 1762). It was believed that these rights could be deduced by man's reason from human nature as created by God, and that they were established in an understood "social contract" between a government and the people. As Neuhaus reminds us, the 17th century in America stressed Providential destiny and a covenant with God, while the 18th century enlightenment had a vision of rational order established through the social contract.[30] The laws of Nature could be discovered by "right reason" and conscience.

Alice M. Baldwin has pointed out the role of the New England clergy in tieing together the thought of America in the 17th and 18th centuries. In *The New England Clergy and the American Revolution*, she endeavors to show "how the New England clergy preserved, extended, and popularized the essential doctrines of political philosophy, thus making familiar to every church-going New Englander long before 1763 not only the doctrines of natural right, the social contract, and the right of resistance but also the fundamental principle of American constitutional law, that government, like its citizens, is bounded by law and when it transcends its authority it acts illegally."[31] After presenting the evidence from the influential clergymen of the period (such as Jonathan Mayhew, 1720–66, and Charles Chauncy, 1705–87), her conclusion is stated as follows:

> The similarity between the political philosophy of the seventeenth century and that of the American Revolution has often been pointed out, but the lines of transmission have never been clearly traced. The teachings of the New England ministers provide one unbroken line of descent. . . . Such principles had been used to divine the relative powers of rulers and people. They had been called upon to strengthen the hands of the colonists against over-bearing governors and councils of church members against the tyranny of pastors, and of governing bodies, both civil and religious, against an unruly people. In such struggles, in defense of Hanoverian against Stuart, in the French and Indian War, these theories had become associated with cherished personal liberties and with the protection of home, church, and country. Thus they had been woven into the warp and woof of New England thought. . . .
>
> A study such as this of the teachings of the ministers proves . . . that a New Englander could not have helped thinking in terms of natural and fundamental law and constitutional right. . . .
>
> They were firmly convinced that civil liberties and religious liberty were inextricably tied together. . . .
>
> With a vocabulary enriched by the Bible they made resistance and at last independence and war a holy cause. . . .
>
> Resistance thus became a sacred duty to a people who still were, on the whole, a religious people. The urge of restless discontent with conditions, with high taxes and hard times, . . . the independent spirit

of the frontier, the travail of a nation in birth, were given legal and religious sanction.[32]

The generally accepted American belief in the legislative freedom of the colonies inside the British Empire was challenged squarely by the direct levying of specific taxes on legal documents in Parliament's Stamp Act of 1765. The Act, which affected all regions in America, brought the colonists together in spirit and action. In October 1765 the Stamp Act Congress, meeting in New York City, resolved, in part: "That it is inseparably essential to the freedom of a people, and the undoubted right of Englishmen, that no taxes be imposed on them but with their own consent, given personally or by their representatives" and "that the people of these colonies are not, and from their local circumstances cannot be, represented in the House of Commons in Great Britain."[33] Bernard Bailyn writes that "it had been the Stamp Act that had led John Adams to see in the original settlement of the colonies 'the opening of a grand scene and design in providence for the illumination of the ignorant and the emancipation of the slavish part of mankind all over the earth.' "[34] Colonial opposition brought about the repeal of the Stamp Act in 1766, but Parliament at the same time declared its power to tax, and in 1767 passed the Townshend Acts levying duties on glass, lead, paint, paper and tea.

British troops began arriving in Boston in 1768, and a confrontation occurred between the army and citizens on March 5, 1770 (the "Boston Massacre") in which five Bostonians were killed (including Crispus Attucks, a black). John Adams himself successfully defended the British soldiers, in the light of colonial provocation. All the Townshend duties were repealed in April 1770, except the one on tea.

The spirit of the times gave rise to high hopes for the future of America. Philip Freneau, then a student at Princeton, had *A Poem on the Rising Glory of America* published in 1772, in part as follows:

This is thy praise America . . .

The seat of empire, the abode of kings,
the final stage where time shall introduce
Renowned characters, and glorious works
Of high invention and of wond'rous art,
which not the ravages of time shall waste
Till he himself has run his long career.[35]

On June 9, 1772, some citizens of Providence burned the revenue sloop *Gaspee*. Britain ordered individuals charged with the act of vandalism to Britain for trial. But it was the Boston Tea Party which brought the crisis to a head; Bostonians had sunk 114 chests of tea in the harbor on December 16, 1773. Parliament responded in February 1774 by passing the so-called Coercive Acts which brought the government of Massachusetts under direct British control and closed the Port of Boston. All the colonies resented and feared the British actions. Patrick Henry expressed the new spirit of union in September 1774: "The distinctions between Virginians, Pennsylvanians, New Yorkers and New Englanders are no more. I am not a Virginian, but an American."[36]

The First Continental Congress met in Carpenter's Hall, Philadelphia, September 5 to October 26, 1774. On the second day the Congress resolved to open the next session with prayers by the Rev. Mr. Duché. He read from Psalm 35: "Plead thou my case, O Lord, with them that strive with me, and fight thou against them that fight against me. Lay hand upon the shield and buckler, and stand up to help me." Catherine Drinker Bowen writes that "the effect was electric. Men bowed their heads and wept. Surely these sacred words had been written for this day, for this company, this hour." He continued with the Psalm: "for they have privily laid their net to destroy me without a cause. . . . False witnesses did rise up." As he continued with an extemporaneous prayer, members fell to their knees, and "when his voice ceased, they took their seats again, renewed, heartened."[37]

The Declaration and Resolves of the First Continental Congress, signed on October 14, 1774, declared:

> That the inhabitants of the English Colonies in North America, by the immutable laws of nature, the principles of the English constitution, and the several charters or compacts, have the following Rights:
>
> 1. That they are entitled to life, liberty, and property & they have never ceded to any sovereign power whatever, a right to dispose of either without their consent.
>
> 2. That our ancestors, who first settled these colonies, were at the time of their emigration from the mother country, entitled to the rights, liberties, and immunities of free and natural-born subjects within the realm of England.
>
> 3. That by such emigration they by no means forfeited, surrendered, or lost any of these rights, but that they were, and their descendants now are entitled to the exercise and enjoyment of all such of them, as

their local and other circumstances enable then to exercise and enjoy.

4. That the foundation of English liberty, and of all free government, is a right in the people to participate in their legislative council; and . . . they are entitled to a free and exclusive power of legislation in their several legislatures, where their right of representation can alone be preserved, in all cases of taxation and internal policy, subject only to the negative of their sovereign, in such manner as has been heretofore used and accustomed. . . .[38]

William Pitt (First Earl of Chatham, Prime Minister during the Seven Years War) on January 20, 1775, praised the spirit of the colonists as he appealed on the floor of Parliament for "conciliation" instead of suppression:

I contend, not for indulgence, but justice in America. . . . Resistance to your acts was as necessary as just; and your vain declaration of the omnipotence of Parliament, and your imperious doctrines of the necessity of submission, will be found equally impotent to convince or to enslave your fellow subjects in America, who feel that tyranny, whether ambitioned by an individual part of the legislature, or by the bodies who compose it, is equally intolerable to all British subjects. . . . Woe be to him who sheds the first, the inexpiable drop of blood, in an impious war with a people contending in the great cause of public liberty! . . . All attempts to enforce servitude upon such men—must be vain, must be futile. We shall be forced ultimately to retract; let us retract while we can, not when we must.[39]

Patrick Henry spoke to the Virginia Convention in St. John's Church in Richmond on March 23, 1775, calling on the colonials to fight, and ending with his most famous words:

. . . Sir, we are not weak, if we make a proper use of the means which the God of nature placed in our power. Three millions of people, armed in the holy cause of liberty, and in such a country as that which we possess, are invincible by any force which our enemy can send against us. Besides, sir, we shall not fight our battles alone. There is a just God who presides over the destinies of nations; and who will raise friends to fight our battles for us. The battle, sir, is not to the strong alone; it is to the vigilant, the active, and the brave. . . . There is no retreat but in submission and slavery! Our chains are forged! Their clanking may be heard on the plains of Boston! The war is inevitable—and let it come! I repeat it, sir, let it come!

It is vain, sir, to extenuate the matter. Gentlemen may cry peace, peace—but there is no peace. The war is actually begun! The next gale that sweeps from the North will bring to our ears the clash of resounding arms! Our brethren are already in the field! Why stand we here idle? What is it that gentlemen wish? What would they have? Is life so dear, or peace so sweet, as to be purchased at the price of chains and slavery? Forbid it, Almighty God! I know what course others may take; but as for me, give me liberty or give me death![40]

When the British moved to take some of the arms of Massachusetts, the battles of Lexington and Concord were fought on April 19, 1775—the "shot heard 'round the world," as Emerson later wrote. The Second Continental Congress met on May 10, 1775, elected George Washington commander-in-chief, and the next day approved a statement on "The Causes and Necessity of Taking Up Arms":

. . . Honor, justice, and humanity forbid us tamely to surrender the freedom which we received from our gallant ancestors, and which our innocent posterity have a right to receive from us. We cannot endure the infamy and guilt of resigning succeeding generations to that wretchedness which inevitably awaits them if we basely entail hereditary bondage upon them.

Our cause is just. Our union is perfect. Our internal resources are great, and, if necessary, foreign assistance is undoubtedly attainable. We gratefully acknowledge, as signal instances of the Divine favor towards us, that his Providence would not permit us to be called into this severe controversy, until we were grown up to our present strength, had been previously exercised in warlike operations and possessed of the means of defending ourselves. With hearts fortified with these animating reflections, we must solemnly, before God and the world, declare that, exerting the utmost energy of those powers which our beneficent creator hath graciously bestowed upon us, the arms we have been compelled by our enemies to assume, we will, in defiance of every hazard, with unabating firmness and perseverance, employ for the preservation of our liberties; being with one mind resolved to die freemen rather than to live slaves. . . .

. . . We have not raised armies with ambitious designs of separating from Great Britain, and establishing independent states. We fight not for glory or conquest. . . .

With an humble confidence in the mercies of the supreme and impartial Judge and Ruler of the Universe, we most devoutly implore his divine goodness to protect us happily through the great conflict, to dispose our adversaries to reconciliation on reasonable terms, and thereby to relieve the empire of the calamities of civil war.[41]

On May 13, the Continental Congress sent a so-called "Olive Branch" Petition to the King: "Most Gracious Sovereign: We, your Majesty's faithful subjects in the Colonies . . . attached to your Majesty's person, family, and government, with all devotion that principle and affection can inspire: connected with Great Britain by the strongest ties that can unite societies, and deploring every event that tends in any degree to weaken them, we solemnly assure your Majesty, that we not only most ardently desire the former harmony between her and these Colonies may be restored, but that a concord may be established between them upon so firm a basis as to perpetuate its blessings, uninterrupted by any future dissensions to succeeding generations in both countries. . . ."[42]

The Battle of Bunker Hill, fought on June 17, 1775, was won by the British, but with heavy losses. The King issued a proclamation on August 23, 1775, for "suppressing rebellion and sedition." Not only had William Pitt been ignored, but also Edmund Burke, who had warned Parliament that Britain should conciliate, not provoke, the freedom-loving Americans:

> In this character of the Americans a love of freedom is the predominating feature which marks and distinguishes the whole; and as an ardent is always a jealous affection, your colonies become suspicious, restive, and untractable whenever they see the least attempt to wrest from them by force, or shuffle from them by chicane, what they think the only advantage worth living for. This fierce spirit of liberty is stronger in the English colonies, probably, than in any other people of the earth, and this from a great variety of powerful causes. . . .
>
> First, the people of the colonies are descendants of Englishmen. England, Sir, is a nation which still, I hope, respects, and formerly adored, her freedom. The colonists emigrated from you when this part of your character was most predominant. . . .
>
> The people are Protestants, and of that kind which is the most adverse to all implicit submission of mind and opinion. . . . This religion, under a variety of denominations agreeing in nothing but in the communion of the spirit of liberty, is predominant in most of the northern provinces. . . .
>
> . . . In the southern colonies . . . there is . . . a circumstance which, in my opinion . . . makes the spirit of liberty still more high and haughty than in those to the northward. It is that in Virginia and the Carolinas they have a vast multitude of slaves. Where this is the case

in any part of the world, those who are free are by far the most proud and jealous of their freedom. Freedom is to them not only an enjoyment, but a kind of rank and privilege. . . .

In no country, perhaps, in the world is the law so general a study. . . . This study renders men acute, inquisitive, dexterous, prompt in attack, ready in defense, full of resources. . . .

Three thousand miles of ocean lie between you and them. No contrivance can prevent the effect of this distance, in weakening government. . . .

The temper and character which prevail in our colonies are, I am afraid, unalterable by any human art. We cannot, I fear, falsify the pedigree of this fierce people, and persuade them that they are not sprung from a nation in which veins the blood of freedom circulates. . . . An Englishman is the unfittest person on earth to argue another Englishman into slavery.[43]

With Americans apparently still in the "extrovert" mood as the colonies prepared to resist the British, a force under Ethan Allen and Benedict Arnold captured Fort Ticonderoga, May 10, 1775, the day the Second Continental Congress convened. Congress then authorized the invasion of Canada: Brigadier General Richard Montgomery occupied Montreal on November 13, but Benedict Arnold's expedition against Quebec on September 13 ended in failure by December (the Americans were forced to retreat from Canada by May 1776).

Benjamin Franklin wrote to a friend in England on October 3, 1775, that unless England changed her policy:

A separation of course will be inevitable. 'Tis a million of pities so fair a plan as we have hitherto been engaged in, for increasing strength and empire with *public felicity*, should be destroyed by the mangling hands of a few blundering ministers. It will not be destroyed; God will protect and prosper it, you will only exclude yourselves with beating us into submission, you know neither the people nor the country.[44]

While Congress deliberated on the problem of independence, Thomas Paine published his famous pamphlet *Common Sense* in January 1776, calling for immediate separation from Britain:

. . . Europe, and not England, is the parent country of America. This new world hath been the asylum for the persecuted lovers of civil and religious liberty from *every part* of Europe. Hither have they fled, not from the tender embraces of the mother, but from the cruelty of the monster; and it is so far true of England, that the same tyranny which drove the first emigrants from home, pursues their descendants still. . . .

. . . It is true interest of America to steer clear of European contentions, which she can never do, while, by her dependence on Britain, she is made the heavyweight in the scale of British politics.

. . . Even the distance at which the Almighty hath placed England and America is a strong and natural proof that the authority of the one over the other, was never the design of heaven. . . .

'Tis repugnant to reason, to the universal order of things, to all examples from former ages, to suppose that this continent can long remain subject to any external power. The most sanguine in Britain doth not think so. The utmost stretch of human wisdom cannot, at this time, compass a plan, short of separation, which can promise the continent even a year's security. Reconciliation is *now* a fallacious dream.[45]

On May 16, Congress proposed that each colony develop its own frame of government. These early state constitutions were accompanied by bills of rights. The Virginia bill of rights (June 12, 1776), written by George Mason and Patrick Henry, declared in its first two sentences:

1. That all men are by nature equally free and independent, and have certain inherent rights, of which, when they enter into a state of society, they cannot by any compact deprive or divest their posterity; namely, the enjoyment of life and liberty, with the means of acquiring and possessing property, and pursuing and obtaining happiness and safety.

2. That all power is vested in, and consequently derived from the people; that magistrates are their trustees and servants, and at all times amenable to them.

And it ended with a statement of basic principles:

15. That no free government, or the blessings of liberty, can be preserved to any people, but by a firm adherence to justice, moderation, temperance, frugality and virtue, and by frequent recurrence to fundamental principles.

16. That religion, or the duty which we owe to our Creator, and the manner of discharging it, can be directed only by reason and conviction, not by force or violence; and therefore all men are equally entitled to the free exercise of religion, according to the dictates of conscience, and that it is the mutual duty of all to practice Christian forbearance, love,

and charity towards each other.[46]

John Adams had written to his wife on February 11, 1776, that he expected some critical event to take place in the spring:

> But the arbiter of events, the sovereign of the world, only knows which way the torrent will be turned. Judging by experience, by probabilities and all appearances, I conclude that it will roll on to dominion and glory, though the circumstances and consequences may be bloody.
>
> In such great changes and commotions, individuals are but atoms. It is scarcely worth while to consider what the consequences will be to us. What will be the effect upon the present and future millions, and millions of millions, is a question very interesting to benevolence, natural and Christian. God grant they may, and I firmly believe they will be happy.[47]

Congress debated a resolution for independence, and appointed a committee on June 11, 1776, to prepare a Declaration: Jefferson, Franklin, John Adams, Robert Livingston, and Roger Sherman. Jefferson's original draft included a statement against the slave trade, but this was deleted—however, Congress had already voted in April 1776 that no slaves be imported into the thirteen colonies (there were estimated to be 500,000 blacks in America in 1774, and 2,100,000 whites). On July 2, Congress voted for independence. The next day John Adams wrote to his wife, Abigail, about the special significance of the event for America and its future:

> Yesterday, the greatest question was decided, which ever was debated in America, and a greater perhaps, never was nor will be decided among men. . . . You will see in a few days a Declaration setting forth the causes which have impelled us to this mighty revolution, and the reasons which will justify us in the sight of God and man. . . .
>
> When I look back to the year 1761 . . . and run through the whole period . . . I am surprised at the suddenness as well as greatness of this revolution. Britain has been filled with folly, and America with wisdom. At least, this is my judgment. Time must determine. It is the will of Heaven that the two countries should suffer calamities still more wasting, and distresses yet more dreadful. . . . The furnace of affliction produces refinement, in States as well as individuals. And the new governments we are assuming in every part will require a purification

from our vices, and an augmentation of our virtues, or they will be no blessings. . . . But I must submit all my hopes and fears to an overruling Providence, in which, unfashionable as the faith may be, I firmly believe. . . .

The second day of July, 1776, will be the most memorable epoch in the history of America. I am apt to believe that it will be celebrated by succeeding generations as the great anniversary festival. It ought to be commemorated as the day of deliverance, by solemn acts of devotion to God Almighty. It ought to be solemnized with pomp and parades, with shows, games, sports, guns, bells, bonfires, and illuminations, from one end of this continent to the other, from this time forward, forevermore.

You will think me transported with enthusiasm, but I am not. I am well aware of the toil, and blood, and treasure, that it will cost us to maintain this declaration, and support and defend those States. Yet, through all the gloom, I can see the rays of ravishing light and glory. I can see that the end is more than worth all the means, and that posterity will triumph in that day's transaction, even although we should rue it, which I trust in God we shall not.[48]

It was on July 4, 1776, that Congress adopted the Declaration of Independence. This turned out to be the more appropriate day for celebration, for the Declaration typified America and its goals from that time forward, summarizing the people's widely held views, by this time, of individual rights, the purpose of government, and the right of revolution, as it begins:

When in the Course of human events, it becomes necessary for one people to dissolve the political bands which have connected them with another, and to assume among the Powers of the earth, the separate and equal station to which the Laws of Nature and of Nature's God entitle them, a decent respect to the opinions of mankind requires that they should declare the causes which impel them to the separation.

We hold these truths to be self-evident, that all men are created equal, that they are endowed by their Creator with certain unalienable Rights, that among these are Life, Liberty, and the pursuit of Happiness. That to secure these rights, Governments are instituted among Men, deriving their just powers from the consent of the governed. That whenever any Form of Government becomes destructive of these ends, it is the Right of the people to alter or to abolish it, and to institute new Government, laying its foundations on such principles and organizing its powers in such form, as to them shall seem most likely to effect their Safety and Happiness. . . .

After listing the alleged abuses of the British Crown against the colonies, the Declaration concluded with the following pledges:

> We, therefore, the Representatives of the united States of America, in General Congress, Assembled, appealing to the Supreme Judge of the world for the rectitude of our intentions, do, in the Name and by the Authority of the good People of these Colonies, solemnly publish and declare, That the United Colonies are, and of Right ought to be Free and Independent States; that they are Absolved from all Allegiance to the British Crown, and that all political connection between them and the State of Great Britain, is and ought to be totally dissolved; and that as Free and Independent States, they have full Power to levy War, conclude Peace, contract Alliances, establish Commerce, and to do all other Acts and Things which Independent States may of right do. And for the support of this Declaration, with a firm reliance on the Protection of Divine Providence, we mutually pledge to each other our Lives, our Fortunes and our sacred Honor.[49]

Bernard Bailyn ends his classic study on the ideological origins of the Revolution with this summary of the ideals of these Americans who were prepared to rebel against British authority:

> . . . Some, caught up in a vision of the future in which the peculiarities of American life became the marks of a chosen people, found in the defiance of traditional order the firmest of all grounds for their hope for a freer life. The details of this new world were not as yet clearly depicted; but faith ran high that a better world than any that had ever been known could be built where authority was distrusted and held in constant scrutiny; where the status of men flowed from their achievements and from their personal qualities, not from distinctions ascribed to them at birth; and where the use of power over the lives of men was jealously guarded and severely restricted. It was only where there was this defiance, this refusal to truckle, this distrust of all authority, political or social, that institutions would express human aspirations, not crush them.[50]

Those who disagreed with the separation from Britain (commonly called Tories) tended to move to Britain, Canada or Florida (owned by Britain from 1763 to 1783).

Thus, 169 years after the first settlement at Jamestown, a new nation—built on moral law and "conceived in liberty and dedicated to the proposition that all men are created equal"—had stepped out on the stage of world history, even as a long and bitter struggle lay ahead with the Mother Country. The Declaration was applied at first to white men in America, but it contained a pledge of ultimate liberty and equality to all people in America—African-Americans, native Americans, Asians, or, in a different category, women.

Notes

1. This covenant relationship has been recently stressed by Richard John Neuhaus in *Time Toward Home: The American Experiment in Revelation* (New York: Seabury Press, 1975). Susan Bercovitch points to the widespread recognition in the colonial period of the concept of Providential judgment, in *The American Jeremiad* (Madison: University of Wisconsin Press, 1978). She regarded the jeremiad as a "political sermon" designed to join social criticism with spiritual renewal, and pointed out that it survived the decline of Puritan New England and contributed to the success of the republic (pp. xi–xv.).

2. William Bradford, *Bradford's History of Plimoth Plantation* (Boston: Wright and Potter, 1899), 79–82.

3. Quoted in Perry Miller, *The American Puritans* (Garden City, N.Y.: Doubleday and Co., 1956), 12.

4. Bradford, 110.

5. John Cotton, *God's Promise to His Plantation* (London: W. Jones for J. Bellamy, 1630), 15–16, 20.

6. Moses Coit Tyler, *A History of American Literature, 1607–1765*, 2 vols. (New York: G. P. Putnam's Sons, 1879), 1:116.

7. John Winthrop, *The History of New England from 1630 to 1649* (Boston: Little, Brown and Co., 1853), 183.

8. Tyler, 1:99–103, 107, 109, 188.

9. Stanley Thomas Williams, *The American Spirit in Letters*, vol. 11 of *The Pageant of America* (New Haven: Yale University Press, 1926), 7.

10. Perry Miller, 155–57, 159, 161–64.

11. Quoted in Tyler, 1:254.

12. Tyler, 2:162–63.

13. Increase Mather, *An Earnest Exhortation to the Inhabitants of New England* (Boston: John Foster, 1676), 6–12, 12–25, 25–26.

14. Quoted in Tyler, 2:225–26.

15. Ibid., 76.

16. Williams, 22 ff.

17. *The New England Primer*, reprint of the earliest known edition. Edited by Paul L. Ford (New York: Dodd Mead, 1899), 1.

18. Tyler, 2:261–62.

19. Perry Miller, 121–37.

20. Tyler, 2:119.

21. *The Works of George Berkeley*, 3 vols. (Oxford: Clarendon Press, 1871), 3:232.

22. Luther A. Weigle, *American Idealism*, vol. 10 of *The Pageant of America* (New Haven: Yale University Press, 1928), 115.

23. Ibid., 118.

24. *The Writings of Benjamin Franklin*, 10 vols. (New York: Macmillan, 1905), 3:71.

25. Benjamin Franklin, 4:4.

26. Ibid., 77.

27. *The Writings of George Washington* (from the Original Manuscript Sources, 1745–1799, Washington, D.C.: U.S. Government Printing Office, 1931–1944), 37 vols., 2:312–13.

28. Quoted in Tyler, 2:129–30.

29. Carl Becker, *The Declaration of Independence: A Study in the History of Political Ideas* (New York: Vintage Books, 1922, 1942), ix–x.

30. Neuhaus, 76.

31. Alice M. Baldwin, *The New England Clergy and the American Revolution* (Durham, N.C.: Duke University Press, 1928), xii.

32. Ibid., 169–71.

33. Hugh T. Lefler, ed., *A History of the United States: From the Age of Exploration to 1865* (Meridian Documents of American History, New York: World Publishing Co., 1960), 161.

34. Bernard Bailyn, *The Ideological Origins of the American Revolution* (Cambridge: Harvard University Press, 1967), 140.

35. Quoted in Carl Bridenbaugh, *The Spirit of '76: The Growth of American Patriotism Before Independence, 1607–1776* (New York: Oxford University Press, 1975), 142.

36. Lefler, 175.

37. Catherine Drinker Bowen, *John Adams and the American Revolution* (Boston: Little, Brown, 1950), 481.

38. Stuart Gerry Brown, ed., *We Hold These Truths*, Documents of American Democracy (New York: Harper, 1941), 19–20.

39. Lefler, 179–80.

40. Brown, 25.

41. Lefler, 185–86.

42. Ibid., 186–87.

43. *Burke's Politics* (New York: Knopf, 1959), 69–72, 77, from his *Speech on Moving Resolution for Conciliation with the Colonies*, March 22, 1775.

44. Franklin, 6:431.

45. Lefler, 189–90.

46. Brown, 34, 36.

47. *The Works of John Adams*, 10 vols. (Boston: Little Brown, 1856), 1:199.

48. John Adams, 9:417–20.
49. Quotations from the Declaration are from Brown, 137, 140.
50. Bailyn, 319.

CHAPTER III

The Revolutionary Period: Independence and a Democratic Republic (1776–1824)

The American colonists were the first people in modern history to announce their independence from an empire. In Seymour Martin Lipset's words, they established the "first new nation"; it was based on equalitarian rather than elitist principles, and was achievement-oriented rather than aristocratic.[1] The Fourth of July, 1776, marked the beginning of one of the great revolutionary periods of Western European and American history (1776–1824), containing the American, French and Latin American Revolutions and their accompanying major wars. It was a time of realism and power-seeking, and considerable secularism, as compared to the rational mood of the "Enlightenment." A time of revolution and war demanded shrewd realistic statesmen in America, to protect the new country's independence, national interests and idealistic goals. These statesmen believed they were working for the rights of mankind as well as for Americans.

This revolutionary period shows rather clear cyclical trends, setting a pattern of *dynamic equilibrium* which has been generally observed ever since. The first 22 years (1776–98) were basically introvert in mood, as the new nation sought to break away from Britain in a generally defensive war. By 1798, the country was stronger and prepared to move forcefully against France (1798) and Britain (1812) because of their interference with American shipping during the French Revolutionary and Napoleonic Wars. The mood had also turned to extroversion (1798–1824).

Both the introvert and extrovert phases were divided about equally between emphases on "liberty" (individual and state's rights) and "union" (strengthened cooperation and central government). The period of liberty (1776–87) contained the weak Articles of Confederation, while the period of union (1787–98) brought in the Constitution and an effective federal government. Similarly, liberty was again emphasized in the basically Jeffersonian period (1798–1811), while the spirit of union was restored in a strong stand against Britain and other European nations (1811–24). Arthur M. Schlesinger has added another cyclical trend, in domestic politics: liberalism (1765–87) and conservatism (1787–1801).[2]

The goals of the American leaders in 1776 were truly revolutionary for their age: (1) a society based on individual freedom (and thus subject to the opposite dangers of anarchy or tyranny); (2) an independent nation in an American continent distant from the sources of power and of civilization—an audacious dream for "mere colonials" in the face of the world's military and naval powers; and (3) the creation of a republic based on a written constitution, rather than on the time-tested institutions of Europe, such as a hereditary monarchy, a powerful state church and the principles of aristocracy. But American leaders (such as Washington, Franklin and John Adams) were inspired with a sense of confidence in their united abilities and of faith in the destiny of the new land under Providential guidance. George Washington proved to be the charismatic leader who kept the new "Americans" together.

The Spirit of Independence: Introversion-Liberty, 1776–87

The very aim of the Declaration of Independence was withdrawal from Britain and from the entangling conspiracies and wars of the European monarchies, with their vast colonial holdings. The mood of "introversion" was thus almost by definition the required mood for creating the new nation. Since, however, the attainment of the ideal required positive action against Britain, the Revolutionary War exhibited a certain degree of "extroversion," as in the alliance with France. Yet basically the war was one of defense—defense of American territory and of American liberty. Great Britain was challenged to take the offensive, if she wished to maintain her colonies. In 1775, when hostilities were commenced, the American colonists were eager to attach Canada to themselves, and launched an expedition which might have imposed a Canadian alliance or union, had it been successful. But by July 1776, the American mood appeared already to have changed to "introversion" as far as the conquest of Canada was concerned—in part perhaps as a natural reaction against the failure by June 1776 of the bold expedition for conquest. Following the Declaration, the Continental Congress endeavored to persuade the Canadians (largely French) to join the Americans, but the only significant plan for further invasion was the thought of a minority who were opposing General Washington's direction of the war.

Surely the mood of introversion was appropriate to the occasion—for the potential dangers to the Americans in their early years would have been vastly increased by an endeavor to break off Canada as well as America from Britain, or by the early incorporation of provinces dominated by the French system of government and culture, or by attempts to conquer other territories while the American experiment itself was young, weak and unstable. Thus, any realistic idea of expansion would have to await the establishment of a stable union, as well as favorable international circumstances.

It was also natural that the original aim of the Americans should be devoted to the achievement of local *liberty*—both from Britain or from any centralized American government—and that the building of a stable *union* should be undertaken as a logical second step, when the relaxation following the successful revolt against Britain demonstrated the weakness at home and abroad of the American union under the Articles of Confederation.

General Washington demonstrated his motivating spirit in the General Orders to his army on July 2, 1776:

> The time is now near at hand which must probably determine, whether Americans are to be, Freemen, or Slaves; . . . The fate of unborn Millions will now depend, under God, on the Courage and Conduct of this army . . . ; if we now shamefully fail, we shall become infamous to the whole world. Let us therefore rely upon the goodness of the Cause, and the aid of the Supreme Being, in whose hands Victory is, to animate and encourage us to great and noble Actions—Eyes of all our countrymen are now upon us, and we shall have their blessings, and praises, if happily we are the instruments of saving them from the Tyranny meditated against them. Let us therefore animate and encourage each other, and shew the whole world, that a Freeman contending for *Liberty* on his own ground is superior to any slavish mercenary on earth.[3]

Even in these early days, Washington often wrote of his *country* and of *America*, as shown in his General Orders of August 1, 1776, in which he warned his soldiers from the different "Provinces" against casting reflections on one another's home areas:

> . . . The honor and success of the army, and the safety of our broad Country, depends upon harmony and good agreement with each other; . . . the Provinces are all United to oppose the common enemy, and all distinctions sunk in the name of an American . . . let all distinctions of Nations, Countries, and Provinces, therefore be lost in the generous contest, who shall behave with the most courage against the enemy, and the most kindness and good humour to each other. . . . [4]

Washington also made it clear that the American aim should be to fight a defensive war—to defend the territory of the 13 states:

> . . . History, our own experience, the advice of our ablest Friends in Europe, the fears of the Enemy, and even the Declarations of Congress demonstrate, that on our Side the War should be defensive. . . . that we should on all Occasions avoid a general Action, or put anything to the Risque, unless compelled by a necessity, into which we ought never to be drawn. [5]

A major aim of the Americans after the decision for independence was to prepare for the expected invasion of the British from Canada. And a second major aim was to secure greatly increased aid from France—the former enemy of the British North American colonies, as well as of the British, in four colonial wars. The Continental Congress resolved on June 12, 1776, to establish a committee to prepare a plan for treaties to be proposed to foreign powers. John Adams was the most influential figure on the committee, and declared that "we ought not to enter into any alliance with [France]":

> which would entangle us in any future wars in Europe. . . . We ought to lay it down, as a first principle and a maxim never to be forgotten, to maintain an entire neutrality in all future European wars. . . . It never could be our interest to unite with France in the destruction of England, or in any measures to break her spirit, or to reduce her to a situation in which she could not support her independence. . . . [6]

Benjamin Franklin arrived in Paris late in 1776 to pave the way for an alliance with France. He stressed the worldwide significance of the War for Independence, as seen by an American patriot, in a letter of

May 1, 1777, to Samuel Cooper:

> All Europe is on our side of the question, as far as Applause and good Wishes can carry them. Those who live under arbitrary Power do nevertheless approve of Liberty, and wish for it; they almost despair of recovering it in Europe. . . . Hence, 'tis a Common Observation here, that our Cause is *the Cause of all Mankind*, and that we are fighting for their Liberty in defending our own. 'Tis a glorious task assign'd us by Providence; which has, I trust, given us Spirit and Virtue equal to it, and will at last crown it with Success.[7]

In addition to the political, commercial, and possibly humanitarian motivations of the French to enter the conflict, one other factor was needful—namely, a convincing demonstration by the Americans of their own capabilities in their defense. France could scarcely tie herself to a "lost cause." The Americans were to give this demonstration at Saratoga in the fall of 1777.

But there were many dark days before Saratoga, as Washington retreated from New York City, and Congress moved from the threatened city of Philadelphia to Baltimore. In this crisis the Continental Congress decided (December 27, 1776) to delegate greater power to General Washington. On December 30, the Congress resolved to send commissions to Vienna, Spain, Prussia and Tuscany. At this very time, Washington was able to restore a measure of American confidence with his coup at Trenton on December 26, in which nearly a thousand Hessians were captured, and his victory at Princeton on January 3, 1777. In the first half of 1777, while the general outlook was doubtful, the Continental Congress adopted a new flag on June 14, with a resolution "that the Union be thirteen stars, white on a blue field, representing a new constellation." The colors appear to represent the three core ideas of America: white for the *moral law*; red for the courage, valor and blood required to achieve and maintain *liberty and union*; and the blue field, where the stars are located, for America's *world mission*.

General Burgoyne's invasion was launched from Canada in June 1777; with initial success, he drove deep into the state of New York. But his reverses in September and October came to a mighty climax at Saratoga on October 17, 1777, when about 6,000 troops, the remnants of his army, surrendered to Major-General Horatio Gates. The stimulating effect of this victory on the morale of the nation is indicated in the resolution of the Continental Congress (November 1) recommending to the several states that December 18 be a "day of thanksgiving" set apart for the signal success.[8]

Now, the Continental Congress, with renewed confidence, could look forward to the establishment of a plan for a union of the states, as well as to the consummation of the vital alliance with France. On November 15, 1777, the Congress adopted and submitted to the states for ratification the Articles of Confederation and Perpetual Union of the United States of America.

General Washington established army headquarters on December 20 at Valley Forge, where the dark hours were lightened somewhat by the expectation of the important French assistance. The American alliance with France was signed in Paris on February 6, 1778, and ratified by the Continental Congress on May 4, 1778. The alliance recognized the sovereign states of the United States, pledged close cooperation in the struggle against England to secure the independence of the United States, and renounced all French claims to Canada. Both parties agreed not to make a separate truce or peace with Britain, without the formal consent of the other. Article XI bound the United States to help guarantee French possessions left in North America (islands), and thus was capable of interpretation as a somewhat permanent military alliance.[9]

The Continental Congress was inspired with great confidence by the conclusion of the French alliance, as is revealed in their address to the "Inhabitants of the United States of Americas" on May 8, 1778. After referring to the cruelties of the British in their conduct of the war, in their treatment of prisoners, and in their incitement of the Indians against the Americans, the address continued:

> Notwithstanding these great provocations, we have treated such of them as fell into our hands with tenderness, and studiously endeavored to alleviate the afflictions of their captivity. This conduct we have pursued so far as to be by them stigmatized with cowardice, and by our friends with folly. But our dependence was not upon man; it was upon Him who hath commanded us to love our enemies, and to render good for evil. and what can be more wonderful than the manner of our deliverances? How often have we been reduced to distress, and yet been raised up? . . . [10]

Washington's high standards of conduct in war are revealed in a message to the Congress on March 7, 1778, opposing their resolution not to exchange prisoners with Lord Howe until certain payments had been made. Washington thought that this resolution was opposed to the spirit and letter of the proposition made by him to General Howe, and acceded to by the latter: ". . . I now conceive, that the public, as well as my own personal honor and faith, are pledged for the Performance. . . ."[11] Congress responded to his rebuke on March 18 by authorizing Washington to proceed with the exchange of prisoners.

Many events favorable to the United States occurred in 1778 and 1779: Washington's victory in the Battle of Monmouth (June 28, 1778); notable naval exploits by Captain John Barry and Captain John Paul Jones; the arrival of a French fleet in American waters; Spain's declaration of war against Britain in June 1779, in alliance with France; and George Rogers Clark's occupation of Kaskaskia (on the Mississippi) and Vincennes (on the Wabash). But dark months lay ahead in 1779 and 1780. The general quality of leadership was high, surmounted by the steadfast figure of Washington; but dissension was widespread, stimulated no doubt by the new spirit of liberty as well as by the rising tide of secularism. Leaders pleaded for a more determined effort and for more cooperation, but the results were usually discouraging. In a letter to James Warren of Massachusetts, March 31, 1779, Washington deplored the degree of speculation and corruption:

> Is the paltry consideration of a little dirty pelf to individuals to be placed in competition with the essential rights and liberties of the present generation, and of Millions yet unborn? . . . And shall we at last become the victims of our abominable lust of gain? Forbid it, heaven! forbid it all and every State in the Union! . . . Our cause is noble, it is the cause of all Mankind! And the danger to it, is to be apprehended from ourselves.[12]

After a military reverse, Washington wrote to Fielding Lewis on July 6, 1780, about the dark outlook after five long years of war. Included is his criticism of the political situation, in which Congress had relinquished most of its powers to the states:

> . . . In a word, our measures are not under the influence and direction of one council, but thirteen, each of which is actuated by local views and politics. . . . The contest among the different States *now*, is not which shall do most for the common cause, but which shall do least. . . . We may rely upon it, that we shall never have Peace till the enemy

are convinced that we are in a condition to carry on the war. It is no new maxim in politics that for a nation to obtain Peace or assure it, it must be prepared for war.[13]

The American troops under General Gates suffered a severe defeat at Camden, South Carolina, on August 16, 1780. And the depths seem to have been reached when General Benedict Arnold decided to commit treason on September 21, 1780, by agreeing to hand over West Point to the British. But the North was saved from possible disaster at this point, because of the capture of the British agent, Major André. Washington was convinced of "providential interposition."[14]

In the meantime, the Continental Congress had been preparing the terms on which it would negotiate peace, with special reference to boundaries (the Mississippi River) and fisheries (off Canada). John Adams was named on September 27, 1779, to negotiate a peace treaty with Britain, when possible.

The year of 1781 was to develop decisive events for the independence of America, but the outlook early in the year was not favorable. The discontent of ill-supplied troops was mounting. Troops from Pennsylvania mutinied on January 1, 1781. Washington ordered Major-General Howe to quell a mutiny of New Jersey troops which had begun on January 20. After the mutiny had been firmly suppressed, the General Orders of January 30 demonstrated the high quality of Washington's leadership:

> The General is deeply sensible of the sufferings of the army. He leaves no expedient unassayed to relieve them. . . . We began a Contest for Liberty and Independence ill provided with the means of war, relying on our own Patriotism to supply the deficiency. We expected to encounter many wants and distresses and we should neither shrink from them when they happen nor fly in the face of Law and Government to procure redress. There is no doubt the public will . . . do ample justice to men fighting and suffering in its defense. But it is our duty to bear present Evils with Fortitude looking forward to the period when our Country will have it in its power to reward our services.
>
> History is full of Examples of armies suffering with patient extremity of distress, which exceed those we have suffered, and this in the cause of ambition and conquest not in that of the rights of humanity, of their country, of their families, of themselves; shall we who aspire to the distinction of a patriot army, who are contending for everything precious in society against everything hateful and degrading

in slavery, shall We who call ourselves citizens discover less Constancy and Military virtue than the mercenary instruments of ambition?[15]

Great preparations were being made for the uncertain future in the first half of 1781. The first "constitution" of the states became effective when the Articles of Confederation were ratified on March 1, 1781, so that Congress met under a new title on March 2 as "The United States in Congress Assembled." The difficulties ahead were recognized in the proclamation of the Congress on March 20, setting apart a day of "humiliation and prayer," and asking the people to pray "that these blessings of peace and liberty may be established on an honorable and permanent basis, and transmitted inviolate to the latest posterity. . . ."[16]

Events were moving toward a mighty climax. In August 1781, Washington suddenly decided to shift American and French troops in the north swiftly to the south, to cooperate with the French fleet in meeting the advancing British threat to Virginia and the other southern states. On August 30, de Grasse arrived off Yorktown, and by September 10 the French fleet had secured command of Chesapeake Bay from the British, thus "bottling up" the British troops under Lord Cornwallis. Washington established his headquarters at Williamsburg on September 15, and immediately expressed his high hopes for the outcome, with the cooperation of the French troops under Major-General Lafayette. The famous siege of Yorktown began on September 28; by October 14, major British redoubts had been captured by the allied armies, so that Washington in his General Orders of October 15 praised the spirit of American-French unity, and its significance for the future[17] Lord Cornwallis surrendered his entire army on October 19, 1781. In his report to Congress, Washington stressed the great help received from the French troops and paid tribute to the French fleet.[18] In his General Orders of October 20, Washington referred to "the recognition of such reiterated and astonishing interposition of Providence. . . ."[19] The Congress issued a fervent Thanksgiving Proclamation, also recognizing the interposition of Providence "in granting remarkable deliverances, and blessing us with the most signal success, when affairs seemed to have the most discouraging appearances. . . ."[20]

General Washington sent a "Circular to the States" on January 31, 1782, calling for continued effort and warning against lethargy.[21] But while Washington was preparing for another campaign in the north, the British decided to make peace (in a Parliamentary action, March 3,

1782). The future of America now depended largely on the diplomatic negotiations in Europe, where Franklin, Adams and Jay labored to build a wide and solid future for the new nation.

With American independence seemingly assured, the Congress, on June 20, 1782, finally adopted the Great Seal which had been discussed ever since 1776. The two parts of this seal are on one side of the dollar bill, with Washington on the other. One side of the seal depicts the American eagle, holding an olive branch on the left and thirteen arrows on the right; in its beak there is a scroll with the motto "E Pluribus Unum" (out of many, one); a crest is placed over its head (made up of a "glory," or breaking through a cloud by thirteen stars); and an escutcheon or shield lies over its breast. According to the resolution of the Congress, the escutcheon's thirteen red and white stripes represented "the several States all joined in one solid compact entire," and the plain blue field above it "unites the whole and represents Congress. . . ." The resolution goes on to explain the rest of this side of the Seal:

> White symbolizes purity and innocence. Red hardiness and valour and Blue . . . signifies vigilance, perseverance and justice. The Olive Branch and arrows denote the power of peace and war which is exclusively vested in Congress. The Constellation denotes a new State taking its place and rank among other sovereign powers. The escutcheon is borne on the breast of the American Eagle without any other supporters, to denote that the United States of America ought to rely on their own virtue.[22]

The other side of the Seal shows an unfinished pyramid, with an eye (of Providence) above it in a triangle, surrounded with a "glory" of light. Over these is the motto: "*Annuit Coeptis*" (He—God—has favored our undertakings). On the base of the pyramid are the Roman numerals for the year 1776, and below that the motto: "*Novus Ordo Seclorum*" (a new order of the ages). The resolution interprets this side as follows:

> The Pyramid signifies strength and direction. The eye over it and the motto allude to the many signal interpositions of providence in favour of the American cause. The date underneath is that of the Declaration of Independence, and the words under it signify the beginning of a new American Era, which commences from that date.[23]

Returning this discussion to diplomacy—Franklin had begun the negotiations for peace with faith in the French and distrust of the

British. John Jay arrived in June 1782, with deep suspicion of French aims. A vital step was taken when the American delegates decided to negotiate on their own, with Franklin presenting his first detailed peace proposals in July without having consulted the French.[24] When Franklin became ill in August, Jay became the chief negotiator; John Adams did not arrive until October. Jay characterized the French attitude toward America as follows: "They are interested in separating us from Great Britain, and on that point we may, I believe, depend upon them; but it is not their interest that we should become a great and formidable people, and therefore they will not help us to become so."[25] Jay informed the Earl of Sherburne, the new British Prime Minister, that by immediately acknowledging American independence, granting America a share in the fisheries, and allowing American access to the Mississippi, England was now in a position "immediately to cut the cords which tied us to France."[26] Formal negotiations between the British and the Americans began on September 27, 1782. John Adams arrived on October 26, and typified the spirit of an American who wanted to be free from all European ties at this time. Adams wrote to Secretary Livingston, November 11, 1782, that the French would perhaps like a French party and an English party in America, to compel the patriotic and independent men to join the French side, and to aid France in a future war.[27]

The preliminary articles of peace between Britain and America were signed on November 20, 1782, without informing the French until later. These articles satisfied the American aims, with the full recognition by England of American independence, of the Mississippi boundary, and of customary fishing rights—a major triumph of American diplomacy. Peace would not finally be secured, however, until France should come to terms with Britain. It was left to Franklin to explain America's unilateral action to Comte de Vergennes (December 17, 1782):

> Nothing has been agreed in the preliminaries contrary to the interests of France; and no peace is to take place between us and England, till you have concurred yourself. Your observation is, however, apparently just, that, in not consulting you before they were signed, we have been guilty of neglecting a point of *bienséance*. But, as this was not from want of respect for the King, whom we all love and honour, we hope it will be excused, and that the great work, which has hitherto been so happily conducted, is so nearly brought to perfection, and is so glorious to his reign, will not be ruined by a single

indiscretion of ours, and certainly the whole edifice sinks to the ground immediately, if you refuse on that account to give us any further assistance.

The English, I just now learn, flatter themselves they have already divided us. I hope this little misunderstanding will therefore be kept a secret, and that they will find themselves totally mistaken.[28]

The American hopes were fulfilled on January 30, 1783, when Britain signed separate preliminary articles of peace with both France and Spain, so that on this date the preliminary articles between the United States and Britain became effective. Spain had to be satisfied with Florida (which the British had held between 1763 and 1782) rather than Gibraltar—this meant that the northern boundary of West Florida was to remain in dispute between the United States and Spain for a number of years. Otherwise, the American dream at that time was well on its way to fulfillment—a large and secure land and sea base of the new and "rising nation."

The attitude of George Washington throughout the year of 1783, as well as in later years, was virtually unprecedented in the annals of military history up to this time, as he prepared the groundwork for the paramount position of the civilian element, rather than the military, in American life. Congress proclaimed the "cessation of hostilities" on April 11, 1783, and ratified the provisional terms of the treaty with Britain on April 15. The "Circular to the States" which Washington sent to the state governments on June 8, 1783, as he was preparing for his retirement, constituted a statement which helped set the pattern and goal for the development of the new nation. The tone of his message is illustrated in these brief excerpts:

. . . The foundation of our Empire was not laid in the gloomy age of Ignorance and Superstition, but at an Epoch when the rights of mankind were better understood and more clearly defined, than at any former period. . . . At this auspicious period, the United States came into existence as a Nation, and if their Citizens should not be completely free and happy, the fault will be entirely their own. . . .

There are four things, which I humbly conceive, are essential to the well being, we may even venture to say, to the existence of the United States as an Independent Power:
1st: An indissoluble Union of the States under one Federal head.
2dly: A Sacred regard to Public Justice.

3dly: The adoption of a proper Peace Establishment, and

4thly: The prevalence of that pacific and friendly Disposition, among the peoples of the United States, which will induce them to forget their local prejudices and policies. . . .

I now make it my earnest prayer, that God would have you and the State over which you preside, in his holy protection . . . and . . . that he would most graciously be pleased to dispose us all to do Justice, to love mercy, and to demean ourselves with that Charity, humility and pacific temper of mind, which were the Characteristics of the Divine Author of our blessed Religion, and without an humble imitation of whose example in these things, we can never hope to be a happy Nation.[29]

Many New England ministers, among others, also looked forward to a successful nation. Luther Weigle summarizes an Election Sermon preached by Ezra Stiles (pastor of the Congregational Church at Newport and President of Yale from 1778 to 1798) before the General Assembly of Connecticut, May 2, 1783, on the subject "The United States Elevated to Glory and Honor":

. . . which is remarkable for its breadth and perspicacity. He set forth in detail the reasons which led him to expect that the states will be drawn to closer union, and will "prosper and flourish into a great American Republic . . . in high and distinguished honor among the nations of the earth." He foretold the dominance of the new nation by English traditions rather than by the traditions of other elements of her mixed people; and predicted a population of fifty million by the close of the first century of national existence, and three hundred millions by the close of the third. And now, my fellow citizens of this independent republic, . . . hear me this day, good audience, the Most High planted our fathers, a small handful, in this Jeshimon, and lo! we, their posterity, have arisen up to three million of people. Our ears have heard, and our fathers have told us, the marvelous things God did for them; but our eyes have seen far more marvelous things done for us, whereby we are glad and rejoice this day. . . . Having fought the good fight, our warfare ended, let us not fail to look through providence up to the God of providence, and give glory to God the Lord of Hosts.[30]

Yet, as in other revolutionary periods, there was a growing secularism. Weigle notes that "the years immediately succeeding the Revolutionary War were marked by a vogue of atheism and infidelity."[31] The Enlightenment of the 18th century, and the confusion of the

Revolutionary War, were important contributing factors, no doubt. An early example of this new emphasis is shown in the title of a book published in 1784, and written by General Ethan Allen: *Reason, the Only Oracle of Man.*[32] Colleges reflected the new trend, according to Weigle:

> At Princeton, in 1782, there were but two students who professed to be Christian leaders. There was but one on Bowdoin. Bishop Meade wrote that the College of William and Mary was regarded as a hotbed of French politics and religion, and that in every educated young man in Virginia he expected to find a sceptic, if not an avowed unbeliever.[33]

Near the end of the year, December 23, 1783, Washington addressed Congress on resigning his commission. The President of the Congress reflected the deep feelings of the participants in his reply:

> The United States in Congress assembled receive with emotions, too affecting for utterance, the solemn resignation of the authorities under which you have led our troops with success through a perilous and doubtful war. . . . You have conducted the great military conquest with wisdom and fortitude, invariably regarding the rights of the civil power throughout all disasters and changes. . . .
>
> Having defended the standard of liberty in this new world; having taught a lesson useful to those who inflict and to those who feel oppression, you retire from the great theatre of action, with the blessings of your fellow-citizens, but the glory of your virtues will not terminate with your military command, it will continue to animate the remotest ages. . . .[34]

Thus, it was with real insight into the nature of America that one of the four paintings of Col. John Trumbull on the walls of the Rotunda of the Capitol should be that of "George Washington resigning his Commission as Commander-in-Chief of the Army," alongside the signing of the Declaration of Independence, the surrender of Burgoyne at Saratoga, and the surrender of Cornwallis at Yorktown.

A final word as to the "core" of America during this Revolutionary period, especially in its early days, may be found in John Adams' beliefs, as he expressed them in a letter to Thomas Jefferson on June 28, 1813, in reference to the Continental Congress:

> The *general principles* on which the fathers achieved independence,

were the only principles in which that beautiful assembly of young men could unite . . . And what were these *general principles*? I answer, the general principles of Christianity, in which all sects were united, and the *general principles* of English and American liberty, in which all those young men united, and which had united all parties in America, in majorities sufficient to assert and maintain her independence. Now I will avow, that I then believed and now believe that those general principles of Christianity are as eternal and immutable as the existence and attributes of God; and that those attributes of liberty are as unalterable as human nature and our terrestrial, mundane society.[35]

While the spirit of "Liberty" was being consolidated in events and institutions, the "Independence" of the United States was also being firmly established. John Adams saw most clearly the need for separation from the interests of Europe at this time.[36] The Congress showed its desire not to be further entangled in European matters by its decision not to participate in the so-called "Armed Neutrality" to which several European nations had become parties. Benjamin Franklin was looking very far into the future, it appears, when he suggested a tripartite alliance to David Hartley in England, October 16, 1783 (just six weeks after the treaty ending the War of the Revolution was signed by the belligerents on September 3):

> What would you think of a proposition, if I sh'd make it, of a family compact between England, France and America? America would be as happy as the Sabine Girls, if she could be the means of uniting in perpetual peace her father and her husband. What repeated follies are these repeated wars! You do not want to conquer and govern one another. . . . You are all Christians. One is *The Most Christian King*, and the other *Defender of the Faith*. Manifest the propriety of these titles by your future conduct. "By this," says Christ, "shall all men know that you are my Disciples, if ye love one another."[37]

The vital question remained as to whether the spirit of liberty could be harnessed to the making of a stable national community, and whether the new nations would receive respect and justice from the leading powers of the world. In general, under the Articles of Confederation stability was not achieved at home, nor was respect secured from abroad. Britain made it clear in March 1784 that no commercial treaty was possible with the American Confederation, nor would she consider giving up the Northwest forts on American soil, until the United States should fulfill its financial obligations pledged in the treaty of peace. John Adams, sent as American Minister to Britain, was unsuccessful in his negotiations with the British, but his faith in the early rise of America was almost unbounded, as shown in a letter of March 2, 1786.[38] Washington noted the likely effect of the stimulation of the spirit of "union" from the refusal to deal with America (letter of June 10, 1785):

> Great Britain, viewing with eyes of chagrin and jealousy the situation of this country, will not, for some time yet if ever, pursue a liberal policy towards it; but unfortunately *for her* the conduct of her Ministers defeats their won ends: their restriction of our trade with them will facilitate the enlargement of Congress' powers in commercial matters, more than half a century wou'd otherwise have effected. The mercantile interests of this Country are uniting as one man, to vest the federal government with ample powers to regulate trade and to counteract the selfish views of other nations: this may be considered as another proof that this Country will ever unite in opposition to unjust or ungenerous measures, whensoever or from whomsoever they are offered.[39]

With the American states in charge of the enforcement of treaties, Britain detailed treaty violations by eight specific states.

The weakness of the United States was also apparent in the negotiations with Spain over the navigation of the Mississippi and the boundaries of Florida (which had been returned to Spain by Britain in the peace of 1783). The financial impotence of Congress was shown by the default of American payments on French loans. Both financial and military weakness are demonstrated in American relations with the Barbary pirates, who demanded ransom and tribute. In 1785, Algiers declared war on the United States, captured two American vessels, and held their crews and passengers for ransom. Congress felt helpless. Only with Morocco could a treaty be made, with intercession from the Spanish government—a "treaty of peace and friendship" which was the beginning of long and friendly relations between the two countries. American negotiators were able to secure only one commercial treaty with a European state—with Prussia in 1785. Trade was opened with China, when Congress, on January 30, 1784, granted sea letters to Captain John Greer for his voyage to Canton on the *Empress of China*.

Not only was American weakness in foreign relations being demonstrated in the critical years between 1783 and 1787, but internal instability was also being widely recognized. The need for a stronger union was especially felt by some of the leaders of the Revolution, notably by Washington himself. There was some violence between states, a depression started in 1784, and Shay's Rebellion of farmers in Massachusetts began in August 1786. Shay's forces were repulsed in January 1787 in an attack on the Federal arsenal in Springfield, and were finally crushed in February by a large body of Massachusetts troops. The spirit of "liberty" seemed to be moving in the direction of anarchy. The weak morale of the Congress was evident in the difficulty in maintaining a quorum. In September 1786, the Annapolis Convention (Virginia, Delaware, Pennsylvania, New Jersey and New York) urged Congress to call a convention for the following May to revise the Constitution. Congress finally endorsed the plan in February 1787.

However, the constructive aspects of the spirit of liberty up to this time should not be overlooked. Individual liberties and state liberties (self-government) had been thoroughly incorporated in the new system of government. Following the Declaration of Independence, each state established its own government. Under the Articles of Confederation as ratified in 1781, each state retained its "sovereign freedom and independence," had one vote in Congress, and kept full power for the *enforcement* of national decisions. The most constructive achievement of Congress under the Articles of Confederation was probably the passage of the Northwest Ordinance, which established the pattern of admitting new states to the Union equal in power to the original thirteen (the original states were giving their western lands to the United States as a whole).

A definite turning point seemed to be reached in the summer of 1787, as American leaders sought both to restrain and consolidate the "Liberty" which had been gained, with a new spirit of cooperation and a political structure for a closer "Union" which could make the United States a respected member of the family of nations. The evidence is seen in the adoption of the Northwest Ordinance on July 13, 1787, and the successful outcome of the Constitutional Convention at Philadelphia, May 25 to September 17, 1787.

The Establishment of the Nation: Introversion-Union, 1787–98

The nature of the growing America was indicated by the requirement of the Northwest Ordinance for "republican" governments in the territories and new states, along with full protection for religious freedom and fundamental legal rights, no slavery or involuntary servitude, and the promotion of education.

This principle of the "co-ordinate state," as Professor Frank Tannenbaum has termed it, seems to have been a logical outgrowth of the unique experiment of the Americans in establishing local self-government under the British and then securing complete independence. Nevertheless, it was not a foregone conclusion. It was a decision based upon a principle, and it strengthened that principle for all future time, it seems. Professor Tannenbaum believed that:

> Next to the formation of the Union itself, the Northwest Ordinance represents the most important single political decision of the American people. The cession of the ill-defined and overlapping claims to western territorial lands was necessary to the establishment of the Union. But the decision to divide this vast area into separate states and admit them, each in turn, upon a footing of equality with the old states was not only something new in territorial policy but was an act of the highest political wisdom. For it is upon this decision that it has been possible to organize a continent into a single federation and have it last until it is now one of the oldest governments in the world, and the most stable.[40]

This general principle was maintained at the Constitutional Convention and was incorporated into the Constitution, but opposition from some of the larger original states, who feared loss of influence, was at first strong. The Supreme Court has consistently held that all states are equal in legal power; further protection of the states was ensured by establishing a U.S. Senate in which each state should have two and only two votes, and providing that treaties be approved by a two-thirds affirmative vote of the Senate. This doctrine of equality of states is basic to general American respect for the rights of all nations, small and large.

Prospects of agreement on a new and stronger union seemed remote after a month of debate in the Constitutional Convention. George Washington, president of the Convention, wrote to Alexander Hamilton, as late as July 10, that "I *almost* despair of seeing a favorable issue to the proceedings of our Convention. . . ."[41] In the midst of the dark situation, some of the spirit of the origins of the nation during the Revolution was recalled to the Convention by its elder statesman, Benjamin Franklin, on June 28. He ended his address by declaring his conviction that without the "concurring aid" of Providence:

. . . we shall succeed in this political Building no better than the Builders of Babel; we shall be divided by our little, partial, local Interests, our Project will be confounded, and we ourselves shall become a Reproach and a Bye-word down to future Ages. And, what is worse, Mankind may hereafter, from this unfortunate Instance, despair of establishing Government by human Wisdom, and leave it to Chance, War, and Conquest.

I therefore beg leave to move.

That henceforth Prayers, imploring the Assistance of Heaven and its Blessing on our Deliberations, be held in this assembly every morning before we proceed to Business; and that one or more of the Clergy of this city be requested to officiate in that Service.[42]

Indicative of the changed spirit of the times since the early Revolutionary days, it was reported that "the convention, except three or four persons, thought prayers unnecessary," and the motion was voted down. Nevertheless, Franklin's speech and motion may well have prompted serious thought by a number of delegates. At least, the spirit of the convention seemed to change within a fairly short time, and real progress was soon made. A committee reported the famous "Connecticut Compromise" (on the House and Senate) on July 5, and the Compromise was adopted in July 16. A rough draft of the Constitution was composed between July 19 and 26.

The Constitution was finally agreed upon and signed by the delegates on September 17, 1787, for submission to the states for ratification. A true national government was envisaged to deal with national problems, notably foreign affairs and foreign and interstate commerce. Professor George Anastaplo has described how this remarkable document was a climax to and was based upon the cultural, political and legal traditions of the British and the Americans.[43]

The chief symbol and agent of the new unity and power of the nation was to be the President—chief executive, commander-in-chief of the armed forces, and chief diplomat, authorized to negotiate treaties. Thus was created a chief executive and head of the state who could lead his country in matching the moves of nations ruled by ancient monarchs or modern dictators.

The Constitution also established a system of Congressional checks on the President, particularly in foreign affairs, such as the power to control all appropriations, Senate approval of appointments and treaties, regulation of foreign commerce, declarations of war, raising and supporting the army and navy, power "to define and punish piracies and felonies committed on the high seas, and offenses against the law of nations," and to remove a President through the impeachment process. The "law of nations" or international law was understood by all three branches of the government—Congress, the President, and the courts——to be a vital part of the obligations of the United States in entering the family of nations as an independent power.

The leaders of the nation, from the very beginning in 1776, had a profound respect for the concept of a just and liberal international law. The most influential treatise on international law in America at this time was *The Law of Nations or The Principles of Natural Law*, written by the Swiss authority, Emmerich de Vattel (1714–67) in 1758. Vattel's principles, with their emphasis on political liberty, seemed almost designed for the new American republic. Vattel stressed the moral rights and obligations of a nation not only toward other nations but also toward its own citizens.[44] He recognized the right of a nation to reform its government, change its constitution, or depose a tyrant.[45] Vattel declared that nations must respect each other's independence and just rights, and are obligated to honor their treaties, to settle their disputes through peaceful means, if possible, and to help one another.[46] Like Grotius, Vattel distinguished between "just" and "unjust" wars: "All the rights of a belligerent are derived from the justice of his cause. . . . Whoever takes up arms without a lawful cause, therefore, has no rights whatsoever; all the acts of hostility which he commits are unjust."[47] He also emphasized the rights of a nation to maintain its neutrality in the wars of others (the United States was to become one of the chief champions of the rights of neutrals).[48]

Vattel concludes his work, which is based on such high standards of international conduct, by stressing peaceful relations among nations and the obligation to cultivate peace:

> Since peace is so salutary to the human race, not only must the sovereign, as representing the Nation, not disturb it on his part, but he must also endeavor to promote it as far as lies in his power, and to dissuade others from violating it, and to inspire in them the love of justice, equity, and public tranquillity—the love of peace. It is one of the most beneficent offices which he can render to Nations and to the world at large.
>
> . . . The love of peace should prevent a sovereign equally from entering upon a war without necessity, and from continuing it when the necessity for it has ceased.[49]

Daniel G. Lang, in his study of early American foreign policy, writes that "Thomas Jefferson held Vattel in high esteem" and that Alexander Hamilton referred to Vattel as "perhaps the most accurate and approved of writer on the law of Nations and regularly invoked his authority. . . ."50

The draft of the new Constitution was submitted to the states for ratification by state conventions on September 28, 1787. After approval by all the states except Rhode Island (which ratified on May 29, 1790), Congress resolved to put the Constitution into effect on September 13, 1788. A new spirit was soon abroad in the land—it was evident that American confidence and morale, which had declined so much following the war, was being restored.

With the basic decision for the Union having been made, the immediate future depended on the quality of the first American leadership, particularly in the Presidency. The nation turned to one man for that post—George Washington, who was inaugurated on April 30, 1789, with John Adams as Vice-President. The Constitution represented the decision for "Union," as the Declaration had been for "Liberty"—now the two principles could move ahead together. In his Inaugural Address in New York City on April 30, after his "fervent supplication to that Almighty Being who rules over the universe, who presides in the Council of Nations, and whose providential aids can supply every defect," Washington urged the application of moral principles to national policy and highlighted America's vital role in the defense of liberty:

> . . . [He trusts] that the foundation of our National policy will be laid in the pure and immutable principles of private morality; and the pre-eminence of a free Government be exemplified by all the attributes which can win the affections of its Citizens and command the respect of the world. . . .
>
> . . . We ought to be . . . persuaded that the propitious smiles of Heaven can never be expected on a nation that disregards the eternal rules of order and right, which Heaven itself has ordained; And . . . the preservation of the sacred fire of liberty, and the destiny of the Republican model of government, are justly considered as *deeply*, perhaps as *finally* staked, on the experiment entrusted to the hands of the American people. . . .51

Under the guidance and prestige of Washington, the new government seemed immediately successful. At the request of Congress, the President issued a Thanksgiving Proclamation on October 3, 1789, in fervent thanks for the new blessing.[52] This was to be Washington's only Thanksgiving proclamation—a sign perhaps of the growing secularism of the times, of the natural proclivity to take such successes for granted once achieved, and also of the growing difficulties which the new Administration was later to face, particularly as a result of the European conflicts which grew out of the French Revolution after July 14, 1789.

Most of the signers of the Constitution did not believe that a "bill of rights" was necessary, since the national government did not seem to have power over "rights," and these rights were protected by the state constitutions. But during the ratification process, many anti-Federalists stressed the need of a separate bill of rights, and secured general approval for the establishment of such rights by the amendment process. Thomas Jefferson, then Minister to France, wrote to James Madison in December 1787, criticizing the omission, and listing some rights that needed direct constitutional protection, such as freedom of the press and religion. He ended his letter: "A bill of rights is what the people are entitled to against every government on earth, general or particular, and what no just government should refuse, or rest on inference."[53] On June 8, 1789, James Madison introduced a proposed bill of rights to the House of Representatives. This became the first ten amendments to the Constitution, ratified by eleven states on December 15, 1791. So the spirit of "liberty" was directly incorporated in the document which created the "union," as specific restraints on the national government. The First Amendment has probably become the most significant: "Congress shall make no law respecting an establishment of religion, or prohibiting the free exercise thereof, or abridging the freedom of speech, or of the press; or the right of the people peaceably to assemble, and to petition the Government for a redress of grievances." Not until the 20th century did the Supreme Court apply these principles to the states, through interpretation of the 14th Amendment adopted in 1868.

The first major test of the new government at home arose in the refusal of western farmers to pay the federal liquor taxes in 1792 and after. The so-called "Whisky Insurrection" finally broke out in July 1794 in western Pennsylvania. President Washington called up the militia, and went to the area himself. In the face of this determination, and the support it received, the rebellion began to collapse. The chief result of the firm action taken by the President was to enhance the prestige of the national government, both at home and abroad, and to strengthen the general spirit of "union."

American foreign problems during this first period of the new Union arose out of the general weakness of the young nation in relation to the great European powers of Britain, Spain and France, and out of the efforts to keep from being involved in their wars. The general mood was one of "introversion," with the aim of making the American continental base secure and of protecting American neutrality.

The moderate character of the French Revolution began to change decisively in 1792, when war came with Austria and Prussia, and the radical Jacobins became triumphant. Conservative opinion in America began to be fearful of the results of the revolution, but Jefferson, Secretary of State, could see the apparent necessity for sweeping changes in France. France declared war on Britain, Holland and Spain on February 1, 1793. Before the news of the actual outbreak of war, President Washington explained the necessity for the non-involvement of the United States as a new and weak nation. American opinion was sharply divided in its sympathies when the war came. Citizen Genet, the new French Minister to the United States, landed in America on April 8, aiming to gain American support for the new French Republic. Washington wrote to Secretary Jefferson on April 12 to prepare plans for strict neutrality. With the unanimous support of the cabinet, including Jefferson, Washington issued a Neutrality Proclamation on April 22, 1793, although the alliance with France during the American Revolution might have been interpreted as to require aid for France. The proclamation contained a pledge to prosecute any who violated the "law of nations with respect to the powers at war." Citizen Genet, however, engaged in arming and equipping vessels in the ports of the United States. The Cabinet decided on August 2 that the French Government should be asked to recall Genet (Genet was replaced in 1794, but stayed on to become an American citizen). Washington was able to maintain the policy of neutrality in the face of strong minority support for France. After he urged Congress to improve the neutrality procedures of the country by law, Congress passed a Neutrality Act in 1794.

America was finally able to make treaties with Britain and Spain. John Jay's controversial treaty with Britain, signed November 19, 1794, was submitted to the Senate on June 8, 1795, and approved by the Senate on June 24, after a long debate, with not a single vote to spare (20 to 10). The Northwest Territory was cleared of all British troops, arbitration arrangements were made for boundary disputes, and commerce was encouraged. Since Britain was the one country most vital to the United States and also the power which could harm or help this country the most, as well as having a general outlook in world affairs the most similar to that of America, Jay's Treaty must be regarded as one of the most significant achievements of the Washington Administration. When peace negotiations with the Indians failed, General Anthony Wayne won the decisive Battle of Fallen Timbers on August 20, 1794, and the Treaty of Greenville, signed on August 3, 1795, between the United States and 20 Indian tribes, secured the vital Northwest for the Americans.

The Administration was also successful in its negotiations with Spain over the Mississippi Rover and the southern boundary. The Treaty of San Lorenzo (commonly called Pinckney's Treaty) was signed on October 27, 1795. Spain recognized the northern boundary of her Florida territory as the 31st parallel, and granted American citizens the right to navigate the whole Mississippi—the long-sought outlet to the sea by the western territories. At the same time, American trade, vital to the nation, was being expanded around the world, with the European war creating an unusual demand for American produce.

There was a continued and ever-growing division in America over the principles represented by Britain and France. In the light of the high internal tension over America's position, and the great pressure from France as well as Britain on American trade, President Washington's warnings in his Farewell Address (September 17, 1796), take on special meaning (the whole address is read in Congress each year on Washington's birthday, February 22):

> Observe good faith and justice towards all nations. Cultivate peace and harmony with all. Religion and morality enjoin this conduct. And can it be that good policy does not equally enjoin it? . . .
>
> To the execution of such a plan nothing is more essential than that permanent, inveterate antipathies against particular nations and passionate attachments for others should be excluded, and that in place of them just and amicable feelings toward all should be cultivated. The nation which indulges toward another an habitual hatred or an habitual fondness is in some degree a slave. It is a slave to its animosity or to its affection, either of which is sufficient to lead it astray from its duty and its interest. . . .
>
> Against the insidious wiles of foreign influence (I conjure you to believe me, fellow-citizens) the jealousy of a free people ought to be *constantly* awake since history and experience prove that foreign influence is one of the most baneful foes of republican government. . . .

The great rule of conduct for us in regard to foreign nations is, in extending our commercial relations to have with then as little *political* connection as possible. So far as we have already formed engagements let them be fulfilled with perfect good faith. Here let us stop.[54]

The President also stressed the importance of staying out of Europe's quarrels and avoiding permanent alliances:

Europe has a set of primary interests which to us have none or a very remote relation. Hence she must be engaged in frequent controversies, the causes of which are essentially foreign to our concerns. . . .

Our detached and distant situation invites and enables us to pursue a different course. If we remain one people, under an efficient government, the period is not far off when we may defy material injury from external annoyances; when we may take such an attitude as will cause the neutrality we may at any time resolve upon to be scrupulously respected; . . . when we may choose peace or war, as our interest, guided by justice, shall counsel.

Why forego the advantages of so peculiar a situation? Why quit our own to stand upon foreign ground? . . .

It is our true policy to steer clear of permanent alliances with any portion of the foreign world, so far, I mean, as we are now at liberty to do it; for let me not be understood as capable of patronizing infidelity to existing engagements. I hold the maxim no less applicable to public than to private affairs that honesty is always the best policy. . . .

Taking care always to keep ourselves by suitable establishments on a respectable defensive posture, we may safely trust to temporary alliances for extraordinary emergencies.

Harmony, liberal intercourse with all nations are recommended by policy, humanity, and interest. But even our commercial policy should hold an equal and impartial hand, neither seeking nor granting exclusive favors or preferences. . . . constantly keeping in view that it is folly in one nation to look for disinterested favors from another. . . .[55]

Secularism continued to grow in the 1780s. Popular deist writers of the time stressed belief only in the God of nature, and dismissed the so-called revelations of the Scriptures. The most influential tract in this direction was Thomas Paine's *The Age of Reason*; the first English edition was printed in France in 1794 and spread broadly throughout America. Materialism was stressed by the noted English scientist, Joseph Priestley, who spent the last ten years of this life (1794–1804) in Pennsylvania. It was reported that by 1800 there were only five student members of the college church at Yale College. Timothy Dwight became President of Yale in 1795, and worked resolutely against the skeptical trend in his addresses and writings (for example, his *Triumph of Infidelity* in 1788, and later addresses, notably 1797).

President Washington's exhortations concerning religion and morality in his Farewell Address were probably inspired in part by the growing tendency to consider high morality attainable without religious foundations:

> Of all the dispositions and habits which lead to political prosperity, religion and morality are indispensable supports. In vain would that man claim the tribute of patriotism who should labor to subvert these great pillars of human happiness—these firmest props of the duties of men and citizens. The mere politician, equally with the pious man, ought to respect and to cherish them. . . . And let us with caution indulge the supposition that morality can be maintained without religion. Whatever may be conceded to the influence of refined education on minds of peculiar strength, reason and experience both forbid us to expect that national morality can prevail in exclusion of religious principle.
>
> It is substantially true that virtue or morality is a necessary spring of popular government. The rule indeed extends with more or less force to every species of free government. Who that is a sincere friend to it can look with indifference upon attempts to shake the foundation of the fabric? Promote, then, as an object of primary importance, institutions for the general diffusion of knowledge. In proportion as the structure of a government gives force to public opinion, it is essential that public opinion should be enlightened.[56]

In the previous month (August 14, 1796), John Adams, who was to be elected President later in the year, expressed his convictions as to the importance of Christianity for political affairs:

> One great advantage of the Christian religion is, that it brings the great principle of the law of nature and nations,—love of neighbor as yourself, and do to others as you would that others should do to you,—to the knowledge, belief, and veneration of the whole people. Children, servants, women, and men are all professors in the science of public and private morality. No other institution for education, no kind of political discipline, could diffuse this kind of necessary information, so universally among all ranks and descriptions of citizens. The duties and rights of the man and the citizen are thus taught from early infancy

to every creature. The sanctions of a future life are thus added to the observances of civil and political as well as domestic and private duties. Prudence, justice, temperance, and fortitude, are thus taught to be the means and conditions of the future as well as present happiness.[57]

This somewhat pragmatic approach to the value of religion may be regarded as rather typical in an age when deeper spiritual motivations were being weakened. And the triumph of the Jeffersonian Republicans in 1800 was to stress the spirit of freedom in general, and temporarily weaken religious sanctions still more.

In the election year of 1796, relations with France grew steadily worse. France demanded more favorable treatment from the United States, under its interpretation of the 1778 treaty, and the French bitterly resented Jay's Treaty between the United States and Britain. Under new decrees issued in July 1796, the French began seizing American ships on an increased scale, and they were looking forward to the defeat of the Federalists in the Presidential election. In the ballots cast on December 7 by the electoral college, John Adams received 71 votes (69 from New England and the Middle states) while Jefferson secured 68 (from the South and Pennsylvania).

President John Adams, in his Inaugural Address on March 4, 1797, stressed his "inflexible determination to maintain peace and inviolable faith with all nations, and that system of neutrality and impartiality among the belligerent powers of Europe which has been adopted by this Government and so solemnly sanctioned by both Houses of Congress and applauded by the legislatures of the States and the public opinion, until it shall be otherwise ordained by Congress." And he referred to his "personal esteem for the French nation, formed in a residence of seven years chiefly among them, and a sincere desire to preserve the friendship which has been so much for the honor and interest of both nations." Furthermore, as if preparing for more difficult challenges to come, he expressed his "unshaken confidence in the honor, spirit, and resources of the American people, on which I have so often hazarded my all and never been deceived."[58]

Tension continued to mount between the two countries. It was reported on June 22, 1797, that 316 American vessels had been captured by French cruisers since July 1796.[59] The President called Congress into special session over the French crisis, sending a message on May 6, 1797, urging an increase in measures for defense, as well as renewed negotiations in the face of French rebuffs. He also sent a special commission to France to negotiate a new treaty—the commission was asked in vain to pay France $240,000 before negotiations. Congress steadily strengthened defenses. The Navy Department was established on May 3, 1798, and commercial intercourse with France was suspended on June 13. Virginia and North Carolina talked of possible secession. Congress passed the Naturalization Act on June 18 which increased the residence requirement from five to fourteen years, and on June 26 the Alien Act which authorized the President to deport dangerous aliens. For the first time the newly created federal union was getting ready to "flex its muscles" in international affairs, so that a new era in American foreign policy can be dated from about the first of July 1798—the beginning of America's first so-called extrovert phase.

Before dealing with this new phase, certain other evidences of introversion during Washington's Administration and the first year of John Adams' should be noted: (1) the emphasis on "peace" in the face of a number of challenges; (2) American submission to pressure from the Barbary states (Congress paid tribute to Tripoli in 1796 and to Tunis in 1797); (3) the lack of interest in building up the Department of State and the foreign service; and (4) Washington's emphasis on American separation from European politics.

The Democratic Republic in a World Aflame: Extroversion-Liberty, 1798–1811

In his farewell address in 1796, Washington had declared that the time would soon come when the increasing strength of America would enable her to support with positive action her desires for independence and non-interference from other nations. Such a time was indeed at hand when French provocation was reaching a peak in the summer of 1798. The French alliance was America's only direct "entanglement" with a foreign power, and, in the face of the strong French challenges, the nation was determined to throw off this yoke and even go to war with France if peaceful alternatives should fail. As in the period just ended (1776–98), the spirit of "liberty" appeared to dominate approximately the first half of the new extrovert phase and the spirit of "union" the last half. The renewed sense of "liberty" was shown in the political victories, in 1800 and after, of the Jeffersonian Republican Party. Accompanying the rising spirit of liberty was a new mood which supported positive action in strengthening America's *independent* position in the family of nations, as the French Revolutionary Wars moved into their prolonged Napoleonic phase (1799–1815).

Congress authorized a limited type of "undeclared war" against France—on May 28 and June 25, 1798—by authorizing the capture of French ships. There was a possibility of real war. On July 2, Adams appointed George Washington as commanding-general of the armies to be raised to meet a possible French invasion. The Congress (still Federalist) passed strong measures against France in quick succession, including the Alien Enemies Act, the Sedition Act, and an increase in the regular army to 13,000. President Adams told Congress on June 21, 1798: "I will never send another Minister to France without assurances that he will be received, respected, and honored as a representative of a great, free, powerful and independent nation."[60] The American Navy had 22 ships and 3,500 men when the undeclared naval war began in November with the French capture of the schooner *Retaliation*. Six newly built frigates, unusually fast, formed the nucleus of an American force which performed some brilliant naval exploits, behind which American wartime commerce with Europe expanded.

A favorable European reaction to America's stand was reported by John Quincy Adams (then Minister to Prussia) in a letter to his mother, September 14, 1798:

> You cannot well imagine how much the attitude which our government and people have taken has raised them in the opinion of the European world. Out of France and the circle of French fanaticism, the clear and unequivocal voice of Europe declares that in this contest we are right and France is wrong. . . .
>
> The French newspapers made no scruple of announcing that a revolution would soon overthrow the American government, and place the affairs of the United States in the hands of patriots devoted to France. . . . But the tone is now totally changed, and the signal of the change was the first show of firmness and a determination to resist on the part of our government.[61]

He added that the French now believed that the differences could be settled amicably.

President Adams publicly acknowledged the new American spirit in his Second Annual Address to Congress on December 8, 1798:

> . . . We have abundant reason to present to the Supreme Being our annual obligations of gratitude for a liberal participation in the ordinary blessings of His providence. To the usual subjects of gratitude I cannot

omit to add one of the first importance to our well-being and safety; I mean that spirit which has arisen in our country against the menaces and aggressions of a foreign nation. A manly sense of national honor, dignity, and independence has appeared which, if encouraged and invigorated by every branch of the Government, will enable us to view undismayed the enterprises of any foreign power and become the sure foundation of national prosperity and glory.[62]

A powerful group in the Federalist Party, under the leadership of Alexander Hamilton, seemed to believe that a war with France was the only choice facing America. But President Adams helped establish a notable precedent in expressing his desire for peace in the message to Congress, while pointing to the role of force in paving the way to peace:

But in demonstrating by our conduct that we do not fear war in the necessary protection of our rights and honor we shall give no room to infer that we abandon the desire for peace. It is peace that we have uniformly and perseveringly cultivated, and harmony between us and France may be restored at her option. But to send another minister without more determinate assurance that he would be received would be an act of humiliation to which the United States ought not to submit.[63]

The election in November 1798 showed major support of the Administration in its strong stand against France and against disloyalty in America. But President Adams squarely opposed the "pro-war" party by nominating William Van Murray on February 18, 1799, as minister and commissioner to France in the hope of negotiating a settlement, when the new French Government had given assurances that the President's representative would be received with proper respect.

The mood of Americans was touched with deep solemnity by the death of Washington on December 14, 1799. President Adams expressed the pride of Americans in their first President, in a message to the Senate on December 23: "His example is now complete, and it will teach wisdom and virtue to magistrates, citizens, and men, not only in the present age, but in future generations as long as our history shall be read."[64] The same spirit was invoked by the President in his next (and last) annual address, November 22, 1800, when the Congress was meeting for the first time in the new Capitol at Washington, D.C.:

It would be unbecoming the representatives of this nation to assemble for the first time in this solemn temple without looking up to the Supreme Ruler of the Universe and imploring His blessing.

May this territory be the residence of virtue and happiness! In this city may that piety and virtue, that wisdom and magnanimity, that constancy and self-government, which adorned the great character whose name it bears be forever in veneration! Here and throughout our country may simple manners, pure morals, and true religion flourish forever![65]

It was difficult for Adams to execute his "peace policy" in the face of Hamilton's supporters in the cabinet, so that Hamilton's loss of control of the New York legislature (which chose Presidential electors as well as Senators) on April 28, 1800, was a notable event. For Adams took the opportunity to move swiftly against his opposition, beginning with his dismissals of Secretary of War James McHenry (May 6) and Secretary of State Timothy Pickering (May 10), and his appointment of John Marshall as the new Secretary of State. Secretary Marshall counselled patience as the delicate negotiations with France continued. Success was achieved when a new treaty was signed with France (under Napoleon) on September 30, 1800.

Thus was ended the "entangling" alliance with France. The United States had demonstrated a spirit of independence with augmented respect from France and other European nations. Peace had been secured with honor. John Adams, writing about the event in 1809, regarded this peaceful solution of the conflict with France as a most "glorious episode" in American history, even as many of his cabinet and the leading Federalists in both houses of Congress had favored war.[66] Jefferson and other leading Republicans regarded the American opposition to France at this time as largely a Federalist experiment in manufacturing hysteria for domestic political purposes. President Adams had taken the middle ground of standing up squarely to France, while seeking an honorable return to peace. His stand took political courage, for it was generally believed that his decision would cost him a second term as President.

A notable result of the limited naval war with France was the virtual creation of the American Navy. Even though the Republicans, who came to power in 1801, moved to reduce military expenditures, especially for the army, the foundations of a regular defense establishment had been solidly laid.

The spirit of "liberty" was given special stimulus by the numerous prosecutions under the Sedition Act of 1798. Jefferson helped write the Kentucky Resolution (November 16 and 22, 1798) and Madison the Virginia Resolution (December 24), both of which declared the Alien and Sedition Acts unconstitutional. Jefferson's Republican Party swept into victory in Congress in the elections of November 1800, and Jefferson won the Presidency by a narrow margin through gaining New York (73 votes for Jefferson, and 65 for Adams). The Federalist Party had already played its great role in establishing the national government. It crumbled rapidly in the elections after 1800. In the Presidential race of 1804, Jefferson defeated Charles Pinckney by a landslide electoral vote of 162 to 14 (Connecticut, Delaware and Maryland).

President Jefferson represented the new emphasis on freedom. Many conservative Federalists regarded Jefferson as the leader of a type of freedom which would promote the decline of religion and morals. Jefferson explained his own position in a letter to Dr. Benjamin Rush (September 23, 1800), in which he expressed his fear of efforts to "establish" one type of religion or another and declared: " . . . I have sworn upon the altar of God, eternal hostility against every form of tyranny over the mind of man."[67]

In his notable First Inaugural Address, March 4, 1801, President Jefferson hoped to strengthen the bonds of the Union by stressing the true principles of Liberty:

> All . . . will bear in mind this sacred principle, that though the will of the majority is in all cases to prevail, that will to be rightful must be reasonable; that the minority possess their equal rights, which equal law must protect, and to violate would be oppression. Let us, then, fellow-citizens, unite with one heart and one mind. Let us restore to social intercourse that harmony and affection without which liberty and even life itself are dreary things. . . . Every difference of opinion is not a difference of principle. We have called by different names brethren of the same principle. We are all Republicans, we are all Federalists.[68]

Jefferson had begun the address with a picture of an unfolding American destiny:

> A rising nation, spread over a wise and fruitful land, traversing all the seas with the rich products of their industry, engaged in commerce with nations who feel power and forget right, advancing rapidly to destinies beyond the reach of mortal eye—when I contemplate these

transcendent objects, and see the honor, the happiness, and the hopes of this beloved country committed to the issue and the auspices of the day, I shrink from the contemplation and humble myself before the magnitude of the undertaking.[69]

Then, following a call to unity, he proceeded to stress the importance of American independence and American principles, and of separation from the turmoil and temptations of the European world, "possessing a chosen country, with room enough for our descendants to the thousandth and thousandth generation" and "acknowledging and adoring an overruling providence, which by all its dispensations proves that it delights in the happiness of man here and his greater happiness thereafter. . . ."[70] With the French alliance coming to an end, and with a full knowledge of all the bitter quarrels which had been occasioned among American citizens over a possible attachment to Britain or to France, Jefferson included among the principles of his administration his famous statement on "entangling alliances": " . . . Peace, commerce, and honest friendship with all nations, entangling alliances with none . . . a well-disciplined militia, our best reliance in peace and for the first moment of war, till regulars may relieve them; and supremacy of the civil over the military authority. . . ."[71]

Throughout his administration, Jefferson pursued peace as a major goal, relying upon the future growth of America as the major assurance that the nation would be able to defend its proper rights.[72] As the European wars continued to increase America's concern with international affairs, Jefferson moved in 1808 to open relations with Russia, whose Czar, Alexander I, was widely admired (John Quincy Adams became Minister to Russia from 1809 to 1814).

The future greatness and world influence of the United States was to depend in part upon its territorial expansion. It was Jefferson who first saw and grasped the opportunity to enlarge America's territorial base enormously, particularly as a means of promoting his generation's major concern: protecting the independence and security of America from interference by any of the major powers of Europe. The vast territory of Louisiana had been transferred from France to Spain by the Treaty of Paris which ended the Seven Years War (French and Indian War) in 1763. But on the very day following the conclusion of the convention by Napoleon with the United States, preliminary articles were signed (October 1, 1800) by which Spain was to transfer Louisiana to France. Napoleon's grandiose dreams then included an American empire as well as a great European one. The Treaty of Madrid on March 21, 1801, confirmed the transfer from weak Spain to a powerful France under this rising military dictator. Jefferson expressed his deep and realistic concern over French possession of Louisiana, in a letter to the American Minister to France, Robert Livingstone (April 18, 1802):

> It completely reverses all the political relations of the United States, and will form a new epoch in our political course. . . . There is on the globe one single spot, the possessor of which is our natural and habitual enemy. It is New Orleans, through which the produce of three-eighths of our territory must pass to market. . . . France, placing herself in that door, assumes to us the attitude of defiance. Spain might have retained it quietly for years. . . . The day that France takes possession of New Orleans . . . seals the union of two nations, who, in conjunction, can maintain exclusive possession of the ocean. From that moment, we must marry ourselves to the British fleet. We must turn all our attention to a maritime force, for which our resources place us on a very high ground. . . .[73]

Early in 1803, Jefferson appointed James Monroe as special envoy to France, to endeavor to purchase Louisiana, telling him that "on the event of this mission depend the future destinies of the republic."[74]

The turn of events in 1802 and 1803 led Napoleon to make the unexpected decision to offer to sell all of Louisiana to the United States. Three special circumstances favored his decision: (1) the terrible casualties suffered by the French forces on Santa Domingo from disease and from the effort to crush the revolt there; (2) the early winter which sealed until spring the European harbor from which a French expedition was being prepared to sail for American; and (3) the imminence of war with Britain, which might be able to seize Louisiana.[75] Napoleon had also become well aware of America's opposition, and of the possible American-British cooperation in this area. The American negotiators, Livingstone and Monroe, exceeded their instructions in agreeing to buy the whole territory, and Jefferson felt that he had to stretch his constitutional powers to approve the transaction—but the statesmen were able to grasp the special significance of the vast territory for the future of America. As Republicans, they could also see the political importance of the new acquisition, which was strongly opposed by most of the New England Federalists. The purchase was altogether a most remarkable event, promoted by specific European developments, and fraught with momentous consequences for the new American nation.

The westward march of the Americans was about to be resumed with new vigor.

The treaty for the Louisiana purchase was signed in Paris, and dated April 30, 1803, with the United States agreeing to pay approximately $15,000,000. Opposition to the addition of the territory grew strong in the Northeast. President Jefferson called Congress into early session, and addressed them on October 17, with special emphasis on the Louisiana treaty and a treaty with Indian tribes (June 7, 1803—opening up important new parts of the Northwest). The Senate approved the Louisiana purchase treaty on October 20 by a vote of 24 to 7, and the House later approved the necessary appropriation. On December 30, 1803, the United States took formal possession of the territory. Although the boundaries were not clear, and were to be subject to much bitter argument with Spain, the territory of the United States was approximately doubled by adding 827,000 square miles to the previous 889,000.

A notable feature of the treaty for the cession of Louisiana is found in Article III, in which the spirit of the Northwest Ordinance was incorporated:

> The inhabitants of the ceded territory shall be incorporated in the Union of the United States and admitted as soon as possible according to the principles of the federal Constitution to the enjoyment of all the rights, advantages and immunities of citizens of the United States, and in the meantime they shall be maintained and protected in the free enjoyment of their liberty, property and the Religion which they profess.[76]

Thus was protected not only the rights of the French inhabitants, but also the rights to self-government of the current and future residents.

Even before the purchase of Louisiana, Jefferson showed his interest in the Far West of America, by asking Congress in January 1803 for appropriations for the Lewis-Clark expedition. On August 31, the expedition started up the Ohio River. Jefferson wrote to Captain Lewis on November 16, 1803, directing him not to undertake a certain winter excursion, but instead to prepare to reach the Pacific:

> Such an excursion will be more dangerous than the main expedition up the Missouri, and would by an accident to you, hazard our main objective, which, since the acquisition of Louisiana, interests everybody in the highest degree. The object of your mission is single, the direct

water communication from sea to sea formed by the bed of the Missouri, and perhaps the Oregon.[77]

The British, who had occupied Florida since 1763, had transferred the territory back to Spain in 1783. The purchase of Louisiana precipitated a boundary dispute with Spain over whether West Florida (extending up to the Mississippi River) was included in the Louisiana purchase, and whetted America's appetite to acquire East Florida as well. Jefferson and Madison, his successor, moved steadily to secure West Florida. Jefferson proposed to Congress preparation for possible hostilities with Spain in his fifth annual message, December 3, 1805.[78] It was quite clear at this time that the Spanish empire in America was not to be feared, and would probably ultimately break up—but that it would never be to America's interest to permit the strong power of France or Britain to replace Spain in any of these areas, as in Cuba. When Cuban delegates visited the United States in 1808 to discuss possible annexation to save them from Napoleon, Jefferson's cabinet expressed its view that it would be extremely unwilling to see Cuba once more under France or Britain, but encouraged a possible declaration of independence if they were threatened.[79]

In addition to Jefferson's contribution to the first enlargements of the territorial base of America, he established two precedents in defense of American rights; (1) using American naval force to protect American shipping against the Barbary pirates in the Mediterranean and (2) employing economic pressure short of war, in an attempt to protect America's commerce.

After Jefferson's inauguration, Tripoli increased its demands for tribute, and declared war on the United States. Jefferson immediately sent a small squadron of frigates into the Mediterranean. An American blockade of Tripoli's ports brought a declaration of war also from Morocco in 1802. In 1803, the *Philadelphia* was grounded, so that its commander and crew of 307 men were taken prisoners and held for nineteen months. It was this ship which Lt. Stephen Decatur and a small band of volunteers succeeded in finding and destroying in the harbor of Tripoli. Even more spectacular, for this period in American history, was the land campaign led by William Eaton, former American consul at Tunis, aiming at replacing the ruler of Tripoli with a rival pretender. With a few American sailors and marines, and several hundred Arabs, he marched with the pretender 500 miles across Libya to capture Derne, with the aid of some American vessels (April 1805). The Pasha of

Tripoli now threatened to slaughter the American prisoners for the *Philadelphia* unless a peace treaty was made. The treaty, drawn up in the summer of 1805, was the most favorable treaty any nation had secured from Tripoli for peace without tribute. But it provided for a ransom of $60,000, and further presents. By comparison with America's previous action in the Mediterranean, one can agree with T. A. Bailey that "Jefferson's courageous action inaugurated a policy that freed American commerce, strengthened American nationality, and awakened a new respect for the United States."[80] American naval forces were withdrawn from the Mediterranean in 1807, because of the growing tension with Britain and France; but they returned after the War of 1812 to end the system of tribute and ransom.

With the renewal of war between Britain and France in 1803, American merchant ships found themselves at the mercy of the powerful belligerents. Britain moved to wipe out any neutral trade with the enemy, and stopped American ships to "impress" seamen (alleged to be British although many were Americans). France likewise seized American vessels trading with the British. American resentment mounted; Jefferson protested and sought to find pressures short of war which could be used to bring increased respect for American rights on the high seas. Jefferson's alternative to war was presented to Congress on December 18, 1807: an embargo on the departure of American vessels from the ports of the United States. The embargo was approved by Congress on December 21. With no goods to be carried out of U.S. ports, the commercial states and cities were indeed hard hit. Many in New England endeavored to evade the embargo. Jefferson felt forced to declare a state of insurrection along the frontier in April 1808. It soon became clear that it was not feasible to continue the "noble experiment" any longer. On March 1, 1809, one of Jefferson's last acts was to sign a new Non-Intercourse Act which replaced the Embargo.

The spirit of "liberty" in the nation was shown not only by the democratic principles of the dominant Republicans, but also by the rising opposition in New England to the Embargo. The growing crisis with Britain was to be left to the new President, James Madison, and it was under Madison, sometimes called the "Father of the Constitution," that the nation would return its main emphasis to "union."

Madison indicated in his First Inaugural Address (March 4, 1809) that he wished to continue Jefferson's policy of peace, but with hints that the nation might rally to resist by force British (or French) pressure too long sustained. Pro-war feelings in America rose rapidly during

1810 and 1811. Madison opened trade with France on November 2, 1810, while trade with England was scheduled to halt early in 1811. The newly elected 12th Congress in the fall of 1810 had 108 Republicans out of 144, and 30 Republican Senators out of 36—it was to develop a spirit which would rather fight than submit to further indignities from Britain. The British established a virtual blockade of New York, and intensified their program of impressment, as their war with Napoleon mounted toward its climax. After a naval engagement on May 18, 1811, British-American relations arrived at an impasse by July.

In the meantime, President Madison authorized the occupation of West Florida on October 1810, as part of the Louisiana Territory. In May 1811, John Jacob Astor founded Astoria at the mouth of the Columbia River. Also in 1811, Joel R. Poinsett, an American, was named Consul-General to the United States from Buenos Aires, Chile, and Peru. Interest in the hoped-for freedom of Latin America and other areas was expressed in a letter of Jefferson on February 12, 1810: "the preservation of the holy fire is confided to us by the world, and the sparks which will emanate from it will ever serve to rekindle it in other quarters of the globe. . . ."[81] Another sign of America's broadening concern in world affairs was the arrival of John Quincy Adams at St. Petersburg in October 1809 as American Minister to Russia. He expressed the common tie of Russia and American during the great war in Europe:

> Unhappily for mankind the present state of the world exhibits the singular phenomenon of two great powers, oppressing the whole species under the color of a war against each other. France and England can do very little harm comparatively speaking to each other, but the armed legions of France lay the continent of Europe under the most enormous contributions to support and enrich them, while the naval force of England extorts the same tribute from the commerce of the world.[82]

It should be noted that there were some special signs of spiritual renewal at this time (1798–1811). Political developments were predominant after the European wars began in 1792–93, and secularism perhaps reached a high point in 1798. There was perhaps a natural reaction of many Americans to the evil fruits of long-continued "worldliness," and the rapid movement west of the frontier presented a continuous challenge to the maintenance of religious institutions and influence. The fear of influences emanating from France increased as

Napoleon became the terror of Europe. John Adams wrote to Benjamin Rush (May 21, 1807): "The ominous dissolution of morality, both in theory and practice, throughout the civilized world, threatens dangers and calamities of a novel species, beyond all calculation, because there is no precedent or example in history which can show the consequences of it."[83]

However, the challenges in America of secularism and violent revolution, of war and the lawless frontier, produced major responses in religious circles around 1798. The Christian churches planned revivals, home missions, new denominations and foreign missions. A so-called Second Great Awakening started among the Congregational churches in New England in 1797, the year in which the first revivals also took place in Kentucky.

The initiation of foreign missions in the early part of the 19th century was another indication of America's growing world concern. The American movement began with a group of students affected by revivals at Williams College (Williamstown, Massachusetts) where a "Haystack Prayer Meeting" resulted in the formation in 1808 by Samuel J. Miller and some of his friends of a secret society whose members pledged themselves to devote their lives to foreign missions. The American Board of Commissioners for Foreign Missions was established in 1810, and in 1812 five of the young men were ordained as ministers and sailed for India. Thus began America's notable worldwide mission program, in cooperation with European missions.

In relation to Europe, politically and militarily, the new republic was ready to bring direct pressure, as the growing spirit of "union" strengthened the new mood of "extroversion."

Challenges to Europe in the Western Hemisphere: Extroversion-Union, 1811–24

The pressure from Britain was strengthening the spirit of union, and was to lead to the "Second War for Independence" from Britain, to be followed by a great outburst of nationalism as well as "good feeling." A new system of transportation was to heighten this growing national feeling: the turnpikes were begun in 1811, and steamboats began to ply the rivers (Fulton's *Clermont* had made its maiden voyage up the Hudson in 1807).

America had tried for a decade to gain respect from Britain and France by means short of war. The population continued to increase—registered at 7,240,000 in the 1810 census. America's patience was nearing the breaking-point as the British continued their system of impressment of American seamen, while the Indians of the Northwest prepared for new advances, and East Florida remained out of America's reach under a weak Spain backed by the major enemy, Britain.

The arrival of a new British Minister (Foster) on July 2, 1811, signified the end of hope for real British concessions. On July 25, President Madison called Congress into early session (November 4) to consider the developing crisis. Public sentiment against Britain was mounting steadily, led by such newspapers as the newly established *Niles' Weekly Register* in Baltimore. The first issue of Niles' paper, with its platform of "peace, liberty, and safety," appeared on September 7, 1811. The Twelfth Congress, which met on November 5, 1811, was dominated by a remarkable group of young men who were destined to become leaders for the generation ahead—such as Henry Clay of Kentucky, John Calhoun of South Carolina, Peter B. Porter of New York, and William Crawford of Georgia. Madison called on Congress for emergency measures of defense against the British "war" on American commerce.

The West was fearing an imminent attack from Tecumseh, allegedly supported by the British in Canada. On November 7, the Indians did attack the force of General William Henry Harrison, but they were beaten back with heavy losses (there were 200 American casualties) and their capital at Tippecanoe was razed. If war with Britain should come, the Westerners hoped to seize Canada, especially to end Indian attacks, and the Southerners expected to take East Florida.

The House Foreign Affairs Committee, on November 29, called on Americans to be worthy of their proper character and destiny, and rise to the defense of their country's rights.[84] Henry Clay, the new Speaker of the House, endeavored to answer those who claimed that Britain was fighting for the liberty of mankind against Napoleon, and should not be opposed by force at such a time:

> . . . Can Great Britain challenge our sympathies, when, instead of putting forth her arms to protect the world, she has converted the war into a means of self-aggrandizement; when, under pretense of defending them, she has destroyed the commerce and trampled on the rights of every nation; when she has attempted to annihilate every vestige of the public maritime code of which she professed to be the champion? Shall

we bear the cuffs and scoffs of British arrogance, because we may entertain chimerical fears of French subjugation? . . . We cannot assure our independence of one power, by a dastardly submission to the will of another. . . .[85]

The opposition to the defense bills spoke vigorously too, upholding the more peaceful side of the American character. Mr. Randolph of Virginia criticized the offensive character of the proposed war.[86]

While Congress was stirring up strong sentiments in favor of preparation for war against Britain, the legislatures or governors of many of the states outside of New England were giving powerful support for this vigorous stand. The rapid growth of a new spirited nationalism was being widely demonstrated. Most striking, perhaps, was the attitude shown in Massachusetts, for New England as a whole was hostile to the idea of war with Britain, since it was expected to stop most American shipping. The Massachusetts House of Representatives passed a resolution, by a vote of 223 to 110, stating that "the period has now come when this country must cease to be an independent power, or reclaim her usurped rights."[87] America was in a general mood which would bring a war soon unless Britain should quickly change her policy of the preceding decade. Little did most Americans realize the darkness and the bitter gloom which lay ahead in a war with Britain. Yet in the struggle to come, the nation was to be re-born, so to speak.

In May 1812, John Quincy Adams wrote of the virtual inevitability of war for America, with the whole world engaged in hostilities, and the possible good effect upon the national character:

> The effect of a war upon our national character and institutions would probably be great and I hope favorable. That we should be destined to enjoy a perpetual peace, however ardently humanity may desire it, cannot reasonably be expected. If war is not the natural state of human society at all times, it is that of the age upon which we have fallen. The spirit of ambition, of glory and of conquest bears in Europe with an intenseness beyond all former example. . . . If we should abandon our commerce to the plundering of Europe, it could not be long before we should be called to defend our territory against them.[88]

It was on June 1, 1812, that President Madison sent his message to Congress asking the body to recognize the state of war which had been thrust upon the United States by Britain. The House voted for war on June 4 by the comfortable margin of 79 to 49, but the Senate debated the issue for two more weeks before voting with the House 19 to 13 (June 18). New England was nearly solidly for peace, and talked of possible secession. But the die was cast for war against the world's strongest sea power, even though this power was engaged in a mighty struggle against Napoleon. Few suspected that the Napoleonic empire was nearing its doom, when its ruler was able to gather 600,000 soldiers to invade Russia on June 24, 1812.

The war with England soon brought deep gloom. Indian Chief Tecumseh joined with the British, and General William Hull surrendered Detroit without firing a shot (he was convicted of cowardice and neglect of duty in a court-martial early in 1814). The grandiose plans for the easy invasion of Canada were thus brought to an early end. America was by no means prepared for a major war. The only hopeful signs were some brilliant single-ship naval victories won by the Americans, and the decision of both America and Britain to open negotiations for a possible armistice.

While the United States was preparing to wage what was now expected to be a long and difficult war, Napoleon was leading his disastrous retreat from Russia. John Quincy Adams saw the Hand of Providence at work in this sudden turn of events: "It has pleased heaven for many years to preserve this man and to make him prosper as an instrument of divine wrath to scourge mankind. The race is now run, and his own turn of punishment has commenced."[89]

America's major successful record in the war continued to be made on the sea. John Adams grasped the significance of the increase in American naval strength for the nation's future world position, as he wrote on January 3, 1813:

> The foundation of an American Navy, which I presume is now established by law, is a grand era in the history of the world. The consequences of it will be greater than any of us can foresee. Look to Asia and Africa, to South America and to Europe for its effects. My private opinion had been for frigates and small vessels, but I rejoice that the ideas of Congress have been greater. The four quarters of the world are in a ferment. We shall interfere everywhere. Nothing but a navy under Heaven can secure, protect, or defend us.
>
> It is an astonishment to every enlightened man in Europe who considers us at all, that we have been so long insensible and inattentive to this great instrument of national prosperity, this most efficacious arm of national power, independence, and safety.[90]

By 1814, over 800 British vessels had been captured by Americans, and several notable naval victories had been won. But on land the outlook was not bright. The darkest hours of the war were to come in 1814. The allies in Europe entered Paris on March 31, 1814, and Napoleon was overthrown on April 6. John Quincy Adams tried to look at these astounding events in perspective (letter to his mother, May 12, 1814):

> The coalition of Europe against France has at length been crowned with complete success. The annals of the world do not, I believe, furnish an example of such a reverse of fortunes as this nation has experienced within the last two years. The interposition of Providence to produce this mighty change has been so signal, so peculiar, so distinct from all human operation, that in ages less addicted to superstition than the present it might have been considered as miraculous. As a judgment of Heaven, it will undoubtedly be considered by all pious minds now and hereafter. . . .[91]

With Napoleon defeated, England was free to turn her great military might against the United States, if she so desired. The U.S. government was near bankruptcy. Even the opening of the peace talks with Britain in Ghent, Belgium, on August 8, 1814, might have been regarded with some dismay, for the British had the upper hand and seemed determined to push their advantage so as to deprive America of some of her Northwest territories, her Canadian fishing rights and the like. The American peace delegation was strong, including Henry Clay, John Quincy Adams, and three others. The depth of humiliation was reached as the British sailed up Chesapeake Bay and marched towards Washington (August 19); the American troops fled at Bladensburg (August 24) to enable the British to march freely into Washington. Resentment and bitterness among Americans reached a high point when they learned of the wanton burning of the Capitol and the White House (August 24–25). A week later, September 1, President Madison issued a fervent appeal to the American people to redouble their energies for the defense of their nation.

The British were preparing attacks upon America from Canada in the north, from their fleet along the eastern coast, and from New Orleans in the south. But especially notable was the effect of the great American naval victory in the Battle of Lake Champlain, September 11, 1814, ending the immediate threat from Canada. On September 13–14, Fort McHenry, guarding Baltimore, held out against the bombardment of the British fleet. It was here that Francis Scott Key wrote the prophetic words of "The Star Spangled Banner" as he felt the new spirit which was beginning to animate the hard-pressed Americans:

> O thus be it even when freemen shall stand
> Between their loved homes and the war's desolation!
> Blest with vict'ry and peace, may the heav'n-rescued land
> Praise the Pow'r that hath made and preserved us a nation!
> Then conquer we must, when our cause it is just,
> And this be our motto: "In God is our trust!"
> And the Star-spangled Banner in triumph shall wave
> O'er the land of the free and the home of the brave.

With the generally dark military outlook and the New England states scheduled to meet in Hartford on December 15 to consider a revision of the Constitution or secession, President Madison issued a proclamation on November 16 for a day of prayer. It seemed that only a miracle could prevent the continuance of the war for an indefinite period. But three major developments were indeed at this very time bringing about a change in the attitude of the British government: (1) the split at the Congress of Vienna which threatened possible war between Britain and Austria on the one side and Prussia and Russia on the other; (2) unrest in France (which was to promote the early return of Napoleon for one last struggle); and (3) the news of the American victory at Lake Champlain which led the Duke of Wellington to recommend making peace without changing the American boundaries. On November 26, the British conceded to the staunchly held view of the American delegation that there should be no territorial changes. The Treaty of Ghent which ended the war was signed on December 24, 1814. It was a "peace without victory" for both sides, as John Quincy Adams described it on January 5, 1815:

> The peace in word and deed has been made upon terms of *perfect reciprocity*, and we have surrendered no one right or pretension of our country. This is the fair side of the treaty. Its darkest side is that is has settled no one subject of dispute between the two nations. . . . The treaty would more properly be called an unlimited armistice than a peace. . . . Certain it is that no other than such a peace could have been made.[92]

Yet this armistice was to prove lasting, and to lay the groundwork for the gradual development of mutual respect and friendship between the two countries whose cooperation could mean most for the liberties of the world. The patience and determination of the American negotiators, in the light of the dark military outlook, had been justified by the sudden turn of events.

Still another major event was to take place before the news of the signing of the treaty was to arrive in America. Many Americans felt the Hand of Providence at work here also. The country seemed to lie in mortal danger from the South. Unknown to General Andrew Jackson, who arrived in New Orleans on December 1, Sir Edward Pakenham had sailed from Jamaica with a large British fleet and 7,500 hardened British veterans, aiming to capture New Orleans and move north up the Mississippi River. Men must have wondered whether the citizen-soldiers of the West would be able to offer any important resistance. The result was to seem nearly incredible, in view of America's previous record in the war in land battles. Without being detected, British advance forces reached a point seven miles below New Orleans, where Jackson had no troops or defense works. Jackson moved swiftly, however, with 5,000 troops to confront this force unexpectedly. The British decided to wait for reinforcements, giving Jackson time to dig in five miles from New Orleans. American artillery won a duel on January 1, 1815. The British decided to attack on January 8, but everything seemed to go wrong for them—heavy fog, delay in the arrival of equipment, and great confusion in general. Pakenham attacked with 5,300 men, to be met by 4,500 entrenched Americans. The British were cut down and driven back, losing 2,035 men killed and wounded. General Pakenham and two other British generals were killed. The American loss was eight killed, and thirteen wounded. It was a tremendous victory for the marksmen of the West, armed with long rifles. A new national hero was created in Andrew Jackson. John William Ward wrote that the speeches in the House of Representatives after his victory showed "national pride apparently resting upon three main concepts, which for brevity may be designated as 'Nature,' 'Providence,' and 'Will' . . . for which Andrew Jackson is *one* symbol."[93]

In Washington, January of 1815 was still one of the darkest months of the war. News was being anxiously awaited from Ghent, from New Orleans, and from the Hartford Convention. On February 4, word arrived of Jackson's crushing defeat of the British at New Orleans. On February 13, copies were received of the Treaty of Ghent which had been signed on December 24. The aims of the extreme Federalists in

New England began to appear as ridiculous in the light of the sudden peace with Britain, but it was reassuring to learn that the moderates had in fact secured control of the Hartford Convention. Thus, it is easy to understand the feeling of immense relief and joy which swept over America. President Madison submitted the "treaty of peace and amity" with Britain to the Senate on February 15; it was approved unanimously on the same day, ratifications were exchanged, and the President proclaimed the treaty in effect on February 17.

America was indeed preparing for a new outburst of confidence and cooperating activity, with a renewed faith in the Providence which had seemed to protect the nation in its darkest hours. President Madison issued a special proclamation for a day of thanksgiving on March 4, 1815, reflecting these sentiments in his review of American history.[94] A wave of confidence and pride swept over the nation. A great destiny seemed to lie ahead for the United States of America. Forty years of internal and external trouble seemed to be nearing an end. The European wars which had been precipitated by the French Revolution were coming to an end after 23 years of nearly continuous fighting, and it was possible that a long period of world peace was about to begin. Americans were gaining a new and real sense of *independence* from Europe. The area of freedom was sure to expand further: south and west. The direction of the future was west: away from Europe. More cement had been added to the foundation of the nation. The sense of union had been strengthened by the intense experience shared by Americans in the dark hours and sacrifices and final elation of the war just ended. Henry Clay spoke of the new European respect for the United States, at a dinner in Lexington, October 7, 1815, honoring him on his return from the peace negotiations in Ghent.

On the other hand, there seemed little possibility of really friendly relations between the United States and Europe. With the partial restoration of the European "old regime," America remained the exceptional country in her devotion to individual liberty. John Quincy Adams (Minister to England) wrote on August 1, 1816, to his father, John Adams, stressing America's need to stand as a nation for liberty and justice at all times:

> . . . The longer I live the stronger I find my national feelings grow upon me and the less of my affections are compassed by partial localities. . . . It is the contemplation of our external relations that makes me especially anxious to strengthen our national government. The conduct

and issue of the late war has undoubtedly raised our national character in the consideration of the world; but we ought also to be aware that it has multiplied and embittered our enemies. This nation (England) is far more inveterate against us than it ever was before. All the restored governments of Europe are deeply hostile to us. The Royalists everywhere detest and despise us as Republicans. . . . How long it will be possible for us to preserve peace with all Europe it is impossible to foresee. Of this I am sure, that we cannot be too well or too quickly prepared for a new conflict to support our rights and our interests. . . . I can never join with my voice in the toast which I see in the papers attributed to one of our gallant naval commanders (Stephen Decatur, Norfolk, Virginia, April 1816: "Our country! in her intercourse with foreign nations, may she always be in the right; but our country, right or wrong"). I cannot ask of heaven success, even for my country, in a cause where she should be in the wrong. . . . My toast would be, may our country be always successful, but whether successful or otherwise always right. I disclaim as unsound all patriotism incompatible with the principles of eternal justice.[95]

The extrovert mood remained dominant for nearly a decade more following the conclusion of the War of 1812. Eyes turned again to the Barbary states, to trade with British possessions, to Florida, and to Oregon and the Pacific.

Algiers had declared war on the United States and seized American ships and sailors during the War of 1812. Stephen Decatur sailed from New York on May 10, 1815, with ten vessels, and secured a treaty on June 20 which ended the system of ransom and tribute. Another American squadron secured similar treaties with Tunis (July 26) and Tripoli (August 5).

The period of the Presidency of James Monroe (1817–25), with John Quincy Adams the Secretary of State, proved to be one of the most significant in American foreign policy—in relation to Britain, Spain, Latin America, the Monroe Doctrine, and the protection of America's worldwide commerce.

A threatened naval race with Britain on the Great Lakes led to negotiations which resulted in the famous Rush-Bagot Agreement of April 28–29, 1817. In agreeing that neither nation should maintain any armed forces on the Great Lakes, except for some small revenue cutters, the pattern was laid for ultimate mutual disarmament on the American-Canadian frontier. The groundwork was also being laid for cooperation between Britain and America in world affairs. In the Convention of

1818 the northern boundary of the United States was extended west of the Great Lakes on the 49th parallel to the Rocky Mountains, and the American claim to the Oregon territory was kept alive.

American claims to Florida and to Texas brought disputes with Spain during this period, and the tension was heightened by American sympathy with the revolting Spanish colonies to the south. American pressure on Spain resulted in Spain's relinquishment of Florida and of claims to the Oregon territory. All Spanish claims north of the 42nd parallel and west of the Rockies were ceded to the United States, so that America's claim to Oregon was strengthened in relation to Britain. Thus the final treaty with Spain, signed on February 22, 1819, is sometimes referred to as the Transcontinental Treaty. Secretary John Quincy Adams referred to the development as "a great epoch in our history" and regarded the result as providential in character.[96] The Senate approved the treaty unanimously only two days after its signature, but the Spanish government delayed month after month. After a Spanish revolution in 1820, ratifications of the treaty were finally exchanged on February 22, 1821.

With Florida securely in American possession, the large adjacent island of Cuba became more important to the security of the United States. Cuban revolutionaries visited the United States in 1822 to ask for governmental encouragement of a revolution and the admission of Cuba into the Union as a new state. President Monroe would have nothing to do with these plans (September 1822), but the Administration was particularly interested in seeing that Cuba would not be transferred to any other European power. Adams felt that the "law of political gravitation" would bring ultimate annexation of Cuba to the United States. The year 1821 was vital not only in "clinching" the treaty with Spain, but also in the successes of the Latin American revolutionists in decisive battles, and in the threat of European intervention which could threaten the peace.

As the United States remained officially neutral, Henry Clay intensified his campaign in behalf of the revolutionary republics. With pressure from Congress, the President recognized Great Columbia, June 18, 1822, Mexico on December 12, and Argentina and Chile on January 27, 1823. On May 27, 1823, Secretary Adams contrasted the European and American attitudes toward the South American colonies, and wrote in eloquent terms of the significance of Spanish American emancipation for future history.[97] (Other states were recognized as they made good their claims to independence—Brazil from Portugal and the Central

American states in 1824, with Peru not recognized until 1826.)

During the year 1823, however, it appeared that the liberation of Latin America might be reversed by action of the continental European powers. The United States had been the only power to recognize the Latin American states. The security of the recently freed New World seemed to be at stake. It was the year of the Monroe Doctrine.

The full significance of the Monroe Doctrine was not to become apparent until many decades after the pronouncement; yet at the time it represented the climax of nearly a half century of effort to establish the independence and security of the United States against the European powers, and an additional effort to champion the freedom of the new states in Latin America. The United States was looking at the whole Western Hemisphere as a "New World" which was set apart from the "Old." There were several vital aspects of Monroe's statement of the American-European relation: (1) the relation of Europe to the American nations; (2) the relation of the United States to Europe; (3) the future of colonization in this hemisphere (directed mainly at Russia); and (4) America's attitude toward Greece in its struggle for independence. Just as important was the practical expression of British-American cooperation in seeking somewhat similar goals.

The spirit of the Holy Alliance in Europe was devoted to the crushing of revolutions. On August 20, 1823, Foreign Secretary Canning of Great Britain proposed that Britain and the United States make a joint declaration to the world that they regarded the recovery of colonies by Spain to be hopeless. President Monroe wrote to Jefferson and Madison for their advice. Jefferson was immensely impressed with the opportunity to stand with Britain in this vital question of the freeing of the Americas, and urged Monroe to accept the British offer. But Secretary Adams urged instead a unilateral declaration so that America would remain free from British restrictions on her policy. The President decided to make the American declaration in his annual message to Congress on December 2, 1823. Near the end of the message was the statement of America's public stand in support of the newly freed states to the south, and of the American challenge to any plans of the Holy Alliance against them: "We owe it . . . to candor and to the amicable relations existing between the United States and those powers to declare that we should consider any attempt on their part to extend their system to any portion of this hemisphere as dangerous to our peace and safety."[98] Although America made the declaration unilaterally, she knew that Britain stood with her in the aim of preventing European intervention against Spain's former colonies. This foreshadowed the ultimate growth of strong Anglo-American cooperation in world affairs for the protection of democratic institutions. But the Monroe Doctrine itself was distinctly American.

Correlative with the principle that Europe should not interfere with political developments in the independent states of America was the statement of President Monroe that the United States would not participate in purely European conflicts and not interfere in European domestic affairs. In relation to the extension of Russian power on the western coast (including a trading post as far south as California), Monroe issued a clear warning in his message: "The American continents, by the free and independent condition which they have assumed, are henceforth not to be considered subject for further colonization by any European power."[99] This dramatic statement was directed to all the European powers—to Britain as well as to Russia. It strengthened America's position on principle against "colonialism." A Russian-American convention was signed on April 17, 1824, in which Russia and the United States agreed to divide their influence at 54 degrees and 40 minutes (the present southern boundary of Alaska).

The question also faced President Monroe as to what America's attitude should be toward the bloody Greek revolution against Turkey which had begun in 1821. A Greek assembly declared independence on January 13, 1822, and drew up a constitution establishing a liberal parliamentary system. Sympathy, which mounted rapidly in America for the little country which was regarded as the birthplace of democracy, reached its peak near the end of 1823 in the form of "sermons, orations, balls, mass meetings, poems . . . the collection of funds . . . and the introduction of resolutions in Congress."[100] Adams' firm stand against any European entanglements helped induce the President to emphasize in his message that the United States would not take any part "in the wars of the European powers in matters related to themselves," but he did include in his message an expression of strong sympathy on behalf of the embattled Greeks and the hope that Greece would soon become an independent nation.

But not all Americans were satisfied with statements of strong sympathy alone. On January 19, 1824, Daniel Webster delivered a notable oration on the Greek Revolution, urging American recognition of Greek independence when the President deemed it expedient:

We are placed, by our good fortune and the wisdom and valor of our ancestors, in a condition in which we *can* play no obscure part. Be it for honor, or be it for dishonor, whatever we do is sure to attract the observation of the world.

. . . Our history, our situation, our character, necessarily decide our position and our course. . . . Our place is on the side of free institutions.

. . . Is it not a duty imposed upon us, to give our weight to the side of liberty and justice, to let mankind know that we are not tired of our own institutions, and to protest against the asserted power of altering at pleasure the law of the civilized world.[101]

On the following day, January 20, 1824, Henry Clay added his weight to Webster's argument, and described the popular sentiment all over the United States in favor of Webster's resolution in Congress.[102] The House of Representatives took no action, although the weight of sentiment was overwhelmingly on the Greek side. As the years went along, Britain, France and Russia moved to help the Greeks, and the London Conference of 1829 decided that Greece should be given complete independence. American interest in the subject had declined by that time, and Greece was not even recognized by the United States until 1833 (an indication of the new introvert phase which had begun around 1824). The most significant feature of the whole episode regarding Greece was not the failure to act more decisively, but the high degree of concern expressed by many Americans and by the Administration in this struggle at the eastern end of the Mediterranean. The seed of America's worldwide concern with the future of democracy and international justice had clearly sprouted.

Among other world interests expressed during Monroe's administration were international trade and its naval protection, and the problem of the slave trade. President Monroe reported in his annual message of 1818 (November 16) that it had been necessary during the year:

to maintain a strong naval force in the Mediterranean and in the Gulf of Mexico, and to send some public ships along the southern coast and to the Pacific Ocean. By these means amicable relations with the Barbary Powers have been preserved, our commerce has been protected, and our rights respected. The augmentation of our Navy is advancing with a steady progress toward the limit contemplated by law.[103]

A large American whaling fleet was created about 1815. After American missionaries arrived in Hawaii from Boston in March 1820,

Monroe appointed an American agent to the islands. The American consul in Manila, under instructions from Monroe, was studying conditions in the Philippines and reporting the prospects for American trade there. The American navy proved to be an invaluable aid in protecting the rights of American commerce against piracy around the world. On May 15, 1820, Congress declared the foreign slave trade to be piracy. A Convention for the suppression of the slave trade, including the right of mutual "visit and search," was signed by the United States and Britain on March 13, 1824. The Senate passed two qualifying amendments to the treaty, under pressure from the South, but since Britain would not accept these the treaty never became effective.

Only one shadow was cast on the spirit of "union" during this period: that of slavery in the struggle over the admission of Missouri. The mood of compromise and cooperation prevailed, however, in the balancing of the slave state, Missouri, by the free state, Maine, and in the establishment of the Mason-Dixon line dividing slave and free states. This Missouri Compromise passed the House of Representatives on March 2, 1820, by the narrow margin of 90 to 87. Secretary of State Adams wrote in his diary the following day, after a talk with Calhoun on slavery: "It establishes false estimates of virtue and vice: for what can be more false and heartless than this doctrine which makes the first and holiest rights of humanity depend upon the color of the skin?"[104]

As in each of the political-cultural periods, this revolutionary period (1776–1824) showed marked signs of the dominant mood of the next period during its final third (1808–24). This next period (of the consolidation of democratic nationalism in America and Western Europe) would exhibit a special mood of moral-spiritual renewal.

Revivals and home missions continued to exert a special influence during this "final third": high points in revivals in the key state of Connecticut occurred in 1807–08, 1812, 1815–16 and 1820–21.[105] A major spiritual awakening at Yale College came in 1815, affecting nearly every individual.[106] The need for more trained ministers was recognized in the establishment of new schools of theology: Andover (1808), Princeton (1812), General (New York, 1817), Auburn (1818), Yale (1822) and Virginia (1823).

Foreign missionary activity was increased, as in the special mission to the Hawaiian (Sandwich) Islands in 1820 and 1822—the king accepted Christianity and made the Ten Commandments basic for the laws of the country in 1825.[107] Special missionary societies were started: by the Presbyterians in 1817, the Methodist Episcopal Church in 1819, and the Protestant Episcopal Church in 1821.

A more liberal spirit was developing in many American Christians during this time. Massachusetts had led the way in establishing a more liberal doctrine in New England with the emphasis on Unitarianism. After the War of 1812, William Ellery Channing became the leader of the growing Unitarian movement, in which he emphasized that the great end of preaching was "to promote a spirit of love, a sober, righteous, and godly life."[108] The American Unitarian Association was formed in 1825.

A special area for Christian expansion was found among the American Negroes (as well as the Indians). By 1828 there were 59,000 Methodist blacks. Negroes formed their own churches in many places. The African Methodist Episcopal Church was begun in 1816. The spreading of Christianity among American Negroes, both before and after the Civil War, is probably a major development in American history as a whole. Many Christians supported movements to aid these African-Americans, as, for example, in the American Colonization Society of 1816, which resulted in the establishment of Liberia on the west coast of Africa in 1822, as an asylum for freed blacks. The anti-slavery movement was getting under way, supported strongly by the Presbyterian General Assembly in 1818 and the new periodical, *Genius of Universal Emancipation* in 1821.

Churches then were not only beginning to oppose slavery, but also many other social evils, such as intemperance and war. Following the end of the War of 1812 and the Napoleonic Wars in Europe, Christians led the way in working for peace. Peace societies were organized in New York and Massachusetts in 1815 (the American Peace Society was not founded until 1828). Henry Adams stressed the American aversion to war as an outstanding trait at this time.[109] But Secretary of State Adams expressed a practical fear of pacifism too zealously sought in a world of powerful princes.[110]

Retrospect in 1824

The power of secularism in America after 1776 has often been underestimated. It remained relatively powerful until around 1824, when the significant moral and spiritual forces which had been building up since 1798 had reached a position of predominance in many quarters. Revolutionary and terribly violent events had shocked a whole generation into a certain degree of humility before fate, history or God, by 1815. And then suddenly the sun began to shine again.

In America, the deep darkness of 1814, which seemed to have been the climax of over twenty years of complicated problems and partisan strife, was dispelled so quickly in 1815 as to be almost unbelievable. Great international events lay ahead for America for another decade, as her territory was still further expanded and she was able to play a significant role in the consolidation of Latin America's liberty. The dark years of 1822–1823, when the Holy Alliance threatened to move on South America, were again followed by the dawning light of 1824, when the New World seemed secure and at peace.

During this time, Dr. C. F. Schmidt-Phiseldek, Counsellor of State for Denmark's King felt strongly that a new age was coming in which America could play a leading role. The introduction to his book of 1820 by the translator, described the author as "animated with the desire of being the humble instrument of imparting to the American nation, that picture of future grandeur and happiness" which he "so prophetically holds out to them. . . ."[111] The author believed that history was based not only on circumstances and conditions, but on the liberty of the human mind, and suggested that a new spark had been kindled in world history:

> . . . As the period just passed away, or in the act of taking leave of us, was subject to the principles of mechanism and of pecuniary calculation, so, can it be expected, that money, for the time to come, will of necessity, be subordinate to a more exalted animated power. . . .
>
> The fourth of July, in the year 1776, points out the commencement of a new period in the history of the world.[112]

The author also saw dangers in America of disunion, extreme commercialism, of possible despotism or licentiousness—but he also saw great hope in religious ties based on religious freedom and on the democratic rule of law: ". . . whatever futurity may have to reserve for the riper ages of these states, they can never fail in attaining their high destination, as long as the fundamental pillars of their happy constitution, the equality of all in the eye of the law, and the publicity of their legislatures as well as their tribunals remain unimpaired."[113]

By 1824 the new nation had been solidly built; its growth in territory and influence had been amazing. The main lines of America's foreign policy had been laid down for the future, particularly under the notable administration of President Monroe and Secretary of State John

Quincy Adams.[114] These principles can be summarized under three headings: (1) the principle of self-determination of nations; (2) American expansion in North America, with no more European colonization in this hemisphere; and (3) international peace and welfare (through negotiation and arbitration), with support for "freedom of the seas" and general freedom of commerce and navigation around the world.

American statesmen at this time grasped the significance of America's new position and example in the world. The general mood around 1824 was one of exaltation, as old problems appeared solved and new ones were not yet obvious or critical. At this time or shortly after, Americans became particularly conscious of the great stream of American history, as special anniversaries of major events were commemorated. Three notable orations were delivered by Daniel Webster. The first was at Plymouth, on the 200th anniversary of the landing of the Pilgrims, December 22, 1820. On January 17, 1825, on the 50th anniversary of the Battle of Bunker Hill, he spoke of world awareness and man's reason building toward peace:

> . . . We may hope that the growing influence of enlightened sentiment will promote the permanent peace of the world. . . . The great principle shall be more and more established, that the interest of the world is peace, and its first great statute, that every nation possesses the power of establishing a government for itself.[115]

The whole country was struck with a remarkable concurrence of events, when on the 50th anniversary of the Declaration of Independence, July 4, 1826, the two chief originators of the document, John Adams and Thomas Jefferson, both died, a few hours apart. Thoughts were naturally focussed on the significance of the Declaration and the nation which was built upon its principles. The two statesmen were virtually the personal embodiment of the spirit of the American nation—its independent Union and its individual Liberty. They were the second and third Presidents, following the revered Washington—one was from the North (Massachusetts) and the other from the South (Virginia). Their strong friendship during the early and later years of their lives was symbolic of the strength of the Union. Their deaths stood out like a comet in the heavens. The President, John Quincy Adams, deeply moved by the death of his father and of Jefferson, confided to his diary: "The time, the manner, the coincidence with the decease of

Jefferson, are visible and palpable proofs of Divine favor, for which I would humble myself in grateful and silent adoration before the Ruler of the Universe."[116] Daniel Webster delivered a discourse on the two great patriots, Adams and Jefferson, in Faneuil Hall in Boston on August 2, 1826, concluding by stressing the idea that a *new age* in human history was being inaugurated in the American experiment:

> It cannot be denied, but by those who would dispute against the sun, that with America, and in America, a new era commences in human affairs. This era is distinguished by free representative government, by entire religious liberty, by improved systems of national intercourse, by a newly awakened and unconquerable spirit of free inquiry, and by a diffusion of knowledge through the community, such as has been altogether unknown and unheard of.
>
> . . . If we cherish the virtues and principles of our fathers, Heaven will assist us to carry on the work of human liberty and human happiness. Auspicious omens cheer us. Great examples are before us.
> . . . [117]

In summary, the first 48 years of the American nation (1776–1824), in a revolutionary age for the West, had set the pattern for America's world role, and determined the basic lines of its future foreign policy. The first five Presidents—Washington, Adams, Jefferson, Madison and Monroe—and Monroe's Secretary of State John Quincy Adams had led the nation in establishing its independence and its government, and had helped enshrine its basic principles in the Declaration of Independence, the Constitution and the Bill of Rights. Out of the ideals in these documents emerged the guidelines for the nation's foreign policy. Future American Presidents would draw inspiration and direction from the ideals and practices of these early statesmen, who were forced to be realists, in a revolutionary time, in support of their idealism.

Yet the work of completion and consolidation of the nation itself was yet to come, as America confronted the rising issues of slavery and disunion, of vast territories to the west, and of the fruits of the secularism which had become so prominent in many citizens.

Notes

1. Seymour Martin Lipset, *The First New Nation: The United States in Historical and Comparative Perspective* (Garden City, N. Y.: Anchor Books, 1967), 244.

2. Arthur M. Schlesinger first published his theory in "Tides of American Politics," *Yale Review* XXIX (December 1939): 217–30; also in his book *Paths to the Present* (New York: Macmillan, 1949).

3. *The Writings of George Washington*, 37 vols. (Washington: U.S. Government Printing Office, 1931–1944), 5:211–12.

4. Washington, 9:362.

5. Message to the Continental Congress, September 8, 1776, Washington, 6:28.

6. *The Words of John Adams*, 2:505, quoted in Richard W. Van Alstyne, *American Diplomacy in Action* (Stanford University Press, 1954), 116–26.

7. *The Writings of Benjamin Franklin*, 10 vols. (New York: Macmillan, 1905), 7:56.

8. Library of Congress, *Journals of the Continental Congress, 1774–1789*. Edited from the original records by Worthington Chauncey Ford, 34 vols. (Washington, D.C.: U.S. Government Printing Office, 1904), 9:854–55 (hereafter designated at *Cont. Cong.*).

9. *Cont. Cong.*, 10:449–52.

10. Ibid., 474–81.

11. Washington, 11:38–42.

12. Washington, 14:311–13.

13. Washington, 19:129–33.

14. Washington, 20:95.

15. Washington, 21:158–59.

16. *Cont. Cong.*, 19:284–85.

17. Washington, 23:223.

18. Ibid., 242.

19. Ibid., 244–47.

20. *Cont. Cong.*, 21:1074–81.

21. Washington, 23:477–79.

22. *Cont. Cong.*, 22:339.

23. Ibid., 339–40.

24. Gerald Stourzh, *Benjamin Franklin and American Foreign Policy* (Chicago: University of Chicago Press, 1954), 173.

25. Quoted in Stourzh, 174.

26. Stourzh, 175.

27. *The Works of John Adams*, 10 vols. (Boston: Little Brown, 1856), 8:8–9.

28. Franklin, 8:642–43.

29. Washington, 26:483–96.

30. Luther A. Weigle, *American Idealism*, vol. 10 of *The Pageant of America* (New Haven: Yale University, 1928), 137.

31. Ibid., 138.

32. Ibid., 140.

33. Ibid., 141.

34. *Cont. Cong.*, 25:838.

35. John Adams, 10:45–46.

36. John Adams, 3:344–45, 365.

37. Franklin, 9:107–8.

38. John Adams, 8:385–86, to Matthew Robinson.

39. Washington, 28:161, to William Carmichael.

40. Frank Tannenbaum, *The American Tradition in Foreign Policy* (Norman: University of Oklahoma Press, 1951), 51.

41. Washington, 29:245–46.

42. Franklin, 9:600–601.

43. George Anastaplo, *The Constitution of 1787: A Commentary* (Baltimore: Johns Hopkins Press, 1989), 1–12, 303. The foundations he discussed for interpreting the Constitution were the language of the English-speaking peoples, the British Constitution, the Declaration of Independence, the common law, the law of public bodies, the state constitutions, the concept of the best temporal regime, the concept of the best spiritual regime, the character of the people, the law of nations, the Articles of Confederation, and the general "world view" in 1787.

44. Emmerich de Vattel. *The Law of Nations or The Principles of Natural Law*, translation of the Edition of 1758 by Charles G. Fenwick, vol. 3 (Washington: Carnegie Institution, 1916), 3a, 7a, 13a.

45. Ibid., 23, 35, 50–54, 57, 68, 78–79.

46. Ibid., 114–18, 131, 162, 188.

47. Ibid., 302.

48. Ibid., 268, 270.

49. Ibid., 343–44.

50. Daniel G. Lang. *Foreign Policy in the Early Republic: The Law of Nations and the Balance of Power* (Baton Rouge: Louisiana State University Press, 1985), 11.

51. Washington, 30:291–96.

52. James D. Richardson, *Messages and Papers of the Presidents, 1789–1902*, 11 vols. (Washington, D.C.: Bureau of National Literature and Art, 1907), 1:64.

53. Ira Glasser, *Visions of Liberty: The Bill of Rights for All Americans* (New York: Arcade Publishing, Little, Brown and Co., 1991), 40–41. He tells the full story of the adoption of the Bill of Rights, pp. 38–61.

54. Richardson, 1:221–22, 224.

55. Stuart Gerry Brown, ed., *We Hold These Truths: Documents of American Democracy* (New York: Harper and Brothers, 1941), 107–8.

56. Richardson, 1:220.

57. John Adams, 3:423–24.

58. Richardson, 1:231–32.

59. Samuel Flagg Bemis, ed., *The American Secretaries of State and Their*

Diplomacy, 10 vols. (New York: Cooper Square Publishers, 1927–29), 2:214.

60. Richardson, 1:266.

61. *The Writings of John Quincy Adams*, 7 vols. (New York: Macmillan, 1913–17), 2:360–62.

62. Richardson, 1:271–72.

63. Ibid., 272–73.

64. Ibid., 299–300.

65. Ibid., 305.

66. *Correspondence between the Honorable John Adams and the Late William Cunningham, Esq., 1803–1812* (Boston: True and Greene, 1823), 93.

67. *The Writings of Thomas Jefferson*, ed. H. A. Washington, 9 vols. (Washington, D.C.: Taylor and Maury, 1853–54), 4:736.

68. Richardson, 1:322.

69. Ibid., 321.

70. Ibid.

71. Ibid., 323–24.

72. Jefferson, 4:414–15.

73. Ibid., 431–34.

74. Ibid., 453–54, letter of January 13, 1803.

75. Bemis, *A Diplomatic History of the United States*, 4th ed. (New York: Holt, 1955), 134.

76. *Treaties and other International Acts of the U.S. of America*, ed. Hunter Miller (Washington: U.S. Government Printing Office, 1946), 2:501.

77. Jefferson, 4:516.

78. Richardson, 1:384.

79. Bemis, *Diplomatic History of the United States*, 197.

80. Thomas A. Bailey, *Diplomatic History of the American People* (New York: Crofts, 1940), 92–93.

81. Jefferson, 5:503.

82. John Quincy Adams, 3:397.

83. John Adams, 9:599.

84. *Niles' Weekly Register* (Baltimore, Md., 3d ed.), vol. 1, December 7, 1811, 253–54.

85. Ibid., January 4, 1812, 333–34.

86. Ibid., December 28, 1811, 317, 319.

87. Ibid., February 1, 1812, 404.

88. John Quincy Adams, 4:327, to William Plumer, May 13, 1812.

89. Ibid., 413.

90. John Adams, 10:24–25, to J. B. Varnum.

91. John Quincy Adams, 5:42–44.

92. Ibid., 261, to L. C. Adams.

93. John William Ward, *Andrew Jackson: Symbol for an Age* (New York: Oxford, 1955), 10.

94. Richardson, 1:560–61.

95. John Quincy Adams, 6:60–62.

96. *The Diary of John Quincy Adams*, ed. Allan Nevins (New York: Longmans Green, 1928), 211–12. Also Samuel Flagg Bemis, *John Quincy Adams and the Foundation of American Foreign Policy* (New York: Knopf, 1949), 338–39.

97. John Quincy Adams, 7:424–25, 466, 486.

98. Richardson, 2:218–19.

99. Ibid., 209.

100. Bailey, 183.

101. *The Works of Daniel Webster*, 6 vols., 18th ed. (Boston: Little, Brown and Co., 1881), 3:65–66, 75–77.

102. *The Works of Henry Clay*, ed. Calvin Colton, 10 vols. (New York: G. P. Putnams, 1904), 6:247.

103. Richardson, 2:46.

104. *The Diary of John Quincy Adams*, 231.

105. Charles Ray Keller, *The Second Great Awakening in Connecticut* (New Haven: Yale University Press, 1942), 42.

106. Ibid., 45.

107. Weigle, 145.

108. Henry Adams, *History of the United States of America, 1801–1817* (Philadelphia: The Blakiston Co., 1945), 9:180.

109. Ibid., 9:226–27.

110. John Quincy Adams, 6:280–81.

111. C. F. von Schmidt-Phiseldek, *Europe and America* (Copenhagen: Bernhard Schlesinger, 1820), p. 1 of Introduction.

112. Ibid., iii–viii, 1.

113. Ibid., 244.

114. Bemis, *John Quincy Adams*, ch. 27.

115. Webster, 1:71, 74–75.

116. *Memoirs of John Quincy Adams*, ed. Charles Francis Adams, 10 vols. (Philadelphia: J. B. Lippincott, 1875), 7:125.

117. Webster, 1:147–48.

CHAPTER IV

Rounding Out the Nation: Liberty, Land and Spirit (1824–1871)

This was the age of the consolidation or "synthesis" of the American democratic union, following its preparation in a time of dominant *rationalism* (1729–76) and the struggle for independence from Britain and Europe as a whole (1776–1824) in a time of *realism*. The consolidation of the nation was to be dominated by a growing *idealism*, with a renewal of the Christian emphasis. The major developments in the United States corresponded to analogous trends in Western Europe, with the rise and ultimate success of democratic (middle-class) nationalism.

This period of consolidation of the American union was begun with a phase of introversion (1824–44), following the success of the "revolutionary" extroversion (1798–1824). As the nation grew in strength, its attention was attracted by the vast tracts of western land loosely held by Mexico (and the native Americans) and by the rising feeling that the American democratic system should be expanded to include them (the period of "Manifest Destiny," 1844–57). Furthermore, the issue of slavery became ever more divisive, so that the very preservation of the union appeared in doubt in the years around the Civil War (or the "War Between the States," as known in the South), 1857–71. America's future world influence would depend largely upon the maintenance of the federal union as a democratic republic, without slavery. The prototype of America during this period was personified in one man—Abraham Lincoln.

Strengthening the New Nation: Introversion, 1824–44

The United States widened its democracy during this phase, especially under President Andrew Jackson (1829–37), paid little attention to foreign affairs, and applied its religious idealism to social issues and foreign missions. Slavery and the treatment of native-American Indians attracted more attention.

By 1824, major foreign problems seemed to have been solved. The world was generally at peace, and there were no visible external threats. The major goal was internal economic and social development.

The introvert phase appears to have begun in the summer of 1824, as bitter personal campaigns were begun for the Presidency. The electoral vote on December 2 gave Andrew Jackson 99 votes; John Quincy Adams, 84; William H. Crawford, 41; and Henry Clay, 37. On February 9, 1825, the House of Representatives elected Adams President, as Henry Clay released his states for Adams (Clay was later named as Adams' Secretary of State). The political struggle was intensified until the Presidential election of 1828, in which all electors were chosen by popular vote except in South Carolina (where the state legislature still made the decision). This popular election gave Jackson 647,000 votes (178 electoral) and Adams 508,000 (83 electoral). A new spirit of liberty was on the march, as Jackson men secured control of both houses of Congress in 1826, and suffrage qualifications were being steadily widened.

Foreign Relations, 1824–44

John Quincy Adams was an able administrator as President from 1825–29, but his policies were unpopular and unsuccessful. He and Secretary of State Clay were frustrated, largely by internal opposition, in their attempts to demonstrate leadership abroad. Americans appeared satisfied with the gains of the past decades. President Monroe, in his final message to Congress on December 7, 1824, pointed out that "we can have no concern in the wars of the European Governments nor in the causes which produce them."[1] President Adams, in his first inaugural address (December 6, 1825), saw America's role as one largely based upon example and moral leadership.[2] The most noteworthy foreign incident in Adams' administration was the Panama Congress in 1826. In December 1824, the great South American liberator, Bolivar, had issued an invitation to all the American nations to a Congress to be held in Panama. President Adams accepted the invitation in December 1825, but opposition developed rapidly in Congress, where fear was expressed of foreign entanglements or alliances, of commercial competition, and of eventual threats to slavery (on the problem of Haiti). Although Congress finally accepted the plan, no American delegate actually reached the Congress. The Pan-American dream was not to be acted upon until 1889.

Britain rebuffed Adams' effort to secure access to the trade of the British West Indies (1825–27); not until 1830 was the United States, under President Jackson, able to secure direct access to these British ports. From 1828 to 1834 there was little concern over foreign relations. Jackson's First Inaugural Address, March 4, 1829, did not even refer to international affairs. In his first annual message, he mentioned America's traditional enemy, Britain, in friendly terms, expressing his hope that "with Great Britain, alike distinguished in peace and war, we may look forward to years of peaceful, honorable and elevated competition."[3]

There was a steady increase in American commerce, particularly in the Pacific. American interest in China was increased by the first arrival of American missionaries there in 1830.[4] In Latin America, little attention was paid to the Monroe Doctrine. In 1833, when Great Britain, over the protests of Argentina, occupied the important Falkland Islands, President Jackson avoided the issue by not questioning the British claim.

Americans moved west into Texas as the Mexican Government encouraged them to settle there by more liberal land laws than those of the United States. Stephen Austin brought in the first Americans in the early 1820s. By 1835 it was estimated that the population of Texas was 30,000, nearly all from the United States and mostly from the slave states. De Tocqueville watched the westward movement in the 1830s, stimulated by European immigration, with awe, and wondered why Americans moved so rapidly to fill up the continent.[5] He pictured the role of the United States in the new world age which he saw coming:

> The time will come when one hundred and fifty millions of men will be living in North America, equal in condition, the progeny of one race, owing their origin to the same cause, and preserving the same civilization, the same language, the same religion, the same habits, the same manner, and imbued with the same opportunities, propagated under the same forms. The rest is uncertain, but this is certain; and it

is a fact new to the world—a fact fraught with such portentous consequences as to baffle the efforts even of the imagination.[6]

De Tocqueville also predicted the rise of both the United States and Russia to world power:

> The Anglo-American relies upon personal interest to accomplish his ends, and gives free scope to the unguided exertion and common sense of its citizens; the Russian centers all the authority of society in a single arm: the principal instrument of the former is freedom, of the latter, servitude. Their starting point is different, and their courses are not the same; yet each seems to be marked by the will of Heaven to sway the destinies of half the globe.[7]

President Jackson had become a successful national leader by 1834, when a spirit of "union" again prevailed, following sharp controversies over slavery (Nat Turner's slave insurrection in Virginia occurred in 1832), conflicts with Indian tribes (the enforced march of the Cherokees from Georgia to Oklahoma, over the "Trail of Tears," did not take place until 1838), the defeat by Jackson of South Carolina's attempted nullification of a tariff in 1832, and his triumph over the United States Bank.

Jackson's spirited stand against France in the French claims dispute (1834–36) aroused a previously apathetic American public opinion, and created somewhat new respect in Europe for America's diplomatic vigor. Jackson stressed the rising rank of America among the nations in his message of December 7, 1835: "The unexampled growth and prosperity of our country having given us a rank in the scale of nations which removes all apprehension of danger to our integrity and independence from external foes, the career of freedom is before us, with an earnest from the past that if true to ourselves there can be no formidable obstacle in the future to its peaceful and uninterrupted pursuit."[8]

When Texas won its independence from Mexico by May 1836, Jackson did not recognize the new nation until March 3, 1837, and President Martin Van Buren rejected the request of Texas for annexation (1837-38). After John Tyler succeeded to the Presidency in 1841 (following the death of William Henry Harrison after only a month in office) and John C. Calhoun became Secretary of State in 1844, a treaty for the annexation of Texas was signed on April 12,

1844. With anti-slavery forces bitterly opposed to the plan and the introvert mood still apparently strong, the Senate voted down the treaty on June 8, 1844—16 for and 35 against. John Quincy Adams, who served in the House of Representatives from 1831 until his death in 1848, saw the Senate vote as a divine deliverance and wrote (June 10, 1844): "The annexation of Texas to this Union is the first step to the conquest of all Mexico, of the West India Islands, of a maritime, colonizing, slave-tainted monarchy, and of extinguished freedom."[9]

A number of disputes developed with Great Britain between 1837 and 1842, but the guiding principle of Secretary of State Daniel Webster during the negotiation of the Webster-Ashburton Treaty of 1842 was "that no differences should be permitted seriously to endanger maintenance of peace with England."[10] One important question was left unsettled—the future of the Oregon territory, still jointly occupied with England. Missionaries sparked interest in the area after 1834, and, beginning in 1841, emigrants moved in ever-increasing numbers over the Oregon Trail (the "Great Migration" was in 1843–44). In the Presidential campaign of 1844, the Whig platform contained nothing on foreign policy, but the Democrats demanded the acquisition of Oregon as well as Texas.

There was a fast-growing American interest in the Pacific. Britain and France were warned in 1842 not to take over the Hawaiian Islands. After the victory of Britain over China in the Opium War (1839–42), President Tyler induced Congress to appropriate money for a commissioner to reside in China and negotiate a treaty of commerce. Secretary of State Webster stressed the friendly and peaceful character of the mission, and the desire of America to be treated as well as the "most-favored-nation."[11] The Treaty of Wanghai was signed on July 3, 1844, opening China more widely to Americans for trade, residence and missions.

Slavery

The problem of slavery and its future was the basic moral challenge to America during this period. By 1827 slavery had been abolished in all the northern states, and church leaders from the north led the opposition. The Presbyterian General Assembly had stated its position squarely in 1818:

We consider the . . . enslaving of one part of the human race by another as a gross violation of the . . . sacred rights of human nature; as utterly inconsistent with the law of God, which requires us to love our neighbor as ourselves; and as totally irreconcilable with . . . the gospel of Christ, which enjoins that "all things whatsoever ye would that men should do to you, do ye even so to them."[12]

William Ellery Channing, the great Unitarian preacher, wrote in his book *Slavery*, published after 1830: "Man cannot justly be held and used as property—He is a Person, not a Thing."[13]

A more aggressive movement against slavery began in the early 1830s, led by men such as William Lloyd Garrison, who started publishing the *Liberator* in 1831. All 12 persons who organized the New England Anti-Slavery Society in 1832 were members of evangelical churches. The region of central New York, heart of the new revivalism, was also the seat of the strongest abolitionist conviction.[14] Nat Turner, a Negro preacher, led an insurrection in 1832 in Virginia which resulted in the deaths of over 50 whites and over 100 Negroes. The American Anti-Slavery Society was begun in 1833; by 1840 it had some 2,000 local chapters, with a total membership of 175,000.[15] The bitterness of the dispute which was developing over slavery was highlighted by the murder of Elijah P. Lovejoy (1802–37), abolitionist editor, by a pro-slavery mob in Alton, Illinois. It had become clear by this time that the colonization of freed Negroes in Africa (the first of some 15,000 freed settlers arrived in Liberia in 1822) would not solve the problem of slavery in America.

The danger and complexity of the problem was grasped by the great French observer de Tocqueville, writing around 1832:

> The danger of a conflict between the white and black inhabitants of the southern states of the Union—a danger which, however remote it may be, is inevitable—perpetually haunts the imagination of the Americans. . . .
>
> Whatever may be the efforts of the Americans of the south to maintain slavery, they will not always succeed. Slavery, which is now confined to a single tract of the civilized earth, which is attacked by Christianity as unjust, and by political economy as prejudicial, and which is now contrasted with democratic liberties and the information of our age, cannot survive. By the choice of the master or the will of the slave, it will cease; and in either case great calamities may be expected to ensue. If liberty be refused to the negroes of the south, they will in the end seize it for themselves by force; if it be given, they will

abuse it ere long.[16]

John Quincy Adams (who had been elected in 1830 to the House of Representatives) recorded on August 11, 1835, the rise of the democratic and moral pressure against slavery:

> There is a great fermentation upon this subject of slavery at this time in all parts of the Union. . . . The theory of the rights of man has taken deep root in the soil of civil society. It has allied itself with the feelings of humanity and the precepts of Christian benevolence. It has armed itself with the strength of organized association. It has linked itself with religious doctrines and religious fervor. . . . there has been recently an alarm of slave insurrection in the State of Mississippi. . . . Add to all this the approach of the Presidential election, and the question whether the President of the United States shall be a slave-holder or not.[17]

The firm establishment of the Underground Railroad by 1840 for the escape of slaves was another significant development. Although America and Britain had agreed in 1842 to cooperate in various ways to suppress the slave trade, each nation was authorized to enforce its own obligations. America's traditional stand against the search of ships at sea helped protect to some extent the illegal slave trade.

As the North's opposition to slavery grew in strength, the South moved to find support in Christianity for the institution. It was a moral issue for the South too. For example, in the 1830s, James Smylie, a Presbyterian minister in Mississippi, argued that the Bible sanctioned slavery. The slave states looked forward to the acquisition of more slave territory, notably Texas.

Idealism

America's growing idealism, as in relation to slavery, was also illustrated in the support of peace movements and international law, in churches and foreign missions, and by major writers and the Presidents.

The American Peace Society was organized in 1828, under the leadership of William Ladd, eventually a Congregational minister. Ladd's successor, Elihu Burritt, was also influential in England and the European continent. American statesmen were deeply impressed with the value and necessity of international law based on moral principles. Daniel Webster, Secretary of State from 1841 to 1843, gave great prestige and publicity to this approach. Vattel's *The Law of Nations*, with his high moral and democratic standards, continued to be the most influential treatise on the subject—twelve American editions had been published by 1854. The first important American treatise on international law was *Elements of International Law* by Henry Wheaton, American diplomatist in Europe, in 1836. Wheaton relied upon Vattel for many general principles.

By the 1820s, a new spiritual day had dawned in America, in contrast to conditions a generation earlier. Great revival movements, especially in the late 1820s and the 1830s, brought large numbers into the churches. This major revival period may be dated from 1826, with the preaching of Charles G. Finney in western New York.[18] De Tocqueville was deeply impressed by the powerful influence of the churches in America:

> . . . There is no country in the whole world in which the Christian religion retains a greater influence over the souls of men than in America, and there can be no greater proof of its utility, and of its conformity to human nature, than that its influence is most powerfully felt over the most enlightened and free nation in the world.
>
> . . . In the United States religion exercises but little influence upon the laws, and upon the details of public opinion; but it directs the manners of the community, and by regulating domestic life, it regulates the state. . . .
>
> The Americans combine the notions of Christianity and of liberty so intimately in their minds, that it is impossible to make them conceive the one without the other; and with them this conviction does not spring from that barren traditionary faith which seems to vegetate in the soul rather than to live.[19]

The Christian vitality of the time was demonstrated in the development of new denominations as well as in the substantial growth of all Christian groups. Although Protestants were most numerous, Roman Catholics and Jews were increasing in numbers. New Christian denominations included the Unitarians in 1825, the Disciples of Christ (Christians) in 1832, and the Church of Jesus Christ of Latter Day Saints (the Mormons) in 1830. The Mormons, with their revelation that Jesus Christ had visited the "new world," saw a great destiny ahead for the United States on the world scene.[20] As American settlers moved west, "home missions" increased in strength. The Rev. Jason Lee, a Methodist, was a pioneer missionary in Oregon, beginning in 1834. The chief stimulus to higher education came from the churches, and religious influences were very significant in elementary and secondary education. At least 25 theological seminaries were established between 1818 and 1840, and scores of denominational colleges were created. The famous McGuffey Readers, first used in schools in 1836, implicitly stressed moral and spiritual teachings.

The Christian renewal in America was vigorous enough to initiate vital concern with missionary activity in Asia and Africa. The same spirit was evident in Western Europe, particularly in England. The first continuing Protestant enterprise in the Near East (then under Turkish sovereignty) was begun by the American Board of Commissioners for Foreign Missions in 1823. This early American religious and educational contact with the Near and Middle East was to prove of vital significance to American influence in the area. American missions to India expanded in the 1830s. The American board began its missionary work in China in 1830; Peter Parker was the first Protestant medical missionary in China, arriving in 1834. Christianity expanded rapidly in Hawaii after 1825.[21] Foreign missions as a whole must be regarded as vital to America's expanding world role.

Writers and Presidents

American writers after 1824 expressed different aspects of the dominant spiritual mood. Many of them interpreted the destiny of America in terms of Providential aims and guidance. Ralph Waldo Emerson (1803–82) was the chief leader in a broader, mystical approach to religion—with his emphasis on the "Universal Spirit," working partly in and through man, and the sacredness and power of the human spirit. His address at Harvard on "The American Scholar," in 1837, called for an indigenous national culture. He emphasized the spiritual basis of nature and history, beginning with his earliest essays (as *Nature* in 1836 and *Essays* in 1841):

> The first and last lesson of religion is, "The things that are seen are temporal; the things that are unseen are eternal. . . ."
>
> . . . Idealism sees the world in God. It beholds the whole circle of persons and things, of actions and events, of country and religion, not as painfully accumulated, atom after atom, act after act, in an aged creeping Past, but as one vast picture which God paints on the instant eternity for the contemplation of the soul.[22]

Along with many other prominent Northern writers, Emerson deplored the existence of slavery and looked forward to the freedom and progress of the Negro, as in his address on "Emancipation in the British West Indies" (August 1, 1844):

> . . . The civility of no race can be perfect whilst another race is degraded. It is a doctrine alike of the oldest and of the newest philosophy, that man is one, and you cannot injure any member, without a sympathetic injury to all its members. America is not civil, whilst Africa is barbarous.
>
> . . . The genius of the Saxon race is friendly to liberty; the enterprise, the very muscular vigor of this nation, are inconsistent with slavery. . . . The sentiment of Right, once very low and indistinct, but ever more articulate, because it is the voice of the universe, pronounces Freedom.[23]

Many writers expressed their belief in the sovereignty of God over history, and in the unique role of America in the growth of human liberty, as part of the march of progress. George Bancroft explained his approach in the introduction to his famous *History of the United States* (first published in 1834):

> The United States of America constitute an essential portion of a great political system, embracing all the civilized nations of the earth. At a period when the force of moral opinion is rapidly increasing, they have the precedence in the practice and defense of the equal rights of man. . . .
>
> It is the object of the present work to explain how the change in the condition of our land has been accomplished; and, as the fortunes of a nation are not under control of blind destiny, to follow the steps by which a favoring Providence, calling our institutions into being, has conducted the country to its present happiness and glory.[24]

Robert J. Breckinridge pictured the United States as the great trustee of the spirit of freedom in the world (1837):

> As Greece gave her literature, and Rome her civilization to the world—it is ours to give it liberty. This vast continent is yet to be crowded from shore to shore with a free, educated, and virtuous population. . . . Our brethren of the races of the Shem and Ham now weeping in our midst, or neglected around our wide frontiers, must yet rejoice under the shadow of our protection, and be repaid for suffering

too long protracted. . . . Yea vast and sublime is the work yet laid up
in store for us; and peerless the glory descendant on its wise and
faithful performance. . . .

 . . . But oh! let us evermore remember that all these paths are beset
by manifold temptations; that these unprecedented mercies are all held
by us as stewards of God, and as trustees for generations of generations,
and so must be accounted before earth and heaven. . . .[25]

In this period of consolidation of the nation, American Presidents
expressed their strong moral and spiritual principles, both reflecting and
guiding the dominant public mood. John Quincy Adams spoke as
follows in his Inaugural Address, March 4, 1825:

 . . . I appear, my fellow-citizens, in your presence and in that of
Heaven to bind myself by the solemnities of religious obligation to the
faithful performance of the duties allotted to me. . . .

 . . . And knowing that "except the Lord keep the city the watchman
waketh but in vain," with fervent supplications for His favor, to His
overruling providence I commit with humble but fearless confidence my
own fate and the future destinies of my country.[26]

Andrew Jackson ended his First Inaugural Address, March 4, 1829, with
these words:

 And a firm reliance on the goodness of that Power whose
providence mercifully protected our national infancy, and has since
upheld our liberties in various vicissitudes, encourages me to offer up
my ardent supplications that He will continue to make our beloved
country the object of His divine care and gracious benediction.[27]

Jackson reminded Americans of their Providential destiny and the
internal dangers in his Farewell Address, March 4, 1837:

 You have no longer any cause to fear danger from abroad; your
strength and power are well known throughout the civilized world. . . .
It is from within, among yourselves—from cupidity, from corruption,
from disappointed ambition and inordinate thirst for power—that
factions will be formed and liberty endangered. . . . You have the
highest of human trusts committed to your care. Providence has
showered on this favored land blessings without number, and has
chosen you as the guardians of freedom, to preserve it for the benefit
of the human race.[28]

Martin Van Buren's Inaugural Address, March 4, 1837, called for divine blessing on the nation. William Henry Harrison, who died a month after assuming the office of President, left his testament to his country in his Inaugural Address, March 4, 1841:

> I admit of no government by divine right, believing that so far as power is concerned, the Beneficent Creator has made no distinction amongst men. . . .
> . . . Sound morals, religious liberty, and a just sense of religious responsibility are essentially connected with all truth and lasting happiness; and to that good Being who has blessed us by the gifts of civil and religious freedom . . . let us unite in fervently commending every interest of our beloved country to all future time.[29]

The new President, John Tyler, issued a proclamation on April 13, 1841, calling for a "day of fasting and prayer" on May 14:

> When a Christian people feel themselves to be overtaken by a great public calamity, it becomes them to humble themselves under the dispensation of Divine Providence, to recognize His righteous government over the children of men, to acknowledge His goodness in times past as well as their own unworthiness, and to supplicate His merciful protection for the future. . . . [30]

Expansion and Civil War: Extroversion, 1844–71

By 1844, after twenty years of general introversion, the nation was again prepared to launch upon a program of expansion, as the concept of "Manifest Destiny" helped sweep the nation's boundaries to the Pacific, while the institution of slavery prompted the nation's greatest crisis in the war between the North and the South.

Manifest Destiny: Extroversion-Liberty, 1844–57

The American international mood was beginning to change in the summer of 1844. The future of Texas and of Oregon were immediate issues; California was seen as an area which the United States ought to possess, and the commerce of the whole Pacific area was showing prospects of rapid expansion. The enlargement of the South would sharpen the issue of slavery, so that the first half of the extrovert period may again be regarded as a phase generally dominated by the spirit of "liberty" and rising internal tension. The growing abolitionist movement in the North likewise typifies another aspect of "liberty," as did the emphasis in the South on states' rights. First, foreign relations in this extrovert phase will be examined, and then the continuing idealism during this period of consolidation or synthesis.

Foreign Relations, 1844–57

In the Presidential campaign of 1844, the expansionist Democrats, under James K. Polk, waged a vigorous emotional campaign. And the Democratic victory opened up the way for a veritable flood of expansion before Polk's four years had ended. President Tyler interpreted the election of Polk over Henry Clay, even though it was close, as a mandate for the annexation of Texas, and urged Congress to approve annexation by a joint resolution in his message of December 3, 1844:

> Since your last session Mexico has threatened to renew the war, and has either made or proposes to make formidable preparation for invading Texas. . . . Mexico has no right to jeopardize the peace of the world by urging any longer a useless and fruitless contest.
> . . . It is the will of both the people and the States that Texas shall be annexed to the Union promptly and immediately. . . . Free and independent herself, she [Texas] asks to be received into our Union. It is a question for our own decision whether she shall be received or not.[31]

The annexation resolution passed the House (elected in 1842) on January 25, 1845, by a vote of 120 to 98 (112 Democrats and 8 Southern Whigs for, and 70 Whigs and 20 Northern Democrats against). The Senate (with 28 Whigs and 25 Democrats) approved an amended version on February 27 by the close vote of 27 to 25; this was accepted by the House on February 28, 132 to 76. The new Senate, taking office on March 4, 1845, had 31 Democrats and 25 Whigs; the House also had a few more Democrats, 143, to 77 Whigs.

President Polk welcomed the decision on Texas in his Inaugural Address on March 4, and implied that no other nation should interfere (whether Britain or France or Mexico):

> I regard the question of annexation as belonging exclusively to the United States and Texas. They are independent powers competent to

contract, and foreign nations have no right to interfere or to take exceptions to their reunion. . . .

. . . None can fail to see the danger to our safety and future peace if Texas remains an independent state or becomes an ally or dependency of some foreign nation more powerful than herself.[32]

Although the "slave interest" may have been a vital element in bringing about the annexation of Texas, the significance of the event was far greater than this. Polk, like many of his countrymen, possessed a concept of the "manifest destiny" of the United States. In his Inaugural Address he answered those who feared the expansion of the United States over too large a territory, by asserting: "it is confidently believed that our system may be safely extended to the utmost bounds of our territorial limits, and that as it shall be extended the bonds of the Union, so far from being weakened, will become stronger."[33] In the summer of 1845, John L. O'Sullivan apparently first used the phrase "manifest destiny" in an article in the expansionist *The United States Magazine and Democratic Review*, where he stated that foreign governments were attempting to prevent the annexation of Texas in order to check "the fulfillment of our manifest destiny to overspread the continent allotted by Providence for the free development of our yearly multiplying millions."[34]

The Congress of Texas voted for annexation on June 23, and a popular referendum approved on October 13. On December 2, 1845, President Polk asked that Texas be admitted to the Union: "We may rejoice that the tranquil and pervading influence of the American principle of self-government was sufficient to defeat the purposes of British and French interference, and that the almost unanimous voice of the people of Texas has given to that interference a peaceful and effective rebuke."[35] Congress acted swiftly; a Congressional resolution admitting Texas as a state was approved by Polk on December 29, 1845. Thus was consummated the first overt act of expansion since 1821 (when East Florida was secured from Spain), increasing the gross area of the United States by 390,000 square miles (the original territory of the United States had been only 889,000 square miles, with the Louisiana Purchase adding 827,000 and Florida 59,000).

Mexico had previously announced that it would regard the annexation of Texas as equivalent to a declaration of war. With annexation, the United States inherited also the disputed boundary question of Texas and Mexico. War threatened throughout 1845, following the joint resolution for annexation on February 28. The new minister to Mexico, John Slidell, was instructed to try to purchase California and New Mexico. The President believed that Great Britain had her eye on California and felt the necessity of securing it for the United States. Mexico had also agreed by treaty to pay claims to American citizens, but most of these had remained unpaid. General Zachary Taylor was ordered to take up positions in the disputed territory; on April 12, 1846, a Mexican general ordered Taylor to leave the area. Mexican forces attacked the American troops on April 25, killing or capturing 63 officers and men. President Polk. supported by his Cabinet, asked Congress on May 11 for a declaration of war. On the same day, the House of Representatives declared that a state of war existed with Mexico, by a vote of 174 to 14. The Senate agreed on May 12 by a vote of 40 to 2. Mexico entered the war with 32,000 troops, while the United States had only 7,400 in its regular army. But there was a growing mood in America to expand westward; early in 1846, William H. Seward stated that "the popular passion for territorial aggrandizement is irresistible."[36]

The Mexican government was doubtless encouraged in its adamant stand by its expectation of possible war between the United States and England over the Oregon question. President Polk had reasserted America's claim to Oregon in his Inaugural Address:

> . . . The world beholds the peaceful triumph of the industry of our emigrants. To us belongs the duty of protecting them adequately wherever they may be upon our soil. The jurisdiction of our laws and the benefit of our republican institutions should be extended over them in the distant region which they have selected for their homes."[37]

Polk directed Secretary of State James Buchanan to offer to divide Oregon at the 49th parallel. When the British declined the proposal without even submitting it to the Foreign Office, Polk decided to demand the whole of Oregon, up to the southern boundary of Alaska (54 degrees, 40 minutes). Expansionist Americans shouted the slogan, "54-40 or fight." The President reaffirmed and amplified the Monroe Doctrine in relation to North America, thereby warning Britain particularly in the areas of Oregon, California and Texas: "It should be distinctly announced to the world as our settled policy that no future European colony or dominion shall with our consent be planned or established on any part of the North American continent."[38]

Congress agreed on April 26, 1848, to recommend the ending of the joint occupation of Oregon. The British finally decided, in the face of the determined American position, to offer the United States the line of 49 degrees. With the war under way against Mexico, the Senate quickly recommended favorable action, 37 to 12. Secretary Buchanan and the British minister signed the convention on June 15, and the Senate formally approved on June 16, 41 to 14. The acquisition of Oregon up to the 49th parallel was a major diplomatic victory for the United States, even though it was a compromise, and the settlement of the question at the beginning of the war with Mexico freed America to look to the southwest. America's title was now clear to 286,000 square miles of Oregon territory, fronting on the Pacific Ocean from 42 to 49 degrees, and including what later became the states of Washington, Oregon, Idaho and portions of Montana and Wyoming.

While the Mexican War was in progress, the President was confronted with the opportunity of gaining important rights over the Isthmus of Panama. New Grenada suddenly offered to guarantee to the Government and citizens of the United States the use of any means of transit across the isthmus, if the United States would guarantee the neutrality of the isthmus and the sovereignty of New Grenada over it. The offer was apparently made to thwart possible British encroachment on the isthmus. The American minister accepted the protocol, and it was included in a treaty which was signed on December 12, 1846. President Polk accepted the offer also, explaining his position as he submitted the treaty to the Senate on February 10, 1847:

> . . . The route by the Isthmus of Panama is the shortest route between the two oceans, and . . . it would seem to be the most practicable for a railroad or canal.
>
> The vast advantages to our commerce which would result from such a communication, not only with the west coast of America, but with Asia and the islands of the Pacific, are too obvious to require any details. Such a passage would relieve us from a long and dangerous navigation of more than 9,000 miles around Cape Horn and render our communication with our possessions on the northwest coast of America comparatively easy and speedy. . . .
>
> . . . The ultimate object . . . is to secure to all nations the free and equal right of passage over the Isthmus. . . . The interests of the world at stake are so important that the security of this passage between the two oceans can not be suffered to depend upon the wars and revolutions which may arise among different nations.[39]

President Polk demonstrated far-sighted vision in this connection, and the Senate finally approved the treaty on June 3, 1848 (after the war was over).

The war against Mexico was being prosecuted with vigor, and Polk was determined, now that war had actually come, to secure California, which he had earlier tried to purchase. The year 1846 saw great events, moving in the direction of an enlarged and strengthened American nation, so that Bernard DeVoto could properly refer to it as "The Year of Decision."[40] Generals John C. Fremont and Stephen W. Kearny were conquering California, the Mormons were on their way to establish a new "empire" in Utah (then still part of Mexico), and plans were being laid to carry the war to the heart of Mexico. The campaigns of the Mexican War, in the 1840s, would seem to be on as large a scale for that period of history as those of the Korean War in the 1950s.

The rising issue of slavery and the growing feeling that the war was turning into a war of conquest brought increasing American opposition to the conduct of the war, particularly in the North. The question of slavery in any new territories which might be secured from the war became a vital issue at once. The House of Representatives passed the so-called "Wilmot Proviso" on August 8, 1846, 87 to 64—declaring that "neither slavery nor involuntary servitude shall ever exist in any part" of the territory secured from Mexico by treaty.

The popular reaction in the North against the war and its conduct helped the Whigs to power by a small margin in the House of Representatives in the election of 1846 (the Whigs moved to 115 seats from 77, while the Democrats dropped to 110 from 143). In his message of December 8, 1846, President Polk endeavored to answer the critics of the war, discussing the matter at great length. He listed all the provocations by Mexico, and affirmed that the United States had made every honorable effort to keep the peace.[41] Most Democrats strongly defended the war as a just one, but Northern Whigs, such as Daniel Webster, attacked it bitterly as an expansionist war. Webster declared: "If any thing is certain, it is certain that the sentiment of the whole North is utterly opposed to the acquisition of territory, to be formed into new slave-holding states, and, as such, admitted into the Union."[42] A young Whig Congressman from Illinois, serving his only term in the House, joined his party fellows in opposing a war for expansion. In the campaign of 1848, Abraham Lincoln said:

> . . . All agree that slavery was an evil, but that we were not

responsible for it and cannot affect it in States of the Union where we
do not live. But, the question of the *extension* of slavery to new
territories of this country, is a part of our responsibility and care, and
is under our control.[43]

President Polk pressed on with the war. General Winfield Scott
occupied Mexico City on September 14, 1847, and a new President of
Mexico soon began negotiating for peace. In his third annual message,
December 7, 1847, Polk praised the courage and skill of the American
army, and insisted that Mexico must make territorial concessions in
satisfaction of claims and as partial payment for the expenses of the
war:

> In proposing to acquire New Mexico and the Californias, it was
> known that but an inconsiderable portion of the Mexican people would
> be transferred with them, the country embraced within these Provinces
> being chiefly an uninhabited region. . . .
> . . . It has never been contemplated by me, as an object of the war,
> to make a permanent conquest of the Republic of Mexico or to
> annihilate her separate existence as an independent nation. On the
> contrary, it has ever been my desire that she should maintain her
> nationality, and under a good government adapted to her condition be
> a free, independent, and prosperous Republic.[44]

The war was nearing its end, for the American commissioner,
Nicholas Trent, who had been recalled from Mexico, defied his
instructions to return and was able to negotiate the Treaty of Guadalupe
Hidalgo on February 2, 1848. The United States secured the territory
desired, and in turn agreed to pay Mexico $15,000,000 and assume the
claims of its citizens against Mexico amounting to $3,250,000. On
February 23, President Polk submitted the treaty to the Senate, which
approved it on March 10, 38 to 14 (26 Democrats and 12 Whigs for, 7
Democrats and 7 Whigs against). Some of the opposition wished to
annex all of Mexico instead. The United States had lost 1,721 killed in
battle, 11,155 dead from disease, and 4,102 were wounded.

The cession of territory amounted to 529,000 square miles, including
the present states of California and New Mexico, and parts of Arizona,
Colorado, Utah and Nevada. In a little over two years, about 1,205,000
square miles had thus been added to the nation, constituting nearly 40
percent of the total area of continental United States (3,022,000 square
miles). The population of the areas began to increase rapidly after

annexation, particularly in California, where gold was discovered on January 24, 1848. Following the exchange of ratifications of the treaty of peace, President Polk expressed to Congress his view of the achievements of the Mexican War, including America's military prestige:

> The extensive and valuable territories ceded by Mexico to the United States constitute indemnity for the past, and the brilliant achievements and signal successes of our arms will be a guaranty of security for the future, by convincing all nations that our rights must be respected. The results of the war with Mexico have given to the United States a national character abroad which our country never before enjoyed. Our power and our resources have become known and are respected throughout the world, and we shall probably be saved from the necessity of engaging in another foreign war for a long series of years. . . .[45]

President Polk also hoped to secure Cuba for the United States, and in 1848 authorized the American minister to Spain to open negotiations for that purpose. But Spain would not consider the proposition. Another possible area of expansion was Yucutan, when the white governor, facing a formidable Indian revolt in the spring of 1848, offered the territory to the United States (as well as Britain and Spain). Polk used the incident to reaffirm the Monroe Doctrine (April 29, 1848), stating that "according to our established policy, we could not consent to a transfer of this 'dominion and sovereignty' either to Spain, Great Britain, or any other European power. . . ."[46] The affair was terminated by an agreement between the whites and Indians in Yucutan.

The American reaction to the war, combined with a split in the Democratic Party, favored the Whigs in the 1848 election. The Whigs were able to stress the value of peace in an honorable way by nominating General Zachary Taylor, a hero of the Mexican War, for the Presidency. The Democratic platform defended the war as just and necessary. In August, the new Free Soil Party nominated former President Martin Van Buren. The Whigs won in a narrow vote, with the Free Soil Party determining the victory by splitting the New York vote so that the Whigs won a plurality (General Taylor, 163 electoral votes; General Lewis Cass for the Democrats, 127).

President Polk's work was done. Although the country was divided on the necessity and value of expansion, the results were accepted without much question. The long-time dream of many Americans to occupy the whole mid-section of the North American continent from the Atlantic to the Pacific had been realized. Although the slave-interest had been a major element in stimulating the expansion and the war with Mexico, yet the very expansion brought the issue of slavery in the territories to a head and thus promoted the early destruction of the institution of slavery in the midst of a great civil war (begun only 13 years after the end of the Mexican War). In his last annual message, December 5, 1848, President Polk reflected the national sentiment for peace, and again reiterated his pride in the military accomplishments of the democratic United States without endangering local liberties. He continued by stressing America's new position and responsibilities in world affairs, arising particularly from the new territories:

> Occupying, as we do, a more commanding position among nations than at any former period, our duties and responsibilities to ourselves and to posterity are correspondingly increased. . . . The addition of seacoast, including Oregon, is very nearly two-thirds as great as all we possessed before. . . . We have now three great maritime fronts—on the Atlantic, the Gulf of Mexico, and the Pacific—making in the whole an extent of seacoast exceeding 5,000 miles. . . .
>
> Upper California . . . holds at this day, in point of value and importance, to the rest of the Union the same relation that Louisiana did when that fine territory was acquired from France forty-five years ago. . . . From its position it must command the rich commerce of China, of Asia, of the islands of the Pacific, of western Mexico, of Central America, the South American States, and of the Russian possessions bordering on that ocean. . . . The deposit of the vast commerce which must exist in the Pacific will probably be at some point on the Bay of San Francisco. . . . [47]

Only one acquisition of territory to the continental United States has been made since the administration of President Polk: the $10,000,000 Gadsden Purchase from Mexico in 1853–54, adding about 30,000 square miles (today the southern part of Arizona and New Mexico) desired as a route for a southern railroad to the Pacific (completed in 1882). President Polk did not seek re-election, and died (June 1849) not long after the inauguration of his successor.

Zachary Taylor's Inaugural Address, March 5, 1849, stressed neutrality and peace in foreign affairs, but America's continued interest in international relations is indicated by the fact that three-fourths of his first annual message (December 4, 1849) was devoted to foreign affairs. The controversy over slavery was to be quieted temporarily by the Compromise of 1850, which included the admission of California as a free state and no restrictions on the other territories. During this so-called "Whig Interlude" (1849–53), America's foreign policy was non-aggressive and cooperative, with special concern for democratic developments in Europe.

President Polk had sent a special message to Congress on April 3, 1848, when he had just recognized the government of the second French Republic: "The world has seldom witnessed a more interesting or sublime spectacle than the peaceful rising of the French people, resolved to secure for themselves enlarged liberty, and to assert, in the majesty of their strength, the great truth that in this enlightened age man is capable of governing himself."[48] President Zachary Taylor stood ready to recognize the independence of Hungary, when Russia intervened to return the people to their previous Austrian control.

This was the period in which the "Young America" movement was inaugurated, supported particularly by Irish and Germans who sympathized with the revolutionary democratic movements in Ireland and Germany, and who urged active American intervention in the affairs of Europe. Secretary of State Webster dispatched a sharp note to Austria in 1850, in reply to the Austrian envoy's complaint over America's diplomatic actions in relation to Hungary. He stressed America's political neutrality, but declared that "as these extraordinary events appeared to have their origin in those great ideas of responsible and popular government, on which the American constitutions themselves are wholly founded, they could not but command the warm sympathy of the people of this country."[49] The great Hungarian patriot, Louis Kossuth, was officially invited to visit America. After his arrival and warm welcome, December 5, 1851, it became clear that he wanted American intervention in Hungary's behalf, and a number of prominent American leaders and the legislature of Massachusetts supported him. The importance of this movement to intervene more actively is suggested by the statement of President Millard Fillmore (President Taylor had died on July 9, 1850), supporting America's historic policy of neutrality and non-interference in the domestic affairs of other nations (message of December 6, 1852).[50]

The Whig Administration maintained America's interest in the future of Hawaii and Central America. America's first treaty with the King of Hawaii was made in 1849; in 1851, the King, alarmed at French designs, tried unsuccessfully to cede the islands to the United States. In the Clayton-Bulwer Treaty with Great Britain in 1850, both nations agreed not to exercise exclusive control of an isthmian canal or occupy any part of Central America. Three private expeditions aimed at the conquest of Cuba (1849, 1850 and 1851) were opposed and disavowed by the Administration. President Fillmore declared: "Our true mission is not to propagate our opinions or impose upon other countries our form of government by artifice or force, but to teach by example and show by our success, moderation, and justice the blessings of self-government and the advantages of free institutions."[51]

The Whig Administration also showed increased concern with the commerce of the Far East. America's first commercial treaty with China had been secured by President Tyler in 1844. In 1852, President Fillmore dispatched a naval squadron under Commodore Matthew C. Perry to Japan, to help open some Japanese ports in a "friendly and peaceful" manner. Perry was able to sign a treaty of peace, friendship, and commerce (the Treaty of Kanagawa) on March 31, 1854 (after the Democrats had been returned to power), opening two ports to American trade and making provision for shipwrecked American seamen.

The Whig platform of 1852 stressed the value of "never quitting our own to stand on foreign ground" and of "teaching by example . . . the blessings of self-government. . . ."[52] But the expansionist Democrats resolved again in their platform that "the war with Mexico . . . was a just and necessary war on our part . . . and we congratulate the American people on the results of that war, which have so manifestly justified the policy and conduct of the democratic party, and assured the United States 'indemnity for the past and security for the future.' "[53] The Democrats were swept back into office, and President Franklin Pierce typified the revived spirit in his Inaugural Address (March 4, 1853), noting that our history had shown we could maintain and even strengthen our liberties while expanding our territory. His address was the first in American history to declare that territorial aggrandizement was an aim of the incoming administration.[54] With widening pressure from the slavery issue, however, the acquisition of territory between 1853 and the opening of the Civil War in 1861 was confined to the Gadsden Purchase of 1853 and the occupation of some uninhabited guano islands in the mid-Pacific (Jarvis and Baker in 1857, and Howland in 1858). Strong diplomatic or military pressure was used in a number of instances, as with Austria, Nicaragua, Britain, Cuba, Hawaii and Japan.

Although the Republican platform of 1856 made no mention of foreign affairs, the Democratic platform continued to stress their importance and explicitly stated for the first time "that we should hold as sacred the principles involved in the Monroe Doctrine." Furthermore, the platform called for American domination over the proposed isthmian canal and the whole Gulf of Mexico (implying also Cuba).[55] The Democratic candidate was James Buchanan, who had held high position under two previous expansionist administrations (Secretary of State under Polk, and Minister to England under Pierce). Buchanan won, although the combined popular vote of the Whig and Republican opponents was considerably larger. In his Inaugural Address of March 4, 1857, Buchanan indicated, following a paragraph extolling peace and justice, that he intended to promote the peaceful expansion of the United States.[56]

By 1857, the future outlook of the American experiment was threatened by slavery and possible secession—the spirit of "union" was to be challenged to the limit. The definition of "liberty" was also at stake. The future influence of the United States in world affairs would hang in the balance for the decade to follow. Although American foreign policy after 1844 showed a great deal of realism, in terms of willingness to use force, the basic spirit of the nation continued to be idealistic. America was regarded as deeply dedicated to democracy and Christianity, even though the role of the Negroes was sharply divisive.

Idealism

The churches continued to maintain their influential position. Evangelism was supplemented by an emphasis on "Christian Nurture," the title of a book published by Horace Bushnell in 1846. The last great wave of revivalism in this period spread across the country in 1857–1858; it was estimated that some 500,000 persons were converted within a year. Charles G. Finney, one of the most prominent evangelists, wrote that "a divine influence seemed to pervade the whole land."[57]

Although there was strong and sometimes violent Protestant opposition to Roman Catholics in the pre-Civil War period (climaxed by riots on 1844), there is much evidence that the Roman Catholics in America were dominated by the American concept of freedom. Brigham Young brought the Mormons into their "promised land" in Utah in 1846–47, beginning an important and successful colonizing effort.

American home missions built solid Christian foundations among three special American groups: the immigrants, the Negroes (African-Americans) and the Indians (native Americans).

Foreign missions continued to thrive. The International Missionary Council dates back in part to the Union Missionary Convention held in New York in 1854. Numbers of schools and universities were established abroad, including the noted Syrian Protestant College (later the American University in Beirut) and Roberts College in Constantinople, both in 1863. Methodists started work in India in 1856; China was a major field for American missionaries, and work was begun in Africa.

This period continued to be one of major social reforms, stimulated by moral and spiritual values. Slavery became a more divisive issue—it was in the middle 1840s that the Methodist and Baptist churches split into northern and southern divisions. The passing of the Kansas-Nebraska Bill in 1854 (authorizing popular referenda on slavery) provoked a storm of opposition in religious circles to the extension of slavery. "Anti-slavery" tended to swallow up other reform movements, such as that for peace. Cole has stated that by 1850 "men who were usually peaceful and peace-loving were ready for war as a means of settling the question."[58] Elihu Burritt led the peace movement, founded the League of Universal Brotherhood in 1846, and organized the first of a series of peace congresses at Brussels in 1848. The American Peace Society, along with many Americans, condemned the Mexican War.

The authors who expressed the "synthesis" of the American idea in a dominant spiritual mood came mainly from New England. Marx and Engels had written the *Communist Manifesto* in 1848, and August Comte's *The Course of Positive Philosophy* (1830–42, stressing the naturalistic social science) was published in an English translation in 1855. But their influence in America was not appreciable until after 1871. Physical and biological sciences were beginning a rapid development, but they seemed to have no conflict with religion. Many of the giants of American literature wrote during the period: Emerson, Hawthorne, Holmes, Longfellow, Lowell, Melville, Poe, Whitman and Whittier. Many writers dealt with the social issues of the day, in poetry or prose, but no other book had the powerful effect of *Uncle Tom's Cabin*, written by Harriet Beecher Stowe in 1852 (translated later into 37 languages).

The "Providential" interpretation of American history and destiny continued to be dominant during this time. J. D. Nourse expressed his opinion in 1847 that "the great mission of the Anglo-Saxon is to solve this highest problem of political philosophy: *the reconciliation of Order and Liberty*."[59] Daniel Webster had become almost a symbol of "Liberty and Union, now and forever, one and inseparable," which he had first affirmed in his debate with Haynes in 1830. The historian George Bancroft expressed his deep faith in Providential purpose and law in a notable oration before the New York Historical Society in 1854, on "The Necessity, the Reality, and the Promise of the Progress of the Human Race":

> . . . Individuals, families, the race, march in accord with the Divine will, and when any part of the destiny of mankind is fulfilled, we see the ways of Providence vindicated. . . . What seemed irrational confusion appears as the web woven by light, liberty and love. But this is not perceived till a great act in the drama of life is finished. . . .
>
> . . . Since the progress of the race appears to be the great purpose of Providence, it becomes us all to venerate the future. We must be ready to sacrifice ourselves for our successors, as they in turn must live for their posterity.[60]

Herman Melville asserted his belief in America, according to Van Wyck Brooks, as the "Israel of our time," and had one of his characters say in *Redburn* (written in 1849):

> We are the heirs of all time, and with all nations we divide our inheritance. On this Western hemisphere all tribes and peoples are forming into one federated whole; and there is a future which shall see the estranged children of Adam restored as to the old hearthstones in Eden. . . . Not a Paradise then, or now; but to be made so, at God's good pleasure, and in the fullness and mellowness of time. The seed is sown, and the harvest must come; and our children's children, on the world's jubilee morning, shall all go . . . to the reaping. Then shall the curse of Babel be revoked, a new Pentecost come, and the language they shall speak shall be the language of Britain.[61]

Faith in the progress of man was at a high point in this youthful American nation. Many were confident of steady moral progress, while some others saw development in spiral form, with some periods of apparent decline. Arthur Ekirch, in a study of the idea of progress in America from 1815 to 1860, states his conclusion that: "generalizing from the results of . . . material and cultural advancement, the American people made the idea of progress both a law of history and the will of a benign Providence."[62] Some of the writers of the time felt that a "new age" was being ushered in for mankind, with a key role to be placed upon the United States. Bancroft stressed the trends toward "unity" and "universality" of the "race" of mankind (1854): "The commonwealth of mankind, as a great whole, was not to be constructed in one generation. But the different peoples are to be considered as its component parts, prepared, like so many springs and wheels, one day to be put together."[63]

The American Presidents continued to reflect the deep religious feeling of the great majority of Americans. James K. Polk began and ended his Inaugural Address of March 4, 1845, with supplications to the "Divine Being":

> In assuming responsibilities so vast I fervently invoke the aid of the Almighty Ruler of the Universe in whose hands are the destinies of nations and of men to guard this Heaven-favored land against the mischiefs which without His guidance might arise from an unwise public policy. With a firm reliance upon the wisdom of Omnipotence to sustain and direct me in the path of duty which I am appointed to pursue, I stand in the presence of this assembled multitude. . . . [64]

The succeeding Presidents spoke in the same vein. After a long section on slavery in his annual message, December 31, 1855, Franklin Pierce ended with these words of faith: "I rely confidently on the patriotism of the people, on the dignity and self-respect of the States, on the wisdom of Congress, and, above all, on the continued gracious favor of Almighty God to maintain against all enemies, whether at home or abroad, the sanctity of the Constitution and the integrity of the Union."[65] But in Pierce's final message, December 2, 1856, for the first time since 1824, there was nothing on Providence or God or religion—the problems of slavery, peace and union seemed to have swallowed up all else. This was the only gap, however, in the Presidential tradition, for James Buchanan appealed desperately for peace and union and Providential guidance during the four years preceding the Civil War. His Inaugural Address, March 4, 1857, called for the "blessing of Divine Providence" upon the people and added: "We ought to cultivate peace, commerce, and friendship with all nations, and this not merely as the best means of promoting our own material interests, but in a spirit of Christian benevolence toward our fellow-men, wherever their lot may be cast. . . ."[66]

By 1857, the land of the continental United States had been "rounded out," and the spirit of the people was strong, but there was great division over the application of the Declaration of Independence to "all men."

Crisis for the Union and America's World Influence: Extroversion-Union, 1857–71

By 1857 or 1858 a new emphasis on the necessity of maintaining the Union was evident in the North. Supported by the Dred Scott decision of March, 6, 1857, the South seemed on its way to the successful extension of slavery to the territories, since Congress was deemed powerless to prohibit it. But the spirit of "liberty" in the South—as expressed in states' rights, the private right of property in slaves, and the freedom to extend slavery into the territories—was producing a powerful reaction toward "union" in the North. Abraham Lincoln became the major spokesman for maintaining the Union, to be composed ultimately of "free men."

In the light of American history and America's later world role, it was almost unbelievable that the spirit of the Declaration of Independence would not be victorious in the momentous struggle to come. But a tremendous effort was necessary to maintain and expand this spirit, and the spirit of "union" had to dominate the North before it would be possible to fight a successful war against the seceding South. Lincoln typified both the spirit of Union and the spirit of the Declaration. By a terrible civil war, the American Union would paradoxically be cemented, the American character tempered in the fires of the struggle, the spirits of Liberty and Equality expanded, and the American nation completed for "all men" so that America could begin to play a great positive role in the new age which was beginning for the whole world.

In relation to the extrovert mood which had become dominant after 1844, this mood continued up to the very eve of the Civil War, was not lost in the North in the midst of the war (although it was partially submerged), and emerged after the war to play a prominent role until about 1871. Some might say that the Civil War indicated a deep introversion, as the nation turned "inward," but rather it would appear that the North directed its extrovert mood with a vengeance toward the conquest of the South, and, in a sense, the South was prepared to conquer part of the North, if possible. Similarly, the sense of "union" was split into two parts, as the South endeavored to become a new nation, while the North was determined to maintain the whole Union.

Union, Slavery, and America's Future, 1857–71

This period is naturally divided into three parts: the coming of war, the Civil War itself, and the restoration of the Union.

The "Irrepressible Conflict," 1857–61

During the 1856 campaign, Lincoln stressed the importance of keeping slavery out of the territories. In his famous speech at Springfield, Illinois, on June 16, 1858, after receiving the Republican nomination for the U.S. Senate, Lincoln used the "house divided" metaphor to state that the Union must ultimately be all free or all slave:

> "A house divided against itself cannot stand."
> I believe this government cannot endure, permanently half *slave* and half *free*.
> I do not expect the Union to be *dissolved*—I do not expect the house to *fall*—but I *do* expect it will cease to be divided.
> It will become *all* one thing, or *all* the other.
> Either the *opponents* of slavery will arrest the further spread of it, and place it where the public mind shall rest in the belief that it is in course of ultimate extinction; or its *advocates* will push it forward, till it shall become lawful in all the States, *old* as well as *new—North* as well as *South*.[67]

The strength of the Union, he felt, lay in its emphasis on the principles of freedom and opportunity proclaimed in the Declaration of Independence. On July 10, at Chicago, Lincoln explained why he believed the nation had endured for 82 years, half-slave and half-free (answering Stephen A. Douglas' criticism of his "house divided" speech):

> I *believe* it has endured because, during all that time, until the introduction of the Nebraska Bill, the public mind did rest, all the time, in the belief that slavery was in course of ultimate extinction. . . . I have always hated slavery. . . . But I have always been quiet about it

until this new era of the introduction of the Nebraska Bill began. . . .

. . . I believe there is no right, and ought to be no inclination in the people of the free States to enter into the slave States, and interfere with the question of slavery at all. I have said that always. . . .[68]

Lincoln continued by explaining the tie that had bound the newer immigrants with the descendants of those in America during the Revolution:

. . . When they look through that old Declaration of Independence they find that those old men say that "We hold these truths to be self-evident, that all men are created equal," and then they feel that that moral sentiment taught in that day evidences their relation to those men, that it is the father of all moral principle in them, and that they have a right to claim it as though they were blood of the blood, and flesh of the flesh of the men who wrote that Declaration . . . and so they are. That is the electric cord in that Declaration that links the hearts of patriotic and liberty-loving men together, that will link those patriotic hearts as long as the love of freedom exists in the minds of men throughout the world.[69]

Lincoln defined democracy (August 1, 1858) in terms of this fundamental equality of men:

As I would not be a *slave*, so I would not be a *master*. This expresses my idea of democracy. Whatever differs from this, to the extent of the difference, is no democracy.[70]

Behind Lincoln's convictions on democracy and slavery stood basic moral principle, as expressed in his notable debates with Stephen A. Douglas (August to October 1858). The Democrats, he alleged, exclude the issue of *wrong* in slavery.[71] Governor William H. Seward of New York saw an "irrepressible conflict" drawing closer (October 25, 1858, at Rochester).[72] President Buchanan endeavored to minimize the significance of the issue over slavery, deploring the refusal of Congress to admit Kansas under the proslavery Lecompton Constitution (December 6, 1858).[73] He was seeking to promote the spirit of compromise.

The Republicans, who gained control of the House of Representatives in the 1858 election, were in no mood for compromise on the extension of slavery. The President's attitude brought increased resentment in the North. The country was electrified by John Brown's capture of the federal arsenal at Harper's Ferry, Virginia, and his unsuccessful attempt to free the slaves by force (October 16–18, 1859). After his execution, his spirit marched on in the North, and excited fear in the South.

Lincoln's moderate but firm position was clarified and strengthened in an address to the Young Men's Republican Union at Cooper Institute in New York City, February 27, 1860:

> Wrong as we think slavery is, we can yet afford to let it alone where it is, because that much is due to the necessity arising from its actual presence in the nation; but can we, while our votes will prevent it, allow it to spread into the National Territories and to overrun us here in the Free States? If our sense of duty forbids this, then let us stand by our duty, fearless and effectively. Let us be diverted by none of those sophisticated contrivances wherewith we are so industriously plied and belabored—contrivances such as grasping for some middle ground between the right and the wrong. . . .
>
> Neither let us be slandered from our duty by false accusations against us, nor frightened from it by menaces of destruction to the Government nor of dungeons to ourselves. *Let us have faith that right makes might, and in that faith, let us, to the end, dare to do our duty as we understand it.*[74]

The Republican National Convention met in Chicago on May 16, 1860. The platform stood squarely on the principles of the Declaration, and the maintenance of the Union. Although Governor Seward of New York led on the first two ballots, Lincoln was nominated on the third. In the general election, Lincoln received a majority of the popular vote in each of the free states, except New Jersey, California and Oregon; this gave him 169 electoral votes by a majority and eleven by a plurality, for a total of 180 out of 303 (with 1,866,000 popular votes). Stephen A. Douglas received 1,377,000 popular votes and 12 electoral for the northern Democrats; John C. Breckinridge 880,000 popular and 72 electoral for the southern Democrats; and John Bell 589,000 popular and 39 electoral for the Constitutional Union Party.

The Civil War (or The War Between the States), 1861–65

When the South Carolina legislature heard of Lincoln's election, it called a state convention to consider immediate secession from the

Union. President Buchanan, in his final message on December 3, 1860, pleaded desperately with the North to save the Union by permitting all states to manage their domestic institutions in their own way, and claimed that the Federal Government was without legal power to deal with the moves of South Carolina or other states toward secession.[75] The South Carolina convention led the way by passing a Secession Ordinance on December 20, 1860. Mississippi, Florida, Alabama, Georgia, Louisiana and Texas followed in order before February 1, 1861. The provisional government of the Confederacy was established on February 8, and Jefferson Davis was elected the President on February 9.

In this dark hour for the United States of America, the President-elect pondered the fate of the nation. He sought for the secret of American strength and prosperity, and found it in "liberty to all," according to his "Fragment on the Constitution and the Union" (dated about January 1861):

> . . . The principle of "Liberty to all" . . . clears the *path* for all—gives *hope* to all—and, by consequence, *enterprize* and *industry* to all.
>
> . . . No oppressed people will *fight* and *endure*, as our fathers did, without the promise of something better, than a mere change of masters.
>
> The assertion of that *principle*, at *that time* was the *word*, "*fitly spoken*," which has proved an "apple of gold" to us. The *Union*, and the *Constitution*, are the *picture of silver*, subsequently framed around it. . . .
>
> So let us act, that neither *picture*, not *apple*, ever be blurred, or bruised or broken.[76]

On February 11, 1861, Lincoln bade farewell to his neighbors in Springfield, Illinois, fully recognizing the magnitude of the task which lay ahead:

> I now leave, not knowing when, or whether ever, I may return, with a task before me greater than that which rested upon Washington. Without the assistance of that Divine Being, who ever attended him, I cannot succeed. With that assistance, I cannot fail.[77]

As Lincoln traveled toward Washington, where he arrived on February 23, the seceding states were building up their moral zeal for their new status. Jefferson Davis concluded his Inaugural Address on

February 18 with these words, grounded in the American principles of liberty and morality:

> It is joyous in the midst of perilous times to look around upon a people united in heart, where one purpose of high resolve animates and actuates the whole, when the sacrifices to be made are not weighed in the balance, against honor, right, liberty, and equality. Obstacles may retard, but they can not long prevent, the progress of a movement sanctioned by its justice and sustained by a virtuous people. Reverently let us invoke the God of our fathers to guide and protect us in our efforts to perpetuate the principles which by His blessing they were able to vindicate, establish, and transmit to their posterity; and with a continuance of His favor, ever gratefully acknowledged, we may hopefully look forward to success, to peace, to prosperity.[78]

At Trenton, New Jersey, on February 21, Lincoln recalled the notable triumph there of Washington in 1776, and felt a Providential destiny at work:

> . . . I am exceedingly anxious that this Union, the Constitution and the liberties of the people shall be perpetuated in accordance with the original idea for which that struggle was made, and I shall be most happy indeed if I shall be an humble instrument in the hands of the Almighty, and on this, his almost chosen people, for perpetuating the object of that great struggle.[79]

Lincoln was deeply impressed by the drama of America in a world setting, as he spoke at Independence Hall in Philadelphia on February 22:

> . . . I have often inquired of myself, what great principle or idea it was that kept this Confederacy so long together. It was not the mere matter of the separation of the Colonies from the mother land; but something in that Declaration giving liberty, not alone to the people of this country, but hope to the world for all future time. . . . It was that which gave promise that in due time the weights should be lifted from the shoulders of all men, and that *all* should have an equal chance. . . .
>
> Now, in my view of the present aspect of affairs, there is no need of bloodshed and war. There is no necessity for it. I am not in favor of such a course, and I may say in advance, there will be no blood shed unless it be forced upon the Government. The Government will not use force unless force is used against it.[80]

At the flag-raising before Independence Hall, Lincoln looked to the distant future with considerable confidence, as he anticipated the adding of new states, "until we shall number as was anticipated by the great historian, five hundred millions of happy and prosperous people."[81]

In his First Inaugural Address, Lincoln exhorted the people of the South to exercise patience and not to use force against the national government:

> Why should there not be a patient confidence in the ultimate justice of the people? Is there any better or equal hope in the world? In our present differences, is either party without faith of being in the right? If the Almighty Ruler of Nations, with His eternal truth and justice, is on the side of the North, or on yours of the South, that truth and that justice will surely prevail by the judgment of this great tribunal of the American people. . . .
>
> My countrymen, one and all, think calmly and *well* upon this whole subject. Nothing valuable can be lost by taking time. . . . Intelligence, patriotism, Christianity, and a firm reliance on Him who has never yet forsaken this favored land are still competent to adjust in the best way all our present difficulty.
>
> In *your* hands, my dissatisfied fellow-countrymen, and not in *mine*, is the momentous issue of civil war. The Government will not assail *you*. You can have no conflict without being yourselves the aggressors. You have no oath registered in heaven to destroy the Government, while *I* shall have the most solemn one to preserve, protect, and defend it.
>
> I am loath to close. We are not enemies, but friends. We must not be enemies. Though passion may have strained it must not break our bonds of affection. The mystic chords of memory, stretching from every battlefield and patriot grave to every living heart and hearthstone all over this broad land, will yet swell the chorus of the Union, when again touched, as surely they will be, by the better angels of our nature.[82]

Earlier in the address, Lincoln had stressed his firm convictions on the nature of the Union:

> I hold that in contemplation of universal law and of the Constitution the Union of these States is perpetual. . . .
>
> . . . The Union is much older than the Constitution. It was formed, in fact, by the Articles of Association in 1774. It was matured and continued by the Declaration of Independence in 1776. . . .
>
> . . . No state upon its own mere motion can lawfully get out of the

Union. . . .

I therefore consider that in view of the Constitution and the laws the Union is unbroken, and to the extent of my ability I shall take care, as the Constitution itself expressly enjoins upon me, that the laws of the Union be faithfully executed in all the States. . . . I trust this will not be regarded as a menace, but only as the declared purpose of the Union that it *will* constitutionally defend and maintain itself.

In doing this there needs to be no bloodshed or violence, and there shall be none unless it be forced upon the national authority.[83]

Lincoln's hand was soon forced, according to his principles. Finally deciding to send provisions to Fort Sumter (near Charleston, South Carolina), he so notified South Carolina on April 6. The government of South Carolina decided to force the surrender of the federal fort at once; when an ultimatum was refused, the shore batteries opened fire on April 12, with the fort surrendering after 34 hours of heavy but bloodless bombardment. South Carolina was in ecstasy. To Lincoln, direct aggression had been committed against the federal government. The long indecision was ended. The die had been cast. Intense indignation was aroused in the North. Lincoln made the decision that force must be used to preserve the Union, and, on April 15, called for 75,000 three-month volunteers. In the same proclamation, Lincoln called Congress to meet in special session on July 4.

President Lincoln's quick decision to use force, following the attack upon Fort Sumter, mobilized strong public opinion in the North in support of the Union. Indecision was replaced by action. Governors and state legislatures vied in proffers of men, money and munitions. Ralph Waldo Emerson wrote: "At the darkest hour in the history of the republic, when it looked as if the nation would be dismembered, pulverized into its original elements, the attack on Fort Sumter chrystallized the North into a unit, and the hope of mankind was saved."[84]

The North doubtless underestimated greatly the immensity of the task which had been undertaken, and considerable dissent was evidenced on the wisdom of the course which had been chosen. The South was fighting for its liberty—for "self-determination," in the phrase of Woodrow Wilson. It would be defending its own land and culture. Pacifism was powerful in the North; the South was more militant, and had secured far more experience in the art of war on land—from the Battle of New Orleans in 1815, through the Texas

Revolution and the Mexican War. Population and resources favored the North (22 million in the North, 9 million in the South, including 3,500,000 slaves), but there was strong reason to expect that the North would be lacking in the spirit to press the war vigorously upon Southern soil.

Yet, under the leadership of Abraham Lincoln, the spirit of Union in the North developed the power to stand in the darkest hours and ultimately to win. Whatever motives inspired the North to carry through this great military endeavor, it became clear in the twentieth century that the future of the free world had been clearly at stake in the bitter struggle. A nation was being preserved, and paradoxically even cemented and strengthened—until the day would come for it to step out on the world scene as the democratic leader. The nation as a whole had to end slavery, and end it speedily if the "rendezvous with destiny" in the twentieth century was to be met worldwide in the spirit of the Declaration. Many Americans seemed to grasp the idea, whether consciously or unconsciously, that it was vital to preserve this new type of *nation* as a unit, and to prevent the further spread of the slave-power, with the aim of its ultimate extinction.

With civil war actually in existence, four other slave states joined the Confederacy: Virginia, April 17; Arkansas, May 6; Tennessee, May 7; and North Carolina, May 20. West Virginia broke away to organize a Union government in June, while four slave states—Delaware, Maryland, Kentucky and Missouri—remained loyal to the Union. Only minor skirmishing had taken place by the time Congress met on July 4, to hear Lincoln's request for the means he considered necessary to prosecute the war (400,000 men and $400 million) and his explanation of the significance of the struggle to preserve the Union.[85]

The rest of the long war is well known. Here it is only necessary to point to some of the other statements of Lincoln about the war and its purposes. In his first annual message to Congress, December 3, 1861, Lincoln stood firm on the principles of the war, and expressed his hope and faith in the future of the Union:

> There are already among us those, who, if the Union be preserved, will live to see it contain two hundred and fifty millions. The struggle of today, is not altogether for today—it is for a vast future also. With a reliance on Providence all the more firm and earnest, let us proceed in the great task which events have devolved upon us.[86]

As the war continued, Lincoln steadily deepened his grasp of the possible world significance of the American nation, and the sovereignty of God in the affairs of men and nation. He spoke of this to a delegation of Evangelical Lutheran ministers on May 13, 1862:

> I accept with gratitude . . . assurances of sympathy and support . . . in an important crisis, which involves, in my judgment, not only the civil and religious liberties of our own dear land, but in a large degree the civil and religious liberties of mankind in many countries and through many ages. . . . You all may recollect that in taking up the sword thus forced into our hands this Government appealed to the prayers of the pious and the good, and declared that it placed its whole dependence upon the favor of God. I now humbly and reverently, in your presence, reiterate the acknowledgement of the dependence, not doubting that, if it shall please the Divine Being who determines the destinies of nations that this shall remain a united people, they will, humbly asking the Divine guidance, make their prolonged national existence a source of new benefits to themselves and their successors, and to all classes and conditions of mankind.[87]

Although Lincoln had hoped that emancipation might be obtained through a plan of public compensation for the financial loss involved, he gradually became convinced that a direct blow at slavery would furnish vital assistance to the war effort, and increase British and other European sympathy for the Union cause. Lincoln could not prudently move to free the slaves while the Union appeared to be losing the war. The Union defeat in the second Battle of Bull Run, August 29–30, 1862, filled Lincoln with deep anguish. Out of this spiritual "depth," Lincoln penned a brief "Meditation on the Divine Will" (September 2, 1862), which Nicolay and Hay believed was not written to be seen by men:

> The will of God prevails. In great contests each party claims to act in accordance with the will of God. Both *may* be, and one *must* be wrong. God can not be *for*, and *against* the same thing at the same time. In the present Civil War it is quite possible that God's purpose is something different from the purpose of either party—and yet the human instrumentalities, working just as they do, are of the best adaptation to effect His purpose. I am almost ready to say this is probably true—that God wills this contest, and wills that it shall not end yet. By His mere quiet power, on the minds of the now contestants, He could have either saved or destroyed the Union without a human

contest. Yet the contest began. And having begun He could give the final victory to either side any day. Yet the contest proceeds.[88]

On September 17, 1862, the 75th anniversary of the signing of the Constitution, the Union forces finally won an important victory at Antietam—the bloodiest day of the war. Although the battle was indecisive, General Robert E. Lee pulled back his forces from Maryland into Virginia. Britain and France, on the verge of recognizing the Confederacy, held back; and Lincoln felt the time had come to issue his Preliminary Emancipation Proclamation, on September 22: "That on the 1st day of January, A.D. 1863, the persons held as slaves within any State or designated part of a State the people whereof shall then be in rebellion against the United States shall be then, thenceforward, and forever, free."[89] This move by the President secured much support from the anti-slavery forces of the North and of England. Lincoln closed his second annual message, December 1, 1862, with an eloquent appeal to Americans to rise to the occasion—in this war of historic significance for the Union and, as it had now become clear, for human freedom. He pleaded with Congress to adopt his plan for compensated emancipation in slave states not in rebellion:

> Fellow-citizens, *we* cannot escape history. We of this Congress and this administration, will be remembered in spite of ourselves. No personal significance, or insignificance, can spare one or another of us. The fiery trial through which we pass, will light us down, in honor or dishonor, to the latest generation. We *say* we are for the Union. The world will forget that we say this. We know how to save the Union. The world knows we know how to save it. We—even we here—hold the power, and bear the responsibility. In *giving* freedom to the *slave*, we *assure* freedom to the *free*—honorable alike in what we give, and what we preserve. We shall nobly save, or meanly lose, the last, best hope of earth. Other means may succeed; this could not fail. The way is plain, peaceful, generous, just—a way, if followed, the world will forever applaud, and God must forever bless.[90]

Although Congress was never to agree to the plan for compensated emancipation, Lincoln issued his famous Emancipation Proclamation on the scheduled date, January 1, 1863.[91] The decision for emancipation added a new moral dimension to the war, and stirred the hearts of many people around the world—especially of free laborers. A message to Lincoln from the workingmen of Manchester, England (the city was the world's greatest manufacturing center, including cotton), praised the President for his stand: "We joyfully honor you, as the President, and the Congress with you, for the many decisive steps towards practically exemplifying your belief in the words of your great founder, 'All men are created free and equal' . . . Accept our high admiration of your firmness in upholding the proclamation of freedom."[92] A new emotional and moral tie was developing between the British and American people, as was recognized by Lincoln in his reply to the citizens of Manchester, January 18, 1863:

> I know and deeply deplore the sufferings which the workingmen of Manchester and in all Europe are called to endure in this crisis. . . . Under these circumstances I can not but regard your decisive utterance upon the question as an instance of sublime Christian heroism which has not been surpassed in any age or any country. It is, indeed, an energetic and reinspiring assurance of the inherent power of truth and of the ultimate and universal triumph of justice, humanity, and freedom. . . . I hail this interchange of sentiment, therefore, as an augury that . . . the peace and friendship which now exists between the two nations will be, as it shall be my desire to make them, perpetual.[93]

As for the war, the outlook was again dark for the North, following the notable Confederate victory at Fredericksburg, on December 13, 1862. At the request of the Senate, Lincoln issued a call on March 30, 1863, for a "day of national humiliation, fasting, and prayer" (for April 30), calling for a spirit of true national repentance.[94] But at 10 o'clock in the morning of July 4, 1863, Lincoln announced the news which had arrived concerning the victory in the decisive Battle of Gettysburg (July 1–3).[95] On the same day, July 4, the bitter siege of Vicksburg was ended by its surrender to the Union forces under General Ulysses S. Grant, and within a few days the Confederacy was split by Union control of the entire Mississippi River. On July 15, Lincoln set apart Thursday, August 6, as a "day of national thanksgiving, praise and prayer." And on October 3, with the tide apparently turning, the President inaugurated the practice of setting aside the last Thursday of November as a national day of thanksgiving, following in the spirit of the Pilgrims, the Continental Congress and of George Washington:

> No human counsel hath devised nor hath any mortal hand worked out these things. They are the gracious gift of the Most High God, who, while dealing with us in anger for our sins, hath nevertheless

remembered mercy.[96]

The war was not over by any means, for some of the severest fighting lay ahead, but at the dedication of the National Cemetery at Gettysburg on November 19, 1863, Lincoln called upon Americans to dedicate themselves "to the great task remaining before us—that from these honored dead we take increased devotion to that cause for which they gave the last full measure of devotion—that we here highly resolve that these dead shall not have died in vain—that this nation, under God, shall have a new birth of freedom—and that government of the people, by the people, for the people, shall not perish from the earth." The address had begun by stressing the spirit of the Declaration of Independence: "Four score and seven years ago our fathers brought forth on this continent, a new nation, conceived in Liberty, and dedicated to the proposition that all men are created equal."[97]

The bitter fighting of 1864 and the heavy Union casualties in Virginia brought near-despair once again to the North. On July 2, Congress asked the President to proclaim a Day of Prayer:

> . . . to implore Him as the Supreme Ruler of the World, not to destroy us as a people, nor suffer us to be destroyed by the hostility or connivance of other nations or by obstinate adhesion to our own counsels, which may be in conflict with His eternal purposes, and to implore Him to enlighten the mind of the nation to know and do His will, humbly believing that it is in accordance with His will that our place should be maintained as a united people among the family of nations.[98]

But on September 3, Lincoln was able to issue a Proclamation of Thanksgiving and Prayer, in celebration of victories in Atlanta (following Sherman's march through Georgia) and at Mobile, Alabama. On October 20, 1864, Lincoln issued his final Thanksgiving Proclamation:

> It has pleased Almighty God . . . to animate and inspire our minds and hearts with fortitude, courage and resolution sufficient for the great trial of civil war into which we have been brought by our adherence as a nation to the cause of Freedom and Humanity. . . .
>
> And I do further recommend . . . penitent and fervent prayers and supplication to the Great Disposer of events for a return to the inestimable blessings of Peace, Union and Harmony throughout the

land, which it has pleased him to assign us as a dwelling place for ourselves and for our posterity throughout all generations.[99]

When the election was held on November 8, 1864, Lincoln, who had felt it probable that he would lose, won a clear-cut victory over General George B. McClellan, the Democratic nominee, with 212 electoral votes to 21, and a popular vote of 2,200,000 to 1,800,000. In his fourth and last annual message, December 6, 1864, Lincoln looked forward confidently to the continued growth and development of the United States:

> I regard our immigrants as one of the principal replenishing streams appointed by Providence to repair the ravages of internal war and its waste of national strength and health. . . .
> . . . The great enterprise of connecting the Atlantic with the Pacific States by railways and telegraph lines has been entered upon with a vigor that gives assurance of success. . . .
> The important fact remains demonstrated that we have *more* men *now* than when the war *began*; . . . that we are *gaining* strength. . . .
> The national resources . . . are unexhausted, and, as we believe, inexhaustible. The public purpose to reestablish and maintain the national authority is unchanged, and, as we believe, unchangeable. . . .[100]

The war was still raging as President Lincoln delivered his brief but famous Second Inaugural Address on March 4, 1865, with its conclusion pointing to a high spiritual objective as a means of promoting peace and union:

> . . . With malice toward none, with charity for all, with firmness in the right as God gives us to see the right, let us strive on to finish the work we are in, to bind up the nation's wounds, to care for him who shall have borne the battle and for his widow and orphan, to do all which may achieve and cherish a just and lasting peace among ourselves and with all nations.[101]

Within six days—from Sunday, April 9, 1865 (Palm Sunday) to April 15 (the day after Good Friday)—the American people, particularly in the North, experienced a drama of terrific intensity. Confederate General Robert E. Lee surrendered his army to Union General Ulysses S. Grant at the Appomattox Courthouse on April 9. The bloody struggle was nearing its end. To a triumphant crowd Lincoln gave his last public address, on Tuesday, April 11, stressing the problem of restoration of the whole Union.[102] On Good Friday, April 14, 1865, the Union flag was hoisted again over Fort Sumter. Then, shortly after 10 p.m. on that same day, the President was struck down by an assassin's bullet.

The prophesy of Secretary of War Stanton at his death—"now he belongs to the ages"—has been fully borne out by subsequent history, in America and in the world. The importance and magnitude of Lincoln's leadership stood forth in the perspective of a later generation (Usher, 1914):

> The greatness of Lincoln's achievement lay in the fact that he made North and South alike realize that the aim of the war was . . . the creation of a mighty nation, powerful in her grasp of a continent and two oceans, rich in the fruits of united endeavor, invincible by reason of her consciousness of a noble and splendid ideal. The war made Southerners and Northerners American.[103]

Lord Charnwood, English biographer of Lincoln, closes his book (1917) with a tribute which helps explain why Lincoln has become a symbol of the finest spirit of America:

> Beyond his own country some of us recall his name as the greatest among those associated with the cause of popular government. . . . He was a citizen of that far country where there is neither aristocrat nor democrat. No political theory stands out from his words or actions; but they show a most unusual sense of the possible dignity of common men and common things. . . .[104]

On the Sunday following Lincoln's death, the Rev. John McClintock (who had been abroad during many of the war years) spoke of the love for Lincoln abroad:

> Abraham Lincoln had come to be . . . the synonyme [sic] of hope . . . not only in every slave cabin in the South, where he is canonized already, but in many a shepherd's lodge in Switzerland—in many a woodman's cabin in the Black Forest—in many a miner's hut of the Hartz Mountains—in many a cottage in Italy, for there, as well as here, the poor had learned to look upon him as the anointed of God for the redemption of the liberties of mankind. It is but lately that Garibaldi named one of his grandchildren Lincoln, little dreaming how soon that

name was to be enrolled among the immortals.[105]

Restoration of the Union, 1865–71

The Civil War was America's most costly war in terms of casualties in relation to the total population. The 1860 census recorded 31,400,000 persons in the United States. The Union dead in the war have been estimated at 350,000 with 275,000 wounded; the Confederate dead at 250,000 with at least 100,000 wounded. These deaths thus amounted to approximately two percent of the total population—a figure equivalent to 5,000,000 in a country of 250,000,000. Yet once the war was over, the nation (particularly the North) moved ahead with vigor and optimism. President Andrew Johnson expressed his confidence in the future of America in the concluding paragraphs of his first Annual Message, December 4, 1865 (the message opened by expressing "gratitude to God in the name of the people for the preservation of the United States" and by referring to the high honor given to the memory of President Lincoln, with "the grief of the nation . . . still fresh."):

> When, on the organization of our Government under the Constitution the President of the United States delivered his inaugural address to the two Houses of Congress, he said to them, and through them to the country and to mankind that—"The preservation of the sacred fire of liberty and the destiny of the republican model of government are justly considered, perhaps as *deeply*, as *finally*, staked on the experiment intrusted to the hands of the American people."
> . . . Who will not join me in the prayer that the Invisible Hand which has led us through the clouds that gloomed around our path will so guide us onward to a perfect restoration of fraternal affection that we of this day may be able to transmit our great inheritance of State governments in all their rights, of the General Government in its whole constitutional vigor, to our posterity, and they to theirs through countless generations.[106]

During the next five years, the three amendments for the protection of the Negro (African-American) were added to the Constitution of the United States, and the states of the South were restored to the Union, following a bitter struggle between the Radical Republican Congress and the moderate President, Andrew Johnson (climaxed by the failure of the Senate to convict the President on charges of impeachment, in a vote on May 16, 1868, just one short of the required two-thirds).

Tennessee was the first Southern state to be restored to the Union —July 24, 1866. Seven more states were re-admitted between June 22 and 25, 1868: Arkansas, Alabama, Florida, Georgia (for a time), Louisiana, North Carolina and South Carolina. In 1870, Mississippi, Texas and Virginia were re-admitted, and Georgia in 1871. The Union troops remained in some states until 1877. Yet by 1871, Southern conservatives were in control of Georgia, North Carolina, Tennessee and Virginia. The federal system, with state self-government, was being re-established in the South. The Supreme Court had stated in 1869 that the American federation was legally indissoluble, the "Constitution, in all its provisions, looks to an indestructible Union, composed of indestructible states."[107] President Johnson had granted full pardon to most of the "rebels" on September 7, 1867, and to all on December 25, 1868.

Other signs of the revival of the Union were shown in political and economic life. General Ulysses S. Grant was elected President in 1868, carrying 26 of 34 states. In the Congressional elections of 1870, the Democrats were able to elect 104 in the House to 134 Republicans (plus five Liberal Republicans). The nation was returning to "normalcy" (in 1874, the Democrats won 170 seats in the House to 107 for the Republicans). The railroad was symbolic of the new economic ties between the East and the West—the Union Pacific and Central Pacific met in 1869, and the first transcontinental railroad trip was completed in 1870, from Boston to Oakland. The development of the West had been greatly stimulated by the Homestead Act of 1862 (160 acres per family) and the homestead bonus of 1864 for veterans.

Thus, by 1871, "Liberty and Union" had been re-won and consolidated. The war had scarcely slowed the normal population growth. The 1870 Census showed nearly 40 million Americans, as compared to 31 million in 1860. The American nation, with strength and character tested and fortified in the terrible Civil War, was ready to march on with renewed vigor. The South faced a very difficult period, indeed, but it too was to recover and join the forward movement of the Union. One unique unfinished problem remained: the future social, economic and political position of the African-Americans, as the South, in particular, moved to establish a system of "white supremacy."

Foreign Relations and Expansion, 1857–71

The extrovert mood continued to dominate during this period in which the issues of slavery and union were so significant. American pressures abroad were strong throughout, even during the Civil War by the North.

Buchanan, 1857–61

President James Buchanan's foreign policy was conducted in a vigorous manner. Jarvis, Baker, and Howland, guano islands in the Pacific, were occupied in 1857. Buchanan looked forward to important acquisitions in North America and nearby islands. In his report to Congress on January 7, 1858, condemning William Walker's filibustering expeditions into Nicaragua, Buchanan described his expectation of American expansion over Central America. He brought continued pressure on Spain to sell Cuba. Civil war in Mexico and border disturbances, with no possibility of collecting claims, caused the President to propose military occupation of the two northern provinces of Mexico in 1858.[108] In his message of December 19, 1859, he urged the necessity of sending troops to Mexico to aid the constitutional forces under Juarez to obtain full control.[109] Buchanan brought pressure on Paraguay and on China. Supporting the goals of Britain and France in their fighting against China in 1857–58, the United States secured by treaty the same privileges in China as did Britain and France. America's first consul to Japan, Townsend Harris, secured a favorable commercial treaty with Japan in 1858, forming the basis for Japan's commercial relations with foreign powers for the rest of the century.

Lincoln, 1861–65

The election of Lincoln in 1860 resulted in the appointment of the expansionist William H. Seward as Secretary of State. Perhaps only in the expansionist atmosphere which had been fostered by the Democrats could Seward have proposed to Lincoln that a foreign war might be undertaken as a means of uniting the nation (especially against Spain, which had violated the Monroe Doctrine in raising her flag over Santo Domingo). Lincoln opposed the plan, but Seward did warn Spain.

With the beginning of the Civil War, the major diplomatic aim of the North was to avert foreign intervention in behalf of the Confederacy, while reserving America's position under the Monroe Doctrine until the war was near a victorious end (especially when French troops occupied Mexico City in June 1862, and installed

Maximilian of Austria on the throne of Mexico, April 10, 1864). Lincoln brought tactful pressure on England which had permitted the construction of two ships for the Confederate Navy in 1862—the *Florida* and the famous *Alabama*. A Russian fleet, fearing it might be bottled up in a possible war with England and France over the Polish revolt, arrived in New York harbor in September 1863; the Russian Pacific fleet reached San Francisco a few weeks later.

In Japan, in 1863, all foreigners were ordered out of the empire, foreigners were attacked, and the British and American legations were burned. The USS *Wyoming* destroyed two vessels which fired on her, and another naval vessel joined British, Dutch and French warships in a punitive bombardment of Shemonoseki in August 1864. In relation to the French in Mexico, the House of Representatives passed a resolution in April 1864, condemning the French occupation. A more immediate threat came from Canada, with raids and threats of raids by Confederate refugees across the border. The continued prestige of the United States in Europe is shown by the high immigration rate from there during the last three years of the war.

Andrew Johnson and Ulysses S. Grant, 1865–71

The extrovert mood, with a partial break in relation to other countries during the Civil War, was to continue for five or six years after the war, in relation to France, the Pacific, the West Indies and England.

President Johnson kept Seward as Secretary of State, and, when the war had ended, brought steady pressure against the empire of Maximilian in Mexico. Secretary Seward, on February 12, 1866, demanded French withdrawal. Napoleon III withdrew his support from Maximilian, bringing his troops home to support his position against Prussia and with a proper regard for the 50,000 American troops in Texas under the command of General Sheridan. When the last of the French troops left Mexico in the spring of 1867, Maximilian's regime tottered, and the Emperor himself was executed in June 1867. Seward also warned Spain which had been involved in war with Peru, Chile, Bolivia and Ecuador—Spain agreed to a formal armistice in 1871.

America's notable expansion during this period occurred in the Pacific with the purchase of Alaska from Russia and the occupation of Midway Island, both in 1867. The international climate which promoted the sale of Alaska was based on American-Russian friendship during and after the Civil War, and on Russia's hostility toward Britain. Russia offered to sell Alaska for $7,200,000. The key to the American decision to accept the offer lay in Secretary Seward's interest in the expansion of America as part of its world destiny, politically and economically. The Senate approved the treaty (April 9, 1867) by a vote of 37 to 2, and the House passed the necessary appropriation (July 14, 1868), 113 to 43. The purchase of Alaska increased American pressure on Britain in Canada, withdrew Russian power from North America, and moved America's potential power clear to Russian Siberia and to Japan's northern island possessions; it added 586,000 square miles to the United States. The uninhabited Midway Islands, a thousand miles west of Hawaii, were occupied on September 30, 1867, while Seward pressed in vain for the annexation of the Hawaiian Islands.

Anson Burlingame was America's minister to China from 1861 to 1867. The United States had feared that the European powers would take advantage of the great Taiping Rebellion (1850–1864) to take new territories, but Burlingame received assurances against this, reporting the general understanding as "a guarantee of the territorial integrity of the Chinese Empire."[110] Burlingame was so respected by the Chinese Government that he was named a member of a three-man commission (with two Chinese) to negotiate for China with the United States and European nations, after he resigned as minister in 1867. In 1868 the United States and China agreed to accept most-favored-nation treatment for the citizens of each country when traveling or residing in the other. This opened the United States to Chinese immigrants, then in demand as cheap labor on the Pacific coast. In June 1867, America landed 181 troops on Formosa to secure satisfaction for the murder of the crew of a shipwrecked American bark.[111] During the revolutionary events in Japan in 1868, 150 sailors were landed in Hiogo, and an armed force went ashore in Nagasaki to protect the foreign settlement there.[112] Korea also felt American influence for the first time, following a number of shipwrecks—1,000 Americans were landed in June 1871, and fought an engagement in which three Americans and perhaps 250 Koreans were killed.[113]

Secretary Seward and later President Grant showed great interest in securing control of the Virgin Islands (the Danish West Indies) and Santo Domingo. Seward signed a treaty with Denmark on October 24, 1867, for the purchase of St. Thomas and St. John; he was also considering the offer of the Dominican Republic for annexation, and gave some attention to the future of Cuba, where a revolution against

Spain had just erupted. As Congress delayed action, President Grant took office on March 4, 1869, appointing as Secretary of State Hamilton Fish, who was less interested in expansion. The Senate Committee on Foreign Relations recommended the rejection of the treaty with Denmark in 1870—thus it was not until 1917 that the Virgin Islands were ceded to the United States. However, President Grant was determined to annex Santo Domingo, if possible, securing two definitive treaties on November 29, 1869; but the Senate rejected the treaty of annexation by a vote of 28 to 28, June 30, 1870. The American mood was beginning to shift away from expansion (or extroversion). The President did not relax his efforts, but it was clear to him by April 1871 that Congress had lost interest.

Until the *Alabama* Claims dispute with Britain was settled in 1871, the United States brought strong pressure against Britain, with many Americans expecting the cession or seizure of Canada. However, after Britain established the self-governing Dominion of Canada, in July 1867, American ideas of annexation declined in importance. But Senator Charles Sumner, long-time chairman of the Foreign Relations Committee, in a climactic speech on April 13, 1869, implied that Britain owed the United States for half the cost of the Civil War (because of the *Alabama* depredations). The President and Secretary Fish moved steadily to reduce the pressure on Canada, while standing firm on Britain's responsibility for the outfitted ship. When Congress met in March 1871, the Republican caucus in the Senate accepted the Administration's insistence that Sumner be removed as chairman of Foreign Relations. American and British representatives then agreed on the notable Treaty of Washington on May 8, 1871, providing for arbitration of the dispute. The Senate approved the treaty on May 24 by a vote of 50 to 12, and cordial relations were restored in 1872, when the arbitrators awarded the United States $15,500,000 in damages and Great Britain $1,400,000.

The summer of 1871 seems to signalize the end of another major period in American history, which began in 1824. The extrovert mood, dominant since 1844, was declining rapidly, with the settlement with Britain and the failure to annex Santo Domingo. Internal problems were again capturing the attention of most Americans. The great era of expansion which had begun in 1844 had come to an end. American democratic government had been consolidated, slavery eliminated, and the Union firmly cemented. "Democratic nationalism" had been triumphant in America as well as in France and Britain. Part of the consolidation was likewise shown in the moral and spiritual emphasis which continued at least until 1871, completing a period of special idealism (1824–71).

Idealism, 1857–71

After 1860, the evangelist was a less important figure, but evangelists had already played a major role in building up the continued strength of American churches. During the period from 1844 to 1871, the sentiment of "manifest destiny," American nationalism, and Christian expansion seemed to reinforce one another.

Much of the progress among African-Americans following emancipation must be attributed to Christianity—both among the Negroes themselves and among helpful white Christians. It has been estimated that there were 520,000 Negroes in Christian churches in 1860, about 12 percent. Similarly, scores of thousands of Indians had become Roman Catholic or Protestant, out of the total of 278,000 in 1870.

Religious influences continued strong in elementary and secondary education. The deep influence of the morally based McGuffey readers in these schools is suggested by the statistics of their sales over a long period: seven million from 1836 to 1860, and 40 million from 1850 to 1870; and the sales continued later, with 60 million from 1870 to 1890, and 15 million from 1890 to 1920.[114] Churches established 73 more colleges from 1860 to 1869.[115] Foreign missions continued to build up steadily—establishing schools, conducting medical work, and training an indigenous clergy. The Women's Union Missionary Society of America began its educational and medical work in 1861; individuals of many denominations cooperated in the China Inland Mission, organized in 1865.[116] Missionaries established themselves in the open ports of Japan after the American-Japanese treaty of 1858.

Social reform continued, as the movement against slavery reached a peak during the Civil War. When the war came, it secured nearly unanimous support from the churches of both sides, as each side defended its principles. Chaplains were appointed for each regiment and hospital, with religion "in the Confederate armies . . . even more conspicuous than in the armies of the Union."[117] The American Temperance Society joined with state societies in 1856 to form the American Temperance Union, and a national Prohibition Party was established in 1869.

The great writers of America continued their moral-spiritual approach. When the Civil War came, Emerson called for the emancipation of the slaves. Julia Ward Howe touched a responsive chord in the American people, with her concept of God's judgments and purposes being furthered through the terrible Civil War ("The Battle Hymn of the Republic"):

Mine eyes have seen the glory of the coming of the Lord;
He is trampling out the vintage where the grapes of wrath are stored;
He hath loosed the fateful lightning of His terrible swift sword;
    His truth is marching on. . . .

In the beauty of the lilies Christ was born across the sea,
With a glory in his bosom that transfigures you and me;
As He died to make men holy, let us die to make men free,
    While God is marching on.

Walt Whitman continued to express his faith in American destiny. He penned "Pioneers! O Pioneers!" in the year the Civil War ended (1865):

    . . . For we cannot tarry here,
We must march my darlings, we must bear the brunt of danger,
We the youthful sinewy races, all the rest on us depend,
    Pioneers! O Pioneers!

After the Civil War, Whitman felt that the United States was entering upon a great new era, with the burden of slavery removed:

It is certain that the United States, by virtue of that war and its results . . . are now ready to enter, and most certainly enter, upon their genuine career in history, as no more torn and divided in their spinal requisites, but a great homogeneous Nation—free states all—a moral and political unity in variety. . . . And I predict that the south is yet to outstrip the north.[118]

Whitman penned two prophetic poems which stressed the rise of freedom among all peoples and the coming growth of world unity and cooperation. The first of these was "Years of the Modern" in 1865:

Years of the modern! Years of the unperform'd!

Your horizon rises, I see it parting away for more august dramas,
I see not America only, not only Liberty's nation, but other nations
preparing,
I see tremendous entrances and exits, new combinations, the solidarity
of races,
I see that force advancing with irresistible power on the world's
stage.[119]

Whitman also emphasized the coming role of East and West, in the
cooperative physical, intellectual and spiritual world of the future, in
"Passage to India" (1868):

. . . .
Passage to India!
Lo, soul, seest thou not God's purpose from the first?
The earth to be spann'd, connected by network,
The races, neighbors, to marry and be given in marriage,
The oceans to be cross'd, the distant brought near,
The lands to be welded together. . . .[120]

The American Presidents continued to stress a moral-spiritual
approach. The burden carried by Abraham Lincoln as President in a
nation split by secession and civil war must have been almost
unbearable. Yet out of the agony and suffering, Lincoln gradually
developed the deep spiritual maturity and faith which have inspired each
generation of Americans since then. During a more recent time of
anguish (the Vietnam War), the noted Quaker writer and preacher, Elton
Trueblood, felt impelled to write a book entitled *Abraham Lincoln:
Theologian of American Anguish.*[121]

Lincoln never joined a church, although he attended the First
Presbyterian Church of Springfield, Illinois, and the New York Avenue
Presbyterian Church in Washington. His faith in Providential guidance
and purpose was deepened and tempered in the anguish of Union
defeats and the death of his son Willie in 1862. In a meeting with a
group brought to see the President by Congressman James F. Wilson of
Iowa, Lincoln expressed his view of the control of God in history, that
God would not abandon us to the foolishness of our own devices:

I also believe that He will compel us to do right in order that He
may do these things, not so much because we desire them as that they
accord with His plan of dealing with this nation, in the midst of which

He means to establish justice. I think He means that we shall do more
than we have yet done in furtherance of His plans, and He will open the
way for our doing it. I have felt His hand upon me in great trials and
submitted to His guidance, and I trust that as He shall further open the
way, I will be ready to walk therein, relying on His help and trusting
in His goodness and wisdom.[122]

Lincoln emphasized the challenges and responsibilities he felt to history,
as he closed his Second Annual Message, December 1, 1862: "Fellow
citizens, we cannot escape history. . . . The fiery trial through which we
pass will light us down in honor or dishonor to the latest generation."[123]
In his call for a day of "thanksgiving and prayer" on the last Thursday
of November 1863, Lincoln asked the American people to pray for the
healing of the nation:

> . . . I recommend to them that while offering up the ascriptions
> justly due to Him for such singular deliverances and blessings they do
> also, with humble penitence for our national perverseness and
> disobedience, commend to his tender care all those who have become
> widows, orphans, mourners, or sufferers in the lamentable civil strife in
> which we are unavoidably engaged, and fervently implore the
> interposition of the Almighty hand to heal the wounds of the nation and
> to restore it, as soon as may be consistent with the divine purposes, to
> the full enjoyment of peace, harmony, tranquility, and union.[124]

It was in 1863 that Congress resolved that the words "In God We
Trust" should be stamped on American coins.

Lincoln reached the height of his spiritual faith in his famous
Second Inaugural Address, March 4, 1865:

> . . . Both parties deprecated war, but one of them would make war
> rather than let the nation survive, and the other would accept war rather
> than let it perish, and the war came.
>
> One eighth of the whole population was colored slaves, not
> distributed generally over the Union, but localized in the southern part
> of it. These slaves constituted a peculiar and powerful interest. All
> knew that this interest was somehow the cause of the war. To
> strengthen, perpetuate and extend this interest was the object for which
> the insurgents would rend the Union even by war, while the government
> claimed no right to do more than to restrict the territorial enlargement
> of it. Neither party expected for the war the magnitude or the duration
> which it has already attained. Neither anticipated that the cause of the

conflict might cease with or even before the conflict itself should cease. Each looked for an easier triumph, and a result less fundamental and astounding. Both read the same Bible and pray to the same God, and each invokes His aid against the other. It may seem strange that any men should dare to ask a just God's assistance in wringing their bread from the sweat of other men's faces, but let us judge not, that we be not judged. The prayers of both could not be answered. That of neither has been answered fully. The Almighty has His own purposes. "Woe unto the world because of offenses, for it must needs be that offenses come, but woe to that man by whom the offense cometh." If we shall suppose that American slavery is one of those offenses which, in the providence of God, must needs come, but which, having continued through His appointed time, He now wills to remove, and that He gives to both North and South this terrible war as the woe due to those by whom the offense came, shall we discern therein any departure from those divine attributes which the believers in a living God always ascribe to Him? Fondly do we hope, fervently do we pray, that this mighty scourge of war may speedily pass away. Yet, if God wills that it continue until all the wealth piled by the bondsman's two hundred and fifty years of unrequited toil shall be sunk, and until every drop of blood drawn with the lash shall be paid by another drawn with the sword, as was said three thousand years ago, so still it must be said, "The judgments of the Lord are true and righteous altogether."

With malice toward none, with charity for all, with firmness in the right as God gives us to see the right, let us strive on to finish the work we are in, to bind up the nation's wounds, to care for him who shall have borne the battle and for his widow and orphan, to do all which may achieve and cherish a just and lasting peace among ourselves and with all nations.[125]

Then on Good Friday, as if to impress the character of this humble and great American President deeply on that generation of Americans and on all generations to come, the Great Emancipator was struck down by the assassin's bullet. His spirit was to help re-mold and re-vitalize the Union, based on Liberty and the Moral Law, and to inspire people in every land on earth. Elton Trueblood summarizes the Lincoln vision as follows:

Nothing in Lincoln's theology made him expect Utopia. He did not claim that the victory of the Union forces would necessarily produce the full liberation of people, black and white. All that he claimed was that such a victory would provide *opportunity*, while defeat would entail unmitigated disaster. He accepted the basic philosophy of the Founding Fathers, including the idea of a special destiny for America, but he was sufficiently acquainted with human failure to know that progress is never certain, as it is never easy. His only certainty lay in the conviction that God will never cease to call America to her true service, not only for her own sake but for the sake of the world. . . . He did not predict an end to American anguish, but he did see the possibility of a determination "to do all which may achieve and cherish a just, and a lasting peace, among ourselves, and with all nations."[126]

In a proclamation of April 25, the new President, Andrew Johnson, called on the people of the United States to observe a special "day of humiliation and mourning . . . again humbling ourselves before the Almighty God, in order that the bereavement may be sanctified to the nation."[127] The President concluded his first annual message, December 4, 1865, with a reaffirmation of faith in Providential guidance of the nation: "Who will not join me in the prayer that the Invisible Hand which has led us through the clouds that gloom our path will also guide us onward to a perfect restoration of fraternal affection. . . ."[128] In his third message, December 3, 1867, shortly before his impeachment trial, Johnson appealed to Congress to work for reconciliation between North and South:

> I have no desire to save from the proper and just consequences of their great crime those who engaged in rebellion against the Government, but as a mode of punishment the measures under consideration are the most unreasonable that could be invented. Many of these people are perfectly innocent; many kept their fidelity to the Union untainted to the last; many were incapable of any legal offense. . . . But these acts of Congress confound them all together in one common doom. . . . Christianity and civilization have made such progress that recourse to a punishment so cruel and unjust would meet with the condemnation of all unprejudiced and right-minded men.[129]

Ulysses S. Grant delivered his First Inaugural Address on March 4, 1869: "In conclusion I ask patient forbearance toward one another throughout the land, and a determined effort on the part of every citizen to do his share toward cementing a happy Union; and I ask the prayer of the nation to Almighty God in behalf of this consummation."[130]

By 1871 it was becoming clear that a new and more secular era was beginning for America. The great "age of faith" in the 19th century was coming to an end, as a "new day" of enlightenment was dawning. The nation was being prepared for the beginning of a new world age.

Notes

1. James D. Richardson, *Messages and Papers of the Presidents, 1769–1902*, 11 vols. (Washington, D.C.: 1907), 2:260–62.

2. Ibid., 316.

3. Ibid., 443.

4. Thomas A. Bailey, *A Diplomatic History of the American People* (New York: F. S. Crofts, 1940); 323–24.

5. Alexis de Tocqueville, *Democracy in America*, 1 vol. (New York: Edward Walker, 1849). 435.

6. Ibid., 470.

7. Ibid., 26–27.

8. Richardson, 3:148.

9. *The Diary of John Quincy Adams*, ed. Allan Nevins (New York: Longmans Green, 1925), 570.

10. Samuel Flagg Bemis, ed. *The American Secretaries of State and Their Diplomacy*, 10 vols. (New York: 1928), 5:15.

11. *The Works of Daniel Webster*, 6 vols. (Boston, 1881), 6:468–69, 471–72.

12. Quoted in Luther A. Weigle, *American Idealism*, vol. 8 of *The Pageant of America* (New Haven: Yale University Press, 1928), 166.

13. Ibid.

14. Charles C. Cole, *The Social Ideas of the Northern Evangelists, 1826–1860* (New York: Columbia University Press, 1954), 194.

15. E. D. Adams, *The Power of Ideals in American History* (New Haven, 1913), 38.

16. de Tocqueville, 412.

17. *Diary of John Quincy Adams*, 462.

18. Cole, 75.

19. de Tocqueville, 331–35.

20. Ezra Taft Benson (Secretary of Agriculture, 1953–61, and a President of the Mormon Council of the Twelve), in his book *This Nation Shall Endure* (Salt Lake City; Deseret Book Co., 1979), states the Mormon conviction that "America is a choice land, a land reserved for God's own purposes" (p. 14). This view is based in part upon passages in the *Book of Mormon*, such as: "And the land shall be a land of liberty unto the Gentiles, and there shall be no kings upon the land" (2 Nephi 10:11); and "it is a land of promise, and whatsoever nation shall possess it shall serve God, or they shall be swept off when the fulness of his wrath shall come upon them" (Ether 2:9).

21. For a full description of American missionary activity, see Kenneth

Scott Latourette, *History of the Expansion of Christianity*, 7 vols. (New York: Harpers, 1941), esp. vol. 4.

22. *The Complete Essays and Other Writings of Ralph Waldo Emerson* (New York: The Modern Library, 1950), 32–33 (on *Nature*).

23. Ibid., 71.

24. George Bancroft, *History of the United States*, 22nd ed., 10 vols. (Boston: Little, Brown and Co., 1867), 1:1, 3–4.

25. Robert J. Breckinridge, *A Discourse on the Formation and Development of the American Mind* (Baltimore: Richard J. Matchett, 1837), 38–40.

26. Richardson, 2:294, 299.

27. Ibid., 438.

28. Richardson, 3: 307–8.

29. Richardson, 4:6, 20.

30. Ibid., 32.

31. Ibid., 341, 343–45.

32. Ibid., 380–81.

33. Ibid., 380.

34. Richard B. Morris, ed. *Encyclopedia of American History* (New York: Harpers, 1953), 193.

35. Richardson, 4:386–87.

36. Bailey, 276.

37. Richardson, 4:381.

38. Ibid., 398.

39. Ibid., 511–13.

40. Bernard DeVoto, *The Year of Decision* (Boston: Little, Brown, 1943).

41. Richardson, 4:494.

42. Webster, 4:254–61.

43. *The Collected Works of Abraham Lincoln*, ed. Roy P. Basler, 8 vols. (Brunswick, N.J.: Rutgers University Press, 1958), 1:514. (referred to as *Lincoln*).

44. Richardson, 4:536–44.

45. Ibid., 587.

46. Ibid., 581–83.

47. Ibid., 633–38.

48. Ibid., 579.

49. Webster, 6:494.

50. Richardson, 5:117.

51. Ibid., 116–17.

52. Kirk H. Porter, *National Party Platforms* (New York: Macmillan, 1942), 26–27.

53. Ibid., 31.

54. Albert K. Weinberg, *Manifest Destiny* (Baltimore: Johns Hopkins Press, 1935). 190.

55. Porter, 46.

56. Richardson, 5:435–36.

57. Cole, 225.

58. Ibid., 218.

59. J. D. Nourse, *Remarks on the Past and Its Legacies to American Society* (Louisville, 1847), 176.

60. George Bancroft, *Literary and Historical Miscellanies* (New York: Harper and Brothers, 1855), 488–91, 516.

61. Van Wyck Brooks, *The Times of Melville and Whitman* (New York: E. P. Dutton, 1947), 158–59.

62. Arthur A. Ekirch, Jr., *The Idea of Progress in America, 1815–1860* (New York: Columbia University Press, 1944), 267.

63. Bancroft, *Miscellanies*, 505–7, 511.

64. Richardson, 4:373–74.

65. Richardson, 5:350.

66. Ibid., 435–46.

67. *Lincoln*, 2:363–64.

68. Ibid., 492.

69. Ibid., 499–500.

70. Ibid., 532.

71. *Lincoln*, 3:315.

72. Horace Greeley, *The American Conflict—A History of the Great Rebellion*, 2 vols. (Hartford: O. D. Case and Co., 1864, 1867), 1:301–2.

73. Richardson, 5:500.

74. *Lincoln*, 3:547–50.

75. Richardson, 5:626–28, 630–31, 633–34.

76. *Lincoln*, 4:168–69.

77. Ibid., 190.

78. Quoted in E. D. Adams, 57.

79. *Lincoln*, 4:236.

80. Ibid., 240–41.

81. Ibid., 241–42.

82. Richardson, 6:11–12.

83. Ibid., 7.

84. E. D. Adams, 20.

85. Richardson, 6:23, 25–30.

86. *Lincoln*, 5:53.

87. Ibid., 212.

88. Ibid., 404.

89. Richardson, 6:96–97.

90. *Lincoln*, 5:537.

91. Richardson, 6:158–59. Professor George Anastaplo reminds us of Lincoln's special statesmanship in this Proclamation, by quoting from an oration

by the distinguished former slave, Frederick Douglass, on April 14, 1876: "His great mission was to accomplish two things: first, to save his country from dismemberment and ruin; and second, to free his country from the great crime of slavery. To do one or the other, or both, he must have the earnest sympathy and powerful co-operation of his loyal fellow-countrymen. Without this primary and essential condition to success, efforts must have been vain and utterly fruitless. *Had he put the abolition of slavery before the salvation of the Union, he would have inevitably driven from him a powerful class of American people and rendered resistance to rebellion impossible.*" Douglass also quoted from Lincoln's letter of April 4, 1864: "I am naturally anti-slavery. If slavery is not wrong, nothing is wrong. I cannot remember when I did not so think and feel." George Anastaplo, *The Emancipation Proclamation*, in Ronald K. L. Collins, ed., *Constitutional Government in America* (Durham, N.C.: Carolina Academic Press, 1980), 421–33, on p. 422.

92. Quoted in *Lincoln*, 6:65.

93. Ibid., 64–65.

94. Richardson, 6:164–65.

95. *Lincoln*, 6:314.

96. Richardson, 6:172–73.

97. From the Gettysburg Address in Stuart Gerry Brown, ed., *We Hold These Truths: Documents of American Democracy* (New York: Harpers, 1941), 229. Garry Wills in *Lincoln at Gettysburg: The Words that Remade America* (New York: Simon and Schuster, 1992) believes that this address helped give America a virtual rebirth of her ideals, stressing "equality" in a nation where slavery had become a powerful institution: "The Civil War *is*, to most Americans, what Lincoln wanted it to *mean*: (p. 38); "In the crucible of the occasion, Lincoln distilled the meaning of the war, of the nation's purpose, of the remaining task, in a statement that is straightforward yet magical"; "By accepting the Gettysburg Address, its concept of a single people dedicated to a purpose, we have been changed" (p. 147); "In his brief time before the crowd at Gettysburg he wove a spell that has not, yet, been broken—he called up a new nation out of the blood and trauma" (p. 175). Wills added that the Gettysburg Address "must be supplemented with his other most significant address, the Second Inaugural, where *sin* is added to the picture" (p. 177).

98. Richardson, 6:221–22.

99. *Lincoln*, 8:55–56.

100. Richardson, 6:244–54.

101. Ibid., 276–77.

102. *Lincoln*, 8:399–403.

103. Roland B. Usher, *The Rise of the American People* (New York: Century, 1914), 9–10.

104. Lord Charnwood, *Abraham Lincoln* (New York: Henry Holt, 1917; Cardinal Edition, 1952), 493–94.

105. From the printed sermon, quoted by Jay Monaghan, *Diplomat in Carpet Slippers* (Indianapolis: The Bobbs-Merrill Co., 1945), 424–25.

106. Richardson, 6:369–71.

107. Texas v. White, 7 Wall. 724.

108. Richardson, 5:413–14.

109. Ibid., 567.

110. Julius W. Pratt, *A History of United States Foreign Policy* (New York: Prentice-Hall, 1955), 276.

111. Lulu Caine, *Conditions Underlying the Minor Wars and Interventions of the United States* (doctoral dissertation, University of Chicago, August 1929), 331.

112. Ibid., 340–41.

113. James A. Callahan, *American Relations in the Pacific and the Far East, 1784–1900* (Baltimore: Johns Hopkins University Press, 1901), 111–12.

114. Richard D. Mosier, *Making the American Mind: Social and Moral Ideas in the McGuffey Readers* (New York: Russell and Russell, 1947), 168.

115. Weigle, 315.

116. Latourette, 4:303, 328–29, 333.

117. William Warren Sweet, *The Story of Religion in America* (New York: Harpers, 1950), 312, 317.

118. *The Whitman Reader*, ed. Maxwell Geismar (New York: Pocket Books, 1955), 421–22.

119. Ibid., 232–34.

120. Ibid., 192–201.

121. Elton Trueblood, *Abraham Lincoln: Theologian of American Anguish* (New York: Harper and Row, 1973).

122. James F. Wilson, *North American Review* (December 1896): 668–69. Quoted in Trueblood, 127.

123. *Lincoln*, 5:537.

124. Richardson, 6:173.

125. Brown, 230–31.

126. Trueblood, 140–41.

127. Richardson, 6:306.

128. Ibid., 370–71.

129. Ibid., 563.

130. Richardson, 7:8.

CHAPTER V

America's Rise as an Industrial World Power: The New Enlightenment (1871–1918)

A new age was beginning for humankind in the latter part of the 19th century—an age in which the United States was ultimately to play a leading role, through its ideals and its power. The sea powers of Europe had for nearly four centuries been expanding their influence around the world—in Africa, in the Americas, and in Asia. By 1871, the steamship and railroad and telegraph were ready to be applied to start the amazing progress toward the creation of a relatively small physical earth.

Similarly, the ideas of the American Revolution—the dignity and freedom of the individual human being and the right of self-government—had been solidly established in the United States. The slaves were freed in America, and the serfs emancipated in Russia (1861). The idea of the "general will," of majority rule, spread widely after the American and French revolutions, but moved toward dictatorship where internal checks and balances were not established. New revolutionary ideas were fermenting in many minds, following their "discovery" in the previous generation: in politics, *The Communist Manifesto* (1848) of Marx and Engels and *Das Kapital* (Marx, 1867); in sociology, the "scientific" secular philosophies of Auguste Comte (*Positive Philosophy*, 1830–42) and Herbert Spencer (*First Principles*, 1862); and in biology, the theory of evolution as developed by Charles Darwin (*Origin of Species* in 1859 and *Descent of Man* in 1871). Men were preparing to launch boldly into uncharted seas of social action. The outlook was exhilarating for those who felt confident that man's progress was now assured.

Walt Whitman was the prophet at this time for the new democratic age he saw ahead, to replace feudalistic principles—a new age in which individuality would be emphasized along with spirituality and brotherhood. These ideas were brought together in *Democratic Vistas*, written between 1868 and 1870 and published in 1871. America would gain material success without doubt, he believed, but the great tests of democracy would come in the mind and spirit.[1] He felt that the re-birth of "spirituality" would be required to redeem and guide America's vaunted materialism: ". . . Faith, very old, now scared away by science, must be restored, brought back by the same power that caused her departure—restored with new sway, deeper, wider, higher than ever."[2] Climaxing his vision, as Whitman surveyed the vistas ahead, was the brotherhood of man, binding all nations together.[3] The words of Whitman show that he was well aware of new difficulties and problems in the making. But he could see a new greatness for America arising from the challenges and suffering, the burdens and sacrifice, and even from evil—in the purposes of Providence.[4] In 1872, Whitman expressed in poetry his concept of the world significance of the American experiment:

> Sail, sail thy best ship of Democracy,
>   of Value is thy freight . . .
> Thou holdest not the venture of thyself alone,
>   nor of the Western continent alone . . .
> With thee time voyages in trust, the antecedent
>   nations sink or swim with thee,
> Theirs, theirs as much as thine, the
>   destination port triumphant.[5]

The third great epoch in American history was beginning. America had been built on the "moral law" (1587–1729) and on individual freedom (1729–1871). She was next to be given an opportunity to demonstrate her possibilities of world leadership. As in the preceding cycles, the first period proved to be one of "preparation" (1871–1918)—America was built as a democratic industrial world power. The second period (1918–67) was a tremendous world revolutionary age again—a new political age in which the dignity of every person in the world seemed ultimately at stake. And, hopefully, America and the world were moving to build a new and more peaceful world order after 1967, made more certain by the apparent ending of the "cold war" between the Soviet Union and the West (1987–91).

This chapter will examine the time of preparation for America's world role—1871–1918. The period had its own special challenges to American democracy. Industrialism raised new problems for a government founded in an agricultural age; new horizons of science brought into question beliefs long unchallenged; and the wounds of the Civil War were yet to be healed before a united nation could be re-established. Industrialism would provide the spur for another wave of American expansionism—this time far outside the continental boundaries. The industrial revolution would make America into a powerful productive machine, uniting the nation—east and west, north and south—with bands of steel and copper, and stimulating the search for access to the new markets and materials of the world. By 1914, America had become a world power, in which the spirit of democracy had developed new progressive forces which brought business and industry under regulation for the common welfare. By 1918, this America had tipped the scales of the European balance of power, and shown the world the power and spirit of a free people at a time when the dreams of Marx and Lenin were being applied to the despairing people of Russia.

Preparation for World Involvement: Introversion, 1871–91

America was again ready for a dominant mood of "introversion," following a quarter of a century in which the continent had been rounded out, national unity had been restored in a bitter military struggle, and American possessions were reaching far into the Pacific. Carl Fish refers to the period from 1872 to 1898 as "the nadir of diplomacy."[6] More logically, perhaps, T. A. Bailey uses the same term to cover the period from 1877 to 1889.[7]

Foreign Relations, 1871–91

Hamilton Fish, President Grant's Secretary of State (1869–77), worked to settle disputes with Spain peacefully, as in the *Virginius* case in 1873, when the Spanish executed 53 "pirates," including some Americans during the rebellion in Cuba (1868–78). Allan Nevins, in his biography of Fish, writes: "Had the event occurred twenty years earlier, when the Southern slave-barons were in power, Cuba would have been immediately conquered."[8] After 1873, Congress began reducing military and naval expenditures steadily. Similarly, in 1876, Congress reduced the appropriations for foreign affairs so much that a number of legations and consulates had to be closed. President Rutherford B. Hayes called Congress into special session on October 15, 1877, since the regular session had adjourned without making any appropriations for the army.[9] The United States was listed as only twelfth in naval strength in the world in 1880. The major attention of Americans during this first decade (1871–81) was focused upon internal problems, industrial development, and the settlement of the West. Political and economic corruption reached a high point in the 1870s. Northern troops were withdrawn from the South in 1877.

A turning point toward greater emphasis upon "union" and cooperation was probably reached in 1881, stimulated by the tragic assassination of President James A. Garfield by a disappointed office-seeker on July 2. As in previous introvert periods, the phase of "union" was characterized by increasing strength and independence in foreign affairs. The navy reached its lowest point in expenditures in the (fiscal) year of 1880. The merchant marine, which had been the pride of America in the 1850s, had likewise almost dropped from the seas. But beginning in 1881, more attention was being given to the development of naval vessels. In 1883, Congress authorized the building of three steel cruisers. The Naval War College was established in 1884.[10] The first sea-going armor-clad vessel was constructed in 1887.[11] Annual naval expenditures reached $26 million in 1891 (fiscal year ending June 30), double the 1880 figure.

Under President Garfield (1881) and Chester Alan Arthur (1881–85), James G. Blaine, Secretary of State for 10 months, followed a more active foreign policy, as in mediation in the War of the Pacific, and trying to call a Pan-American Conference. A treaty was signed with Korea in 1880, recognizing its independence (ratified in 1883). The Hawaiian reciprocity treaty of 1875 was renewed in 1884, with an important additional clause giving the United States the exclusive right to a fortified naval base in Pearl Harbor. The United States was also interested in protecting trading rights during this introvert period, and sent delegates to the Berlin Conference on the Congo Territory in 1884, as well as to a conference in Morocco in 1880.

Grover Cleveland was elected in 1884 as the first Democratic President since the Civil War. One of his first acts was to withdraw from the Senate a treaty negotiated with Nicaragua in 1884, authorizing construction of a canal, railroad and telegraph line across the country. He also refused to submit to the Senate the treaty which American delegates had signed in the 1884 Berlin Conference, holding it to be "an alliance whose responsibility we are not in a position to assume."[12]

Republican Benjamin Harrison became President on March 4, 1889, with James G. Blaine as Secretary of State for the second time. Bailey uses the phrase "spirited diplomacy" to characterize this administration.[13] These were the years which appear to constitute the prelude to an extrovert phase.

Tension mounted among Britain, Germany and the United States over the future of the Samoan Islands, as a unilateral German occupation was feared, when a terrific hurricane wrecked or sank three American and three German warships there (March 16, 1889). The three powers worked out at Berlin a complicated tripartite condominium, with the independence and neutrality of the islands also pledged.[14]

Congress had authorized the calling of a Pan-American Conference in 1888, and Secretary Blaine was able to welcome the delegates in Washington, and preside as chairman in October 1889. Most notable was the establishment in Washington of a permanent secretariat for the International Union of American Republics (later called the Pan-American Union). Secretary Blaine took a strong stand in relation to the disputes with Britain over Canadian seal fishing in the Bering Sea—an arbitral tribunal settled the case in 1893. American delegates attended the Conference at Brussels in 1890, to devise means for suppressing the slave trade and liquor traffic in Africa. The revival of anti-Semitic laws in Russia and occasional pogroms, resulting in a large Jewish emigration, caused the United States to protest strongly in 1891. It was also during this year, 1891, that America took a firm stand in serious diplomatic incidents with Chile and Italy, so that this year may be regarded as the turning point toward extroversion.

Expectations of America's World Leadership

In the decade of the 1880s, the American mind was being prepared for another period of expansionism and wider concern with world affairs. John Fiske, American philosopher and historian, stressed the growing influence and power of the English-speaking peoples in lectures first given in Boston in 1879, in London in 1880, and then all over the United States.[15] Bismarck, Chancellor of Germany from 1871 to 1890, regarded the common language of Britain and America as the most important fact for the world's political future. Fiske saw that English might ultimately become the language of mankind. His goal was world order and peace and prosperity, with power necessary for peace at the stage of civilization then:

> . . . A general diminution of warfare is rendered possible only by the union of small political groups into larger groups that are kept together by community of interests, and that can adjust their mutual relations by legal discussion without coming to blows. . . .
>
> . . . In order that the pacific community may be able to go on doing its work, it must be strong and warlike enough to overcome its barbaric neighbors who have no notion whatever of keeping peace. This is another of the seeming paradoxes of the history of civilization, that for a very long time the possibility of peace can be guaranteed only through war. Obviously the permanent peace of the world can be secured only through the gradual concentration of the preponderant military strength into the hands of the most pacific communities.[16]

Federation would be the means, Fiske wrote, of bringing peace to larger and larger areas. He saw European federation in response to relative European weakness, with the United States becoming so strong. Fiske concluded his lecture on "Manifest Destiny" with a vision of world peace and ultimate world federation:

> Indeed, only when such a state of things has begun to be realized, can Civilization, as sharply demarcated from Barbarism, be said to have fairly begun. Only then can the world be said to be become truly Christian. Many ages of toil and doubt and perplexity will no doubt pass by before such a desideratum is reached. Meanwhile it is pleasant to feel that the dispassionate contemplation of great masses of historical facts goes far towards confirming our faith in this ultimate triumph of good over evil.[17]

Thousands of Christians in America were electrified by the message of Josiah Strong's book, published in 1885: *Our Country, Its Possible Future and Its Present Crisis*. Rev. Strong was the General Secretary of the Evangelical Alliance for the United States, and appealed strongly for the speedy "Christianization" of the American West, so that America could fulfill her Providential destiny in world affairs. Strong felt that a new age was dawning for the world:

> Many are not aware that we are living in extraordinary times. Few suppose that these years of peaceful prosperity, in which we are quietly developing a continent, are the pivot on which is turning the nation's future. And fewer still imagine that the destinies of mankind, for

centuries to come, can be seriously affected, much less determined, by the men of this generation in the United States. But no generation appreciates its own place in history.[18]

Like many of his generation, Strong saw the Anglo-Saxon playing the key role in the world's future as the chief representative of two great ideas—civil liberty and a pure *spiritual* Christianity.[19] It may be true, as Gabriel suggests, that Strong "spoke for what was, in world outlook, a smug and self-righteous generation."[20] Yet perhaps some dramatic concept of world mission, such as Strong's, was vital in helping prepare the nation for the world role which was to come. Strong had a vision of the future in which a Christian America would lead toward a better world—if America would become predominantly Christian in all its parts.[21] He ends his book with an appeal for action—for faith and sacrifice:

> And our plea is not America for America's sake, but America for the world's sake. For, if this generation is faithful to its trust, America is to become God's right arm in his battle with the world's ignorance and oppression and sin. . . .[22]

One of the most notable writers in paving the way for America's future world influence was Captain Alfred Thayer Mahan, friend of Theodore Roosevelt and Henry Cabot Lodge. His first book, in 1890, was a detailed study of the decisive role of sea power in affecting the world influence of the western European nations from 1660 to 1783. Mahan described the role of sea power in a possible war, and the value of a larger merchant marine:

> The eyes of the country have for a quarter of a century been turned from the sea. . . . It may safely be said that it is essential to the welfare of the whole country that the conditions of trade and commerce should remain, as far as possible, unaffected by an external war. In order to do this, the enemy must be kept not only out of our ports, but far away from our coasts. [23]

To help rouse the people from their naval lethargy, Mahan wrote an article, "The United States Looking Outward," for the *Atlantic Monthly* (December 1890). He stressed the changing attitude which he detected, in the light of America's business enterprise and growing productive capacity:

The interesting and significant feature of this changing attitude is the turning of the eyes outward, instead of inward only, to seek the welfare of the country. To affirm the importance of distant markets, and the relation of them to our own immense powers of production, implies logically the recognition of the link that joins the products and the markets,—that is, the carrying trade. . . . We shall not follow far this line of thought before there will dawn the realization of America's unique position, facing the older worlds of the East and West, her shores washed by the oceans which touch the one or the other, but which are common to her alone.[24]

Mahan concluded his article by pointing to the desirability and possibility of close cooperation with Britain as America became involved in world affairs:

. . . While Great Britain is undoubtedly the most formidable of our possible enemies . . . it must be added that a cordial understanding with that country is one of the first of our external interests. Both nations doubtless, and properly, seek their own advantage; but both, also, are controlled by a sense of law and justice, drawn from the same sources, and deep-rooted in their instincts. Whatever temporary aberration may occur, a return to mutual standards of right will certainly follow. Formal alliance between the two is out of the question, but a cordial recognition of the similarity of character and ideas will give birth to sympathy, which in turn will facilitate a co-operation beneficial to both; for if sentimentality is weak, sentiment is strong.[25]

Theodore Roosevelt met Mahan in 1887, and was soon to be one of his ardent disciples in the field of political action on the world stage. Roosevelt came to Washington in 1889 as a member of the Civil Service Commission. Woodrow Wilson was a young professor of history and political science at Wesleyan University in 1889, when he expressed his faith in America and its ideals, speaking at a celebration of the hundredth anniversary of the first inauguration of George Washington:

We are here only to renew our vows at the altar of Liberty. . . . The tasks of the future are not to be less but greater than the tasks of the past: it is our part to improve even the giant breed of which we came—to return to the high-statured ages: to weld our people together in a patriotism as pure, a wisdom as elevated, a virtue as sound as those of the greater generation whom to-day we hold in special and grateful remembrance. . . .[26]

Rationalism, 1871–91

The period which saw the rise of America as a democratic industrialized world power was dominated by intellectual and economic forces which inaugurated an era of increasing secularism like the "enlightenment" of the 18th century. Industrialization and the new horizons in science brought into question beliefs which had long gone unchallenged. For many, the old religious outlook seemed much too narrow.

European thought was influential among Americans during this time of increased travel and communication; many young Americans studied abroad, particularly at the noted German universities. Professor Carlton J. H. Hayes has expressed what he regarded as the dominant theme in Europe during the period from 1871 to 1900 in the title of his historical essay on *A Generation of Materialism*, where he perceived "a nemesis lurking in the era of 1871. . . ."[27] The time was one of growing "realistic rationalism," yet the ethical ideals of the previous period had a continuing momentum, at least in theory. But many Christian beliefs were subject to attack on every front, on a scale never witnessed since the formation of the Christian Church.[28]

People were dreaming of steady progress toward perfection, as they did in the middle of the 18th century, through education and science and reason. Material problems came to occupy the center of attention. After the Civil War in America, the acquisition of property and wealth became the touchstone of success.

Yet Christianity and Judaism in America continued to show real vitality. American churches engaged in a great deal of foreign missionary activity after 1871, when many areas of Africa and Asia were being opened up to Western influence (Stanley "found" Livingstone in 1871). One new American denomination was established at this time—Christian Science, particularly appropriate, perhaps, in an age of science. Mary Baker Eddy "discovered" its principles in 1866, published *Science and Health* in 1875, organized the Christian Science Association in 1876, and established the Church of Christ, Scientist, in 1879. Probably the most significant development in American religion was the rise of the "social gospel"—the application of Christian principles to the social order. Rev. Washington Gladden is often credited with starting the movement, with his book entitled *Being A*

Christian," in 1876. So-called institutional churches were started by 1883, aiming at helping people living in city neighborhoods to solve their problems.

But the basic trend of the new "enlightenment" was rationalistic, rather than idealistic or spiritual, with particular faith in material progress. Science began replacing religion and philosophy for many intellectual pioneers.

A New World Power: Extroversion, 1891–1918

The Spanish-American War of 1898 is commonly regarded as the turning point in the development of America as a world power. Although 1898 is a key year, nevertheless the new extrovert mood was clearly evident in 1895, and was somewhat prominent as early as 1891. A rising sense of world responsibility for Americans was evident after 1905.

The New Imperialism, 1891–1904

The rising industrialism, it is often said, needed markets and raw materials abroad, coaling stations, and secure trade routes on the oceans—perhaps even colonies. The European powers were staking out their claims in Asia and Africa, setting a possible example for the United States, even though anti-imperialism had been a powerful force in America as compared to Europe.

The occasion in which the nation demonstrated the new extrovert attitude was precipitated by the civil war which had erupted in January 1891 in Chile. Before the affair had ended, the two countries were on the verge of war. An American cruiser chased a Chilean ship all the way from California to Chile, and seized it. But the Chilean rebels won by August. In October, Chilean groups attacked American sailors, killing 2 and wounding 17; 36 sailors were arrested. American opinion was outraged; no expression of regret was received from the Chilean government. The Administration sent a sharp note of protest; war fever rose in the United States. The Chilean navy was superior to the American in some departments, and the vulnerable Pacific coast was near panic for a time. The Navy Department made energetic preparations for war.[29] The ultimatum, along with a change in the Chilean government in December, finally brought a conciliatory reply, and Chile paid a reparation of $75,000. President Harrison described his satisfaction in his last annual message, December 6, 1892, and stated his desire for friendship with all Latin America:

> I have endeavored in every way to assure our sister Republics of Central and South America that the United States Government and its people have only the most friendly disposition toward them all. We do not covet their territory. We have no disposition to be oppressive or exacting in our dealings with any of them, even the weakest.[30]

A second diplomatic incident occurred in 1891, with Italy—and this too occasioned some war talk. In this case, the United States bore some major responsibility for the initial trouble. With members of the Mafia Black Hand Society (made up mostly of Italian subjects) accused of murdering the chief of police in New Orleans in 1890, a mob of several thousand Americans lynched 11 Italian subjects on March 14, 1891. The Italian Government protested strongly, demanding punishment for the offenders and an indemnity. Secretary of State Blaine insisted the national government was powerless to act in matters under local police jurisdiction. Italy withdrew its minister on March 31, and the United States called its minister home from Rome. There was some discussion in America of the possibility of war, with the Italian navy much larger than the American. The affair was suddenly ended by Secretary Blaine's note of April 12, 1892, admitting American responsibility for "the lamentable massacre at New Orleans" and offering to pay a sum of $25,000 for the families. His hope of the restoration of friendly relations was reciprocated by the Italian Government, in accepting the indemnity and restoring full diplomatic relations.[31] Both the Chilean and Italian incidents reminded Americans of their relatively weak navy, and helped stimulate Congress to raise the naval appropriations.

A third major event of Harrison's last two years was the near annexation of the Hawaiian Islands. The phrase "manifest destiny" reappeared in the Republican platform of 1892.[32] The Democratic platform denounced the Republican policies as creating the danger of hostility and war.[33] Grover Cleveland was again elected President in November 1892, although the combined Republican and Populist vote was considerably larger. But Harrison still had four months in office. John L. Stevens, minister to Hawaii, favored annexation. Queen Liliuokalani suddenly revoked the liberal constitution of 1887, and issued a new autocratic constitution on January 14, 1893. A revolutionary pro-American committee was ready for action, apparently assured of the help of the American Minister, who ordered marines landed on January 16 and recognized the revolutionary regime the next day. The new Secretary of State, John W. Foster, negotiated a treaty of annexation with Hawaiian commissioners, signed it on February 14, and transmitted it to the Senate on February 15. But the Senate failed to act before the 52nd Congress ended on March 4.

This sudden proposed annexation of overseas territory offended the anti-expansionist President Cleveland, who took office on March 4. On March 9, he withdrew the annexation treaty from the Senate, sent a special representative to Hawaii who investigated and had the American flag over Hawaii hauled down. In the meantime, Republicans denounced Cleveland's action. Captain Mahan wrote an article in March 1893, stressing the need for Hawaii as a base for an enlarged American navy. Theodore Roosevelt expressed his philosophy in a letter in April as follows:

> I . . . feel very strong about . . . Hawaii. . . . I am a bit of a believer in the manifest destiny doctrine. . . . I don't want to see our flag hauled down where it has been hauled up. . . .
>
> It was a crime against the United States, it was a crime against white civilization, not to annex it.[34]

President Cleveland sent a special message to Congress on December 18, 1893, denouncing the part played by the preceding administration in the annexation.[35] Cleveland's action was another example of American idealism, but the Provisional Government in Hawaii refused to surrender power. It became clear that only American force could restore the Queen. On July 4, 1894, the Republic of Hawaii was formally proclaimed, and President Cleveland recognized it on August 7, while the government of Hawaii continued to seek annexation.

President Cleveland, in spite of his anti-imperialist views, felt impelled to follow a rather strong foreign policy, seeking justice. He pressed China in 1893 to pay reparation for the murder of Swedish missionaries.[36] Secretary of State Walter Gresham played an active role in the Sino-Japanese War of 1894–95, in seeking assurances from Japan concerning the independence of Korea (acting under the American-Korean treaty of 1882), in tendering American good offices to both sides to help end the conflict, and in helping induce Japan to make an early peace.[37] Marines were landed in China and Korea in 1894, for the protection of Americans.

During a civil war in Nicaragua in 1894, Cleveland sent a warship there and reported that "our naval commanders at the scene of these disturbances by their consistent exhibition of firmness and good judgment contributed largely to the prevention of more serious consequences and to the restoration of quiet and order."[38] Cleveland's role in the Brazilian civil war (1893–95) demonstrated special firmness. A major crisis had been created by a revolution led by monarchists, who secured control of the Brazilian navy in September 1893. An American cruiser fired on a rebel vessel, which was attacking a merchant ship. The firm American position helped end the naval revolt and the monarchist uprising. Bemis testifies as to the significance of this event in Brazilian-American relations: "The policy of the United States at that decisive hour of trial was an earnest to Brazil of the real feelings of the American people and laid the foundations for a persistent cordiality between the two republics ever since."[39] President Cleveland, in his first message to Congress, December 4, 1893, recognized America's special international obligations, a new American dignity in diplomacy, and the growing naval strength of the nation:

> Since the passage of the act of March 3, 1893, authorizing the President to raise the grade of our envoys to correspond with the rank in which foreign countries accredit their agents here, Great Britain, France, Italy, and Germany have conferred upon their representatives at this capital the title of ambassador, and I have responded by accrediting the agents of the United States in those countries with the same title. A like elevation of mission is announced by Russia, and when made will be similarly met. This step fittingly comports with the position the United States holds in the family of nations.[40]

Cleveland noted then that four first-class battleships would be completed by February 1, 1896, and in 1894 he called on Congress to provide for more battleships and torpedo boats.

A turning point in America's development as a world power was reached in 1895, when President Cleveland, noted for his concepts of international justice and fairness, electrified the nation with his strong stand against Britain in the boundary dispute between Venezuela and British Guiana. Cleveland's sense of justice had been offended by the refusal of Britain to arbitrate the dispute. He had shown his firmness at home in a crisis by calling out federal troops in the Pullman strike of 1894 (June 21–July 20). Richard Olney, the strong-minded Attorney-

General, became Secretary of State on June 8, 1895, and sent a sharp note to Britain on July 20. Britain's position was squarely challenged as an affront to the role of the United States as the power capable of defending justice in the Americas and as a direct violation of the Monroe Doctrine. The blunt dispatch called on Britain for a definite decision as to arbitration of the dispute with Venezuela.[41] When Congress convened on December 2, 1895, to hear the President's message, no reply from England had yet been received. Tension had mounted in the United States, as the British position appeared to be a studied insult. The reply from Britain (dated November 26) turned out to be a flat refusal to arbitrate. President Cleveland decided to accept the challenge to the American position, and to follow through. He closed his message to Congress on December 17, 1895, by asking Congress to move directly toward the settlement of the boundary dispute, with the United States prepared to defend the settlement.[42]

Cleveland realized the seriousness of this virtual ultimatum to Great Britain, and that war was a possible result, even though he entertained high hopes of a peaceful result when Britain became aware of the determination of the American nation:

> In making these recommendations I am fully alive to the responsibility incurred and keenly realize all the consequences that may follow.
>
> I am, nevertheless, firm in my conviction that while it is a grievous thing to contemplate the two great English-speaking peoples of the world as being otherwise than friendly competitors in the onward march of civilization and strenuous and worthy rivals in all the arts of peace, there is no calamity which a great nation can invite which equals that which follows a supine submission to wrong and injustice and the consequent loss of national self-respect and honor, beneath which are shielded and defended a people's safety and greatness.[43]

Congress unanimously appropriated the money for the expenses of a boundary commission. War fever swept over the country. Theodore Roosevelt was typical of those who were prepared to fight. He wrote to Henry Cabot Lodge on December 20, 1895: "Let the fight come if it must; I don't care whether our sea coast cities are bombarded or not; we would take Canada."[44] But American forces for peace began to make themselves heard, particularly the financial interests, church leaders, and certain academic circles. Roosevelt was deeply perturbed by the peace talk, when he wrote to Lodge on December 27:

> Our peace at any price men, if they only knew it . . . are rendering
> war likely, because they will encourage England to persist; in the long
> run this means a fight. Personally I rather hope the fight will come
> soon. The clamor of the peace faction has convinced me that this
> country needs a war.[45]

Two major factors brought a peaceful issue to the matter, by inducing
the British to "back down" and submit the boundary dispute to
arbitration: (1) the strong British desire not to fight America over a
boundary dispute in South America; and (2) British resentment against
Germany when the Kaiser congratulated the South African Republic on
the Boer success against Britain on January 3, 1896. (The arbitral
tribunal, on October 3, 1899, gave most of the disputed territory to
Britain.)

The paradoxical result of the Venezuelan crisis was the sudden
strengthening of British-American friendship. Statesmen of both sides
seemed to become aware of the need for friendship and the possibility
of close cooperation in a world growing more dangerous. The United
States was now recognized as a Great Power, and felt herself to be
such. Her friendship would be worth cultivating. Britain proved to be
America's only friend among the powers during the Spanish-American
War, and the two cooperated in the developing crisis over the future of
China. Two future Presidents publicly approved Cleveland's strong
stand in the Venezuelan crisis: Theodore Roosevelt and Woodrow
Wilson.

The Cuban Revolution against Spain, beginning in 1895, continued
while America was beginning to feel a new sense of international power
and responsibility. Cuba was the most important colony still existing in
the Americas, and Americans were much disturbed by what was
regarded as Spanish misrule and the attempted ruthless suppression of
the uprising. Tension in America mounted rapidly, particularly when
General ("Butcher") Weyler began the establishment of "concentration
camps" after February 10, 1896. The Republican Party, which emerged
victorious in the election, devoted nearly half of its platform to foreign
relations, with a vigorous, expansionist tone, suggesting the possibility
of ultimate American intervention in the Cuban struggle, if it continued
much longer.[46] Cleveland offered the "good offices" of the United
States in vain to help promote peace on the basis of home rule for Cuba
(December 1896). McKinley apparently felt the necessity of urging
some moderation upon the American people in relation to Cuba in his

Inaugural Address, March 4, 1897, and continued to appeal for moderation and patience in his first annual message, December 6, 1897, while referring to the possible necessity of forceful action, if peaceful conditions were not restored.[47]

Theodore Roosevelt, who had been appointed Assistant Secretary of the Navy, was particularly important during this period in helping get the Navy ready for possible war. An apparent shift in Spanish policy came too late to change the growing tide of sentiment in America for forcible intervention to free Cuba. Humanitarian groups and newspaper sensationalism kept feeding the desire for action. Several events early in 1898 brought the tension in America to a high point: the publication on February 9 of a confidential letter from the Spanish Minister, belittling President McKinley and revealing a degree of bad faith on the Minister's part; above all, the tragic and sensational sinking of the American warship *Maine* in Havana harbor on February 15, with the loss of 260 men (the *Maine* had arrived on January 15 on a "courtesy call," following rioting in Havana in January); and Senator Proctor's report of the appalling conditions in Cuba, as observed on a private trip of inspection. Although the responsibility for the explosion which sank the *Maine* has never been placed, most Americans naturally tended to blame the Spanish for it.

The mood of the American people and Congress was virtually forcing the President to call for strong action. Early in April, he decided to ask Congress for authority to use the military forces of the United States to end the hostilities in Cuba. He requested Congress for authority to help establish a stable government in Cuba and to distribute food and supplies to the starving people there[48] Congress hammered through a series of resolutions giving the President the authority he wished, and stressing that "the people of Cuba are, and of right ought to be free and independent." The Teller Amendment was adopted without a dissenting vote: "The United States hereby disclaims any disposition or intention to exercise sovereignty, jurisdiction, or control over said Island except for the pacification thereof, and asserts its determination, when that is accomplished, to leave the government and control of the Island to its people." The war resolutions were approved by the Senate 67 to 21 (although the final vote was 42 to 35 because of House changes) and by the House 311 to 6, on April 19.[49] Spain broke off diplomatic relations on April 21, and declared war on April 24. Congress declared war on Spain on April 25, making it retroactive to April 21.

The war was brought to a quick conclusion by the clear-cut victories of the American Navy. Most astonishing and exhilarating to the American people was Admiral George Dewey's decisive victory at Manila in the Philippines on May 1: the Spanish ships were all lost or disabled and 381 men killed; no American ships were seriously damaged, and the American casualties were eight wounded. The President sent a special message to Congress on May 9, expressing the national sense of tremendous pride in this achievement.[50] The Spanish fleet in the Caribbean was destroyed on July 3, Santiago surrendered on July 13, and an armistice was agreed to on August 12. Peace negotiations were opened in Paris on October 1. By the Treaty of Paris, signed on December 10, 1898, Spain relinquished "sovereignty over and title to" Cuba, and ceded Puerto Rico, Guam, and the Philippines to the United States. The United States agreed to pay Spain $20,000,000 for public works and improvements in the Philippines. President McKinley had made the decision to ask for the Philippines only after long and prayerful consideration convinced him that it was the obligation of the United States to help the Filipinos.[51] Other factors which influenced the Administration seemed to have been the desire to end Spanish rule there, the belief that the islands were not ready for independence, the fear that Japan or Germany would secure them, and the value of a secure commercial base in the developing Far East. If the Senate would approve the Treaty, and if the people would support the Republican Party in the election of 1900, the United States would clearly be launched upon its career as a great world power.

The brief Spanish-American War had electrified the American people. Archibald Coolidge wrote in 1908 that "suddenly, and without warning, the whole situation changed, and the country found itself engaged in a foreign war, and presently, without preparation or design, launched on a career of conquest and expansion."[52] Americans launched into a "great debate" over their future policy. On February 4, 1899, a revolt broke out in the Philippines, aiming at independence. Two days later, the Senate approved the treaty with Spain by a vote of 57 to 27 (with only 2 votes more than the necessary two-thirds). The Senate then rejected a resolution promising ultimate independence to the Philippines, when Vice President Hobart broke a tie with a negative vote. The decision was thus made to make sure that the Philippines were secured (not until 1902 was the revolt crushed) before the problem of independence was again discussed.

In the debate over America's future foreign policy, the predominant opinion favored pressing toward the wider influence which was opening up. There was a strong economic impetus in this direction, and the newly felt pride of power was subtly tempting; but withal there was a strong undercurrent of the idealism which had distinguished American development. These ideals sometimes promoted the idea of expansion, but at other times they stood as warnings against the extremes of patriotic pride and imperial power.

Could America rule other peoples without surrendering its own ideals? Many influential leaders of opinion did not believe it would be possible. David Starr Jordan, President of Stanford University, urged the withdrawal of the American fleet from the Philippines, speaking on the day after Dewey's great victory. If we held the Philippines, he felt that "we should be committing the folly and crime which has always lain at the foundation of empire, and which is the cause of its ultimate disintegration everywhere."[53] The Anti-Imperialist League included such well-known men as Senator George F. Hoar of Massachusetts, Carl Schurz, Andrew Carnegie and Felix Adler. The debate in the Senate revealed a powerful sentiment looking forward to the time of full self-government for the Philippines.

Some Americans warned against the dangers of entering an arms race with the imperial powers—with its threats of war and dictatorship. Carl Schurz was one of these, speaking on "Militarism and Democracy" at the meeting of the American Academy of Political and Social Science, April 7, 1899.[54] But most of the speakers at the meeting welcomed the new world responsibilities that were devolving upon America, and looked forward to increased trade with China.[55] Frederick W. Williams (Yale University) dealt with a topic which was beginning to be widely discussed in circles concerned with international affairs: "The Real Menace of Russian Aggression" in Asia.[56]

The year 1900 was marked by the publication of several significant books discussing these problems, particularly those by Giddings, Reinsch, Mahan and Brooks Adams. Early in January, Senator Albert J. Beveridge had delivered an oration in the Senate on the destiny of America under Providence:

> And of all our race He has marked the American people as His chosen nation to finally lead in the regeneration of the world. This is the divine mission of America, and it holds for us all the profit, all the glory, all the happiness possible to man. We are the trustees of the world's progress, guardians of its righteous peace. The judgment of the

Master is upon us: "Ye have been faithful over a few things; I will make you ruler of many things. . . . "[57]

Franklin Henry Giddings, Professor of Sociology at Columbia University, wrote the preface for his book, *Democracy and Empire*, in January 1900:

> . . . I became convinced . . . that the future of civilization will depend largely, and perhaps chiefly, upon the predominant influence of either the English-speaking people of the world or of the Russian Empire, according as one or the other of these two gigantic powers wins the advantage in the international struggle for existence. At the same time, I remained convinced that the democratic tendencies of the nineteenth century are not likely to be checked or thwarted in our own or future generations.[58]

The United States, Giddings believed, would have to do its share in the attempt "to bring tropical regions under efficient government and a sound industrial organization, which is the only ultimate possibility to be thought of by humane and far-seeing men." The goal was world "democratic empire."[59]

Paul S. Reinsch, Professor of Political Science at the University of Wisconsin, saw the United States entering the world scene as one of the great powers, and as one which would need to live up to its professed ideals.[60] He was one of the few writers who seemed to look forward to the possibility of friendly relations with Russia, as American ideals were applied to the cause of free men.[61] Admiral Mahan's new book in 1900 stressed the common interest of the United States in Asia with Great Britain in particular, but also with Germany and Japan, as Russian power pressed upon China. American influence in China was for the good, he felt, in helping keep it open to European and American processes of life and thought.[62] Brooks Adams, in his book entitled *America's Economic Supremacy*, saw Britain and America necessarily standing together, with the Philippines constituting America's base in the Pacific.[63] The economic center of the world was crossing the Atlantic from England to America, according to Adams, and America would have to bear the burden of leadership.[64] Adams foresaw either social revolution in Russia or great pressure for expansion, and stressed the importance of helping guide the development of China.[65]

All walks of life in America were struck by the country's new opportunities and responsibilities. In 1901, Lyman Abbott, an outstanding clergyman and editor, in his book entitled *The Rights of Man*, expressed his confidence that America could and would retain its idealism in its new world role.[66] He believed that America's new position was inescapable, under its Providential destiny.[67] In working toward American goals, Abbott felt that the Philippines would give the United States an opportunity to test its ideals, for its work would be to develop in a people the power of self-government.[68] The new president of Princeton University, Woodrow Wilson, during his first year in the new post (1902), wrote an article for the *Atlantic Monthly* entitled "The Ideals of America":

> It is by the widening of vision that nations, as men, grow and are made great. We need not fear the expanding scene. It was plain destiny that we should come to this, and if we have kept our ideals clear, unmarred, commanding through the great century and the moving scenes that made us a nation, we may keep them also through the century that shall see us as a great power in the world. Let us put our leading characters at the front; let us pray that vision may come with power; let us ponder our duties like men of conscience and temper our ambitions like men who seek to serve, not to subdue, the world; let us lift our thoughts to the level of the great tasks that await us, and bring a great age in with the coming of our day of strength.[69]

America was indeed "looking outward" in 1898 and afterwards, with important annexations: the Hawaiian Islands in 1898; the Philippines, Guam and Puerto Rico (with ratification of the treaty with Spain on February 6, 1899); Wake Island (previously unoccupied); and the Samoan Islands (divided with Germany, December 2, 1899). Also in 1899, Secretary of State John Hay secured the support of the powers for his first "open door" note (keeping the door open for trade in China, then threatened with partition), and the United States played an important role in the First Hague Peace Conference (with its establishment of the Permanent Court of International Arbitration).

When the Boxer Rebellion of 1900 brought a great anti-foreign onslaught in China, American marines participated in the international expedition which relieved the besieged diplomats and foreign citizens in Peking on August 14. Secretary Hay expressed America's policy toward China in his second note (approved in general by the other powers for themselves): "The policy of the Government of the United

States is to seek a solution which may bring about permanent safety and peace to China, preserve Chinese territorial and administrative entity, protect all rights guaranteed to foreign powers by treaty and international law, and safeguard for the world the principle of equal and impartial trade with all parts of the Chinese Empire. . . ."[70]

The major issue of the 1900 Presidential campaign was "imperialism." The Democratic platform denounced the war of "criminal aggression" against the Filipinos.[71] The Republican platform gloried in the achievements and results of the Spanish-American War.[72] President McKinley was re-elected, defeating William Jennings Bryan for the second time, 292 to 85 electoral votes. The assassination of McKinley on September 6, 1901, brought the dynamic Theodore Roosevelt, with his vision of strong American influence in world affairs, to the presidency. A major development in the foreign position of America was the conclusion (November 18) of the second Hay-Pauncefote Treaty, which abrogated the Clayton-Bulwer Treaty of 1850 with Britain, and gave the United States alone the right to construct and control an isthmian canal.

President Roosevelt's second annual message, December 2, 1902, acclaimed the end of the Philippine insurrection and emphasized America's significant world role:

> As a people we have played a large part in the world, as we are bent upon making our future even larger than the past. In particular, the events of the last four years have definitely decided that, for woe or for weal, our place must be great among the nations. We may either fail greatly or succeed greatly; but we can not avoid the endeavor from which either great failure or great success must come. Even if we would, we can not play a small part. If we should try, all that would follow would be that we should play a large part ignobly and shamefully.[73]

Before the President's next message to Congress, three major events illustrated America's positive international role: (1) strong pressure against Germany in a Venezuelan crisis (December 1902 to February 1903); (2) the threat of force in the Alaskan boundary dispute with Britain; and (3) support of the successful revolution in Panama and the American treaty with Panama for the lease in perpetuity of the Panama Canal zone (November 1903). In May 1904, Perdicaris, believed to be a naturalized American citizen, was kidnapped by a Moroccan chieftain,

Raisuli. The Republican National Convention, meeting in Chicago, was stirred and excited by the message which the President had Secretary Hay send—that the United States must have "Perdicaris alive or Raisuli dead"[74] (Perdicaris was released with ransom, later repaid by the Moroccan Government). The general popularity of Roosevelt's policies is suggested by the large popular majority he received in the election in November 1904 (7.6 million to 5.1 million, with 336 to 140 electoral votes), and in the increase of Republican strength in Congress.

In his fourth annual message (December 6, 1904), President Roosevelt emphasized his philosophy of positive action and force in behalf of just international relations.[75] In it he also stated what has come to be known as the Roosevelt Corollary to the Monroe Doctrine:

> . . . If a nation shows that it knows how to act with reasonable efficiency and decency in social and political matters, if it keeps order and pays its obligations, it need fear no interference from the United States. Chronic wrongdoing, or an impotence which results in a general loosening of the ties of civilized society, may in America, as elsewhere, ultimately require intervention by some civilized nation, and in the Western Hemisphere the adherence of the United States to the Monroe Doctrine may force the United States, however reluctantly, in flagrant cases of such wrongdoing or impotence, to the exercise of an international police power.[76]

When the Dominican Government could see no other way to handle its debts, it signed a protocol with the American Minister, on February 4, 1905, giving the United States charge of its customs houses and financial administration, as well as the authority to guarantee the territorial integrity of the Dominican Republic. Economic conditions in the island steadily improved, bringing American withdrawal in 1907. A precedent had been laid for similar actions later in other unstable countries of the Caribbean.

It may be noted that the spirit of "liberty" dominated the first part of this extrovert period (1891–1904). It was a time of economic struggle and discontent. President McKinley was assassinated by an anarchist in 1901. In 1902 there was a major coal strike, in which popular and Presidential sympathies lay with the miners. The "Muckrakers" began to expose economic and political evils on a broad scale in 1903 and after.

America's Rising Sense of World Responsibility:
Extroversion-Union, 1905–14

America's "imperialistic" tendencies appeared to be diminishing by 1905. After Roosevelt's inauguration in March, world peace, a stable balance of power and international cooperation were stressed. This shift in foreign policy coincided roughly with the new emphasis in the country on "union"—on duties, cooperation and promotion of the general welfare.

The three Presidents of this period emphasized three different aspects of America's techniques of world influence: Theodore Roosevelt, the role of military force and the importance of a world balance of power in the maintenance of peace; William Howard Taft, the role of capital, investment and trade—"dollar diplomacy"; and Woodrow Wilson, the role of ideals and just principles—the power of world opinion. With each aspect vital, America secured special experience in applying them in turn, until the day would come when all were stressed simultaneously (as in World War I).

American ties with the rest of the world were steadily increasing through immigration and trade. The chief source of immigration at this time, well over a million a year, was from central, eastern and southern Europe. America's nationality base was being significantly broadened, especially after adding the Asians (in Hawaii and the Philippines) and Latin Americans (in Puerto Rico).

In his Inaugural Address of March 4, 1905, President Roosevelt emphasized his concept of America using its new-found strength with a special sense of duty and responsibility in world affairs:

> Much has been given us, and much will rightfully be expected from us. We have duties to others and duties to ourselves; and we can shirk neither. . . . We wish peace, but because we think it is right and not because we are afraid. No weak nation that acts manfully and justly should ever have cause to fear us, and no strong power should ever be able to single us out as a subject for insolent aggression.[77]

The new attitude of America in international affairs was emphasized in the meeting of the American Academy of Political and Social Science at Philadelphia, April 7–8, 1905, on "The United States as a World Power." The Honorable Seth Low of New York City delivered the "annual address" on "The Position of the United States Among the

Nations," and set the idealistic theme of the conference:

> The influence and power of a nation . . . depend, not so much upon
> its population and resources, as upon the character, the capacity, and,
> especially, the ideals of its people.
>
> . . . [America's] presence in the Philippines is almost certain to
> make for international peace in the Far East, because it throws actively
> into the scale as a factor making for peace there, on the basis of justice,
> the great moral force of the United States. The United States opened
> Japan to intercourse with the western world by peaceful negotiation. It
> has stood like a rock, during recent troubles, for the integrity of China;
> for its neutrality during the present war between Japan and Russia; and
> for the "open door" in China for the commerce of all nations. . . .
>
> . . . No one begins to understand America who does not appreciate
> its earnestness and its idealism. The old Puritan doctrine may have been
> modified, but the Puritan spirit remains. . . . It is a spirit to which men
> are of more moment than things; before which there shines always the
> ideals of a nation built upon righteousness; of a nation whose aim in the
> world is to stand for justice and liberty, at home and abroad. . . . Such
> a country as a world power may make mistakes, but its influence at
> large can not but be elevating; and the more so because its policies
> represent the free action of the largest body of free men on the face of
> the globe. . . .[78]

In a more realistic vein, perhaps, John Hays Hammond of New York
City predicted a period of bitter commercial and naval rivalry between
the United States and Japan.[79]

Theodore Roosevelt's emphasis on the "balance of power" and
peace was shown in his mediation in the Russo-Japanese War
(1904–05), for which he received the Nobel Peace Prize in 1906, and
in his influence in bringing France and Germany to the Algeciras
Conference to settle the future of Morocco (1905–06). An American
effort to improve relations with China was made in the important
decision of January 1907 to remit a portion of the Chinese Boxer
Indemnity to a special fund for the education of Chinese students in the
United States. After the San Francisco decision in October 1906 to
segregate Oriental children in separate schools, the President was able
to work out a compromise through a "Gentleman's Agreement" with
Japan, February 24, 1907 (the school board then withdrew its order).
Partly to keep the Japanese from feeling that his concessions were due
to American weakness, the President sent the battle fleet on a famous

world cruise (December 16, 1907, to February 22, 1909). American delegates played a prominent role in the Second Hague Peace Conference in 1907, where important conventions on the international law of war and of neutrality were adopted; they worked in vain, however, for a favorite dream of Secretary of State Elihu Root, to establish a permanent court of international justice (this was not to become a reality until after World War I). Secretary Root was able to negotiate arbitration treaties with 25 nations, after the 1907 conference.

Under William Howard Taft's presidency (1909–13), the expansion of the world's peaceful pursuits seemed to be the main goal of America. The major task was to build American prosperity and influence through the expansion of international trade and investment, encouraged and protected by the United States Government. President Taft explained, December 7, 1909, that this policy would bring peoples and governments closer together and so form bonds of peace and mutual dependency.[80] Two disputes were settled in 1910 by the Permanent Court of International Arbitration—one with Britain over the important North Atlantic fisheries, and one with Venezuela. Congress authorized the President to appoint a commission of five members to consider plans for an international police force, made up of the navies of the world.[81] The fourth Pan-American Conference met in 1910, and a new building was constructed in Washington for the organization. Loan arrangements for China were nearing completion in 1911 (in cooperation with French, British and German interests), and a new and important commercial treaty was concluded with Japan. After a revolt in Nicaragua, American marines were landed on August 14, 1912, at the request of the Nicaraguan government, to supervise financial arrangements—a small detachment of marines remained until 1925. The Senate passed the "Lodge Corollary" (1912) of the Monroe Doctrine, 51 to 4, to show American opposition to the effort of a Japanese syndicate to secure a site in Mexico (where a revolution had begun in 1910).

Foreign issues were overshadowed in the campaign of 1912 by the progressive movement in domestic politics; the split of the Republicans between President Taft and Theodore Roosevelt's "Bull-Moose" party ensured the election of Woodrow Wilson in November 1912.

Woodrow Wilson was the first President to lead America into world affairs on a big scale. However, when he entered the presidency, he expected to be concerned mostly with domestic affairs, in terms of his concept of the "New Freedom." But external pressures caused him to play a major role in foreign policy, especially after the Great War began in Europe. Although the general age in Europe and America had stressed rationalism and imperialism, Wilson was motivated largely by the idealistic principles of the American democratic republic along with a sense of realism (in terms of willingness to use force).

He moved quickly in the direction of reversing the policy of so-called "dollar diplomacy," and although he stood theoretically against "intervention" as such, he was soon to find himself impelled by his democratic convictions to intervene in Mexico. In his first 17 months in the presidency, before the European war, Wilson laid down the general international principles which he would develop and apply during the war.

Wilson saw America as a servant of humanity. To a graduating class at the United States Naval Academy he expressed America's goal as he saw it:

> We are all of us in the world, as I understand it, to set forward the affairs of the whole world, though we play a special part in that great function.
> The idea of America is to serve humanity. . . .[82]

At the dedication of Congress Hall in Philadelphia, Wilson was inspired by the founders of the nation: ". . . looking east and west, north and south, let us remind ourselves that we are the custodians, in some degree, of the principles which have made men free and governments just."[83] His last major address before the Great War began was at Independence Hall on July 4, 1914: "My dream is that . . . America will come into the full light of day when all may know that she puts human rights above all other rights and that her flag is the flag not only of America but of humanity. . . ." He added: "If I did not believe that the moral judgment would be the last judgment, the final judgment, in the minds of men as well as at the tribunal of God, I could not believe in popular government."[84]

Wilson was concerned with democracy abroad and with peace. During the month before his inauguration, Mexico's democratically minded President, Francisco Madero, was murdered, and the reactionary regime of Victoriano Huerta took over. Here was an immediate challenge to the President's democratic concepts. As tension mounted and some American sailors were arrested for a time, Wilson asked Congress for authority to use force if necessary to secure respect for the American flag and nation:

> . . . Our feeling for the people of Mexico is one of deep and generous friendship, and everything that we have so far done or refrained from doing has proceeded from our desire to help them.
>
> . . . We seek to maintain the dignity and authority of the United States only because we wish always to keep our great influence unimpaired for the uses of liberty, both in the United States and wherever else it may be employed for the benefit of mankind.[85]

Vera Cruz was bombarded and captured on April 21, with a loss of 19 American lives, and a German munitions ship was seized. To prevent war, Wilson accepted the mediation offer of Argentina, Brazil and Chile. Huerta went into voluntary exile on July 15. Although Wilson's acts had been quite controversial, the President had clearly shown his desire to support democracy abroad, by force if necessary.

The American people were gratified when the United States became the first Great Power to recognize the new Republic of China (May 2, 1913). Secretary of State William Jennings Bryan was negotiating treaties of "conciliation" with many nations, and Wilson, on December 2, 1913, stressed the importance of these "cooling-off" treaties and the bright prospects for general peace in the world.[86]

Wilson demonstrated his opposition to the practice of continued Western colonialism by his attitude toward the Philippines and China. Governor-General Francis B. Harrison expressed Wilson's view on October 6, 1913:

> We regard ourselves as trustees acting not for the advantage of the United States but for the benefit of the people of the Philippine Islands. Every step we take will be taken with a view to the ultimate independence of the islands and as a preparation for that independence; and we hope to move toward that end as rapidly as the safety and the permanent interests of the islands will permit.[87]

Wilson signed the Jones Act on August 29, 1916, pledging to recognize the independence of the Philippines when a stable government was established. On March 18, 1913, he withdrew the support of the United States Government from the proposed six-power loan to China, believing it to be an infringement on the "administrative independence" of China.[88]

Wilson similarly demonstrated his support for international law and the faithful observance of treaties. As the time drew near in 1914 for the opening of the Panama Canal, Wilson saw a stain on the national honor and on America's moral principles in the legislation passed in 1912 exempting American coastwise shipping from paying any tolls, in violation of the Hay-Pauncefote Treaty with Great Britain (1901) providing that the canal was to be free and open to ships of all nations on equal terms. The President made a personal explanation to Congress on March 5, 1914, to urge the repeal of this legislation which gave American ships a special advantage:

> We consented to the treaty, its language we accepted . . . and we are too big, too powerful, too self-respecting a nation to interpret with a too strained or refined reading the words of our own promises just because we have power enough to give us leave to read them as we please. . . . We ought to reverse our action without raising the question whether we are right or wrong, and so once more deserve our reputation for generosity and the redemption of every obligation without quibble or hesitation.
>
> . . . I shall not know how to deal with other matters of even greater delicacy and nearer consequence if you do not grant it to me in ungrudging measure.[89]

The House repealed the 1912 legislation by a sizeable majority, but the Senate debated the question bitterly for three months before it finally supported the President on June 11, 1914, 50 to 35. The Panama Canal was opened on August 15, 1914, in accordance with the treaty terms.

American Ideals and Power during World War I, 1914–18

The American people were shocked by the outbreak of the war in Europe, July 28–August 4, 1914, and deeply disturbed by the German invasion, on August 4, of Belgium, whose neutralization had been pledged by the Great Powers in 1839. President Wilson issued a proclamation of neutrality on August 4. The development of his policies during this period stressed insistence on the international law of "freedom of the seas," hopes of American mediation to bring the war to an end, and later the goal of a world "league of nations" to help guarantee a just peace. On October 22, the Commission for Relief in Belgium was established, with Herbert Hoover as chairman.

Wilson's firm diplomacy forced Germany twice to end its submarine warfare in violation of recognized international law, after the sinking of the British *Lusitania* (with the loss of 1,200 lives, including

124 Americans), May 7, 1915, and the French *Sussex*, March 24, 1916. Col. Edward M. House was sent as his personal representative to Europe in February 1915 and after to explore the possibility of American mediation. On May 27, 1916, Wilson presented his ideas on world organization to the League to Enforce Peace, which had been founded in 1915:

> . . . The principle of public right must henceforth take precedence over the individual interests of particular nations, and . . . the nations of the world must in some way band themselves together to see that the right prevails as against any sort of selfish aggression. . . .
> . . . I am sure that I speak the mind and wish of the people of America when I say that the United States is willing to become a partner in any feasible association of nations formed to realize these objects and make them secure against violation.[90]

After his victory over Charles Evans Hughes in a very close election, Wilson felt a powerful mandate to make another strong effort to bring the war to an end, despite the unfavorable outlook. On December 18, 1916, he asked the belligerent powers for specific statements of their war aims. When the answers were vague and unsatisfying, the President decided to present his own principles for a peace settlement—one that would have to be, in his words, a "peace without victory" to be lasting (January 22, 1917):

> . . . So far as our participation in guarantees of future peace is concerned, . . . the treaties and agreements which bring it to an end must embody terms which will create a peace that is worth guaranteeing and preserving, a peace that will win the approval of mankind. . . .
> . . . First of all . . . it must be a peace without victory. . . . Victory would mean peace forced upon the loser, a victor's terms imposed upon the vanquished. It would be accepted in humiliation, under duress, at an intolerable sacrifice, and would leave a sting, a resentment, a bitter memory. . . . Only a peace between equals can last.[91]

The President's hopes for peace with Germany were dashed by the German decision on January 31, 1917, that German submarines would sink all ships in a specified zone. His hand was forced, at a time when he was pushing hard for peace and believed "that the aspirations of the Allies were as selfish as those of Germany."[92] Diplomatic relations were broken with Germany on February 3, and, when American ships were attacked, March 12 and 19, the President called Congress into special session for April 2. At the same time, the first (democratic) phase of the Russian revolution was taking place, climaxed by the abdication of Czar Nicholas II on March 15.

On April 2, the President appeared before Congress to explain to that body and to the people the necessity of war, especially to those who had supported him as the leader who had kept America out of the war:

> . . . The present German submarine warfare against commerce is a warfare against mankind. . . .
>
> Our motive will not be revenge or the victorious assertion of the physical might of the nation, but only the vindication of right, of human right, of which we are only a single champion.
>
> . . . There is one choice we cannot make, we are incapable of making: we will not choose the path of submission and suffer the most sacred rights of our Nation and our people to be ignored or violated. The wrongs against which we now array ourselves are not common wrongs; they cut to the very roots of human life.[93]

In discussing America's ultimate purposes, Wilson remained true to his earlier concept of the United States as a mediator and guarantor of peace and right:

> Our object . . . is to vindicate the principles of peace and justice in the life of the world as against selfish and autocratic power and to set up amongst the really free and self-governed peoples of the world such a concert of purpose and of action as will henceforth insure the observance of these principles. . . .
>
> . . . We are glad, now that we see the facts with no veil of false pretense about them, to fight thus for the ultimate peace of the world and for the liberation of its peoples, the German peoples included: for the rights of nations great and small and the privilege of men everywhere to choose their way of life and of obedience. The world must be made safe for democracy. Its peace must be planted upon the tested foundations of political liberty. We have no selfish ends to serve. We desire no conquest, no dominion. We seek no indemnities for ourselves, no material compensation for the sacrifices we shall freely make. We are but one of the champions of the rights of mankind. We shall be satisfied when those rights have been made as secure as the faith and the freedom of nations can make them.[94]

The President closed his eloquent address with moving words which expressed his deep concern over the suffering which the war would bring, and which reflected his firm conviction that America, under the Providence of God, was being given a special opportunity to serve mankind:

> To such a task we can dedicate our lives and our fortunes, everything that we are and everything that we have, with the pride of those who know that the day has come when America is privileged to spend her blood and her might for the principles that gave her birth and happiness and the peace which she has treasured. God helping her, she can do no other.[95]

Wilson's message won tremendous support from Americans—it appealed both to the "militant idealists" and the "pacific idealists."[96] The war resolution passed the Senate on April 4 by a vote of 82 to 6, and the House on April 6 by 373 to 50. When Wilson finally recommended war, it seemed almost an inevitable choice, as he had prepared the American mind by interpreting the issues in an idealistic manner. The *New Republic* emphasized this point in an editorial on April 14, 1917:

> When one considered the obstacles to American entrance into the war, the more remarkable and unprecedented does the final decision become. . . . For the first time in history a wholly independent nation has entered a great and costly war under the influence of ideas rather than immediate interests and without any expectation of gains, except those which can be shared with all liberal and inoffensive nations.[97]

During the rest of 1917, Wilson combined his talents for practical organization and for moral inspiration. He soon established *The Inquiry*, made up of scholars and other specialists to study the basic problems of peace in Europe and Asia. The Bolshevik coup of November 6 and the Russian revelation of the secret treaties of the European Allies for dividing up the "spoils of victory" prompted Wilson to state America's war and peace aims specifically in his famous "Fourteen Points" address to Congress on January 8, 1918, stressing "open covenants of peace, openly arrived at," freedom of the seas, international trade, reduction of armaments, self-determination for the peoples of Europe and the Near East, and a "general association of nations."[98] He then summarized the American Government's attitude toward Germany, in what Arthur S.

Link calls his "fifteenth point": that America wished Germany "only to accept a place of equality among the peoples of the . . . new world in which we now live,—instead of a place of mastery."[99] The President concluded his address with a final paragraph which stated the basic moral principle behind the peace program: "justice to all peoples and nationalities, and their right to live on equal terms of liberty and safety with one another, whether they be strong or weak."[100] Thus Wilson gave his answer both to Soviet propaganda and to German militarism.

As the war on the Western Front mounted in fury, Wilson began stressing with new conviction the interests of the common man and of the whole world in the peace to come. When the final offensive was opened on September 26, with 1,200,000 American soldiers involved, Wilson's emphasis upon fair and just peace terms had a powerful effect in undermining the will of Germany and Austria-Hungary to resist, when the tide began turning definitely against them. A new German chancellor took office on October 2, and, on October 6, requested Wilson for an armistice preliminary to a peace based on the Fourteen Points. There followed one of the great dramatic developments of the war, for, within a little over a month, Wilson was able to negotiate an armistice which deprived Germany of any further effective power to carry on the war. The President, through Col. House, also secured the support of the Allies for the Fourteen Points (with reservations on "freedom of the seas" and on reparations).

German territory had not been invaded, but Wilson saw that too much Allied success might prevent a just and durable peace.[101] The Kaiser abdicated on November 9. Suddenly, on November 11, 1918, the war was over, amid uncontrollable rejoicing. Wilson knew that his task was only half-finished, and announced on November 18 that he would personally lead the American delegation to the Paris Peace Conference. He explained his position in his annual message on December 2:

> The peace settlements which are now to be agreed upon are of transcendent importance both to us and to the rest of the world, and I know of no business or interest which should take precedence of them. The gallant men of our armed forces on land and sea have consciously fought for the ideals which they knew to be the ideals of their country. I owe it to them to see to it, so far as in me lies, that no false or mistaken interpretation is put upon them, and no possible effort omitted to realize them. It is now my duty to play my full part in making good what they offered their life's blood to obtain. I can think of no call .

. . which could transcend this.[102]

On December 4, 1918, the President sailed for Europe on the *George Washington*. He was welcomed by enthusiastic crowds in Europe as a veritable "savior." Yet it was the personal tragedy of Wilson to be asked to lead America and the world to peace at the beginning of a new phase of political revolution, deepened secularism, and intensified selfishness. He would not succeed at once, but he would plant the seeds. But even before Wilson had sailed for Europe he had successfully achieved three great steps in the eventual building of peace: he had brought a united America into the war for great idealistic purposes; he had organized and inspired the nation and the Allies for victory; and, above all, he had planted deeply in men's hearts the vision of a peace of justice, freedom and brotherhood. The preparation of America for a new world age had been completed. It would require further hammer-blows from history before Americans would be ready to accept the role of free world leadership on a grand scale.

The New "Enlightenment" (continued), 1891–1918

America's industrial production and international trade continued to mount during this extrovert period. Prominent industrialists and business leaders provided the initiative. Economic power was concentrated; business and industrial enterprises were growing larger. The spirit of American democracy was being challenged as an agrarian democracy was turning into an industrial society. The political question was whether the American people could control or regulate society in the machine age.

The economic interpretation of the major movements of history gained popularity, following the impetus given by Karl Marx. Realistic-naturalistic trends were evident in literature and art. The "fundamental law" was tending to become a purely "natural law," believed to contain an inherent principle of progress. William James stressed the appealing philosophy of "pragmatism"—the test of a principle or an idea was whether or not it "worked." The growing rationalism helped promote the steady rise of "relativism" in place of more absolute standards. Education became more secular.

Probably the most significant development in American religion after 1871 was the rise of the "social gospel"—the application of Christian principles to the social order, following the general humanitarian trend, but with a theistic foundation. The emphasis was placed on cooperation and brotherhood, as a means of eliminating the evils of competition and selfishness. The most important prophet of the social gospel was a professor at Rochester Theological Seminary, Walter Rauschenbusch (1861–1918), who wrote such books as *Christianity and the Social Order* (1907), *Christianizing the Social Order* (1912), and *A Theology for the Social Gospel* (1917). Ephraim Adams, Professor of History at Stanford, believed (1913) that the "social gospel" had restored the vitality of American religion, by emphasizing the "service of man to man," along with faith in divine purpose and in immortality.[103]

The rational "enlightenment" and the "social gospel" combined to strengthen the progressive forces of the country. The federal government was moving steadily to improve the position of the consumer and the laborer. By the year 1912, the progressives were dominant, with Wilson receiving 42 percent of the popular vote; Theodore Roosevelt, 28 percent; and the Socialist candidate Eugene V. Debs, 6 percent. This left only 23 percent for the somewhat more conservative Republican candidate, President Taft. The traditional forces of American democracy had triumphed. As Theodore Roosevelt had emphasized the "Square Deal," Woodrow Wilson was to stress the "New Freedom" and to win the Presidency again in 1916 in a straight two-party vote. As William Allen White expressed it, Wilson took the ideals of Bryan and Theodore Roosevelt and made them into law.[104] In 1913, two constitutional amendments were added—the federal income tax and the direct election of Senators. Then came the Federal Reserve Act (1913), the Federal Trade Commission Act (1914), the Clayton Anti-Trust Act (1914), and the Federal Farm Loan Act (1916). Mass production contributed to an expanding market and higher wages for the workers; Henry Ford doubled the wages of the laboring men of the Ford Motor Company on January 1, 1914.

Thus, through governmental and private actions, the foundations were solidly laid by 1917 for a *democratic* industrial society—at a moment in history when America's concept of freedom and America's productive genius were to be thrown into the international balance of power. In the very year in which communism captured Russia, the lie had been given to the prophesy of Karl Marx and Nicolai Lenin that in a capitalist society the rich will grow richer and the poor become poorer until the whole society is overturned by violent revolution on behalf of the working classes. Communist groups were seeking to heighten the "class struggle," but Wilson declared that "the problem of the next generation, if America were really to release her energy" was to "reach a real, genuine, fundamental reconciliation between capital and labor."[105]

In terms of the "rationalist-realist-idealist" thesis outlined in this study, the period from 1871 to 1918 (rationalist and increasingly materialist) can be seen as prelude and preparation both for the revolutionary age to follow (1918–67) and for the age of consolidation and synthesis which followed. Woodrow Wilson himself stressed international ideals which the nation was not ready to implement in his time.

Notes

1. *The Complete Poetry and Prose of Walt Whitman*, intro. Malcolm Cowley, 2 vols. (New York: Pellegrini and Cudahy, 1948), 2:208–9.

2. Ibid., 255.

3. Ibid., 223.

4. Ibid., 256–57.

5. "As a Strong Bird on Pinions Free," Commencement Poem, Dartmouth College, June 26, 1872, quoted in Ralph Henry Gabriel, *The Course of American Democratic Thought*, 2nd ed. (New York: Ronald Press, 1956), 137.

6. Carl R. Fish, *American Diplomacy*, 4th ed. (New York: Henry Holt, 1923), 3.

7. Thomas A. Bailey, *A Diplomatic History of the American People* (New York: F. S. Crofts, 1940), 92–93.

8. Allan Nevins, *Hamilton Fish* (New York: Dodd, Mead, 1937), 674, 689.

9. James D. Richardson, *Messages and Papers of the President, 1789–1902*, 11 vols. (Washington, D.C.: Bureau of National Literature and Art, 1907), 7:452.

10. E. B. Potter, ed., *The United States and World Sea Power* (Englewood Cliffs, N.J.: Prentice Hall, 1955), 398 ff.

11. Bernard Brodie, ed., *Sea Power in the Machine Age*, 2nd ed. (Princeton: Princeton University Press, 1947), 147.

12. Richardson, 8:330.

13. Bailey, 443.

14. Samuel Flagg Bemis, *A Diplomatic History of the United States* (New York: Henry Holt, 1955), 350.

15. John Fiske, *American Political Ideals Viewed from the Standpoint of Universal History* (New York: Harpers, 1885), 9–10.

16. Ibid., 107–9.

17. Ibid., 151–52.

18. Josiah Strong, *Our Country, Its Possible Future and Its Present Crisis*

(New York: Baker and Taylor, 1885), 1.

19. Ibid., 161.

20. Gabriel, 372.

21. Strong, 179–80.

22. Ibid., 217–19.

23. Captain Alfred Thayer Mahan, *The Influence of Sea Power upon History, 1660–1783* (Boston: Little, Brown, 1897), 87.

24. Mahan, *The Interest of America in Sea Power, Present and Future* (Boston: Little, Brown, 1897), 3–6.

25. Ibid., 27.

26. *Selected Literary and Political Papers and Addresses of Woodrow Wilson*, 3 vols. (New York: Grosset and Dunlap, 1925–1926), 1:30–31.

27. Carlton J. H. Hayes, *A Generation of Materialism, 1871–1900*, 2nd ed. (New York: Harper and Brothers, 1941), 339.

28. Ibid., 123–24.

29. Bailey, 452–55.

30. Richardson, 9:315–16.

31. Bemis, ed., *American Secretaries of State and Their Diplomacy*, 10 vols. (New York: Cooper Square Publishers, 1926), 8:155.

32. Porter, 174–75.

33. Ibid., 161.

34. Howard K. Beale, *Theodore Roosevelt and the Rise of America to World Power* (Baltimore: Johns Hopkins University Press, 1956), 47.

35. Richardson, 9:469–72.

36. Ibid., 436.

37. Bemis, *American Secretaries of State*, 8:263–66.

38. Richardson, 9:528.

39. Bemis, *Diplomatic History*, 755.

40. Richardson, 9:436–51.

41. Bemis, *American Secretaries of State*, 8:307.

42. Richardson, 9:658.

43. Ibid.

44. Beale, 51.

45. Ibid., 52.

46. Porter, 204–5.

47. Richardson, 10:38.

48. Ibid., 67.

49. Julius W. Pratt, *A History of United States Foreign Policy* (New York: Prentice Hall, 1955), 380.

50. Richardson, 10:74.

51. Bailey, 520.

52. Archibald Cary Coolidge, *The United States as a World Power* (New York: Macmillan, 1908), 39.

53. Quoted in Gabriel, 384.

54. American Academy of Political and Social Science, *The Foreign Policy of the United States: Political and Commercial*, Addresses and Discussion, April 7–8, 1899 (Philadelphia: American Academy, 1899), 77, 88, 102.

55. Ibid., 152–53.

56. Ibid., 184, 189, 196-97.

57. *Congressional Record*, 56th Congress, First Session (Senate), January 9, 1900, vol. 33, pt. 1, p. 711.

58. Franklin H. Giddings, *Democracy and Empire* (New York: Macmillan, 1900), p. v.

59. Ibid., 285, 357.

60. Paul S. Reinsch, *World Politics at the End of the 19th Century, as Influenced by the Oriental Situation* (New York: Macmillan, 1900), 311, 324, 356–57.

61. Ibid., 359–62.

62. Mahan, *The Problem of Asia and its Effects upon International Policies* (Boston: Little, Brown, 1900), 172–73.

63. Brooks Adams, *America's Economic Supremacy*, with a New Evaluation by Marquis W. Childs (New York: Harpers, 1947), 70–71.

64. Ibid., 104–5, 135, 169–79.

65. Ibid., 191–93.

66. Lyman Abbott, *The Rights of Man, A Study of Twentieth Century Problems* (Boston: Houghton Mifflin, 1901), 214–15.

67. Ibid., 260–62.

68. Ibid., 276–77.

69. *Selected Literary and Political Papers and Addresses of Woodrow Wilson*, 1:168–69.

70. Quoted in Frank Tannenbaum, *The American Tradition in Foreign Policy* (Norman: University of Oklahoma Press, 1951), 100.

71. Porter, 210, 220.

72. Ibid., 229, 233–34.

73. Richardson, 10:527–28.

74. Bailey, 560.

75. Richardson, 10:829–31.

76. Ibid., 831.

77. Ibid., 838–39.

78. American Academy of Political and Social Science, *The United States as a World Power* (Philadelphia, 1905), 2, 9, 13–15.

79. Ibid., 87.

80. 52nd Congress, *A Compilation of the Messages and Papers of the Presidents*, 16 vols. (New York: Bureau of National Literature), 15:7415.

81. Ibid., 7494.

82. *The Public Papers of Woodrow Wilson*, Authorized Edition, 6 vols., ed.

Ray Stannard Baker and William E. Dodd; *College and State*, 2 vols.; *The New Democracy*, 2 vols., *War and Peace*, 2 vols. (New York: Harpers, 1925, 1926, 1927). In *The New Democracy* 1:127 (June 5, 1914).

83. Ibid., 63 (October 25, 1913).

84. Ibid., 146–47.

85. Ibid., 100–2 (April 20, 1914).

86. Ibid., 70–71.

87. Ibid., 53.

88. See N. Gordon Levin, *Woodrow Wilson and World Politics: America's Response to War and Revolution* (New York: Oxford University Press, 1968), 19.

89. Wilson, *The New Democracy*, 1:93.

90. Ibid., 2:186.

91. Ibid., 408–10.

92. Charles Seymour, ed., *The Intimate Papers of Col. House*, 4 vols. (Boston: Houghton Mifflin, 1926), 2:433–34.

93. Wilson, *War and Peace*, 1:8–9.

94. Ibid., 11, 14.

95. Ibid., 16.

96. See Robert Osgood, *Ideals and Self-Interest in American Foreign Relations* (Chicago: University of Chicago Press, 1953), 256–59.

97. *The New Republic*, 10:308–9.

98. Wilson, *War and Peace*, 1:159–61.

99. Ibid., 161–62.

100. Ibid., 162.

101. See Arthur S. Link, *Wilson the Diplomatist* (Baltimore: Johns Hopkins University Press, 1957), 107–8.

102. Wilson, *War and Peace*, 1:322–23.

103. Ephraim Adams, *The Power of Ideals in American History* (New Haven: Yale University Press, 1913), 119–24.

104. William Allen White, *Some Cycles of Cathay* (Chapel Hill: University of North Carolina Press, 1925), 83. White refers to the period from 1870 to 1917 as the "Populist Cycle," following the two preceding periods, the "Revolutionary Cycle" and the "Anti-Slavery Cycle," pp. 80–81.

105. Wilson, *The New Democracy*, 2:203–4 (September 23, 1916).

CHAPTER VI

World Crisis for Freedom: Revolution and Realism (1918/19–1966/67)

An age was at hand which would ultimately see the expansion of freedom in great waves, but there would first be furious counter-waves which would appear to threaten freedom as never before in modern history. The First World War had apparently helped unleash forces which would threaten the very life of freedom for decades to come—the Communists were in power in Russia after 1917, Mussolini established fascism in Italy in 1922, and Hitler created a Nazi Germany in 1933.

Woodrow Wilson felt the necessity for and the inevitability of America's world leadership. But the American people began moving toward introversion during the final years of Wilson's administration. Then three Republican Presidents guided American policy during the following twelve years of so-called "normalcy," boom and depression—Harding, Coolidge and Hoover. Isolationism appeared to reach its deepest point during the first term of Franklin D. Roosevelt (1933–37). Beginning in 1937, however, Roosevelt, who had been Wilson's Assistant-Secretary of the Navy and the Democratic Vice-Presidential candidate in 1920, gradually helped prepare the American mind for the day when extroversion would again be the dominant American mood.

As a result of World War II and the subsequent Communist challenges, the American nation found itself involved and ultimately committed for the defense and development of the "free world," first in Europe, and then in the Far East and the Middle East, in addition to the area of the Monroe Doctrine (Latin America). By 1966/67, the democratic nations again appeared predominant, at a time when the United States was feeling the strong tug of introversion, following 27 years of deep involvement in world affairs.

American Introversion, 1918/19–40

This phase was introduced by a "great debate" over America's future role, as Wilson helped create the League of Nations and fought valiantly, but vainly, for American membership and leadership in the world organization.

Wilson's Vision of Peace, 1918–20

Woodrow Wilson was the pioneer in leading America into special involvement in world affairs, and became the prophet of America's new sense of world responsibility—developed later in the successful struggles against fascist and communist power. A common explanation of Wilson's defeat by personal and party rancor is much too simple and incomplete, and at least partially incorrect.[1] The full story is complicated and perhaps not fully understood. Yet the result was quite clear: America did move for the fourth time since 1776 into a mood of sustained political-military introversion. The American people acted as if they had grown tired of world responsibility after a quarter of a century of expanding world involvement, climaxed by sending two million American soldiers to engage in the bloodiest battles on the European continent since the time of Napoleon.

Even before America's entry into the war, the groundwork appeared to have been laid for possible introversion after the war. American idealism itself, as interpreted by Wilson, helped prepare the way for isolationism. In the first place, Wilson's international ideals repelled many America "realists"—particularly those who felt that American should long before have joined the Allies in crushing an ambitious and dangerous Germany. More important, perhaps, was Wilson's success in calling forth American idealism in relation to world problems, and raising hopes which could not possibly be fulfilled at that time, at least. For example, the *New Republic*, an influential weekly journal, supported Wilson in his liberal ideals before and during the war. Yet along with the *Nation*, it led liberal opinion in repudiating the Treaty of Versailles and the League of Nations as a betrayal of the Wilsonian dreams. American idealists saw European motivations as too selfish, and opposed Wilson's compromises. Wilson had himself, in January 1917, pledged American support in enforcing a "just peace," implying that the United States could not join in helping guarantee any other kind of peace.

Some realistic students of international affairs, such as Senator Henry Cabot Lodge and Elihu Root, were fearful of the all-inclusive commitments against aggression to which Wilson seemed ready to pledge the American people. Robert Lansing, Wilson's Secretary of State, believed Wilson emphasized the possible use of force too much; he was thinking in a more traditional American manner, in stressing diplomatic negotiations, arbitration and possible judicial settlement—with force as a last resort if seen as desirable under the particular circumstances.[2]

The decisive struggle developed between those who favored American leadership without hesitation or reservations, as Wilson proposed, and those who believed in somewhat more limited international commitments by the United States (to be secured by certain American reservations to the Treaty, which the other powers might well be expected to approve in order to secure American participation in the League).[3] Neither side, it turned out, was able to secure the required two-thirds vote in the Senate; and the majority of the American people then approved the negative decision, at least on "Wilson's League," by turning the Democratic Party out of power in 1920. But Wilson's words supporting American international leadership became more acceptable during and after World War II.

President Wilson arrived in France on December 14, 1918. Since the first formal meeting of the Peace Conference was not held until January 12, 1919, Wilson had time to travel in France, Britain and Italy. He was welcomed everywhere by enthusiastic throngs; the hope of millions of common people for future peace seemed concentrated upon him In these early talks, Wilson stressed the role of moral force, the necessity of the League, and the new friendship of nations brought together under Providential purposes.

Wilson brought all his influence and powers of persuasion to bear upon the Peace Conference of Paris in securing the acceptance of a satisfactory League of Nations Covenant. When, as chairman of the commission to draft the Covenant, he presented the Covenant to the Conference (February 14), he emphasized the role of public opinion and the spirit of world brotherhood essential to its success.[4] On his return (February 24) for the end of the Congressional session, he appealed to all Americans to be aware of their responsibility and of the trust which others had in America as the "hope of the world."[5] Yet on March 4, when Wilson expressed firm confidence in America on the eve of his return to Paris, 39 Senators or Senators-elect signed a famous "Round-

Robin" letter strongly criticizing the proposed league, particularly as a part of the treaty of peace.

Back in Europe, Wilson was faced with determined demands by French and Italian leaders. The French effort to create a buffer state out of the German Rhineland, or a permanent Allied occupation of it, apparently led, on April 7, to Wilson's order to have the *George Washington* come to Europe, presumably to take him home. The French finally yielded, but Wilson in return agreed to a temporary Allied occupation of the Rhineland and to a special treaty binding Britain and America to defend France against future attack. Wilson's appeal to the Italian people to desert their leaders, and press for a peace of justice only, caused the Italian delegates to leave the conference from April 23 to May 6. On April 28, Wilson finally compromised with the Japanese, permitting them to succeed to the special rights of Germany in the Chinese province of Shantung, in return for their pledge to give Shantung back to China later. The Chinese responded by refusing to sign the Treaty, and many Americans resented the compromise with Japan. In the meantime, Wilson was able to secure a number of modifications in the League Covenant which he believed answered the major objections which had been raised by American critics. Wilson's experience was convincing him of the need to cultivate a spirit of patience and mutual understanding in planning changes in the world's political structure, and of the importance of the development of international law.[6]

The treaty as agreed upon by the Allies was presented to the Germans on May 7, 1919. The German delegates were able to secure a few modifications to the treaty before finally accepting it (under the Allied threat of further military force), on June 28. On May 30, Wilson delivered an address under moving circumstances, speaking on Memorial Day at the cemetery for American dead at Suresnes, France:

> No one with a heart in his breast, no American, no lover of humanity, can stand in the presence of these graves without the most profound emotion. These men who lie here are men of a unique breed. Their like has not been seen since the far days of the Crusades. Never before have men crossed the seas to a foreign land to fight for a cause which they did not pretend was peculiarly their own, but knew was the cause of humanity and of mankind. And when they came, they found fit comrades for their courage and their devotion. They found armies of liberty already in the field. . . .

It is our privilege and our high duty to consecrate ourselves afresh on a day like this to the objects for which they fought. . . . It is for us, particularly for us who are civilians, to use our proper weapons of counsel and agreement to see to it that there never is such a war again. The nation that should now fling out of this common concord would betray the human race.

. . . The League of Nations is the covenant of governments that these men shall not have died in vain. . . .[7]

The Treaty of Versailles was signed by the victorious powers and by Germany on June 28, 1919. Wilson had fought hard for the principles he believed in, and had secured a substantial proportion of his aims. There had indeed been compromises—mutual compromises required between men and nations of different viewpoints—but Wilson had secured his major aim: a League of Nations which he believed could maintain the peace and remedy injustices. The President regarded Article 10 as the heart of the League Covenant, with Articles 11 and 19 also exceedingly important in preventing war or successful aggression:

Article 10. The Members of the League undertake to respect and preserve as against external aggression the territorial integrity and existing political independence of all Members of the League. In case of any such aggression or in case of any threat or danger of such aggression, the Council shall advise upon the means by which this obligation shall be fulfilled.

It should be recalled that the rule of voting in both the Council and the Assembly of the League was one of "unanimity" (with the important exception of an alleged aggressor).

Wilson presented the Treaty to the Senate with high hopes, on July 10, believing that it deserved the full support of Americans and that the compromises "nowhere cut to the heart of any principle."[8] He waited until July 29 to present the more definite commitment of the tripartite defensive treaty with France, by which Britain and the United States pledged immediate military assistance to France in case of unprovoked German aggression.[9]

In speaking to the Senate on July 10, Wilson had expressed his conception of America's destiny under Providence—in having entered the war and in American leadership for peace, in the new world age, within the League of Nations:

. . . Our isolation was ended twenty years ago; and now fear of us is ended also, our counsel and association sought after and desired. There can be no question of our ceasing to be a world power. The only question is whether we can refuse the moral leadership that is offered us, whether we shall accept or reject the confidence of the world.

. . . The stage is set, the destiny disclosed. It has come about by no plan of our conceiving, but by the hand of God who led us into this way. We cannot turn back. We can only go forward, with lifted eyes and freshened spirit, to follow the vision. It was of this that we dreamed at our birth. America shall in truth show the way. The light streams upon the path ahead, and nowhere else.[10]

But it became clear in August that Senate approval of the Treaty was indeed in danger. The Republican Party controlled the Senate by two votes (since the November 1918 election), and a majority of the Senators were in favor of amendments, or at least specific American reservations to the Treaty. Those Senators "irreconcilably" opposed to the League were planning speaking tours in the Middle West and Far West, after the Treaty was reported out of the Committee.[11] The President decided that he himself, despite the opposition of his physician, must take the case for the League and the Treaty directly to the American people.

Wilson's addresses from September 4 to 25, 1919, may be regarded as his "farewell addresses" to the American people on their international obligations. He warned America of the future dangers of aggression and war if the Treaty should be repudiated; he explained the principles of justice involved; and he appealed to American citizens, with deeply felt conviction, to honor the pledges which had been made to those who died on the field of battle.

The President acknowledged that the peace terms with Germany were severe, but he affirmed his belief that they were just, in the light of Germany's actions (Columbus, September 4).[12] He also realized that potential forces of aggression still existed in Germany and perhaps in other nations (St. Paul, September 9).[13] The result of the almost inconceivable failure of America to participate in helping guarantee the peace would be a new and more terrible war within a generation:

. . . And the glory of the Armies and Navies of the United States is gone like a dream in the night, and there ensues upon it, in the suitable darkness of the night, the nightmare of dread which lay upon the nations before this war came; and there will come sometime, in the vengeful Providence of God, another struggle in which, not a few hundred thousand fine men from America will have to die, but as many millions as are necessary to accomplish the final freedom of the peoples of the world.[14]

Without America in the League, the forces of aggression and evil would be immediately encouraged (Coeur D'alene, Idaho, September 12); the guarantees of peace would "not be sufficient without America."[15]

Wilson repeatedly pointed out certain high principles of the League, and the best spirit of mankind which the League sought to mobilize (Columbus, September 4):

> . . . In drawing the humane endeavors of the world together it makes a league of the fine passions of the world, of its philanthropic passions, of its passion of pity, of its passion of human sympathy, of its passion of human friendliness and helpfulness, for there is such a passion. It is the passion which has lifted us along the slow road of civilization. It is the passion which has made ordered government possible, It is the passion which has made justice and established it in the world.[16]

The basic principle of the League—the protection of the rights of all nations, large or small—was, he affirmed, a traditional and powerful American belief (Portland, September 15).[17] Wilson stressed the new attitude toward the "colonial" question, as demonstrated in the "mandate" system for the former German and Turkish colonies.[18] When former colonies should become self-governing, as the United States had promised the Philippines in 1916, they could begin their independent existence with a sense of security, inside the League (Kansas City, September 6).[19] Wilson clearly foresaw that one of the major problems of the generation ahead lay in the field of labor relations and the welfare of the workingman, and he reminded his audiences of Article 23 of the League Covenant which laid the groundwork for the establishment of the International Labor Organization (Columbus, September 4).[20] He saw the need for democratic and constructive solutions to the human problems of an industrial society, and reacted strongly against the communist program in Russia (referring to the "political poison" spreading from Russia into Europe—Des Moines, September 6).[21]

European problems were the major concern of the Peace Conference of Paris, but the League could ultimately help rectify the injustices around the world (Columbus, September 4).[22] Throughout the whole tour of the West, Wilson emphasized his faith in America's idealism and moral purpose in world affairs:

> . . . If by any mysterious influence of error America should not take the leading part in this new enterprise of concerted power, the world would experience one of those penetrating chills of reaction, which would lead to a universal cynicism. For if America goes back upon mankind, mankind has no other place to turn. It is the hope of Nations all over the world that America will do this great thing. (Sioux Falls, North Dakota, September 8).[23]

He looked forward to the time, which he then apparently felt must be near at hand, when America would respond to the great moral challenges of the time like an "army of God" (Seattle, September 13):

> America responds to nothing so quickly or unanimously as a great moral challenge. . . . America is unaccustomed to military tasks, but America is accustomed to fulfilling its pledges and following its visions.
> . . . I look forward to the day when all this debate will seem in our recollection like a strange mist that came over the minds of men here and there in the Nation, like a groping in the fog, having lost the way, the plain way, the beaten way, that America had made for itself for generations together; and we shall then know that of a sudden, upon the assertion of the real spirit of the American people, they came to the edge of the mist, and outside lay the sunny country where every question of duty lay plain and clear and where the great tramp of the American people sounded in the ears of the whole world, which knew that the armies of God were on their way.[24]

In his talks across the nation, Wilson painted word pictures of the thousands of white crosses above American soldiers in France, and reminded the people of the sacred pledge to be redeemed.[25] In his last speech, at Pueblo, September 25, he declared that his "clients" were the children of America, in the case he was presenting for America's full participation in the organization designed to maintain peace:

> . . . My clients are the children; my clients are the next generation. They do not know what promises and bonds I undertook when I ordered the armies of the United States to the soil of France, but I know, and I intend to redeem my pledges to the children; they shall not be sent upon a similar errand.[26]

The President was thus expressing his belief that American leadership could prevent another great war. Wilson's confidence was ultimately grounded in his faith in God—in the Providential purpose of peace on earth (San Francisco, September 17):

> My fellow citizens, I believe in Divine Providence. If I did not, I would go crazy. If I thought the direction of the disordered affairs of this world depended upon our finite intelligence, I should not know how to reason my way to sanity, and I do not believe that there is any body of men, however they concert their power or their influence, that can defeat this great enterprise, which is the enterprise of divine mercy and peace and good will.[27]

In his last two sentences at Pueblo, just before the collapse which ended his remarkable speaking tour, Wilson prophesied his expectation of what his beloved country would do:

> . . . There is one thing that the American people always rise to and extend their hand to, and that is the truth of justice and of liberty and of peace. We have accepted that truth and we are going to be led by it, and it is going to lead us, and through us the world, out into pastures of quietness and peace such as the world never dreamed of before.[28]

Cancelling the rest of his engagements, Wilson returned to Washington, where he suffered a severe stroke which left him partially paralyzed. The leader of the pro-League forces was thus stricken at a critical time in the struggle for Senate approval of the Treaty. Wilson decided to oppose the Senate reservations, particularly on Article 10. Two key votes were taken by the Senate on November 19. The first vote was on the Treaty with the Lodge reservations: 39 for, 55 against. The second vote for unconditional approval of the original Treaty was 38 for to 53 against. Only 15 Senators—12 Republicans and 3 Democrats—were opposed to the Treaty and League under any conditions. The others favored approval with either mild or strong reservations.

If the Senate should again reject the Treaty (another vote was scheduled for early in 1920), Wilson was convinced that the American people would rally to it in the election, which would take the form of a "great and solemn referendum."[29] The final Senate vote came on March 19, 1920, when the Treaty with the Lodge reservations received 49 votes for and 35 against. The 35 negative votes included the 15 "irreconcilables" and 20 Democratic Senators who stayed solidly with the President. Had only seven more switched their vote, the Treaty would have been approved (56 to 28).

This meant the end of the League for America unless the American people should rally behind Wilson's position in the forthcoming election. At the Republican Convention in Chicago, June 8, 1920, the platform strongly criticized the Wilson Administration, but pledged support of international cooperation in general.[30] On the tenth ballot, Senator Warren G. Harding of Ohio was nominated for President; Governor Calvin Coolidge of Massachusetts was chosen for Vice-President. The Democratic Convention, meeting at San Francisco on June 28, adopted a platform plank squarely in favor of the League. On the 44th ballot, Governor James M. Cox of Ohio received the Presidential nomination; Franklin D. Roosevelt, Assistant-Secretary of the Navy, was nominated for Vice-President.

Harding maintained an equivocal position on world organization. His speech accepting the Republican nomination, July 22, opposed a world "super-government" as he seemed to regard the League, but favored an association of nations to "preserve peace through justice rather than force."[31] From time to time, Harding pointed out the possibility of an entirely new association or of a revised League. A clear-cut referendum on the international issue was almost completely ruled out by the "Statement of the Thirty-One" on October 14. Written by the eminent international lawyer and statesman, Elihu Root, it was signed by 30 other leading Republicans, all well-known public figures:

> . . . We have reached the conclusion that the true course to bring America into an effective league to preserve peace is not by insisting with Mr. Cox upon the acceptance of such a provision as Article X . . . but by frankly calling upon the other nations to agree to changes in the proposed agreement. . . .
>
> For this course we can look only to the Republican Party and its candidate. . . .
>
> . . . We therefore believe that we can most effectively advance the cause of international organization to promote peace by supporting Mr. Harding for election to the Presidency.[32]

In the election on November 2, with women voting on a national scale for the first time, Harding was swept into the Presidency by a huge majority of the popular vote: 16,150,000 to 9,150,000 for Cox

(404 electoral votes to 127). President-elect Harding seemed to forget at once his vague promises concerning modification of the League Covenant, as when he spoke to a victory celebration in his home town on November 4:

> You just didn't want a surrender of the United States of America; you wanted America to go on under American ideals. That's why you didn't care for the League which is now deceased.[33]

Mark Sullivan characterized the new mood in terms of opposition to Wilson and his principles:

> . . . Wilson, in short, was the symbol both of the war we had begun to think of with disillusion, and of the peace we had come to think of with cynicism. And Cox, by identifying himself with Wilson, took on Wilson's liabilities.
>
> Rarely has any national mood been so definite or so nearly universal as the American one which followed on the heels of the Great War.[34]

A word should be added about Wilson's strong convictions in the rightness of the cause he had undertaken to further and which he believed would ultimately triumph. In an article published in the *Atlantic Monthly* for August 1923, he felt that "the road away from revolution" in the world would be found in the spiritual redemption of democracy:

> The sum of the whole matter is this, that our civilization cannot survive materially unless it be redeemed spiritually. It can be saved only by becoming permeated with the spirit of Christ and being made free and happy by the practices which spring out of that spirit. Only thus can discontent be driven out and all the shadows lifted from the road ahead.
>
> Here is the final challenge to our churches, to our political organizations, and to our capitalists—to everyone who fears God or loves his country. Shall we not all earnestly cooperate to bring in the new day?[35]

Wilson's last public address was delivered over the radio on the eve of the fifth anniversary of the signing of the Armistice, November 10, 1923, emphasizing America's world political duties:

The only way in which we can worthily give proof of our appreciation of the high significance of Armistice Day is by resolving to put self-interest away and once more formulate and act upon the highest ideals and purposes of international policy.

Thus, and only thus, can we return to the true traditions of America.[36]

Wilson never broke faith with his ideals. Death came to him quietly on February 3, 1924.

If the United States had joined the League of Nations, and if all the major democracies had given the League full support, World War II might well have been prevented. But, according to the cyclical nature of American moods, the American decision appears to follow the past or normal pattern of change. A natural reaction in the direction of introversion was taking place, following nearly three decades of extroversion which had ended in this major war. The growing trend of secularism was beginning to produce cynicism about ideals in international affairs. It is probably also true that the Americans were not ready for prolonged world leadership in 1920. They knew too little about the world, its peoples and its problems, for one thing. Perhaps, too, America would not participate effectively in a system of collective security without feeling insecure herself—in 1920, America felt relatively secure. Furthermore, a world in which America could lead with full moral vigor would need to be a "free world" or a world moving in the direction of freedom; "imperialism" and "colonialism" were still widely accepted in the West in the 1920s. Many Americans hesitated to support the so-called "imperial powers"—Britain and France—in the League.

As it turned out, the failure of the League, with America outside it, doubtless helped convince the American people in the 1940s of the necessity for their vigorous leadership in the United Nations and in regional organizations for collective security. Many Americans had deep feelings of guilt or remorse stemming from the failure of their nation to participate in the plan which might have prevented the tragedy of the second World War. Much college education in the 1920s tended to stress Wilsonian principles, and to be critical of the American decision to remain outside the League.[37] America was to be given a second, even though more costly, chance in the 1940s. Suddenly Woodrow Wilson's ideas would seem singularly appropriate again. The challenges of 1917–18 had not proved sufficient to bring an American commitment, but they had started a train of thought which would heighten the positive responses to the greater challenges to come after 1940—at a time when Americans were ready for a new mood of extroversion.

American Isolationism, from Harding to Roosevelt, 1921–40

In view of the growing world interdependence and mutual concern by 1918–19, America's fourth movement into introversion seems somewhat paradoxical. It was to be another "leveling-off" of America's international mood, but at a much higher stage of international involvement than in the previous introvert phase. Business was "in the saddle" after the war, and the spirit of economic "liberty" was predominant until the Great Depression (beginning in 1929–30).

The new introvert mood was demonstrated by various events and decisions of Presidents Harding, Coolidge and Hoover, and seemed to be intensified during President Franklin D. Roosevelt's first term, following the intense phase of the depression. Yet, as in the previous introvert periods, the coming extrovert period was foreshadowed during the last half of the introvert period with its greater emphasis on "union." This phase of "union" seemed to have begun in 1929, under President Hoover, with his wide international and humanitarian experience, and was strengthened by the challenge of the depression. Then, with the national government under the dynamic leadership of President Roosevelt, America was prepared internally, better than it knew, for the mighty challenges to come from abroad in 1940 and 1941.

Harding and Coolidge, 1921–29

President Harding and Secretary of State Charles Evans Hughes were determined to ignore the League of Nations—for six months mail from the League to the Department of State was not even acknowledged.[38] A separate treaty of peace was signed with Germany on August 25, 1921—reserving to the United States all its rights under the Treaty of Versailles, but with none of its obligations. This treaty was accepted by the Senate on October 18 by a vote of 66 to 20. America's continued humanitarianism was illustrated by President Harding's call to Congress to appropriate money for the relief of 15 million Russians on the Volga in the midst of famine (December 6, 1921).[39]

The answer of the Harding Administration to the desire for some moves by America to promote peace came in the call, on July 11, 1921, for a great disarmament conference. The aim was to avert a possible naval race with Britain and Japan, and to achieve greater stability in the Far East. In general, the conference succeeded in its aims. However, the total result probably illustrates the growing mood of American withdrawal from world politics—not only by the special American stress on disarmament at a time when international political cooperation on other subjects was being refused, but particularly by the American-British pledge to Japan not to increase their fortifications in the Western Pacific. Such a pledge could only encourage the military group inside Japan which looked forward toward expansion by force. Yet at the time, the Great Power agreement was seen as promoting only peace and freedom.

President Harding died on August 2, 1923, before the financial scandals involving some of his appointees had come to light. He had helped bring the country to what he had called "normalcy," and his successor, Calvin Coolidge, was to continue to hold the nation steady and relatively unconcerned about the world's difficulties, while prosperity mounted. President Coolidge was a man of high ideals who encouraged American cooperation in building processes of peace—notably in promoting the Dawes Plan (1924), which included American loans to Germany; urging the Senate to approve the Statute of the World Court (the Senate's reservations caused this to fail); and stressing the (Kellogg-Briand) Pact of Paris (1928) for the outlawry of war. In the election of November 4, 1924, Coolidge had won an overwhelming victory, with 15,700,000 popular votes to 8,400,000 for John W. Davis and 4,800,000 for Robert LaFollette (Progressive)—the electoral votes were 382, 136, and 13.

Relations with Japan had grown definitely worse in 1924, when Congress excluded Japanese completely from immigration. This action overshadowed the warm response given by the Japanese to the generous relief furnished by Americans following the disastrous earthquake in Japan in September 1923. In January 1929 the Senate approved the Pact of Paris by a vote of 85 to 1. American expectation of great results from the pact (which made aggressive war "illegal") is probably another sign of growing introversion—for the pact had no means of enforcement. When wars came in the 1930s and 1940s, Americans came to view the pact with cynicism.

President Coolidge continued to follow the policy of the withdrawal of the marines from the Caribbean and to promote friendlier relations with Latin American nations. The American mood against intervention was steadily growing in strength, as illustrated in the official State Department Clark Memorandum of December 17, 1928, repudiating the Roosevelt Corollary of the Monroe Doctrine under which some interventions had been justified. In an address on Washington's birthday, February 22, 1929, the President explained the value he saw in America's detached position in world politics, whereby the nation was enabled to render service and help wherever needed.[40] Yet the rest of the world seemed far away, with only one major event dramatizing that a "shrinking" of the world was occurring: the heroic solo flight of Charles A. Lindbergh in The Spirit of St. Louis from New York to Paris in 33 hours (May 20–21, 1927). But this seemed to be an isolated incident which would not change America's pattern of "complacency." This mood of complacency was doubtless strengthened by the widespread emphasis upon material gain and individual comfort.

Herbert Hoover, 1929–33

The nomination and election of a man like Herbert Hoover was probably an indication of a new trend toward a spirit of "union." In the election on November 6, 1928, Hoover received 21,400,000 popular votes and 444 electoral votes; Governor Alfred E. Smith of New York, 15,000,000 popular and 87 electoral votes. Hoover's reputation had been built largely through his efficient organization of major humanitarian enterprises during and after World War I. With the coming of the depression, Hoover moved quite energetically in fostering public works and promoting relief, while trying to stimulate greater individual and local responsibility for the common good. He had also been prepared for his somewhat larger role in international affairs (a characteristic of "union") by his world-wide mining and engineering activities (1895–1914), his humanitarian work in Europe during and after the war, his former support of the League of Nations, and his deep concern for peace (fostered by his Quaker faith). The general introvert mood in America, however, prevented any strong positive action in world affairs, while the Great Depression had the ultimate effect of turning America's attention inward far more than in the 1920s.

Hoover continued to strengthen America's growing friendly relations with Latin America. Shortly after his election, he undertook a good-will tour of eleven Latin-American countries.[41] In his first annual message, December 3, 1929, Hoover indicated his wish to withdraw American marines from Nicaragua, Haiti and China as soon as possible.[42] He also abandoned Wilson's policy of using recognition as a means of weakening, opposing, or overthrowing revolutionary dictatorial governments—returning to the normal policy of recognizing de facto regimes in Latin America. The Administration also cooperated closely with the League of Nations in making preparations for the Disarmament Conference which met in Geneva on February 2, 1932, to deal with land armaments (in view of rising international tension, no agreements were to be reached).

The stock market crash in October 1929 was a sign of the coming Great Depression. The first response of Congress which affected international affairs was to raise American tariffs to unusually high rates in the Smoot-Hawley Act, approved by the Senate on June 13, 1930, by the narrow margin of 44 to 42. This marked the beginning of the intensification of American introversion in response to the depression. Hoover, however, stressed the importance of international cooperation in helping overcome the economic downturn,[43] and pledged American support of the London Economic Conference called by the League and scheduled to meet in 1933.

Japanese troops precipitated a major international crisis in Manchuria on September 18, 1931—the first significant military aggression since the World War. Secretary of State Henry L. Stimson sent a note of protest in September, and gradually moved to cooperate with the League of Nations on the problem. When Japan crushed Chinese resistance in Manchuria by January 1932, Stimson sent identical notes to Japan and China, stating that the United States would not recognize any situation brought about by means contrary to the Pact of Paris. This was as far as America would consider going, however. When the League issued a rather mild condemnation of Japan and adopted the Stimson "Non-Recognition" Doctrine in February 1933, Japan withdrew from the League on March 27, keeping outright the Pacific islands which she held as mandates from the League. Power politics was thus clearly back in the saddle in the Pacific.

The United States, however, was far more concerned about the domestic depression, and turned away from world events to a deeper introversion. The leading Democratic candidate for the Presidency, Governor Franklin D. Roosevelt of New York, made it clear in a speech of February 2, 1932, that the League of Nations had become a dead issue for him.[44] He was nominated on the fourth ballot in Chicago on

June 27, and was swept into power on November 8 by a huge popular and electoral majority (27,800,000 to 15,800,000 for President Hoover, and 472 to 59 electoral votes), along with large Democratic majorities in Congress.

The American people were so deeply immersed in their own domestic predicament that they paid little attention to events in Germany as well as Japan. On January 30, 1933 (the birthday of President-elect Roosevelt), Adolf Hitler was named Chancellor of Germany; he dissolved the Reichstag on February 1 and was granted full dictatorial powers by a new Reichstag on March 23 (Roosevelt had been inaugurated on March 4).

Franklin D. Roosevelt: Recovery and Peace, 1933–37

In his Inaugural Address of March 4, 1933, President Roosevelt's ringing words helped overcome the deep "crisis of confidence" in America:

> This great nation will endure as it has endured, will revive and will prosper. So, first of all, let me assert my firm belief that the only things we have to fear is fear itself. . . .[45]

The President moved quickly, by word and deed, to initiate governmental programs which would alleviate suffering and pave the way for economic recovery and renewed growth. Domestic problems were given top priority; foreign policy emphases were placed on the "good neighbor" (Latin America), politically and economically, and on peace and neutrality.

On December 26, 1933, at the Seventh International Conference of American States at Montevideo, the United States joined the other states in general opposition to intervention: "No state has the right to intervene in the internal or external affairs of another." The Platt Amendment, which authorized intervention in Cuba under certain circumstances, was abrogated by an agreement of May 29, 1934; and all troops were withdrawn from Haiti in August 1934. By a new treaty with Panama, signed in March 1936, the United States renounced its right to intervene in Panama's affairs.

The spirit of the "good neighbor" also probably helped prompt the opening of diplomatic relations with the Soviet Union on November 16, 1933, after Soviet pledges of non-interference and an agreement on claims. The American people were ready for this move, after 15 years of non-recognition, and the re-establishment of political contacts with this country seemed particularly desirable to many in the face of the menacing signs emerging from Japan and Germany.

President Roosevelt regarded the international economic area as secondary to the domestic economy. The London Economic Conference (June 12–July 27, 1933) was unable to reach any agreement, when the United States would not consider the proposed international currency stabilization. Instead, the Administration concentrated on stimulating the national economy and promoting its export trade, through the abandonment of the gold standard and the devaluation of the dollar. Close cooperation with the social work of the League of Nations was continued and strengthened, however: the most significant step taken was to join the International Labor Organization in June 1934, by a joint Congressional resolution at the suggestion of the President.

The World Disarmament Conference ended in complete failure in June 1934, following Hitler's withdrawal from the Conference and from the League of Nations (Germany had joined in 1926). As tension mounted in Europe as well as Asia, Congress tried to remove America's economic interest from future foreign wars, when the Nye Committee in the Senate concluded that America had been involved in the World War by selfish economic interests. The Johnson Debt Default Act (April 1934) prohibited loans to any foreign governments in default (only Finland had kept up its payments). With war threatening between Italy and Ethiopia, the Neutrality Act of August 1935 authorized the President to prohibit arms shipments to all belligerents in a recognized war, and forbade American travel on the ships of belligerents. Although President Roosevelt's proposal to join the World Court had powerful press support, enough strength was mobilized against the Court (particularly by Father Coughlin of radio fame, Senators Hiram Johnson and Huey Long, and the Hearst papers) to help cause the Senate vote on January 29, 1935, to be seven votes short of the required two-thirds (52 to 36).[46]

When the Italo-Ethiopian War broke out on October 5, 1935, the President applied the new Neutrality Act to Italy and to Ethiopia, thereby treating aggressor and victim alike. As the international outlook continued to darken, Congress strengthened the Act in February 1936, shortly before Hitler suddenly reoccupied the demilitarized Rhineland (March 7). By summer, Mussolini had conquered Ethiopia.

The Democratic Party, meeting in Philadelphia on June 23, 1936, renominated President Roosevelt, and devoted little space in its platform to foreign affairs—the platform stressed peace, neutrality, and insulation from any motivations for war.[47] The President stressed his opposition to war at Chautauqua, New York, August 14, 1936:

> I have seen war. . . . I hate war.
> . . . I wish I could keep war from all nations; but that is beyond my power. I can at least make clear that the conscience of America revolts against war and that any Nation which provokes war forfeits the sympathy of the people of the United States.
> . . . If we face the choice of profits or peace, the Nation will answer—must answer—"We choose peace."[48]

President Roosevelt won an enormous victory in the election for his "New Deal" concepts: 27,750,000 popular votes to 16,700,000 for Governor Alfred M. Landon of Kansas (the electoral vote was 523 to 8).

After the fascist threat moved to Spain, where a civil war had broken out on July 18, 1936, Congress extended the Neutrality Act to Spain in January 1937, thus forbidding arms shipments to Madrid as well as to the fascist rebels under General Franco.

By the summer of 1937, more apprehension was being felt about the world outlook, in view of the opening of the new Sino-Japanese War and the possibility that the Spanish Civil War might spread (as Hitler and Mussolini violated their international pledges not to intervene). Millions of Americans began to show concern and uneasiness, for never before had world events been reported with such complete coverage by press and radio. President Roosevelt suggested the possibility of cooperative action by the democratic nations against international lawlessness in his famous "quarantine" speech at Chicago, October 5, 1937.[49] But the public reaction was strongly critical, and the President's outspoken opponents began to raise doubts as to his ultimate intentions. The President himself later (July 10, 1941) described the American reaction as he saw it:

> Unfortunately, this suggestion fell upon deaf ears—even hostile and resentful ears. The pronouncement became the subject of bitter attack at home and abroad. It was hailed as war mongering; it was condemned as attempted intervention in foreign affairs; it was even ridiculed as a nervous search "under the bed" for danger of war which did not exist.[50]

When the Japanese deliberately sank the American gunboat Panay in Chinese waters, December 12, 1937, with two Americans killed and thirty wounded, American opinion remained relatively calm and many Americans showed their fear of the Administration and of Congress by urging passage of the "Ludlow Amendment," which would require a popular referendum before war could be declared. Although a Gallup Poll in October had shown 73 percent in favor of the amendment,[51] the House of Representatives finally returned it to committee on January 10, 1938, by the narrow margin of 209 to 188.

Hitler occupied Austria on March 12, 1938, and increased pressure on Czechoslovakia for the annexation of the German-speaking Sudetenland. The President and Congress had been moving steadily but slowly, ever since 1935, to increase expenditures for the Army and Navy. When Hitler moved to seize the Sudetenland and war seemed almost certain, President Roosevelt sent a message on September 26, 1938, to all the nations concerned, urging a peaceful solution. The Munich Conference on September 30 gave the Sudetenland to Hitler, preserving the peace and breaking the morale of the Czechs. Americans breathed more freely for the moment, but the huge black headlines and dramatic radio broadcasts of the Czech crisis filled most citizens with ominous forebodings. Although American influence in world affairs was small at the time, Walter Lippman was predicting a coming shift in America's position and attitude, in his 1938 lectures at the University of Chicago:

> In our time, we shall witness the dawning realization that a new power exists which is destined to be a successor of Rome and of Britain as the giver of peace, and that its mission is to prepare itself for the accomplishment of that destiny. I refer, of course, to the United States of America. . . . It is better to play the part knowingly than to drift. . . . However much Americans today may dislike it, they cannot refuse it. Their greatness, their position and their power among the peoples of the earth imply that they must accept their destiny. They must accept the enormous burdens and the heavy responsibilities.[52]

In the President's annual message on January 4, 1939, there was a new note of urgency concerning the growing dangers to the ideals which America prized, and new warnings to Americans against encouraging aggressive nations.[53]

The President's secret approval of the sale of American planes to

France (the Neutrality Act applied only to belligerents) was revealed by an accidental plane crash in California (January 1939). The President was unwilling, it seemed to take the American public into his confidence, fearing that it was not prepared to grasp the dangerous world situation. He did not wish to get too far ahead of public opinion.[54] America's hesitancy to act was dramatized in February 1939, when Congress defeated an appropriation of $5,000,000 for harbor works on the unfortified island of Guam.

After Hitler seized the remainder of Czechoslovakia (March 15, 1939) in violation of his pledges at Munich, and Mussolini occupied Albania on April 7 (Palm Sunday), President Roosevelt sent notes (April 15) to Hitler and Mussolini asking them to give pledges against the invasion of 31 independent countries, and ordered the American fleet from the Atlantic to the Pacific (Japan had just occupied Hainan Island, east of French Indo-China). Although the President hoped to secure Congressional repeal of the "arms embargo," he was unwilling to press strongly for a change for fear of arousing isolationist sentiment still further.[55] On July 11, the Senate Foreign Relations Committee voted 12 to 11 to postpone consideration of the arms embargo, partly because of Senator William E. Borah's strong assurance that there would be no war in 1939.[56]

American opinion did mount against the continuance of private trade to Japan in materials which were aiding her war against China. On July 26, 1939, the U.S. Government gave the required six-months' notice for the termination of the commercial treaty of 1911. Then, on August 23, came the "bombshell" announcement of the signing of a German-Soviet pact of friendship and non-aggression. Hitler thereupon attacked Poland on September 1, and Britain and France honored their pledges to help the Poles by their declarations of war against Germany on September 3. While the Germans were crushing Warsaw, the Russians moved in to take over the eastern half of Poland (September 17).

The President proclaimed America's neutrality under the Neutrality Act on September 3 (thereby stopping the shipment of millions of dollars of war materials already ordered by Britain and France), but on September 13 he called for a special session of Congress to meet in September 21 to consider revision of the Neutrality Act. A notable American debate began at once on America's proper role in relation to the war. The pressure to keep America isolated was strong, coming from such sources as the eminent historian Charles A. Beard,[57] and the famed young aviator, Charles A. Lindbergh. After Congress met, sentiment gradually mounted in favor of repealing the arms embargo, on a "cash-carry" basis, in the hope that peace for America could best be maintained by encouraging a speedier Allied victory, while keeping American ships and citizens out of danger. The new "cash-carry" act was passed by Congress on November 3, 55 to 24 in the Senate and 243 to 172 in the House (only 6 Republicans voted for the bill in the Senate and 19 in the House).[58]

All American plans seemed to be set on a relatively small scale, with little realization of the possibility of an intense crisis for the free world. Then, suddenly, there followed three months of disastrous news from abroad—events which had a terrific impact on the American mood, beginning with the German invasion of neutral Denmark and Norway on April 9. After these nations fell, the Nazis struck without warning at Luxembourg, the Netherlands and Belgium on May 10. In Britain, Prime Minister Chamberlain was replaced by the dynamic Winston Churchill (May 11). The Germans struck into France on May 15, Brussels fell on May 18, and the Nazi armies reached the French coast by May 21, splitting the armies of the defense. With the collapse of Western Europe suddenly appearing possible, President Roosevelt summoned the American people, in a "fireside chat" on May 26, to rise to the occasion, to prepare to build 50,000 planes a year, and to strengthen themselves to defend a "way of life" for future generations, while praying for peace.[59]

France and Britain appealed frantically for more aid from America. William Allen White and others organized the influential Committee to Defend America by Aiding the Allies (to counteract the organization, America First). Voices grew ever stronger calling upon Americans to play a greater role. For example, Henry R. Luce, publisher of *Time*, *Life*, and *Fortune*, delivered an address on May 22, in which he declared:

> America is now confronted by a greater challenge to its survival as a land of liberty than any it has had to face in eighty years.
>
> . . . If Great Britain and France fall, we know that we and we only among the great powers are left to defend the democratic faith throughout the world. . . . We know now that, fundamentally, their struggle is our struggle.
>
> The frame of mind of the American people has changed amazingly in the last few weeks.[60]

Belgium surrendered on May 28. The almost miraculous evacuation of 340,000 British and French troops from Dunkirk occurred between May 28 and June 4. Winston Churchill raised the morale of Americans, as well as Britons, with his ringing words on June 4:

> We shall go on to the end. We shall fight in France, we shall fight on the seas and oceans. We shall fight with growing confidence and growing strength in the air, we shall defend our island, whatever the cost may be, we shall fight on the beaches, we shall fight on the landing-grounds, we shall fight in the fields and in the streets, we shall fight in the hills; we shall never surrender, and even if, which I do not for a moment believe, this Island or a large part of it were subjugated and starving, then our Empire beyond the seas, armed and guarded by the British Fleet, would carry on the struggle, until, in God's good time, the New World, with all its power and might, steps forth to the rescue and the liberation of the old.[61]

As the British were thus being summoned to demonstrate the courage and spirit of "their finest hour," Americans too were reminded of the great role they might be called upon to play.

The full Nazi attack upon France commenced on June 5, 1940. When Italy attacked France on June 10, President Roosevelt, in an address at the University of Virginia, referred to it by saying that "the hand that held the dagger has struck it into the back of its neighbor," and compared the challenge for Americans to that of the War of the Revolution, or of the Civil War, pledging full support, in terms of supplies, to Britain and France.[62]

Events moved rapidly to a climax. Paris surrendered on June 14, while Premier Reynaud appealed vainly to America for "clouds of airplanes" (Reynaud resigned on June 16). On June 15, President Roosevelt established the National Defense Research Committee under Dr. Vannevar Buish—one of its major aims was to seek to build an "atomic bomb" as rapidly as possible.[63] With France near collapse, on June 17, the President requested Congress to appropriate funds for a "two-ocean" navy, and sent a note to the French government at Bordeaux, warning against the surrender of the French fleet to Germany.[64] On June 17 and 18, Congress passed a joint resolution declaring its stand against the transfer of any European possession in the New World (the vote was unanimous in the Senate, and 380 to 8 in the House). The President strengthened his Cabinet on June 20 in a bipartisan direction, by naming two prominent Republicans: Henry L.

Stimson (former Secretary of State under Hoover and Secretary of War under Taft) as Secretary of War, and Frank L. Knox (Republican Vice-Presidential candidate in 1936) as Secretary of the Navy. France, under Marshal Pétain, signed an armistice with Germany on June 22 (the French National Committee in London, under General Charles de Gaulle, had pledged continuing French resistance on June 28), and with Italy on June 24. President Roosevelt, on June 24, issued an order that all weapons which could be spared should be shipped to Britain.[65] A poll on June 25 showed that 59 percent of Americans already favored military conscription.[66] "Introversion" was beginning to appear out of date.

Secularism, 1918–40

The period from 1918 to 1966 seems analogous to that from 1776 to 1824 in Europe—an age of tremendous violence (especially after 1940) in which the "old order" is torn from its roots. A "new age" is apparently being born in great travail. The Communists arose on the left to pervert the democratic dream, even as they adopted part of it. The Fascists were determined to crush both the democratic "dreamers" and the Communists.

Robert T. Handy designated the period from 1920 to 1940, in a spiritual sense, as "the age of conflict and doubt."[67] "Atheistic" Communism was established as the official ideology of Russia, and a general agnosticism spread steadily throughout much of the Western world. Ralph H. Gabriel has called the period from 1918 to 1941 the "Great Liberation."[68] The age began in America in an exhilarated, as well as a disillusioned, mood—with the old restraints beginning to be thrown off and a new sense of freedom in the exploration of a "new world" of activity and passion. Self-expression became an important goal, and sex was a preoccupation for many. The pragmatic test of "success" took the place of earlier moral and religious authority. "Debunking" was a favorite "sport." Parental restraint and family ties were weakened. Crime intensified. It is true that orthodox Christianity had a strong hold on many Americans, and that its influence appeared strengthened for a time in the "Fundamentalism" of the early 1920s (particularly before the Scopes trial in Tennessee in 1925), but by the end of the 1920s the prestige of religion had dropped to a low point. Church membership remained rather high, but much religion was only nominal and there was a tendency to be so narrowly "individualistic" that it may have heightened certain social problems. Nevertheless, there was kept alive, more in America than anywhere else, a basic Judeo-Christian "flame" which was always significant.

Most writers in the 1920s saw little hope in religion. By the year 1925, literature had become more frank, more free and, in a sense, more pessimistic—"naturalistic," so to speak. Relativism in morals, as in physics, was a growing concept. Charles A. Beard's 1928 symposium, *Whither Mankind?*, dealt with the "historic trend toward secularization," although it stressed faith in the cooperative spirit as well as in science in building the world of the future.[69]

As the depression deepened in 1930 and 1931, bitter criticism of the "American way of life" mounted, and radical changes appeared to many to be desirable. Samuel B. Schmalhausen's symposium, *Behold America* (1931), was filled with such condemnation. The editor wrote that the aim was "to probe the malady called American civilization."[70]

After the inauguration of Roosevelt on March 4, 1933, his assertion of leadership restored an important measure of confidence in the capacity of a democracy to solve the economic problems of an industrial age. Yet many Americans assumed that their nation, along with many others, was heading in the ultimate direction either of communism or fascism. A significant number of intellectuals were communist sympathizers.[71]

When Harold E. Stearns collected a second symposium on America, in 1938, he included two articles on religion (there was none in his 1922 symposium). H. Paul Douglass, prominent Protestant minister and philosopher, criticized the superficiality of America's popular religious feeling.[72] Francis X. Talbot, Jesuit priest, described the battle of the Catholic Church against a growing worldliness and immorality.[73]

Some writers in the 1920s and 1930s not only pointed out elements of moral-spiritual decline, but also helped keep spiritual forces alive—these included Harry Emerson Fosdick (Protestant minister), Reinhold Niebuhr (to become an outstanding theologian), and Europeans like Albert Schweitzer (the Alsatian physician and philosopher) and Nicholas Berdyaev (Russian-born philosopher). Berdyaev saw (1919 and 1923) a "new barbarism" at hand, but he was confident that it would be followed at some time by a Christian renaissance.[74] As Arnold J. Toynbee, British historian, questioned the future of Western Civilization in 1939, he saw the possibility of a rebirth of Christianity, but the hour was dark and he believed the issue was in doubt.[75]

In America in 1940, the challenge of the European war was

powerfully felt by many writers. Lewis Mumford wrote *Faith for Living* in that year, appealing to Americans to defend freedom against the Axis assault and calling for a "conversion" to new values.[76] Other notable books were written to re-stimulate confidence in a world of freedom and faith, such as Ralph Barton Perry's *And Shall Not Perish from the Earth*.

In the public statements of the President, there was little direct moral-spiritual emphasis from 1930 to 1939, except for Calvin Coolidge and for Franklin D. Roosevelt in December 1936. Coolidge was a man of deep and simple faith which he expressed in a number of addresses. With world peace threatened in 1936, President Roosevelt was moved to speak out to the delegates at the Inter-American Conference in Buenos Aires (December 1936) concerning the importance of religious faith in the Western world.[77]

The fruits of extreme secularism continued to be harvested for many decades after 1940, but the war itself helped start a reaction toward deeper moral and spiritual concerns.

America's Major World Involvement: Extroversion, 1940–66/67

In the months after the fall of France to Hitler (June 1940) and before Pearl Harbor (December 7, 1941), the American mood was visibly shifting, while during the American direct participation in the war the Republicans joined the Democrats in supporting the concept of an America strong in world affairs, with active membership in a new international organization designed to keep the peace. At the end of the war, American troops occupied Japan and portions of Germany, Austria and Italy. The response of America to the increasing pressure of the Soviet Union in the eastern Mediterranean and in Europe was a decision in 1947 to stand with economic, political and military strength in these areas. When mainland China came under Communist control in 1949 and South Korea was attacked in 1950, the United States became deeply involved in all the areas of the Far East which seemed threatened. The importance of the Western Hemisphere was highlighted by Premier Castro's Communist control in Cuba after 1959, while Southeast Asia moved into the center of attention in the middle 1960s. With land warfare beginning in 1965, opposition to the American role began to mount significantly in 1966 and 1967, so that these years seem to indicate a shift of America toward a more introvert policy—that is, a leveling-off of America's direct pressure on the outside world. Early signs of such a shift were apparent by 1963. But it was clear that the nation's involvement would nevertheless remain at a very high level, since American armed forces were still stationed around the world and the United States was a party to political and military agreements with 42 other nations.

There is some evidence that the extrovert period from 1940 to 1966/67 may be divided about equally, as in previous cases, into phases of "liberty" and "union." There was considerable domestic disunity even during World War II, including race riots and labor strikes. After the war, internal divisions continued throughout most of President Harry S Truman's Presidency. President Dwight D. Eisenhower became a symbol of a new "consensus" for a majority of Americans during his two terms in office (1953–61). This spirit continued for six years or so under Presidents John F. Kennedy and Lyndon B. Johnson. Not until 1966 was there an important break in the general spirit of "union," over such problems as the war in Vietnam, the Great Society programs, and the civil rights movement (with the rise of so-called "black power." The years 1966 and 1967 seem to inaugurate an important new era in American life—in foreign policy, in domestic struggles and reorientation, and probably also in spiritual outlook.From 1940 onward, there were great expectations of America's coming positive role as a world leader, both in war and in the peace to follow.

America's World Leadership, 1940–66/67

During this phase of extroversion, America was blessed with far-sighted leaders who all had "positive expectations" about America's world role: President Roosevelt and Secretary of State Cordell Hull; President Harry S Truman and Secretaries James F. Byrnes, George Marshall and Dean Acheson; President Dwight D. Eisenhower and Secretary John Foster Dulles; President John F. Kennedy, Secretary Dean Rusk and National Security Assistant McGeorge Bundy; and President Lyndon B. Johnson, Secretary Rusk and Bundy (who resigned on February 28, 1966, to be replaced by Walt W. Rostow on April 1) The victory in World War II made the world "safe for democracy," in the words of Woodrow Wilson, but also safe for communism. The major direction for the world as a whole was yet to be determined. The Soviet Union proved to be a powerful stimulus or catalyst (as Arnold J. Toynbee once suggested) for the continued renewal or revitalization of the democratic world. The American people confounded many prophets of a return at some stage to "isolationism" by supporting increased world commitments with what could be regarded as remarkable steadiness and patience.

Franklin D. Roosevelt, 1940–45

The tide of public opinion was shifting toward extroversion in the summer of 1940. The Republicans nominated their only "internationalist" contender for President, Wendell Willkie, on June 28. The Democratic National Convention met in Chicago on July 15. Its platform was entitled "We Must Strengthen Democracy Against Aggression":

> . . . It is America's destiny, in these days of rampant despotism, to be the guardian of the world's heritage of liberty and to hold aloft and aflame the torch of Western civilization.
> Firmly relying upon a continuation of the blessings of Divine Providence upon all our righteous endeavors to preserve forever the priceless heritage of American liberty and peace, we appeal to all. . . .[78]

The platform also made it clear that the United States would not send troops outside the Americas, except in case of attack. President Roosevelt was then renominated for an unprecedented third term, as the leader who had warned against the fascist threats. With the beginning of Hitler's aerial "blitz" against Britain in August 1940, a Gallup Poll showed for the first time that a majority of those with opinions favored aiding Britain "even at the risk of war," and the size of this majority continued to increase during the following months.

The deeply serious concern of America with the critical state of European affairs was dramatized by the President's proclamation on August 7, 1940, of a day of prayer for Sunday, September 8:

> . . . When every succeeding day brings sad news of suffering and disaster abroad, we are especially conscious of the Divine Power and our dependence upon God's merciful guidance. . . .[79]

While the Battle of Britain was getting under way, President Roosevelt traded fifty over-age American destroyers to Britain in return for 99-year leases on eight British territories, from Newfoundland to British Guiana, for the construction of American naval bases. This constituted

America's first territorial expansion since the purchase of the Virgin Islands (1916–17). Roosevelt stressed the significance of this executive agreement, when he informed Congress of it on September 3:

> This is the most important action in the reinforcement of our national defense that has been taken since the Louisiana Purchase. Then as now, considerations of safety from overseas attack were fundamental.
>
> The value to the Western Hemisphere of these outposts of security is beyond calculation. . . . They are essential to the protection of the Panama Canal, Central America, the Northern portion of South America, the Antilles, Canada, Mexico, and our own eastern and Gulf seaboards. Their consequent importance in hemispheric defense is obvious. For these reasons I have taken advantage of the present opportunity to acquire them.[80]

America's first peace-time Selective Service Act (favored by both Presidential candidates) became law on September 16. The international picture for America was darkened by the formation of the tripartite pact of Germany, Italy and Japan on September 27, 1940—directed chiefly at the United States.

President Roosevelt gained a fresh mandate for his policy, when he was re-elected on November 2 for a third term of four years (27.2 million popular and 49 electroal votes to Wendell Willkie's 22.3 million popular and 82 electoral votes). Britain still stood, as the British Air Force continued to repel Hitler's air attacks. Many Americans were wondering how America could further help the gallant British nation, under its remarkable war-time leader, Winston Churchill. The President suggested the "lend-lease" idea at a press conference on December 17, and explained the need for it in a dramatic "fireside chat" on December 29, just before the opening of the new Congressional session:

> Never before since Jamestown and Plymouth Rock has our American civilization been in such danger as now.
>
> For, on September 27, 1940, by an agreement signed at Berlin, three powerful nations, two in Europe and one in Asia, joined themselves together in the threat that if the United States of America interfered with or blocked the expansion program of these three nations—a program aimed at world control—they would unite in ultimate action against the United States.
>
> . . . There is far less chance of the United States getting into war if we do all we can now to support the nations defending themselves

against attack by the Axis than if we acquiesce in their defeat, submit tamely to an Axis victory, and wait our turn to be the object of attack in another war later on.

. . . We must be the great arsenal of democracy. For us this is an emergency as serious as war itself.[81]

At every point in the President's moves following the fall of France, the majority of the American people and the Congress gave their approval and support. The annual message to Congress, January 6, 1941, included the President's formulation of his famous "Four Freedoms," as he called upon Congress to send arms to Britain and Greece (attacked by Italy in October 1940) and any other nation "in actual war with aggressor nations":

. . . In the future days, which we seek to make secure, we look forward to a world founded upon four essential freedoms.

The first is freedom of speech and expression—everywhere in the world.

The second is freedom of every person to worship God in his own way—everywhere in the world.

The third is freedom from want—which, translated into world terms, means economic understandings which will secure to every nation a healthy peace time life for its inhabitants—everywhere in the world.

The fourth is freedom from fear—which, translated into world terms, means a world-wide reduction of armaments to such a point and in such a thorough fashion that no nation will be in a position to commit an act of physical aggression against any neighbor—anywhere in the world.

That is no vision of a distant millennium. It is a definite basis for a kind of world attainable in our own time and generation.[82]

While the Lend-Lease Bill was still being debated in Congress, Henry R. Luce published an essay on "The American Century" in *Life* (February 17, 1941), painting an inspiring picture of America's possible role as a world leader in the service of mankind:

It [the 20th Century] is America's first century as a dominant power in the world. . . . No other century has been so big with promise for human progress and happiness. And in no century have so many men and women and children suffered such pain and anguish and bitter death.

. . . The world of the 20th Century, if it is to come to life in any nobility of health and vigor, must be to a significant degree an American Century.

. . . It is meaningless to say that we reject isolationism and accept the logic of internationalism. What internationalism? Rome had a great internationalism.

. . . It must be a sharing with all peoples of our Bill of Rights, our Declaration of Independence, our Constitution, our magnificent industrial product, our technical skills. It must be an internationalism of the people, by the people and for the people.

. . . As America enters dynamically upon the world scene, we need most of all to seek and to bring forth a vision of America as a world power which is authentically American and which can inspire us to live and work and fight with vigor and enthusiasm.

. . . We are the inheritors of all the great principles of Western civilization—above all Justice, the love of Truth, the ideal of Charity. . . . It now becomes our time to be the powerhouse from which the ideals spread throughout the world.

. . . America as the dynamic center of ever-widening spheres of enterprise, America as the training center of the skillful servants of mankind, America as the Good Samaritan, really believing again that it is more blessed to give than to receive, and America as the powerhouse of the ideals of Freedom and Justice—out of these elements surely can be fashioned a vision of the 20th Century to which we can and will devote ourselves in joy and gladness and vigor and enthusiasm.[83]

The Lend-Lease Act became law on March 11, 1941—passing the Senate on March 8 by a vote of 60 to 31, and the House on March 11, 317 to 71. America thus pledged its material and moral support to the nations which were fighting or which would fight against Axis aggression. A major decision was reached on June 24, when President Roosevelt promised to send "lend-lease" aid to Soviet Russia (Hitler had launched his mighty attack on the Eastern Front on June 22). During this period, the President and Prime Minister Churchill were moving steadily toward a closer understanding of purpose and will. After Japan occupied French Indo-China, on July 24, the United States and Britain froze all Japanese credits and funds (July 26)—the result would be to force Japan to choose between peace in the Far East or all-out war. Roosevelt and Churchill met in the Atlantic on August 14 to draw up the eight principles of the famous Atlantic Charter, stressing the goals of a free world in which territorial and governmental changes should be based on the "freely expressed wishes of the peoples concerned." They joined in their desire for full economic collaboration among the nations, and for a secure peace in which the world would abandon the "use of force."[84]

Japan's momentous decision for war was made clear on December 7, 1941, with the treacherous attack on Pearl Harbor. Congress accepted the challenge by a declaration of war against Japan on December 8, with only one dissenting vote (cast by a sincere pacifist), after President Roosevelt had concluded his ringing call to action with the words: "With confidence in our armed forces—with the unbounded determination of our people—we will gain the inevitable triumph—so help us God."[85] That the war was indeed to be a "war for survival" was made clear when Germany and Italy honored the terms of their alliance with Japan, by declaring war on the United States on December 11. Congress in turn declared war on Germany and Italy on the same day, as the President reminded Americans of the mortal dangers facing the nation:

> The long-known and the long-expected has thus taken place. The forces endeavoring to enslave the entire world now are moving toward this hemisphere.
>
> Never before has there been a greater challenge to life, liberty, and civilization.
>
> Delay invites greater danger. Rapid and united effort by all the peoples of the world who are determined to remain free will ensure a world victory of the forces of justice and of righteousness over the forces of savagery and of barbarism.[86]

The Axis powers had finally sealed their own doom, without knowing it—for the American giant was suddenly thoroughly aroused and determined to mobilize its full power to overcome the combined Japanese-German-Italian threat. But this immense mobilization of American resources was yet to come—no one could be sure of its outcome in advance. The hour was dark like that of 1861 or 1775. President Roosevelt, in his "Christmas Address to the American People" on December 24, quoted from his Proclamation of a Day of Prayer for January 1:

> "We are confident in our devotion to country, in our love of freedom, in our inheritance of courage. But our strength, as the strength of all men everywhere, is of greater avail as God upholds us.

"We need His guidance that this people may be humble in spirit but strong in conviction of the right; steadfast to endure sacrifice, and brave to achieve a victory of liberty and peace."

Our strongest weapon in this war is that conviction of the dignity and brotherhood of man which Christmas Day signifies—more than any other day or any other symbol.

Against enemies who preach the principles of hate and practice them, we set our faith in human love and in God's care for us and all men everywhere.[87]

The representatives of the 26 nations at war with the Axis powers met in Washington on January 1, 1942, to sign the United Nations Declaration—subscribing to the purposes and principles embodied in the Atlantic Charter, and pledging to use their full resources for the war and not to make a separate armistice or peace with the enemies. This second World War of the 20th century was to be fought virtually over the whole earth. American troops were to appear—by land, sea and air—on most of the battlefields. The early months of the war saw great Axis victories, but by February 1943 the tide had definitely turned—in the Pacific (with the capture of Guadalcanal), in Russia (at Stalingrad), and in North Africa.

The first of the Axis capitals to fall to the Allies was Rome—on June 4, 1944. Two days later, June 6, came the mighty amphibious invasion of Normandy in France, under the Allied Commander, General Dwight D. Eisenhower. As millions of young Americans joined in this great "crusade," with its enormous hazards, President Roosevelt called upon Americans "in this poignant hour" to join with him in a "D-Day Prayer."[88]

While the Battle of France was getting under way, and shortly after the Battle of the Philippine Sea (June 19–20) which opened the campaign for the recapture of the Philippines under General Douglas MacArthur, the Republican National Convention met in Chicago, on June 26. By 1943, the major leaders of the Republican Party had shifted their stand toward internationalism. The two party platforms in 1944 were considerably alike in foreign relations. Governor Thomas E. Dewey of New York received the Republican nomination, and expressed a viewpoint in his acceptance speech which apparently reflected a new growth of general American confidence in the future destiny of the United States:

... We shall never build a better world by listening to ... counsels of defeat. ... I say to you: Our country is just finding its way through to new horizons. The future of America has no limit.

True, we now pass through dark and troubled times. Scarcely a home escapes the touch of dread anxiety and grief; yet in this hour the American spirit rises, faith returns—faith in our God, faith in our fellow man, faith in the land our fathers died to win, faith in the future, limitless and bright, of this, our country.[89]

The Democratic National Convention, also meeting in Chicago, on July 1, adopted a platform with a strong international position, including support of a new international organization, and nominated for a fourth term "our beloved and matchless leader and President, Franklin D. Roosevelt." In his acceptance speech broadcast from a naval base on the Pacific coast, July 20, the President stressed the need for an American "world view": "The American people now know that all nations of the world—large and small—will have to play their appropriate part in keeping the peace by force, and in deciding peacefully the disputes which might lead to war."[90] During the campaign, in a radio address on October 21, the President reminded Americans of the lesson they had been forced to learn since 1919:

A quarter of a century ago we helped save our freedom, but we failed to organize the kind of world in which future generations could live—with freedom. Opportunity knocks again. there is no guarantee that opportunity will knock a third time.

... I speak to the present generation of Americans with a reverent participation in its sorrows and in its hopes. No generation has undergone a greater test, or has met that test with greater heroism and I think greater wisdom, and no generation has had a more exalted mission.

For this generation must act not only for itself, but as a trustee for all those who fell in the last war—a part of their mission unfulfilled.

It must act also for all those who have paid the supreme price in this war—lest their mission, too, be betrayed.

And finally it must act for the generations to come. They must be granted a heritage of peace.[91]

On November 7, 1944, President Roosevelt was re-elected to his fourth term, with Senator Harry S Truman as Vice-President. (Roosevelt received 25.6 million popular and 432 electoral votes; New York Governor Thomas E. Dewey, 22.0 million popular and 89 electoral votes.) In his last annual message, January 6, 1945, the President called upon Americans and all the allied people to work together in constructing a lasting peace, but not to expect perfection.[92] Four days later, Senator Arthur Vandenberg of Michigan, ranking Republican member of the Foreign Relations Committee, captured the imagination of many Americans in a Senate speech stressing the necessity of strong American international commitments, particularly in view of doubts about Soviet intentions. Vandenberg had moved steadily from "isolationism" after Pearl Harbor, but it was this address which marked the beginning of his remarkable leadership of the majority of Congressional Republicans into bipartisan cooperation in foreign affairs. Governor Dewey also selected John Foster Dulles, his foreign policy adviser, to serve as a consultant to Secretary of State Cordell Hull.

The final conference of the three great wartime leaders—Roosevelt, Churchill and Stalin—was held at Yalta in Russia, February 4–11, 1945. Pledges of cooperation were solemnly undertaken for the defeat of Germany and Japan, for the holding of a great conference to establish the United Nations as a permanent organization, and for the liberation of Eastern Europe.[93] In his last report to Congress, on March 1, 1945, the President was enthusiastic about the results of the Yalta Conference: "I am confident that the Congress and the American people will accept the results of this Conference as the beginning of a permanent structure of peace upon which we can begin to build, under God, that better world in which our children and grandchildren—yours and mine, the children and grandchildren of the whole world—must live, and can live."[94]

No one knows how President Roosevelt would have handled relations with the Soviet Union, had he lived. He was determined to cooperate as fully as possible, but he could not help being disquieted by certain reports from the area following the Yalta Conference, particularly from the American Ambassador to the Soviet Union, W. Averill Harriman.[95] The peoples of the world were stunned by the announcement of the sudden death of President Roosevelt on April 12, 1945. It was a shock to Americans somewhat comparable to the assassination of Abraham Lincoln 80 years earlier, on April 14, 1865.

Although there was a general feeling that no one could take the place of Franklin D. Roosevelt, perhaps his great work was truly finished. The mighty Axis effort to conquer the world was facing certain defeat, the American people had been truly awakened to a large concept of world responsibility and leadership, and the plans for "permanent peace" were far along, including the United Nations. The President left one final legacy—a brief undelivered address prepared for Jefferson Day, April 13, 1945:

> . . . Today this nation which Jefferson helped so greatly to build is playing a tremendous part in the battle for the rights of man all over the world.
>
> . . . We, as Americans, do not choose to deny our responsibility.
>
> Nor do we intend to abandon our determination, that, within the lives of our children and our children's children, there will not be a third world war.
>
> We seek peace—enduring peace. More than an end to war. We want an end to the beginnings of all wars—yes, an end to this brutish, inhuman, and thoroughly impractical method of settling the differences between governments.
>
> . . . Today, we are faced with the preeminent fact that, if civilization is to survive, we must cultivate the science of human relationships—the ability of all peoples, of all kinds, to live together and work together, in the same world, at peace.
>
> . . . The only limit to our realization of tomorrow will be our doubts of today. Let us move forward with strong and active faith.[96]

Harry S Truman, 1945–53

The Vice-President, Harry S Truman, took the oath of office as President and, in an address to Congress, on April 16, pledged his full effort to lead America in the march toward peace:

> Today, the entire world is looking to America for enlightened leadership to peace and progress. Such a leadership requires vision, courage, and tolerance. It can be provided only by a united Nation deeply devoted to the highest ideals.[97]

The next few weeks and months were filled with momentous events in human history. The San Francisco Conference of the United Nations opened on schedule on April 25—Franklin D. Roosevelt was present in spirit, if not in person as he had intended. Within two weeks, Germany had surrendered (V-E Day, May 8)—the dreaded war in Europe was finally over, after nearly six long years. The defeat of Japan still lay ahead, with the expectation of many months of hard fighting (as already shown in the Japanese defense of many small islands). The Charter of the United Nations was agreed upon and signed by the delegates of 51 nations, on June 26. Hopes of all peoples were raised to a high pitch.

Known to but a few, an atomic bomb was successfully tested on July 16, 1945, at the Alamogordo air base in New Mexico. Preparations were under way for the invasion of Japan, when, on August 6, Hiroshima, Japan, was virtually destroyed by one "small" atomic bomb. A second such bomb was exploded over Nagasaki on August 9. The Japanese will to resist was broken in the face of this new terror. The Soviet Union declared war on Japan on August 8. Allied peace terms were accepted by Japan on August 14 (V-J Day in the United States was on August 15). In World War II, perhaps 350,000 Americans had been killed, and twice that number wounded—and countless millions more from other nations.

World War II had come to an end, but a lurid light had been cast over the world by the mushrooming clouds over Hiroshima and Nagasaki. Did the atomic bomb portend the destruction of man and civilization, or was a great new age for good being opened up? The hopes of some for peace were expressed by General Eisenhower, as he described his reaction to the news of the atomic bomb during the early occupation of Germany: "I gained increased hope that this development of what appeared to be the ultimate in destruction would drive men, in self-preservation, to find a way of eliminating war."[98]

By the end of the war American troops had been stationed around the world. But when the fighting had ceased, the natural desire of Americans was to have the soldiers come home as soon as possible. President Roosevelt apparently stated at Yalta that America could not be expected to keep troops in Europe for more than two years. But it turned out that, particularly in the face of a new Soviet challenge in Eastern Europe, the United States, then still in the early part of an extrovert phase, was apparently prepared to "stay the course," at least for another generation.

America's first basic commitment was to join and support the United Nations and all its specialized agencies. The Senate voted 89 to 2, on July 28, 1945, to join the United Nations, and world trust in American leadership was shown in the establishment of the headquarters of the organization in New York City. The basic hope of a successful United Nations lay in the expectation that the United States and the Soviet Union would cooperate inside the organization—but this hope failed to be fulfilled. Nevertheless, the United Nations was able to play an important role in world affairs, especially during its first 20 years, under American leadership.

The generally friendly Western attitude toward the Soviet Union was apparently interpreted as a signal to Russian and Communist imperialists to press forward on plans for expansion into areas of weakness. On February 9, 1946, during the election campaign, Premier Stalin stressed Russia's great new military and industrial power, as demonstrated by the victory in the war, and reminded Soviet listeners of the "necessity" for "capitalist" nations to seek war. The implication was that the Soviet Union still remained in great danger, and must rebuild and greatly strengthen its military and industrial might as rapidly as possible.[99] The American people did not find it easy to accept this new possibility, and many were shocked by Winston Churchill's "iron curtain" speech at Westminster College, Fulton, Missouri, on March 5, 1946, in which he called for much closer American-British cooperation in the face of the rising Russian threat.[100]

When the Soviet threat was focused on Greece and Turkey, major keys to the defense of the Mediterranean and the whole Middle East, a major crisis was created by the British decision, in 1947, to withdraw most of its support from the area, because of growing British economic difficulties. The Greek Government sent an urgent appeal to Washington for aid. The American people were electrified when President Truman appeared before a special session of Congress on March 12, 1947, to present the case for what came to be called the "Truman Doctrine":

> I believe that it must be the policy of the United Stats to support free peoples who are resisting attempted subjugation by armed minorities or by outside pressures.
>
> I believe that we must assist free peoples to work out their own destinies in their own way.
>
> I believe that our help should be primarily through economic and financial aid which is essential to their economic stability and orderly political processes.
>
> . . . In helping free and independent nations to maintain their freedom, the United States will be giving effect to the principles of the Charter of the United Nations.[101]

The Senate passed the bill for $400 million of aid, plus civilian and military personnel, for Greece and Turkey, 67 to 23 on April 23; the House 287 to 107 on May 8; and the President signed the bill on May 22, 1947. Thus was launched America's great peacetime program of "foreign aid" in the developing "cold war" with the Soviet Union.

In the meantime, a stalemate was reached with the Soviet Union on the future of Germany and Austria. Secretary of State George Marshall indicated the critical condition of Europe in his report to the nation on April 28:

> The recovery of Europe has been far slower than had been expected. Disintegrating forces are becoming evident. The patient is sinking while the doctors deliberate. So I believe action cannot await compromise through exhaustion.[102]

Finally, Secretary Marshall, in an address at Harvard University on June 5, made the original public suggestion which eventuated in the famous "Marshall Plan" (or European Recovery Program) for a large unprecedented humanitarian program for the countries of Europe (the Soviet Union was invited but soon dropped out of the planning). On December 19, following the creation by the European leaders of a cooperative organization, President Truman submitted his request for a 17 billion dollar program (for four years), concluding with a statement of the fundamental purposes involved:

> In providing aid to Europe we must share more than goods and funds. We must give our moral support to those nations in their struggle to rekindle the fires of hope and strengthen the will of their people to overcome their adversities. We must develop a feeling of teamwork in our common cause of combating the suspicions, prejudices, and fabrications which undermine cooperative effort, both at home and abroad.
> This joint undertaking . . . is proof that free men can effectively join together to defend their free institutions against totalitarian pressures, and to promote better standards of life for all their peoples.[103]

Congress passed an emergency appropriation to help Europe during the severe winter. With the growing Communist pressure in Europe dramatized by the complete seizure of power by the Communists in Czechoslovakia, on February 24, 1948, the House passed the "Marshall Plan" by a vote of 329 to 76, and the Senate supported it 69 to 17. President Truman's signature on the bill on April 3 buoyed the democratic forces of all Western Europe, particularly in the critical former Axis areas of Italy and Germany.

Western Europe was relatively defenseless at this time against the

Red Army. On June 11, 1948, the Senate passed the Vandenberg Resolution, 64 to 4, giving the Administration its support in advance for negotiating a pact for military cooperation in the Atlantic area.[104] The seriousness of the Soviet threat became more apparent when the major "Berlin Blockade" was clamped on the Allied-occupied West Berlin on June 24. Suddenly, scarcely more than three years after the end of the war against Germany, a major European war again loomed as a real possibility. The decision was quickly made by the Allies to build a great "airlift" into Berlin, by bringing to Europe the available transportation planes from bases all over the world.

While the Berlin Blockade continued, the national campaign and election of 1948 took place. Governor Thomas E. Dewey, the Republican candidate for a second time, gave his solid support to America's position of strong international leadership, as in an address on September 30.[105] President Truman expressed his faith in the "world mission" of America in his election-eve appeal on November 1, 1948:

> I believe with all my heart and soul that Almighty God has intended the United States of America to lead the world to peace.
> . . . This time, we must live up to our opportunity to establish a permanent peace for the greatest age in human history.[106]

President Truman's surprising victory in the election meant that there was to be no break in the continuity of American foreign policy during the critical winter period of the Berlin Blockade. (Truman received 24.1 million popular and 304 electoral votes, while Governor Dewey had 22.0 million popular and 189 electoral votes.)

It was on April 4, 1949, that the Foreign Ministers of 12 countries of the North Atlantic area met in Washington to sign the famous North Atlantic Treaty, in which the United States and Canada joined hands in a mutual security pact with many of the European nations which had peopled the New World. The twelve nations stressed their common ties in the Preamble:

> The Parties to this Treaty reaffirm their faith in the purposes and principles of the United Nations and their desire to live in peace with all peoples and all governments.
> They are determined to safeguard the freedom, common heritage and civilization of their peoples, founded on the principles of democracy, individual liberty and the rule of law.
> They seek to promote stability and well-being in the North Atlantic

area.

They are resolved to unite their efforts for the collective defense and for the preservation of peace and security.[107]

The Treaty dramatized a major shift in American foreign policy, with its peacetime pledge of support to its European friends (who, in turn, promised their support for the United States). Secretary of State Dean Acheson stressed the fundamental values which underlay the agreement in his address at the signing ceremony:

> . . . The reality which is set down here is not created here. The reality is the unity of belief, of spirit, of interest of the community of nations represented here. It is the product of many centuries of common thought and of the blood of many simple and brave men and women.
> The reality lies not in the common pursuit of a material role or of a power to dominate others. It lies in the affirmation of moral and spiritual values which govern the kind of life they propose to lead and which they propose to defend, by all possible means, should that necessity be thrust upon them. . . . This purpose is a fact which has been demonstrated twice in this present century.[108]

It remained to be seen whether the Senate would approve the unprecedented Treaty, and whether the margin would be decisive. Following the strong speech of Senator Tom Connally (Democratic chairman of the Foreign Relations Committee), Senator Arthur Vandenberg delivered an impressive two-hour oration in support of the new policy:

> There is not one aggressive syllable in the entire contract. There is nothing but peace in the aspirations which give it being and in the self-help and mutual aid which give it life. . . . It is built to stop wars before they start. . . . This is the logical evolution of one of our greatest American idioms, "United we stand, divided we fall."[109]

When the vote was taken in the Senate on July 21, 1949, the Treaty was approved by a large majority, 82 to 13. The United States was thus definitely and deeply involved in the future defense of Western Europe—with the aim of deterrence of any attack. Secretary of State Acheson wrote later how a virtual new "creation" had been called for in these basic changes in American foreign policy, 1947–49. It was, he wrote:

. . . the product of enormous will and effort. Its hero is the American people, led by two men of rare quality, President Truman and General Marshall, served by lieutenants of which I had the good fortune to be one. The enormity of the task before all of them, after the wars in Europe and Asia ended in 1945, only slowly revealed itself. As it did so, it began to appear as just a bit less formidable than that described in the first chapter of Genesis. That was to create a world out of chaos; ours, to create half a world, a free half, out of the same material without blowing the whole to pieces in the process. The wonder of it is how much was done.[110]

The basic decisions for a broad American leadership in world affairs had been made—in the Truman Doctrine, the Marshall Plan, and the North Atlantic Treaty. In the meantime, the Soviet Union had decided to lift the eleven-month-old Berlin Blockade, on May 12, 1949, having failed in its effort to drive the Allies out of West Berlin, while inducing them to form a defensive treaty instead (thereby also defending West Germany, which was itself to join NATO in May 1955). For at least 17 more years, the American people would continue to demonstrate their decisive extrovert mood in support of an expanding American role on the world scene.

On October 1, 1949, the Chinese Communists proclaimed at Peiping the establishment of the Peoples Republic of China; the Nationalists under Chiang Kai-shek escaped to the island of Formosa on December 8. On February 14, 1950, the Soviet Union and Communist China announced a 30-year Treaty of Alliance and Mutual Assistance. The fear that the Communist nations would use military force in their program of expansion was brought to reality when Communist North Korea launched its attack on South Korea (thereby also threatening Japan) on June 25, 1950. By June 27, President Truman announced the decision of the United States to stand with the South Koreans:

> The attack upon Korea makes it plain beyond all doubt that Communism has passed beyond the use of subversion to conquer independent nations and will now use armed invasion and war.
>
> . . . I have ordered the Seventh Fleet to prevent any attack on Formosa.
>
> I know that all members of the United Nations will consider carefully the consequences of this latest aggression in Korea in defiance of the Charter of the United Nations. A return to the rule of force in international affairs would have far-reaching effects. The United States

will continue to uphold the rule of law.[111]

The United Nations Security Council then recommended, also on June 27, that members of the United Nations furnish assistance to South Korea. So, for the first time in modern history, a major military action was authorized by an international organization. Fifty-three members of the United Nations (out of 60 at the time) publicly supported South Korea; 24 made offers of military assistance (in addition to the United States and South Korea), of which 15 were accepted; and many others gave material assistance of many kinds. Senator Vandenberg gave his opinion of the American decision in a note to President Truman on July 3:

> I think you have done a courageous and indispensable thing in Korea. . . . When the time came for you to act in behalf of free men and a free world you did so with a spectacular courage which has revived the relentless purpose of all peaceful nations to deny aggression.[112]

With the might of Communist China thrown into the struggle in December 1950, following the defeat of the North Koreans by the forces of the United Nations, under General Douglas MacArthur, the free world was soon galvanized into decisive action in Europe and the Middle East as well as in Asia. General Dwight D. Eisenhower was named Supreme Commander of NATO forces on December 19, 1950. The challenge of Communist China had also given rise to another important debate in American foreign policy—with ex-president Hoover and Senator Robert Taft suggesting the possibility of making a "Western Hemisphere Gibraltar," without sending American land troops abroad. With America in a temporary mood of uncertainty, General Eisenhower helped urge Congress to extend the full cooperation of the United States in building up NATO defenses in Europe:

> . . . What nation is more capable, more ready for providing this leadership than the United States? We have been spared much of the discouragement, the defeatism, the destruction that has been visited upon Europe. We are younger, we are fresher, and a further important point is that we are farther removed from the immediate threat.
> . . . The point I make is that Western Europe is so important to our future, our future is so definitely tied up with them, that we cannot afford to do less than our best in making sure it does not go down the

drain.

> . . . The true defense of a nation must be found it its own soul, and you cannot import a soul. We must make sure that the heart and soul of Europe is right. . . .[113]

Here a new champion for America's international leadership was emerging on the public stage. Senator Vandenberg, weakened from cancer, "listened enthusiastically to General Eisenhower's address." He told a newspaper reporter: "I feel as though a great load had just been lifted from my back. Things will be all right with Ike at the helm."[114] The Senate voted on April 4, 1951, to approve President Truman's decision to send four additional divisions to Germany for NATO defense.

It should also be noted that the increasing threat of Communism and poverty in the underdeveloped nations led President Truman to propose his famous "Point Four" program in his Inaugural Address of January 20, 1949:

> I believe that we should make available to peace-loving peoples the benefits of our store of technical knowledge in order to help them realize their aspirations for a better life. And, in cooperation with other nations, we should foster capital investment in areas needing development.
>
> . . . Democracy alone can supply the vitalizing force to stir the peoples of the world into triumphal action, not only against their human oppressors, but also against their ancient enemies—hunger, misery, and despair.[115]

This statement gave special encouragement to the United Nations in its plans for a mutual technical assistance program.

The Communist military threat in Asia stimulated the United States to strengthen its general Pacific position. By July 1951, John Foster Dulles, working for many months at the request of President Truman, had completed the draft of an acceptable treaty between Japan and the Allies, This just and generous treaty of peace with Japan was signed by the Allies (except for the Soviet Union) and Japan at San Francisco on September 8, 1951, and the United States and Japan agreed to the maintenance of American bases in Japan for its defense.[116] A treaty for mutual defense was signed with the Philippines (which had been given its independence on schedule in 1946); and a similar treaty on September 1 with Australia and New Zealand (the ANZUS Pact).[117]

With the war in Korea continuing into 1952, the Republican National Convention met on July 7 to nominate General Dwight D. Eisenhower for the Presidency (in a close vote with Senator Robert Taft). The Democratic Convention on July 21 named Governor Adlai Stevenson of Illinois as its candidate. When Eisenhower was elected on November 4, in a landslide (33.9 million popular and 442 electoral votes to Stevenson's 27.3 million popular and 89 electoral votes), he appeared to have a mandate either to seek a Korean truce or an all-out victory. His accession to office seemed a symbol of the growing determination of the American people to use their military power, if necessary, to a more effective degree in the world-wide struggle against aggressive Communism. At the same time, Eisenhower was widely trusted as a man who would consider the use of force with proper democratic and moral restraint, as a "man of peace," so to speak.

Dwight D. Eisenhower, 1953–61

Eisenhower and Secretary of State John Foster Dulles saw the need to stress the "long haul" which might lie ahead for America—to maintain American military power in readiness as long as necessary. The administration kept the commitments already made by President Truman in Europe, consolidated and strengthened the new American stand in the Far East, and also became deeply involved in a third vital strategic area, the Middle East (where Israel had been created in 1948). A truce with Communist China and North Korea was signed on July 26, 1953, after over 50,000 American deaths in the fighting. A mutual defense pact with South Korea was signed on October 1, 1953. To deter the Communists from future attacks, the President and the National Security Council made a decision on "retaliatory power," reported publicly by Secretary Dulles on January 12, 1954:

> A potential aggressor must know that he cannot always prescribe battle conditions that suit him. . . .
> The basic decision [is] to depend primarily upon a great capacity to retaliate, instantly, by means and at places of our choosing.[118]

This approach was commonly labeled the "massive retaliation" doctrine. After Vietnam was divided at the 17th parallel on July 20, 1954, the United States took the initiative to establish the Southeast Asia Treaty Organization (SEATO), designed in part to defend South Vietnam. Both in 1955 and 1958, the Eisenhower Administration, supported by Congressional resolutions, apparently deterred attempts by Communist China to take over the "Republic of China" on the island of Formosa (Taiwan).

The United States helped promote a pact for the Middle East—the Baghdad Pact—in 1955, with Turkey, Iraq, Iran, Pakistan and Britain, while the United States joined only some committees. After Egypt nationalized the Suez Canal in July 1956, Israel, Britain and France attacked Egypt on October 29. President Eisenhower stood squarely with the United Nations General Assembly, in helping force the withdrawal of the attacking forces and the introduction of a United Nations Peacekeeping Force for the first time. The President explained America's purpose on October 31:

> My fellow citizens, as I review the march of world events in recent years, I am ever more deeply convinced that the United Nations represents the soundest hope for peace in the world. For this very reason I believe that the processes of the United Nations need further to be developed and strengthened.
>
> I speak particularly of increasing its ability to secure justice under international law
>
> . . . The peace we seek and need means much more than mere absence or war. It means the acceptance of law and the fostering of justice in all the world.[119]

Eisenhower was re-elected, again defeating Adlai E. Stevenson by a decisive majority a few days later. After the withdrawal of British, French and Israeli troops, the Administration felt it was imperative to take a strong defensive stand in the Middle East—under the so-called Eisenhower Doctrine, January 5, 1957, which Congress supported, authorizing "the employment of the armed forces of the United States to secure and protect the territorial integrity and political independence of such nations requesting such aid against overt armed aggression from any nation controlled by international communism."[120] Under this authority, Eisenhower sent troops to Lebanon in July 1958.

Throughout his Administration, President Eisenhower endeavored to seek cooperation with the Soviet Union where possible. After Stalin's death in March 1953, Eisenhower expressed America's hopes, April 16, 1953, for some signs of a shift in Soviet policy, so that savings through disarmament could be sought for a "fund for world aid and reconstruction."[121] One of Eisenhower's most notable suggestions was the "atoms-for-peace" plan, valued especially after the Soviet Union had exploded its first H(hydrogen)-bomb on August 12, 1953. On December 8, 1953, at the invitation of Secretary General Dag Hammarskjöld, President Eisenhower explained his plan for the peaceful uses of some atomic stockpiles, in an impressive televised address before the General Assembly of the United Nations:

> . . . The United States pledges before you—and therefore before the world—its determination to help to solve the fearful atomic dilemma—to devote its entire heart and mind to find the way by which the miraculous inventiveness of man shall not be dedicated to his death, but consecrated to his life.[122]

The United States made an initial pledge of 220 pounds of fissionable material. The charter of the International Atomic Energy Agency was signed at a conference of 80 nations in New York City in October 1956. When the United States ratified this charter on July 29, 1957, Eisenhower announced that 220,000 pounds of fissionable material had been made available for peaceful uses.

With Austria finally freed from all occupying troops in May 1955, a summit meeting was held, July 18–23, 1955, in Geneva, where the President failed to get the Soviet Union to accept his proposal for mutual aerial inspection (the "open skies" plan). There was hope again in the Soviet Union after Chairman Khrushchev denounced the dead Stalin in February 1956, but before the year was over Soviet troops had crushed a hopeful Hungarian uprising.

Washington had announced its plans in July 1955 to launch an earth satellite between July 1957 and December 1958. Many Americans were shocked when Moscow announced the Soviet's successful firing of an inter-continental ballistic missile (ICBM) on August 26, 1957, and the launching of a satellite (the first Soviet "Sputnik") on October 4. American satellites were not ready for launch until February and March 1958. At the same time, America reacted by pressing for more intensive scientific education.

The special challenge in Latin America came in the island of Cuba, always of major concern to the United States. Fidel Castro and his forces took control on January 2, 1959, leading soon to his open espousal of Communism.

After the death of Secretary Dulles in 1959, the President decided to use his own personal prestige to "wage peace." Khrushchev accepted an invitation to visit the United States in September 1959, and Eisenhower was expected to visit the Soviet Union the following year. After Khrushchev's successful visit, President Eisenhower made a series of triumphant visits to Europe, the Middle East, and southern Asia. But Khrushchev torpedoed the summit conference scheduled for Paris in May 1960, after the Soviet capture of the American aerial spy, Gary Powers, and resumed the Soviet pressure on Berlin.

The popular vote in the Presidential election on November 8, 1960, was the closest in 76 years, with Senator John F. Kennedy receiving 34,227,000 popular votes and Vice-President Richard M. Nixon 34,108,000 (49.7 percent to 49.59); the electoral vote was 303 to 219.

At the end of 1960, the major problems to face the United States in the next few years were all foreshadowed—Cuba, Laos, Berlin, nuclear arms, South Vietnam and others. Yet for the ten months preceding May 1960, hopes had soared high for a possible breakthrough to a more peaceful world. In his 1965 memoirs, Eisenhower records his disappointment: "One of my major regrets is that as we left the White House I had to admit little success in making progress in global disarmament or in reducing the bitterness of the East-West struggle."[123] He also expressed his faith then in the future of the American people and their leaders: "Imbued with sense and spirit we will select future leaders who, proud of the character and riches bequeathed to us, will have the vision and selflessness to keep a firm, sure hand on the rudder of this splendid ship of state, guiding her through future generations, to the great destiny for which she was created."[124]

President Eisenhower delivered a Farewell Address to the nation, televised from the White House on the evening of January 17, 1961. He called upon America to live for purposes worthy of a "free and religious people": " . . . America's leadership and prestige depend, not merely upon our unmatched material progress, riches and military strength, but on how we use our power in the interests of world peace and human betterment." Calling upon Americans to be prepared to maintain the struggle against Communist aggressive purposes as long as necessary, he warned, however, that "we must guard against the acquisition of unwarranted influence, whether sought or unsought, by the military-industrial complex." Expressing his disappointment that a "lasting peace" was not yet in sight, he ended by praying that "all peoples will come to live together in a peace guaranteed by the binding force of mutual respect and love."[125]

John F. Kennedy, 1961–63

The American nation was yet to be even more fully involved on the world scene under the youthful, dynamic new Democratic President. America and the free world were thrilled by his stirring Inaugural Address (January 20, 1961). He began with a solemn pledge:

> We observe today not a victory of party but a celebration of freedom, symbolizing an end as well as a beginning, signifying renewal as well as change. For I have sworn before you and Almighty God the same solemn oath our forebears prescribed nearly a century and three-quarters ago.
>
> The world is very different now. For man holds in his mortal hands the power to abolish all forms of human poverty and all forms of human life. And yet the same revolutionary belief for which our forebears fought is still at issue around the globe, the belief that the rights of man come not from the generosity of the state but from the hand of God.
>
> We dare not forget that we are the heirs of that first revolution. Let the word go forth from this time and place to friend and foe alike, that the torch has been passed to a new generation of Americans, born in this century, tempered by war, disciplined by a hard and bitter peace, proud of our ancient heritage, and unwilling to witness or permit the slow undoing of those human rights to which this nation has always been committed, and to which we are committed today at home and around the world.
>
> Let every nation know, whether it wishes us well or ill, that we shall pay any price, bear any burden, meet any hardship, support any friend, oppose any foe to assure the survival and success of liberty.[126]

"Let us never negotiate out of fear," he continued, "but let us never fear to negotiate." He recognized fully the dangers of the hour and expressed his strong faith in what Americans could do:

> In the long history of the world, only a few generations have been granted the role of defending freedom in its hour of maximum danger. I do not shrink from this responsibility. I welcome it. I do not believe that any of us would exchange places with any other people or any other generation. The energy, the faith, the devotion which we bring to this endeavor will light the country and all who serve it, and the glow from that fire can truly light the world.
>
> And so, my fellow Americans, ask not what your country can do for

you; ask what you can do for your country.

My fellow citizens of the world, ask not what America will do for you, but what together we can do for the freedom of man.

Finally, whether you are citizens of America or citizens of the world, ask of us here the same high standards of strength and sacrifice which we ask of you. With a good conscience our only sure reward, with history the final judge of our deeds, let us go forth to lead the land we love, asking His blessing and His help, but knowing that here on earth God's work must truly be our own.[127]

Early in his administration, March 1, 1961, the President proposed a distinctive supplemental program in the area of foreign aid: a permanent Peace Corps—"a pool of trained men and women sent overseas by the United States Government or through private organization and institutions to help foreign countries meet their urgent needs for skilled manpower. . . ."[128] He was encouraged by the early support given to the plan. Another proposal, May 25, which captured the American imagination was the program intended to land a man on the moon "before this decade is out," at an estimated cost of about 20 billion dollars:

No single space project in this period will be more impressive to mankind or more important . . . [or] so difficult or expensive to accomplish. . . .

. . . In a very real sense, it will not be one man going to the moon . . . it will be an entire nation, for all of us must work to put him there. . . . This is not merely a race. Space is open to us now; and our eagerness to share its meaning is not governed by the efforts of others. We go into space because whatever mankind must undertake, free men must fully share.[129]

On February 20, 1962, Americans were thrilled by Lt. Col. John H. Glenn's three-orbit flight around the globe in a *Mercury* capsule.

After the failure of the "Bay of Pigs" invasion of Cuba by exiles (trained under the Eisenhower Administration, but not supported by American force), the President's answer to the rising threat of Communism in the hemisphere was a call (March 13) for a new cooperative "Ten-Year Plan for the Americas," to be named the Alliance for Progress. In relation to the Soviet Union itself, President Kennedy met personally with Chairman Khrushchev in Vienna (May 30), where Khrushchev delivered a virtual ultimatum on Berlin. The

President pledged on July 29 that "we cannot and will not permit the Communists to drive us out of Berlin, either gradually or by force."[130] On August 1, Congress authorized the recall of 250,000 reservists. For their part, the Communists closed the boundary between East and West Berlin, and started building the famous "Berlin Wall" (August 13, 1961).

The President gave full support to the United Nations force in helping end the secession movement in the Congo (1961–63). By the end of 1961, with American aid increasing to South Vietnam, President Kennedy finally decided that the United States must commit itself more fully, by sending military and economic advisers to President Ngo Dinh Diem.

By September 1962, Communist pressure on Berlin was mounting again, just as Cuba signed a definite economic and military assistance agreement with the Soviet Union, on September 2. Kennedy warned against making Cuba an offensive military base for the Soviet Union (September 13), but not until October 16 were photographs received of Soviet offensive missiles being introduced into Cuba. It was a solemn and chilling moment when the President, on October 22, spoke by television and radio on the necessity of demanding the removal of the missiles and for a naval "quarantine" of Cuba:

> . . . It shall be the policy of this nation to regard any nuclear missiles launched from Cuba against any nation in the Western Hemisphere as an attack by the Soviet Union on the United States, requiring a full retaliatory response upon the Soviet Union. . . .
>
> The path we have chosen for the present is full of hazards, as all paths are, but it is the one most consistent with our character and courage as a nation and our commitments around the world. The cost of freedom is always high, but Americans have always paid it. And one path we shall never choose, and that is the path of surrender or submission.
>
> Our goal is not the victory of might, but the vindication of right; not peace at the expense of freedom, but both peace and freedom, here in this hemisphere, and, we hope, around the world. God willing, that goal will be reached.[131]

During a week of climactic tension, a courageous and almost confident calm seemed to pervade the American nation. After the week of anxious waiting, and with the aid of the United Nations, the high tension was finally broken by Khrushchev's decision, on October 28, 1962, to withdraw the "offensive" missiles.

The result of the Cuban missile crisis apparently prevented a new threat to Berlin at this time The President received a tumultuous welcome when he visited West Berlin on June 26, 1963. The people of West Berlin were heartened as he spoke to a huge crowd in what has been renamed "Kennedy Platz":

> There are many people in the world who really don't understand, or say they don't, what is the great issue between the free world and the Communist world. Let them come to Berlin. . . . "Lasst sie nach Berlin kommen."
>
> . . . In eighteen years of peace and good faith, this generation of Germans has earned the right to be free, including the right to unite their families and their nation in lasting peace with good will to all people.
>
> . . . Freedom is indivisible, and when one man is enslaved, all are not free. . . .
>
> All free men, wherever they may live, are citizens of Berlin, and, therefore, as a free man, I take pride in the words, "Ich bin ein Berliner."[132]

Beginning in September 1961, the Soviet Union and the United States engaged in the resumption of nuclear testing (including a Soviet 60-megaton explosion in the atmosphere on October 30). After the Cuban "nuclear" confrontation in October 1962, however, Khrushchev gradually began to change his approach, and President Kennedy referred to hopeful "winds of change" at the close of his State of the Union message on January 14, 1963. The President alerted the American people to new possibilities in a notable address at The American University in Washington, D.C., on June 10, 1963:

> . . . Let us re-examine our attitude toward the Soviet Union.
>
> . . . No government or social system is so evil that its people must be considered as lacking in virtue.
>
> . . . Among the many traits the people of our two countries have in common, none is stronger than our mutual abhorrence of war. Almost unique among the major world powers, we have never been at war with each other. . . .
>
> . . . In short, both the United States and its allies, and the Soviet Union and its allies, have a mutually deep interest in a just and genuine peace and in halting the arms race.
>
> . . . And if we cannot end now our divisions, at least we can help

make the world safe for diversity.

. . . We must . . . persevere in the search for peace in the hope that constructive changes within the Communist bloc might bring within reach solutions which now seem beyond us. We must conduct our affairs in such a way that it becomes in the Communists' interest to agree on a genuine peace.[133]

Negotiations for a test-ban treaty began in Moscow on July 14, 1963, among representatives of America, Britain and the Soviet Union. (One should note that between July 5 and 20, Soviet-Chinese negotiations in Moscow ended in what seemed to be a definite "parting of the ways.") The three powers officially signed the treaty banning nuclear tests in the atmosphere, in outer space and under water, August 5. President Kennedy viewed the treaty as a "first step" in the "path to peace." By August 30, a "hot-line" (for instantaneous direct communication) was established between Washington and Moscow.

Kennedy appeared before the United Nations General Assembly a second time, on September 20, 1963, to appeal for further acts of cooperation, following the test-ban treaty:

. . . In a field where the United States and the Soviet Union have a special capacity—in the field of space—there is room for new cooperation. . . . I include among these possibilities a joint expedition to the moon. . . . Why should man's first flight to the moon be a matter of national competition?

. . . Let us strive to build peace, a desire for peace, a willingness to work for peace, in the hearts and minds of all our people. I believe that we can.[134]

The U.S. Senate approved the test-ban treaty on September 24 by the substantial margin of 80 to 19. President Kennedy ratified it for the United States on October 7, and it was later ratified by practically all the nations of the world except Communist China and France.

The President spoke fervently about his hopes for peace throughout the last few months of his life. To the Irish Parliament, on June 28, 1963, he affirmed his belief that "the supreme reality of our time is our indivisibility as children of God and our common vulnerability on this planet."[135] At the Mormon Tabernacle in Salt Lake City, September 26, he emphasized his view that America's world involvement is "irreversible."[136] To the Protestant Council of the City of New York, November 8, he spoke repeatedly of "The Family of Man," at a time when the foreign aid proposals were encountering heavy opposition in Congress:

> The rich must help the poor. The industrialized nations must help the developing nations.
>
> . . . The dignity and liberty of all free men, of a world of diversity where the balance of power is clearly on the side of the free nations, is essential to the security of the United States.
>
> . . . It is essential . . . that the word go forth from the United States to all who are concerned about the future of the Family of Man that we are not weary in well-doing. And I am confident, if we maintain the peace, we shall in due course reap the kind of world we deserve and deserve the kind of world we shall have.[137]

President Kennedy also worked for the strengthening of the nation internally. He moved slowly but steadily at first to fulfill the Democratic Party's pledge to broaden civil rights for the American blacks (or African-Americans). But a challenging climax was reached in the ugly racial incident at Birmingham, Alabama, in May 1963. The President felt impelled to speak out to the nation over television, on June 11:

> We are confronted primarily with a moral issue. It is as old as the Scriptures and is as clear as the American Constitution.
>
> The heart of the question is whether all Americans are to be afforded equal rights and equal opportunities, whether we are going to treat our fellow Americans as we want to be treated. . . .
>
> . . . One hundred years of delay have passed since President Lincoln freed the slaves, yet their heirs, their grandsons, are not fully free.
>
> . . . This is one country. It has become one country because all of us and all the people who came here had an equal chance to develop their talents.[138]

On June 19, President Kennedy asked Congress to pass a new Civil Rights Act to promote equal rights and to help end segregation in education. On August 28, about 200,000 Americans of both races staged an impressive, orderly civil rights march in Washington, D.C., where Dr. Martin Luther King, Jr., delivered his famous "I Have A Dream" address.

Near the end of his administration, the President felt forced to turn against President Diem of South Vietnam. Diem was a Catholic who was beginning to lose popular support, especially from the Buddhists. When Diem declared martial law, August 21, and ordered his troops to seize hundreds of Buddhist priests, the United States denounced his action. The result was a military coup which overthrew and killed Diem and his autocratic brother, November 1 and 2. The outlook for South Vietnam became even more uncertain.

In an undelivered speech for Dallas on November 22, 1963, President Kennedy gave his last interpretation of America's goals in the world—a truly farewell speech to the country:

> The success of our leadership is dependent upon respect for our mission in the world as well as our missiles—on a clearer recognition of the virtues of freedom as well as the evils of tyranny.
>
> . . . It should be clear by now that a nation can be no stronger abroad than she is at home. Only an America which practices what it preaches about equal rights and social justice will be respected by those whose choice affects our future.
>
> . . . Now we have the military, the scientific and the economic strength to do whatever must be done for the preservation and promotion of freedom.
>
> That strength will never be used in pursuit of aggressive ambitions; it will always be used in pursuit of peace. It will never be used to promote provocations; it will always be used to promote the peaceful settlement of disputes.
>
> We in this country, in this generation, are, by destiny rather than choice, the watchmen on the walls of world freedom. We ask, therefore, that we may be worthy of our power and responsibility, that we may exercise our strength with wisdom and restraint, and that we may achieve in our time and for all time the ancient vision of "peace on earth, good will toward men." That must always be our goal—and the righteousness of our cause must always underlie our strength. For as was written long ago: "Except the Lord keep the city, the watchman waketh but in vain."[139]

The indelible date was November 22, 1963: as John Fitzgerald Kennedy rode through cheering crowds in Dallas on his way to speak at a luncheon meeting, he was assassinated, presumably by Lee Harvey Oswald. The revulsion of the nation against this horrible act of violence and other such acts would ensure the passage of a strong Civil Rights Act. It became apparent only after his death that he and his wife had captured the imagination and hope of much of the world, particularly among the youth—King Arthur's Camelot seemed to have been reborn for them. There is little doubt that the miracle of modern communication heightened the sense of personal loss which for a moment tied the world together. The President's tragic assassination, as in the case of Lincoln, would impress the words he spoke and his spirited style more deeply upon the American people.

Lyndon B. Johnson, 1963–66/67

Lyndon B. Johnson became President in the midst of a deep national tragedy, as the nation mourned for the fallen President and felt sharp anguish that the deed had been committed. In the face of the past bitterness over civil rights, the new President appealed for cooperation when he addressed a joint session of Congress on November 27, 1963:

> The time has come for Americans of all races and creeds and political beliefs to understand and to respect one another. So, let us put an end to the teaching and preaching of hate and evil and violence, let us turn away from the fanatic, from the far left and the far right, from the apostles of bitterness and bigotry, from those defiant of the law, and those who pour venom into our nation's bloodstream.[140]

In his Thanksgiving Day address, on November 28, he called upon the United States to "move toward a new American greatness," to "banish rancor from our words and malice from our hearts," and "to hasten the day when bias of race, religion and region is no more and to bring the day when our great energies, and decencies and spirit will be free of the burden that we have borne so long."[141] Thus did a President from the South join to support the on-going "black revolution" in America.

The President was able to sign the civil rights bill supported by President Kennedy on July 2, 1964. Following riots and police confrontations, Johnson called upon Congress for a much stronger voting rights bill (March 19, 1965), and this was signed on August 6. Only nine days later, the nation was shocked and horrified by the black riot in Watts, a Los Angeles suburb, with 35 killed and $40 million of property destroyed.

In the meantime, the challenge from North Vietnam was increasing, and two American destroyers were allegedly attacked in August in the Gulf of Tonkin. Congress supported the President immediately by passing a strong resolution, August 7, 1964, authorizing the President to "take all necessary measures to repel any armed attack against the forces of the United States and to prevent further aggression" in Southeast Asia (the House vote was 416 to 0, the Senate 88 to 2).[142] (This Tonkin Gulf Resolution was used as Congressional authorization by the President in 1965 to order American armed forces into the conflict.)

In the national election on November 3, 1964, the President swamped Senator Barry M. Goldwater by 43 million votes to 27 million (486 to 52 electoral votes). The campaign had had the effect of making President Johnson appear as a "dove" as compared to the "hawk-like" approach of Senator Goldwater. Thus the Communists in North Vietnam might well have been misled as to America's intentions, while they may also have been buoyed by the first nuclear explosion in Communist China on October 6. President Johnson stressed the domestic scene in his State of the Union message on January 4, 1965, emphasizing the historical view that America was entering the third century of its pursuit of American union (opening in 1765 with the Stamp Act Congress, and followed by the compact of union finally sealed in 1865). His pledge to the world was in line with America's democratic traditions, stressing "diversity" as did his predecessor:

> We seek not fidelity to an iron faith, but a diversity of belief as varied as man himself. We seek not to extend the power of America but the progress of humanity. We seek not to dominate others but to strengthen the freedom of all.[143]

The President's Inaugural Address, January 20, 1965, was an appeal to the faith of Americans in relation to America's destiny as a whole: "Our destiny in the midst of change will rest in the unchanged character of our people—and on their faith." Those who came to America, he continued:

> made a covenant with this land. Conceived in justice, written in liberty, bound in union, it was meant one day to inspire the hopes of all mankind. And it binds us still. And if we keep its terms we shall flourish.
> . . . We can never again stand aside, prideful in isolation. . . .How incredible it is in this fragile existence we should hate and destroy one another. . . .
> If we succeed, it will not be because of what we have, but what we are; not because of what we own but rather of what we believe.[144]

President Johnson used the phrase, the "Great Society," to symbolize his domestic goals. He stressed a "war on poverty" and the promotion of health and education, along with the stimulation of business (he signed his notable "Medicare" bill on June 3, 1965).

He stood firm in the Caribbean as well as in Southeast Asia. The Administration believed there was a possibility of a second "Cuba" when the civilian junta in the Dominican Republic was overthrown on April 25, 1965. American troops were landed to protect the lives of Americans, and an Inter-American Force, including a majority from the United States, was established on May 6. By August 31, mediation by the Organization of American States brought about a political settlement.

In South Vietnam, just before the American election in 1964, several American soldiers were killed in a Vietcong raid on American bases near Saigon—these soldiers were serving as advisers. When seven more American soldiers were killed and over 100 wounded at Pleiku, February 5, 1965, the President was ready for retaliatory air attacks on the southern portion of North Vietnam. Rising criticism by some Americans of this new involvement may have encouraged the President to announce that the United States was ready for "unconditional" talks with North Vietnam (April 7). A major statement by President Johnson on July 28 announced America's increased commitment to actual ground fighting by American soldiers, with the troop level raised from 75,000 to 125,000; and again he called for peace negotiations. The war kept "escalating" slowly and steadily, as American forces engaged in heavy fighting and casualties mounted. Thailand began to furnish bases, and South Korea, Australia and New Zealand sent troops (in contrast to the Korean War, the United Nations was not involved).

In the midst of the enlarging struggle, the President explained America's goals carefully and appealed for peace, in his third annual address, January 12, 1966:

> An America mighty beyond description—yet living in a hostile and despairing world—would be neither safe, nor free to build a civilization to liberate the spirit of man.
>
> . . . History is on the side of freedom. It is on the side of societies shaped from the genius of each people.
>
> . . . We will stay because in Asia—and around the world—are countries whose course of independence rests, in large measure, on confidence in American protection.

. . . Our decision to stand firm has been matched by our desire for peace.

. . . To all those caught up in this conflict, we . . . say again: Let us choose peace, and with it the wondrous works of peace, and beyond that, the time when hope reaches unchained toward consummation, and life is the servant of life.[145]

America's impact on the world, the President (as well as Secretary of State Dean Rusk) came more and more to believe, would depend in the future largely upon the fulfillment of American ideals at home and the application of those ideals to the world scene. Thus Johnson spoke at the University of Denver on August 26, 1966:

The overwhelming rule which I want to affirm is that our foreign policy must always be an extension of our domestic policy. Our safest guide to what we do abroad is always what we do at home.

The great creative periods of American foreign policy have been the great periods of domestic achievement. Lincoln, Wilson and Franklin Roosevelt—to mention but three—projected their image of concern and accomplishment to the entire world.

. . . Our foreign policy, like our domestic policy, is all those things from education, to jobs, to order, to health, to justice for all our people.[146]

The President left for an Asian trip on October 17, 1966, and was warmly welcomed in the seven nations he visited, including American troops when in South Vietnam (there were over 350,000 American troops there by this time). He reaffirmed and strengthened America's commitment to the defense of South Vietnam, to a negotiated solution if possible, and to the future development of Asia. His trip was widely regarded as symbolic of a new commitment for America to aid in the development of an independent "emerging" Asia. Johnson spoke in these terms to the Korean National Assembly on November 1:

The world has turned its eyes to Asia and begun to understand the goals, the problems and the energies of this region where almost two-thirds of humanity lives.

A new, young generation of Asian leaders is determined that there shall be security and order and progress in this region. These are men who are prepared to stake their lives on that proposition.

The new Asia will remain loyal to its own traditions and culture and values, even as it works constructively with the United States and other nations throughout the world.

> . . . I have seen millions of faces—friendly and well-wishing. And
> I have been deeply encouraged. I leave today with a deep sense of
> confidence in the future of Asia and the Pacific.[147]

Only a short time before his trip to Asia, President Johnson made a
plea to the Russian people and government, September 27, 1966, in an
interview published in the magazine *Amerika*, and distributed by the
U.S. Information Agency in the Soviet Union:

> The United States and the Soviet Union still have an agenda of
> unresolved difficulties, some of them quite serious. I believe we can
> settle these disputes, honorably and peacefully. We in the United States
> are determined to try.
> . . . As great powers, our two nations will undoubtedly have
> commitments that will conflict. But there is one commitment I hope we
> both share: the commitment to a warless world. However you define it,
> this is mankind's age of greatest promise. We must move toward
> it—not toward war. We must find ways toward disarmament and an
> international rule of law strong enough to take the place of arms.[148]

President Johnson had sought a negotiated peace throughout the war
in Vietnam, stopping the bombing for several rather long periods to
encourage negotiation, or mediation by others. But the North
Vietnamese, with aid from Communist China and the Soviet Union, had
confidence in their staying power. In America, however, the war was
seen as a bitter stalemate with heavy casualties on both sides, half way
around the world. The opposition to the war increased steadily in the
United States. According to Chester L. Cooper, American diplomatist
close to the events in Southeast Asia: "in November, 1966, the Johnson
Administration embarked on a sustained search for 'a way out.' "[149]
The extrovert mood of America, which had stayed relatively strong for
26 years, was showing definite signs of changing. The last time
America had reacted against "extroversion" was in 1918/19, when 27
years had ended in a foreign war, even though America was victorious.
This time, the United States was still deeply involved in a far-off war
which seemed to have no end in sight.

Yet, at this very time, after the 26 or 27 years of American military
and economic pressure around the world, it appears that America had
already helped achieve, far more than was perceived at the time, a high
degree of security and strength for the "free world." The contrast was

remarkable between the world in 1966 and in 1940, when the Fascists seemed on the verge of world domination; or 1949, when the Communists of the Soviet Union and China apparently had great hopes of expansion. By 1966/67, Western Europe (particularly West Germany) and Japan had become major democratic centers of prosperity and potential power; South Korea and the Republic of China (Taiwan) were on the verge of rapid economic development; the vast region of Southeast Asia outside former French Indochina remained independent and was growing strong—Thailand, Malaysia, Indonesia, Singapore, the Philippines and Burma—because of the American stand in South Vietnam; no country in Africa had gone Communist, and only one in Latin America (Cuba). In addition, the Soviet Union and Communist China seemed to have been irrevocably split, while in 1966 Communist China turned inward in the "Great Proletarian Cultural Revolution." The United States had also helped the United Nations to play an important role in protecting freedom, preventing major war, and encouraging economic development. The world crisis for freedom seemed to have been largely overcome by 1966/67.

Little of this major success of America and its allies seemed apparent to the American people at the time, with the nation deeply bogged down in the unpopular Vietnam War. By 1967, a new wave of relative introversion appeared ready to move over America (for the fifth time since 1776), even while the nation saw no easy or honorable way to withdraw from Vietnam. In fact, among some Americans there had been preliminary signs of a mood favoring considerable withdrawal from such deep world involvement ever since 1963.

Preliminary Signs of Introversion, 1963–66

After the virtual "nuclear" confrontation over Cuba in October 1962, both the United States and the Soviet Union appeared to "back off," as shown in the Nuclear Test Ban Treaty signed in August 1963. Problems with American allies began to appear in 1963, raising doubts in the minds of some Americans about the strength of American ties abroad. A serious split in NATO loomed as a possibility, following President De Gaulle's veto (January 14, 1963) of the British application for admission to the European Common market. By February 1966, De Gaulle had removed French military forces from the NATO command, and on July 1, 1966, had all foreign troops and bases removed from French soil. France and West Germany were both looking toward improved relations with the Soviet Union. Considerable American opinion was represented by the resolution introduced by 13 Senators (including Senate majority leader Mike Mansfield) proposing a reduction in the size of American forces in Europe (August 31, 1966).

Many Americans were also turning against deeper involvement in Vietnam during the summer of 1963, as they watched the increasingly repressive regime of President Diem. After the death of President Diem, the government of South Vietnam remained unstable and rather ineffective. It is not clear what President Kennedy would have done in Vietnam, had he lived, but his death on November 22, 1963, was a powerful blow to America's general morale, especially among the youth.

At the same time, domestic problems were attracting increased attention. In the year 1963, racial tension rose dramatically, as a new day appeared to be dawning for black influence. Americans also became aware of increased crime, poverty, urban problems, the "youth revolt," and educational inadequacies, as well as over race. Jules David wrote that "a striking evidence of change could be observed in the nation's 'mood' in 1964, with Americans more perturbed by domestic than international problems."[150] The President responded positively by getting Congress to enact legislation for the "Great Society." Even so, major confrontations of black marchers and police, and black riots, occurred in 1965, 1966 and 1967. A "black revolution" was under way, supported by many white Americans.

Step by step, President Johnson was to find himself forced deeper into Vietnam, despite his pledge for peace in the 1964 election campaign, somewhat analogous to the position of Woodrow Wilson after the campaign of 1916. The President desired peace, but the North Vietnamese leaders apparently interpreted the election of Johnson as a sign of no direct American involvement or American weakness, and thus attacked the bases of American advisers. The American decision to help South Vietnam, however, seemed virtually required by the spirit of the Truman Doctrine, and by the terms of the Southeast Asian Treaty Organization. However, the rising uneasiness over the Vietnam War was reflected rather strongly in the decision of Senator James W. Fulbright (Chairman of the Foreign Relations Committee) to hold critical hearings on the question of the war before his committee, beginning on January 28, 1966. Signs of generally weakening "consensus" were especially evident in the summer of 1966, not only in opposition to the war, but particularly in the field of race relations. The concept of "black power" began to split the civil rights movement, which had stressed "non-violence" under the leadership of Dr. Martin Luther King, Jr. Dr. King also began to oppose the war in Vietnam. A wave of racial riots swept over the country in July 1966, shortly after heavy bombing of the Hanoi and Haiphong areas in North Vietnam. The impressive gains of the Republicans in the November 8, 1966, Congressional elections, were widely interpreted as representing growing dissatisfaction—for both "hawks" and "doves"—with the continuance of the inconclusive war. The numbers, especially of college students, who participated in major (with over 1,000 persons) anti-war demonstrations grew steadily: 100,000 in 1966, and 160,000 in 1967. Public opinion around the world also seemed to grow more hostile to America's role, as the heavy bombing was continued and intensified. By October 1967, a majority of the American people (46 to 44 percent) already believed that the United States had made a mistake in sending troops to Vietnam (Gallup Poll).

In retrospect, the outlook in 1966/67 might have seemed fundamentally hopeful in the world as a whole, yet Americans had perhaps never felt more confused, uncertain, or frustrated about what their policy ought to be, as the war in Vietnam dragged on. It appears also that the American people were beginning to react against their prolonged deep military and political involvement in the world, by a trend toward "withdrawal" or "leveling-off," with the aim of "no more Vietnams."

Realism and the Rise of Moral Concerns, 1940–66/67

Realism (stressing the role of military force) in international affairs and secularism tended to dominate this period. World War II was fought to the bitter end, with unrestrained bombing of cities and with the requirement by the Allies of unconditional surrender by the Axis powers. The international law of war was given little consideration, contrary to the American approach before World War I.

After World War II and the beginning of the "cold war," John H. Hallowell, political philosopher, wrote squarely (1950) of the "crisis of our times" in the world:

> It requires no great seer or prophet to discern today the signs of decadence that are everywhere manifest. Only the most stubborn would venture optimistic prediction for the future of the world and its civilization. The complacent optimism of the last century has given way

to a deep-rooted despair and men everywhere are gripped by fear and insecurity. . . .

The sickness of the modern world is the sickness of moral confusion, intellectual anarchy, and spiritual despair. . . . Having alienated himself from God, having discredited the reason with which he was endowed by God, unable or unwilling to identify the evil with which the world of man is infected—modern man oscillates between extravagant optimism and hopeless despair. . . . In his anxiety to escape from utter futility and meaningless existence he is tempted to give up his most priceless heritage—his freedom—to any man who even promises deliverance from insecurity. . . .[151]

Material goals were stressed. Max Lerner, a liberal writer, saw a basically secular America in 1957, when his exhaustive study of American civilization was published. He noted, among other things, that a new sexual freedom had replaced the centuries-old "Puritan heritage of repression," and that "the reigning moral deity in America is 'fun.' "[152] He described the mixture of secular and religious elements in American culture:

America is as secular as a culture can be where religion has played an important role in its origins and early growth and has been intertwined with the founding and meaning of the society. It is also as religious as a culture can be whose life goals are worldly and whose daily strivings revolve not around God but around man.[153]

Cynicism grew as motives of political and business leaders were suspect. When the hopeful President Kennedy was assassinated in 1963, many people, especially among the young, felt a sense of despair about the future. Crime increased. Racial animosity continued. The fighting in Vietnam brought bitter opposition.

Yet World War II and its aftermath, including nuclear weapons, induced a reaction toward rising moral and spiritual concern, particularly among American statesmen and various influential writers. Thus American realism and secularism was tempered by a renewed idealism, especially in terms of the purposes of the nation on the world scene.

Notable in its impact, at the beginning of the war, was the appearance of the first of two volumes by Dr. Reinhold Niebuhr, theologian: *Human Nature*, 1941. He carefully distinguished the "classical" and "modern" views of man from the "Christian" view, and was becoming the leader of a group of influential theologians (neo-orthodox) and writers who were trying the reinterpret history and culture in the light of Judeo-Christian principles and to apply these principles to political and social life. In 1943, Niebuhr's second volume, *Human Destiny*, was published, with a concluding section on the meaning of history and its fulfillment "beyond history."[154] Niebuhr had led the way for many Christians to support the war against Hitler, but when peace came he warned the super-power America against the temptations and dangers of excessive pride and power (1952):

> If virtue becomes vice through some hidden defect in the virtue; if strength becomes weakness because of the vanity to which strength may prompt the mighty man or nation; if security is transmuted into insecurity because too much reliance is placed upon it; if wisdom becomes folly because it does not know its own limits—in all such cases the situation is ironic.[155]

He thought that the urgencies of the struggle against communism should be "subordinated to a sense of awe before the vastness of the historical drama in which we are jointly involved; to a sense of modesty about the virtue and wisdom and power available to us for the resolution of its perplexities; to a sense of contrition about the common human frailties and foibles which lie at the foundation of both the enemy's demonry and our vanities; and to a sense of gratitude for the divine mercies which are promised to those who humble themselves."[156]

Among the notable preachers of the day was Dr. Peter Marshall in Washington, D.C. (where he served for a time as Chaplain of the U.S. Senate). He spoke before overflowing crowds in the late 1940s, and in "The American Dream," stressed the idea that the United States was a "Covenant Nation":

> . . . A Covenant Nation is one which recognizes that God and His purposes stand over and above the nation . . .
>
> that the highest role a nation can play is to reflect God's righteousness in national policy.
>
> . . . There have been periods in our history when the American Dream has faded and grown dim.
>
> Today there is real danger that the American Dream will become the Forgotten Dream.
>
> . . . The price of world leadership is high.
>
> . . . I believe that the dream has been glimpsed by enough people

and is deep enough in the heart of the average citizen to shape America's future and make the dream come true.

. . . America may be humanity's last chance.

Certainly it is God's latest experiment.[157]

While the Senate was considering whether devastated Europe should be sent greatly needed food, Peter Marshall prayed before the Senate, March 3, 1947:

> Lord God of Heaven, who hath so lavishly blessed our beloved land, keep us humble. Forgive our boasting and our pride, and help us to share what Thou hast given. Impress us with a sense of responsibility, and remind us, lest we become filled with conceit, that one day a reckoning will be required of us.[158]

Dr. Marshall died young, but a new figure appeared on the scene when Dr. Billy Graham addressed a crowd of 40,000 from the steps of the Capitol in 1952, and went on to cover the nation and the world. The spirit of expectancy which many Americans felt, as the new year of 1953 began, was expressed poetically by Carl Sandburg:

> I see America, not in the setting sun of a black night of despair ahead of us. I see America in the crimson light of a rising sun fresh from the burning, creative hand of God. I see great days ahead, great days possible to men and women of will and vision. . . .[159]

The most noted Christian leader of America toward racial reconciliation and international peace was Dr. Martin Luther King, Jr., who summarized the results of his "nonviolent" approach as follows:

> The nonviolent approach does not immediately change the heart of the oppressor. It first does something to the hearts and souls of those committed to it. It gives them new self-respect; it calls up resources of strength and courage that they did not know they had. Finally it reaches the opponent and so stirs his conscience that reconciliation becomes a reality.
>
> I suggest this approach because I think it is the only way to re-establish the broken community. . . .
>
> . . . This is a great hour for the Negro. The challenge is here. To become the instruments of a great idea is a privilege that history gives only occasionally. Arnold Toynbee says in *A Study of History* that it may be the Negro who will give the new spiritual dynamic to Western

civilization that it so desperately needs to survive. I hope this is possible. The spiritual power that the Negro can radiate to the world comes from love, understanding, good will, and nonviolence. . . . The eternal appeal takes the form of a warning: "All that take the sword will perish by the sword."[160]

Many Americans, white and black, were deeply impressed by King's fervent "I Have a Dream" address in Washington, D.C., August 28, 1963, before the Lincoln Memorial, ending with these words:

> And when we allow freedom to ring, when we let it ring from every village and hamlet, from every state and city, we will be able to speed up that day when all of God's children—black men and white men, Jews and Gentiles, Catholics and Protestants—will be able to join hands and to sing in the words of the old Negro spiritual, "Free at last, free at last; thank God Almighty, we are free at last."[161]

King received the Nobel Peace Prize in 1964. His principles ultimately led him to oppose the war in Vietnam, tying the peace movement to the civil rights movement in his address, "A Time to Break Silence," at Riverside Church in New York City, April 4, 1967.[162]

American statesmen continued to point the way to the nation's moral leadership on the world scene. President Roosevelt inspired the American people during World War II with his statements and his impressive prayers. He ended his Fourth Inaugural Address, January 20, 1945, with a prayer which concluded: "So we pray to Him now for the vision to see our way clearly—to see the way that leads to a better life for ourselves and for our fellowmen—to the achievement of His will, to peace on earth."[163] The sudden death of the President, on April 12, 1945, had a deep psychological and spiritual impact on the people of America and the whole world. His spirit marched on, so to speak, at the United Nations Conference which opened in San Francisco on April 25.

The "blinding light" of two atomic bombs preceded the surrender of Japan on August 14, 1945. General Douglas MacArthur perceived the beginning of a "new age" as he stood on the Battleship *Missouri* to accept the surrender:

> A new era is upon us. . . .
> Men since the beginning of time have sought peace. . . . Military alliances, balance of power, league of nations all in turn failed, leaving the only path to be by way of the crucible of war.

The utter destructiveness of war now blots out this alternative. If we do not devise some greater and more equitable system Armageddon will be at our door. The problem basically is theological and involves a spiritual recrudescence and improvement of human character that will synchronize with our almost matchless advance in science, art, literature, and all material and cultural developments of the past two thousand years. It must be of the spirit if we are to save the flesh.[164]

When the "cold war" with the Soviet Union developed in 1947 and after, President Truman stressed a new note in his message to Congress, January 7, 1948: "The basic source of our strength is spiritual. . . . This is the hour to rededicate ourselves to the faith in God that gives us confidence as we face the challenge of the years ahead."[165] And so the President continued to speak, particularly during the dark days of the Korean War (1950–53). (The year 1950 was already two-thirds of the way through the revolutionary period from 1918 to 1966 with moral-spiritual signs more evident in the last third.)

In relation to the relations between the Soviet Union and America, the most notable prophecy or expectation of the time was written by George F. Kennan (former official in the American Embassy in Moscow, and a member of the Policy Planning Staff of the Department of State at the time) in 1947, as he explained the importance of the proposed policy of the "containment" of Soviet expansion:

> . . . The United States has it in its power to increase enormously the strains under which Soviet policy must operate, to force upon the Kremlin a far greater degree of moderation and circumspection than it has had to observe in recent years, and in this way to promote tendencies which must eventually find their outlet in either the break-up or the gradual mellowing of Soviet power. . . .
>
> Thus the decision will really fall in large measure in this country itself. The issue of Soviet-American relations is in essence a test of the over-all worth of the United States as a nation among nations. To avoid destruction the United States need only measure up to its own best traditions and prove itself worthy of preservation as a great nation.
>
> . . . The thoughtful observer of Russian-American relations will find no cause for complaint in the Kremlin's challenge to American society. He will rather experience a certain gratitude to a Providence which, by providing the American people with this implacable challenge, has made their entire security as a nation dependent on their pulling themselves together and accepting the responsibilities of moral and political leadership their history plainly intended them to bear[166]

(It appears that both parts of Kennan's "prophecy"—break-up and mellowing—were being fulfilled 40 long years later, in the later 1980s.)

It seems that the United States did rise to the challenge which Kennan perceived, as its leaders continued to show a high degree of idealism, as well as realism, in the "realistic" age of the "balance of terror" in nuclear arms. Among those to witness publicly to their spiritual conviction in 1950 and after were Dwight D. Eisenhower, then President of Columbia University, and John Foster Dulles, Republican consultant to the Department of State (during World War II, Dulles had been Chairman of the Commission on a Just and Durable Peace, established by the Federal Council of Churches, and in 1950 he published a widely-read book on *War or Peace* in which he stressed America's "spiritual need").[167] President Truman asked Dulles in 1950 to negotiate a peace treaty between the Allies and Japan. Dulles (who had been present at Versailles in 1919 when a considerable spirit of "revenge" was evident) affirmed that he had made an effort "to invoke the principles of the moral law" in order to make a peace of reconciliation, "the spirit of forgiveness to overcome the spirit of vengefulness; the spirit of magnanimity to overcome the spirit of hatred; the spirit of humanity and fair play to overcome the spirit of competitive greed; and the spirit of fellowship to overcome the spirit of arrogance and discrimination; and the spirit of trust to overcome the spirit of fear."[168] After a year of negotiation, the Japanese Peace Conference assembled at San Francisco in September 1951. Delegates of nations representing the major religions of the world stood to express their belief that the treaty was in line with the highest traditions of their religions. The Japanese Prime Minister declared: "It is not a treaty of vengeance, but an instrument of reconciliation. All Japanese delegates gladly accept this fair and generous treaty." Dulles continued: "the chairman of the conference, Dean Acheson, concluded it with a benediction which had never before been pronounced at such a gathering, but which had been made appropriate by all that had gone before. . . ."[169] The treaty was signed by representatives of all the nations present except the Soviet Union.

When Eisenhower became President and Dulles Secretary of State in 1953, the two men inaugurated one of the most open commitments to religious faith in American political history. Dulles died in May 1959, leaving behind a vital legacy of faith. President Eisenhower symbolized the spirit he hoped to demonstrate by opening his Inaugural Address with a personal prayer. His cabinet meetings were also opened with silent or spoken prayer. Secretary Dulles stressed the need for people to learn to sacrifice for peace as they did for war.[170] Both Eisenhower and Dulles expressed their faith in the people behind the "Iron Curtain." Eisenhower spoke in this manner in 1956:

> . . . Hundreds of millions who dwell there still cling to their religious faith; still are moved by aspirations for justice and freedom that cannot be answered merely by more steel or by bigger bombers; still seek a reward that is beyond money or place or power; still dream of the day that they may walk fearlessly in the fullness of human freedom.
>
> The destiny of man is freedom and justice under his Creator. Any ideology that denies this universal faith will ultimately perish or be recast. This is the first great truth that must underlie all our thinking, all our striving in this struggling world.[171]

Dulles expressed his conviction (as in 1957) that dictatorial communism was a passing phase in China:

> We know that the materialistic rule of international communism will never permanently serve the aspirations with which human beings are endowed by their Creator.
>
> Communism is repugnant to the Chinese people. They are, above all, individualists. . . .
>
> . . . We can hopefully look forward to the day when those in Asia who are yet free can confidently remain free and when the people of China and the people of America can resume their long history of cooperative friendship.[172]

Dulles spoke in West Berlin on May 8, 1958, paying tribute to the spirit of the people and recalling the surprise decision of the Russians to liberate Austria:

> It shows that we need not despair for Germany and for Berlin. The day will come when, probably unexpectedly and without predictability, the Geneva promises of 1955 will be fulfilled and Germany will again be reunified in freedom.
>
> . . . Berlin teaches . . . that man is a spiritual being able, by faith, to perform miracles. . . .[173]

The President opened his 1959 State of the Union Address (January 9) with a question, and affirmed his faith in a positive answer:

Can government based upon liberty and the God-given rights of man permanently endure when ceaselessly challenged by a dictatorship, hostile to our mode of life, and controlling an economic and military strength of great and growing power?

For us the answer has always been found, and is still found, in the devotion, the vision, the courage, and the fortitude of our people. . . .

. . . If we make ourselves worthy of America's Ideals, if we do not forget that our Nation was founded on the premise that all men are creatures of God's making, the world will come to know that it is free men who carry forward the true promise of human progress and dignity.[174]

Secretary Dulles made his last public appearances in January 1959. To the Senate Foreign Relations Committee, January 14, he stressed his hope in freedom and in America for the long-run future:

. . . As we look ahead, we see freedom as a predominant force, shaping our 20th-century world. As Americans, we have faith that the aspiration, deep within the soul of man, to live freely and with dignity in a just and peaceful world is stronger than all the material forces which the Communists invoke as the pledge and promise of their power. . . . [175]

In 1959 and 1960, when President Eisenhower undertook his trip to many nations, everywhere he went he carried with him a message of common moral and religious values which he believed could lead the world to peace.

After 1960, there appeared to be rising signs in America which many interpreted as the practical harvest of a long period of moral and spiritual decline or apathy among a large part of the citizenry, but both Presidents John F. Kennedy and Lyndon B. Johnson delivered strong moral and spiritual appeals on a number of occasions. President Kennedy stressed activism, as when he concluded his Inaugural Address with the words: "knowing that here on earth God's work must truly be our own."[176] His final words in his undelivered speech scheduled for Dallas, November 22, 1963, were:

. . . the righteousness of our cause must always underlie our strength. For as was written long ago, "Except the Lord keep the city, the watchman waketh but in vain."[177]

President Johnson also spoke strongly in terms of spiritual faith, as in his Inaugural Address on January 20, 1965:

> Under this covenant—of justice, liberty and union—we have become a nation; prosperous, great, and mighty. We have kept our freedom.
> But we have no promise from God that our greatness will endure.
> We have been allowed by Him to seek greatness with the sweat of our hands and the strength of our spirit.[178]

After emphasizing the spirit of service, the President ended his State of the Union message on January 12, 1966, by deploring the necessity of the war in Vietnam:

> . . . I must order the guns to fire, against all the most inward pulls of my desire. For we have children to teach and sick to be cured and men to be freed. There are poor to be lifted up and cities to be built and a world to be helped.[179]

Annual Presidential Prayer Breakfasts were begun in 1953 and have been held ever since, along with weekly prayer breakfasts for Senators and Representatives. At such a Presidential Breakfast, February 17, 1966, President Johnson spoke in conclusion:

> . . . In private prayer at unusual moments, I have found courage to meet another day in a world where peace on earth is still only an empty dream. The prophet Isaiah tells us, "they that wait upon the Lord shall renew their strength". . . .
> I believe that with all my heart.
> . . . I am sustained by the prayers of hundreds of Americans who daily take the time to look up from their own problems in order to try to give me a little encouragement in mine.[180]

In the face of such events as the assassination of a President, the war in Vietnam, and the race riots in Watts, the response of some Americans was to become more cynical and fatalistic than before. But there were many others who began to seek new spiritual answers—to seek for the meaning of these events in an assumed spiritual universe. Polls showed that Americans as a whole retained or had regained their faith in religion as a vital force, although they judged in 1965 that religion was losing some of its influence relatively (65 percent saw it losing, 33 percent gaining).[181]

In relation to the "world crisis for freedom" which had lasted since 1918, the "free world" led by the United States seemed to have, in a sense, "won" the struggle against totalitarianism by 1966/67. But this result was not evident at this time to most Americans, as the continuing stalemated war in Vietnam strengthened an American reaction toward introversion.

Notes

1. The emphasis on personal and party factors is stressed in the widely read study by Denna F. Fleming, *The United States and the League of Nations, 1918–1920* (New York: G. P. Putnam's, 1932), especially ch. 3, "The Plan of Opposition," and ch. 19, "Wilson and Lodge."

2. See Robert Lansing, *The Peace Negotiations: A Personal Narrative* (Boston: Houghton Mifflin, 1921), 34–35, 71.

3. See Arthur S. Link, *Wilson the Diplomatist* (Baltimore: Johns Hopkins University Press, 1957), 153–55.

4. Woodrow Wilson, *War and Peace*, 2 vols. of *Presidential Messages, Addresses, and Public Papers*, eds. Ray Stannard Baker and William E. Dodd (New York: Harpers, 1927), 1:425–26, 429.

5. Ibid., 433–34, 436–37, 439.

6. *Selected Literary and Political Papers of Woodrow Wilson*, 3 vols. (New York: Grosset and Dunlap, 1927), 2:326–29.

7. Ibid., 334, 336–37, 340.

8. Wilson, *War and Peace* 1:549.

9. Ibid., 555–56.

10. Ibid., 550–52.

11. Fleming, 325–26.

12. *Selected . . . Papers of Wilson*, 2:351.

13. Wilson, *War and Peace*, 2:83.

14. Ibid., 1:633.

15. Ibid., 2:142.

16. *Selected . . . Papers of Wilson*, 2:336.

17. Wilson, *War and Peace*, 2:211–12.

18. *Selected . . . Papers of Wilson*, 2:364–65.

19. Wilson, *War and Peace*, 2:11.

20. *Selected . . . Papers of Wilson*, 2:363–64.

21. Wilson, *War and Peace*, 2:15.

22. *Selected . . . Papers of Wilson*, 2:359.

23. Wilson, *War and Peace*. 2:52, 56–57.

24. Ibid., 181, 194.

25. Ibid., 137.

26. *Selected . . . Papers of Wilson*, 2:386–87.

27. Ibid., 262.

28. Ibid., 390.

29. Wilson, *War and Peace*, 2:453, 455–56.

30. Kirk H. Porter, *National Party Platforms*, (New York: Macmillan, 1942), 449, 451–52.

31. Warren G. Harding, "Speech of Acceptance of Republican Party Nomination," (Marion, Oh., July 22, 1920, issued by the Republican National Committee), 5–7.

32. Fleming, 461–63.

33. Ibid., 471.

34. Mark Sullivan, *Our Times: The United States, 1900–1925*, 6 vols. (New York: Scribner's, 1926–1935), 6:111.

35. *Selected . . . Papers of Wilson*, 2:395, 397–98.

36. Ibid., 399–400.

37. See Quincy Wright, *The Study of International Relations* (New York: Appleton-Century-Crofts, 1955), 69–70.

38. Denna F. Fleming, *The United States and World Organization, 1920–1933* (New York; Columbia University Press, 1938), 70.

39. 52nd Congress, *A Compilation of the Messages and Papers of the Presidents*, 18 vols. (New York: Bureau of National Literature), 18:9030.

40. "Address of President Coolidge at the Commencement of George Washington University," Washington, D.C., February 22, 1929 (Washington, D.C.: U.S. Government Printing Office, 1929), 7.

41. William Starr Myers, ed. *The State Papers and Other Public Writings of Herbert Hoover*, 2 vols. (Garden City, N.Y.: Doubleday Doran, 1934), 1:9–10.

42. Ibid., 140.

43. Ibid., 42–43.

44. See Charles A. Beard, *American Foreign Policy in the Making, 1932–1940: A Study in Responsibilities* (New Haven: Yale University Press, 1946), 76–77.

45. *The Public Papers and Addresses of Franklin D. Roosevelt*, ed. Samuel I. Rosenman, 13 vols. (New York: Random House, I-V; Macmillan, VI-IX; Harpers, X-XIII, 1938–1950), 2:11.

46. Denna D. Fleming, *The United States and the World Court* (Garden City, N.Y.: Doubleday Doran, 1945), 117–37.

47. *The Campaign Book of the Democratic Party* (Democratic National Committee, 1936), 5–6.

48. F. D. Roosevelt, *Public Papers*, 5:286, 288–89, 291–92.

49. Ibid., 407–11.

50. Ibid., 8:xxviii.

51. *Public Opinion Quarterly*, 3 (October 1939): 599.

52. Quoted in Paul G. Hoffman, *Peace Can Be Won* (Garden City, N.Y.: Doubleday, 1951), 26.

53. F. D. Roosevelt, *Public Papers*, 8:1–4, 12.

54. Walter L. Langer and S. Everett Gleason, *The Challenge to Isolation, 1937–1940* (New York: Harpers, 1952, 26–27.

55. Ibid., 81.

56. Ibid., 140–44.

57. See Charles A. Beard, *Giddy Minds and Foreign Quarrels* (New York: Macmillan, 1939), 68–70, 73–74.

58. Langer and Gleason, 230–31.

59. F. D. Roosevelt, *Public Papers*, 9:239–40.

60. *Life*, June 3, 1940, 40.

61. Langer and Gleason, 497.

62. F. D. Roosevelt, *Public Papers*, 9:260–62.

63. Langer and Gleason, 678–79.

64. Ibid., 550–51.

65. Ibid., 567.

66. Ibid., 680.

67. Robert T. Handy, "The American Scene" in *Twentieth Century Christianity*, ed. Bishop Stephen Neill (Garden City, N.Y.: Doubleday-Dolphin Books, 1963), 190.

68. Ralph Henry Gabriel, *The Course of American Democratic Thought*, 2nd ed. (New York: Ronald Press, 1928), 407.

69. Charles E. Beard. ed., *Whither Mankind: A Panorama of Modern Civilization* (New York: Longmans, Green, 1928), 403–4, 406.

70. Samuel D. Schmalhausen, ed., *Behold America* (New York: Farrar and Rinehart, 1931), p. x.

71. Frederick Lewis Allen, *Since Yesterday: The 1930s in America* (New York: Harpers, 1940), 158–59.

72. Harold E. Stearns, ed., *America Now: An Inquiry into Civilization in the United States* (New York: Scribner's, 1938), 508–9.

73. Ibid., 536–37, 540.

74. Nicholas Berdyaev, *The End of Out Time*, trans. Donald Atwater (New York: Sheed and Ward, 1933).

75. Arnold J. Toynbee, *A Study of History*, 10 vols. (London: Oxford University Press, 1933, 1939, 1955), 5:193–94, 6:319–21.

76. Lewis Mumford, *Faith for Living* (New York: Harcourt, Brace and Co., 1940), 193, 195–96, 331, 333.

77. F. D. Roosevelt, *Public Papers*, 5:609–10.

78. *Democratic Campaign Handbook* (Democratic National Committee, 1940), 84–85, 90.

79. F. D. Roosevelt, *Public Papers*, 9:327–28.

80. Ibid., 391–92.

81. Ibid., 634–36, 640, 643–44.

82. B. D. Zevin, ed., *Nothing to Fear: The Selected Addresses of Franklin D. Roosevelt, 1932–1945* (Cambridge: Houghton, Mifflin, 1946), 264–67.

83. Henry R. Luce, "The American Century," *Life* (February 17, 1941), 61–65.

84. Francis O. Wilcox and T. V. Kalijarvi, *Recent American Foreign Policy: Basic Documents, 1941–1945* (New York: Appleton-Century-Crofts, 1952), 2.

85. *The War Messages of Franklin D. Roosevelt, December 1941–October 1942* (Washington, D.C.: U.S. Government Printing Office, 1942), 6.

86. Ibid., 13.

87. Ibid., 26.

88. F. D. Roosevelt, *Public Papers*, 13:152–53.

89. *Official Report of the Proceedings of the 23rd Republican National Convention (1944)*, 240.

90. F. D. Roosevelt, *Public Papers*, 13: 203–4.

91. Ibid., 342–43, 353–54.

92. Ibid., 497–500.

93. Ibid., 531–37.

94. Ibid., 577–86.

95. See Walter Millis, ed., *The Forrestal Diaries* (New York: Viking Press, 1951), 39.

96. F. D. Roosevelt, *Public Papers*, 13:613–16.

97. *Congressional Record*, 91:3389.

98. Dwight D. Eisenhower, *Crusade in Europe* (Garden City, N.Y.: Doubleday and Co., 1948), p. 456.

99. Text of Stalin's speech in *New York Times*, February 10, 1946, 30.

100. See Winston Churchill, "The Cold 'Peace' and Our Future," *Look*, April 29, 1958, 24.

101. *New York Times*, March 13, 1947, 2.

102. *New York Times*, April 29, 1947, 4.

103. Wilcox and Kalijarvi, 833–34.

104. Ibid., 867–68.

105. *St. Louis Globe-Democrat*, October 1, 1948.

106. Ibid., November 2, 1948.

107. Wilcox and Kalijarvi, 868–69.

108. *New York Times*, April 5, 1949, 6.

109. *Congressional Record*, 81st Congress, First Session, vol. 95, part 7, pp. 8891–93.

110. Dean Acheson, *Present at the Creation: My Years in the State Department* (New York: W. W. Norton and Co., 1969), p. iii.

111. Department of State, *United States Policy in the Korean Crisis*,

Publication 3922, July 1950, 18.

112. Arthur H. Vandenberg, *The Private Papers of Senator Vandenberg* (Cambridge: Houghton Mifflin, 1952), 543.

113. Wilcox and Kalijarvi, 894–901.

114. Vandenberg, 575.

115. Wilcox and Kalijarvi, 906–7.

116. Samuel Flagg Bemis, *A Diplomatic History of the United States*, 4th ed. (New York: Henry Holt and Co., 1955), 936–37.

117. Ibid., 938.

118. Quoted in Robert J. Donovan, *Eisenhower, the Inside Story* (New York: Harpers, 1956), 326.

119. *New York Times*, 1 November 1956.

120. "Middle East Proposals," Department of State Publication 6440 (Washington, D.C.).

121. *New York Times*, April 17, 1953, 4.

122. "Atoms for Peace," Address by President Eisenhower, Department of State Publication 5314, 1953.

123. Dwight D. Eisenhower, *Waging Peace, 1956–1961* (Garden City, N.Y.: Doubleday, 1965), 624.

124. Ibid., 658.

125. *New York Times*, January 18, 1961, 22.

126. John F. Kennedy, *To Turn the Tide*, ed. John W. Gardner (New York: Harpers, 1962), 6–7.

127. Ibid., 10–11.

128. Ibid., 156, 158.

129. Quoted in Theodore G. Sorenson, *Kennedy* (New York: Harper and Row, 1965), 526.

130. Kennedy, *To Turn the Tide*, 191.

131. John F. Kennedy, *The Burden and the Glory: Public Statements and Addresses in 1962 and 1963*, ed. Allan Nevins (New York: Harper and Row, 1964), 89, 93, 95–96.

132. Ibid., 98–100.

133. Ibid., 53, 55–58.

134. Ibid., 68–69, 71, 76.

135. Ibid., 132.

136. Ibid., 141.

137. Ibid., 145–46, 148.

138. Ibid., 182–84.

139. Ibid., 275–77.

140. *New York Times*, November 28, 1963, 20.

141. Ibid., November 29, 1963, 20.

142. *Department of State Bulletin*, March 28, 1966, 12–13.

143. *St. Louis Globe-Democrat*, January 5, 1965, 6A.

144. *New York Times*, January 21, 1965, 16.

145. *St. Louis Globe-Democrat*, January 13, 1966, 8A.

146. *New York Times*, August 27, 1966, 10.

147. *New York Times*, November 2, 1966, 16.

148. Ibid., September 28, 1966, 14.

149. Chester L. Cooper, *The Lost Crusade: America in Vietnam* (New York: Dodd, Mead and Co., 1970), 238–44.

150. Jules Davids, *The United States in World Affairs: 1964* (New York: Harper and Row, 1965), 5.

151. John H. Hallowell, *Main Currents in Modern Political Thought* (New York: Henry Holt, 1950), 618–19.

152. Max Lerner, *America as a Civilization: Life and Thought in the United States Today* (New York: Simon and Schuster, 1957), 666, 675–76, 678, 684, 698.

153. Ibid., 703–4, 709.

154. Reinhold Niebuhr, *The Nature and Destiny of Man*, 2 vols., vol. 1, *Human Nature*; vol. 2, *Human Destiny* (New York: Scribners, 1941, 1943), 2:299, 319–21.

155. Reinhold Niebuhr, *The Irony of American History* (New York: Scribners, 1952), viii.

156. Ibid., 174.

157. Catherine Marshall, *A Man Called Peter* (New York: McGraw-Hill, 1951), 280–83, 285, 299–92.

158. *The Prayers of Peter Marshall*, ed. Catherine Marshall (New York: McGraw-Hill, 1954), 144–45.

159. *This Week Magazine*, January 4, 1953, 16.

160. Martin Luther King, Jr., *Stride Toward Freedom: The Montgomery Story* (New York: Harpers, 1958), 210–11, 213–14, 219, 224.

161. *A Testament of Hope: The Essential Writings and Speeches of Martin Luther King, Jr.*, ed. James M. Washington (New York: Harper Collins Paperback, 1991), 220.

162. Ibid., 231–44.

163. *Congressional Record*, 79th Congress, First Session, vol 91, part 1, 364.

164. Frank Kelly and Cornelius Ryan, *MacArthur: Man of Action* (Garden City, N.Y.: Doubleday and Co., 1950), 188–89.

165. *New York Times*, January 8, 1948, 4.

166. X, "The Sources of Soviet Conduct," *Foreign Affairs* 25, no. 4 (July 1974): 582. "X" was later revealed to be George F. Kennan.

167. John Foster Dulles, *War or Peace* (New York: Macmillan, 1950), 253–56, 258–61, 266.

168. *Christian Century*, March 19, 1952, 336–38.

169. Ibid.

170. John Foster Dulles, "The Cost of Peace," Address at Iowa State College Commencement, June 9, 1956 (Department of State, Series S-No. 48).

171. *New York Times*, May 26, 1956, 6 (Eisenhower address at Baylor University commencement).

172. *New York Times*, June 29, 1957, 6 (Dulles address at San Francisco).

173. Ibid., May 9, 1958, 4.

174. "Foreign Affairs: Excerpts from the State of the Union Message by President Eisenhower," January 9, 1959 (Department of State Publication 6763).

175. John Foster Dulles, "Freedom—The Predominant Force," statement before the Senate Foreign Relations Committee, January 14, 1959 (Department of State, Series—No. 77).

176. Kennedy, *To Turn the Tide*, 11.

177. Kennedy, *The Burden and the Glory*, 277.

178. *St. Louis Globe-Democrat*, January 21, 1965, 4A.

179. Ibid., January 13, 1966, 8A.

180. Reprinted from the *Congressional Record*, 89th Congress, Second Session, February 23, 1966.

181. Gallup Poll, Southern Illinoisan [Carbondale, Ill.], April 18, 1965.

CHAPTER VII

The Search for World Peace, Justice and Freedom: Idealism (1966/67–)

One of the greatest shifts in world history occurred in 1989–91, when Eastern European nations were peacefully freed from Soviet and communist domination and the communist system in the Soviet Union collapsed, followed by the dissolution of that nation (or empire) into 15 separate republics.

A partial explanation seems to lie in the gradual appearance of a new wave of relative idealism in the world in reaction to a half-century of ideological and military struggles (1918–66, World War II and the "cold war").

As more and more Americans began to react negatively to involvement in the Vietnam War by 1966 and 1967, American Presidents sought détente with the two great communist powers, as well as disarmament and peace in general. Lyndon B. Johnson (1966–69) tried to end the war in Vietnam, and hoped to negotiate arms reduction with the Soviet Union. Richard Nixon (1969–74) opened relations with the Peoples Republic of China in 1972, after over 20 years of complete estrangement, secured a strategic arms limitation agreement (SALT I) with the Soviet Union that same year, brought America's armed forces in Vietnam home by January 1973, and reopened relations with some Arab countries, notably Egypt. His declared goal was a generation or more of peace. Gerald Ford (1974–77) was restrained by Congress in foreign policy leadership, but he sought international cooperation in the United Nations and other international organizations.

Jimmy Carter (1977–81) emphasized human rights and good relations with the nations of the so-called "third world," while the Soviet Union continued to expand again into areas of weakness. But when the Soviets invaded Afghanistan in December 1979, the spirit of the "cold war" was renewed among Americans, first under Carter and then, more strongly, under Ronald Reagan (1981–89). America then moved to strengthen its military arm and to support democracy and market economics on a world scale. This approach apparently helped bring Mikhail Gorbachev to power in 1985 in the Soviet Union, with his plans for greater cooperation with the West. By 1986/87 the United States, after 20 years of relative introversion, was prepared to support the anti-communist forces struggling in Afghanistan, Angola, Cambodia and Nicaragua, and in general to extend its new military strength outward as the extrovert mood was revived.

The American stand brought a stalemate to the Soviet plans for expansion, and helped promote a mutual desire for strategic arms reduction and for cooperation in general. Hopes for world peace among the great powers and for a "new world order" soared under the first three years of the presidency of George Bush (1989–93). President Bill Clinton (1993–) believed that America's continued world leadership depended in large part on strengthening the American economic and social systems, as he faced the problems of aid to Russia and the "ethnic cleansing" in Bosnia.

The presumed end of the "cold war" encouraged greater use of the United Nations and other international organizations, and, along with the recession, helped bring about the election of Bill Clinton as President in November 1992. At the same time, a new type of world challenge had been developing as dictatorial controls were removed in Eastern Europe and the former Soviet Union—namely, ethnic and religious clashes, most notably in Yugoslavia. Civil war and widespread famine, particularly in Somalia, dramatized another type of world challenge.

Especially noteworthy during this whole period since 1966 has been the emphasis of each President on America's desire for peace, justice and freedom. Surely this consistency in promoting such ideals helped pave the way for the breakthrough toward peace and freedom in Eastern Europe and then the Soviet Union. These recent American Presidents, from President Johnson onward, have been so controversial during their time in office, that most Americans have probably overlooked their basic idealism in explaining America's goals on the world scene. During this time, America's search for peace can be divided into three periods: (1) seeking peace during relative introversion (1966/67–80)—the reduction of America's military involvement; (2) return of the "cold war" spirit (1980–86/87)—America's military buildup in response to Soviet expansionism, though most Americans remained in an introvert mood; and (3) America's renewed leadership as the "cold war" ends (1986/87–)—a revived extrovert mood.

Seeking Peace during Relative Introversion, 1966/67–80

Henry Brandon captured the mood of the American people in the 1970s in the title of his 1973 book, *The Retreat of American Power.*[1] Noting America's apparent inability or unwillingness to win the war against North Vietnam, American Presidents sought "negotiation instead of confrontation," to use President Nixon's phrase.

Lyndon B. Johnson, 1966–69

President Johnson continually sought peace in Vietnam, particularly after 1966, while steadily increasing the military pressure on North Vietnam until early in 1968. Numerous American bombing pauses (there was one for 37 days early in 1966) were ordered to encourage negotiations, but to no avail. The President's talk with General William Westmoreland in August 1966 confirmed his conviction that "the single most important factor now is our will to prosecute the war until the Communists, recognizing the futility of their ambitions, either end the fighting or seek a peaceful settlement."[2] But the American public's support of the war was already beginning to decline rapidly. To show the Chinese backing of North Vietnam, Johnson quoted China's Defense Minister Marshal Lin Piao, who called the conflict a "war of liberation": "the people in other parts of the world will see . . . that what the Vietnamese people can do, they can do, too."[3] At the Manila summit conference, October 24, 1966, seven Pacific nations declared their goals of freedom in Vietnam and in the Asian and Pacific area, and the President stated that, when peace comes, "we will extend the hand of reconciliation."[4] Looking ahead, when he spoke in Korea, the President foresaw a great future for Asia and the Pacific, as he pledged American support.[5]

Although the President's major goal had been to build the "Great Society" in America, he maintained his concern with the world's people, as in signing the Food for Peace Act of 1966, November 12, and announcing agreement on the Outer Space Treaty (peaceful uses only), December 8, 1966 (signed on January 27, 1967). His Christmas message to the armed forces on December 18 ended: "We shall reaffirm our determination to secure a world at peace, and we shall hold fast to our faith in the brotherhood of man, everywhere on earth."[6]

In his State of the Union message, January 10, 1967, the President looked forward to the early ending of the cold war: "We are in the midst of a great transition—a transition from narrow nationalism to international partnership; from the harsh spirit of the cold war to the hopeful spirit of common humanity on a troubled and threatened planet."[7] He also noted that the other nations of Southeast Asia had already been protected by the American stand in Vietnam.[8] He sent a special message to Congress, February 2, 1967, on Food for India and the International War on Hunger:

> Last February I proposed that all mankind join in a war against man's oldest enemy: hunger. . . .
>
> . . . We have never stood idly by while famine or pestilence raged among any part of the human family. America would cease to be America if we walked by on the other side when confronted by such catastrophe.[9]

In the meantime, racial disorders were climaxed by the week of riots in Detroit in July, leading to the appointment of a special Advisory Commission on Civil Disorder. The President was definitely encouraged when the Eighteen-Nation Disarmament Committee agreed on a draft of the vital Nuclear Non-Proliferation Treaty (NPT) on August 24, 1967 (signed July 1, 1968).

By 1967, after two years of the inconclusive fighting in Vietnam, the American people were definitely turning against the war as well as against America's general deep involvement abroad. By October 1967, Gallup Polls showed the American people voting 46 to 44 percent that the United States made a mistake in sending troops to Vietnam, a figure which increased to 53 to 35 percent by August 1968. Congress had begun to question the Vietnam policy as early as February 1966, when critical hearings were held by the Senate Foreign Relations Committee (under its chairman, J. W. Fulbright). Senator Mike Mansfield introduced a resolution signed by 13 Senators to reduce the size of American forces in Europe (this was introduced each year for several more years). In signing the Foreign Assistance Act of 1967 in December, the President deplored the Congressional cut of an "austere request."[10]

Although major attention was focused on Vietnam through most of 1967, the Middle East ("Six-Day") War in June was a sensational event with ominous as well as hopeful implications. The United Arab Republic (Egypt and Syria together for a short time) immediately broke off diplomatic relations with the United States, and the Soviet Union again began rearming the defeated Arab states and moving a large number of warships into the Mediterranean, where the U.S. Sixth Fleet was stationed. The United States supported the unanimous recommendation of the U.N. Security Council for peace in the Middle East (the famous resolution 242, November 22, 1967, aimed at the return of the conquered territory for the assurance of peace). The President sent planes in July to help the President of the Congo (Zaire), threatened by mercenary forces, but there was such determined opposition from the Senate that the planes were withdrawn as soon as possible.

In his State of the Union message on January 17, 1968, the President stated that America's goal was peace at the earliest possible moment. The American people were not psychologically prepared for the military shocks in January and February 1968: (1) the seizure of the American espionage vessel, the *Pueblo*, by North Korea on January 26; and (2) the surprise TET offensive by North Vietnam and the Vietcong on January 30. Although General Westmoreland announced within a few days that the Communists had suffered a severe military defeat (apparently the Vietcong had been decimated), the American people lost their heart for a continuation of the fighting, without hope of an early victory. Still, the nation was astonished on March 31, when President Johnson renounced any further Presidential ambitions and announced a unilateral reduction of the American war effort—stopping all attacks above the 20th parallel, where 90 percent of the North Vietnamese lived, in the hope of starting negotiations for peace. He planned to devote full time to securing peace. North Vietnam shortly agreed to open negotiations, but the discussions remained procedural throughout the year, while heavy fighting continued. It is clear in retrospect that America was set at this point upon an irreversible course toward de-escalation and ultimate withdrawal from the war.

Professor Robert W. Tucker, in a 1968 book, noted the depth of the changes in public opinion:

> In a period of a few weeks in the spring of 1968 what had been the verities of postwar American foreign policy suddenly seemed to become the great uncertainties. . . . There appeared the prospect of a change in mood and policy as great as preceding changes the nation had

experienced in this century.[11]

Tucker observed in 1970 that the most important new influence in public opinion did not come from the critics of the "new left" but from "the substantive defection of those who have formed a critical part of this consensus for the past generation."[12] Many leaders of America as well as the general public had thus moved decisively toward relative "introversion," after the extroversion which had dominated since 1940.

Nevertheless, withdrawal from Vietnam in an "honorable" way would take five more years (after 1968). The North Vietnamese were determined to fight for victory, apparently believing that public opinion in the United States would force the Americans to withdraw, sooner or later. In his memoirs, President Johnson gave his opinion "that we perhaps tried too hard to spell out our honest desire for peace: these numerous appeals through so many channels may well have convinced the North Vietnamese that we wanted peace at any price."[13] Yet he concluded that when he turned the problem over to President Nixon:

> We had kept our word to Southeast Asia. We had exposed and defeated aggression, as we promised we would. We had given 17 million South Vietnamese a chance to build their own country and own institutions, and we had seen them well down the road.[14]

Walt Rostow, Johnson's National Security Adviser, wrote in 1972 that if "the Asian efforts . . . move forward in economic and social modernization, . . . Johnson's Vietnam policy will be vindicated in history. For without his dispatch of American forces in 1965, no such Asia could have evolved."[15] Secretary of State Dean Rusk recently gave his estimate of the problem:

> As Secretary of State I made two serious mistakes with respect to Vietnam. First, I overestimated the patience of the American people, and second, I underestimated the tenacity of the North Vietnamese. They took frightful casualties. In relation to our own population, their total casualties throughout the war were roughly equivalent to ten million American casualties.[16]

The year 1968 held much American tragedy, with two assassinations of American leaders (Dr. Martin Luther King, Jr., on April 4, and Senator Robert Kennedy, candidate for President, on June 5–6), rioting by blacks in 125 cities, and major demonstrations against the war (particularly at the Democratic National Convention in Chicago, during the last week in August). Congress and the President continued to strengthen civil rights in the Civil Rights Act of 1968, in April, stressing fair housing for all. When the President joined others in signing the Nuclear Non-Proliferation Treaty in Washington on July 1, 1968, he expressed his hope for the future:

> Man can still shape his destiny in the nuclear age, and learn to live as brothers.
> Toward that goal—the day when the world moves out of the night of war into the light of sanity and security—I solemnly pledge the resources, the resolve, and the unrelenting efforts of the people of the United States and their Government.[17]

Also on July 1, the United States and the Soviet Union agreed to enter into discussions on the limitation and reduction of both offensive and defensive nuclear weapons. But these plans were postponed following the Warsaw Pact invasion of Czechoslovakia on August 20, just before the Democratic Convention. The United States, deeply involved in Vietnam, could only protest verbally.

Richard Nixon, who declared he had a plan to "end the war" in Vietnam, won the close election for President in November, with 43.4 percent of the popular vote (302 electoral votes), while Vice President Hubert Humphrey received 42.7 percent (191 electoral), and George Wallace 13.5 percent (45 electoral). In his annual message on the State of the Union, President Johnson spoke of his deep "regret, more than any of you know, that it has not been possible to restore peace to South Vietnam," but added that "the free nations of Asia know what they were not sure of . . . that America cares about their freedom, and it also cares about America's own vital interests in Asia and throughout the Pacific." He concluded that "I deeply believe in the ultimate purpose of this Nation—described by the Constitution" and "tempered by history."[18]

Richard M. Nixon, 1969–74

At the time of the election of Richard Nixon as President, America appeared almost on the verge of a "revolution" against the three-year old Vietnam War, with its virtual stalemate and heavy casualties, halfway around the world. Only once before had America fought a war during an introvert phase—namely, during the American Revolution, where there was deep dissension. But that war was fought on American soil, and was basically a war of defense against British power based mainly across the Atlantic Ocean. In 1968, many of America's youth, especially those in college, were revolting to some extent against all authority; similar outbreaks occurred in other countries, notably in France. Thus the new Administration faced a most difficult situation, as the President, who had made his reputation as a determined anti-Communist, planned how to restore stability to America as well as continue to give the South Vietnamese a chance to save themselves.

Nixon had perceived the changing mood of the American people in foreign policy in 1967, when he wrote in *Foreign Affairs*:

> One of the legacies of Viet Nam almost certainly will be a deep reluctance on the part of the United States to become involved once again in a similar intervention on a similar basis. . . . Other nations must recognize that the role of the United States as a world policeman is likely to be limited in the future.
>
> Weary with war, disheartened with allies, disillusioned with aid, dismayed at domestic crises, many Americans are heeding the call of the new isolationism, and they are not alone; there is a tendency in the whole Western world to become parochial and isolationist—dangerously so. But there can be neither peace nor security a generation hence unless we recognize the massiveness of the forces at work in Asia. . . .
>
> . . . Without turning our backs on Europe, we have now to reach westward to the East, and to fashion the sinews of a Pacific community.[19]

He also saw the possibility for a positive policy in relation to Communist China:

> The world cannot be safe until China changes. Thus our aim, to the extent that we can influence events, should be to induce change. The way to do this is to persuade China that it *must* change: that it cannot satisfy its imperial ambitions, and that its own national interest requires a turning away from foreign adventuring and a turning inward toward the solution of its own domestic problems.[20]

After Nixon was nominated by the Republican National Convention on August 8, 1968, he pledged in his acceptance speech to bring an "honorable end to the Viet Nam War" and declared to the Soviet Union and China that "the time has come for an era of negotiation. . . . We extend the hand of friendship to all people—to the Russian people—to the Chinese people." After his inauguration, Nixon was determined to try to seek détente and peace with the two great Communist powers. As an admirer of Woodrow Wilson, he saw the opportunity to achieve these goals, at a time when the American people were turning away from military involvement abroad. To help him, he named Henry Kissinger his National Security Adviser; Kissinger felt the importance of building a more stable balance of power with the Soviet Union and China. The two made a powerful team, with Nixon determined to wield Presidential power and Kissinger possessing the skills of a diplomatist with a keen sense of history (including his special study of Austrian Chancellor Metternich, who had built a "structure of peace" after the Napoleonic Wars).

In his Inaugural Address on January 20, 1969, President Nixon dramatized his hope for peace:

> . . . The times are on the side of peace.
>
> The greatest honor history can bestow is the title of peacemaker. This honor now beckons America—the chance to help lead the world at last out of the valley of turmoil and onto the high ground of peace that man has dreamed of since the dawn of civilization. . . .
>
> After a period of confrontation, we are entering an era of negotiation. . . .
>
> We seek an open world—open to ideas, open to exchange of goods and people—a world in which no people, great or small, will live in angry isolation. . . .
>
> Those who would be our adversaries, we invite to a peaceful competition—not in conquering territory or extending dominion, but in enriching the life of man. . . .
>
> But to all those who would be tempted by weakness, let us leave no doubt that we will be as strong as we need to be for as long as we need to be. . . .
>
> . . . I shall consecrate my office, my energies, and all the wisdom I can summon to the cause of peace among nations.
>
> The peace we seek . . . is not victory over any other people, but the peace that comes with "healing in its wings"; with compassion for those who have suffered; with understanding for those who have opposed us; with the opportunity for all people of this earth to choose their own destiny.[21]

To achieve peace, Nixon believed it was essential to maintain enough American power along with strong allies, in order to discourage further aggression. He went to Europe late in February to reaffirm America's support of NATO.[22] In Berlin, he praised the spirit of the people:

> Berlin is known as a four-power city. But there is a fifth power in Berlin . . . the determination of the free people of Berlin to remain free and the determination of free people everywhere to stand by those who desire to remain free. . . .
>
> I stand here today as a symbol of that fifth power, the power which will not be intimidated by any threat, by any pressure from any direction.[23]

In the meantime, negotiations with North Vietnam proved unsuccessful and the war continued, accompanied by massive campus protests. As the President prepared to limit America's role in Vietnam and the world, he continued to stress the need of American leadership, as in his address to the Air Force Academy on June 4, 1969:

> . . . I believe a resurgence of American idealism can bring about a modern miracle, and that modern miracle is a world order of peace and justice. . . .
>
> I believe this above all: That this Nation shall continue to be a source of world leadership, a source of freedom's strength, in creating a just world order that will bring an end to war.[24]

Henry Kissinger, in his memoirs, characterized the problem which the Nixon Administration faced:

> Even as we entered office, it was clear that the agony of Vietnam threatened a new disillusionment with international affairs that could draw America inward to nurse its wounds and renounce its world leadership. This would be a profound tragedy. . . . Therefore the Nixon Administration saw it as its task to lay the foundation for a long-range American foreign policy, even while liquidating our Indochina involvement.[25]

Just before leaving on a world tour, the President spoke to the Apollo 11 astronauts who had just fulfilled President Kennedy's dream by landing on the moon (July 20, 1969):

> For every American this has to be the proudest day of our lives, and

> . . . people all over the world . . . join with Americans in recognizing what an immense feat this is.
>
> . . . For one priceless moment in the whole history of man all the people on this earth are truly one—one in their pride in what you have done and one in our prayers that you will safely return to the earth.[26]

World press and polls showed that this peaceful and sensational scientific achievement had raised the prestige of the United States around the world to a surprising extent.

While the President was on Guam on July 25, he first described a new American policy which was later labelled the "Nixon Doctrine":

> . . . We must avoid the kind of policy that will make countries in Asia so dependent upon us that we are dragged into conflict such as the one in Viet Nam.
>
> . . . I want to be sure that our policies in the future, all over the world, in Asia, Latin America, Africa, and the rest, reduces American involvement. One of assistance, yes, assistance in helping them solve their own problems, but not going there and just doing the job ourselves because that is the easier way to do it.[27]

Later, President Nixon evaluated the general purpose of the Doctrine (apparently in view of America's growing reluctance to be deeply involved militarily):

> The Nixon Doctrine announced in Guam was misinterpreted by some as signaling a new policy that would lead to total American withdrawal from Asia and from other parts of the world as well. . . . The Nixon Doctrine was not a formula for getting America *out* of Asia, but one that provided the only sound basis for America's staying *in* and continuing to play a responsible role in helping the non-Communist nations and neutrals as well as our Asian allies to defend their independence.[28]

Nixon was moving toward the steady "Vietnamization" of the war, accompanied by a gradual withdrawal of the American troops. In Saigon, on July 20, he spoke to the American troops of the hope for peace in Vietnam:

> We have stopped the bombing of North Vietnam. We have withdrawn 25,000 American troops. . . . We have made . . . a peace offer that is as generous as any ever made in the history of warfare. It

is a peace of reconciliation that is offered.[29]

In India, on July 31, he stressed America's goal of a generation of peace, as Prime Minister Nehru had earlier urged: "I am certain that this new era will be one in which the ancient goal of dwelling together in peace finds inspiration in the title of a collection of the writings of Mahatma Gandhi: *All Men Are Brothers*."[30] In the communist nation of Romania, where he was warmly welcomed on August 2, Nixon implied America's desire to improve relations with the communist nations:

> Nations can have widely different internal orders and live in peace. Nations can have widely differing economic interests and live in peace. . . .
>
> My country has already taken initiatives to reduce the tensions that exist in the world. . . . Every nation, of whatever size and whatever region of the world, will find us receptive to realistic new departures on the path of peace.[31]

The President was thus prepared to stress American leadership for peace at a time when the American people were becoming steadily more "introvert," while being willing to maintain the nation's commitments to the defense of Western Europe and Japan. As early as February 1, 1969, President Nixon had asked Henry Kissinger to employ every possibility for opening relations with Communist China.[32] Preparations were also begun early to open arms talks with the Soviet Union (the Strategic Arms Limitation Talks, SALT, were officially opened in Helsinki on November 17, 1969). In his address to the United Nations General Assembly, September 18, 1969, the President pledged that America would work for reconciliation and peace with Vietnam and the other Communist states.[33]

The President's emphasis on peace, along with the rising American mood of relative introversion, may well have had a subtle effect on opinion in the Soviet Union and in China in reducing their fear of Western attack, and in fostering their own hopes for peace and cooperation. For North Vietnam, however, the American mood was doubtless a sign that South Vietnam could ultimately be defeated, when the Americans fully withdrew their own troops.

The President clarified the "Nixon Doctrine" and his concept of American destiny in an address to the nation on November 3:

First, the United States will keep all of its treaty commitments.

Second, we shall provide a shield if a nuclear power threatens the freedom of a nation allied with us or a nation whose survival we consider vital to our security.

Third, in cases involving other types of aggression, we shall furnish military and economic assistance when requested, in accordance with our treaty commitments. But we shall look at the nation directly threatened to assume the primary responsibility of providing the manpower for its defense. . . .

. . . The wheel of destiny has turned so that any hope the world has for the survival of peace and freedom will be determined by whether the American people have the moral stamina and the courage to meet the challenge of free world leadership.

And so tonight—to you, the great silent majority of my fellow Americans, I ask for your support.[34]

On the same day, the United States released the reply (August 25) of the North Vietnamese leader, Ho Chi Minh, to a Nixon letter of July 15. He called the conflict a "war of aggression of the United States against our people, violating our fundamental national rights." In order to achieve peace, he continued, "the United States must cease the war of aggression and withdraw their troops from South Vietnam."[35] Nixon concluded his annual message to Congress on the State of the Union in 1970 by referring to the challenges to come in the last third of the century: "May God give us the wisdom, the strength, and above all, the idealism to be worthy of that challenge, so that America can fulfill its destiny of being the world's best hope for liberty, for opportunity, for progress, and peace for all peoples."[36]

While President Nixon was responding to the national mood by reducing America's military commitments abroad, he desired to maintain America's influence on the world scene, using military pressure if needed, as Vietnam continued the war and the Soviet Union increased its strength in the Arab world, the Mediterranean, and the Indian Ocean. This is at least a partial explanation for the attack upon the North Vietnamese forces in Cambodia (April 30 to June 30, 1970)—an event which virtually caused American college campuses to "explode" in opposition to what seemed to the students a widening of the war (four students were killed at Kent State, and two at Jackson State). A similar case was the threat of American intervention after Syrian troops temporarily invaded Jordan in September 1970 (Syria withdrew). In defending the attack on North Vietnamese forces in

Cambodia, as a means of protecting the continuing American withdrawal, Nixon spoke in broad terms: "If, when the chips are down, the world's most powerful nation, the United States of America, acts like a pitiful, helpless giant, the forces of totalitarianism and anarchy will threaten free nations and free institutions throughout the world."[37] In the case of the Syrian invasion of Jordan, the President later visited the Sixth Fleet in the Mediterranean, and spoke to its officers and men (September 29):

> I have often described our forces . . . as the peace forces of the world. And the Sixth Fleet was certainly in that great tradition during this period of tension. The power and mobility, the readiness of the Sixth Fleet in this period was absolutely indispensable in keeping the peace in the Mediterranean. . . .
> . . . What we desire, all of us, is a full generation of peace, and more, for the American people and the world.[38]

Nixon again emphasized the American goal of peace in his address to the 25th session of the U.N. General Assembly, October 23, 1970):

> . . . What we seek is not a Pax Americana, not an American Century, but rather a structure of stability and progress that will enable every nation, large or small, to chart its own course. . . .
> We seek good relations with all the people of the world. We respect the right of each people to choose its own way.[39]

Perhaps to the astonishment of many, President Nixon's words were backed up by deeds, particularly evident in the diplomatic negotiations of Henry Kissinger, squarely directed and backed by the President. He foreshadowed the breakthrough toward more national unity and to the Communist powers in his annual message of 1971 (January 22).[40] Nixon sent a special message to Congress on the need to protect the environment (February 8—the first Earth Day had been celebrated in 1970):

> I call upon all Americans to dedicate themselves during the decade of the seventies to the goal of restoring the environment, and reclaiming the earth for ourselves and our posterity. And I invite all peoples everywhere to join us in this great endeavor. We hold this good earth in trust.[41]

Nixon had a chance to extol the vision of Woodrow Wilson in remarks at the dedication of the Woodrow Wilson International Center for Scholars (February 18, 1971):

> . . . The Wilsonian vision, the American passion for peace with freedom . . . is on the verge of triumph.
> . . . The strong likelihood exists that there will be no need for a war to end wars, that indeed, by taking one careful step at a time, by making peace for one full generation, we will get this world into the habit of peace.
> By his example Woodrow Wilson helped make the world safe for idealism.
> By following that example, by not fearing to be idealist ourselves, we shall make the world safe for free men to live in peace.[42]

In his message to Congress, February 25, concerning his Administration's long second report on U.S. foreign policy, the President stressed the importance of *partnership* both with America's allies and with her adversaries "on the paramount world interest—to rid the earth of the scourge of war."[43]

Such appeared to be the purposes of President Nixon, as he and Henry Kissinger moved toward closer relations with the Peoples Republic of China and the Soviet Union. Following secret negotiations in Beijing by Dr. Kissinger, the President made a dramatic TV announcement on July 15, 1971, accepting Premier Chou En-lai's invitation to visit China before May 1972 (the visit was later scheduled to begin on February 21, 1972):

> Our action in seeking a new relationship with the Peoples Republic of China will not be at the expense of our old friends. It is not directed against any other nation. We seek friendly relations with all nations.[44]

In a Veterans Day address on October 24, 1971, Nixon held out the hope "that this generation of veterans might truly be the last; that the world will see a new dawn of hope for the old ideal of human brotherhood; and that men and nations will find at last a larger purpose in peace than they ever found in war."[45] Not long before, on August 23, the Big Four Ambassadors to Berlin (including the Soviet Union's) reached an agreement on Berlin, essentially defusing the Berlin situation after 24 years of confrontation there. In his 1972 State of the Union address, January 20, Nixon spoke of China and the Soviet Union: "We shall continue to have great differences, but peace depends on the ability of great powers to live together on the same planet despite their differences."[46]

In his first toast at a banquet in Peking on February 21, as the world watched on TV with deep fascination, President Nixon stated his hope for the unprecedented negotiations:

> . . . Let us, in these next five days, start a long march together, not in lockstep, but on different roads leading to the same goal, the goal of building a world structure of peace and justice in which we may stand together with equal dignity and in which each nation, large or small, has a right to determine its own form of government, free of outside interference or domination.
>
> This is the hour, this is the day for our two peoples to rise to the heights of greatness which can build a new and better world.[47]

Premier Chou En-lai responded in like fashion: "taking this opportunity to extend on behalf of the Chinese people cordial greetings to the American people on the other side of the great ocean" and looking toward "normal state relations on the basis of the Five Principles of mutual respect for sovereignty and territorial integrity, mutual nonaggression, noninterference in each other's internal affairs, equality of mutual benefits, and peaceful coexistence. . . ."[48]

The meetings were cordial and basically successful in beginning the process of "normalization" of relations. At the end of the talks, President Nixon averred: "We have demonstrated that nations with very deep and fundamental differences can learn to discuss those differences calmly, rationally, and frankly, without compromising their principles."[49]

The détente between the United States and China doubtless stimulated the Soviet Union also to seek better relations with the United States . The President arrived in Moscow on May 22, toasting the Soviet nation in these words:

> The Soviet Union and the United States are both great powers. Ours are both great peoples. In the long history of both of our nations, we have never fought one another in war. Let us make decisions now which will help ensure that we shall never do so in the future.
>
> The American people want peace, I know from my travels through the Soviet Union, the people of the Soviet Union want peace.[50]

Then, preceded by two years of careful preparation by negotiators, President Nixon and Chairman Brezhnev were able to sign the first Strategic Arms Limitation Treaty (SALT I), along with an agreement on twelve "Basic Principles of Mutual Relations." In a radio and TV address to the Soviet people (May 28), the President declared that "these agreements can start us on a new road of cooperation for the benefit of our people, for the benefit of all peoples."[51]

On the way home from Moscow, Nixon and Kissinger stopped in Iran on May 30 to strengthen ties to the Shah. Iran was perceived as a vital nation for the application of the Nixon Doctrine, in terms of building up Iran's military strength as a friend in helping maintain Persian Gulf stability. Stopping also in Warsaw, the friendship between the Polish and American people was stressed. Reporting on his trip to a joint session of Congress on June 1, the President endeavored to build up American morale and pride: "if the new age we seek is ever to become a reality, we must keep America strong in spirit—a nation proud of its greatness as a free society, confident of its mission in the world." He concluded:

> An unparalleled opportunity has been placed in American hands.
> . . . We have made a good beginning, and because we have begun,
> history now lays upon us a special obligation to see it through. We can
> seize the moment or we can lose it. . . .[52]

It appears, however, that the American people were not ready at this time for true world leadership, and especially that the Soviet Union was not ready to give up its dreams of far wider influence and control. Fifteen more years would go by before a spirit of true cooperation began to develop on both sides. Nevertheless, two major steps had been taken by America—one toward China and one toward the Soviet Union. The American people approved. Following the Administration's breakthrough to mainland China, the SALT agreement with the Soviet Union, and the expectation of an imminent cease-fire in Vietnam, President Nixon gained a landslide victory over Senator George McGovern in the election in November 1972 (the electoral votes were 521 to 17, and the popular vote 47 million to 29 million). In his Second Inaugural Address (January 20, 1973), Nixon emphasized his hopes for peace: "Let us continue to bring down the walls of hostility which have divided the world for so long ,and to build in their place bridges of understanding—so that despite profound differences between systems of government, the people of the world can be friends."[53]

Only three days later (January 23), following months of strong pressure on both North and South Vietnam (including the "Christmas" bombing of Hanoi and Haiphong), the President was able to announce that agreement had been reached on ending the war and restoring peace in Vietnam, with the formal signing by Kissinger and Le Duc Tho on January 27. It was a time of major rejoicing in America, after eight years of war, with the soldiers and POWs coming home. President Nixon expected to be able to enforce the terms of the peace should the North Vietnamese violate them, but the North Vietnamese noted the complete withdrawal of the American troops and the fact that their own troops were allowed to keep their positions in Vietnam (although they pledged to leave South Vietnam later). After April 1973, President Nixon's prestige at home dropped markedly as a result of the Watergate scandal disclosures. Congress had also been moving since 1969 to diminish the powers of the Presidency in foreign affairs (to limit the "imperial Presidency," in the words of Arthur Schlesinger, Jr.). In 1970, Congress had barred the use of American combat troops in Laos and Thailand, and (even though the Communist forces in Cambodia refused to accept a truce) ended (August 15, 1973) all appropriations for military action anywhere in Indochina. The War Powers Act, designed to limit the President further, was passed over the President's veto (November 7, 1973). All these measures had strong public support.

Nixon welcomed Brezhnev to the United States (June 18–25, 1973), and reached broad new agreements on many subjects. In an address to the nation, the President deplored the effect of the Watergate investigations: "a continued backward-looking obsession with Watergate is causing this Nation to neglect matters of far greater importance to all of the American people."[54] When Kissinger was given the additional post of Secretary of State on September 22, he stated America's major goal, as he saw it:

> When we speak of a structure of peace, we mean a world which has not just eased tensions, but overcome them; a world not based on strength, but on justice; a relationship among nations based on cooperation and not an equilibrium of force alone. That kind of a world is the task, as the President has pointed out, of all Americans.
>
> As we work for a world at peace with justice, compassion, and humanity, we know that America is fulfilling man's deepest aspirations, fulfilling what is best within it.[55]

On the same day, the President wrote to the Senate, deploring Congressional reductions in the defense budget: "All our efforts to secure a more peaceful and prosperous world will be endangered if we unilaterally erode our defense posture."[56]

Despite the pressure of the public and Congress toward more introversion, President Nixon was able to use the threat of force in the October 1973 Yom Kippur War, in which Egypt's surprise attack first broke through Israel's lines. America furnished large quantities of weapons by air to Israel, and then called a world-wide military alert (October 25) when the Soviet Union threatened to intervene to save Egyptian troops. The United States and the Soviet Union were able to work out a compromise for peace talks through the U.N. Security Council, including the authorization of U.N. peacekeeping forces. The Arab oil embargo after the war dramatized America's energy weakness in its reliance on Middle East oil.

For eight months in 1974, as "Watergate" pressure mounted against the President, he was still able to play a significant role in the Middle East and with the Soviet Union. He felt strongly the basic idealism of the American people, as he spoke on April 18, 1974:

> . . . I believe, as Jefferson believed and as Lincoln believed and as Wilson believed, that America came into the world not just for ourselves but for the contribution that we as Americans could make to all of mankind, not in terms of what we could give to them materially, but more importantly, in terms of the leadership we could provide to those forces in the world which are essential if we are to have and to enjoy a world of peace, peace meaning more than the absence of war.[57]

On June 5, he warned Americans of the danger of "turning inward": "This threat of a new wave of isolationism, blind to both the lessons of the past and the perils of the future, was and remains today one of the greatest potential dangers facing our country. . . ."[58]

After the U.N.-sponsored peace for the October 1973 Yom Kippur War, Secretary Kissinger ardently pursued mediation between Israel and Egypt, and Israel and Syria. By April 1974, President Sadat of Egypt had made the decision to break with the Soviet Union and cooperate with the United States. President Nixon was welcomed warmly in Egypt on June 12. Sadat gave much of the credit to Nixon: "Your visit marks the opening of a new phase which will go down in history as one of your major achievements."[59] Nixon also visited Saudi Arabia, Syria, and Israel (under Prime Minister Yitzhak Rabin at the time). To the Israelis the President stressed the goal of a just and enduring peace in the area, and added: "Under no circumstances does the fact that the United States is seeking better relations with some of Israel's neighbors mean that the friendship of the United States and the support for Israel is any less."[60] Finally he visited Jordan and Portugal.

Nixon went to the Soviet Union for the third summit meeting with Brezhnev, June 27–July 2, 1974, although the American people's attention was concentrated on Watergate. The President had another opportunity to deliver a radio and TV address to the Soviet people: "Our two nations bear a shared responsibility toward the entire world, and we, too, must plant so that future generations will reap a harvest of peace—a peace in which our children can live together as brothers and sisters. . . ."[61] On his return, Nixon spoke to the American people about their responsibilities and opportunities (July 3):

> Our generation, which has known so much war and destruction—four wars in this century—now has an opportunity to build for the next generation a structure of peace in which we hope war will have no part whatever.
> This is the great task before us, and this is the greatest task in which any people can be summoned. . . .[62]

Finally, on the verge of a probable impeachment trial, Nixon announced to the nation on August 8 his intention to resign the office of President. Then he discussed future American goals, in a kind of "farewell address":

> . . . As we look to the future, the first essential is to begin healing the wounds of this Nation, to put the bitterness and divisions of the recent past behind us and to rediscover those shared ideals that lie at the heart of our strength and unity as a great and as a free people. . .
>
> . . . I would say only that if some of my judgments were wrong—and some were wrong—they were made in what I believed at the time to be the best interest of the Nation.
> We must keep a structure of peace so that it will be said of this generation, our generation of Americans, by the people of all nations, not only that we ended one war but that we prevented future wars.
> We must now ensure that the one quarter of the world's people who live in the Peoples Republic of China will be and remain not our

enemies, but our friends.

In the Middle East, 100 million people in the Arab countries, many of whom have considered us as their enemies for nearly 20 years, now look on us as their friends. We must continue to build on that friendship so that peace can settle at last over the Middle East and so that the cradle of civilization will not become its grave.

Together with the Soviet Union, we have made the crucial breakthroughs that have begun the process of limiting nuclear arms. But we must set as our goal not just limiting but reducing, and, finally, destroying these terrible weapons so that they cannot destroy civilization and so that the threat of nuclear war will no longer hang over the world and the people.

We have opened the new relations with the Soviet Union. We must continue to develop and expand that new relationship so that the two strongest nations of the world will live together in cooperation, rather than confrontation.

. . . We must keep as our goal turning away from production for war and expanding production for peace so that people everywhere on this Earth can at last look forward in their children's time, if not in our own time, to having the necessities of a decent life.[63]

Finally, he foreshadowed the role he hoped to perform as an ex-President (which turned out to be that of giving advice on American foreign policy through many writings).

President Nixon was setting goals for the long run, since at the time the majority of the American people and Congress wished to concentrate on domestic affairs, and perhaps believed that the world situation was no longer dangerous. The spirit of introversion was deepened also by the Watergate scandal, as the President had lost the support of the majority of the American people. They felt betrayed by Nixon's deceptive effort to cover up his role in the Watergate affair, although he had the mistaken belief that he could strengthen the Presidency by doing so. Yet the President had already paved the way to peace, by his decisive breakthroughs to China, to the Soviet Union, and to the Middle East. The effect of the Watergate affair and the bitter political struggle which accompanied it, however, was to reduce to a marked degree America's effectiveness as a world leader for a number of years to come.

Gerald R. Ford, August 9, 1974–January 20, 1977

Some continuity in American foreign policy was maintained under President Ford by his decision to keep Henry Kissinger as Secretary of State, but American political-military weakness was reflected in events in the eastern Mediterranean, Southeast Asia, the Middle East and Africa. Following Turkey's occupation of part of Cyprus, Greece withdrew its forces from NATO on August 14, 1974, and Greek Cypriots attacked the U.S. Embassy in Nicosia, killing the American Ambassador (August 19). When Congress, responding to pressure from Greek-Americans, cut off arms transfers to Turkey (February 5, 1975), Turkey suspended America's use of vital bases there.

When North Vietnam launched a broad-scale attack on South Vietnam, Congress refused President Ford's January (1975) request for American aid; South Vietnam and Cambodia collapsed quickly. All Americans were evacuated in a rather humiliating fashion from Cambodia (April 12) and South Vietnam (April 29), with thousands of native supporters of the United States left behind to face their fate. The great American naval base in Camranh Bay, South Vietnam, was ultimately taken over by the Soviet Union.

It took Secretary Kissinger nearly 17 months after the Israeli-Syrian agreement to secure a second Israeli-Egyptian agreement (September 1, 1975) for further Israeli withdrawal from a small part of the Sinai. America appeared to have no influence in Lebanon, where a bloody civil war began in the spring of 1975, followed by Syrian intervention.

After Portugal freed its African colonies, a civil war ensued in Angola, and it was revealed, in December 1975, that the United States had been sending a limited amount of aid to anti-Communist forces there. The Senate immediately voted to stop all covert or other aid to these forces (54 to 22, December 19), and the House followed suit (323 to 99, January 27, 1976). By February 12, the pro-Western forces in Angola had been thrown out of their major positions by intervening Cuban troops supported by the Soviet Union. Cuban troops were also used to support the new government in Ethiopia, where America's friend, Emperor Haile Selassie, had been overthrown on September 12, 1974.

President Ford pledged himself to follow American ideals in foreign policy in his address to a joint session of Congress on August 12, 1974:

> To the entire international community—to the United Nations, to the world's nonaligned nations, and to all others—I pledge continuity in our dedication to the humane goals which throughout our history

have been so much of America's contribution to mankind.

So long as the people of the world have confidence in our purposes and faith in our word, the age-old vision of peace on Earth will grow brighter.[64]

To reduce America's preoccupation with a potential trial of former President Nixon, President Ford granted him a full pardon for all offenses he may have committed, on September 8, 1974.[65]

President Ford and Secretary Kissinger gave special support to United Nations conferences for general humanitarian problems: Population Conference ((Bucharest, August 1974); World Food Conference (Rome, November 1974—Nixon had taken a special initiative on this); Women's Rights (Mexico City, June–July 1975); Trade and Development (New York City, May 1976); and Human Settlements (Vancouver, June 1976). Secretary Kissinger began in 1974 to lead the way toward closer relations with the nations of Latin America (including a pledge to Panama for a new treaty), of Europe, of Africa, and with the United Nations. Ford met with Brezhnev in Vladivostok, November 24, 1974, following his visit to Japan, and initialed a preliminary agreement which became part of SALT II. At Helsinki, August 17, 1975, he signed the important pact on Security and Cooperation between NATO and the Warsaw Pact (establishing the Conference on Security and Cooperation in Europe, CSCE); and in December 1975 visited Peking, where he received a warning to beware of the Soviet Union's growing military strength.

The general opposition between the Administration and Congress brought a kind of paralysis for a time into American foreign policy, and a major decline in American prestige abroad. On March 1, 1976, Secretary Kissinger called "division at home" the nation's biggest foreign policy problem.[66] Flora Lewis reported on March 31, 1976, that "concern is spreading in Europe about the willingness and ability of the United States to sustain a coherent foreign policy as leader of the West."[67] Erwin D. Canham commented on March 14, after an official trip to the Far East that "the friendliest nations in the Pacific part of the world are filled with uncertainty about the United States. . . . They wonder whether the American sense of purpose in the world is still strong and clear. . . . They see a weakened executive, a beleaguered Secretary of State, an always unpredictable but powerful Congress."[68] As an example of the conflict between the President and Congress, rather typical of an introvert mood phase, President Ford condemned the

Senate action in suspending military assistance to Turkey, October 1, 1974. This action, he declared, "would destroy any hope for the success of the initiative the United States has already taken or might take in the future to contribute to a just settlement of the Cyprus dispute."[69] Another example was Congressional insistence in a trade agreement with the Soviet Union for a Soviet pledge to increase the number of Jews allowed to emigrate; thereupon the Soviet Union turned down the proposed agreement, January 10, 1975, and reduced the number of Jews permitted to leave (from 35,000 in 1973 to 13,500 in 1975).

A new spirit of "union" began to be restored under President Ford, especially as the nation began to celebrate its bicentennial. On July 17, 1975, the President spoke by telephone with the crews of the joined American and Soviet spacecraft:

> Your flight is a momentous event and a very great achievement, not only for the five of you but also for the thousands of American and Soviet scientists and technicians who have worked together for 3 years to ensure the success of this very historic and very successful experiment in international cooperation.[70]

On June 29, 1976, the President proclaimed Bicentennial Independence Days:

> We face the future with renewed dedication to the principles embodied in our Declaration of Independence. . . .
>
> . . . In keeping with the wishes of Congress, I ask that all Americans join in an expanded period of celebration, thanksgiving, and prayer on the second, third, fourth, and fifth Days of July . . . so that people of all faiths, in their own way, may give thanks for the protection of Divine Providence through 200 years, and pray for the safety and happiness of our Nation.[71]

On July 4, he spoke at Valley Forge on the need to sacrifice:

> Americans will remember the name of Valley Forge as long as the spirit of sacrifice lives within our hearts.
>
> Here the vein of iron in our national character was forged.
>
> . . . The patriots of Valley Forge and the pioneers of the American frontier . . . send us this simple message: Though prosperity is a good thing, though compassionate charity is a good thing, though institutional reform is a good thing, a nation survives only so long as the spirit of

sacrifice and self-discipline is strong within its people.[72]

Finally, on July 7, the President welcomed a special visit from Queen Elizabeth II of the United Kingdom:

> Your Majesty's visit symbolizes our deep and continuing commitment to the common values of Anglo-American civilization. . . . As democrats we continue our quest for peace and justice. . . .
>
> At stake is the further extension of the blessings of liberty, to all humanity in the creation of a better world.
>
> Something wonderful happened to America this past weekend. A spark of unity and togetherness deep within the American soul sprang to the surface in a way we had almost forgotten. People showed again that they care, that they want to live in peace and harmony with their neighbors, that they want to pull together for the good of the Nation and for the good of mankind.[73]

In a fairly close election in November 1976, Governor Jimmy Carter of Georgia won over President Ford, with 291 to 241 electoral votes and 51 to 48 percent of the popular vote. Ford ended his State of the Union address, January 12, 1977, with a prayer:

> My fellow Americans, I once asked you for your prayers and now I give you mine: May God guide this wonderful country, its people, and those they have chosen to lead them. May our third century be illuminated by liberty, blessed with brotherhood, so that we and all who come after us may be the humble servant of thy peace. Amen.[74]

President Carter himself, at the Inauguration on January 20, 1977, summed up President Ford's special contribution to America's role, as described by Ford in his memoirs:

> Carter's first words were, "For myself and for our nation I want to thank my predecessor for all he has done to heal our land."
>
> That was so unexpected, such a gracious thing for him to say. The crowd began to applaud, and I bit my lip to mask my emotion. I didn't know whether to remain seated or to stand. But when the cheers continued I decided to stand, and I reached over to clasp Carter's hand.[75]

Thus, too, was symbolized the normal friendly spirit and basic unity of Americans when the torch is passed from one party to the other.

Jimmy Carter, 1977–80

America's general political-military introversion continued during President Carter's first three years in office, but the President added a special American emphasis by placing "human rights" and moral principles (grounded in a deep religious faith) at the center of his goals. The inauguration of the Governor from Georgia as President also broadened the sense of unity in the nation by his representation of the deep South, his reconciling influence on African-Americans, and his closeness to the growing number of evangelical Christians. He maintained some of the emphases of Nixon and Ford, such as less military involvement, non-intervention, negotiation and mediation. Jerel A. Rosati summarizes Carter's broad approach in the title of his book: *The Carter Administration's Quest for Global Community.*[76] In his emphasis on fairness and justice, on American mediation, and on greater cooperation in the United Nations, President Carter continued to impress upon the mind of the world's peoples some of the fundamental characteristics of the American idealistic tradition in world leadership. But the leaders of the Soviet Union must have been more impressed by America's apparent weakening political-military influence on the total world scene. On the other hand, there must also have been a deep and subtle positive influence toward peace on the part of millions on every continent—especially in the Soviet Union, in China, in the Middle East, and in Africa.

President Carter showed his new approach in his Inaugural Address, January 20, 1977:

> Ours was the first society to define itself in terms of both spirituality and human liberty. It is that unique self-definition which has given us an exceptional appeal, but it also imposes upon us a special obligation to take on those moral duties which, when affirmed, seem invariably to be in our own best interests.
>
> . . . The passion for freedom is on the rise. Tapping this new spirit, there can be no nobler nor more ambitious task for America to undertake on this day of new beginning than to help shape a just and peaceful world that is truly humane. . . .
>
> We will be ever vigilant and never vulnerable, and we will fight our wars against poverty, ignorance, and injustice. For those are enemies against which our force can be honorably marshaled.
>
> We are a proudly idealistic nation, but let no one confuse our idealism with weakness. . . .[77]

Then he stressed his hope for the ultimate elimination of nuclear weapons:

> . . . We pledge perseverance and wisdom in our effort to limit the world's armaments to those necessary for every nation's own domestic safety, and we will move this year a step toward our ultimate goal—the elimination of all nuclear weapons from this Earth. We urge all other people to join us, for success can mean life instead of death.[78]

On the same day, Carter took the unusual step of making "remarks to people of other nations":

> I want to assure you that the relations of the United States with the other countries and peoples of the world will be guided during my own administration by our desire to shape a world order that is more responsive to human aspirations. The United States will meet its obligation to help create a stable, just, and peaceful world order.
> . . . In these endeavors, we need your help, and we offer ours. We need your experience; we need your wisdom.
> We need your active participation in joint efforts to move the reality of the world closer to the ideals of human freedom and dignity.[79]

On the next day, January 21, Carter proclaimed a pardon for the violators of the Selective Service Act, from August 4, 1964, to March 28, 1973. To strengthen America's international ties, he sent Vice-President Walter Mondale to Europe and Japan, Secretary of State Cyrus Vance to the Middle East, and America's Ambassador to the United Nations, Andrew Young, to Africa. Similarly, he stressed his strong support for the United Nations and especially for human rights, in an address to the U.N. General Assembly, March 17, 1977.[80]

Carter faced the continuing problems of Panama, the Middle East, the Soviet Union and China. He immediately showed his respect for small nations by engaging in negotiations with Panama. After the massive Panamanian rioting on January 9, 1964 (four American soldiers and 20 Panamanians had been killed), Presidents Johnson, Nixon and Ford all carried on talks with Panama, but with no agreement. President Carter wrote later:

> . . . I believed that a new treaty was absolutely necessary. I was convinced that we needed to correct an injustice. . . .
> . . . Our military leaders came to tell me and also testify to

Congress that the Canal could not be defended permanently unless we were able to maintain a working partnership and good relations with Panama.[81]

Negotiations were begun by Secretary of State Vance within two weeks of the inauguration, and, despite considerable American criticism, the two new treaties were completed and signed on September 7. The President analyzed the treaties as follows:

> We have never had sovereignty over the Panama Canal Zone. . . . We had control of the Zone, as though we had sovereignty, but we have recognized the sovereignty of Panama down through the years.
>
> I believe that the most important consideration is that the canal be open to the ships from all countries, that the canal be well operated, that there be harmony between us and the Panamanians, and that we, in case of emergency in this century and in perpetuity, have the right to protect the canal as we see is fit. . . . And all these elements have been written into the treaty.[82]

The President put the two treaties into a larger context at the signing ceremony, with representatives of 27 nations of the Americas present:

> . . . This has been a bipartisan effort, and it is extremely important for our country to stay unified in our commitment to the fairness, the symbol of equality, the mutual respect, the preservation of the security and defense of our own Nation, and an exhibition of cooperation which sets an example that is important to us all before this assembly tonight and before the American people in the future.[83]

Many observers noted the contrast between this negotiation and the Egyptian seizure of the Suez Canal in 1956, followed by war. Yet the Senate would still need to approve the treaty by a two-thirds vote. The opposition would tend to follow California Governor Ronald Reagan's approach in 1976: ". . . we built it, we paid for it, its ours and we should tell Torrijos and Co. that we are going to keep it."[84]

President Carter was determined to continue the search for peace in the Middle East, and was perhaps the first President to stress the need for a Palestinian "homeland." At a meeting in Washington on April 4, President Anwar Sadat of Egypt spoke publicly of the new idealism of President Carter. It was at a news conference on May 12 that the President declared: "I do not think that there can be any reasonable hope for a settlement of the Middle East question . . . without a homeland for the Palestinians." He added that our number one commitment is to "protect the right of Israel to exist, to exist permanently, and to exist in peace. It is a special relationship."[85] On July 19, 1977, Carter held his first meeting with the newly elected Prime Minister of Israel, Menachem Begin, who praised the moral greatness of America.[86]

Although the Carter Administration was working hard to convene a Middle East peace conference in Geneva under joint American and Soviet chairmanship, President Sadat announced, November 9, 1977, that he would be willing to go directly to Jerusalem for talks. Prime Minister Begin issued an invitation on November 15, and most observers were astonished by the dramatic visit of Sadat to Jerusalem, November 1977. Carter praised the arrival of Sadat on November 19: "The hopes and prayers of all Americans are with these two men as they seek progress toward peace for the people of the Middle East and, indeed, for the entire world."[87] By November 30, Carter spoke of the hopes for peace which lay ahead because of the "historic breakthrough."[88] As the negotiations continued, President Carter was able to play the decisive mediating role in securing a successful conclusion.

The President, from the beginning, hoped to develop more cooperative relations with the Soviet Union, and particularly to work on an agreement to reduce armaments substantially. However, on March 30, 1977, the Soviets rejected outright such proposals submitted by Secretary of State Cyrus Vance, making clear that the Soviet Union wished to move slowly in limiting strategic weapons. In a major foreign policy address on May 22, Carter declared that the democracies were strong enough that they did not need to fear communism:

> Democracy's great recent successes—in India, Portugal, Spain, Greece—show that our confidence in this system is not misplaced. Being confident of our own future, we are now free of that inordinate fear of communism which once led us to embrace any dictator who joined us in that fear. I am glad that this is being changed. . . .
>
> I believe in détente with the Soviet Union. . . . We hope to persuade the Soviet Union that one cannot impose its system of society upon another, either through direct military intervention or through the use of client state's military force, as was the case with Cuban intervention in Angola. . . . [89]

In search of peace and cooperation, Carter visited Poland, Iran, India, Saudi Arabia, France, Belgium and Egypt, December 29, 1977–January 6, 1978. In India he stressed the values which tied the two countries together:

> The world's two greatest and largest democracies are bound together with a profound commitment to the importance of moral values. . . .
>
> [Gandhi] was, indeed, and still is a spiritual leader of the whole world, and he represents principles that I try to keep ever present in my own mind—a hope for peace, for nonviolence, for pure truth, for dedication, for compassion, for understanding, for love, for simplicity.[90]

The year 1978 saw the fruition of several of President Carter's hopes in foreign affairs. After a long popular debate and a 22-day Senate debate, the first Panama treaty (providing for continuing U.S. defense of the canal) was passed by the Senate on March 16 by a vote of 68 to 32, only one vote above the required two-thirds. And on April 18, the Senate approved the second treaty (turning the canal over to Panama after 2000). Two months later, on June 18, the President was given an enthusiastic welcome in Panama, for the exchange of the treaty ratifications. His National Security Adviser, Zbigniew Brzezinski, reports in his notes on the significance of the reception:

> An enormous outpouring of emotion. Two hundred thousand people in the street; a real sense of national liberation and this thanks to the efforts of Carter and his team. I believe that we have set in motion a different pattern of relations with Latin America.
>
> . . . It was a new beginning, and I was proud of our achievement.[91]

To expedite, if possible, the Egyptian-Israeli peace talks, President Carter invited President Sadat and Prime Minister Begin to Camp David. What followed was a highlight of Carter's term in office, as he mediated their discussions for 13 days, September 4–17, ending with their signatures of "The Framework for Peacemaking in the Middle East" and the "Framework for the Conclusion of a Peace Treaty Between Egypt and Israel." The high moral-spiritual character of the talks are suggested by the joint statement issued at Camp David on September 6:

After four wars, despite vast human effort, the Holy Land does not yet enjoy the blessings of peace.

Conscious of the grave issues which face us, we place our trust in the God of our fathers, from whom we seek wisdom and guidance.

As we meet here at Camp David we ask people of all faiths to pray with us that peace and justice may result from these deliberations.[92]

The vital role played by the American President was attested to by both Sadat and Begin.[93] President Carter addressed a joint session of Congress on September 18: "Today we are privileged to see the chance for one of the seemingly rare, bright moments in human history—a chance that may offer the way to peace."[94] Although it would take some months and further friendly pressure by President Carter before the Egyptian-Israeli Peace Treaty was signed, the special role of the United States, as sometimes an indispensable mediator, had been dramatized.

A third major achievement in 1978 was the completion of negotiations with the Peoples Republic of China which brought the announcement on December 15 of the full establishment of diplomatic relations between the United States and China on January 1, 1979. At the same time diplomatic relations with Taiwan (Republic of China) were terminated, and the required year's notice given for the end of the defense treaty; existing cultural and trade relations were to be maintained with Taiwan through non-governmental means, under Congressional authorization. The new relations with China were cemented by the visit of China's leader, Deng Xiaoping, to Washington, January 29–31, 1978. Deng particularly expressed his concern about the rapid increase in Soviet military strength, and characterized Vietnam as a "Cuba of the East." [95]

President Carter also indicated his growing concern about future relations with the Soviet Union in his foreign policy address at the U.S. Naval Academy (June 1978). He reported good prospects for a SALT II agreement, but added:

To the Soviet Union, détente seems to mean a continued aggressive struggle for political advantage and increased influence in a variety of ways. . . .

As became apparent in Korea, in Angola, and also . . . in Ethiopia more recently, the Soviets prefer to use proxy force to achieve their purposes.

. . . The Soviet Union can choose either confrontation or

cooperation. The United States is adequately prepared to meet either choice.

We would prefer cooperation through a détente that increasingly involves similar restraint for both sides. . . .

. . . We hope eventually to lead an international system into a more stable, more peaceful, and a more hopeful future.[96]

Finally, on June 18, 1979, Carter and Brezhnev signed the SALT II Treaty in Vienna. Carter spoke to a joint session of Congress on the same day:

The truth of the nuclear age is that the United States and the Soviet Union must live in peace, or we may not live at all. . . .

From the beginning of history, the fortunes of men and nations were made and unmade in unending cycles of war and peace. . . . My fellow Americans, that pattern of war must now be broken forever. . . .

. . . The ultimate future of the human race lies not with tyranny, but with freedom; not with war, but with peace.[97]

However, relations with the Soviet Union grew cooler, especially when the Soviet Union placed new intermediate missiles in Eastern Europe; NATO agreed, on December 12, 1979, to deploy similar missiles in Europe by 1983, if negotiations failed. SALT II was never ratified, but its terms were followed nevertheless by both sides.

President Carter expressed his view of what unites Americans, in his remarks, December 6, 1978, commemorating the 30th anniversary of the Universal Declaration of Human Rights (December 10, 1948):

The American people want the actions of their government, our government, both to reduce human suffering and to increase human freedom. That's why . . . I have sought to rekindle the beacon of human rights in American foreign policy.

What unites us—what makes us Americans—is a common belief in peace, in a free society, and a common devotion to the liberties enshrined in our Constitution.[98]

The Carter Administration had been steadily working for human rights and independence in Zimbabwe and Namibia, among other places.

The year 1979 brought both triumph and tragedy. Triumph appeared to come in the Middle East, where the treaty was not yet signed. The President flew to Egypt on March 8, 1979, talking with Sadat and addressing the Egyptian Parliament; then to Israel, talking with Begin and addressing the Israeli Knesset (Parliament); finally back to Egypt on March 13. Sadat accepted the President's proposals, based on his discussions with Begin, and Begin accepted on March 14. On March 25, Sadat, Begin and Carter met in Washington and issued an unprecedented joint statement:

> Our trust in God was well placed. On Monday [March 26] a peace treaty will be signed between Egypt and Israel within the framework of a comprehensive peace settlement in the area. We are grateful to the people around the world who joined us in prayer. We now ask people of all faiths to join again in a day of prayer and thanksgiving for what has been accomplished, and then ask God to guide our nations in the days ahead as we continue to work for a cooperative, just and lasting peace. With God's help, we and generations to come will know peace between our peoples. To this end, we ask that Monday, March 26, be a day of prayer around the world.[99]

After signing the treaty, President Sadat again spoke of President Carter's role, after thanking all those who worked for the treaty:

> But the man who performed the miracle was President Carter. Without any exaggeration, what he did constitutes one of the greatest achievements of our time. He devoted his skill, hard work and, above all, his firm belief in the ultimate triumph of good against evil to ensure the success of our mission.[100]

Prime Minister Begin likewise praised President Carter. Thus peace was brought between Egypt and Israel. The comprehensive peace had not yet come by September 1995, but a giant step toward it had been taken (despite the general Arab opposition to Egypt's stand at the time).

Despite the idealism of President Carter, the Soviet leaders did not appear impressed. And a poll on March 24, 1979 (AP/NBC), showed that 58 percent of Americans believed that the United States had lost its power to influence events around the world; other polls showed the dominant desire of the voters to concentrate on problems chiefly domestic in character. The President himself noted an inner threat to America, as he addressed the nation on July 15, 1979:

> The threat is nearly invisible in ordinary ways. It is a crisis of confidence. It is a crisis that strikes at the very heart and soul and spirit

of our national will. We can see this crisis in the growing doubt about
the meaning of our lives and in the loss of a unity of purpose for our
Nation.

The erosion of our confidence in the future is threatening to destroy
the social and political fabric of America. . . .

. . . In a nation that was proud of hard work, strong families, close-
knit communities, and our faith in God, too many of us now tend to
worship self-indulgence and consumption.

We simply must have faith in each other, faith in our ability to
govern ourselves, and faith in the future of this Nation.[101]

The special foreign tragedies of 1979 were to come in Iran and
Afghanistan. The Shah, on whom the United States had depended for
many years, was forced out on January 16; the Ayatollah Khomeini
returned as leader on February 1. On October 20, the Shah was
admitted to the United States for medical treatment, and, on November
4, the U.S. Embassy in Iran was overrun, with the staff imprisoned as
hostages. The whole approach of the Administration, and of the
American people, was changed by the Soviet invasion of Afghanistan
on December 27, 1979—the first use of Soviet troops outside its own
territory except in its Eastern European puppets (Hungary in 1956 and
Czechoslovakia in 1968).

Return of the "Cold War" Spirit, 1980–86/87

Although the mood of introversion remained dominant for the next
several years, there was a bipartisan effort to rebuild America's military
and economic strength—preparatory, as in the past, to a later mood of
extroversion. President Carter found it necessary to change his approach
toward the Soviet Union, but the American people turned again (in the
1980 election) to a "cold warrior" for its next President—Ronald
Reagan. Nevertheless, President Carter's emphasis on peace, justice and
human rights would leave a major legacy in America's developing role.

Jimmy Carter, 1980–January 20, 1981

A sign of a changing approach to the Soviet Union came on October
1, 1979, when the President spoke to the nation about a Soviet combat
brigade which had been in Cuba for several years and about Cuban
forces which threatened various countries in Africa and Central

America. He warned that "no Soviet unit in Cuba can be used as a combat force to threaten the security of the United States or any other nation in this hemisphere," and added that he was establishing "a permanent, full-time Caribbean joint task force with headquarters in Key West, Florida." He also declared that a "rapid deployment force" would be strengthened, and that the American naval presence in the Indian Ocean would be reinforced.[102]

The seizure of American diplomats by a mob in Iran on November 4 added a deep sense of disquiet to Americans, as the Administration sought a peaceful solution through the United Nations and every other available channel. But the biggest shock was the December 27 Soviet invasion of Afghanistan, allegedly to support the pro-Soviet regime, established by coup in 1978, against opposition forces. The invasion constituted a potential threat to Pakistan, Iran and the whole Persian Gulf area. Carter spoke to the nation on January 4 to announce sanctions against the Soviet Union.

In his State of the Union message of January 23, 1980, the President warned the Soviet Union against any direct threat to the Persian Gulf region (the new "Carter Doctrine"):

> The implication of the Soviet invasion could pose the most serious threat to the peace since the Second World War. . . . No action of a world power has ever been so quickly and so overwhelmingly condemned. . . . The Soviet Union must pay a concrete price for their aggression.
>
> The region which is now threatened by Soviet troops in Afghanistan is of great strategic importance: it contains more than two-thirds of the world's exportable oil.
>
> Let our position be absolutely clear: An attempt by any outside force to gain control of the Persian Gulf region will be regarded as an assault on the vital interests of the United States, and such an assault will be repelled by any means necessary, including military force.
>
> It is imperative that Congress approve this strong defense budget for 1981, encompassing a 5 percent real increase in authorizations, without any reduction.[103]

The President went on to name a number of measures to strengthen the American position, such as reconfirming the 1959 agreement to help Pakistan preserve its independence and its integrity, and revitalizing the Selective Service System. Other modest sanctions would be imposed later, such as a grain embargo and a refusal to attend the Summer

Olympics in Moscow. Carter stressed peace on February 13: "We must convince the Soviet Union, through peaceful means, *peaceful* means, that they cannot invade an innocent country with impunity and they must suffer the consequences of their action."[104]

In relation to Iran, the President also imposed sanctions and secured the support of all United Nations organizations against the holding of the hostages. After the ultimate release of the hostages, who were held for 444 days, the President praised the approach of the American people:

> During this time the nation acted with patience, a willingness to sacrifice for the national good, and a complete dedication to peace. Confronted with outrageous behavior abroad, we as a nation never strayed from the great value we place on human life and human freedom.[105]

But the President himself lost his patience by April, and ordered an attempt by the military to rescue the hostages. Secretary of State Vance submitted his resignation in opposition to the move, three days before the failed rescue attempt (April 24), called off after eight men were killed in an air collision. Vance was replaced by Senator Edmund Muskie.

Ronald Reagan was nominated by the Republicans on July 16, and Carter was renominated on August 13. In his acceptance address, Carter restated his faith in the search for peace:

> I see a future of peace—a peace born of wisdom and based on a fairness toward all countries of the world, a peace guaranteed both by America's military strength and by America's moral strength as well.
> . . . If the world is to have a future of freedom as well as peace, America must continue to defend human rights.[106]

Throughout the campaign, Carter continued his emphasis on peace, and implied that Reagan appeared to propose a new arms race with the Soviet Union. In a foreign policy radio address on October 19, 1980, the President spoke as follows:

> For the past 4 years, the United States has been at peace. . . . This is no accident. This is the result of a careful exercise of the enormous strength of America. . . .
> As we raise our shield against war, let us also hear the stricken

voice of the homeless refugee, the cry of the hungry child, the weeping of the bereaved widow, the whispered prayer of the political prisoner. We are one with the family of all people. . . .

We seek a world in which the rule of law, not the threat of force, is the language of statecraft. We seek a world in which nations put aside the madness of war and nuclear arms races and turn their energies instead to the conquest of our common global enemies—dwindling resources, ecological decay, ignorance, and hunger.

We will keep our Nation strong, but this I can say to you: Peace is my passion.[107]

President Carter was looking far ahead, it seems, in terms of America's highest ideals.

In the Presidential debate on October 28, Governor Reagan stressed military strength as the way to world peace at that time:

I believe with all my heart that our first priority must be world peace, and that use of force is always and only a last resort, when everything else has failed, and then only with regard to our national security.

. . . To maintain that peace requires strength. America has never gotten in a war because we were too strong. We can get into a war by letting events get out of hand, as they have in the last three and a half years under the foreign policy of this administration. . . .[108]

Many Americans felt that the world was becoming more dangerous. On September 22, Iraq had invaded Iran. A Harris Survey (September 8, 1980) showed 60 to 29 percent believing that President Carter "had lost the respect of the world abroad." Many writers in 1980 deplored the allegedly low state of America's military readiness. In his memoirs, President Reagan stated his belief that in 1980 "America had lost faith in itself":

We were told there was a "malaise" in our nation and America was past its prime. . . .

We were told we would have to lower our expectations. . . .

. . . I saw no national malaise. I found nothing wrong with the American people.

We had to recapture our dreams, our pride in ourselves and our country, and regain that unique sense of destiny that had always made America different from any other country in the world.

If I could be elected president, I wanted to do what I could to bring about a spiritual revival in Americans.

    I believed—and I intended to make it a theme of my campaign—that . . . we had to . . . decide what had gone wrong, and then put it back on course.[109]

It appears that Ronald Reagan was elected President in part because of his clear-cut stand for increased defense against Communist dangers and for greater internal strength. He won by an impressive electoral majority on November 4, 1980, 489 to 49, with a popular vote of 43 million to 38 million for President Carter and 5.6 million for Representative John Anderson (independent). Republicans also gained control of the Senate, 54 to 46.

President Carter delivered an impressive Farewell Address to the nation on January 14, 1981:

    . . . I want to . . . speak to you as a fellow citizen of the world about three issues, three difficult issues: the threat of nuclear destruction, our stewardship of our planet, and the preeminence of the basic rights of human beings.

    National weakness, real or perceived, can tempt aggressors and thus cause war. That is why the United States can never neglect its military strength. . . . But with equal determination, the United States and all countries must find ways to control and to reduce the horrifying danger that is posed by the enormous stockpile of nuclear arms.

    . . . We see our Earth as it really is—a small and fragile and beautiful blue globe, the only home we have. We see no barrier of race or religion or country. We see an essential unity of our species and our planet. And with faith and common sense, that bright vision will prevail.

    The struggle for human rights overrides all divisions of color or nation or rank. Those who hunger for freedom, who thirst for human dignity, and who suffer for the sake of justice, they are the patriots of this cause.

    I believe with all my heart that America must always stand for these basic human rights, at home and abroad. That is both our history and our destiny.

    . . . Our social and political progress has been based on one fundamental principle: the value and importance of the individual. . . . The love of liberty is the common blood that flows in our American veins.

    . . . We should take pride that the ideals which gave birth to our Nation still inspire the hopes of oppressed people around the world. We have no cause for self-righteousness or complacency, but we have every reason to persevere, both within our own country and beyond our borders.

If we are to serve as a beacon for human rights, we must continue to perfect here at home the rights and values which we espouse around the world. . . .

. . . Our common vision of a free and just society is our greatest source of cohesion at home and strength abroad. . . .

. . . We know that democracy is always an unfinished creation. Each generation must renew its foundations. Each generation must rediscover the meaning of this hallowed vision in the light of its own modern challenges. . . .

As I return home to the South . . . I intend to work as a citizen, as I have worked here in this office as President, for the values this Nation was founded to secure.[110]

Not until January 18, 1981, were the final terms negotiated for the release of the American hostages in Iran, and not until the inaugural ceremonies were over on January 20 were the 52 hostages actually released. President Reagan graciously had President Carter fly over to Wiesbaden, Germany, on January 21 to meet the released hostages. In his diary entry on January 20, Carter reported a visit from the Administrator of Veterans Affairs, a Vietnam veteran and amputee:

Max Cleland came to tell me good-bye. He brought me a plaque with a quote from Thomas Jefferson:
"I HAVE THE CONSOLATION TO REFLECT
THAT DURING THE PERIOD OF MY
ADMINISTRATION NOT A DROP
OF THE BLOOD OF A SINGLE CITIZEN
WAS SHED BY THE SWORD OF WAR."
This is something that I shall always cherish.[111]

Ronald Reagan, 1981–86/87

Ronald Reagan proved to be one of America's most popular Presidents according to public opinion polls, at least until 1986 when the Iran-Contra scandal was revealed. He was confident and hopeful about the future of America in the world, stressing economic as well as political freedom. He described his approach in his first Inaugural Address, January 20, 1981:

If we look to the answer as to why for so many years we achieved so much, prospered as no other peoples on Earth, it was because here in this land we unleashed the energy and individual genius of man to a greater extent than has ever been done before. Freedom and the dignity of the individual have been more available and assured here than in any other place on Earth.

. . . As we renew ourselves here in our own land, we will be seen as having greater strength throughout the world. We will again be the exemplar of freedom and a beacon of hope for those who do not now have freedom.

He also stressed peace, based on physical and moral strength:

As for the enemies of freedom, those who are our potential adversaries, they will be reminded that peace is the highest aspiration of the American people. We will negotiate for it, sacrifice for it; we will not surrender for it, now or ever.

Above all, we must realize that no arsenal or new weapon in the arsenals of the world, is so formidable as the will and moral courage of free men and women.

I am told that tens of thousands of prayer meetings are being held on this day, and for that I am deeply grateful. We are a nation under God, and I believe God intended us to be free.[112]

When Reagan welcomed the freed American hostages from Iran, on January 27, he warned terrorists:

Let terrorists be aware that when the rules of international behavior are violated, our policy will be one of swift and effective retaliation. We hear it said that we live in an era of limits to our power, Well, let it also be understood, there are limits to our patience.[113]

In answer to a question at a news conference, on January 29, the President squarely criticized the Soviet Union:

. . . So far détente has been a one-way street that the Soviet Union has used to pursue it own aims. . . . I know of no leader of the Soviet Union since the revolution, and including the present leadership, that has not more than once repeated in the various Communist congresses . . . their determination that their goal must be the promotion of world revolution and a one-world Socialist or Communist state. . . .

Now as long as they do that and as long as they, at the same time, have openly and publicly declared that the only morality they recognize is what will further their success, meaning they reserve unto themselves the right to commit any crime, to lie, to cheat, in order to attain that . . . I think when you do business with them . . . you keep that in mind.[114]

President Carter had talked of reducing the number of American troops in South Korea. President Reagan's first foreign visitor (February 2, 1981) was President Chun Doo Hwan of the Republic of Korea, and Reagan stressed again the American commitment:

Our special bond of freedom and friendship is as strong today as it was . . . 30 years ago.

. . . Our meeting here today is a sign to all the people of Asia as well as to the people of Korea, that the United States has a long standing interest and enduring commitment to that part of the world.[115]

When British Prime Minister Margaret Thatcher visited on February 26, the ties between the United States and Britain were stressed. The President declared:

Great Britain and the United States are kindred nations of like-minded people and must face their tests together. We are bound by common language and linked in history. We share laws and literature, blood, and moral fiber. The responsibility for freedom is ours to share.
. . .
. . . Together we'll strive to preserve the liberty and peace so cherished by our peoples. No foe of freedom should doubt our resolve. We will prevail, because our faith is strong and our cause is just.

Mrs. Thatcher spoke in turn:

Mr. President, you've spoken of a time of renewal. . . . We must have the courage to reassert our traditional values and the resolve to prevail against those who deny our ideals and threaten our way of life.[116]

The nation was shocked by the attempted assassination of President Reagan on March 30 by John Hinckley. It was a narrow escape—the bullet was in the President's lung, less than an inch from his heart. The President felt he had been granted a new lease on life: "After I left the hospital and was back in the White House, I wrote a few words about the shooting in my diary that concluded: 'Whatever happens to me now I owe my life to God and will try to serve Him in every way I can.'"[117] This experience doubtless deepened his concern over the attempted assassination of Pope John Paul II on May 13, 1981, after which the President issued a statement:

> We are grateful that he has been spared. We pray that all of us will heed Pope John Paul's call for a "world of love, not of hate"; that we will hear his words reminding us that all men are brothers, that they must forever forsake an occasion of violence and live together in peace.[118]

The President wished to steel Americans for a period of new tension with the expanding Soviet Union. He had named a General, Alexander Haig, as Secretary of State (Haig was replaced by George Shultz in July 1982). On a realistic vein he sent a five-year rearmament program to Congress. At a May 17 commencement, he asked whether Americans would rise to the current challenges:

> When it is written, history of our time won't dwell long on the hardships of the recent past. But history will ask—and our answer determines that fate of freedom for a thousand years—Did a nation born of hope lose hope? Did a people forged by courage find courage wanting? Did a generation steeled by hard war and a harsh peace forsake honor at the moment of great climactic struggle for the human spirit?
>
> . . . The world will soon know and history some day record that in its third century, the American Nation came of age, affirmed its leadership of free men and women serving selflessly a vision of man with God, government for people, and humanity at peace.
>
> A few years ago an Australian Prime Minister John Gorton said, "I wonder if anybody ever wrote what the situation for the comparatively small nations in the world would be if there were not in existence the United States. if there were not this grand country prepared to make so many sacrifices." This is the noble and rich history rooted in the great civil ideas of the West, and it is yours.[119]

On May 27, Reagan quoted Pope Pius XII at the end of World War II: "America has a great genius for great and unselfish deeds. . . . Into the hands of America God has placed afflicted mankind."[120]

During this period, President Reagan stated his belief that communism was weakening and that its last passages in history were being written, that "communism is an aberration," and that "it's not a normal way of living for human beings, and I think we are seeing the first beginning cracks, the beginning of the end."[121] At the same time, Reagan pointed out that "I have said many times I would like to enter into negotiations toward a definite, verifiable reduction of strategic nuclear weapons world-wide."[122] On the 20th anniversary of the Berlin Wall, on August 13, 1981, Reagan looked forward to the freedom of Eastern Europe:

> All who treasure freedom and human dignity should never accept nor take for granted this lethal barrier to freedom that stands today in the heart of Europe. . . .
> . . . Today throughout the world men and women who cherish freedom pray for the day when the Berlin Wall and other such monuments to tyranny are only a bitter memory—a day when the people of Eastern Europe can once again enjoy free contact with their neighbors in the West.[123]

The President also stressed the important role of a much enlarged Navy, when he spoke to the crew of the *Constellation* and signed the John Barry Day Resolution:

> We're committed to a 600-ship Navy that is big enough to deter aggression wherever it might occur. Let friend and foe alike know that America has the muscle to back up its words, and ships like this and men like you are that muscle.
> . . . There's a new spirit, I can tell you, sweeping America, and you're part of it.
> . . . I know, today your ship's motto, "The Spirit is Old; the Pride is New" fits this Nation as well as the vessel.[124]

As the United States began to increase its supply of nuclear weapons, critics of the President wondered if he was preparing for the possibility of a nuclear war. He was asked, "Is there a winnable nuclear war?" and he replied:

> It's very difficult for me to think that there's a winnable nuclear war, but where our great risk falls is that the Soviet Union has made it very plain that among themselves, they believe it is winnable. And

believing that, that makes them constitute a threat, which is one of the reasons why I'm dedicated to getting them to a table not for arms limitation talks, but for arms reduction talks.[125]

Talk of nuclear war stimulated a new and strong peace movement in the United States and in Europe, seeking in particular a "nuclear freeze." This movement remained influential until Reagan was finally able to meet with Gorbachev in 1985 (following the successive deaths of Soviet leaders—Brezhnev in 1982, Andropov in 1984, and Chernenko in 1985).

Reagan also wished to show that he had the will to use force against nations who encouraged terrorists. On August 20, 1981, two Libyan aircraft, which had fired on American jets 60 miles off the coast of Libya, were shot down. When Egypt's President Anwar al-Sadat was assassinated on October 6, the President called the deed an act of "cowardly infamy": "America has lost a great friend; the world has lost a great statesman, and mankind has lost a champion of peace."[126] When martial law was declared in Poland (as *Solidarity* was gaining in strength and the Soviet Union was threatening to intervene), the President praised the spirit of the Polish people (December 17, 1981):

> The Polish nation, speaking through Solidarity, has provided one of the brightest, bravest moments in modern history. The people of Poland are giving us an imperishable example of courage and devotion to the values of freedom in the face of relentless opposition.
>
> Two Decembers ago, freedom was lost in Afghanistan; this Christmas it is at stake in Poland. But the torch of liberty is hot. It warms those who hold it high. It burns those who try to extinguish it.[127]

On December 23, he further encouraged the Polish people: "We the people of the Free World stand as one with our Polish brothers and sisters. Their cause is ours, and our prayers and hopes go out to them this Christmas."[128] (It was revealed by Carl Bernstein in *Time*, February 24, 1992, that President Reagan and Pope John Paul II, especially after their meeting on June 7, 1982, "secretly joined forces to keep the Solidarity union alive," with the ultimate hope of freeing Eastern Europe.)

President Reagan was getting ready to endeavor to strengthen the opposition to communism which was rising in a number of countries, and to strengthen governments which were resisting rebel forces supported by communist nations. This controversial policy was first applied early in 1981 to El Salvador, where the rebels were supported with weapons from Cuba, Nicaragua and the Soviet Union. When military advisers were sent to help the government of El Salvador, Congress showed its restraint by requiring that not more than 55 be sent. Reagan noted that the Afghan people were still resisting two years after the Soviet invasion, and implied American support for the rebels: "As long as the Soviet Union occupies Afghanistan in defiance of the international community, the heroic Afghan resistance will continue, and the United States will support the cause of free Afghanistan."[129]

On January 1, 1982, the President broadcast New Year's Day remarks to the people of foreign nations, explaining the American position of growing military strength and continued devotion to freedom:

> During my lifetime, I have seen the rise of fascism and communism. Both philosophies glorify the arbitrary power of the state. . . . Both deny those God-given liberties that are the inalienable right of each person on this planet; indeed they deny the existence of God. Because of this fundamental flaw, fascism has already been destroyed, and the bankruptcy of communism has been laid bare for all to see—a system that is efficient in producing the machines of war, but cannot feed its people.
>
> Americans begin this new year with a renewed commitment to our ideals and with confidence that the peace will be maintained and that freedom for all men will ultimately prevail. . . . To all who yearn to breathe free, who long for a better life, we think of you; we pray for you; we're with you always.[130]

The President appealed to the American people in similar fashion in his State of the Union Address on January 26, 1982:

> Our foreign policy is a policy of strength, fairness, and balance. By restoring America's military credibility, by pursuing peace at the negotiating table whenever both sides are willing to sit down in good faith, and by regaining the respect of America's allies and adversaries alike, we have strengthened our country's position as a force for peace and progress in the world.[131]

Speaking to the Permanent Council of the Organization of American

States on February 24, Reagan expressed his hopes for the whole Western Hemisphere:

> I have always believed that this hemisphere was a special place with a special destiny. I believe we are destined to be the beacon of hope for all mankind. With God's help we can make it so. We can create a peaceful, free, and prospering hemisphere based on our shared ideals and reaching from pole to pole of what we proudly call the New World.[132]

A climax for the President's support of freedom around the world was reached in his trip to Europe, June 2–11, 1982. He commemorated the 38th anniversary of the Normandy invasion (June 5), attended the Versailles economic summit, visited the Pope (June 7), and addressed the British Parliament on June 8, where he pledged a crusade for democracy, in a deeply hopeful spirit:

> I believe we live now at a turning point. . . . It is the Soviet Union that runs against the tide of history, by denying human freedom and human dignity to its citizens. It also is in deep economic difficulty.
>
> Around the world today, the democratic revolution is gathering new strength. . . .
>
> If the rest of this century is to witness the gradual growth of freedom and democratic ideals, we must take actions to assist the campaign for democracy.
>
> We cannot ignore the fact that even without our encouragement there has been and will continue to be repeated explosions against repressive dictatorships. The Soviet Union is not immune to this reality. . . .
>
> We must be staunch in our conviction that freedom is not the sole prerogative of a lucky few, but the inalienable and universal right of all human beings. . . .
>
> The objective I propose is quite simple to state: to foster the infrastructure of democracy, the system of a free press, unions, political parties. . . .
>
> It is time that we committed ourselves as a nation—in both the public and private sectors—to assisting democratic development. . . .
>
> . . . What I am describing now is a plan and a hope for the long term—the march of freedom and democracy which will leave Marxism-Leninism on the ashheap of history as it has left other tyrannies which stifle the freedom and muzzle the self-expression of the people.
>
> Our military strength is a prerequisite of peace, but let it be clear

we maintain this strength in the hope it will never be used, for the ultimate determinant in the struggle that now goes on in the world will not be bombs or rockets, but a test of wills and ideas, a trial of spiritual resolve, the values we hold, the beliefs we cherish, the ideals to which we are dedicated.

The British people know that, given strong leadership, time and a little bit of hope, the forces of good ultimately rally and triumph over evil. . . .

. . . I've often wondered about the shyness of some of us in the West about standing for these ideals that have done so much to ease the plight of man and the hardships of our imperfect world. . . . The emergency is upon us. Let us be shy no longer. Let us go to our strength. Let us offer hope. Let us tell the world that a new age is not only possible but probable.

. . . The task I've set forth will long outlive our own generation. But together, we . . . have come through the worst. Let us now begin a major effort to secure the best—a crusade for freedom that will engage the faith and fortitude of the next generation. For the sake of peace and justice, let us move toward a world in which all people are at last free to determine their own destiny.[133]

Prime Minister Thatcher, at a luncheon in honor of the President, praised his "magnificent speech to members of both Houses of Parliament":

We are grateful to you for putting freedom on the offensive, which is where it should be. You wrote a new chapter in our history. . . .[134]

The President spoke to the German Bundestag in Bonn, June 9, stressing peace as well as democracy:

Earlier, I said the German people had built a remarkable cathedral of democracy. But we still have other work ahead. We must build a cathedral of peace, where nations are safe from war and where people need not fear for their liberties. . . .

Let us build a cathedral as the people of Cologne built theirs—with the deepest commitment and determination. Let us build as they did—not just for ourselves but for the generations beyond. For if we construct our peace properly, it will endure as long as the spires of Cologne.[135]

Finally he spoke to the people of Berlin:

Our forces will remain here as long as necessary to preserve the peace and protect the freedom of the people of Berlin. For us the American presence in Berlin, as long as it is needed, is not a burden, it is a sacred trust.

Ours is a defensive mission. . . . But we do extend a challenge, a new Berlin initiative to the leaders of the Soviet bloc. It is a challenge for peace. We challenge the men in the Kremlin to join with us in the quest for peace, security, and lowering of the tensions and weaponry that could lead to future conflict.

. . . I call on President Brezhnev to join me in a sincere effort to translate the dashed hopes of the 1970's into the reality of a safer and freer Europe in the 1980's.

I am determined to assure that our civilization averts the catastrophe of a nuclear war.[136]

By the middle of 1982, President Reagan had clearly set out his own ideals and goals, and he maintained them: the buildup of America's military strength in the expectation that communist power could be deterred and also rolled back in nations where rebels were opposing it, and that nuclear armaments could be reduced by agreement with the Soviet Union. He was one of the few observers who spoke of the weakness and decline of communism, and he had positive expectations about America's future world role, as the leader for democracy and for a market economy. A special characteristic of the Reagan Administration was America's "unilateralism" in foreign policy. One such indication came in the decision by President Reagan (July 9, 1982) not to sign the new Law of the Sea Treaty, adopted after eight years of negotiation on April 30, 1982. Another was the strong criticism of the United Nations (partly because many U.N. delegates were very critical of the United States) and its Specialized Agencies (which often appeared "politicized" until world conditions changed after 1987).

Little progress seemed possible with the Soviet Union, as there were three Soviet leaders in succession—Brezhnev died on November 11, 1982, Andropov on February 10, 1984, and Chernenko on March 11, 1985. Then occurred one of the great surprises of history—the naming of Mikhail Gorbachev, at the age of 54, as General Secretary of the Soviet Communist Party. Gorbachev almost immediately urged arms control and the strengthening of the economic and intellectual vigor of his country. But it took two years or so before his hopeful policies became clear to others.

In the meantime, the Reagan Administration continued to support growing military force, while using it with restraint—as in peacekeeping operations in Lebanon (1982–1984, climaxed by the terrorist killing of 241 marines on October 23, 1983), and in the small island-state of Grenada (where the pro-Communist government, permitting another Soviet-Cuban base in the Caribbean, was overthrown on October 25–26, 1983). Reagan spoke often of his faith in America's future, as on September 9, 1982:

> Let's reject the nonsense that America is doomed to decline, the world sliding toward disaster no matter what we do. . . .
> In a world racked by hatred, economic crisis, and political tension, America remains mankind's best hope. The eyes of mankind are on us, counting on us to protect the peace, promote new prosperity, and provide for them a better world.[137]

Despite considerable American opposition, Reagan was determined to continue aid to the government of El Salvador in resisting the rebels, and to give support to the "Contras" who were fighting the pro-Communist regime in Nicaragua. In an address before a joint session of Congress on Central America, April 27, 1983, the President warned: "If the United States cannot respond to a threat near our own borders, why should Europeans or Asians believe that we're sincerely concerned about threats to them?"[138] Congress, however, held back, and in 1984 cut off U.S. aid for the Contras (for the next two years). Whereupon the President urged other countries and civilians to help the Contras (leading to the Iran-Contra scandal revealed in late 1986).[139]

Reagan continued to speak squarely in opposition to communism and to stress its weakness (March 8, 1983):

> I believe that communism is another sad, bizarre chapter in human history, whose last passages even now are being written. I believe this because the source of our strength in the quest for human freedom is not material but spiritual. And because it knows no limits, it must . . . ultimately triumph over those who would enslave their fellow man.[140]

On March 23, the President indicated his support for research on the controversial Strategic Defense Initiative (SDI or "Star Wars"), aimed at destroying nuclear missiles flying toward the United States.[141] Tension with the Soviet Union reached a high point when the Soviets shot down a Korean civilian plane, off course over Soviet territory, on September 3, 1983, killing all 269 on board. The President condemned the attack but urged restraint.[142]

Reagan visited Japan and South Korea, November 10–13, 1983. He made a special appeal to the Soviet Union in his State of the Union address, January 25, 1984:

> People of the Soviet Union, there is only one sane policy, for your country and mine, to preserve our civilization in this modern age: A nuclear war cannot be won and must never be fought. . . .
> . . . Americans are people of peace. If your government wants peace, we can come together in faith and friendship to build a safer and far better world for our children and their children's children. And the whole world will rejoice.[143]

Relations with China were improved as the President was warmly received there on his visit, April 26–30, 1984. Reagan told the American people that "our two nations are poised to take a historic step forward on the path of peaceful cooperation and economic development."[144] In June he visited Ireland, France and Britain, and helped the London Economic Summit submit a Declaration on Democratic Values (June 8).

In the election in November against former Vice President Walter Mondale, Reagan carried 49 states (525 electoral votes to 13, and 59 percent popular vote to 41). His Inaugural Address, January 21, 1985, was filled with confidence:

> My fellow citizens, our nation is poised for greatness. We must do what we know is right, and do it with all our might. . . .
> There must be no wavering by us, nor any doubt by others, that America will meet her responsibility to remain free, secure, and at peace.
> We seek the total elimination one day of the nuclear weapons from the face of the earth. . . .
> . . . Human freedom is on the march, and nowhere more so than in our own hemisphere.
> America must remain freedom's staunchest friend, for freedom is our best ally, and it's the world's only hope to conquer poverty and preserve peace.[145]

Mikhail Gorbachev became the leader of the Soviet Union on March 11, 1985. In his message to the Soviet Union on the death of Konstantine Chernenko, Reagan added: "I hope that the Soviet leadership will join with me with renewed dedication to create a firm and durable basis for better relations between our two countries."[146] Vice-President George Bush took a letter from Reagan to Gorbachev at the Chernenko funeral, inviting him to the United States for a summit conference. Gorbachev wrote a friendly reply in two weeks, beginning a continuing correspondence between the two leaders, while arms talks were carried on in Geneva.[147] Secretary of State George Shultz also met from time to time with Soviet Foreign Secretary Eduard Shevardnadze.

After the Bonn Economic Summit, Reagan spoke on May 8 to a special session of the European Parliament in Strasbourg, France:

> The United States is committed not only to the security of Europe. We are committed to the re-creation of a larger and more genuinely European Europe. The United States is committed not only to a partnership with Europe, the United States is committed to an end to the artificial division of Europe.[148]

On that same day, the 40th anniversary of the end of World War II in Europe, Reagan wrote a letter to Gorbachev about his future hopes:

> Together with our other allies, our two countries played a full part in that long struggle. We demonstrated that despite our differences we can join together in successful common effort.
>
> I believe we should also see this solemn occasion as an opportunity to look forward to the future with vision and hope. I should like our countries to join in rededication to the task of overcoming the divisions and resolving the problems between us, and in renewed progress toward the goals of making peace more stable and eliminating nuclear weapons from the face of the earth.[149]

In his address to the U.N. General Assembly on October 24, 1985 (the 40th anniversary of the United Nations), Reagan spoke of the Geneva summit to come with Gorbachev in November: "Let both sides go committed to walk together on a safer path into the 21st century and to lay the foundations for enduring peace."[150]

The summit meetings in Geneva, on November 19–20, were expected to be largely exploratory; they proved to be friendly and hopeful, and the two leaders planned to meet again, in Washington in 1986 and in Moscow in 1987. Reagan said he had explained his proposal to Gorbachev for a peace process to stop the wars in Afghanistan, Nicaragua, Ethiopia, Angola and Cambodia, and added: "I have made it clear to Mr. Gorbachev that we must reduce the mistrust and suspicion between us if we are to do such things as reduce arms, and this will take deeds, not words alone, and I believe he is in agreement."[151]

In a radio address to the nation on December 21, Reagan noted the new stand of Congress in July in support of "freedom fighters" abroad (the "Reagan Doctrine"):

> The final legislative achievement I want to mention concerns foreign affairs. It involves the emergence in the Congress of a new mood, a new point of view, during this past year. The Congress repudiated isolationism and weakness and reasserted America's legitimate world role on behalf of freedom. Indeed in July, Congress voted aid to freedom fighters in Cambodia, Afghanistan, Nicaragua, and elsewhere, and repealed the ban on aid to the freedom fighters in Angola. . . . I'm convinced that a new, bipartisan foreign policy consensus is emerging, one based upon realism and which unites Democrats and Republicans alike in support of a strong national defense and help for freedom fighters around the globe.[152]

By agreement, Reagan and Gorbachev sent unprecedented and hopeful New Year's messages to each other's countries (January 1, 1986).[153] As 1986 began, the President became more determined and more confident in pressing for democracy abroad, as in his State of the Union message on February 4.[154] The Reagan Administration finally helped the Filipino people overthrow President Marcos, after the February fraudulent election in which he was declared the victor, and recognized President Aquino on February 25. Reagan sent a special foreign policy message to Congress on March 14, in which he urged the Soviet Union to change its policies, and stressed American support for human rights not only in dictatorships of the left but also of the right.[155]

President Carter in 1980 and President Reagan, from 1981 to 1986, had paved the way for the shift to a new dominant mood of extroversion combined with an emphasis on internationalism, especially when it became clear that Soviet policy was indeed changing toward cooperation. Economic and psychological pressures were mounting inside the communist system of East Europe and the Soviet Union, but few expected the major breakthrough which was only a few years away. The United States was getting ready to increase its direct diplomatic and military pressure abroad, while the Soviet Union was preparing to retrench and to withdraw. By 1986/87 President Reagan's more active policy began receiving majority support (in spite of the Iran-Contra problem), so that it appeared that an extrovert phase was beginning.

America's Renewed Leadership as the Cold War Ends: Extrovert Internationalism, 1986/87–

One of the special features of extroversion in the past had been the application of American military force from time to time. Although the Soviet challenge was due to be sharply minimized, there were three rising challenges or opportunities for the use of pressure abroad: (1) military pressure from small strategic states (such as Iraq or Iran); (2) terrorist bombings encouraged by some states (such as Libya or Syria); and (3) spreading democratic moves against authoritarian governments (as in the Philippines) or against communist regimes. Increasing American economic and diplomatic pressures on other nations were also signs of a growing mood of extroversion, while the continuing idealist trend encouraged negotiations for disarmament, cooperation and peace.

Ronald Reagan, 1986/87–January 1989

Three extrovert acts with public support occurred in 1986: (1) the American bomber attack on five targets in Libya (April 14), following evidence that Libya had been involved in the bomb explosion in West Berlin which killed two, including an American soldier, and injured 155 (April 5); (2) the first clear House vote (June 25) to give military aid to the Nicaraguan Contras, 221 to 209 ($70 million military and $30 million humanitarian aid), followed by Senate support 53 to 47 (August 14); and (3) Congressional passage of sanctions against South Africa over the President's veto (House vote of 313 to 83, September 29, and Senate vote 78 to 21, October 2). It is believed that the delivery of *Stinger* missiles to Afghan rebels in June of 1986 may have turned the tide in the civil war in their favor. Reagan's prestige was lowered by the revelation, in November 1986, of the secret shipment of arms to Iran via Israel (1985–86), partly in the hope that some of the hostages held in Lebanon would be released (as three of them were in time); some of the Iranian payments were diverted to the Contras in Nicaragua.

Reagan and Gorbachev agreed to meet in Reykjavik, Iceland, on October 11–12, 1986, in an attempt to accelerate the continuing arms talks in Geneva, working on a proposed 50 percent reduction of strategic nuclear weapons. Surprisingly, they came close to a historic agreement on the dramatic reduction or even elimination of nuclear weapons, if the United States would have been willing to give up its "Star Wars" program, and this Reagan refused to do. In an address to the nation on October 13, Reagan concluded: "The door is open, and the opportunity to begin eliminating the nuclear threat is within reach."[156]

After the Venice economic summit (June 9, 1987), where the allies called for closer East-West relations, Reagan gave a sharp challenge to Gorbachev at the Brandenburg Gate, between East and West Berlin:

> There is one sign the Soviets can make that would be unmistakable, that would advance dramatically the cause of freedom and peace. General Secretary Gorbachev . . . come here to this gate! Mr. Gorbachev, open this gate! Mr. Gorbachev, tear down this wall![157]

Gorbachev's 1987 book, *Perestroika*, increased Western confidence in his ultimate aims.[158] In his conclusion, however, Gorbachev wrote that he was still motivated by "the ideas of Lenin."[159]

Extrovert indications in 1987 focused on the Persian Gulf, where the United States gave naval protection to Kuwaiti ships transferred to the American flag (March 23) and carrying supplies to and from Iraq. After Iranian provocation, American ships or helicopters fired on Iranian vessels or off-shore platforms (September 21, October 8, October 19). Aid to the Nicaraguan Contras was maintained in 1988, when the Senate voted to keep it (52 to 48).

The major internationalist event of the year was the Reagan-Gorbachev meeting in Washington, December 8, 1987, with the signing of the Intermediate-Range Nuclear Forces (INF) Treaty eliminating these weapons from Europe. Both sides felt this was a major step toward peace in Europe and toward the future reduction of strategic weapons.

A number of American writers by 1987 had stressed the likelihood of the decline of America's influence in the world, especially if the nation followed previous great powers in overextending its role. Part of this evaluation was perhaps based upon the evidence of America's introversion between 1967 and 1987. Paul Kennedy's popular book, *The Rise and Fall of the Great Powers*, dramatized the possibility of America's weakness.[160] This point of view was strongly refuted in 1988 by other writers.[161] Former National Security Adviser Zbigniew

Brzezinski declared that "in the years to come no alternative to a leading American role is likely to develop and America's partners will continue to want the United States to play that role."[162]

The new spirit in Soviet-American relations was demonstrated again when Reagan and Gorbachev exchanged New Year's messages to each other's countries. Gorbachev referred to the impact on his thinking of his visit to Washington:

> I did understand what is most important about the American people, and that is their enormous stock of good will. Let me assure you that Soviet people, too, have an equally good stock of good will. Putting it to full use is the most noble and responsible task of governmental and political leaders in our two countries.[163]

In his State of the Union message on January 25, 1988, Reagan referred to the "startling hope of giving our children a future free of both totalitarian and nuclear terror."[164] A few days before a special meeting with the heads of governments of NATO, Reagan addressed the citizens of Western Europe directly (February 27):

> The Atlantic community is the house of democracy. The Atlantic alliance is the guardian of Europe's greatest legacy to the ages—human freedom and democratic rule. This is the challenge before the alliance now: to remain strong so that generations to come will know peace and freedom just as we do.[165]

In 1988, the United States expanded its protection in the Persian Gulf to neutral ships (April 29), and, unfortunately, shot down an Iranian airliner (July 3), in the mistaken belief it was a military plane (the 290 passengers were killed). In response to an alleged Nicaraguan invasion of Honduras, the President dispatched a 3,200-man force to Honduras (March 17).

The Senate approved the important INF Treaty, 93 to 5, on May 27, just a few days before the successful summit meeting of Reagan and Gorbachev in Moscow (May 30–June 1, 1988), where the ratifications of the INF Treaty were exchanged and the proposed 50 percent reduction of nuclear weapons was accelerated. Reagan was able to speak to religious leaders at the Danilov Monastery, to Soviet dissidents, to artistic and cultural leaders, and finally to students and faculty at Moscow State University. At the University, he spoke of the growing friendship between the two peoples and extolled the values of freedom—freedom of thought, freedom of information, and freedom of communication:

> Your generation is living in one of the most exciting, hopeful times in Soviet history. It is a time when the first breath of freedom stirs the air and the heart beats to the accelerated rhythm of hope, when the accumulated spiritual energies of long silenced years break free.[166]

On his return, Reagan spoke to the American people about the momentous events of the previous week, and its relation to American ideals:

> . . . Our strategy is based on faith in the eventual triumph of human freedom.
> That faith in freedom, that abiding faith in what the unfettered human spirit can accomplish, defines us as a people and a nation.
> . . . That faith in freedom, that belief in the unalienable rights of man begun in Carpenter's Hall in Philadelphia, traveled last week to the Lenin Hills in Moscow.
> The judgment of future generations will be harsh upon us if, after so much sacrifice and now at the hour of hope, we falter or fail. Let us resolve to continue, one nation, one people, united in our love of peace and freedom, determined to keep our defenses strong, to stand with those who struggle for freedom across the world, to keep America a shining city, a light unto the nations.[167]

With the new spirit of Soviet-American and Chinese-American cooperation, the United Nations Security Council was able to work for peace in 1988, and various nations moved to end their conflicts. Among the major events were: (1) a truce agreement between the Sandinista government of Nicaragua and the Contras (March 24); (2) the Soviet accord signed with the United States, Pakistan and Afghanistan to pull out its troops from Afghanistan (April 14); (3) the Vietnam plan to withdraw 50,000 troops from Cambodia (May 25); (4) Iran's acceptance of a cease-fire in the Iran-Iraq War (July 18), followed by direct talks under United Nations auspices to bring the war to an end; (5) agreement by South Africa, Cuba and Angola for the withdrawal of all foreign troops in Angola, and on independence for Namibia under United Nations supervision (August 5); (6) an intensive effort by Secretary of State George Shultz to encourage peace negotiations between Israel and the Palestinians, after the Palestinian uprising (*intafada*) in December 1987; (7) and the award of the Nobel Peace Prize to the U.N. Peacekeeping Forces (September 24). Reagan announced that the United States would pay its back U.N. assessments (September 19) and praised the work and role of the U.N. in his farewell address to the U.N. General Assembly on September 26.

One of the most dramatic developments in 1988 was Gorbachev's special address to the U.N. General Assembly on December 7, in which he appealed for international cooperation (almost in words like Woodrow Wilson's) and pledged a large unilateral reduction of Soviet military forces, implying a "clearly defensive stand in Europe."[168] A special symbol of the new era was a photograph of President Reagan, President-elect Bush (who had won the November 8 election against Governor Michael Dukakis, 426 to 112 electoral votes, and 54 to 46 percent popular vote), and General Secretary Gorbachev with the Statue of Liberty in the background.

To move ahead the spirit of peace in the Middle East, the United States agreed on December 14 to talk with the PLO (Palestine Liberation Organization), after their leader, Yasir Arafat spoke for the Organization in recognizing Israel, accepting the appropriate U.N. Security Council resolutions, and renouncing terrorism. In his Farewell Address to the nation on January 11, 1989, President Reagan referred to the many moves toward peace across the globe, and stressed the importance of a knowledge of American history:

> Once you begin a great movement, there is no telling where it will end. We meant to change a nation, and instead we changed a world.
>
> We've got to do a better job of getting across that America is freedom—freedom of speech, freedom of religion, freedom of enterprise. And freedom is special and rare. It's fragile; it needs protection.
>
> I'm warning of an eradication of American memory, that could result ultimately, in an erosion of the American spirit.
>
> I have spoken of the shining city all my political life. . . . In my mind it was a tall, proud city built on rocks, stronger than oceans, windswept, God-blessed, and teeming with people of all kinds living in harmony and peace; a city with free ports that hummed with commerce and creativity.
>
> . . . After 200 years she's still a beacon, still a magnet for all who must have freedom. . . .[169]

George Bush, January 1989–January 1993

President Bush's Inaugural Address expressed hope in the future along with a pledge of America's continued strength for "good" in the world:

> I come before you and assume the Presidency at a moment rich with promise. . . . For a new breeze is blowing, and a world refreshed by freedom seems reborn. For in man's heart, if not in fact, the day of the dictator is over. The totalitarian era is passed. . . .
> Great nations of the world are moving toward democracy through the door to freedom. . . .
> . . . We know in our hearts, not loudly and proudly, but as a simple fact, that this country has meaning beyond what we see, and that our strength is a force for good.
> . . . America is never wholly herself unless she is engaged in high moral principles. We as a people have such a purpose today. It is to make kinder the face of the Nation and gentler the face of the world.
> . . . To the world . . . we offer new engagement and a renewed vow. We will stay strong to protect the peace. The offered hand is a reluctant fist; once made—strong, and can be used with great effect.[170]

In an address to Congress (February 1) on the goals of his Administration, he said "there are voices who say that America's best days have passed" and then added: "We Americans have only begun on our mission of goodness and greatness."[171]

The President himself went to the funeral of the late Emperor of Japan (February 24), and took the opportunity to go also to Beijing, where he was given a warm reception (February 25). At a banquet he spoke of the growing closeness in relations between America and China, and encouraged the move toward greater freedom in China: "There is a world-wide movement toward greater freedom: freedom of human creativity and freedom of economic opportunity. . . . China was one of the first nations to feel this new breeze. . . ."[172] This was just two months before the Chinese students and others marched in Beijing in defiance of their government (April 27–June 3), only to be crushed at the end.

In Central America and Eastern Europe, democracy was clearly on the march. Democratic and Republican leaders in Congress signed an accord with President Bush (on March 24), uniting in support of the peace process developed first by President Oscar Arias Sanchez of

Costa Rica and then by President Bush in cooperation with the United Nations, for Central American nations. The United States welcomed Gorbachev's words in Havana, Cuba, about not exporting revolution (April 5). Solidarity and the Communist Party in Poland agreed on democratic reforms (April 5)—this was the beginning of the "unraveling" of communism in Eastern Europe in the year 1989. The United States applauded Prime Minister Yitzhak Shamir's proposal to hold elections for the Palestinians in the occupied territories (April 6).

Two setbacks occurred in May and June. General Noriega voided the election in Panama on May 7, although observers believed the opposition had won by a three-to-one margin. President Bush declared: "The United States will not recognize nor accommodate with a regime that holds power through force and violence at the expense of the Panamanian people's right to be free."[173] When the Chinese Government crushed the nearly six-week occupation of the central Tiananmen Square on June 3, with heavy loss of life, Bush expressed his dismay, and urged continued political and economic reform in China:

> It is clear that the Chinese Government has chosen to use force against Chinese citizens who were making a peaceful statement in favor of democracy. I deeply deplore the decision to use force against peaceful demonstrators and the consequent loss of life. . . . I urge a return to nonviolent means for dealing with the current situation. . . . I hope that China will rapidly return to the path of political and economic reform and conditions of stability so that this relationship so important to both our peoples can continue its growth.[174]

The United States stopped the shipment of government arms to China, as a first sanction.

After this, from June to December 1989, came the rapid elimination of communist control in Eastern Europe. Gorbachev paved the way by his United Nations address in December 1988, his visit to Bonn to sign a declaration on "healing the wounds" (June 12), his address to the Council of Europe in Strasbourg spurning armed aggression (July 6), his announcement in Finland disavowing any right of regional intervention (October 26), and his visit to the Pope on December 1, when he promised religious freedom in the Soviet Union.

After the huge victory by Solidarity in the Polish election of June 4, President Bush visited Poland and Hungary (July 9–12). At his welcome in Warsaw, he expressed America's satisfaction and hopes (July 9):

> . . . Here in the heart of Europe, the American people have a fervent wish—that Europe be whole and free.
> . . . History, which has so often conspired with geography to deny the Polish people their freedom, now offers up a new and brighter future for Poland.
> . . . The world is inspired by what is happening here.
> . . . My prayers and the prayers of the American people remain with Poland, as they have throughout its long struggle.[175]

To the Polish National Assembly in Warsaw (July 10), he reflected on the spirit of change, which was sweeping "the world from Poland to the Pacific."[176] Then he outlined a program of modest American help. He expressed similar hopes in Budapest (July 11–12), where signs of a coming revolution were already apparent, before going to the Economic Summit of the seven major industrial powers (G-7, Group of Seven) in Paris (July 13–15), where more aid was pledged to Eastern Europe.

On August 12, Bush made a statement on the 28th anniversary of the building of the Berlin Wall: "As we now mark the day the wall was built, so shall we inevitably celebrate a day when it no longer divides Berlin, the German people, and the nations of Europe."[177] The American people were pleased with the Soviet announcement of the end of arms shipments to Nicaragua (September 6). In his address to the U.N. General Assembly (September 25), the President spoke of the new hope for freedom and international cooperation.[178]

Events moved in rapid succession in Eastern Europe. On September 10, Hungary allowed 7,000 East Germans to emigrate to West Germany; large East German rallies were held on October 9; Hungary declared itself a republic (October 23); 500,000 rallied in East Berlin (November 4); and on November 9 East Germany astonished the world by opening the Wall to the West; the Communist leaders of Bulgaria resigned on November 10; and the leaders of East Germany did the same on December 3.

President Bush reflected the widespread American amazement and hope at these astonishing events taking place in Europe, in his special Thanksgiving address to the nation on November 22:

> This is not the end of the book of history. But it's a joyful end to

one of history's saddest chapters.

Not long after the wall began to open, West German Chancellor Kohl telephoned, and he asked me to give you, the American people, a message of thanks. He said that the remarkable change in Eastern Europe would not be taking place without the steadfast support of the United States . . . for 40 years. We have not wavered in our commitment to freedom.

After praising all the American Presidents from Truman to Reagan for their firm stands, Bush continued:

And now we are at the threshold of the 1990's, and as we begin this new decade I am reaching out to President Gorbachev, asking him to work with me to bring down the last barriers to a new world of freedom. Let us move beyond containment and once and for all end the cold war.[179]

Although no final agreement had yet been reached between the United States and the Soviet Union on the proposed 50 percent nuclear arms reduction, Bush and Gorbachev held informal cordial meetings off the island of Malta, December 3.[180] Bush then presented his expectations for the future at NATO headquarters in Brussels:

We stand on the threshold of a new era. We know that we are contributing to a process of history driven by peoples determined to be free. . . . Yet the outcome is not predestined. It depends upon our continuing strength and solidarity as an alliance.[181]

The democratic contagion in Eastern Europe continued to spread in November and December: the Communist leaders of Bulgaria quit after 35 years (November 10); Czechoslovakian party leaders resigned (November 24, as 350,000 demonstrated in the "Velvet Revolution") and Alexander Dubcek was picked as leader of the Parliament (December 28); and the bloody Romanian revolution came December 22–25 (climaxed by the execution of party leader Nicolai Ceausesco). All of these major events in Eastern Europe had occurred in President Bush's first year in office.

America's extrovert approach was further demonstrated in December 1989, in the Philippines and especially in Panama. On December 1, the United States used fighter jets to save President Aquino from a rebel revolt and siege. On December 20, the President addressed the nation to explain the military invasion of Panama:

> Last Friday, Noriega declared his military dictatorship to be in a
> state of war with the United States and publicly threatened the lives of
> Americans in Panama. The very next day, forces under his command
> shot and killed an American serviceman, wounded another, and arrested
> and brutally beat a third. . . . This was enough, General Noriega's
> reckless threats and attacks upon Americans in Panama created an
> imminent danger to the 35,000 American citizens in Panama.
>
> The brave Panamanians elected by the people of Panama in the
> election last May . . . have assumed the rightful leadership of their
> country. . . . The United States today recognized the democratically
> elected government under President Endara.
>
> I hope that the people of Panama will put this dark chapter of
> dictatorship behind them and move forward together as citizens of a
> democratic Panama with this government that they themselves have
> elected.[182]

The war was virtually over in three days, while President Noriega
waited until January 4 before coming out of diplomatic asylum to
surrender himself to the United States.

The year 1990 was to be dominated by the continued spread of
democracy, the unification of the two Germanies (inside NATO), and
particularly by the stand of the United States and the U.N. Security
Council against Iraq's invasion of Kuwait (August 2). The American
leadership against Iraq was a major extrovert event, strongly supported
by the American people. In his New Year's Day message to the Soviet
people (January 1, 1990), Bush contrasted the past with the hopeful
future:

> . . . As we look back to nine decades of war, of strife, of suspicion,
> let us also look forward to a new century and a new millennium of
> peace, freedom and prosperity.
>
> Our nations have produced Abraham Lincoln, Leo Tolstoy, Martin
> Luther King, and Andrew Sakharov. We have persevered as allies in a
> terrible war. The challenges we face today are no less daunting, but
> with good will and determination on both sides, I am confident our two
> peoples will be equal to the task. . . .[183]

In his State of the Union address (January 31), the President spoke of
the "remarkable events . . . that fulfill the long held hopes of the
American people . . . based on a single shining principle: the cause of

freedom." He announced a major new step in the reduction of American and Soviet forces in Eastern Europe, 195,000 on each side, and then noted the possible dangers ahead:

> In many regions of the world tonight, the reality is conflict, not peace. Enduring animosities and opposing interests remain. And thus the cause of peace must be served by an America strong enough and sure enough to defend our interests and our ideals. It's this American idea that for the past four decades helped inspire the Revolution of '89.[184]

America was inspired by the address of Vaclav Havel, President of Czechoslovakia, to Congress on February 21. In welcoming President Havel, President Bush pledged America's continued stand in Europe.[185] In a joint news conference with Chancellor Helmut Kohl in Washington, February 25, Bush stood squarely for a unified Germany as a full member of NATO. Chancellor Kohl paid tribute to America's strong position in this regard: ". . . when the day of unity is drawing near for us Germans, we are conscious with profound gratitude of the fact that all of this would not have been possible without the close friendship and the confident partnership with the United States of America."[186]

Many Americans were surprised at the clear victory won by the opposition over the ruling Sandinistas in the Nicaraguan election on February 25–26, 1990, with Violeto Chamorro becoming the new President. Soviet troops began to withdraw from Hungary on March 12, and pro-democratic parties won the election there on April 8.

Bush and Gorbachev held a warm summit meeting in Washington, May 31–June 4, signing major accords on missiles, chemical weapons, and trade. Bush praised Gorbachev for his positive role, and Gorbachev noted the close relationship being built between the two powers: "the fog of prejudice, mistrust, and animosity is vanishing."[187] They hoped to be able to sign a Strategic Arms Reduction Treaty (START) before the end of the year, and to expedite the reduction of conventional armed forces in Europe.

The African National Congress leader, Nelson Mandela, received a warm welcome in New York City on June 20, and met President Bush (June 25), who pledged his support to the new movements in South Africa against apartheid:

> As Martin Luther King said on the steps of the Lincoln Memorial,

we cannot walk alone. Sir, we here in America walk in solidarity with all in South Africa who seek through nonviolent means democracy, human rights, and freedom.[188]

Meanwhile, the two Germanies agreed on unification (June 26), with Germany to be in NATO. President Bush and the other NATO leaders agreed on a London Declaration (July 6), proclaiming the end of the cold war, pledging closer relations between West and East, and also a mutual reduction of military forces. The Big Seven industrial powers met in Houston on July 9, and issued a special Political Declaration, "Securing Europe." Gorbachev cleared the way for German unification on July 16, by dropping opposition to the new Germany's membership in NATO. Thus a new spirit of cooperation and hope was evident, just before the major Iraqi challenge to peace and security in the Middle East. (To complete German unification, the four Allies of World War II signed a treaty giving up their rights in Germany, September 21, and the two Germanies were officially united on October 3.)

When Iraq, led by Saddam Hussein, suddenly occupied Kuwait on August 2, Bush called for an immediate withdrawal of Iraq's forces, as did the U.N. Security Council under American leadership. U.N. sanctions were established against Iraq on August 6. After meeting with Prime Minister Thatcher (August 2 and 6), with the Secretary General of NATO, talking to Saudi Arabian leaders, and making other diplomatic soundings, President Bush ordered American forces into Saudi Arabia on August 7. The President explained his stand in an address to the nation on August 8:

. . . The acquisition of territory by force is unacceptable. No one, friend or foe, should doubt our desire for peace; and no one should underestimate our determination to confront aggression.

. . . My administration, as has been the case with every President from President Roosevelt to President Reagan, is committed to the security and stability of the Persian Gulf.

. . . Iraq has massed an enormous war machine on the Saudi border capable of initiating hostilities with little or no additional preparation.

. . . To assume Iraq will not attack again would be unwise and unrealistic.

. . . The sovereign independence of Saudi Arabia is of vital interest to the United States.

. . . America has never wavered when her purpose is driven by principle.[189]

Thus began what proved to be preparation for a major military effort in the Middle East, in which the U.N. Security Council passed over a dozen resolutions and 28 nations moved military forces into the area. It was widely recognized that President Bush was largely responsible for this successful diplomatic effort, and that only the United States was prepared to send a major force. The new American mood of extroversion was clearly evident, as a strong majority of the American people stood behind the President. Furthermore, for the passage of the Security Council resolutions, it was vital that neither the Soviet Union nor China would cast a veto. Bush and Gorbachev issued a joint statement in Helsinki, Finland, on September 9:

> We are united in the belief that Iraq aggression must not be tolerated. No peaceful international order is possible if larger states can devour their smaller neighbors.
>
> Today, we once again call upon the Government of Iraq to withdraw unconditionally from Kuwait. . . .
>
> We must demonstrate beyond any doubt that aggression cannot and will not pay[190]

On September 11, the President spoke to a special joint session of Congress, emphasizing the "new world order" that he saw in the making:

> If there ever was a time to put country before self, and patriotism before party, the time is now. . . .
>
> No longer can a dictator count on the East-West confrontation to stymie concerted United Nations action against aggression. A new partnership of nations has begun.
>
> . . . The crisis in the Persian Gulf, as grave as it is, also offers a rare opportunity to move toward an historic period of cooperation. Out of these troubled times, our fifth objective—a new world order—can emerge: a new era—freer from the threat of terror, stronger in the pursuit of justice, and more secure in the quests for peace. . . . Today that new world is struggling to be born. . . .
>
> . . . Once again, Americans have stepped forward to share a tearful goodbye with their families before leaving for a strange and distant shore. At this very moment, they serve together with Arabs, Europeans, Asians, and Africans in defense of principle and the dream of a new world order.[191]

President Bush delivered another dramatic address to the 45th session of the U.N. General Assembly on October 1:

> . . . Not since 1945 have we seen the real possibility of using the United Nations as it was designed: as a center for international collective security. . . . When the Soviet Union agreed with so many of us here in the United Nations to condemn the aggression of Iraq, there could be no doubt . . . that we had, indeed, put four decades of history behind us.
>
> . . . Let me . . . emphasize that all of us here in the United Nations hope that military force will never be used. We seek a peaceful outcome, a diplomatic outcome.[192]

The President also expressed his hope for peace throughout the Middle East, including the conflict between Israel and the Arabs.

On the eve of another striking event, the unification of West and East Germany after 45 years of separation, Bush gave an address to the German people (October 2, 1990):

> The United States is proud to have built with you the foundations of freedom; proud to have been a steady partner in the quest for one Germany, whole and free. America is proud to count itself among the friends and allies of free Germany, now and in the future. . . .
>
> . . . The last remnants of the Wall remain at the heart of free Berlin, a ragged monument in brick and barbed wire, proof that no wall is ever strong enough to strangle the human spirit, that no wall can ever crush a nation's soul.[193]

With no sign of Iraq's willingness to withdraw from Kuwait, in spite of U.N. sanctions, the President, on November 8, ordered a major buildup of U.S. forces in the Gulf (ultimately doubling its size to half a million troops), to permit an "adequate offensive military option should that be necessary."[194]

After that, the President took steps to strengthen America's ties, first with Europe and the Middle East, and then with South America. A highlight was the President's address to the Federal Assembly in Prague, Czechoslovakia, on November 17, the first anniversary of the "Velvet Revolution," when he spoke of a new "commonwealth of freedom."[195] The President met with other leaders of Europe, and participated in the signing of two major instruments: (1) Joint Declaration of Twenty-Two States (November 19), stressing partnership and friendship between Eastern and Western European nations; and (2) the Charter of Paris for a New Europe (November 21), signed by the heads of 34 member states of the Conference on Security and Cooperation in Europe (CSCE), proclaiming a new era of democracy, peace and unity, and establishing a permanent Council and Secretariat Thus the cold war came officially to an end.

On November 29, the U.N. Security Council voted (with China abstaining) to give Iraq until January 15, 1991, to withdraw from Kuwait, after which the 28 nations would be free to use "all necessary means" to force the withdrawal. Bush added his own warning on November 30:

> I want peace, not war. But if there must be war, we will not permit our troops to have their hands tied behind their backs. . . . I will never—ever—agree to halfway efforts.[196]

On December 3, the President began a five-nation, six-day trip to South America (Brazil, Uruguay, Argentina, Chile and Venezuela), speaking to the Congress in each of the first four visits. His address in Brasilia, with its hope for freedom, was typical:

> To fulfill the New World's destiny, all of the Americas and the Caribbean must embark on a venture for the coming century: to create the first full democratic hemisphere in the history of mankind, the first hemisphere devoted to the democratic ideal—to unleash the power of free people, free elections, and free markets.
> . . . It is also within our power to make this hemisphere the largest free-trade partnership of sovereign nations in the world.
> . . . I salute your leadership in the world community and united stand against Iraq's aggression and in defense of the rule of law.[197]

After Congress agreed with the U.N. Security Council in authorizing the use of force against Iraq (January 12), the war against Iraq proved to be short and decisive in driving the Iraqi forces from Kuwait January 16–February 27.

During the rest of 1991, Bush and Gorbachev signed the Strategic Arms Reduction Treaty (July 31); Yugoslavia began to split apart and most unexpected of all, the Soviet Union, following a brief failed coup, broke up into 15 independent republics, and Gorbachev resigned as the last Soviet leader (December 25). Russia became the major successor state to the Soviet Union, under President Yeltsin (elected on June 13, 1991). Although Gorbachev was eliminated, largely because of the decline of the domestic economy, he had already played an indispensable and successful role in the rise of the Eastern European states to independence and in the major changes (Glasnost—openness, and Perestroika—restructuring) in the Soviet Union. President Bush continued to be the major world leader, even as the American domestic economy moved into a recession.

As 1991 opened, President Bush sent another message to the people of the Soviet Union (January 1), and then a message to the Allied nations in the Persian Gulf crisis (January 8). Also on January 8, he urged Congress to support the U.N. Security Council's resolution authorizing the use of force after January 15, hoping it would bring about a shift in Iraq's policy.[198] After a serious Congressional debate, between those who favored continued sanctions and those who were ready to use military force, Congress supported the Security Council's position on January 12 (52 to 47 in the Senate, and 250 to 183 in the House).

On January 16, President Bush addressed the nation as the Allied forces opened an air attack on military targets in Iraq and Kuwait:

> This is an historic moment. We have in this past year made great progress in ending the long era of conflict and cold war. We have before us the opportunity to forge for ourselves and for future generations a new world order—a world where the rule of law, not the law of the jungle, governs the conduct of nations . . . an order in which a credible United Nations can use its peacekeeping role to fulfill the promise and vision of the United Nations' founders.
>
> . . . I am convinced not only that we will prevail but that out of this horror of combat will come the recognition that no nation can stand against a world united, no nation will be permitted to brutally assault its neighbor.
>
> . . . No President can easily commit our sons and daughters to war. They are the Nation's finest. Ours is an all-volunteer force, magnificently trained, highly motivated.[199]

Thus began America's first major military operation since President Johnson's decision 26 years earlier to commit large forces in South Vietnam. The President and Secretary of State James Baker III had shown high diplomatic skill in arranging for the coalition of 28 nations, acting under the authority of Security Council resolutions.

The President stressed the "hard work of freedom" and the "community of conscience" in his State of the Union message to

Congress on January 29.[200] On January 30 Bush spoke to Americans on the occasion of the 50th Anniversary Observance of Franklin D. Roosevelt's Four Freedoms: "We hope that . . . the liberty bell of the four freedoms will ring for all people in every nation of this world."[201]

When Iraq ignored a deadline to withdraw by noon on February 23, the allied military coalition moved its ground forces against the Iraqi troops. A swift decisive victory followed in three days, as the Iraqis were driven from Kuwait, retreating with heavy losses. Americans felt a sense of euphoria, as the allies suffered only light casualties. President Bush spoke on February 27 on the suspension of the allied offensive:

> Kuwait is liberated.
>
> It was not only a victory for Kuwait but a victory for all the coalition partners. This is a victory for the United Nations, for all mankind, for the rule of law, and for what is right.
>
> This war is now behind us. Ahead of us is the difficult task of securing a potentially historic peace. Tonight though, let us be proud of what we have accomplished. Let us give thanks to those who risked their lives. Let us never forget those who gave their lives.[202]

To a joint session on Congress (March 6), the President declared:

> . . . Enduring peace must be our mission.
>
> Americans are a caring people, a good people, a generous people. Let us always be caring and good and generous in all we do.[203]

In welcoming some of the troops home to Sumter, South Carolina, on March 17, the President declared that the successful war had established a new and strong American spirit, filled with courage and confidence.[204] On March 22, he proclaimed National Days of Thanksgiving for April 5 and 7.[205]

The President and most Americans seemed to expect a successful revolt in Iraq to overthrow Saddam Hussein, after Iraq's catastrophic defeat. But instead Hussein held on, and moved ruthlessly to crush the revolts from the Kurds in the north and the Shiites in the south. Bush expressed America's humanitarian instincts on April 5, as he ordered planes to fly in aid to the refugees who had fled their homes in the north:

> The human tragedy unfolding in and around Iraq demands immediate action on a massive scale. At stake are not only the lives of

hundreds of thousands of innocent men, women, and children but the peace and security of the Gulf.[206]

By April 16, Bush went further by ordering American troops, in cooperation with others, to build camps for refugees in northern Iraq. America was beginning to use its armed forces for humanitarian action on an unprecedented scale. Bush also sent American troops, with helicopters, to aid Bangladesh after a catastrophic cyclone (May 11, 1991).

At Maxwell Air Force Base War College in Montgomery (April 13), President Bush further defined his concept of a "new world order," and ended by describing America's unique character as he saw it:

> . . . Never before has the world looked more to the American example. Never before have so many millions drawn hope from the American idea. And the reason is simple: Unlike any other nation in the world, as Americans we enjoy profound and mysterious bonds of affection and idealism. We feel our deep conviction to community, to family, to our faith.
> . . . What makes us Americans is our allegiance to an idea that all people everywhere must be free.
> . . . The new world facing us . . . it's a wonderful world of discovery, a world devoted to unlocking the promise of freedom. . . . If we strive to engage in the world that beckons us, then and only then will America be true to all that is best in us.[207]

At the University of Michigan commencement on May 4, the President again stressed the nation's humanitarian impulse (mentioning Bangladesh as well as Iraq): "Dare to serve others, and future generations will never forget the example you set."[208]

When the President welcomed Queen Elizabeth II to Washington (May 14), the two leaders stressed the continued strength of the American-British ties.[209] In his Yale commencement address, May 27, Bush explained why he wished to continue to give the most-favored-nation (MFN) trading rights to China, when many critics were urging more sanctions instead:

> . . . If we pursue a policy that cultivates contacts with the Chinese people, promotes commerce to our benefit, we can help create a climate for democratic change. . . . Just as the democratic idea has transformed nations on every continent, so, too, change will inevitably come to

China.[210]

On June 20, President Bush welcomed Boris Yeltsin (who had been elected Presodent of the Russian Republic on June 13), to the White House, pledging to work both with the Russian Republic and with the Soviet Government under President Gorbachev: "Let's not forget that it was President Gorbachev's courageous policies of *glasnost* and *perestroika* that were the pivotal factors enabling us to end the cold war and make Europe whole and free." President Yeltsin expressed his faith that the Russian people would stand firm in their new direction.[211]

During this time, the United States gave its support to several peacemaking efforts. It was the principal party in arranging a cease-fire in the Ethiopian civil war (in London, May 27), with the rebels taking over on June 13. The White House urged peace in Yugoslavia (July 2). President Bush went to Greece and Turkey partly to urge a Cyprus settlement (July 19–21). On July 18, Syria approved the Bush-Baker plan for a Middle East peace conference, and Israel accepted on August 1 (the conference met in Madrid on October 30, under joint U.S.-Soviet chairmanship).

Democracy spread steadily in Latin America, Eastern Europe and South Africa (where Prime Minister F. W. de Klerk moved to end all apartheid laws, February 1, June 17). President Bush lifted American sanctions on South Africa on July 10.

American public opinion showed wide support for U.S.-Soviet rapprochement and for mutual disarmament agreements, as well as for U.S. leadership and cooperation in world affairs in general. Presidents Bush and Gorbachev held a successful summit meeting in Moscow, July 29–31, signing the long-sought START (Strategic Arms Reduction Talks) Treaty, providing for a 30 percent mutual reduction of such weapons, and four other accords.[212]

Then, suddenly came the shock of a KGB-Army coup in Moscow which overthrew President Gorbachev (he was arrested and flown to the Crimea on August 19). But at this time occurred one of the most dramatic developments in Russian history, as the people of Moscow stood against the coup. The hero of the hour was Boris Yeltsin, who showed tremendous courage as tens of thousands of Muscovites rallied around him at the Russian Parliament. The soldiers lacked the nerve to massacre the Russian people who stood with Yeltsin. Gorbachev had built far better than he knew, in giving so much freedom to the Soviet people. When the coup came, most of the people seemed to realize that they did not wish to go back to the days of dictatorship, even though the economic outlook was so bad. On the third day, the coup collapsed, and Gorbachev returned. The next day, in an interview with Robert MacNeil, former Ambassador George F. Kennan called the event a turning-point of the most momentous historical significance, as the Russian people for the first time in history turned their backs on the manner in which they had been ruled for centuries. He also pointed to the dangers which lay ahead for Russia.

President Bush had spoken to President Yeltsin on August 20, and assured him of continued U.S. support for the goal of the restoration of Gorbachev as the constitutionally chosen leader. Yeltsin expressed his gratitude. On August 21, the President spoke to Gorbachev, who "stated his sincere appreciation to the people of the United States and others around the world for their support of democracy and reform."[213] Ambassador Robert Strauss read the President's message of support at the funeral (August 24) of the few who had died in standing up to the attempted coup.[214]

Mikhail Gorbachev had apparently expected slow reform and the continuity of the Soviet Union in some form under the Communist Party. But Boris Yeltsin, the elected Russian President, moved quickly against the Communist Party, and Gorbachev resigned as the General Secretary on August 24, keeping his post as President of the Soviet Union. On August 25, the Ukraine and Byelorussia declared their independence, and the Soviet Congress yielded rule to the republics on September 4. President Bush, too, had apparently hoped to be able to deal with a united Soviet state—he had gone to Kiev (capital of the Ukraine) at the end of July to express this hope. But the Soviet Union was breaking up rapidly into its 15 separate republics, creating an atmosphere of uncertainty.

President Bush spoke of a "Pax Universale" to the U.N. General Assembly On September 23:

> Communism held history captive for years. . . . As it has dissolved, suspended hatreds have sprung to life. . . .
>
> This revival of history ushers in a new era, teeming with opportunities and perils.
>
> You may wonder about America's role in the new world that I have described. Let me assure you that the United States has no intention of striving for a "Pax Americana." However, we will remain engaged. We will not retreat and pull back into isolationism. We will offer friendship

and leadership. In short, we seek a "Pax Universale" built upon shared
responsibilities and aspirations.

. . . We can build a future more satisfying than any our world has
ever known. The future lies undefined before us—full of promise,
littered with peril. We can choose the kind of world we want. . . .[215]

A few days later, on September 27, Bush, in a major unilateral
action, announced that the United States would eliminate all short-range
nuclear weapons on land and sea in Europe and Asia, in the expectation
that the Soviet Union would do the same, and he offered to negotiate
with the Soviet Union for further sharp reductions in long-range
missiles. Gorbachev welcomed the American plan, and indicated the
Soviet Union would make the same reductions; Britain and France
announced they would follow. Deputy Secretary of State Lawrence
Eagleburger pointed out the necessity for American engagement in
facing the problems of a post-Cold War world (October 3, 1991).[216]

The well-planned Middle East conference met in Madrid, Spain,
on October 30, 1991, under joint American-Soviet auspices. Both
President Bush and President Gorbachev were present. Bush expressed
America's hope for a comprehensive peace, and promised American
guarantees, if needed.[217] The changing world situation was also
dramatized by the freeing, from October 21 to December 4, of the
hostages held in Lebanon, with a United Nations official mediating the
operation.

A NATO summit (heads of government) was held in Rome to help
renew the strength of the alliance under the new conditions in Europe.
President Bush pledged continued American involvement (November 7):

> This alliance has been more successful than any of us dared to
> dream. It was designed to defend our freedom, but, in fact, it triumphed
> over totalitarianism. What we have built is not some military pact but
> a community of values and trust—unique in history, perpetual, and vital
> for the new order.[218]

As the President prepared to go to Asia later in the month, Secretary of
State Baker was in Tokyo (November 11) speaking of the United States
and Japan as global partners in a growing "Pacific community." Bush,
who was being criticized at home for spending too much time on
foreign affairs while the domestic economy was in recession, stressed
the importance of foreign relations as he spoke of the importance of

Asia (November 13):

> . . . The Asia-Pacific region has become our largest and fastest growing trade partner. We conduct more than $300 billion worth of two-way trade annually.
> . . . We will deepen our partnership with our Asian friends in building democracy and freedom.[219]

As the year 1991 was ending, the Soviet Union was breaking up into its 15 sovereign republics. The Ukrainian people voted for independence on December 1, by a 90 percent margin. On December 8, Russia, the Ukraine and Belarus (formerly Byelorussia) formed the Community of Independent States (CIS)—there were eleven members by December 21. Secretary of State Baker dramatized the collapse of the Soviet empire, and stressed the need to work together (December 12):

> For the third time this century, we have ended a war—this time a cold war—between the Great Powers.
> . . . Today, after the Cold War, we *again* stand at history's precipice. If, during the Cold War, we faced each other as two scorpions in a bottle, now the Western nations and the former Soviet republics stand as awkward climbers on a steep mountain. Held together by a common rope, a fall toward fascism or anarchy in the former Soviet Union, will pull the West down, too. Yet, equally as important, a strong and steady pull by the West now can help them to gain their footing so that they, too, can climb above to enduring democracy and freedom. Surely, we must strengthen the rope, not sever it.[220]

On the day when President Gorbachev resigned as the last Soviet leader, December 25, 1991, President Bush spoke to the nation, as he welcomed the new Commonwealth of Independent States:

> This is a day of great hope for all Americans. Our enemies have become our partners, committed to building a democratic and civil society. They ask for our support, and we will give it to them. We will do it because as Americans we can do no less.[221]

The year 1992 was dominated in America by the campaign for President, with rising criticism of President Bush for his concentration on America's world role while the nation was in a recession. So the President postponed his Asian trip from November 1991 until December

31 to January 9, and publicly stressed its major aim as American jobs (taking the top automobile executives with him). Up until the election, the President, as reported by the press, appeared rather hesitant in foreign affairs, even though he continued to play a positive role.

The President's trip to Asia stressed the need for increased trade. He visited Australia, Singapore, South Korea and Japan. Speaking to the Korean National Assembly in Seoul (January 6, 1992), he praised the people of South Korea, and supported again their desire for reunification with North Korea as well as their security.[222] At the state dinner in the Imperial Palace in Tokyo, January 8, the President emphasized American-Japanese cooperation: ". . . in this changing world where the walls that once divided whole nations from each other are crumbling, we all must become both bridges to and partners in a new world order."[223]

On January 22–23, a Coordinating Conference on Assistance to the New Independent States (of the former Soviet Union) was held in Washington. Proposals were agreed upon, and the United States announced Operation Provide Hope, which began a major short-term airlift of emergency humanitarian assistance on February 10. Presidents Bush and Yeltsin met at Camp David on February 1, issuing a six-part Camp David Declaration with the first two points reading as follows:

> . . . Russia and the United States do not regard each other as potential adversaries. From now on, their relationship will be characterized by friendship and partnership, founded on mutual trust and respect and common commitment to democracy and economic freedom.
> . . . We will work to remove any remnants of Cold War hostility, including taking steps to reduce our strategic arsenals. . . .[224]

In his State of the Union address (January 28), the President thanked the American people for their stand which helped, "by the grace of God," end the Cold War, and noted that the world did not fear American power:

> . . . The world trusts us with power—and the world is right. They trust us to be fair and restrained; they trust us to be on the side of decency. They trust us to do what's right.[225]

On January 31, the U.N. Security Council held an unprecedented meeting of the heads of governments, and asked the new Secretary

General, Boutros Boutros-Ghali of Egypt, to draw up plans to strengthen the Security Council in working for peace. President Bush pledged American support for a strengthened United Nations, especially in helping to prevent armed conflicts ("preventive diplomacy").[226] On April 3, after some pressure from Presidential candidate Governor Clinton and from former President Richard Nixon, Bush submitted a major proposal for aid to the republics of the former Soviet Union (the Freedom Support Act of 1992), and pledged to cooperate with the other G-7 (Group of Seven) nations in a $24 billion package.[227] (Congress did not approve the act until October 25). Secretary of State Baker delivered a major address on April 21, calling upon Americans to recognize and maintain their role of world leadership: "We must live up to the greatness of our ideals—to win a democratic peace."[228]

The nation's attention was again concentrated more deeply on domestic affairs, especially in the inner cities, by the Los Angeles riots over the acquittal of four policemen in the beating of Rodney King (April 30–May 2)—the death toll was over 50 and the damage estimated at $1 billion. The President ordered 5,000 federal troops to the city. Another domestic challenge was produced by Hurricane Andrew which swept through Florida on August 24, killing 15, with damages estimated at $20 billion. Under some pressure from environmentalists, the President spoke on June 12 to the notable U.N. Conference on Environment and Development in Rio de Janeiro, Brazil, and signed a Convention on Climatic Change.[229]

A highlight of the year was the summit conference with Russian President Yeltsin in Washington, June 16–17. The two Presidents signed a number of very significant documents, including "A Charter for American-Russian Partnership and Friendship," a "Joint Understanding on Reductions in Strategic Offensive Arms" (paving the way for START II, reducing nuclear warheads by 75 percent, signed by Bush and Yeltsin on January 3, 1993), and agreements on cooperation in space, chemical weapons, defense conversion, trade relations and investment, and on an American Peace Corps in the Russian Federation. Bush announced at the signing ceremony that Russia would receive most-favored-nation trade status immediately, and stressed America's economic support for Russia (June 17).[230] President Yeltsin was cheered and given 13 standing ovations when he spoke to Congress (June 17). He declared the end of Communism, and announced he was deactivating the major nuclear missiles aimed at the United States.[231]

On the way to two important international meetings in Europe,

President Bush stopped in Warsaw, July 5, to hold discussions with President Lech Walesa. At the G-7 summit in Munich, July 6–8, their political declarations dealt with the problems of aid to Russia and war in Yugoslavia. Finally, Bush attended the summit meeting of 52 nations of the Conference on Security and Cooperation in Europe (CSCE), including now the 15 republics of the former Soviet Union, in Helsinki, Finland, July 9–10. It was agreed that the Treaty on Conventional Armed Forces in Europe (CFE) would be applied provisionally on July 17, with its major reduction in weapons ceilings from the Atlantic to the Urals.

The prospects for successful Israeli-Arab negotiations were improved by the election of Yitzhak Rabin as Prime Minister on June 23. He and President Bush met in Maine on August 11, and agreed on general principles (including American support for $10 billion in loan guarantees, in return for an Israeli pledge to build no new settlements in the occupied Palestinian areas). On August 12, negotiations were completed for a North American Free Trade Agreement (NAFTA), with the United States, Canada and Mexico the partners (the treaty was initialed on October 7). The Senate again approved (September 30) the START I treaty, 93 to 6, this time applied to the four former Soviet republics holding strategic nuclear weapons. The Freedom Support Act for Russia and other republics was signed into law on October 25. During 1992, the Administration supported the U.N. move to send 22,000 peacekeepers to Cambodia.

Foreign policy did not seem to play a significant role in the campaign for President between Governor Bill Clinton of Arkansas (nominated by the Democrats on July 17, along with Albert Gore) and President Bush (renominated on August 20 along with Dan Quayle). In the election on November 3, Clinton carried 370 electoral votes to Bush's 168, with the popular vote 43 percent to 38, while Ross Perot, independent, had 19 percent. Governor Clinton had emphasized the point that American leadership abroad depended largely on strengthening America's economic base.

After the election, President Bush seemed to feel freer to act on the international scene, as he carried out four major initiatives, continuing his extrovert approach: for Somalia, NAFTA, START II, and Iraq. A special event, not particularly desired by the United States, was the closure of the Subic Bay Naval Base at the request of the Philippines, November 24, 1992, ending 94 years of the American military presence on the islands.

Throughout 1992, the situation in Somalia had grown steadily more critical, as perhaps two million Somalis were facing possible starvation from famine and civil war. The U.N. Security Council on December 3 voted unanimously in favor of an unprecedented armed humanitarian rescue attempt, authorizing a force led by over 20,000 American troops. As the President ordered the troops into Somalia on December 4, he addressed the nation:

> These and other American forces will assist in Operation Restore Hope. They are America's finest. We will perform this mission with courage and compassion, and they will succeed.
>
> The people of Somalia, especially the children of Somalia, need our help. We're able to ease their suffering. We must help them live. We must give them hope. America must act.
>
> . . . Only the United States has the global reach to place a large security force on the ground in such a distant place quickly and efficiently and thus save thousands of innocents from death.
>
> . . . To every sailor, soldier, airman, and marine who is involved in this mission, let me say, you're doing God's work. We will not fail.[232]

Most Somalis seemed to welcome the American troops, when they began arriving on December 8. The North American Free Trade Agreement was signed on December 17 in the three capitals of the United States, Canada and Mexico. Bush spoke of the possible long-run significance of the pact.[233]

Secretary of State Eagleburger (who had succeeded James Baker III when Baker became the President's Chief of Staff, August 13, 1992) and Foreign Minister Andrei Kozyrev of Russia announced agreement (December 29) on the drastic cuts in the second nuclear arms reduction agreement (START II), cutting them by over two-thirds. After President Bush visited Somalia and the American troops there on December 31, he flew to Moscow, where he and President Yeltsin signed this historic treaty on January 3. At the signing, Bush stressed the growing friendship and partnership between the two great nations:

> Today, the Cold War is over, and, for the first time in history, an American President has set foot in a democratic Russia. And together we're now embarked on what must be the noblest mission of all, to turn an adversarial relationship into one of friendship and partnership [234]

Then on January 13, just a week before the end of his term, Bush ordered American planes to bomb Iraqi missile sites (French and British planes also joined in) because of Saddam Hussein's defiance of U.N. commands. At the same time, he sent 1,250 U.S. troops to Kuwait as a deterrent to Iraqi incursions. The American public approved these air strikes by 83 percent (Gallup Poll). Further attacks were made on January 17.

In addition to these actions, the President and Secretary Eagleburger delivered some addresses to show their expectations of America's proper world role (a type of farewell address). Secretary Eagleburger spoke to the Conference on Security and Cooperation in Europe (CSCE) in Strasbourg, December 14, on "A New Role for a New Europe," noting the struggle between democracy and disorder:

> . . . We have it within our power to decide whether historians will call this an age of democracy or an age of disorder.
> . . . The challenge we have yet to face is the need to develop new international structures to manage global change in this new era.
> Yugoslavia is a shocking reminder that barbarities exist within our midst and that we cannot call the new Europe either civilized or secure until we have developed stronger mechanisms for dealing with this and similar crises.[235]

President Bush, on December 15, called upon Americans to continue their role of world leadership:

> History is summoning us once again to lead. Proud of its past, America must once again look forward, and we must live up to the greatness of our forefathers' ideals and in doing so secure our grandchildren's future.[236]

The President spoke of the necessity for America to be ready to use force, if needed (at West Point, January 5, 1993).[237] And Secretary Eagleburger praised the American legacy, as the United States faces a major time of transition, in an address to the Council on Foreign Relations in Washington, D.C., January 7, 1993:

> . . . It is abundantly clear that we are in the midst of a global revolution—a period of change and instability in modern times equaled only by the aftermath of the French and Russian revolutions.
> . . . The question is whether we will, in the coming decades, deal with the new challenges of the post-Cold War era with the wisdom and strength of

character that, on the whole, marked our international passage over the course of the past half century.[238]

Bill Clinton, January 1993–

By June 1, 1993, President Bill Clinton appeared to be continuing America's extrovert, idealist, internationalist policies—with special emphasis on human rights. During his campaign for President, Governor Bill Clinton of Arkansas had called for more aid to Russia and for a strengthened stand against the "ethnic cleansing" in Bosnia, especially by the Serbs. The new Secretary of State-designate, Warren Christopher (who had been Deputy Secretary of State under President Carter), gave the Administration's position at his confirmation hearings before the Senate Foreign Relations Committee on January 13, 1993:

> I believe we have arrived at a uniquely promising moment. . . . The Cold War is over. . . . We now have the opportunity to create a new strategy that directs American resources to something other than superpower confrontation. . . .
>
> . . . While we are alert to this era's dangers, we nevertheless approach it with an underlying sense of optimism.
>
> Not since the late 1940s has our nation faced a challenge of shaping an entire new foreign policy for a world that has fundamentally changed.

Specifically, he emphasized the great importance of "helping Russia demilitarize, privatize, invigorate its economy, and develop representative political institutions." In relation to China, he said "our policies will seek to facilitate a peaceful evolution of China from communism to democracy by encouraging the forces of economic and political liberalization in that great country." Similarly, he supported cooperation with Japan and South Korea, a just and lasting peace in the Middle East, the North American Free Trade Agreement, the development of Africa, and the ending of apartheid.[239]

President-elect Clinton gave an address to the Diplomatic Corps at Georgetown University on January 18:

> While we cannot yet discern all the contours of the new age in which we are living, we know it is clearly an era of both peril and promise . . . when the dreams of freedom and democracy and economic prosperity and human rights can become real—but they may or

not—depending on what we do.

He indicated his administration would "build on the successes of my predecessor in specific areas," and that "the foreign policy of my Administration will be built upon three pillars": economic security, the prudent use of armed force, and democratic principles. He concluded: "Finally, I want to assure all of you—the members of the diplomatic corps—that, as President, I will work closely with the international community through the United Nations and other vital institutions to resolve contentious disputes and to meet the challenges of the next century."[240]

The new President's Inaugural Address on January 20 stressed America's renewal and continuing world leadership, in terms of its idealistic principles:

> Today, as an old order passes, the new world is more friendly and less stable. Communism's collapse has called forth old animosities and new dangers. Clearly America must continue to lead the world we did so much to make.
>
> While America rebuilds at home, we will not shrink from the challenges, nor fail to seize the opportunities of this new world.
>
> Where our vital interests are challenged, or the will and conscience of the international community is defied, we will act—with peaceful diplomacy whenever possible, with force when necessary. The brave Americans serving our nation today in the Persian Gulf, in Somalia and wherever else they stand are testament to our resolve.
>
> But our greatest strength is the power of our ideas, which are still new in many lands. Across the world, we see them embraced—and we rejoice. Our hopes, our hearts, our hands are with those on every continent who are building democracy and freedom. Their cause is America's cause.

The President ended with an appeal for the ideal of service and the idea of America:

> I challenge a new generation of young Americans to a season of service. . . .
>
> . . . Today we do more than celebrate America: we rededicate ourselves to the very idea of America.
>
> An idea born in revolution and renewed through two centuries of challenge.
>
> An idea tempered by the knowledge that, but for fate we—the

fortunate and the unfortunate—might have been each other.

An idea ennobled by the faith that our nation can summon from its myriad diversities the deepest measure of unity.

An idea infused with the conviction that America's long heroic journey must go forever upward.

And so, my fellow Americans, as we stand at the edge of the 21st century, let us begin with energy and hope, with faith and discipline, and let us work until our work is done. The Scripture says, "And let us not be weary in well-doing, for, in due season, we shall reap if we faint not."

From this joyful mountaintop of celebration, we hear a call to serve in the valley.

We have heard the trumpet. We have changed the guard. And now—each in our own way, and with God's help—we must answer the call.[241]

In a major address at the American University in Washington, on February 26, Clinton stressed "the great challenge of this day: the imperative of American leadership in the face of global change":

The world clearly remains a dangerous place. Ethnic hatreds, religious strife, the proliferation of weapons of mass destruction, the violation of human rights flagrantly in altogether too many places around the world call on us to have a sense of national security in which our national defense is an integral part. And the world still calls on us to promote democracy. . . .

. . . Now we are woven inextricably into the fabric of a global economy. . . .

Capital clearly has become global. Some $3 billion of capital races around the world every day. . . .

. . . The truth of our age is this . . . : Open and competitive commerce will enrich us as a nation.

. . . For now and for the foreseeable future, the world looks to us to be the engine of global growth.

The President stressed the importance of helping democracy succeed in Russia and other former Soviet republics, and ended by challenging Americans to live up to their heritage:

. . . Here we are again, ready to accept a new challenge, ready to seek new change because we're curious and restless and bold. It flows out of our heritage. It's engrained in the soul of America. It's no accident that our nation has steadily expanded the frontiers of democracy, of religious tolerance, of racial justice, of equality for all people, of environmental protection and technology and, indeed, the cosmos itself. For it is our nature to reach out, and reaching out has served not only ourselves, but the world as a whole.[242]

President Clinton made his attitude clear by acting in several areas, such as Iraq, Bosnia, Somalia, Russia and the Middle East. Air attacks on Iraq continued until January 25, and on February 16 Clinton stated the necessity of continuing the sanctions against Iraq. Bosnia remained his most difficult problem. On February 10, the Administration announced a more active role in seeking peace and help for Bosnia. By March 1, American planes began dropping food and medicine to the people of East Bosnia, largely Muslim, under siege by Serb forces. By May, the President was prepared to bring military pressure by air against the Bosnian Serbs, but Secretary Christopher found in Europe that America's allies would rather move more slowly; finally the United States, Russia, Britain, France and Spain, meeting in Washington, May 22, agreed to try to establish "safe havens" in six cities for the Bosnian Muslims, protected by U.N. forces, who in turn would be protected by American air power, if desired (the plan needed U.N. Security Council support).

American troops in Somalia strengthened their position, while preparing to turn over their mission to U.N. forces in May. The United States continued to maintain a military presence in Somalia, to help protect the international forces there.

To prepare for decisions in relation to Russia and other areas, Clinton met with British Prime Minister John Major (February 24), the U.N. Secretary General Boutros Boutros-Ghali (February 25), and President Mitterand of France (March 7). With Russian President Boris Yeltsin facing strong opposition from the old Parliament, both Secretary Christopher (March 22 in Chicago) and President Clinton (March 23) emphasized their support for Russian democracy and Russian reforms under President Yeltsin. Clinton gave a major address on the subject on April 1, in which he said that "Russian reforms offer us the opportunity to complete the movement from having an adversary in foreign policy to having a partner in global problem solving." He also addressed the Russian people directly:

You are a people who understand patriotic struggle. . . . I speak for

Americans everywhere when I say: We are with you. For we share this
bond: the key to each of our futures is not in clinging to the past but in
having the courage to change.[243]

Presidents Clinton and Yeltsin met for the first time in Vancouver,
Canada, April 3–4. Clinton regarded the results as hopeful:

> . . . I believe we have laid the foundation for a new democratic
> partnership between the United States and Russia. . . .
> . . . Now it is in the self-interest and the high duty of all of the
> world's democracies to stand by Russian democratic reforms in its new
> hour of challenge.[244]

Clinton pledged Yeltsin firm support and at least $1.6 billion in aid. On
April 15, the foreign and finance ministers of the G-7 countries,
meeting in Tokyo, pledged at least $28 billion in aid, under certain
conditions. Doubtless these pledges helped Yeltsin win a favorable vote
of 59 percent in the Russian referendum on April 25.

To show his concern for renewing peace negotiations between Israel
and the Arabs, the President sent Secretary Christopher to six nations
in the Middle East, February 17–24. He announced this mission with a
statement on February 3:

> Those who are willing to make peace will find in me and my
> Administration a full partner. This is an historic moment. It can slip
> away too easily. But if we seize the opportunity, we can begin now to
> construct a peaceful Middle East for future generations.[245]

Clinton met with Israeli Prime Minister Yitzhak Rabin in Washington
on March 15, and with Egyptian President Hosni Mubarak on April 6.
With American pressure on both sides and with continued Russian
cooperation, the Middle East peace conference reopened in Washington
on April 27, with the United States taking a more active role. After
meeting for three weeks, the next session was scheduled for June.

In a significant shift, on May 19, the Clinton Administration
recognized the government of Angola, which had won the election of
September 1992 against the UNITA party under Jonas Savimbi
(Savimbi, who had received American support for many years, had
taken up arms again). On May 27, it was indicated that the United
States would continue to extend most-favored-nation (MFN) trading
status to China for another year, with a further extension dependent

upon conditions, such as improved human rights. It was also reported that American policy was being redirected more positively toward African states, to encourage democracy and development there. Similarly, the foreign aid program in general was expected to promote democracy, cleaner environment, quicker response to disasters like famines, and population control.[246] Thus the Clinton Administration appeared to be staying squarely in the path of pragmatic American idealism in its foreign policy. Clinton's appointment, on May 29, 1993, of the highly respected editor and commentator, David Gergen (who had held high posts in the White House under Presidents Reagan, Ford and Nixon), as Counselor to the President and director of communications, implied an effort by the Administration to create a more effective and more bipartisan policy in general.

From June 1993 onward, the challenges America faced abroad became somewhat clearer, but both President Clinton and the American people were uncertain as to what counter-steps should be undertaken. Polls in 1993 demonstrated America's continued international concern. Dr. Al Richman, Office of Research in the U.S. Information Agency, concluded (March 29, 1994):

> Polls which present just two response options . . . have found that about two-thirds of the public continue to favor a generally active, cooperative U.S. role in world affairs, compared to less than one-third who oppose active involvement.
> Both the American public and elites support the idea of the U.S. acting in concert with other major countries to exert leadership in world affairs. . . . Most elite favor an assertive U.S. leadership role . . . ; most of the public favor a more cautious approach—sharing the leadership role more or less equally with other major countries.[247]

Similarly, another study expresses the view: "While the American public now accords domestic needs higher priority, little suggests that Americans are more inward looking."[248] A major poll (Chicago Council on Foreign Relations and Gallup) near the end of 1994 showed that the United Nations was supported by 74 percent of Americans, and that 65 percent of the general public and 98 percent of leaders believed that the United States should take an active part in world affairs. Also 51 percent favored strengthening the United Nations, and 82 percent stressed the importance of stopping the spread of nuclear weapons.[249] A June 1995 nation-wide poll showed that two-thirds of the public thought that U.N. peacekeeping was a good idea and that the U.S. should contribute troops to it.[250]

On May 5, 1994, the Administration issued a "National Security Study of Engagement and Enlargement," stressing policies of "engagement" in international affairs in a leadership role and "enlargement" of democracies and open markets around the world.

President Clinton's policies can be summarized under eight headings: (1) military power and the United Nations; (2) supporting Russia and Europe in general; (3) the enlargement of democracy and human rights; (4) stopping the spread of nuclear weapons; (5) expanding international trade and investment; (6) promoting peace (especially in the Middle East); (7) humanitarian aid; and (8) strengthening diplomatic relations.

Military Power and the United Nations

President Clinton's extrovert approach, though moderate in general, was indicated in his emphasis on the vital role of American military force, including its humanitarian actions, in his State of the Union message on January 25, 1994:

> But nothing, nothing is more important to our security than our nation's armed forces. We honor their contribution, including those who are carrying out the longest humanitarian airlift in history in Bosnia, those who will complete their mission in Somalia this year, and their brave comrades who gave their lives there.
>
> Our forces are the finest military our nation has ever had, and I have pledged that as long as I am President they will remain the best-equipped, the best-trained, and the best-prepared fighting force on the face of the earth.
>
> Last year, I proposed a defense plan that maintains our post-cold war security at lower cost. . . . We must not cut our defense further. . .
>
> Ultimately . . . the basic strategy to insure our security and to build a durable peace is to support the advance of democracy elsewhere. . . [251]

Nevertheless, the Pentagon admitted on November 17, 1994, that one-fourth of the U.S. Army divisions were not fully ready for combat. On December 1 the President asked Congress for $25 billion more for defense over the next six years to improve military readiness. And the new Republican Congress was prepared to increase defense expenditures much more.

President Clinton used military force to deter Iraq, in Yugoslavia, and in Haiti. American planes bombed Iraq on June 26, 1993, in retaliation for evidence that Iraq had been responsible for a plot on the life of former President George Bush when he visited Kuwait. When Iraq massed 50,000 troops on the border of Kuwait, the President, on October 7, 1994, began sending 36,000 troops and more planes to Kuwait, until Iraq withdrew its forces in December.

Also in June 1993, the United States sent 300 American soldiers to Macedonia (in former Yugoslavia) to join other U.N. forces in deterring possible Serbian aggression there. In relation to Yugoslavia, the situation was extremely complicated. When Croatia and Bosnia had declared their independence, the Serbs living in those areas, backed by the Serb government of Yugoslavia, wished to take their territories into Serbia proper or at least be independent. Thus the fighting began, with the Serbs engaging in what was called "ethnic cleansing," especially against the dominant Bosnian Muslims. Not until August 1995 were the Croatians able to invade and return some of their Serb-conquered territory. The Bosnians had lost 70 percent of their area to the Serbs. The aims of the Clinton Administration, the West and the United Nations appeared to be: to keep the war from spreading; to get supplies through to major civilian centers; to give some protection to six "safe havens"; and to obtain a negotiated peace as soon as possible (although their formula gave 49 percent of Bosnia to the Serbs, the Bosnian Serbs rejected it).

The United Nations installed troops, mainly British and French, to pursue these goals, while the United States used its air power with other NATO countries to keep Serb planes out of Bosnia, and to bomb some Serb positions if they threatened the "safe havens." The general feeling in the United States was that no American ground forces should be introduced except for the purposes of helping remove the U.N. forces or possibly re-position them—President Clinton had offered 25,000 soldiers. As early as March 10, 1994, the President ordered an end to the enforcement of the arms embargo against the Bosnian government.

By July 21, 1995, the Allies (the United States, Britain and France) warned the Bosnian Serbs of "substantial and decisive" air strikes if the U.N. enclave at Gorazde were attacked. Five days later, a restive U.S. Senate, frustrated at the inability of the West thus far to change the situation, voted 69 to 29 to override the U.N. arms embargo (which had been applied to all sides) against the Bosnian government. The House supported lifting the embargo on August 1, 298 to 128. The President vetoed the measure on August 11. Pressure against the Serbs mounted in two directions: the U.N. and NATO agreed, August 1, to protect the four remaining "safe havens," aided by a British-French strike force being introduced; and a large Croatian army (apparently given some indirect U.S. training) reconquered Krajina (August 4–7), which the Serbs had held since their occupation in 1991. Hope remained that these two moves might restore a balance of power so that the Serbs could be induced to end the terrible war by negotiation, before the fighting spread even further.

The Clinton Administration, under mounting pressure to use force against the military government of Haiti, which had overthrown the elected President Aristide, sought a negotiated solution. On July 8, 1993, the Haitian government signed an agreement to restore President Bertrand Aristide to power in October. When the President sent a small force to prepare for the shift, the force never landed because of some Haitian opposition on the shore. The U.N. Security Council voted additional sanctions, and six American warships helped enforce them. Finally, the Security Council authorized "all means necessary," including the use of force, to remove the Haitian rulers (July 31, 1994—the vote was 12 to 0, with China and Brazil abstaining and Rwanda absent). On September 15, 1994, the President addressed the nation on the American determination to invade Haiti, since diplomatic efforts had been fruitless. He said that the message of the United States was clear: the dictators' time was up, and they should leave now or be forced from power. Over 20,000 American troops were poised to invade. Twenty nations had offered troops to help in the U.N occupation. Polls showed that a majority of the American public opposed invasion, and the Administration did not ask Congress for a vote on the issue.

Then on September 18 occurred a striking demonstration of a policy which combined realism and idealism. With an American invasion force on the way, a negotiating team—led by former President Jimmy Carter, along with General Colin Powell and Senator Sam Nunn—was able to convince the Haitian military junta to cooperate with an American force to start arriving on September 19, and then to step down later (deadline of October 15) so President Aristide could be restored.

The results were quite successful. On October 13, Lt. General Raoul Cedras went into exile, and the elected President Aristide returned on

October 15 to a joyful reception. President Clinton was welcomed on March 3, 1995, as a U.N. force of 6,000 (including 2,400 American soldiers) under an American commander moved in. A fairly successful election was held on June 23. Thus far, this has been regarded as one of the major successes in the establishment of a democracy under a military occupation.

The military forces which had been introduced into Somalia for humanitarian purposes were thwarted in various ways by General Aidid. When American forces, attempting to build a stable government, unsuccessfully attacked the troops of General Aidid, 12 Americans were killed (October 4, 1993). President Clinton strengthened the American forces temporarily, but vowed to withdraw them by March 31. In the meantime, he had urged a note of caution about intervention, when he spoke to the U.N. General Assembly on September 27, 1993:

> The United Nations simply cannot become engaged in every one of the world's problems. If the American people are to say yes to U.N. peace-keeping, the United Nations must know when to say no. The United Nations must also have the technical means to run a modern, world-class peace-keeping operation.[252]

The U.S. Representative to the United Nations, Madeleine Albright, spoke directly on conditions governing the American use of force:

> The Administration believes that whether an operation is multilateral or unilateral, whether the troops are U.S. or foreign, young men and women should not be sent in harm's way without a clear mission, competent commanders, sensible rules of engagement, and the means required to get the job done. . . .
>
> Under the Clinton Administration, our nation will not retreat into a post-cold war foxhole. Under the President's leadership, we are all to work together . . . to protect America and build a better world.[253]

In relation to the United Nations in general, the President emphasized the American role of leadership to the General Assembly:

> The United States intends to remain engaged and to lead. We cannot solve every problem, but we must and will serve as a fulcrum for change and a pivot point for peace.
>
> . . . As a country that has over 150 different racial, ethnic, and religious groups within our borders, our policy is and must be rooted in

a profound respect for all the world's religions and cultures. But we must oppose everywhere extremism that produces terrorism and hate, and we must pursue our humanitarian goal of reducing suffering, fostering sustainable development, and improving health and living standards, particularly for our world's children.

. . . Let us ensure that the tide of freedom and democracy is not pushed back by the fierce winds of ethnic hatred. Let us ensure that the world's most dangerous weapons are safely reduced and denied to dangerous hands. Let us ensure that the world we pass to our children is healthier, safer, and more abundant than the one we inherit today. I believe—I know, that together we can extend this moment of miracles into an age of great and new wonders.[254]

On May 25, 1994, the White House released a summary of the "Policy on Reforming Multilateral Peace Operations," setting conditions, urging reduced U.S. costs, and strengthening the U.N.'s capabilities.[255]

Russia and Europe

President Clinton appeared to take particular pride in cooperating with the Russian Government under President Yeltsin (including the crushing of the revolt of Parliament on October 4, 1993), and urging Russia, as well as other Eastern European countries, to join NATO's Partnership for Peace (Russia joined on June 21, 1994, after the others). The United States pledged economic aid to Russia and other former Soviet republics, as well as to the independent countries in the East, notably Poland, the Czech Republic and Hungary. Special attention was given to the successful removal of nuclear weapons from Ukraine, Kazhakistan and Belarus.

The President presented his proposed "Partnership for Peace" in a major address at NATO Headquarters in Brussels, January 10, 1994:

. . . If democracy in the East fails, the violence and disruption from the East will once again harm us and other democracies.

I believe our generation's stewardship of this grand alliance will be judged most critically by whether we succeed in integrating the nations of the East within the compass of Western security and Western values. For we have been granted an opportunity without precedent.

To seize the great opportunity before us, I have proposed that we forge what we have decided to call the Partnership for Peace, open to all the former communist states of the Warsaw Pact, along with other non-NATO states. . . .

The Partnership for Peace . . . enables us to prepare and to work toward the enlargement of NATO when other countries are capable of fulfilling their NATO responsibilities.[256]

The President reasserted America's commitment to Europe and NATO in this summit meeting in Brussels, and returned to Europe in June 1994 to help commemorate the 50th anniversary of the D-Day invasion in 1944. Returning again, July 6–14, he delivered a significant address to the French National Assembly, attended the G-7 meeting in Naples, and spoke in Berlin (July 12) at the Brandenburg Gate:

> . . . In our own time, you, courageous Berliners, have again made the Brandenburg what its builders meant it to be—a gateway. Now, together, we can walk through that gateway to our destiny, to a Europe united—united in peace, united in freedom, united in progress for the first time in history. Nothing will stop us. *Nichts wird uns aufhalten. Alles ist moeglich. Berlin ist frei.* Berlin is free.[257]

Russian President Yeltsin met President Clinton again in Washington, September 27–28, 1994, where they stressed nuclear disarmament and signed agreements on trade and investment. On December 16, Yeltsin ordered an invasion of the breakaway Russian republic of Chechnya. As the conflict continued with heavy casualties, much American and world opinion became critical of the Russian President and his actions. With peace talks under way, President Clinton and Prime Minister John Major of Britain joined President Yeltsin in Moscow, May 9–10, 1995, to celebrate the 50th anniversary of the end of World War II. A preliminary peace pact was reached between Russia and Chechnya on June 21. A further hopeful development in American-Russian relations occurred with two special American space shuttle dockings with the Russian space station *Mir* (February 6, 1995 and June 29)—an American astronaut lived for four months on the Russian station. Russia was welcomed into active engagement in the Partnership for Peace with NATO on May 31, 1995.

Enlargement of Democracy

American emphasis on the expansion of democracy was shown in special help to the nations of Eastern Europe and the former Soviet

Union, as they moved from dictatorship to democracy, and in bringing pressure on many nations to hold elections and respect human rights, as in Haiti. Particularly encouraging were the peaceful elections in South Africa on April 26, 1994, and the installation of Nelson Mandela as President on May 10 (attended by Vice-President Albert Gore and First Lady Hillary Rodham Clinton). President Mandela visited the United States, and asked (October 4, 1994) for American help in the re-birth of his nation. The Clinton Administration pledged, through help from the Overseas Private Investment Corporation, to generate a billion dollars in investment there.

The Administration gave special support to moves toward democracy in Africa, with diplomatic pressure on the Nigerian military to restore democracy in Nigeria. Anthony Lake, Assistant to the President for National Security Affairs, pledged U.S. support for democracy in Africa when he spoke to the Organization of African Unity (OAU) at Addis Ababa, Ethiopia, December 15, 1994:

> As we look into the future of this continent—which I believe does hang in the balance—I hope that we never forget how far Africa has come. . . . They are the reasons why reasonable men and women in far-away capitals should continue to invest in the future of Africa.
>
> That, I believe, is the basis for a new "Afro-realism"—an Afro-realism that commits us to the hard work that can strengthen the partnership between Africa and America. For if we let that partnership weaken, Africa will lose a crucial source of support, and America will have lost the chance to participate in what could be—and what must be—one of the great adventures of our time: fulfilling the dreams of Africa's greatness that animated the leaders of its independence all those years ago.[258]

Anthony Lake had previously stated (September 21, 1993) the general policy of America as the dominant power in the post-cold war world to be "enlargement" instead of "the previous policy of containment":

> . . . It is a moment of unparalleled opportunity. We have the blessing of living in the world's most powerful and respected nation at a time when the world is embracing our ideals as never before. We can let this moment slip away. Or we can mobilize our nation in order to enlarge democracy, enlarge markets, and enlarge our future.[259]

Freedom House reported in December 1994 that 45 percent of the world's people lived in democracies, far more than ever before. Of the world's 191 nations, 114 were formal democracies in 1994, up from 63 in 1984.[260] On December 7–8, Namibia gave a boost to African democracy by holding a tranquil election to keep the party in power which favored democracy.

Nuclear Weapons

The United States worked with the International Atomic Energy Agency to try to induce North Korea to live up to its obligations under the Non-Proliferation Treaty (NPT) not to manufacture nuclear weapons. After long and unsuccessful talks, with the threat of possible U.N. sanctions against North Korea, former President Carter met the Korean leader, Kim Il Sung, and helped induce him (June 23, 1994) to hold talks with the United States and to meet with the President of South Korea. Negotiations were postponed when Kim Il Sung unexpectedly died on July 8, but the talks were resumed in August. A hopeful initial agreement was reached on August 12. On October 19, 1994, the two countries agreed in Paris on a ten-year program which eliminated the expectation of nuclear weapons in North Korea. Not until June 12, 1995, did North Korea finally agree to the supply of modern nuclear reactors, for peaceful purposes, from South Korea.

When the United Nations opened a conference on the expiring Non-Proliferation Treaty in New York City on April 17, 1995, the United States pressed strongly for an indefinite continuation of the treaty. On May 11, 170 nations signed a pact for this indefinite extension. Both Russia and the United States have ended the targeting of each other with nuclear weapons. In May 1995, President Clinton indicated he would seek a world-wide ban on nuclear testing by the end of 1996. The START II treaty for the reduction of American and Russian nuclear weapons was submitted to the Senate by President Clinton that same month.

International Trade and Investment

The Clinton Administration's emphasis on international trade and world prosperity was emphasized in many ways: (1) the summit meetings of the Group of Seven (G7—1993 in Tokyo, 1994 in Naples, 1995 in Halifax); (2) the North Atlantic Free Trade Agreement

(NAFTA—the U.S., Canada and Mexico), approved by Congress in November 1973 (the House vote was 224-200, November 17); (3) the pressure for open markets at the Asian-Pacific Conferences (November 20, 1993, November 15, 1994—when, with President Clinton in attendance, 18 nations agreed to establish some free trade by 2010 and all by 2020); (4) the U.S. signing of the General Agreement on Trade and Tariffs (GATT), creating the World Trade Organization (WTO), along with 108 other nations (April 15, 1994—the House approved, 288 to 148, on November 29, and the Senate, 76 to 24, December 1); (5) the maintenance of the Most-Favored-Nation (MFN) clause with China (May 26, 1994 and June 2, 1995, with a special agreement to reduce piracy of copyrighted materials, February 26, 1995) and the President's separation of trade in the future from China's record in human rights; (6) opening Vietnam to American trade, and later agreeing to exchange diplomatic missions (May 26, 1994); (7) a "Western Hemisphere" meeting in Miami, where 34 nations decided to create a free trade zone beginning in 2005 (December 9, 1994); (8) the Clinton emergency offer of $20 billion to Mexico for the rescue of the devalued peso; (9) and seeking agreements with Japan to open its market wider to American goods, climaxed by an agreement, June 28, 1995, which obviated planned American tariffs on Japanese luxury cars.

President Clinton demonstrated his positive attitude on the expansion of trade in his comments on NAFTA, GATT, and China. He signed the NAFTA side agreements in September 1993, in the presence of former Presidents Carter, Ford and Bush:

> I believe that NAFTA will create 1 million jobs in the first 5 years of its impact.
>
> In a few moments, I will sign side agreements to NAFTA that will make it harder than it is today for businesses to relocate solely because of very low wages or lax environmental rules. . . .
>
> . . . This is our opportunity to provide an impetus to freedom and democracy in Latin America and create new jobs for America as well.[261]

The President announced the successful completion of the GATT negotiations on December 15, 1993, calling it "the most comprehensive trade agreement in history":

> Not since the end of World War II has the United States pushed to

completion trade agreements of such significance as NAFTA and GATT. We've shown leadership by example. We've set forth a vision for a thriving global economy. And our trading partners, to their credit, have also rallied to that cause.[262]

In relation to China, President Clinton announced he was de-linking "human rights" from the annual extension of most-favored-nation trading status for China:

Will we do more to advance the cause of human rights if China is isolated or if our nations are engaged in a growing web of political and economic cooperation and contacts? I am persuaded that the best path for advancing freedom in China is for the United States to intensify and broaden its engagement with that nation.

. . . In three decades and three wars during this century, Americans have fought and died in the Asia-Pacific to advance their ideals and their security. Our destiny demands that we continue to play an active role in this region.

. . . I believe . . . this is in the strategic, economic, and political interest of both the United States and China. . . .[263]

Promoting Peace

Continuing friendly pressure was put on the peoples of the Middle East to bring peace between Israel and the Arabs. After successful secret negotiations mediated by Norwegian officials in Norway, Prime Minister Yitzhak Rabin and Chairman Yasir Arafat signed an Israel-Palestine accord in Washington, September 13, 1993, for Israeli withdrawal from the Gaza Strip and Jericho, as a first step; the two leaders finally confirmed agreements on the details in Cairo (May 4, 1994), and Arafat moved into Gaza on July 1. A Washington conference brought together nations who pledged two billion dollars of aid to the Palestinians (September 20, 1993). King Hussein of Jordan and Prime Minister Rabin signed a Washington Declaration of Principles for peace (July 25, 1994), and both of them were accorded warm emotional ovations when they addressed Congress. The United States is expected to write off $702 million of Jordanian debt. Secretary of State Christopher was active in promoting peace in his several trips to the Middle East, including Syria.

President Clinton spoke first at the Israeli-Palestinian ceremony at the White House (September 13, 1993):

Today, we bear witness to an extraordinary act in one of history's defining dramas. . . . That hallowed piece of earth, that land of light and revelation is the home to the memories of Jews, Muslims, and Christians throughout the world.

. . . Let us salute, also, today, the Government of Norway for its remarkable role in nurturing this agreement. But of all, above all, let us today pay tribute to the leaders who had the courage to lead their people toward peace. . . .

. . . Mr. Prime Minister, Mr. Chairman, I pledge the active support of the United States of America to the difficult work that lies ahead.

The children of Abraham, the descendants of Isaac and Ishmael, have embarked together on a bold journey. Together, today, with all our hearts and all our souls, we bid them *shalom, salaam,* peace.

After the signing ceremony, the President concluded:

We have been granted the great privilege of witnessing this victory for peace. . . .

Now let each of us here today return to our portion of that effort, uplifted by the spirit of the moment, refreshed in our hopes and guided by the wisdom of the Almighty, who has brought us to this joyous day.

Go in peace. Go as peacemakers.[264]

The United States helped Israel and Jordan improve their relations over many months, partly by the work of the U.S.-Jordanian-Israeli Trilateral Committee, which held its fourth meeting in Washington on July 6–7, 1994. President Clinton spoke at the signing ceremony on July 25:

The Washington Declaration is the product of much hard work. . . . Together, with the wise counsel and persistent energy of the Secretary of State, Warren Christopher, Israel and Jordan . . . have pursued peace, and we are all in their debt.

. . . Today, King Hussein and Prime Minister Rabin give their people a new currency of hope and the chance to prosper in a region of peace.[265]

President Clinton attended the final signing of the pact by King Hussein and Prime Minister Rabin at the Israel-Jordan border (October 26, 1994). Peace talks between Israel and the PLO were constantly being delayed by Palestinian terrorist attacks on Israelis (as on October 14, 1994, November 12, and January 22, 1995), but, on July 4, 1995, the two parties reached a general agreement on the beginning of Israeli withdrawal from the West Bank, scheduled for July 25. Another large terrorist attack occurred on July 24, but it was planned that the peace talks would continue. Preliminary agreements were reached on August 8 and 11. The United States continued its steady pressure on all parties for peace. President Clinton visited President Assad of Syria twice in 1994, and talks between Israelis and Syrians were held regularly in Washington.

The Clinton Administration directly encouraged peace negotiations in Northern Ireland, and was heartened by the Irish Republican Army (IRA) declaration of a cease-fire on August 31, 1994, with the militant Protestants following suit on October 13. In Angola, where the U.S. was also involved, the government and the rebels pledged peace on May 6, 1995. Former President Carter mediated a two-month cease-fire in the civil war in Sudan (May 28, 1995), partly to treat disease. On September 8, 1994, the troops of the United States, Britain and France left Berlin, to complete the freedom of Germany.

Humanitarian Aid

In 1993 and 1994, American aid abroad continued much as in the past. For example, the House approved a $13.7 billion aid package on August 4, 1994, with $700 million in loan forgiveness for Jordan, $50 million emergency aid for Rwanda, $850 million for the former Soviet republics, $330 million for East European and Baltic states, $80 million for the Development Fund for Africa, $3 billion for Israel, and $2.1 billion for Egypt. On July 12, 1995, the new Republican House approved (333 to 89) a bill with major reductions, 20 percent below the Clinton request, except for maintaining the grants for Israel and Egypt.

The novel type of aid begun by American military forces under President Bush was continued under President Clinton and later enlarged, enabling America to use its direct pressure abroad to try to save lives. In Somalia, when 12 American soldiers were killed, the troops there were almost completely withdrawn by March 25, 1995. In the meantime, however, the United States, the United Nations and private agencies had saved thousands of lives.

Aid was continued to the Kurds in northern Iraq, it was increased to the besieged Bosnians (flying in food), and President Clinton asked the Pentagon to begin a huge aid effort for more than a million Rwandan refugees who had fled to Zaire (July 22, 1994). Over 200 soldiers were sent to Goma, Zaire, 900 were running an airlift in Entebbe, Uganda, and a sizeable force was sent to secure the Kigali airport in Rwanda itself.

With so many tragic events in Africa—civil war, famine and disease—the President arranged for a White House Conference on Africa, June 26–27, 1994 (before the decision to send troops to help the Rwandans). His address stressed America's humanitarian goals:

> The United States is currently supporting seven peace-keeping efforts in Africa.
>
> [In Rwanda] we have provided material, financial, and statistical support for the U.N. peace-keeping mission—more than $100 million in humanitarian relief.
>
> It seems to me that in the face of all the tensions that are now gripping the continent, we need a new American policy based on the idea that we should help the nations of Africa identify and solve problems before they erupt.
>
> . . . As Africans turn away from the failed experiments of the past, they're also embracing new political freedoms. . . . As we meet today, more than a dozen African nations are preparing for elections. . . . The lights of freedom shine brighter.
>
> I think South Africa has given us great cause for hope, not only on the African continent but throughout the world.[266]

Strengthening Diplomatic Relations

The Clinton Administration endeavored to improve relations with many nations, including some who had been hostile. Notable have been the steady moves toward opening relations with Vietnam, where the trade embargo was lifted in 1994 and full diplomatic relations were opened on July 11, 1995. The President declared this was a "time for healing":

> By helping to bring Vietnam into the community of nations, normalization also serves our interest in working for a free and pacific Vietnam in a stable and peaceful Asia. . . .
>
> I believe normalization and increased contacts between America and Vietnam will advance the cause of freedom in Vietnam just as it did in Eastern Europe and the former Soviet Union. . . .
>
> I am proud to be joined in this view by distinguished veterans of the Vietnam War. They served their country bravely. . . .
>
> Whatever we may think about the political decisions of the Vietnam

era, the brave Americans who fought and died there had noble motives. They fought for the freedom and the independence of the Vietnam people. Today the Vietnamese are independent, and we believe this step will help to extend the reach of freedom in Vietnam. . . .

This step will also help our own country to move forward on an issue that has separated Americans from one another for too long now. Let the future be our destination. We have so much work ahead of us. This moment offers us the opportunity to bind up our own wounds. . . . Let this moment in the words of Scripture, "Be a time to heal, and a time to build."[267]

Difficulties were encountered with the other Communist nations—China, Cuba and North Korea. China resented America's relations with Taiwan and its criticism of "human rights." Relations with Cuba improved as Cuba ended its encouragement of "emigration," and the United States agreed to accept 20,000 Cubans with visas annually (September 9, 1994). The outlook with North Korea was somewhat more hopeful after the agreement of June 12, 1995, on nuclear reactors from South Korea. Relations with Iraq, Iran and Libya remained tense.

An indication of deep American world involvement was given in the dedication of the new National Foreign Affairs Training Center at Arlington, Virginia, on October 13, 1993. Secretary of State Christopher said: "This exceptional center will train 15,000 students annually. . . . students will come from some 47 U.S. Government agencies, and they will study 300 courses, including 63 languages."[268] A major step forward in the development of international law was taken on July 28, 1994, when the United States signed the Law of the Sea Treaty, after renegotiation had occurred on the protection of mining rights on the sea floor. The Treaty was submitted to the U.S. Senate on October 7, 1994.

Conclusion

In spite of a common impression that President Clinton was little concerned with international relations, he and his Administration continued to play an active role on the world scene, with clear extrovert tendencies. Nevertheless, there was a fairly widespread feeling, at home and abroad, that the President had not been a strong and consistent leader in world affairs. Then in 1995, the new Republican Congress desired to reduce foreign aid and America's support of the United

Nations. So the debate proceeded as to the nature of America's leadership—especially whether it should be dominated by multilateralism (cooperating with other countries and the United Nations) or unilateralism (leading alone, with an emphasis on America's own basic interests).

In his 1995 State of the Union address, President Clinton stressed the close relation between America's domestic and international strength:

> Our security still depends upon our continued world leadership for peace and freedom and democracy. We still cannot be strong at home unless we're strong abroad.
>
> We have proudly supported peace and prosperity and freedom from South Africa to Northern Ireland, from Central and Eastern Europe to Asia, from Latin America to the Middle East. All these endeavors are good in those places, but they make our future more confident and more secure. . . .[269]

The coming struggle with the Republican Congress was highlighted by a letter from Secretary of State Warren Christopher and Secretary of Defense William Perry to Speaker of the House Newt Gingrich (February 20, 1995):

> This week the House of Representatives will consider legislation that would undermine this and every future President's ability to safeguard America's security and to command our armed forces. The National Security and Revitalization Act, or H.R. 872, is deeply flawed and, if adopted, would endanger national security.

They particularly opposed the bill's emphasis on a National Missile Defense, which would drain "billions from more pressing needs"; for its constrictions on the President's authority to use American troops (particularly in conjunction with the United Nations); its abrogation of "our treaty obligations to the United Nations to pay our share"; and its favor toward a reckless expansion of NATO membership.[270] The House passed the measure, largely unchanged.

Three months later, Deputy Secretary of State Strobe Talbott stressed the foreign policy debate in America, in an address on "American Leadership in the Post-Cold War World":

> Now more than ever, the world looks to our country for leadership.

Now more than ever, the rewards for providing that leadership abroad will be realized here at home.

. . . For at least the third time in this century, we face a great national debate—a debate over America's role in the world and over what it takes to play the role we should. . . .

. . . Let us get on with the great debate, but let its starting point be a shared recognition of our nation's three greatest strengths: *first*, the strength and global appeal of our democratic values and institutions; *second*, the strength of our economy, which depends on global peace and stability; and *third*, the strength of our military power. In short, we have the heart, the brains, the wallet, and the muscle to exercise international leadership, and to do so on behalf of our interests as well as those of humanity as a whole.[271]

A month later, Secretary Christopher appealed to the Senate Foreign Relations Committee not to slash the International Affairs budget:

Slashing our International Affairs budget would represent, both substantively and symbolically, an abdication of . . . leadership. Refusing to work in alliances and institutions would undermine our influence abroad. If we cast aside half a century of American engagement, there is no other country with the strength or the vision to replace us. But there are plenty of forces that would like to exploit the vacuum that we would leave behind.

Last November's elections . . . did not change—indeed they enhanced—our responsibility to cooperate on a bipartisan basis in foreign affairs.[272]

In addition to America's other goals, Secretary Christopher emphasized the importance of fighting terrorism, narcotics and international crimes.

Senate Majority Leader Bob Dole and Speaker of the House Newt Gingrich remain influential in determining American policy. Thus their approaches should be included. In a *Foreign Policy* article On "Shaping America's Global Future," Senator Dole wrote as follows:

. . . Never before . . . has America been so alone at the pinnacle of world leadership.

. . . We have witnessed two efforts to "reinvent" American foreign policy since the end of the Cold War: President George Bush's New World Order and the Assertive Multilateralism, or Engagement and Enlargement, of President Bill Clinton. Unfortunately, neither effort has been successful.

. . . In the minds of many, U.S. foreign policy has been marked by inconsistency, incoherence, lack of purpose, and a reluctance to lead. . . . From Bosnia to China, from North Korea to Poland, our allies and our adversaries doubt out resolve and question our commitments.

. . . American leadership . . . can overcome the challenges of building a just and durable peace after the Cold War. The words of President Dwight Eisenhower's first inaugural address are as true today as they were in 1953: "To meet the challenge of our time, destiny has laid upon our country the responsibility of the free world's leadership. . . ."

. . . Put American interests first and lead the way. The future will not wait for America, but it can be shaped by an America second to none.[273]

Speaker Newt Gingrich stressed defense, leadership and service in his book *To Renew America*:

While I am a cheap hawk, I remain a hawk. I believe the world is a dangerous place. I believe there are active enemies who would love to destroy the United States. I believe our opponents are clever and determined and deserve our respect. I believe we need to have a much bigger investment in intelligence and make a much bigger effort to stop terrorism. When in doubt, I favor a stronger rather than a weaker America.

. . . The challenge to our generation is enormous. No country has ever had the potential to lead the entire human race the way America does today. No country has ever had as many people of as many different backgrounds call on it as we do today. No country has ever had as many neighbors who suspect, distrust, and, in some cases, hate one another call on it to help achieve peace and help transform conflict into community. No country has ever had as many former dictatorships call on it for advice about how to create free governments, free markets, and a military that can operate within the rule of law and under civilian control

The simple fact is that with the end of the Cold War and the collapse of the Soviet empire, the need for American leadership has become greater.[274]

Secretary Warren Christopher summarized the Administration's basic approach in *Foreign Policy*, **"America's Leadership, America's Opportunity":**

The United States has a remarkable opportunity to help shape a world conducive to American interests and consistent with American values: a more secure and prosperous world of open markets and open societies that will improve the lives of our people for generations to come. This is an American foreign policy that should command bipartisan support.[275]

Some Special Signs of Idealism Since 1966

Perhaps the major sign of idealism in America since 1966 has been seen in the steady march toward peace and freedom by the Presidents, supported by the majority of the people and by millions more around the world. With the nuclear stalemate nearly two decades old, the decision was made to seek disarmament and "peaceful coexistence" with the Soviet Union and the Peoples Republic of China, without compromising on America's principles of justice and freedom.

Although the Cold War did not end officially until 1991 or 1992, it showed signs of moving toward an end after 1966. Both France and Germany paved the way by seeking closer relations with the Soviet Union. Peace was envisaged between powers with vastly different ideologies, with the very survival of humanity threatened by nuclear weapons. Furthermore, the steady development of closer unity in the European Community (now the European Union) was another idealist sign.

All the American Presidents sought peace, with justice and freedom. Johnson tried almost desperately to bring peace in Vietnam, while helping the South Vietnamese defense against the Communist North aided by the Soviet Union and China. Nixon broke through the barriers to communist China and to the Soviet Union, seeking, he said, a generation or more of peace, while improving relations with several Arab states. Ford cooperated with the United Nations on global economic and social problems. Carter improved relations with Panama, helped secure peace between Egypt and Israel, opened full relations with China, and supported independence and human rights in Africa and elsewhere. Reagan felt the necessity of increasing America's military and economic strength as a prelude to talks with the expanding Soviet Union, but was ready to negotiate true arms reduction and friendly cooperation after Gorbachev shifted the Soviet approach. Bush sought, after the fall of communism, to build a "new world order" through collective security against an aggressor state like Iraq, through using

American troops for humanitarian purposes as in Somalia, and through pressure for peace between Israel and the Arab peoples. Clinton has likewise been seeking peace and justice in the Middle East and in Yugoslavia, encouraging the new coalition government in South Africa under President Nelson Mandela, and promoting the moves toward peace in Northern Ireland. He has also been determined to help the Russian people achieve a measure of democracy and market economics.

A further sign of idealism was evident in the special role which morally dedicated people around the world, as well as in America, played in working toward justice, welfare and peace. There was widespread emphasis on the "moral crisis" in America and elsewhere. Pope John Paul II urged several hundred thousand young people, at the World Youth Day in Denver, August 15, 1993, to work for a moral renewal (President Clinton met with him). His encyclical *Veritatis Splendor* (The Splendor of Truth), October 1993, insisted that morality cannot exist independent of faith. His notable book in 1994, *Crossing the Threshold of Hope*, was an inspiration to many, as he called for people to cultivate in their hearts "that true fear of God, which is the beginning of wisdom" and declared that "Andre Malraux was certainly right when he said that the twenty-first century would be the century of religion or it would not be at all."[276] *Time* magazine had the Pope's picture on the cover of its issue of December 26, 1994–January 2, 1995, as it named him "Man of the Year."

Vaclav Havel, noted President of the Czech Republic, issued "A Call for Sacrifice: The Co-Responsibility of the West," in *Foreign Affairs*:

> We are concerned about the destiny of the values and principles that communism denied, and in whose name we resisted communism and ultimately brought it down.
>
> . . . I have in mind . . . a willingness to sacrifice for the common interest some of one's own particular interest, including even the quest for larger and larger domestic production and consumption.
>
> Why has the West lost its ability to sacrifice?
>
> . . . People today know that they can only be saved by a new type of global responsibility. Only one small detail is missing: that responsibility must genuinely be assumed.[277]

In an address at Independence Hall in Philadelphia, July 4, 1994. President Havel stressed the need for "self-transcendence," for faith in the Creator:

The central task of the final years of this century . . . is the creation
of a new model of coexistence among the various cultures within a
single international civilization. . . .

Politicians may reiterate a thousand times that the basis of the new
world order must be universal respect for human rights, but it will mean
nothing as long as this imperative does not derive from the respect of
the miracle of being, the miracle of the universe, the miracle of nature,
the miracle of our own existence. . . .

The Declaration of Independence, adopted 218 years ago, states that
the creator gave man the right to liberty. It seems man can realize that
liberty only if he does not forget the one who endowed him with it.[278]

When Havel delivered the commencement address at Harvard University
on June 8, 1995, he spoke of the hope for mankind that grows out of
the "genuine spiritual roots hidden beneath the skin of our common,
global civilization":

Our conscience must catch up to our reason, otherwise we are lost.
. . . It is obvious that those who have the greatest power and
influence also bear the greatest responsibility. Like it or not, the United
States of America now bears probably the greatest responsibility for the
direction the world will take. The United States, therefore, should
reflect more deeply on this responsibility.
. . . What is now at stake is saving the human race.[279]

When Aleksandr Solzhenitsyn, who had spent many years in
America in exile, arrived in Vladivostok on May 27, 1994, he stressed
Russia's need for repentance and reconciliation, and believed Russia
was ready to search for a new order based on "Russian history, tradition
and spirit" and that "there cannot be national reconciliation without
spiritual cleansing."[280]

In America there were numerous calls for greater ethical-moral-
spiritual concern. Notable books were written, 1993–1995, by William
J. Bennett, Stephen L. Carter, Gertrude Himmelfarb, Douglas Johnston,
George A. Marsden, James Q. Wilson and Robert Wuthnow.[281] Andrew
Young, former U.S. Ambassador to the United Nations, was asked
where a renewed sense of purpose and leadership would come from:

The purpose and idealism of the U.N.'s postwar period came from
the churches; renewal will come from the same place.
. . . Global vision has to come from the people of God because

ultimately it flows out of a religious ideal—that all humans are children of the same God.

. . . Investment, education, jobs, economic opportunity, economic justice—they are the weapons we have to employ against the serious threat to our nation posed by poverty. And America has to provide global leadership along the same lines.[282]

A most notable example of individual dedication to peace and justice, inspired by spiritual values, is the work of former President Jimmy Carter, as in his mediation in the conflicts related to North Korea, Haiti, Yugoslavia and the Sudan. *Newsweek, Time* and *U.S. News and World Report* all had special sections in 1994 and 1995 devoted to the contemporary religious situation, noting the relative vitality of religion among the majority of Americans. The so-called "religious right" played an important role in the elections in 1994. At the same time, the nation was worried about extremists prepared to use violence, notably in the terrible bombing of the federal building in Oklahoma City, April 19, 1995, with more than 160 killed.

All the Presidents seemed to feel deep religious motivation, even though some of their decisions may have fallen short. Robert N. Bellah wrote a widely read (though controversial) article early in 1967 entitled "Civil Religion in America," arguing that "this religion—or perhaps better, this religious denomination—has its own seriousness and integrity and requires the same care in understanding as any other religion does." He regarded this civil religion as "an understanding of the American experience in the light of ultimate and universal reality," and believed that it was "still very much alive."[283] Elton Trueblood's book *Abraham Lincoln: Theologian of American Anguish* is also a reminder of the special role of moral-spiritual leadership which has been played by some American presidents both during and after their presidencies.[284] This concept of an American "civil religion" appears related to a belief in America's "world mission," stressed by Ralph Henry Gabriel as one of America's dominant historical convictions.

The American Presidents since 1966 all seemed to feel that America was the nation that must lead, if the world was to move toward peace and freedom and justice. This feeling was associated with strong religious convictions, especially expressed by Presidents Carter and Reagan. All the Presidents spoke of their personal religious convictions in the annual Presidential Prayer Breakfasts (started by President Eisenhower in 1953). President Nixon (February 5, 1970) stressed the idea that "America is a Nation under God":

> We do have a destiny, not a destiny to conquer the world or to
> exploit the world, but a destiny to give something more to the world .
> . . to give to other nations of the world an example of spiritual
> leadership and idealism which no material strength or military power
> can provide.[285]

At the Christmas Pageant of Peace, December 15, 1977, President
Carter summarized part of his faith:

> . . . Almost 2000 years ago the Son of Peace was born to give us
> the vision of perfection, a vision of humility, a vision of unselfishness,
> a vision of compassion, a vision of love.
>   . . . And I hope that we'll make every effort this Christmas season
> . . . to look to the family of humankind . . . that we forgive one
> another, and, indeed, form a worldwide family where every human
> being on Earth is our brother or our sister.[286]

On October 3, 1978, Carter spoke at the Martin Luther King Center in
praise of this leader:

> He brought together the conscience of white Americans and the
> courage of black Americans in a bond of love that broke down the
> barriers which had existed for centuries. He helped us overcome our
> ignorance of one another and our fear of doing what many of us knew
> was right.[287]

At the 1983 Presidential Prayer Breakfast, President Reagan spoke
of America:

> I also believed this blessed land was set apart in a very special way,
> a country created by men and women who came here not in search of
> gold, but in search of God. They would be free people, living together
> under the law with faith in their Maker and their future.[288]

On January 6, 1986, Reagan sent a message to the Soviet people on the
date of the observance of Christmas by the Orthodox Catholic Church:

> We are told that there are up to 100 million believers in the Soviet
> Union alone. . . . Please know that we in America join you, as one
> family under the Fatherhood of God, binding ourselves in a communion

of hearts, for today and tomorrow and for all time. Know, too, our heartfelt desire that this day will kindle in all men that spirit which alone can bring real peace on earth.[289]

In an address to the Royal Institute of International Affairs in London on June 3, 1988, Reagan stated his belief that "our Maker, while never denying us free will, does over time guide us with a wise and provident hand, giving direction to history and slowly bringing good from evil—leading us ever so slowly but ever so relentlessly and lovingly to a moment when the will of man and God are each one again."[290]

President Bush spoke of the higher spiritual values, June 28, 1991, to the Annual Convention of National Religious Broadcasters:

> . . . I speak of the teachings which uphold moral values like tolerance, compassion, faith, and courage, that remind us that . . . men cannot live without God. His love and His justice inspire in us a yearning for faith and a compassion for the weak and oppressed, as well as the courage and conviction to oppose tyranny and injustice.[291]

At his first Presidential Prayer Breakfast, February 4, 1993, President Clinton asked God for "the humility to walk by faith and not by sight," and spoke of "the living example of Jesus Christ, who was so at ease with the hurting and hungry and lonely, and, yes, the sinner."[292] *Time* magazine described Clinton's deep faith (next to an article about the rapid growth of his denomination, the Southern Baptists, as well as the Roman Catholics, the Mormons, and more evangelical churches in the United States).[293]

Clinton made a notable address (November 13, 1993) to black ministers in the Church of God in Christ, Memphis, Tennessee (where Martin Luther King, Jr., delivered his last address). He spoke of the "great crisis of the spirit that is gripping America today," and asked what Martin Luther King would say if he were here. After having King say, "You did a good job in opening opportunity," then King would add:

> "I did not live and die to see the American family destroyed. . . . I fought for freedom, but not for the freedom of people to kill each other with reckless abandonment, nor for the freedom of children to have children and the fathers of the children to walk away from them and abandon them, as if they don't amount to anything.
> ". . . I fought to stop white people from being so filled with hate

that they would wreak violence on black people. I did not fight for the right of black people to murder other black people."

Clinton added:

> . . . I tell you it is our duty to turn it around. . . . And now, I think, finally we have a chance. . . . There are some changes we're going to have to make from the inside out. . . . I don't believe we can repair the basic failures of our society until people who are willing to work have work. Work organizes life.
>
> . . . We won't make all the work that has gone on here benefit a few. We will do it together by the grace of God.[294]

In his State of the Union address on January 26, 1994, the President stressed the importance of a renewal of family life:

> We can't renew our country until we realize that governments do not raise children, parents do.
>
> . . . Let us by our example teach them to obey the law, respect our neighbors and cherish our values.[295]

At the Presidential Prayer Breakfast, February 2, 1995, Clinton stressed the importance of the communications revolution that "gives words not only the power to lift up and liberate [but] the power to divide and destroy as never before."[296] On July 12, the President outlined the various ways in which religion can be introduced in a constitutional manner into the public schools.[297] He supported "affirmative action" in a major address on July 19: "When affirmative action is done right, it is flexible, it is fair, and it works."[298]

Two bills which the President felt were vital for changing America were passed by Congress in 1994: (1) "Goals 2000: Educate America Act" (signed April 10, 1994); and (2) the Crime Act (signed September 13). He also placed special emphasis on the creation of new opportunities for service, notably in the establishment of the AmeriCorps (September 12), for youth service to communities, with special money for college education (20,000 expected to participate the first year, and probably 100,000 by the end of 1996, unless Congress reduces the appropriation). In addition he signed a law (August 23, 1994) making Martin Luther King's birthday, January 17, a day for special national and community service.

The renewed interest of Americans in religious values after 1966 was symbolized by several special publications: a Winter 1967 issue of *Daedalus* devoted to "Religion in America": a 1,200-page book on *The Religious Situation, 1968*[299]; an 1,150-page book on *The Religious Situation, 1969*[300]; and a 1972 study entitled *The Religious Awakening in America*.[301] Church concerns with social, economic and political problems were increased from this time forward—particularly for the mainline churches. Evangelical groups became more significant by 1976 and after. The influential evangelist Billy Graham spoke in the Soviet Union in 1982 and in later years, as well as around the world. He held a huge meeting in Moscow, October 23–25, 1992, and another in Essen, Germany, March 17–21, 1993, broadcast to 59 countries and territories in 44 languages. His meetings in Puerto Rico, March 14–18, 1995, were broadcast around the world in 116 languages to 185 countries. Two significant movements began in 1990: (1) the organization of "Promise Keepers," appealing to conservative religious men, with a typical meeting of 65,000 in an Atlanta stadium, July 4, 1995; and (2) an annual "March for Jesus," observed by 12 million people in 178 countries, June 25, 1995.

Polls in 1993 and after show high support for religion in the United States: over 90 percent believe in God; 70 percent report they are church members (up from 65 percent in 1990); and 58 percent in 1992 said religion was important in their lives.[302] Furthermore, many Americans have high ethical and spiritual standards without an institutional religious base.

Support for peace in America was stimulated by the terrible destruction and high casualties in the Vietnam War, shown on television in the nation's homes almost every night from 1965 to 1973. Churches and clergy, especially mainline, took a leading role in criticizing the war. Martin Luther King, Jr., tied together the search for civil rights and for peace in Vietnam. The movement for world peace received special support from the World Conference on Religion and Peace (with its headquarters in New York City, beginning with a conference attended by representatives of the world's major religions in Tokyo in 1970 and its Sixth General Assembly in Italy, November 2–10, 1994), the World Council of Churches, and the National Council of Churches. The Parliament of World Religions met 100 years after the first one, again in Chicago, and this time from August 25 to September 5, 1993. Over 250 religious leaders from around the world approved "The Declaration of a Global Ethic," drafted by the Swiss-born Catholic theologian, Hans Küng, and affirming "a common set of core values found in the teaching of the religions," forming the basis of a "global ethic," stressing non-violence, solidarity, tolerance and truthfulness.[303]

The peace movement was encouraged by the efforts of Presidents Nixon and Carter to build détente with the communist powers. When President Reagan led the way in building up America's military power in 1981 and after, the peace movement in America and Western Europe was revitalized, largely because of a revived fear of nuclear war. On June 12, 1982, it was estimated that 750,000 people marched in Central Park, New York City, for arms control, at the time of the U.N. Second Special Session on Disarmament. The National Conference of Catholic Bishops presented a "Pastoral Letter on War and Peace" in 1983, condemning the use of nuclear weapons:

> Under no circumstances may nuclear weapons or other instruments of mass slaughter be used for the purpose of destroying population centers or other predominantly civilian targets. Retaliatory action which would indiscriminately and disproportionately take many wholly innocent lives . . . must also be condemned.
>
> We do not perceive any situation in which the deliberate initiation of nuclear war, on however restricted a scale, can be morally justified.[304]

As the debate in the churches continued, an "American Catholic Committee" issued a somewhat more moderate view, stressing the concept of "just war" and including the approach that "in the battle for peace, we as Christians should rely most heavily on our one unanswerable weapon: prayer."[305]

After 1985, when President Reagan and General Secretary Gorbachev began to agree on plans for the reduction of nuclear weapons and on cooperation toward peace in many areas, a real breakthrough had occurred in moving toward the ideal of peace and in permitting more effective use of the United Nations.

Along with peace, major progress was made toward freedom and justice in the continuing "black revolution" in America, and the movement toward equal rights for women. The danger to the environment from modern technology was dramatized after 1970, when the first Earth Day was observed. The pictures from space of "Spaceship Earth" also heightened popular concern over the future of this unique planet and the possibility of peace.

Televised pictures of starvation and disease in Africa stimulated large humanitarian programs, both private and public. American contributions worldwide were planned by such organizations as Bread for the World (a Christian citizens' group of 44,000 members designed to press Congress for appropriations at home and abroad, founded by the Rev. Arthur Simon in 1970), Project HOPE, World Vision, CARE, the Red Cross, and hundreds of others. Finally, American armed forces were used on a big scale to help furnish or protect humanitarian aid—as in Iraq, Bangladesh, Somalia, Bosnia and Rwanda.

Eastern European movements against dictatorial communist control were often led and supported by Christians, most notably in Poland. Similarly, the Christian pressure in Russia, Ukraine and Byelorussia (Belarus) has been widely recognized. The idealist mood seems to have bypassed many in former Yugoslavia, where ethnic and religious groups have been engaged in bitter fighting and so-called "ethnic cleansing." Yet there are reports of considerable cooperation among many individuals of these groups, as in bringing aid.[306] A special breakthrough toward peace with deep religious motivation took place in Egyptian-Israeli relations, mediated by President Carter, with the leaders representing the reconciling spirit present in the three great religions which came from the Middle East—Judaism, Christianity and Islam.

Certain idealist principles were also promoted by young people during the Vietnam War and after. Extremists, however, supported a "revolt" against the "establishment" and against authority in general. There was a reaction against the materialism, racism and militarism which some of them came to believe dominated American society. Charles A. Reich called this movement "the greening of America" and "the revolution of the new generation." He declared that "its ultimate creation will be a new and enduring wholeness and beauty—a renewed relationship of man to himself, to other men, to society, to nature, and to the land."[307] Some of this generation, represented by President Bill Clinton and Vice-President Al Gore, obtained positions of leadership in 1992, giving them a chance to try to improve the "health" of American society and to further America's idealistic purposes on the world scene. After the elections of November 1994, it can be hoped that the best ideals of both the newer and older generations can be combined.

Notes

1. Henry Brandon, *The Retreat of American Power* (Garden City, N.Y.: Doubleday and Co., 1973).

2. Lyndon B. Johnson, *Public Papers of the Presidents of the United States, 1966, Book II* (Washington, D.C.: U.S. Government Printing Office, 1967), 821 (August 14, 1966).

3. Ibid., 936, August 30, 1966.

4. Ibid., 1258.

5. Ibid., 1292, November 2, 1966.

6. Ibid., 1445.

7. Johnson, *Public Papers, 1967, I*, 2.

8. Ibid., 12.

9. Ibid., 121–22, 128.

10. Johnson, *Public Papers, 1968–69, I*, 476.

11. Robert W. Tucker, *Nation or Empire? The Debate over American Foreign Policy* (Baltimore: Johns Hopkins University Press, 1968), 138.

12. Robert E. Osgood, Robert W. Tucker and others, *America and the World: From the Truman Doctrine to Vietnam* (Baltimore: Johns Hopkins University Press, 1970), 58, footnote.

13. Lyndon B. Johnson, *The Vantage Point: Perspectives on the Presidency, 1963–1969* (New York: Holt, Rinehart and Winston, 1971), 250.

14. Ibid., 529.

15. W. W. Rostow, *The Diffusion of Power* (New York: Macmillan, 1972), 530.

16. Dean Rusk, *As I Saw It*, as told to Richard Rusk (New York: W. W. Norton, 1990), 497.

17. Johnson, *Public Papers, 1968–69, II*, 765.

18. Ibid., 1268, 1270.

19. Richard M. Nixon, "Asia After Viet Nam," *Foreign Affairs*, vol. 46, no. 1 (October 1967), 113–14, 123–24.

20. Ibid., 121.

21. Nixon, *Public Papers, 1969*, 1, 3–4.

22. Ibid., 136, February 24, 1969.

23. Ibid., 153, February 27, 1969.

24. Ibid., 434–35, 437.

25. Henry Kissinger, *White House Years* (Boston: Little, Brown and Co., 1979), 65.

26. Nixon, *Public Papers, 1969*, 520.

27. Ibid., 548, 554.

28. *The Memoirs of Richard Nixon* (New York: Grosset and Dunlap, 1978), 395.

29. Nixon, *Public Papers, 1969*, 566.

30. Ibid., 589, 591.

31. Ibid., 605.

32. Brandon, *Retreat*, 183.

33. Nixon, *Public Papers, 1969*, 727, 730–1.

34. Ibid., 905, 909.
35. Ibid., 910.
36. Nixon, *Public Papers, 1970*, 16.
37. Ibid., 408.
38. Ibid., 782.
39. Ibid., 930.
40. Nixon, *Public Papers, 1971*, 51.
41. Ibid., 140.
42. Ibid., 187–88.
43. Ibid., 218.
44. Ibid., 820.
45. Ibid., 1064.
46. Nixon, *Public Papers, 1972*, 37.
47. Ibid., 368–69.
48. Ibid., 370.
49. Ibid., 382.
50. Ibid., 619.
51. Ibid., 630.
52. Ibid., 661, 666.
53. Nixon, *Public Papers, 1973*, 13.
54. Ibid., 697.
55. Ibid., 816.
56. Ibid., 820.
57. Nixon, *Public Papers, Jan. 1–Aug. 9, 1974*, 368 (address to D.A.R.).
58. Ibid., 467 (address to U.S. Naval Academy).
59. Ibid., 490.
60. Ibid., 522.
61. Ibid., 562.
62. Ibid., 578.
63. Ibid., 629.
64. Gerald R. Ford, *Public Papers, August 9 to December 31, 1974*, 12–13.
65. Ibid., 103.
66. *Christian Science Monitor*, March 12, 1976, 2.
67. *New York Times*, March 14, 1976, 1.
68. *Christian Science Monitor*, March 15, 1976, 31.
69. Ford, *Public Papers, 1974*, 213.
70. Ford, *Public Papers, 1975, I*, 1001.
71. Ford, *Public Papers, 1976–77, II*, 1928.
72. Ibid., 1963, 1965.
73. Ibid., 1982–83.
74. Ford, *Public Papers, 1976–77, III*, 2926.
75. *A Time to Heal: The Autobiography of Gerald R. Ford* (New York: Harper and Row, 1979), 441–42.

76. Jerel A. Rosati, *The Carter Administration's Quest for Global Community* (Columbia: University of South Carolina Press, 1987).

77. Jimmy Carter, *Public Papers, 1977, I* (Washington, 1977), 1–3.

78. Ibid., 3.

79. Ibid., 5.

80. Ibid., 444–48.

81. Jimmy Carter, *Keeping Faith: Memoirs of a President* (New York: Bantam Books, 1982), 155.

82. Carter, *Public Papers, 1977, II*, 1526.

83. Ibid., 1543.

84. Carter, *Keeping Faith*, 154.

85. Carter, *Public Papers, 1977, II*, 861.

86. Ibid., 1289–90.

87. Ibid., 2042.

88. Ibid., 2053, news conference.

89. Carter, *Public Papers, 1977, I*, 956–57.

90. Carter, *Public Papers, 1978, I*, 3–4, January 1, 1978.

91. Zbigniew Brzezinski, *Power and Principle: Memoirs of the National Security Adviser, 1977–1981* (New York: Farrar, Straus, Giraux, 1983), 139.

92. Carter, *Keeping Faith*, 319.

93. Carter, *Public Papers, 1978, II*, 1520–21, September 17, 1978.

94. Ibid., 1537.

95. Carter, *Keeping Faith*, 203–4.

96. Carter, *Public Papers, 1978, I*, 1054, 1057.

97. Carter, *Public Papers, 1979, I*, 1087, 1092.

98. Carter, *Public Papers, 1978, II*, 2162, 2164.

99. Carter, *Public Papers, 1979, I*, 470–71.

100. Ibid., 519.

101. Carter, *Public Papers, 1979, II*, 1237–38.

102. Ibid., 1802–4.

103. Carter, *Public Papers, 1980, I*, 197.

104. Ibid., 307.

105. Ibid., p. v. (Foreword).

106. Carter, *Public Papers, 1980–81, II*, 1534, 1536.

107. Carter, *Public Papers, 1980–81, III*, 2336, 2339–40.

108. Ibid., 2477.

109. Ronald Reagan, *An American Life* (New York: Simon and Schuster, 1990), 219.

110. Carter, *Public Papers, 1980–81, III*, 2890–93.

111. Carter, *Keeping Faith*, 596.

112. Ronald Reagan, *Public Papers, 1981*, 1–3.

113. Ibid., 41.

114. Ibid., 57.

115. Ibid., 66, 68.

116. Ibid., 164–65, 168.

117. Reagan, *An American Life*, 263.

118. Reagan, *Public Papers, 1981*, 423.

119. Ibid., 435 (commencement address at the University of Notre Dame, May 17, 1981).

120. Ibid., 461 (commencement address at U.S. Military Academy, May 27, 1981).

121. Ibid., 519–20, June 18, 1981 (news conference).

122. Ibid., 521.

123. Ibid., 713.

124. Ibid., 724.

125. Ibid., 871.

126. Ibid., 898.

127. Ibid., 1162.

128. Ibid., 1187.

129. Ibid., 1200.

130. Reagan, *Public Papers, 1982, I*, 1–2.

131. Ibid., 78.

132. Ibid., 215.

133. Ibid., 744–47.

134. Ibid., 748.

135. Ibid., 759.

136. Ibid., 766–67.

137. Ibid., 1119–20 (at Kansas State University).

138. Reagan, *Public Papers, 1983, I*, 605.

139. Reagan explained his approach in his memoirs: Reagan, *An American Life*, 484–85.

140. Reagan, *Public Papers, 1983, I*, 364 (to National Association of Evangelicals).

141. Ibid., 437–43.

142. Ibid., 1224.

143. Reagan, *Public Papers, 1984, I*, 93.

144. Ibid., 594.

145. Reagan, *Public Papers, 1985, I*, 56–58.

146. Ibid., 271.

147. A number of Gorbachev's letters are quoted in Reagan, *An American Life*, 612–719.

148. Reagan, *Public Papers, 1985, I*, 587.

149. Ibid., 589.

150. Reagan, *Public Papers, 1985, II*, 1289.

151. Ibid., 1413.

152. Ibid., 1497.

153. Reagan, *Public Papers, 1986, I,* 2.

154. Ibid., 129.

155. Ibid., 243.

156. Reagan, *Public Papers, 1986, II,* 1369.

157. Reagan, *Public Papers, 1987, I,* 635.

158. Mikhail Gorbachev, *Perestroika: New Thinking for our Country and the World* (New York: Harper and Row, 1987), 12.

159. Ibid., 253.

160. Paul Kennedy, *The Rise and Fall of the Great Powers: Economic Changes and Military Conflicts from 1500 to 2000* (New York: Vintage Books, 1989, first published by Random House, 1987).

161. See, e.g., W. W. Rostow, "Beware of Historians Bearing False Analogies," review of Kennedy's book, *Foreign Affairs* 66 (Spring 1988): 863–68; Richard N. Haas, "The Use (and Mainly Misuse) of History," review of Kennedy's book, *Orbis* 32 (Summer 1988): 411–19; and Joseph S. Nye, Jr., "Understanding U.S. Strength," *Foreign Policy* 73 (Fall 1988): 105–29.

162. Zbigniew Brzezinski, "America's New Geostrategy," *Foreign Affairs* 66 (Spring 1988): 699.

163. Reagan, *Public Papers, 1988, I,* 3.

164. Ibid., 85.

165. Ibid., 244.

166. Ibid., 687.

167. Ibid. 722–23.

168. *New York Times,* December 8, 1988, 6.

169. Reagan, *Public Papers, 1988, II,* 1720, 1722. Secretary of State George Shultz recently described the change of spirit at the United Nations, September 26, 1988, after Reagan spoke to the General Assembly: "As I went from meeting to meeting . . . seeing foreign ministers and heads of government from every part of the world, I could hear echoes of the president's refrain. It was as if the whole world had breathed a deep sigh of relief. An immense tension had gone out of the system." George P. Shultz, *Turmoil and Triumph: My Years as Secretary of State* (New York: Scribner's, 1993), 1131.

170. George Bush, *Public Papers, 1989, I,* 1–3.

171. Ibid., 81.

172. Ibid., 143.

173. Ibid., 556.

174. Ibid., 669.

175. Bush, *Public Papers, 1989, II,* 917.

176. Ibid., 920–21.

177. Ibid., 1080.

178. Ibid., 1249.

179. Ibid., 1581–82.

180. Ibid., 1620.

181. Ibid., 1646.

182. Ibid., 1722–23.

183. Bush, *Public Papers, 1990, I*, 1.

184. Ibid., 134.

185. Ibid., 243.

186. Ibid., 265.

187. Ibid., 730–32.

188. Ibid., 865.

189. Bush, *Public Papers, 1990, II*, 1107–9.

190. Ibid., 1203–4.

191. Ibid., 1218–22.

192. Ibid., 1331.

193. Ibid., 1348.

194. Ibid., 1581.

195. Ibid., 1623–26.

196. Ibid., 1720.

197. Ibid., 1738, 1740.

198. Bush, *Public Papers, 1991*, 13.

199. Ibid., 44.

200. Ibid., 79.

201. Ibid., 81.

202. Ibid., 187–88.

203. Ibid., 222.

204. Ibid., 279.

205. Ibid., 297.

206. Ibid., 331.

207. Ibid., 366–68.

208. Ibid., 472.

209. Ibid., 510, 512–13.

210. Ibid., 566.

211. Ibid., 703.

212. *Department of State Dispatch*, published by the Bureau of Public Affairs of the Department of State, Washington, D.C. (hereafter called *Dispatch*), 12 August 1991, 596.

213. *Dispatch*, August 19, 1991, 615–17.

214. *Dispatch*, September 2, 1991, 647.

215. *Dispatch*, September 30, 1991, 718, 720–21.

216. *Dispatch*, October 7, 1991, 739–40.

217. *Dispatch*, November 4, 1991, 803–4.

218. *Dispatch*, November 11, 1991, 824.

219. *Dispatch*, November 18, 1991, 839 (address to the Asia Society, New York City).

220. *Dispatch*, December 16, 1991, 893 (address at Princeton University).

221. *Dispatch*, December 30, 1991, 911–12.

222. *Dispatch*, January 13, 1992, 23–25.

223. *Dispatch*, January 20, 1992, 38.

224. *Dispatch*, February 3, 1992, 78.

225. Ibid., 73.

226. Ibid., 76.

227. *Dispatch*, April 6, 1992, 263–66.

228. *Dispatch*, April 27, 1992, 325 (address before Chicago Council on Foreign Relations).

229. *Dispatch*, June 15, 1992, 461–62; and July 1992, vol. 3, suppl. 4, pp. 1–35.

230. *Dispatch*, June 22, 1992, 488. See also pp. 481–504.

231. *New York Times*, June 15, 1992, A8.

232. *Dispatch*, December 7, 1992, 865–66.

233. *Dispatch*, January 4, 1993, 2.

234. *Dispatch*, January 11, 1993, 21.

235. *Dispatch*, December 28, 1992, 913.

236. *New York Times*, December 16, 1992, C18 (at Texas A&M University).

237. *Dispatch*, January 11, 1993, 13–14.

238. Ibid., 16, 19.

239. *Dispatch*, January 25, 1993, 45–49.

240. *Dispatch*, February 1, 1993, 57–58.

241. *St. Louis Post-Dispatch*, January 21, 1993, C1.

242. *Dispatch*, March 1, 1993, 114–15, 118.

243. *Dispatch*, April 5, 1993, 193.

244. *Dispatch*, April 12, 1993, 225.

245. *Dispatch*, February 8, 1993, 74.

246. See *Christian Science Monitor*, May 13, 1993, 3.

247. Al Richman, "American Public Attitudes Toward U.S. International Involvement in the Post-Cold War Era," paper at 1994 Annual Meeting of the International Studies Association, Washington, DC, March 29, 1994 (in the Summary).

248. In Abstract of Ronald H. Hinckly and Eugene R. Wittkopf, "The Domestication of American Foreign Policy: Public Opinion in the Post Cold War Era," paper at the Annual Convention of the International Studies Association, Washington, D.C., March 28–April, 1, 1994.

249. John E. Rielly, "The Public Mood at Mid-Decade," *Foreign Policy*, no. 98 (Spring 1995): 76–93.

250. Steven Kull, "The U.S. Isn't Averse to Peacekeeping," *Christian Science Monitor*, June 21, 1995, 19. Kull's University of Maryland program polled 1,204 Americans nation-wide. He reported that a *Newsweek* poll found that 61 percent supported sending U.S. ground troops to Bosnia "to join U.N.

forces in the efforts to maintain peace and protect relief operations." A later poll showed that a majority would be willing to see the loss of life by 3,500 American soldiers in a successful U.N. effort to pacify Bosnia and stop ethnic cleansing (*St. Louis Post-Dispatch*, July 25, 1995, 13B).

251. *New York Times*, January 26, 1994, A17.

252. *Dispatch*, September 27, 1993, 652.

253. Ibid., 667–68 (address to the National War College, September 23, 1993).

254. Ibid., 650, 653.

255. *Dispatch*, May 16, 1994, 321.

256. *Dispatch Supplement*, January 9–16, 1994, 3–4.

257. *Dispatch*, August 1, 1994, 517.

258. *Dispatch*, January 9, 1995, 17.

259. *Dispatch*, September 27, 1993, 664 (address to Johns Hopkins University School of Advanced International Studies, Washington, DC, 21 September 1993).

260. *Christian Science Monitor*, December 15, 1994, 3.

261. *Dispatch*, September 13, 1993, 622–24.

262. *Dispatch*, December 20, 1993, 873.

263. *Dispatch*, May 30, 1994, 345–46.

264. *Dispatch Supplement*, September 1993, 7–8, 11.

265. *New York Times*, July 26, 1994, A5.

266. *Dispatch*, July 4, 1994, 445–46.

267. *New York Times*, July 12, 1995, A7.

268. *Dispatch*, October 18, 1993, 718.

269. *Dispatch*, January 30, 1995, 53.

270. *Dispatch*, February 20, 1995, 118–19.

271. *Dispatch*, May 1, 1995, 372–76 (address to Foreign Policy Association, New York City, April 24, 1995).

272. *Dispatch*, May 22, 1995, 416 (statement of May 18, 1995).

273. Bob Dole, "Shaping America's Global Future," *Foreign Policy* (Spring 1995): 29, 33, 34, 41

274. Newt Gingrich, *To Renew America* (New York: HarperCollins Publishers, 1995), 185–87.

275. Warren Christopher, "America's Leadership, America's Opportunity," *Foreign Policy* (Spring 1995): 6.

276. Pope John Paul II, *Crossing the Threshold of Hope*, ed. Vittorio Messori, trans. Jenny McPhee and Martha McPhee (New York: Alfred A. Knopf, 1994), 185–87.

277. Vaclav Havel, "A Call for Sacrifice: The Co-Responsibility of the West," *Foreign Affairs* (March/April 1994): 2–7.

278. *St. Louis Post-Dispatch*, July 10, 1994, 3B.

279. *Christian Science Monitor*, June 9, 1995, 18.

280. *New York Times*, May 18, 1994.

281. William J. Bennett, *The Book of Virtues: A Treasury of Great Moral Stories* (New York: Simon and Schuster, 1993); Stephen L. Carter, *The Culture of Disbelief: How American Law and Politics Trivializes Religious Devotion* (New York: Harper Basic Books, 1993); Gertrude Himmelfarb, *The De-Moralization of Society: From Victorian Virtues to Modern Values* (New York: Knopf, 1995); Douglas Johnston and Cynthia Sampson, *Religion: The Missing Dimension of Statecraft* (New York: Oxford University Press, 1994); George A. Marsden, *The Soul of the American University: From Protestant Establishment to Established Nonbelief* (New York: Oxford University Press, 1994); James Q. Wilson, *The Moral Sense* (New York: Free Press, 1993); Robert Wuthnow, *Sharing the Journey: Support Groups and America's New Quest for Community* (New York: Free Press, 1994).

282. Andrew Young, "Global Vision: An Interview with Andrew Young," *Christian Century*, June 21–28, 1995, 638–41.

283. Robert N. Bellah, "Civil Religion in America," in *The Religious Situation, 1968* (Boston: Beacon Press, 1973), 330–56; first published in *Daedelus*, vol. 96, no. 1 (Winter 1967).

284. Elton Trueblood, *Abraham Lincoln: Theologian of American Anguish* (New York: Harper and Row, 1973), written during the Vietnam War.

285. Nixon, *Public Papers, 1970*, 82.

286. Carter, *Public Papers, 1977, II*, 2127.

287. Carter, *Public Papers, 1978, II*, 1703.

288. Reagan, *Public Papers, 1982, I*, 109.

289. Reagan, *Public Papers, 1986, I*, 11.

290. Reagan, *Public Papers, 1988, I*, 719.

291. Bush, *Public Papers, 1991, I*, 70–71.

292. *Christian Century*, May 3, 1993, 234–35.

293. *Time*, April 5, 1993, 49–51, 43–48.

294. *New York Times*, November 14, 1993, Y19.

295. *New York Times*, January 27, 1994, A11.

296. *Christian Science Monitor*, February 17, 1995, 19.

297. *New York Times*, July 13, 1995, A1, A10.

298. *Christian Science Monitor*, July 24, 1995, 19.

299. *The Religious Situation, 1968* (Boston: Beacon Press, 1968).

300. *The Religious Situation, 1969* (Boston: Beacon Press, 1969).

301. U.S. News and World Report Book, *The Religious Awakening in America* (Washington, D.C., 1972).

302. Reported in *Christian Science Monitor*, May 3, 1993, 14.

303. Hans Küng, "The Declaration of a Global Ethic," *National Catholic Reporter*, September 24, 1993, 11–14.

304. National Conference of Catholic Bishops, *The Challenge of Peace: God's Promises and Our Response* (Washington, D.C.: United States Catholic

Conference, 1983), p. v.

305. American Catholic Committee, *Justice and War in the Nuclear Age* (Lanham, Md.: University Press of America, 1983).

306. Elizabeth Salater, "The Serbian Orthodox Church: Space for Reconciliation," *One World*, May 1993 (World Council of Churches).

307. Charles A. Reich, *The Greening of America* (New York: Bantam Books, 1970, originally published by Random House), 2.

CHAPTER VIII.

Conclusion:
America's Record and Outlook

This conclusion will summarize the record of America, note the current challenges briefly, and speculate on the outlook as guided by past history. The last three centuries seem to have paved the way for the hoped-for "new world order," first in the creation of democratic nationalism in the West (1729–1871) and then in the struggle for a liberal internationalism since 1871. Perhaps there is, as Americans often believe, an innate desire in the majority of human beings for freedom, dignity, basic welfare and peace.

The Record

Two characteristics of American foreign policy have been noted in this study as especially impressive: (1) the strong thread of idealism as expressed throughout by leaders, particularly the Presidents; and (2) the regularity of the cyclical trends, extending America's world involvement and expanding American and world democracy.

Positive Expectations

Much American history since 1776 seems almost contemporary. And the "founding fathers" felt too that they were building on foundations already there. Lincoln's position came from the Declaration of Independence—from Jefferson and Washington. Wilson built on Lincoln, and Franklin D. Roosevelt and his successors were inspired by Wilson's vision of peace. So the positive expectations of many American leaders often seem timely for today and tomorrow. In a Biblical sense, Americans can feel "surrounded by so great a cloud of witnesses" (Hebrews 12:1), watching whether America will live up to its promise and even surpass past expectations.

American leaders stressed freedom and moral principle and great hope for their country. A few of their statements should be repeated. In 1776, John Adams felt that the adoption of the Declaration of Independence should be celebrated each year "from one end of the continent to the other, from this time forward, forevermore." Franklin wrote from France in 1777 that it was a "Common Observation here, that our Cause is the *Cause of all Mankind*, and that we are fighting for their Liberty in defending our own." Washington, in his First Inaugural Address in 1789, declared that "the preservation of the sacred fire of liberty, and the destiny of the Republican Model of Government are justly considered as *deeply*, perhaps as *finally*, staked on the experiment entrusted to the hands of the American people." Jefferson, in his First Inaugural, spoke of "a rising nation, spread over a wide and fruitful land . . . advancing rapidly to destinies beyond the reach of mortal eye. . . ."

John Adams wrote in 1813 that "the foundation of an American Navy . . . is a grand era in the history of the world. The consequences of it will be greater than any of us can foresee." John Quincy Adams, when Minister to England in 1816, gave a toast: ". . . May our country always be successful, but whether successful or otherwise always right. I disclaim as unsound a patriotism incompatible with the principles of eternal justice."

Dr. C. F. Schmidt-Phiseldek, from Denmark, predicted in 1820 a picture of "future grandeur and happiness" for the American nation, believing that July 4, 1776, "pointed out the commencement of a new period in the history of the world," based especially on the liberty of the human mind. Daniel Webster in 1826 averred that "if we cherish the virtues and principles of our fathers, Heaven will assist us to carry on the work of human liberty and human happiness." De Tocqueville in the 1830s saw the rise of America "as a fact new to the world—a fact fraught with such portentous consequences as to baffle the efforts even of the imagination." Andrew Jackson, in his Farewell Address (1837), said: "Providence has showered on this favored land blessings without number, and has chosen us as the guardians of freedom, to preserve it for the benefit of the human race."

Lincoln said in February 1860: "Let us have faith that right makes might, and in that faith, let us, to the end, dare to do our duty as we understand it." He felt (1861) that the "great principle" of America "was that which may promise that in due time the weight should be lifted from the shoulders of all men, and that *all* should have a equal chance." Lincoln asked America in 1863 to resolve "that this nation under God shall have a new birth of freedom" and in his Second Inaugural he urged Americans "to do all which may achieve and cherish a just and lasting peace among ourselves and with all nations."

Woodrow Wilson was perhaps the most idealistic of the Presidents, expressing his view that "the idea of America is to serve humanity." He declared that "the world must be made safe for democracy" and that all nations, large or small, should be protected by a system of collective security so that there "never is such a war again." But America was not ready in 1919 to follow his leadership, turning inward again instead. Wilson responded by writing that "our civilization cannot survive materially unless it be redeemed spiritually."

Walter Lippman in 1938 asserted that "a new power exists which is destined to be a successor of Rome and of Britain as the giver of peace, and that its mission is to prepare itself for the accomplishment of that destiny." President Roosevelt, early in 1941, asked that the "Four Freedoms" be established "everywhere in the world." That year, Henry R. Luce called on America to be the "Good Samaritan, really believing again that it is more blessed to give than to receive," and to be "the powerhouse of the ideals of Freedom and Justice. . . ." At the end of his life in 1945, Roosevelt asserted his goal of peace: "We seek peace— enduring peace. More than an end to war. We want an end to the beginning of all wars. . . ."

General Douglas MacArthur, in accepting the surrender of Japan after the atom bombs were dropped in 1945, called for a "spiritual recrudescence and improvement of human character": "It must be of the spirit if we are to save the flesh." George F. Kennan affirmed in 1947 his belief that Providence had made the American people's "entire security dependent on their pulling themselves together and accepting the responsibility of moral and political leadership their history plainly intended them to bear."

President Eisenhower and Secretary of State Dulles both expressed their faith in the people behind the "Iron Curtain," believing that freedom would come to them. Eisenhower predicted in 1959 that "if we make ourselves worthy of America's ideals . . . the world will come to know that it is free men who carry forward the true promise of human progress and dignity."

The youthful President Kennedy, in his Inaugural Address, pledged the nation to "assure the survival and success of liberty." In Berlin in 1963, he declared that "freedom is indivisible, and when one man is enslaved, all are not free." His final words were: "We in this country, in this generation, are, by destiny rather than by choice, the watchmen on the walls of world freedom," and "the righteousness of our cause must always underlie our strength, for as was written long ago, 'Except the Lord keep the city, the watchmen waketh but in vain.'" Dr. Martin Luther King, Jr., called for peace and reconciliation among races and nations, based on non-violence and love.

Similarly, all the Presidents since Kennedy have expressed their moral and spiritual values (as shown under "Idealism" in the last chapter). Many Presidents and other leaders have been virtual "prophets" of American democracy and American destiny. Thus, the traditional values of America, based on a Judeo-Christian foundation, have ever remained strong, and continue to be powerful in our own time.

"The First Universal Nation"

Ben J. Wattenberg used this term as the title for his 1991 book. This title implies the immigration into the United States from all areas of the world, the expanding use of the English language, the widespread intellectual and cultural impact of America (as through its universities and universal television like CNN), the world impact of many American corporations, and the spread of democracy and the market system. Similarly, America includes the major religions of the world, with the great majority Christian (Catholic and Protestant), but with significant numbers of other religions (as six million Jews and three or four million Muslims). All this continues as the world as a whole becomes more interdependent. Wattenberg believes that "for five hundred years, America has been the biggest story in the world," and reminds us of the recent influx of Hispanics (now 9 percent) and Asians (5 percent), in addition to the Europeans and African-Americans (12 percent).[1]

Wattenberg mentions also that Alexis de Tocqueville coined the phrase "'American Exceptionalism' to express the idea that Americans were different."[2] This concept of the unique quality of America is in contrast to the belief that America was becoming an "ordinary country," especially in foreign relations. This idea was rather common in the 1970s, perhaps partly because of the impact of the dominant introvert mood (1967–87).[3]

This exposition as a whole has concentrated on the positive aspects of American development, in relation to America's expanding role. Although negative aspects are often pointed out, these can be regarded as challenges which Americans have endeavored to overcome in trying to fulfill the ideals of liberty, justice and equality. The evil institution of slavery brought Africans in chains to the continent, but other Americans moved to eliminate slavery and ultimately enable many African-Americans to achieve the ideals. Similarly, native Americans have often been mistreated as other Americans or immigrants moved west. Immigrants to America were also often discriminated against by those already here, but they too were later assimilated and granted relative equal positions of opportunity. The ideal goals of America are probably not completely attainable by imperfect human beings, but remain as challenges to be met. Samuel Huntington's study, *American Politics: The Promise of Disharmony*, leads him to aver that "the United States has no meaning, no identity, no political culture or even history apart from its ideals of liberty and democracy and the continuing effort of Americans to realize their ideals."[4]

America's World Involvement (Introversion-Extroversion)

Although the United States began as a small independent nation of 2.8 million people in the eastern part of the continent, with a desire to be separated from the rest of the world in a political and military sense, yet the course of history created a huge continental nation between the Atlantic and Pacific, ever more deeply involved around the world. The census of 1990 showed nearly 249,000,000 people.

Outside challenges especially brought American responses which resulted in the expansion of American territory and power. Another part of American influence abroad has been based on the desire to trade (pressing "freedom of the seas" and an "open door" policy) and on humanitarian motives (led by church missionaries building schools, colleges and hospitals, and by philanthropic organizations). It was during the extrovert phases that America pushed outward diplomatically and militarily, often with a sense of "manifest destiny." In the first extrovert phase (1798–1824) after independence, the challenges from Europe prompted the huge Louisiana Purchase, the further expansion of the West (after the War of 1812 with Britain), the cession from Spain of Florida and its claims to part of the Oregon Territory, and the

Monroe Doctrine which warned Europe against any further intervention or colonization in the Western hemisphere.

In the second extrovert phase (1844–71), America secured the whole Southwest, half of the Oregon Territory, and Alaska, rounding out the continental territory. The third phase (1891–1918) saw the United States pushing overseas—freeing Cuba and adding the Philippines, Guam, Puerto Rico, American Samoa, and later the Virgin Islands. In World War I, closer relations were established with Britain and France, and Americans were made more aware of the international problems of the world.

The fourth phase (1940–66/67) covered World War II and its aftermath. American troops occupied Japan and parts of Korea, Germany, Italy and Austria, and America received the Japanese-mandated Pacific islands under United Nations trusteeship. The United States felt impelled to help Europe recover from the war (the Marshall Plan), and to pledge itself to defend Western Europe (through NATO) in the face of a Soviet communist threat. The Korean War stimulated the United States to pledge itself to the defense of South Korea, Japan, Formosa and Southeast Asia. American military and naval bases circled the globe. The Vietnam War, beginning in 1965, helped defend the rest of Southeast Asia, even though South Vietnam, Laos and Cambodia were conquered by communist North Vietnam.

During the subsequent introvert phase (1966/67–86/87), it was partly the challenge and danger of the nuclear arms race which induced the efforts for détente with the Soviet Union and China, and for the limitation of nuclear arms. The fifth extrovert phase (1986/87–   ) opened as the communist system was beginning to collapse in Eastern Europe and the Soviet Union. With the "cold war" apparently ending, new challenges arose from Iran, Iraq, the breakup of the Soviet Union and especially Yugoslavia (with its bitter fighting and "ethnic cleansing"), the famine and civil war in a number of African countries (notably Somalia, as shown on American television), and the continuing and rising tension between Israel and the occupied Palestinians. These challenges seemed to arise almost immediately, contrary to the common expectation of peace and tranquillity following the end of the tension with the Soviet Union. America seemed somehow to be involved by her ideals in almost all areas of the world, even as domestic problems captured major attention. The world seemed close, through instantaneous communication, swift transportation, and growing trade.

America's Tripartite Development

America, along with Western Civilization, has reached its major goals in a succession of moods of rationalism ("enlightenment"), realism (struggle), and idealism (consolidation). In the first "grand period" (1587–1729), the Americans built a Protestant Christian society, emphasizing faith and justice. In the second such period (1729–1871), an independent democratic republic was created, stressing liberty and equality (the democratic "middle class" nationalism of the West).

The third grand period, beginning in 1871, saw the United States stepping out more clearly on the world stage, apparently seeking to fulfill its concept of "world mission," based on its own foundation principles of moral justice and responsible freedom. This portended a search for a liberal democratic internationalism, as the industrial revolution created a new laboring class and began tying the world more closely together physically. In terms of the tripartite development, the *rational* preparation of America's world power took place from 1871 to 1917–18. Then the democratic powers faced a tremendous *realist* struggle (1917/18–66/67) against, first, the expanding fascist states and, then, the communists. By 1967, the "cold war" between democracy and communism was showing signs of coming to an end; as the period progressed, *idealist* hopes for peace developed among the major powers, along with the dream of a safe, just and free "world order." To secure such a dream, American power and will seemed essential. America and its allies had held the line for 40 years against the communist threat, and then they were astonished that this communist "world" began to break up without a major war. This left the United States as the only superpower in the political and military sense, as many nations moved toward democracy.

The Expansion of Democracy

One of the most encouraging developments for America and for peace has been the establishment of other democratic nations, particularly since World War II. Democratic states seldom go to war with one another. The three defeated fascist states moved steadily toward democracy and free enterprise—with Japan under American occupation and West Germany under American-British-French occupation.

Samuel Huntington describes three waves of democracy since

American independence: (1) 1828–1926, (2) 1943–62, and (3) since 1974.[5] In the first wave, the United States influenced the slow democratic trend by example. During the second wave, direct American and allied power was vital in the spread of democracy. The third wave (with 30 countries moving to democracy by 1990) seems to have been promoted by the steady success of the major democratic powers, particularly the United States, the nations of Western Europe, and Japan, and by rising idealism worldwide. An important factor was democratic broadcasting, as by the British Broadcasting Corporation (BBC), the Voice of America, Radio Free Europe, and Radio Liberty.

Western Europe, the United States and Canada brought special pressure on Eastern Europe at the Helsinki Conference, August 1975, where a permanent Conference on Security and Cooperation in Europe (CSCE) was established. The U.S. Congress in 1974 had stopped aid to nations which engaged in gross violations of human rights. President Carter placed special emphasis on human rights. President Reagan urged a crusade for democracy in his June 1982 address to the British Parliament, and Congress created the National Endowment for Democracy in 1984, designed to encourage and support both private and public help for democratic institutions abroad. Huntington estimates that the percentage of democratic states increased from 25 percent in 1973 to 45 percent in 1990.[6] Joshua Muravchik similarly covers systematically the evidence for the recent virtual explosion of democracy around the world, with the exception of much of Africa.[7] The moves toward democracy in Eastern Europe and in the former republics of the Soviet Union were particularly encouraging. Latin America has, for the first time, become almost completely democratic (Peru moved toward temporary dictatorship in 1992, and Guatemala tried late in May 1993).

The expansion of democracy has also naturally encouraged more freedom of religion. The growing influence of Christianity has been prominent in Eastern Europe and the European states of the former Soviet Union. Political democracy and religious freedom often combine to promote peace at home and abroad. However, religious intolerance promotes fighting, especially when combined with long-standing ethnic conflicts (as in the former Yugoslavia).

Inside the United States, the basic principles of democracy appear strengthened when the liberal phase of the liberal-conservative cycle appears. According to the Schlesingers, liberalism has come seven times since 1765, at approximately 30-year intervals. The inauguration of Bill

Clinton as President on January 20, 1993, seemed to mark the beginning of a 15- to 17-year phase of liberalism, with stronger emphasis on human rights, the general welfare and peace. President Bush may already have started in a liberal direction, at home with higher taxes, and abroad as in sending troops to Somalia for humanitarian purposes. The success of the Republicans in the 1994 election raises questions as to whether a liberal phase may not yet have begun, or whether perhaps a "new liberalism" contains some conservative values in an age of idealism.

Current Challenges

After World War II and the 40 years of "cold war" in the nuclear age (including the Korean and Vietnamese Wars), most Americans were filled with a sense of euphoria when communism in Europe seemed to collapse.

But it soon became clear that new challenges were arising or being perceived, and that the United States would be involved, especially as the only remaining superpower and also as a nation with democratic ideals and certain guiding moral principles. These challenges were internal as well as external, and it was widely felt that America's prestige and influence would partly depend on the degree of respect given by others to American culture and power, as well as America's own self-esteem.

When the superpower "cold war" was ended and the communist dictatorships collapsed, many political-military restraints were lifted. This enabled small nations to dream of unopposed expansion (for example, Iraq), or ethnic groups within a nation to dream of independence (as Croatia or Bosnia) or wider control (as Serbia). The ethnic-racial tension in the world has caused Senator Daniel Moynihan to describe the result in the title of his 1993 book *Pandaemonium*.[8] Zbigniew Brzezinski (President Carter's national security adviser) gives his estimate of the situation in the title of his 1993 book *Out of Control*:

> This book is not a prediction but an urgent warning. It is about the state of global politics today, about what may happen by the onset of the twenty-first century, and also about *what must not be allowed to happen*.[9]

John Lewis Gaddis depicts a growing struggle between two ideas:

fragmentation (as in Yugoslavia) versus integration (as in the European Community or the United Nations).[10]

Among some of the political-military challenges America and the world face are: the ethnic fighting in Yugoslavia and elsewhere, the future of Cambodia (which appears quite hopeful after the success of the elections, May 23–28, 1993, under the supervision of 22,000 United Nations peacekeepers), dealing with the Communist states (China, Vietnam, North Korea, Cuba), the political-economic crisis in Russia and the other former Soviet republics as they seek to change their societies fundamentally, dangerous international crises (as between Israel on the one hand and the Arab states and the Palestinians on the other, with much hope and slow progress since the Israeli-Palestinian agreement of September 13, 1993), and the threat of further nuclear proliferation. The *New York Times* recently identified 48 ethnic wars in progress: 9 in Europe, 7 in the Middle East and North Africa, 15 in Africa south of the Sahara, 13 in Asia, and 4 in Latin America.[11] Many struggling nations—such as Somalia, Cambodia (successful U.N. operation), Liberia, Zaire, or Haiti (current U.N. operation)—have been or are in need of international "tutelage," to use Robert I. Rotberg's term.[12]

Special global problems include strengthening the United Nations, protecting the environment (atmosphere, oceans, land resources), dealing with the population explosion in the third world, reducing disease epidemics (as AIDS), and caring for the millions of refugees.

In the economic area, there is the growing inequality between the rich and poor nations, the problems of maintaining and increasing international trade (along with the challenge of the huge U.S. trade deficit), and the improvement of America's foreign aid programs.

In the cultural sphere, there are religious-cultural conflicts (especially sharpened by the extremists), lack of understanding among the great religious groups (such as Islam and Christianity), the continuance of illiteracy and poor education, and the power of extreme secularism. Many observers seem to agree with Brzezinski when he writes: "*The global crisis of the spirit has to be overcome if humanity is to assert command over its destiny,*" and "the recognition both of the complexity and the contingency of the human condition thus underlies the *political* need for shared moral consciousness."[13]

The crisis of the spirit is also reflected in America's internal challenges, such as the danger of excessive materialism, racism, or militarism. There is abuse of drugs, frightening crime rates, too much immorality, and the decline of the family. There are sharp problems of poverty and unemployment, inadequate health care, and defective education. Since the end of the cold war, there is also the difficult task of converting a defense economy to civilian production.

Speaking in positive terms, America faces the special "domestic" problem of realizing the necessity of American leadership in establishing five types of needed international order:

(1) An international order of *force*, with as much international authority (especially United Nations) as possible, along with a large degree of disarmament; in the meantime, the United States and its allies must "hold the line" against aggression.

(2) An international order of *peaceful settlement*, stressing "preventive diplomacy" as much as possible and using mediation, arbitration, and the United Nations instrumentalities (the Security Council, the International Court of Justice, panels of the General Assembly, and the Secretary General and his staff).

(3) An international *legal* order, covering the oceans, outer space, human rights, and the rights and duties of nations in general.

(4) An international economic-social order, to deal with hunger, disease, education, and the promotion of wider prosperity.

(5) An international cultural-moral-spiritual order, in which the contributions of different nations, cultures, and religions are better understood and prized, along with ideals of a world community, freedom for the spirit of man, the importance of the individual, the spiritual nature of humanity and the universe, and motivations toward justice, reconciliation, and compassion.

Finally, America may face the temptation of a new "imperialism" as it continues to be the major world leader.[14] This could include the danger of "overextension" which has promoted the ultimate decline of Great Powers in the past.[15] Or, on the other hand, the United States could consider partial withdrawal from world leadership to concentrate on its domestic problems, in reaction to the long and successful effort to defeat fascist and communist totalitarianism.

The Outlook: Extrovert Democratic Internationalism

A nation (like an individual) is probably created for a worthwhile purpose outside of itself. Its development would depend on strong and usually successful responses to powerful challenges (as Arnold J. Toynbee has stressed in his *Study of History*). America has faced many challenges successfully, with its leaders focusing on "positive expectations" throughout. Thus the current challenges, though numerous, can be welcomed, in a sense, by a nation which believes in seeking worthwhile goals for humanity as well as for itself.

These problems to be faced are not expected to be solved in the short run, but rather in the long run, and then only provisionally. The cycles of American history point toward the expectation that the American people will stand strong in world affairs for the next 20 years or so, at least (in a mood of extroversion), long enough to help lead the world, in partnership with like-minded nations, to some hopeful solutions.

Furthermore, the goals America is expected to seek are *idealist* in nature—greater peace, wider justice, and more responsible freedom. American leaders have usually maintained these idealist goals, but this is a time of special hope as it is a world-involved idealist period in American history (since 1967, and especially since 1982)—by the end of which the ideal of "liberal democratic internationalism" can be expected to be consolidated. This goal began in its age of preparation (1871–1918) and then precipitated a sharp international struggle (1918–67). This is the time for synthesis (1967 to, say, 2014), according to the length of such past cycles—a time for achieving a progressive balance of the forces which make for peace, justice and freedom.

In a period of idealism, it is proper to expect some "good surprises," such as the trip of President Sadat of Egypt to Jerusalem in 1977 which led to the Egyptian-Israeli peace, or even to huge hopeful surprises, such as the collapse of the Berlin Wall or, even greater, the collapse of communism. In contrast, in the preceding revolutionary power struggle, "bad surprises" seemed more common—such as the American decision to reject the League of Nations in 1919, or the rise of Hitler to world power along with the Holocaust, or the development of the atom bomb. Yet even these "evil" events could help lead to provisional solutions to some problems. For example, Hitler and Tojo awakened America to its worldwide responsibilities; and the nuclear weapons seem to have promoted the probable end of war between the major powers, since the knowledge of nuclear bombs and their terror will remain in spite of disarmament.[16] "Bad surprises" also seem to come in the time of idealism, but then the responses may usually be positive or "good," as when the Iraqi aggression in 1990 brought about the world's first real "collective security" response through the United Nations, or the famine and civil war in Somalia which resulted in a major military effort for humanitarian purposes Perhaps even the Bosnian crisis can bring a hopeful response in terms of preventing future similar crises.

As the United States presses outward in an idealist period, international cooperation and partnership is the likely approach, rather than unilateralism or imperialism, although unilateralism was given some increased influence by the Republican Congressional victory in 1994. Woodrow Wilson again seems to be the prophet for our times, as the United Nations becomes more important and more efficient and the United States is in a position of unchallenged power. The extrovert mood should enable America to use its military force when needed, and America's idealism should guide such force into prudent uses and often for humanitarian purposes (as in Somalia). Furthermore, America's influence should also be based much more on the elements of "soft power," to use the term coined by Joseph F. Nye, Jr., to cover such influences as ideology (democratic principles) and cultural attraction.[17]

Recent polls have shown majority public support for extrovert actions, particularly when undertaken for humanitarian purposes. In April 1993, the use of U.S. military force for "primarily humanitarian reasons" was supported by 84 percent, as opposed to "vital military and economic interests" of the United States. Those who believe the United States had done a good job in Somalia numbered 77 percent, and 57 percent supported the United Nations intervention in Cambodia (where 22,000 U.N. peacekeeping forces were placed). Even more, 79 percent said they would back U.S. intervention on humanitarian grounds in Haiti or Afghanistan. U.N. peacekeeping in Bosnia so far was supported by 52 percent. Only 43 percent supported cuts in defense spending as compared to 63 percent in December 1991.[18] Walter Russell Mead supports America's current idealist position in his arguments against the belief that the United States is a "modern secular state":

> Nothing could be farther from the truth: the overwhelming majority of Americans are obsessed with questions of value and spirit. It is not just that 40 percent of the American population goes to church; the roots of American individualism and the national "pursuit of happiness" go back to the radical transcendent Protestantism of thinkers like Emerson and Thoreau. . . . American society has as messianic and as transcendental views of its role in the world as any country in history.[19]

Positive Expectations (continued)

Many current observers have special hope in America's continuing world role, while they recognize the sharp challenges. In the economic area, Henry R. Nau sees the United States continuing to lead the world economy, rather than going into decline.[20] Joseph F. Nye, Jr., believes the historical situation makes American leadership essential in this new global age:

> The United States has both the traditional hard power resources and the new soft power resources to meet the challenges of transnational interdependence. The critical question is whether it will have the political leadership and strategic vision to convert these power resources into real influence in a transitional period of world politics. . . .
> . . . The United States remains the largest and richest power with the greatest capacity to shape the future. And in a democracy, the choices are the people's.[21]

Eric Sevareid sees the hope for America in its idealism:

> The puzzle of America's destiny will not be found in outer space, but in inner space, terra firma inner man. . . .
> . . . Is it possible that we can see the emergence of Altruistic Man? The instinct for it is there among us. There *is* a thread of goodness running through the American system. There is a chance that it can be woven into a fabric.[22]

A pastor and mission volunteer challenges America from India:

> Does my country know its awesome power? Does my country know its remarkable opportunity? Do my brothers and sisters in the United States sense the impact they have on others—such as those I meet in India? Does my country know its responsibility?[23]

He also notes that many "see us as people who can make the difference for good in our time."

Former President Nixon reminded Americans that "while the communists have lost, we have not won until we prove that the ideas of freedom can provide the peoples of the former Soviet Union with a better life."[24] In his 1992 book *Seize the Moment*, he calls for "the renewal of America":

If we meet the challenge of peace, our legacy will be not just that we saved the world from communism but that we helped make the world safe for freedom.

.... America preeminently represents three values: freedom, opportunity, and respect for the individual human being. These values transcend our borders. They rise from the human spirit, and they speak directly to that spirit.

... The world needs U.S. leadership militarily, politically, and economically. Most of all, it needs our leadership in the critical area of ideas.

... We are privileged to live at a moment of history like none most people have ever experienced or will ever experience again. We must seize the moment not just for ourselves but for others.[25]

With Bosnia and Somalia in mind, James N. Wall, in a memo to George Bush and Bill Clinton during the Presidential campaign, urged the new President to seek a new vision:

... I write to say that as president in a post-cold-war era you have a rare opportunity to move toward a new vision—one in which you could seek to transform the world from a collection of warring ethnic and national groups into a coalition of communities willing to reach out and serve others.[26]

Former Ambassador Robert G. Neumann envisions the new role of the United Nations, but adds that if the Security Council is to act collectively, "there has to be a catalyst" and "that catalyst is, and for a long time to come, can only be, the United States. . . ." He adds:

Firm, constructive leadership by an American president is capable of arousing, over time, pride in the role that the United States is called upon to take. This is not "manifest destiny." . . . It is only sheer necessity to move, gradually, haltingly, messily toward a somewhat more orderly and less murderous world.[27]

James W. Hoge, Jr., Editor of *Foreign Affairs*, refers to the topics fully examined in the 1992/93 "turn-of-the-year" issue:

The picture of the world that emerges is unsettling and hardly allows the United States to relax or withdraw. The United States can turn inward to address domestic problems, but as a complement—not a substitute—for the guiding American hand in a still dangerous world.[28]

General Colin L. Powell, Chairman of the Joint Chiefs of Staff, felt at the end of 1992 that America is obligated to lead and wondered "what Lincoln would think were he here to see us and marvel at our strength":

> America is still the last best hope of earth, and we still hold the power and bear the responsibility for its remaining so. This is an enormous power and a sobering responsibility, especially since America is no longer alone but is accompanied by a free world growing ever larger and more interconnected.
>
> . . . No other nation on earth has the power we possess More important, no other nation on earth has the trusted power that we possess. We are obligated to lead. If the free world is to harvest the hope and fulfill the promise that our great victory in the Cold War has offered us, America must shoulder the responsibility of its power. . . .
>
> . . . Today, unlike that December day in 1862 when President Lincoln spoke to Congress, the prospects for America are anything but bleak. . . .
>
> I believe Mr. Lincoln would be especially excited by the prospects that now lie before his nation. Only three times in our history have we had a 'rendezvous with destiny,' as President Franklin D. Roosevelt called our challenge in World War II. . . .
>
> The summons to leadership that we face at present is our fourth rendezvous with destiny. Answering this summons does not mean peace, prosperity, justice for all and no more wars in the world—any more than the American Revolution meant all people were free, the Civil War meant an end to racial inequality, or World War II and our great victory in the Cold War meant the triumph of democracy and free markets. What our leadership in the world does mean is that these things have a chance. We can have peace. We can continue moving toward greater prosperity for all. We can strive for justice in the world. We can seek to limit the destruction and the casualties of war. We can help enslaved people find their freedom. This is our fourth rendezvous with destiny: to lead the world at a time of immense opportunity—an opportunity never seen in the world before. As Lincoln said in 1862, America could not escape history. In 1992, we must not let history escape us.[29]

Charles L. Maynes, Editor of *Foreign Policy*, expects America to continue moving outward:

> Although the world may worry about a post-Cold War America turning inward, the rhetoric of the last presidential campaign followed by the December 1992 decision to intervene in Somalia suggests that

America is poised for a new burst of foreign policy activism. The victor, Bill Clinton, in his April 1, 1992, speech before the Foreign Policy Association, had called for America "to lead a global alliance for democracy as united and steadfast as the global alliance that defeated communism."[30]

In 1991, Joseph Muravchik stressed the necessity for America's future support of democracy, especially for the critical nations of Russia and China:

> For our nation, this is the opportunity of a lifetime. Our failure to exert every possible effort to secure this outcome would be unforgivable.
>
> If we succeed we will have forged a Pax Americana unlike any previous peace, one of harmony, not of conquest. Then the twenty-first century will be the American century by virtue of the triumph of the humane idea born in the American experiment: all men are created equal and endowed with unalienable rights. Ironically America's relative power in such a world—measured in the old-fashioned coin of guns and dollars—would diminish as other nations imitated the secrets of our success. Yet we would stand triumphant for achieving by our model and our influence the visionary goal stamped by the founding fathers on the seal of the United States: *novus ordo seclorum*, a new order of the ages.[31]

Since 1991, the terrible conflict in former Yugoslavia has resulted in a general rise of pessimism, highlighting the weakness of the West, and especially of America, in dealing with such a complex ambiguous problem. Nevertheless, the experience of Yugoslavia could challenge and stimulate the United States and others to move more quickly to detect such rising crises in advance, with the hope of solving them or ending them by the early moderate use of force.

Democratic and Liberal World Views

America's future leadership will be enhanced by the current spread of democracy (liberty and equality) and liberalism (concern with justice for all people, especially for the so-called "common man"). A number of political scientists have recently added their voices to the idealism of the 1990s. Hayward R. Alker, Jr., sees a new "humanistic moment" emerging in international studies, especially as he recalls the role of the Spanish bishop and writer Bartolomé de las Casas (1474-1566) with his "striving for universal recognition of human dignity," having in mind justice for the natives of the New World. A similar approach, he said, was shown by Martin Luther King, Jr.:

> The standards of a universalist, multicultural humanism are powerfully articulated in King's call that "every nation must now develop an overriding loyalty to mankind as a whole in order to preserve the best in their individual societies." King recognizes a syncretic Hindu-Moslem-Christian-Jewish-Buddhist belief in love as the "unifying principle of life."[32]

Charles W. Kegley, Jr., points out that the threats of international anarchy and environmental dangers "require leaders who contemplate substituting an ethic of 'shared sovereignty' and mutual assistance for the conventional realpolitik ethic of self-help and national competition":

> An ethic predicated on reciprocity and mutuality would place the Golden Rule—that states treat others as they wish to be treated in return—at the center of their strategies for enhancing their security and welfare.
>
> . . . History suggests that when the threat of external attack has receded, as it now has, America's historic commitment to fostering such liberal values as protection of human rights, free markets, civil liberties, and democratic institutions will intensify.[33]

In his Presidential Address to the International Studies Association in 1993, Kegley implies that the early 1990s may be a "neoidealist" moment:

> . . . As the Cold War has ended, the emergent conditions at this "defining moment" . . . transcend the *realpolitik* that has dominated discussion of international affairs for the past five decades and invite a reconstructed paradigm, perhaps one inspired by the idealist ideas associated with the Wilsonian vision. The question I examine, in short, is whether the early 1990s is a "neoidealist" moment.
>
> . . . In place of realism, there is today a visibly enthusiastic resurgence of interest in the Wilsonian program. In fact, his philosophy defines the issues that have risen to the top of the agenda. . . .
>
> . . . To claim that international mechanisms are needed to resolve ethnic conflicts and alleviate human suffering is to rediscover an approach that Wilson proposed to confront the ethnic and religious strife and structural violence that plagues the post-colonial, post-Cold

War world. And it is to restore a place for morality in foreign policy.
. . .

. . . Four decades ago John Herz (1951) suggested that idealism was
realism—that cooperation was advantageous and served national
interests. Principled behavior and moral purpose can enhance a nation's
power and competitive advantage—they are compatible and need not be
in tension.[34]

One of America's traditional major ideals, also emphasized by
Woodrow Wilson, has been the broadening and strengthening of
international law, as the normal method of maintaining peaceful
relations among nations. A popular book by Senator Daniel Patrick
Moynihan has recently given a sharp impetus to the importance of a
new emphasis on international law in the practice of American
diplomacy.[35]

The apparent revival of "liberalism" around 1992–93, following 15
or so years of conservatism (in the Schlesinger pattern), led to the
expectation of greater American support for democracy, justice, peace
and the general welfare. Arthur Schlesinger, Jr., interpreted the election
of President Clinton in this fashion:

The thesis is that American politics alternates at roughly thirty[-]
year intervals between conservative and liberal periods.
. . . President Clinton will have one salient advantage: the turning
of the cycle will coincide with his own personal convictions. This has
not always been the case. . . .
. . . In 1993, President and Zeitgeist should meet in warm embrace.
. . . The next generation of political leaders, in the White House and
in Congress, will have no more than the opportunity to move the
republic in new directions.
. . . No doubt the nation will continue in a spirit of public purpose
for fifteen years or so.[36]

The new liberalism, after the experiences of the 20th century, seems to
stress some elements of conservatism, such as the concept of individual
responsibility under high moral standards (in an age of idealism) and
much reliance on private enterprise. This could especially be true after
the year 2000, when a spirit of "union" might be more evident.

If the past "liberty-union" alternation continues, the current extrovert
period would be divided approximately in half by a phase of liberty
from 1986 to around 2000, followed by a dominant mood of union from

2000 to 2014 or so. With "liberty," one expects emphasis on individual and group rights, with marked dissension, and a major debate about America's proper goals in world affairs. Under a "union" mood, a strong consensus might be achieved on what America's foreign policy ought to be, along with a general spirit of cooperation on current divisive issues, such as race, sex, and the role of government in economic life. The Schlesinger alternation overlaps the liberty-union alternation, with liberalism expected to dominate from 1993 to around 2008, and then conservatism from 2008 to, say, 2023.

A liberal idealist period should help transmute some of the alleged evils, when carried to extremes (such as militarism, racism and materialism), into forces for good. For example, there is a positive value to the prudent use of military force, in order to establish and maintain justice (Pascal urged combining justice and force). Cultural, religious, racial and national diversity can be sources of strength, as each different group makes its special contribution. A democratic liberal approach will prize and respect this diversity. Particularly do the adherents of the great monotheistic religions of the West—Judaism, Christianity and Islam—need to seek deeper understanding of one another's highest principles (so close together in many fundamentals)) as a path to peace. Father Roger Karban describes the philosophy for such a search, as he writes of the growing number of conversations among Jews, Christians and Muslims:

> If we truly believe God's rays shine through all religions, then those faiths which have encompassed the most people over the longest periods of time demand our unbiased attention and inquiry. If we rely just on the few God-experiences with which we are comfortable, we are as limiting of the divinity as those who believe the Lord is distinctively male or Caucasian.[37]

With over a billion Muslims around the world in many countries, and three to four million in the United States, relations between Christians and Muslims (as well as with Jews) are exceedingly vital to America and the world. A hopeful event was the Parliament of World Religions in Chicago, August 28–September 5, 1993. With major challenges coming from the intolerant extremists in the major religions, hope for reconciliation depends upon tolerant moderates becoming more committed and more active. Finally, in relation to the abuse of materialism, it is recognized that material values are exceedingly useful, if kept in proper perspective—especially for those in great need, and also for those who are well-off and thus able to help others.

Another liberal approach to world understanding is suggested by the concept of a "civil religion" for the world, to help tie the world together peacefully. Leroy S. Rouney asks the question: "Can Christianity, which helped establish an American civil religion in order to fashion a national community out of great diversity, now shape the civil religion essential to a world community?" He refers, for example, to a "christianization" of Hinduism, "not in terms of theological convictions, but in regard to the ethical values and practices, based on a new sense of the dignity of the individual human being."[38] It is possible that all the higher religions can contribute to a sense of oneness in humanity as their contacts with one another increase.

A Major Turning Point in History?

America's future world leadership is stimulated by its prominent role in the new economy of the world, sometimes termed the "global village." Professor Robert Harper stressed this point in an address on "The Post-Industrial World and its Impact on the United States." The technological revolutions in transportation and especially communication (information) have tied the world together economically and culturally. Global operations can be managed from a single place. A global urban network is being built; New York, London and Tokyo do world business on a 24-hour basis. International trade has become enormous, with the United States becoming the largest market. The power of multinational corporations is immense, as they can shift production, markets and management from one place to another. One of the reasons for the fall of communism, Harper said, was its inability to play in the international economic game. He also believes we are only in the early stages of this technological revolution, and challenges the American people to become more aware of these changes.[39] Strobe Talbott believes that we are witnessing the virtual "birth of the global nation," with integration prevailing over disintegration and fragmentation in the long run.[40] Boutros Boutros-Ghali, Secretary General of the United Nations, sees the United Nations in a more hopeful global position: "Despite the news of wars, hunger, homelessness and disease affecting millions, the world is moving towards a new, more participatory, people-centered way of conducting international affairs. . . . The first truly global era has begun."[41]

The coming of a new millennium in the year 2000 also builds a sense of suspense in many people, especially among "apocalyptic" Christians. Henry Grunwald challenges the will of Americans, as he asks the question "The Year 2000: Is it the End or Just the Beginning?" and concludes "The year 2000 could very well open a second American Century, given a major national effort of will. Absent that, it could also be the beginning of the end of the United States as a significant power."[42]

The cycle of democratic liberal internationalism, as used in this study, is currently in the period of synthesis or consolidation, in which idealism and moral-spiritual forces should become more prominent, leading to provisional solutions to many world problems. As for America, Paul Johnson felt in 1985 that the nation was in the midst of a fourth Great Awakening which "has gathered speed slowly but now appears to be maturing." He saw a "popular ecumenicalism" developing:

> based upon a common reassertion of traditional moral values and of belief in the salient articles of Christianity not as symbol but as plain historical fact. What is unusual about this fourth Awakening is that for the first time it embraces Catholics. Indeed it appeals to many non-practicing Christians and even non-Christians who feel that the Judeo-Christian system of ethics and morals which underlies American republican democracy is in peril, and in need of reestablishment. The phenomenon has no counterpart in Europe.[43]

Religious historian William G. McLoughlin in 1978 identified the cyclical succession of religious revivals, cultural awakenings and practical reform. He estimated that the fourth cultural awakening which began around 1960 would continue to around 1990, lasting 30 years as did previous ones. He predicted that "at some point in the future, early in the 1990s at best, a consensus would emerge that will thrust into political leadership a president with a platform committed to the kinds of fundamental restructuring that have followed in previous awakenings —in 1776, in 1830, and in 1932." Prior to this restructuring must come an ideological reorientation which will likely include "a new sense of the mystical unity of all mankind and of the vital power of harmony between man and nature."[44] Richard John Neuhaus, a close observer of American culture, noted in 1992 that "there are signs of a resurgence of religion and religiously based moral concern in our public life," and stressed the importance of moral-spiritual laws which are unenforceable:

Civilization depends upon obedience to the unenforceable. Public law deals with the enforceable. Because the unenforceable—virtue, honor, discernment, decency, compassion, and hope—is ever so much more important, the sphere of law must be limited as much as possible.[45]

The collapse of communism in the Soviet Union, thus far at least, is one of the most striking turning points in history. It was largely unpredicted, especially for such an early time. Ambassador George F. Kennan had seen the possibility in 1947, if the West followed a persistent policy of "containment," but 40 years had gone by with no special sign of collapse. Aleksandr Solzhenitsyn believed in 1980 that "a Russian national reawakening and liberation would mark the downfall of Soviet and with it of world communism," and he noted that a "religious and national renaissance" was under way in Russia.[46] But Vaclav Havel, the noted President of the Czech Republic, has seen a far larger significance in the end of communism, believing it to be a sign of the "end of the modern era":

The end of Communism is, first and foremost, a message to the human race. It is a message we have not yet fully deciphered and comprehended. In its deepest sense, the end of Communism has brought a major era in human history to an end. It has brought an end not just to the 19th and 20th centuries, but to the modern age as a whole.

. . . The end of Communism is a serious warning to all mankind. It is a signal that the era of arrogant, absolutist reason is drawing to a close and it is high time to draw conclusions from that fact.

Communism was not defeated by military force, but by life, by the human spirit, by conscience, by the resistance of Being and man to manipulation. It was defeated by a revolt of color, authenticity, history in all its variety and human individuality against imprisonment within a uniform ideology.

. . . It is my profound conviction that we have to release from the sphere of private whim such forces as . . . an elementary sense of justice, the ability to see things as others do, a sense of transcendental responsibility, archetypical wisdom, good taste , courage, compassion and faith in the importance of particular measures that do not aspire to be a universal key to salvation. Such forces must be rehabilitated.[47]

Arnold J. Toynbee implied that the end of modern history in the West began as long ago as 1875, with Western civilization marked by shifts every 400 years[48]:

Dark Ages	675–1075
Middle Ages	1075–1475
Modern	1475–1875
Post-Modern	1875–

Toynbee's division of periods suggests that our age of transition is as significant as that of the late Renaissance and Reformation. He has also divided the history of civilizations into four periods: the Heroic Age (based on moral-spiritual values); a Time of Troubles (wars and revolutions); the Universal State (created through conquest by the strongest power); and Disintegration, along with the rise of a Universal Religion. Western Christian Civilization, which now affects the whole world, still stood (he wrote in 1948) in the Time of Troubles, which began at the time of the Reformation.[49] Since a civilization's decline is prompted largely by an emphasis on militarism, Toynbee saw the possibility that the West could be saved from the Universal State and thus from destruction through a revival of religion: "this happier spiritual prospect was at least a possibility in which a dispirited generation of Western men and women might catch a beckoning gleam of kindly light."[50] Two special hopeful developments have occurred since Toynbee wrote: (1) the United States has become the only power which might be able to conquer the world and try to create a "universal state," but it wishes instead to build a cooperative world order; and (2) a revival of moral-spiritual principles does seem under way, in the United States and in much of the world.

Another vital transition which especially involves America is the idea that the victory of democratic internationalism in the struggle with fascism and communism foreshadows the end of the major struggle of man throughout history for freedom and recognition. The German philosopher Hegel, lecturing and writing in the 1820s, interpreted the whole of world history (guided by the "Universal Spirit") as showing "the development of the Idea of Freedom," and demonstrating "the justification of God in History."[51] Hegel believed that the end of this historical trend was near, in Western Europe, when he wrote. Francis Fukuyama dramatized Hegel's approach, as Communism was unraveling, by writing an article entitled "The End of History" in *The National Interest* (Summer 1989), and developing it into a book in 1992. Fukuyama stresses the point that after the defeat of the "military-authoritarian Right" and the "communist-totalitarian Left," "liberal democracy remains the only coherent political aspiration that spans different regions and cultures around the globe," as a special goal of a "Universal History of Mankind." He concludes:

> It is possible that if events continue to unfold as they have over the past few decades, that the idea of a universal and directional history leading up to liberal democracy may become more plausible to people, and that the relativist impasse of modern thought will in a sense solve itself.[52]

At least this approach suggests that the United States should promote the goal of "liberal democracy" with a great deal of confidence that the spirit of man will continue to move in this direction, in spite of temporary setbacks. It is interesting to note again that Hegel referred to the United States in 1820 as "the land of the future, where in the ages that lie before us, the burden of the World's History shall reveal itself. . . ."[53]

Another possible major transition in our time would support the concept of a change as significant as the "Axial Period" which the philosopher Karl Jaspers, writing in 1953, identified as occurring about 2,500 years ago (when special changes occurred, with other changes between 800 B.C. and 200 B.C.). This was the time, he wrote, when man as we know him today came into being—when he became conscious of Being, of himself and his limitations, when the great world religions began, almost simultaneously.[54] Jaspers believed that another Axial Age was probably developing—a basic transformation of man's historical consciousness, prompted by a "real unity of mankind on the earth" for the first time in human history, moving toward either world empire or world order.[55] Toynbee and other observers have attached special hopeful significance to the meeting of the cultures and religions of the East and West in the 20th century.[56] Toynbee too has emphasized the principles which are common to all the higher religions. Van Leeuwen, Dutch professor of world religions, has written (1964) of the present period as the second "axial age," with world revolution really beginning, along with the nuclear age, and an interpenetration of cultures and cross-fertilization in a planetary world.[57]

Brzezinski seems to feel the challenge of a new age in his 1993 book:

> A significant portion of humanity thus finds itself on the brink of an entirely new era in human affairs. The philosophical implications of

human history being on the edge of a new and mysterious age are almost mind-boggling. Ultimately, that raises the question of what is the essence of the human being.

. . . And all will have to seek a more explicitly defined balance in the modern world between the material and the spiritual dimensions of life, especially if the purpose of global politics is increasingly defined as the progressive shaping of a common global community, with gradually equalizing opportunities for human fulfillment.[58]

A major National Commission (1992), which proposed principles for American foreign policy, introduced its study by emphasizing the importance of the "present moment" for action:

> Now America once again faces a rare opportunity, an open but fleeting moment in world history. We must seize it now. This is our chance to ensure that recent enemies become future friends and that present allies don't become new antagonists. This is our chance to shape new forms of leadership before the fluid trends of the moment harden into something not to our liking. Above all, this is the time for us to change the way we think about the world and the way we conduct our affairs at home and abroad.
>
> The world we have known for half a century is rapidly receding into history. A new world is emerging as a strange shape, unformed, yet forming fast. Familiar landmarks are changing before we can adjust our thinking.
>
> . . . Creating a more democratic world has long been an American ideal. Today, when we can work with an expanding community of democracies, it is an ideal both more feasible and more important. So, too, is the goal of environmental protection. Preserving a habitable planet is an urgent addition to our foreign policy agenda.
>
> . . . We must also keep faith with our ideals. When brave Chinese citizens died in Tiananmen Square, they fell before a "Goddess of Democracy" that evoked the Statue of Liberty. If their faith in democracy struck some as naive, it expressed the spirit of the age and possibilities for the future.[59]

Meaning and Purpose in History

A final word should be written about the meaning of history, especially as applied to America. Some see historical processes as self-contained, so to speak, probably based upon fundamental tendencies of human nature and lessons from a long human history. Others note the special role of moral purpose and ethical principles. Yet it is even more typical of Americans throughout their history to see the Creator-God or Providence at work in history, helping move people and nations, along with their freedom of choice, toward long-run goals of justice and peace. The Judeo-Christian doctrine recognizes God as the sovereign of history as well as the Creator of the universe, of life, and of human beings.

Hegel stressed God or Universal Spirit active in history for Freedom. Jaspers saw great patterns in history leading toward the unity of humankind. Herbert Butterfield, British historian, stressed the ultimate control of God even as man exercises his freedom of choice:

> Either you trace everything back in the long run to sheer blind Chance, or you trace everything to God. Some of you might say there is a third alternative—namely that everything just happens through the operation of the laws of nature. But that is not an explanation at all and the mind cannot rest there, for such a thesis does not tell us where the laws themselves have come from.[60]

Glenn Tinder, political scientist, gives his Christian view:

> For Christians, and for all who in any way have faith in human destiny, the ultimate future does not depend on the practical efficacy, or even on the wisdom, of nations and individuals. Our responsibility is only to be attentive to God, or transcendence, to the deepest necessities of history, and to human beings everywhere, and to be available for the future that is given us. We must watch and—if we are Christians—pray. Paul's statement . . . "When I am weak, then I am strong" bears on this situation. In the face of world disorder and suffering, all of us are weak. Prophetic hope rests on the faith that in admitting this, we are paradoxically strong.[61]

Peter C. Hodgson, theologian, builds on Hegel and Jaspers, noting Hegel's "helical spiral" of advance toward freedom (thesis, antithesis, synthesis) and Jaspers' three basic tendencies (socialism or sense of community, world unity and faith) which "converge in the goal of accomplished human freedom": "In God the many shapes of freedom are transfigured into one encompassing shape, which is God, the One who loves in freedom."[62]

Many observers have believed that God is at work in the major events of history. Matthew Bender writes of Reinhold Niebuhr:

He believed . . . that great historical events, such as the defeat of Nazism and Communism, owe more to divine providence than human virtue. He knew that the agency of the free world was really the instrument of a good greater than itself.[63]

Joseph D. Small writes: "God speaks through the signs of the times. . . . The living God is always at work in the world to bring about God's reign."[64]

God (or Providence, or Universal Spirit, or Transcendence, or Being, or History) seems to work through individuals—like Washington, Jefferson, Lincoln, Wilson, Martin Luther King, Jr.—and through nations—like the Hebrews, Greece, Rome, Britain, and, now especially, the United States (to name only one group). God works in history through challenges and through judgments, as Lincoln believed about the Civil War. And God appears to work through historical patterns or cycles in the dominant motivations of humankind, as generations succeed one another. In the rational-realist-idealist cycle, which establishes a new order in the life of nations, there is a time of preparation or planting; a time of intense struggle, violence and sacrifice; and, finally, a time of consolidation or harvest, as in the current phase (1967 to, say, 2014). The American nation has also alternated between phases of introversion and extroversion, liberalism and conservatism, liberty and union. The general regularity of these cycles in the past gives one reason to expect their continuation in the future, since human nature remains stable and generations still have approximately the same length. Inside each phase of a cycle, there are many "ups and downs," but the general average demonstrates the current dominant mood (an analogy is the variation in temperatures during one of the seasons). Cycles may come and go with regularity, but specific events appear unpredictable and often surprising.

One long-range goal of history may be implied by all the higher religions, especially by the Christians—the brotherhood of man under the fatherhood of God. The special goal of the next two decades may be the establishment of peace among nations and inside nations, with a minimum of force, aided by a moral-spiritual motivation of respect, concern, compassion, forgiveness and reconciliation.[65] And perhaps humanity, in the nuclear age, will move away from the cyclical return of hegemonic wars which have been prominent for the last 500 years.[66]

Brzezinski in 1993 continues to stress a "moral imperative": "It is noteworthy that the need for an enhanced moral consciousness is advocated not only by religious authorities but also by reflective political leaders."[67]

Conclusion

America indeed appears to be entering a new phase of history, with challenges such as Rwanda, Haiti and Bosnia, and domestic divisions and moral problems. Mark Sommers (University of California-Berkeley) stresses "a bold new view on defense" for the United States:

> Instead of drilling its soldiers to refight past wars, the U.S. military needs to retrain them for an era of still precarious peace, to perform the highly specialized work of monitoring cease-fires and arms agreements, providing relief supplies for human and natural disasters, assistance in environmental cleaning, and mediating conflicts before they erupt into violence.[68]

Daniel J. Boorstin notes the divisions in the United States and calls on Americans to renew a sense of "community":

> There has been so much emphasis recently on the diversity of our people, I think it's time that we reaffirm the fact that what has built our country is community and that community is not dependent on government. It depends on the willingness of people to build together.[69]

Boorstin also reminds Americans of their world responsibilities and opportunities: "The uniqueness that Jefferson and Lincoln claimed for us, we must remember, was for the sake of *all* mankind."[70]

Brent Scowcroft, National Security Adviser for President Bush, sees the necessity of a leadership role for the United States:

> A better world can emerge only as a result of strong and enlightened leadership. Whether we like it or not, the U.S. alone can provide that leadership. No other power, no international organization, has the global view, respect and the reach to touch every corner of the world. Left to its own devices, history will sooner or later serve up another nasty surprise. . . . We do not have the luxury of putting our leadership on hold until we get our domestic house in order.[71]

Henry Kissinger, Secretary of State for Presidents Nixon and Ford, calls upon Americans to show a realist patience as they seek idealist goals:

> The fulfillment of American ideals will have to be sought in the patient accumulation of partial successes. . . . The Wilsonian goals of America's past—peace, stability, progress and freedom for mankind—will have to be sought in a journey that has no end.[72]

Former President Nixon in his last book, written just before his death, challenges Americans to lead the world toward high goals:

> The United States must lead. We must lead to open the eyes of those still blinded by despotism, to embolden those who remain oppressed, and to bring out from the dungeons of tyranny those who still live in darkness.
>
> . . . History thrusts certain powers at certain times onto center stage. In this era, the spotlight shines on the United States. How long it stays on us—and how brightly it shines—will be determined by us alone.
>
> We cannot lead solely by example or solely by power but must combine the best elements of both. Today we must find the moral equivalent of war to unify and inspire us. . . . When the people of the world look to us, they should see not just our money and our arsenal but also our vast capacity as a force for good.
>
> . . . We stand at a great watershed in history, looking back on a century of war and bloodshed and looking forward to a century we can make one of peace and freedom. The future beyond peace is in our hands.[73]

Professor Tony Smith reminded Americans in a major work in 1994 that "America's mission" throughout the 20th century had been devoted to the "worldwide struggle for democracy." He asked whether the United States would continue in this direction:

> Is democracy's current victory limited and momentary, soon to be reversed by some new challenge, or can the momentum of liberal democratic internationalism be preserved? After two world wars and the collapse of Soviet communism, is the world finally safe for democracy?[74]

Smith sees America's historical approach combining the best elements of idealism with realism, and calls upon America to keep its democratic vision and apply it with a high degree of patience:

> . . . Given the established character of other people and the obvious limits of American power, Wilsonianism will not everywhere be a

relevant framework for action.

. . . What the historical record nonetheless shows is that this country's greatest triumphs in foreign affairs have been the result of liberal democratic internationalism, and that American national security would surely suffer were this vision to be forgotten today, when nationalist and religious extremism are breeding anarchy and militarism in a world whose increasing political fragmentation calls for determined American leadership.[75]

Former Secretary of State Henry Kissinger, regarded as a realist, also stresses idealist goals and realist judgment for Americans, in his major study entitled *Diplomacy*:

In traveling along the road to world order for the third time in the modern era, American idealism remains as essential as ever, perhaps even more so. But in the new world order, its role will be to provide the faith to sustain America through all the ambiguities of choice in an imperfect world. Traditional American idealism must combine with a thoughtful assessment of contemporary realities to bring about a usable definition of American interests.[76]

George Weigel, president of the Ethics and Public Policy Committee in Washington, D.C., likewise combines idealism and realism in his book entitled *Idealism Without Illusions*:

. . . My hunch . . . is that the American people are eager . . . for a leadership that is commensurate with the realities of the West's recent victory in the Fifty-Five Years' War and the responsibility that victory has laid upon us. So far, an extraordinary opportunity to shape a world order more reflective of humankind's nobler instincts is being botched, in part because of sheer inattention.[77]

Weigel's conclusion refers to "The Responsible Superpower":

The new democracies . . . do not expect the United States to shoulder the entire burden or responsibility for defining and enforcing the ground rules of world politics in the 1990s. But they fear the chaos they believe will fill the vacuum if the United States, the lone superpower, abdicates the responsibility of leadership.

. . . Powerful motives of economic and political self-interest ought to impel the American people and their leaders to seize the opportunities for responsible leadership in world affairs that history . .

. has set before us.[78]

Professor Stanley Hoffmann perceives a need for the reconstruction of "liberal internationalism":

> Marxism is discredited. Realism promises only the perpetuation of the same old game and is no better equipped to face the politics of chaos than is liberalism. Liberalism remains the only comprehensive and hopeful vision of world affairs, but it needs to be thoroughly reconstructed—and that task has not proceeded very far either in its domestic or its international dimension.[79]

Arthur Schlesinger, Jr., warns Americans of the neo-isolationist impulse:

> In the United States, neo-isolationism promises to prevent the most powerful nation on the planet from playing any role in enforcing the peace system. . . . We are not going to achieve a new world order without paying for it in blood as well as in words and money.
> . . . If we cannot find ways of implementing collective security, we must be realistic about the alternative: a chaotic, violent, and ever-more dangerous planet.[80]

If America is to play a truly beneficent role on the world scene, its own society must be strengthened in the moral, educational, economic and political areas. As Robert Hormats has written, "the nation's capacity to maintain a strong economy and a healthy society will be critical to its global prospects—and will be severely tested."[81] The period for the consolidation of "democratic liberal internationalism" would, if history repeats itself, cover from 1967 to about 2014, with American extroversion dominant during the last 27 years of this period. The United States should be able, in the next two decades, to demonstrate special leadership qualities in working with other nations in a spirit of partnership—hopefully with Russia and China, as well as Western Europe and Japan, Latin America, Eastern Europe, and other countries around the world. Doubtless there will be difficult challenges and temporary setbacks, but leaders should move ahead toward worthy goals with long-run confidence. (It should be remembered that the consolidation of democratic nationalism in the United States, France and Britain was not provisionally completed until near the end of the period of synthesis, 1824–71.) One should expect more novel and hopeful events from time to time as the positive impact of a more widespread "idealism" is felt.

The introvert-extrovert cycle throughout American history enables one to predict with some assurance that America will remain fundamentally extrovert and involved for the next 20 years or so—long enough to help establish, with the aid of the other major democratic powers, a provisional peaceful world, based on the ideals of justice, freedom and cooperation.

The somewhat less clear cycle of the alternation of a spirit of "liberty" with a spirit of "union" suggests that by the year 2000 a decisive majority of the American people, including the so-called minorities, will agree on an appropriate world leadership role for the nation, stimulated by a "vision" of worthy goals, articulated by its leaders. A mood supporting "union" and "community," in an age of idealism, should help create a new vibrant liberalism, including contributions from conservatism.

After the new world order of peace is, hopefully, constructed, one would expect a continuation of the "harvest" of peace even as the preparation for a new age takes place over the subsequent half-century or so. This next "grand period" (perhaps from 2014 to 2161, if history repeats) might well be concentrated in the realm of economic, cultural and spiritual progress, growing out of the increasing contacts among peoples with their different religions and cultures, aided by further scientific and technological advances. Although a significant struggle may well come in the next definite realist (political power) period, it could be hoped that it might not precipitate major Great Power wars as in the past, and that the warning of Samuel P. Huntington about "The Clash of Civilizations" will not come to pass. Huntington concludes his article with this challenge: "For the relevant future, it will be no universal civilization, but instead a world of different civilizations, each of which will have to learn to coexist with the others."[82]

A wider awareness of the cyclical trends discussed in this study could perhaps help reduce a possible dangerous magnitude of future shifts, such as too much introversion, or too much force (realism), or too little idealism.[83] The current cyclical trends (extroversion, idealism, liberalism-liberty) suggest there is real hope that the United States will respond positively to the challenges and opportunities which lie ahead and that much of the world will join in working toward a just and stable peace.

For 40 years after 1947, America and the West were motivated by opposition to communism. With the totalitarian challenges apparently gone, or at least sharply reduced, future goals for America may have a special moral quality. The major source of America's "moral imperative" for the next decades still remains the spirit of the Declaration of Independence, adopted nearly 220 years ago and still not fulfilled for all the people in the United States (or in the world):

> We hold these truths to be self-evident, that all men are created equal, that they are endowed by their Creator with certain unalienable Rights, that among these are Life, Liberty and the Pursuit of Happiness. That to secure these rights, governments are instituted among men, deriving their just powers from the consent of the governed.

American goals are also symbolized in the Preamble to the Constitution of the United States, beginning "We, the people of the United States, in order to form a more perfect Union," and in the Preamble to the Charter of the United Nations, beginning "We the Peoples of the United Nations, determined to save succeeding generations from the scourge of war, which twice in our lifetime has brought untold sorrow to mankind." To fulfill America's mission provisionally in the next two decades, Americans need to seek a proper balance between idealism (the search for the good of all, at home and abroad, in this interdependent world) and realism (the prudent use of force in this extrovert period), inspired by the efforts of past generations of Americans and confident hopes for the future.

Notes

1. Ben J. Wattenberg, *The First Universal Nation: Leading Indicators and Ideas about the Surge of America in the 1990s* (New York: The Free Press, 1991), 25, and also see 7–25.

2. Ibid., 367–69.

3. See, e.g., Richard Rosecrance, ed., *America as an Ordinary Country: U.S. Foreign Policy in the Future* (Ithaca, N.Y.: Cornell University Press, 1976).

4. Samuel P. Huntington, *American Politics: The Promise of Disharmony* (Cambridge: Harvard University Press, 1981), 262.

5. Samuel P. Huntington, *The Third Wave: Democratization in the Late Twentieth Century* (Norman: University of Oklahoma Press, 1991), 16 ff.

6. Ibid., 26.

7. Joseph Muravchik, *Exporting Democracy: Fulfilling America's Destiny* (Washington, D.C.: The AEI Press, American Enterprise Institute, 1991).

8. Daniel Patrick Moynihan, *Pandaemonium: Ethnicity in International Politics* (New York: Oxford University Press, 1993), 24. (Pandaemonium was the capital of hell in *Paradise Lost*.)

9. Zbigniew Brzezinski, *Out of Control: Global Turmoil on the Eve of the 21st Century* (New York: Scribner's, 1993), ix.

10. John Lewis Gaddis, *The United States and the End of the Cold War* (New York: Oxford University Press, 1992), esp. 198–200.

11. *New York Times*, February 7, 1993, 1, 12.

12. Robert I. Rotberg, "Struggling Nations Need Guidance," *Christian Science Monitor*, May 14, 1993, 19. Rotberg is President of Lafayette College. Paul Johnson wrote of the need for some international trusteeships in "Colonialism's Back—and Not a Moment Too Soon," *New York Times Magazine*, April 18, 1993, 22, 43–44. He declares that some countries are not currently fit to govern themselves.

13. Brzezinski, 230–31.

14. Robert W. Tucker and David C. Hendrickson, *The Imperial Temptation: The New World Order and America's Purpose* (New York: Council on Foreign Relations Press, 1992).

15. See Paul Kennedy, *The Rise and Fall of the Great Powers* (New York: Vintage Books-Random House, 1987, 1989), and *Preparing for the Twenty-First Century* (New York: Random House, 1993).

16. See, e.g., Werner Levi, *The Coming End of War*, vol. 117, Sage Library of Social Research (Beverly Hills, Calif.: Sage Publications, 1981).

17. Joseph F. Nye, Jr., *Bound to Lead: The Changing Nature of American Power* (New York: Basic Books, 1990), 188–201.

18. *New York Times*, May 11, 1993, 8A, reporting on polls by *Americans Talk Issues*, Washington-based foundation. See also the foreign affairs polls from 1940 to 1993 in *The American Enterprise*, March/April 1993, 94–104.

19. Walter Russell Mead, review of Brzezinski's *Out of Control*, *New York Times Book Review*, April 4, 1993, 10. Mead is senior counselor of the World Policy Institute of the New School.

20. Henry R. Nau, *The Myth of America's Decline: Leading the World Economy into the 1990s* (New York: Oxford University Press, 1990).

21. Nye, *Bound to Lead*, 260–61.

22. Eric Sevareid, "A New Stage," *Modern Maturity*, April–May 1991, 76.

23. James G. Emerson, Jr., "A Theology of Responsibility: The Challenge to My Country," *Presbyterian Outlook*, March 9, 1992, 6. Among religious groups, the Church of Jesus Christ of Latter-Day Saints (Mormons) is the most devoted to the United States; e.g., Ezra Taft Benson has written: "It is a part of my religious belief that American is a land choice above all others, that we are not just another of the family of nations, but that we have been singled out to

perform a divine mission for liberty-loving people everywhere," in *God-Family-Country: Our Three Great Loyalties* (Salt Lake City: Deseret Book Co., 1974), 305. Similarly Paul H. Dunn acclaims America in *The Light of Liberty* (Salt Lake City: Bookcraft, 1987).

24. Richard Nixon, "We Are Ignoring Our World Role," *Time*, March 16, 1992, 74.

25. Richard Nixon, *Seize the Moment: America's Challenge in a One Superpower World* (New York: Simon and Schuster, 1992), 273, 288, 299, 305.

26. James N. Wall, ed., "To Stem the Tide of World Affairs," *Christian Century*, August 29, 1992, 763.

27. Robert G. Neumann, "This Next Disorderly Half Century: Some Proposed Remedies," *The Washington Quarterly* (Winter 1993): 33, 35.

28. James G. Hoge, Jr., "Preface: The Year Ahead," *Foreign Affairs, America and the World, 1992/93*, xii.

29. Colin L. Powell, "U.S. Forces: Challenges Ahead," *Foreign Affairs*, (Winter 1992/93): 32–33, 44–45.

30. Charles William Maynes, "Containing Ethnic Conflict," *Foreign Policy*, No. 90 (Spring 1993): 3.

31. Muravchik, 227.

32. Hayward R. Alker, Jr., "The Humanistic Moment in International Studies: Reflections on Machiavelli and las Cases," 1992 Presidential Address for the International Studies Association in Atlanta, *International Studies Quarterly* 36 (December 1992): 347–71, esp. 365.

33. Charles W. Kegley, Jr., "The New Global Order: The Power of Principle in a Pluralistic World," *Ethics in International Affairs*, vol. 6 (1992): 21–40., esp. 27, 30, 36.

34. Kegley, "The Neoidealist Moment in International Studies? Realist Myths and the New International Realities," address at Acapulco, Mexico, March 25, 1993, *International Studies Quarterly* 37 (1993): 131–46, esp. 131–32, 134, 138, 142.

35. Daniel Patrick Moynihan, *On the Law of Nations* (Cambridge: Harvard University Press, 1990).

36. Arthur M. Schlesinger, Jr., "The Turn of the Cycle," *The New Yorker* (November 16, 1992), 46–54, esp. 53–54.

37. Father Roger Karban of Belleville, Illinois, "Interfaith Conversation: Expanding Our Minds and Hearts," *Jews, Christians and Muslims in Conversation* (Carbondale, Ill.: Religious Studies Department, Southern Illinois University), vol. 1, no. 2 (November 1992), 4. For true reconciliation, theologian Henry Nelson Wieman has stressed the importance of what he calls "creative interchange" which includes: "(1) interchange which creates appreciative understanding of unique individuality; (2) integration within each individual of what he gets from others in this way, thus progressively creating his own personality in power, knowledge, and capacity to appreciate more

profoundly diverse individuals, peoples, and things," in *Man's Ultimate Commitment* (Carbondale, Ill.: Southern Illinois University Press, 1958), 305.

38. Richard E. Wentz, review of Leroy S. Rouner, *To Be At Home: Christianity, Civil Religion, and World Community* (Boston: Beacon Press, 1991) in *Christian Century*, September 4–11, 1991, 823.

39. Robert Harper (geographer, University of Maryland and Southern Illinois University), address on "The Post-Industrial World and its Impact on the United States," Southern Illinois University, February 2, 1993.

40. Strobe Talbott, "The Birth of the Global Nation," *Time*, July 20, 1992, 70–71.

41. *UN Chronicle*, Winter (March) 1993, 1. UN Day message, October 24, 1992.

42. *Time*, March 30, 1992, 75–76.

43. Paul Johnson, "The Almost-Chosen People: Why America is Different," the first annual Erasmus Lecture, January 24, 1985 (New York: Rockford Institute, 1985), 12.

44. William G. McLoughlin, *Revivals, Awakenings, and Reform: An Essay on Religious and Social Change in America, 1607–1977* (Chicago: University of Chicago Press, 1978), 214–16.

45. Richard John Neuhaus, *America Against Itself: Moral Vision and the Public Order* (South Bend, Ind.: University of Notre Dame Press, 1992), 68, 189.

46. Aleksandr Solzhenitsyn, "Misconceptions about Russia are a Threat to America," *Foreign Affairs*, vol. 58, no. 4 (Spring 1980): 814, 832, 834.

47. Vaclav Havel, "The End of the Modern Era," *New York Times*, March 1, 1992, E15.

48. Arnold J. Toynbee, *A Study of History*, Abridgement of vols. I–VI by D. C. Somerwell (New York: Oxford University Press, 1946), 39.

49. Ibid., 12–13.

50. Toynbee, *A Study of History*, abridgement of vols. 7–10 by Somerwell, 349.

51. Georg Wilhelm Friedrich Hegel, *Lectures on the Philosophy of History* (London: G. Ball and Sons, 1890), 476–77.

52. Francis Fukuyama, *The End of History and the Last Man* (New York: The Free Press, 1992), xiii–xiv, 338.

53. Hegel, *The Philosophy of History*, rev. ed. (New York: Wiley Book Co., 1904), 86.

54. Karl Jaspers, *The Origin and Goal of History* (New Haven: Yale University Press, 1953), 1–21.

55. Ibid., 126.

56. Arnold J. Toynbee, *An Historian's Approach to Religion* (New York: Oxford University Press, 1956), 284.

57. Arend Th. Van Leeuwen, *Christianity in World History: The Meeting*

of the Faiths of East and West, trans. H. H. Hoskins (New York: Scribner's, 1964), 26, 35, 409, 426, 432.

58. Brzezinski, *Out of Control*, 219, 221.

59. Carnegie Endowment for International Peace National Commission, *Changing Our Ways: America and the New World* (Carnegie Endowment for International Peace, 1992), 1, 4.

60. Herbert Butterfield, *Writings on Christianity and History*, ed. C. T. McIntire (New York: Oxford University Press, 1979), 8.

61. Glenn Tinder, *The Political Meaning of Christianity: An Interpretation* (Baton Rouge: Louisiana State University Press, 1989), 243.

62. Peter C. Hodgson, *God in History: Shapes of Freedom* (Nashville, Tenn.: Abingdon Press, 1989), 243, 247, 251.

63. Matthew Berke, "The Disputed Legacy of Reinhold Niebuhr," *First Things*, November 1992, 42. Berke is the Managing Editor.

64. *Presbyterian Survey*, January–February 1993, 36.

65. See Frank L. Klingberg, "Hope for Peace," *Presbyterian Outlook*, November 12, 1984, 6–8.

66. For a description of the theories of hegemonic wars, see Jack S. Levy, "Long Cycles, Hegemonic Transitions, and the Long Peace," in Charles W. Kegley, ed., *The Long Postwar Peace: Contending Explanations and Projections* (New York: HarperCollins, 1991), 147–76.

67. Zbigniew Brzezinski, "Power and Morality," *World Monitor*, March 1993, 28.

68. *Christian Science Monitor*, September 28, 1993, 19.

69. Tad Szulc, "The Greatest Danger We Face," *Parade*, July 25, 1993, 4.

70. Daniel Boorstin, "I am Optimistic about America," *Parade*, July 10, 1994, 6.

71. Brent Scowcroft, Op. Ed., *New York Times*, July 2, 1993, A12.

72. Henry Kissinger, "How to Achieve the New World Order," *Time*, March 14, 1994, excerpt from *Diplomacy* (New York: Simon and Schuster, 1994).

73. Richard Nixon, *Beyond Peace* (New York: Random House, 1994), 24–25.

74. Tony Smith, *America's Mission: The United States and the Worldwide Struggle for Democracy in the Twentieth Century* (A Twentieth Century Fund Book, Princeton, N.J.: Princeton University Press, 1994), xiv.

75. Ibid., 345.

76. Henry Kissinger, *Diplomacy* (A Touchstone Book, New York: Simon and Schuster, 1994), 836.

77. George Weigel, *Idealism Without Illusions* (Ethics and Public Policy Center, Grand Rapids, Mich.: William B. Eerdman's Publishing Co., 1994), 106–7.

78. Ibid., 231–33.

79. Stanley Hoffmann, "The Crisis of Liberal Internationalism," *Foreign*

Policy (Spring 1995): 177.

80. Arthur Schlesinger, Jr., "Back to the Womb? Isolationism's Renewed Threat," *Foreign Affairs* (July/August 1995): 8.

81. Robert D. Hormats, "The Roots of American Power," *Foreign Affairs* (Summer 1991): 149.

82. Samuel P. Huntington, "The Clash of Civilizations?" *Foreign Affairs* (Summer 1993): 22–49.

83. Jack E. Holmes discusses the educational problems involved in helping smooth out the cycles, in the conclusion of his book *The Mood/Interest Theory of American Foreign Policy* (Lexington: University Press of Kentucky), 168.

Bibliography

Books

Abbott, Lyman. *The Rights of Man: A Study of Twentieth Century Problems.* Boston: Houghton Mifflin, 1901.

Acheson, Dean. *Present at the Creation: My Years in the State Department,* New York: W. W. Norton, 1969.

Adams, Brooks. *America's Economic Supremacy,* with a New Evaluation by Marquis W. Childs. New York: Harpers, 1947.

Adams, Ephraim D. *The Power of Ideals in American History.* New Haven: Yale University Press, 1913.

Adams, Henry. *History of the United States of America, 1801-1817.* Vol. 9. Philadelphia: The Blakiston Co., 1945.

Adams, John. *Correspondence between the Honorable John Adams and the late William Cunningham, Esq., 1803-1812.* Boston: True and Greene, 1822.

———. *The Works of John Adams.* 10 vols. Boston: Little Brown, 1856.

Adams, John Quincy. *The Diary of John Quincy Adams.* Edited by Allan Nevins. New York: Longmans Green, 1928.

———. *Memoirs of John Quincy Adams.* 10 vols. Edited by Charles Francis Adams. Philadelphia: J. B. Lippincott, 1875.

———. *The Writings of John Quincy Adams.* 7 vols. New York: Macmillan, 1913–17.

Allen, Frederick Lewis. *Since Yesterday: the 1930s in America.* New York: Harpers, 1940.

American Academy of Political and Social Science. *The Foreign Policy of the United States: Political and Commercial, Addresses and Discussions.* Philadelpha: American Academy, 1899.

———. *The United States as a World Power.* Philadelphia: American Academy, 1905.

American Catholic Committee. *Justice and War in the Nuclear Age.* Lanham,

Md.: University Press of America, 1983.

Anastaplo, George. *The Constitution of 1787: A Commentary.* (Baltimore: Johns Hopkins University Press, 1989.

————. "The Emancipation Proclamation." In *Constitutional Government in America.* Ronald K. L. Collins, ed. Durham, N.C.: Carolina Academic Press, 1980.

Bailey, Thomas A. *A Diplomatic History of the American People.* New York: Crofts, 1940.

Bailyn, Bernard. *The Ideological Origins of the American Revolution.* Cambridge: Harvard University Press, 1967.

Baldwin, Alice M. *The New England Clergy and the American Revolution.* Durham, N.C.: Duke University Press, 1928.

Bancroft, George. *History of the United States* . 10 vols. 22nd Edition. Boston: Little, Brown, 1867.

————. *Literary and Historical Miscellanies* New York: Harper and Brothers, 1855.

Beale, Howard K. *Theodore Roosevelt and the Rise of America to World Power.* Baltimore: Johns Hopkins University Press, 1956.

Beard, Charles A. *American Foreign Policy in the Making, 1932-1940: A Study in Responsibilities.* New Haven: Yale University Press, 1946.

————. *Giddy Minds and Foreign Quarrels.* New York: Macmillan, 1939.

Beard, Charles A., editor. *Whither Mankind: A Panorama of Modern Civilization.* New York; Longmans, Green, 1928.

Becker, Carl. *The Declaration of Independence: A Study in the History of Political Ideas.* New York: Vintage Books, 1922, 1942.

Bellah, Robert N. "Civil Religion in America." In *The Religious Situation, 1968.* Boston: Beacon Press, 1968.

Bemis, Samuel Flagg, ed. *The American Secretaries of State and their Diplomacy.* 10 vols. New York: Cooper Square Publishers, 1926–29.

————. *A Diplomatic History of the United States.* 4th ed. New York: Henry Holt, 1955.

————. *John Quincy Adams and the Foundation of American Foreign Policy.* New York: Knopf, 1949.

Bennett, William J. *The Book of Virtues: A Treasury of Great Moral Stories.* New York: Simon and Schuster, 1993.

Benson, Ezra Taft. *God--Family--Country: Our Three Great Loyalties.* Salt Lake City: Deseret Book Co., 1974.

————. *This Nation Shall Endure.* Salt Lake City: Deseret Book Co., 1979.

Bercovitch, Susan. *The American Jeremiad.* Madison: University of Wisconsin Press, 1978.

Berdyaev, Nicholas. *The End of Our Time.* Translated by Donald Atwater. New York: Sheed and Ward, 1933.

Berkeley, George. *The Works of George Berkeley.* 3 vols. Oxford: Clarendon

Press, 1871.

Billington, Ray Allen. *Westward Expansion: A History of the American Frontier.* New York: Macmillan, 1949.

Bowen, Catherine Drinker. *John Adams and the American Revolution.* Boston: Little, Brown, 1950.

Bradford, William. *Bradford's History of Plimoth Plantation.* Boston: Wright and Potter, 1899.

Brandon, Henry. *The Retreat of American Power.* Garden City, New York: Doubleday and Co., 1973.

Breckinridge, Robert J. *A Discourse on the Formation and Development of the American Mind.* Baltimore: Richard J. Matchett, 1837.

Bridenbaugh, Carl. *The Spirit of 76: The Growth of American Patriotism Before Independence, 1607-1776.* New York: Oxford University Press, 1975.

Brodie, Bernard. *Sea Power in the Machine Age.* 2nd ed. Princeton: Princeton University Press, 1947.

Brooks, Van Wyck. *The Times of Melville and Whitman.* New York: E. P. Dutton, 1947.

Brown, Stuart Gerry, ed. *We Hold These Truths: Documents of American Democracy.* New York: Harper and Brothers, 1941.

Brzezinski, Zbigniew. *Power and Principle: Memoirs of the National Security Adviser, 1977-1981.* New York: Farrar, Straus, Giraux, 1983.
———. *Out of Control: Global Turmoil on the Eve of the 21st Century.* New York: Scribner's, 1993.

Burke, Edmund. *Burke's Politics.* New York: Knopf, 1949.

Butterfield, Herbert. *Writings on Christianity and History.* Edited by C. T. McIntire. New York: Oxford University Press, 1979.

Callahan, James A. *American Relations in the Pacific and the Far East, 1784–1900.* Baltimore: Johns Hopkins University Press, 1901.

Canfield, D. Lincoln. *East Meets West South of the Border.* Carbondale: Southern Illinois University Press, 1968.

Carnegie Endowment for International Peace National Commission. *Changing Our Ways: America and the New World.* Carnegie Endowment for International Peace, 1992.

Carter, Jimmy. *Keeping Faith: Memoirs of a President.* New York; Bantam Books, 1982.

Carter, Stephen L. *The Culture of Disbelief: How American Law and Politics Trivializes Religious Devotion.* New York: Harper Basic Books, 1993.

Charnwood, Lord. *Abraham Lincoln.* New York: Henry Holt, 1917; Cardinal Edition, 1952.

Clay, Henry. *The Works of Henry Clay.* Edited by Calvin Colton. 10 vols. New York: G. P. Putnams, 1904.

Cole, Charles C. *The Social Ideas of the Northern Evangelists, 1826-1860.*

New York: Columbia University Press, 1954.

Coolidge, Archibald Cary. *The United States as a World Power*. New York: Macmillan, 1908.

Cooper, Chester L. *The Lost Crusade: America in Vietnam*. New York: Dodd, Mead and Co., 1970.

Cotton, John. *God's Promise to His Plantation*. London: W. Jones for J.Bellamy, 1630.

Crabb, Cecil V., Jr. *American Diplomacy and the Pragmatic Tradition*. Baton Rouge: Lousiana State University Press, 1989.

Crèvecoeur, J. Hector St. John. *Letters from an American Farmer*. New York, 1904; reprinted from the Original Edition, London, 1782.

Davids, Jules. *The United States in World Affairs: 1964*. New York; Harper and Row, 1965.

DeVoto, Bernard. *The Year of Decision*. Boston: Little, Brown, 1943.

Donovan, Robert J. *Eisenhower, the Inside Story*. New York: Harpers, 1956.

Dulles, John Foster. *War or Peace*. New York: Macmillan, 1950.

Dunn, Paul H. *The Light of Liberty*. Salt Lake City: Bookcraft, 1987.

Eisenhower, Dwight D. *Crusade in Europe*. Garden City, New York: Doubleday and Co., 1948.

———. *Waging Peace, 1956–61* New York: Doubleday and Co., 1965.

Ekirch, Arthur A. Jr. *The Idea of Progress in America, 1815–1860*. New York: Columbia University Press, 1944.

Emerson, Ralph Waldo. *The Complete Essays and Other Writings of Ralph Waldo Emerson*. New York: The Modern Library, 1950.

Fallows, James. *More Like Us: Making America Great Again*. Boston: Houghton Mifflin, 1989.

Fish, Carl R. *American Diplomacy*. 4th ed. New York: Henry Holt, 1923.

Fiske, John. *American Political Ideas Viewed from the Standpoint of Universal History*. New York: Harpers 1885.

Fitch, Robert E. *A Certain Blind Man*. New York: Scribner's 1944.

Fleming, Denna F. *The United States and the League of Nations, 1918–1920*. New York: G. P. Putnam's, 1932.

———. *The United States and the World Court*. Garden City, New York: Doubleday, Doran, 1945.

———. *The United States and World Organization, 1920-1933*. New York: Columbia University Press, 1938.

Ford, Gerald R. *A Time to Heal: The Autobiography of Gerald R. Ford*. New York: Harper and Row, 1979.

Ford, Paul L., ed. *The New England Primer*, reprint of the earliest known edition, New York: Dodd Mead, 1899.

Forrestal, James V. *The Forrestal Diaries*. Edited by Walter Millis. New York: Viking Press, 1951.

Franklin, Benjamin. *The Writings of Benjamin Franklin*. 10 vols. New York:

Macmillan, 1905.

Fukuyama, Francis. *The End of History and the Last Man*. New York: Free Press, 1992.

Furay, Conal. *The Grass Roots Mind in America: The American Sense of Absolutes*. New York: New Viewpoints, Franklin Watts, 1977.

Gabriel, Ralph Henry. *The Course of American Democratic Thought*. New York: Ronald Press, 1940 (First Edition) and 1956 (Second Edition).

Gaddis, John Lewis. *The United States and the End of the Cold War*. New York: Oxford University Press, 1992.

Gibbs, Philip. *People of Destiny: Americans as I Saw Them at Home and Abroad*. New York: Harpers, 1920.

Giddings, Franklin H. *Democracy and Empire*. New York: Macmillan, 1900.

Gingrich, Newt. *To Renew America*. New York: HarperCollins, 1995.

Glasser, Ira. *Visions of Liberty: The Bill of Rights for All Americans*. New York: Arcade Publishing, Little, Brown and Co., 1991.

Gorbachev, Mikhail. *Perestroika: New Thinking for Our Country and the World*. New York: Harper and Row, 1987.

Greeley, Horace. *The American Conflict: A History of the Great Rebellion*. 2 vols. Hartford: O.D. Case and Co., 1864 and 1867.

Hallowell, John H. *Main Currents in Modern Political Thought*. New York: Henry Holt, 1950.

Handy, Robert T. "The American Scene." In *Twentieth Century Christianity*, edited by Bishop Stephen Neill. Garden City, New York: Doubleday-Dolphin Books, 1963.

Hayes, Carlton J.H. *A Generation of Materialism, 1871-1900*. 2nd ed. New York, 1941.

Hegel, Georg Wilhelm Friedrich. *Lectures on the Philosophy of History*. London: G. Ball and Sons, 1890.

———. *The Philosophy of History*. Rev. ed. New York: Willey Book Co., 1904.

Himmelfarb, Gertrude. *The De-Moralization of Society: From Victorian Virtues to Modern Values*. New York; Knopf, 1995.

Hodgson, Peter C. *God in History: Shapes of Freedom*. Nashville, Tenn.: Abingdon Press, 1989.

Hoffman, Paul G. *Peace Can Be Won*.Garden City, N.Y.: Doubleday, 1951.

Holmes, Jack E. *The Moood/Interest Theory of Foreign Policy*. Lexington: University Press of Kentucky, 1985.

Hoover, Herbert. *The State Papers and Other Public Writings of Herbert Hoover*. 2 vols. Edited by William Starr Myers. Garden City, N.Y.: Doubleday, Doran, 1934.

House, Col. Edward M. *The Intimate Papers of Col House*. 4 vols. Edited by Charles Seymour. Boston: Houghton Mifflin, 1926.

Huntington, Samuel P. *American Politics: The Promise of Disharmony*.

Cambridge, Mass.: Belknap Press of Harvard University Press, 1981.

―――. *The Third Wave: Democratization in the Late Twentieth Century.* Norman: University of Oklahoma Press, 1991.

Jaspers, Karl. *The Origin and Goal of History.* New Haven: Yale University Press, 1953.

Jefferson, Thomas. *The Writings of Thomas Jefferson.* 9 vols. Edited by H. A. Washington. Washington, D.C.: Taylor and Maury, 1853-54.

Johnson, Lyndon Baines. *The Vantage Point: Perspectives on the Presidency, 1963–1969.* New York: Holt, Rinehart and Winston, 1971.

Johnston, Douglas and Cynthia Sampson. *Religion: The Missing Dimension of Statecraft.* New York: Oxford University Press, 1994.

Kegley, Charles W., Jr., ed. *The Long Post-War Peace: Contending Explanations and Projections.* New York: HarperCollins, 1991.

Keller, Charles Ray. *The Second Great Awakening in Connecticut.* New Haven: Yale University Press, 1942.

Kelly, Frank and Cornelius Ryan. *MacArthur: Man of Action.* Garden City, N.Y.: Doubleday and Co., 1950.

Kennan, George F. *American Diplomacy, 1900–1950* Chicago: University of Chicago Press, 1951.

Kennedy, John F. *The Burden and the Glory: Public Statements and Addresses in 1962 and 1963.* Edited by Allan Nevins. New York: Harper and Row, 1964.

―――. *To Turn the Tide.* Edited by John W. Gardner. New York: Harpers, 1962.

Kennedy, Paul. *Preparing for the Twenty-First Century.* New York: Random House, 1993.

―――. *The Rise and Fall of the Great Powers: Economic Changes and Military Conflicts from 1500 to 2000.* New York: Vintage Books, 1989, first published by Random House, 1987.

King, Martin Luther, Jr. *Stride Toward Freedom: The Montgomery Story.* New York, Harpers, 1958.

―――. *A Testament of Hope: The Essential Writings and Speeches of Martin Luther King, Jr.* Edited by James M. Washington. New York: HarperCollins Paperback, 1991.

Kissinger, Henry. *Diplomacy.* New York: Simon and Schuster, 1994.

―――. *White House Years.* Boston: Little, Brown, 1979.

Klingberg, Frank L. *Cyclical Trends in American Foreign Policy Moods: The Unfolding of America's World Role.* Lanham, Md.: University Press of America, 1983.

Lang, Daniel G. *Foreign Policy in the Early Republic: The Law of Nations and the Balance of Power.* Baton Rouge: Louisiana State University Press, 1985.

Langer, Walter L. and S. Everett Gleason. *The Challenge to Isolation, 1937–1940.* New York: Harpers, 1952.

Lansing, Robert. *The Peace Negotiations: A Personal Narrative.* Boston: Houghton Mifflin, 1921.

Lasswell, Harold D. *The Analysis of Political Behavior.* New York: Oxford University Press, 1949.

Latourette, Kenneth Scott. *History of the Expansion of Christianity.* 7 vols. New York: Harpers, 1941.

Lefler, Hugh T., ed. *A History of the United States from the Age of Exploration to 1865.* Meridian Documents of American History. New York: World Publishing Co., 1960.

Lerner, Max. *America as a Civilization: Life and Thought in the United States Today.* New York: Simon and Schuster, 1957.

Levi, Werner. *The Coming End of War.* Vol. 117, Sage Library of Social Research. Beverly Hills, Calif.: Sage Publications, 1981.

Levin, N. Gordon. *Woodrow Wilson and World Politics: America's Response to War and Revolution.* New York: Oxford University Press, 1968.

Levy, Jack S. "Long Cycles, Hegemonic Transitions, and the Long Peace." In Charles W. Kegley, ed. *The Long Postwar Peace: Contending Explanations and Projections.* New York: HarperCollins, 1991.

Lincoln, Abraham. *The Collected Works of Abraham Lincoln.* Roy P. Basler, ed. 8 vols. Brunswick, N. J.: Rutgers University Press, 1958.

Link, Arthur S. *Wilson the Diplomatist.* Baltimore: Johns Hopkins University Press, 1957.

Lipset, Seymour Martin. *The First New Nation: the United States in Historical and Comparative Perspective.* Garden City, New York: Anchor Books, 1967.

McLoughlin, William G. *Revivals, Awakenings, and Reform: An Essay on Religious and Social Changes in America, 1607–1977.* Chicago: University of Chicago Press, 1978.

Mahan, Captain Alfred Thayer. *The Influence of Sea Power upon History, 1660–1783.* Boston: Little, Brown, 1890.

———. *The Interest of America in Sea Power, Present and Future.* Boston: Little, Brown, 1897.

———. *The Problem of Asia and its Effect upon International Policies.* Boston: Little, Brown, 1900.

Marsden, George A. *The Soul of the American University: From Protestant Establishment to Established Non-Belief.* New York: Oxford University Press, 1994.

Marshall, Catherine. *A Man Called Peter.* New York : McGraw-Hill, 1951.

Marshall, Peter. *The Prayers of Peter Marshall.* Edited by Catherine Marshall. New York: McGraw-Hill, 1964.

Mather, Cotton. *Magnalia Christi Americana, or The Ecclesiastical History of New England from its first planting in the year 1620, unto the year of our Lord 1698.* 2 vols. 1702.

Mather, Increase. *An Earnest Exhortation to the Inhabitants of New England*. Boston: John Foster, 1676.

Miller, Perry. *The American Puritans*. Garden City, N.Y.: Doubleday and Co., 1956.

Monaghan, Jay. *Diplomat in Carpet Slippers*. Indianapolis: Bobbs-Merrill Co., 1945.

Morris, Richard B., ed. *Encyclopedia of American History*. New York: Harpers, 1953.

Mosier, Richard D. *Making the American Mind: Social and Moral Ideas in the McGuffey Readers*. New York: Russell & Russell, 1947.

Moynihan, Daniel Patrick. *On the Law of Nations*. Cambridge. Mass.: Harvard University Press, 1990.

———. *Pandaemonium: Ethnicity in International Politics*. New York: Oxford University Press, 1993.

Mumford, Lewis. *Faith for Living*. New York: Harcourt, Brace and Co., 1940.

Muravchik, Joseph. *Exporting Democracy: Fulfilling America's Destiny*. Washington, D.C.: The AEI Press--American Enterprise Institute--1991.

National Conference of Catholic Bishops. *The Challlenge of Peace: God's Promises and Our Response*. Washington, D.C.: United States Catholic Conference, 1983.

Nau, Henry R. *The Myth of America's Decline: Leading the World Economy into the 1990s*. New York: Oxford University Press, 1990.

Neuhaus, Richard John. *America Against Itself: Moral Vision and the Public Order*. Notre Dame: University of Notre Dame Press, 1992.

———. *Time Toward Home: The American Experiment in Revelation*. New York: Seabury Press, 1975.

Nevins, Allen. *Hamilton Fish*. New York: Dodd, Mead, 1937.

Niebuhr, Reinhold. *The Irony of American History*. New York: Scribner's, 1952.

———. *The Nature and Destiny of Man.*. 2 vols. Vol. 1, *Human Nature*. Vol. 2, *Human Destiny*. New York: Scribner's, 1941 and 1943.

Nixon, Richard. *Beyond Peace*. New York: Random House, 1994.

———. *The Memoirs of Richard Nixon*. New York: Grosset and Dunlap, 1978.

———. *Seize the Moment: America's Challenges in a One Superpower World*. New York: Simon and Schuster, 1992.

Nourse, J. D. *Remarks on the Past and its Legacies to American Society*. Louisville, 1847.

Nye, Joseph F.,Jr. *Bound to Lead: The Changing Nature of American Power*. New York: Basic Books, 1990.

Osgood, Robert E., and others. *America and the World: From the Truman Doctrine to Vietnam*. Baltimore: Johns Hopkins University Press, 1970.

Osgood, Robert E. *Ideals and Self-Interest in American Foreign Relations*. Chicago: University of Chicago Press, 1953.

Pope John Paul II. *Crossing the Threshold of Hope*. Edited by Vittorio Messori, translated by Jenny McPhee and Martha McPhee. New York: Alfred A. Knopf, 1994.

Porter, Kirk H. *National Party Platforms.* New York: Macmillan, 1942.

Potter, E. B., ed. *The United States and World Sea Power.* Englewood Cliffs, N.J.: Prentice Hall, 1955.

Pratt, Julius. *A History of United States Foreign Policy.* New York: Prentice Hall, 1955.

Reagan, Ronald. *An American Life.* New York: Simon and Schuster, 1990.

Reich, Charles A. *The Greening of America.* New York: Bantam Books, 1970; originally published by Random House.

Reinsch, Paul S. *World Politics at the End of the 19th Century, as Influenced by the Oriental Situation.* New York: Macmillan, 1900.

The Religious Situation, 1968. Boston: Beacon Press, 1968.

The Religious Situation, 1969. Boston: Beacon Press, 1969.

Roosevelt, Franklin D. *Nothing to Fear: The Selected Addresses of Franklin D. Roosevelt, 1932–1945.* Edited by B. D. Zevin. Cambridge, Mass.: Houghton, Mifflin, 1946.

———. *The Public Papers and Addresses of Franklin D. Roosevelt.* 13 vols. Edited by Samuel I Rosenman. New York: Random House, I-V; Macmillan, VI-IX; Harpers, X to XIII, 1938–1950.

Rosati, Jerel A. *The Carter Administration's Quest for Global Community.* Columbia, S.C.: University of South Carolina Press, 1987.

Rosecrance, Richard, ed. *America as an Ordinary Country: U.S. Foreign Policy in the Future.* Ithaca, N.Y.: Cornell University Press, 1976.

Rostow, W. W. *The Diffusion of Power.* New York: Macmillan, 1972.

Rusk, Dean. *As I Saw It,* as told to Richard Rusk. New York: W. W. Norton, 1990.

Schlesinger, Arthur M. *Paths to the Present.* New York: Macmillan 1949.

Schlesinger, Arthur M., Jr. *The Cycles of American History.* Boston: Houghton Mifflin, 1986.

Schmalhausen, Samuel D., ed. *Behold America.* New York : Farrar and Rinehart, 1931.

Shultz, George P. *Turmoil and Triumph: My Years as Secretary of State.* New York: Scribner's, 1993.

Siegfried, André. *Nations Have Souls.* New York: Putnam's, 1932.

Smith, Tony. *America's Mission: The United States and the Worldwide Struggle for Democracy in the Twentieth Century.* A Twentieth Century Fund Book. Princeton, N.J.: Princeton University Press,1994.

Sorensen, Theodore G. *Kennedy.* New York: Harper and Row, 1965.

Stearns, Harold E., ed. *America Now: An Inquiry into Civilization in the United States.* New York: Scribner's, 1938.

Stourzh, Gerald. *Benjamin Franklin and American Foreign Policy.* Chicago: University of Chicago Press, 1954.

Strong, Josiah. *Our Country: Its Possible Future and its Present Crisis.* New York: Baker and Taylor, 1885.

Sullivan, Mark. *Our Times: The United States, 1900–1925.* 6 vols. New York: Scribner's, 1926–1935.

Sweet, William Warren. *The Story of Religion in America.* New York: Harpers, 1950.

Tannenbaum, Frank. *The American Tradition in Foreign Policy.* Norman: University of Oklahoma Press, 1951.

Tinder, Glenn. *The Political Meaning of Christianity: An Interpretation.* Baton Rouge: Louisiana State University Press, 1989.

Tocqueville, Alexis de. *Democracy in America.* One Volume Edition. New York: Edward Walker, 1849.

Toynbee, Arnold J. *An Historian's Approach to Religion.* New York: Oxford University Press, 1956.

———. *A Study of History.* 10 vols. London: Oxford University Press, 1933, 1939, 1955.

———. *A Study of History,* abridgement of vols. I-VI by D. C. Somervell. New York: Oxford University Press, 1946.

———. *A Study of History,* abridgement of vols. VII-X by D. C. Somervell. New York: Oxford University Press, 1957.

Trueblood, Elton. *Abraham Lincoln: Theologian of American Anguish.* New York: Harper and Row, 1973.

Tucker, Robert W. *Nation or Empire? The Debate over American Foreign Policy.* Baltimore: Johns Hopkins University Press, 1968.

Tucker, Robert W. and David C. Hendrickson. *The Imperial Temptation: The New World Order and America's Purpose.* New York: Council on Foreign Relations Press, 1992.

Tyler, Moses Coit. *A History of American Literature, 1607–1765.* 2 vols. New York: G. P. Putnam's, 1879.

Usher, Roland B. *The Rise of the American People.* New York: Century, 1914.

U.S. News and World Report. *The Religious Awakening in America.* Washington, D.C., 1972.

Van Alstyne, Richard W. *American Diplomacy in Action.* Stanford University Press, 1954.

Van Dyke, Henry. *The Spirit of America.* New York: Macmillan, 1910.

Van Leeuwen, Arend Th. *Christianity in World History: The Meeting of the Faiths of East and West.* Translated by H. H. Hoskins. New York: Scribner's, 1964.

Vandenberg, Arthur H. *The Private Papers of Senator Vandenberg.* Cambridge: Houghton Mifflin, 1952.

Vattel, Emerich de. *The Law of Nations or the Principles of Natural Law.* Translation of the edition of 1758 by Charles G. Fenwick, Vol. III. Washington, D.C.: Carnegie Institution, 1916.

Vico, Giambattista. *The New Science of Giambattista Vico*. Ithaca, N.Y.: Cornell University Press, 1948.

Von Schmidt-Phiseldek, D. C. F. *Europe and America*. Copenhagen: Bernhard Schlesinger, 1820.

Ward, John William. *Andrew Jackson: Symbol for an Age*. New York: Oxford University Press, 1955.

Wattenberg, Ben J. *The First Universal Nation: Leading Indicaators and Ideas about the Surge of America in the 1990s*. New York: Free Press, 1991.

Webster, Daniel *The Works of Daniel Webster*. 18th ed., 6 vols. Boston: Little, Brown, 1881.

Weigel, George. *Idealism Without Illusions*. Ethics and Public Policy Center. Grand Rapids, Mich.: Wiliam B. Eerdmans, 1994.

Weigle, Luther A. *American Idealism*. Vol. 10 of *The Pageant of America*. New Haven: Yale University Press, 1928.

Weinberg, Albert K. *Manifest Destiny*. Baltimore: Johns Hopkins University Press, 1935.

White, William Allen. *Some Cycles of Cathay*. Chapel Hill: University of North Carolina Press, 1925.

Whitman, Walt. *The Complete Poetry and Prose of Walt Whitman*. Introduction by Malcolm Cowley, 2 vols. New York: Pellegrini and Cudahy, 1948.

———. *The Whitman Reader*.Edited by Maxwell Geismar. New York: Pocket Books, 1955.

Wieman, Henry Nelson. *Man's Ultimate Commitment*. Carbondale, Ill.: Southern Illinois University Press, 1958.

Wilcox, Francis O. and T. V. Kalijarvi. *Recent American Foreign Policy: Basic Documents, 1941–1951*. New York: Appleton-Century-Crofts, 1952.

Williams, Stanley Thomas. *The American Spirit in Letters*. Vol. 11 of *The Pageant of America*. New Haven: Yale University Press, 1926.

Wills, Garry. *Lincoln at Gettysburg: The Words that Remade America*. New York: Simon and Schuster, 1992.

Wilson, James Q. *The Moral Sense*. New York; Free Press, 1993.

Wilson, Woodrow. *The Public Papers of Woodrow Wilson*. Authorized Edition. 6 vols. Edited by Ray Stannard Baker and William E. Dodd. *College and State*, 2 vols.; *The New Democracy*, 2 vols.; *War and Peace*, 2 vols. New York: Harpers, 1925, 1926, 1927.

———. *Selected Literary and Political Papers and Addresses of Woodrow Wilson*. 3 vols. New York: Grosset and Dunlap, 1925, 1926, 1927.

Winthrop, John *The History of New England from 1630 to 1649*. Boston: Little, Brown, 1853.

Wright, Quincy. *The Study of International Relations*. New York: Appleton-Century-Crofts, 1955.

Wuthnow, Robert *Sharing the Journey: Support Groups and America's New Quest for Community*. New York: Free Press, 1994.

Articles

Alker, Hayward R., Jr. "The Humanistic Moment in International Studies: Reflections on Machiavelli and las Casas," *International Studies Quarterly* 36 (December 1992).

Bellah, Robert N. "Civil Religion in America." in *The Religious Situation, 1968*. Boston: Beacon Press, 1968.

Berke, Matthew. "The Disputed Legacy of Reinhold Niebuhr." *First Things*, November 1992.

Boorstin, Daniel. "I Am Optimistic about America." *Parade*, July 10, 1994.

Brzezinski, Zbigniew. "America's New Geostrategy." *Foreign Affairs* 66, no. 4 (spring 1988).

———. "Power and Morality." *World Monitor*, March 1993.

Christopher, Warren. "America's Leadership, America's Opportunity." *Foreign Policy*, Spring 1995.

Churchill, Winston. "The Cold 'Peace' and Our Future." *Look*, April 29, 1958.

Dole, Bob. "Shaping America's Global Future." *Foreign Policy*, Spring 1995.

Emerson, James G.Jr. "A Theology of Responsibility: The Challenge to My Country." *Presbyterian Outlook*, March 9, 1992.

Haas, Richard N. "The Use (and Mainly Misuse) of History." Review of Paul Kennedy's *The Rise and Fall of the Great Powers*. *Orbis* 32, no. 3, (summer 1988).

Havel, Vaclav. "A Call for Sacrifice: The Co-Responsibility of the West." *Foreign Affairs*, March/April 1994.

———. "The End of the Modern Era." *New York Times*, March 1, 1992.

Hoffman, Stanley. "The Crisis of Liberal Internationalism." *Foreign Policy*, Spring 1995.

Hoge, James G. Jr. "Preface: The Year Ahead." *Foreign Affairs, America and the World, 1992–93*.

Hormats, Robert D. "The Roots of American Power." *Foreign Affairs*, Summer 1991.

Huntington, Samuel P. "The Clash of Civilizations?" *Foreign Affairs*, Summer 1993.

Johnson, Paul. "Colonialism's Back—and Not a Moment Too Soon." *New York Times Magazine*, April 18, 1993.

Karban, Father Roger. "Interfaith Conversation: Expanding Our Minds and Hearts." *Jews, Christians and Muslims in Conversation* (Carbondale, Ill.: Religious Studies Department, Southern Illinois University) 1, no. 2 (November 1992).

Kegley, Charles W., Jr. "Neo-Idealism: A Practical Matter." Carnegie Council on Ethics and International Affairs: *Ethics and International Affairs* 2 (1988).

———. "The Neo-idealist Moment in International Studies? Realist Myths and the New International Realities." *International Studies Quarterly* 37 (1993).

———. "The New Global Order: The Power of Principle in a Pluralistic World." *Ethics and International Affairs* 6 (1992).

Kennan, George F. [pseudonym X], "The Sources of Soviet Conduct." *Foreign Affairs* 25, no. 4 (July 1947).

Kissinger, Henry. "How to Achieve the New World Order." *Time*, March 14, 1994.

Klingberg, Frank L. "The Historical Alternation of Moods in American Foreign Policy." *World Politics* 4, no. 2 (January 1952).

———. "Hope for Peace." *Presbyterian Outlook*, November 12, 1984.

Kull, Steven. "The U.S. Isn't Averse to Peacekeeping." *Christian Science Monitor*, June 21, 1995.

Küng, Hans. "The Declaration of a Global Ethic." *National Catholic Reporter*, September 24, 1993.

Layne, Christopher. "Why the Gulf War Was Not in the National Interest." *Atlantic Monthly*, July 1991.

Luce, Henry R. "The American Century." *Life*, February 17,1941.

Mead, Walter Russell, review of Brzezinski's *Out of Control. New York Times Book Review*, April 4, 1993.

Maynes, Charles William. "Containing Ethnic Conflict." *Foreign Policy,* Spring 1993.

Neumann, Robert G. "The Next Disorderly Half Century: Some Proposed Remedies." *Washington Quarterly*, Winter 1993.

Nixon, Richard M. "Asia After Viet Nam." *Foreign Affairs* 46, no. 1 (October 1967).

———. "We Are Ignoring Our World Role." *Time*, March 16, 1992.

Nye, Joseph S. Jr. "Understanding U.S. Strength." *Foreign Policy*, no. 73 (fall 1988).

———. "Why the Gulf War Served the National Interest." *Atlantic Monthly,* July 1991.

Powell, Colin L. "U.S. Forces: Challenges Ahead." *Foreign Affairs* Winter 1992/93.

Rielly, John E. "The Public Mood at Mid-Decade." *Foreign Policy*, no. 98 (Spring 1995).

Rostow, W. W. "Beware of Historians Bearing False Analogies," review of Paul Kennedy's *The Rise and Fall of the Great Powers. Foreign Affairs*, Spring 1988.

Rotberg, Robert I. "Struggling Nations Need Guidance." *Christian Science Monitor*, May 14, 1993.

Salater, Elizabeth. "The Serbian Orthodox Church: Space for Reconciliation." *One World*, May, 1993 (World Council of Churches).

Schlesinger, Arthur M. "Tides in American Politics," *Yale Review* 29 (December 1939).

Schlesinger, Arthur M., Jr. "Back to the Womb? Isolationism's Renewed Threat." *Foreign Affairs*, July/August 1995.

————. "The Turn of the Cycle." *New Yorker*, November 16, 1992.

Sevareid, Eric. "A New Stage." *Modern Maturity*, April/May, 1991.

Solzhenitsyn, Aleksandr. "Misconceptions About Russia are a Threat to America." *Foreign Affairs* 58, no. 4 (spring 1980).

Szulc, Tad. "The Greatest Danger We Face." *Parade*, July 25, 1993.

Talbott, Strobe. "The Birth of the Global Nation." *Time*, July 20, 1992.

Tonelson, Alan. "What is the National Interest?" *Atlantic Monthly*, July 1991.

Wall, James N. "To Stem the Tide of World Affairs." *Christian Century*, August 26, 1992.

Wentz, Richard E. Review of Leroy S. Rouner's *To Be at Home: Christianity, Civil Religion, and World Community* (Boston: Beacon Press, 1991), in *Christian Century*, September 4–11, 1991.

Young, Andrew. "Global Vision: An Interview with Andrew Young." *Christian Century*, June 21–28, 1995.

U.S. Government Documents

Congressional Record. 1900, 1945, 1949, 1966.

Department of State Bulletin. 1950 to 1966.

Department of State Dispatch. 1991 to 1995.

Fifty-second Congress. *A Compilation of the Messages and Papers of the Presidents,* 16 vols. New York: Bureau of National Literature.

Library of Congress. *Journals of the Continental Congress, 1774-1789*. 34 vols. Edited from the original records by Worthington Chauncey Ford. Washington: Government Printing Office, 1904.

Miller, Hunter, ed. *Treaties and other International Acts of the United States of America.* Washington, D.C.: U.S. Government Printing Office, 1946– .

Public Papers of the Presidents of the United States, Washington: U.S. Government Printing Office, 1966-1992 (Presidents Johnson, Nixon, Ford, Carter, Reagan and Bush).

Richardson, James D. *Messages and Papers of the Presidents, 1789-1902.* 11 vols. (Washington, D.C.: Bureau of National Literature and Art, 1907).

Roosevelt, Franklin D. *The War Messages of Franklin D. Roosevelt, December, 1941–October, 1942.* Washington, D.C.: U.S Government Printing Office, 1942.

Texas v. White, 7 Wall. 724. U.S. Supreme Court, 1869.

Washington, George. *The Writings of George Washington (from the Original Manuscript Sources), 1745-1799.* 37 vols. Washington, D.C.: U.S. Government Printing Office, 1931-1944.

Miscellaneous

Beard, Charles A. "Memorandum on Beard's Laws of History," given to Professor George Counts, Southern Illinois University, 1966.

Caine, Lulu. "Conditions Underlying the Minor Wars and Interventions of the United States." Doctoral dissertation, University of Chicago, August 1929.

Coolidge, Calvin. Address at Commencement of George Washington University, February 22, 1929. U.S. Government Printing Office, 1929.

Democratic National Committee. *The Campaign Book of the Democratic Party*, 1936.

———. *Democratic Campaign Handbook*, 1940.

U.S. Department of State. Publication 6440, "Middle East Proposals," 1957.

———. Publication 3922, "United States Policy in the Korean Crisis," July 1950.

Dulles, John Foster. Address at San Francisco. *New York Times*, June 29, 1957.

———. "The Cost of Peace." Address at Iowa State College Commencement, June 9, 1956. Department of State, Series S, no. 48.

———. "Freedom--the Predominant Force " Statement before the Senate Foreign Relations Committee, January 14, 1959. Department of State, no. 77.

Eisenhower, Dwight D. Address at Baylor University Commencement, *New York Times*, May 26, 1956.

———. "Atoms for Peace" address. U.S. Department of State Publication 5314, 1953.

———. "Foreign Affairs: Excerpts from the State of the Union Message, January 9, 1959. U.S. Department of State Publication 6763.

Harding, Warren G. "Speech of Acceptance of Republican Party Nomination," Marion, Oh., July 22, 1920. Issued by the Republican National Committee.

Harper, Robert. "The Post-Industrial World and its Impact on the United States." Address at Southern Illinois University at Carbondale, February 2, 1992.

Hinckly, Ronald H. and Eugene R. Wittkopf, "The Domestication of American Foreign Policy Public Opinion in the Post-Cold War Era." Paper at annual convention of the International Studies Association, Washington, D.C., March 28–April 1, 1994.

Johnson, Paul. "The Almost-Chosen People: Why America is Different." The first annual Erasmus Lecture, January 24, 1985. New York: Rockford Institute, 1985.

Republican National Committee. "Official Report of the Proceedings of the 23rd Republican National Convention," 1944.

Richman, Al. "American Public Attitudes Toward U.S. International Involvement in the Post-Cold War Era." Paper at annual convention of the International Studies Association, Washington, D.C., March 29, 1994.

Scowcroft, Brent. Op. Ed., *New York Times*, July 2, 1993.
Stalin, Josef. Text of Stalin's speech, in *New York Times*, February 10, 1946.

Magazines and Newspapers

American Enterprise, Nov.–Dec. 1990 and March–April, 1993.
Christian Century, March 19, 1952, and May 3, 1993.
Christian Science Monitor.
Life, June 3, 1940.
New Republic. vol. 10 (April 14, 1917).
New York Times.
Presbyterian Survey, January–February, 1993.
Public Opinion Quarterly, October 1939.
Southern Illinoisan, Carbondale, Ill.
St. Louis Globe-Democrat, published up to 1966.
St. Louis Post-Dispatch.
Time, March 30, 1992, and April 5, 1993.
United Nations Chronicle, Winter (March) 1993.

Index

Persons

Subjects

About the Author

Frank L. Klingberg received his A.B. and A.M. degrees from the University of Kansas, and his Ph.D., under Professor Quincy Wright, from the University of Chicago. After teaching at Millikin University and Knox College, he served in the Department of Political Science at Southern Illinois University at Carbondale, where he is now Professor Emeritus.

He pioneered in three areas: psychometric methods and factor analysis in measuring relations among nations (*Psychometrika*, December 1941); the relation of casualties to the ending of wars (research in the Department of War in 1945 and *Journal of Conflict Resolution*, June 1966); and the study of cyclical trends in American foreign policy, including:

> *World Politics*, January 1952
> *Journal of Conflict Resolution*, December 1970
> Chapter 2 in Kegley and McGowan, *Challenges to America: U.S. Foreign Policy in the 1980s*, (Sage, 1979).
> *Cyclical Trends in American Foreign Policy Moods: The Unfolding of America's World Role* (University Press of America, 1983).

The present study is a sequel to the 1983 book, stressing the "positive expectations" of leaders in the context of the continuing cyclical trends (up to August 1995).